The Macedonian Knot

Hans-Lothar Steppan

The Macedonian Knot

The Identity of the Macedonians, as Revealed
in the Development of the Balkan League
1878 – 1914

The Role of Macedonia in the Strategy
of the Entente Before the First World War

Revised and Supplemented Edition

PETER LANG
Frankfurt am Main · Berlin · Bern · Bruxelles · New York · Oxford · Wien

Bibliographic Information published by the Deutsche Nationalbibliothek
The Deutsche Nationalbibliothek lists this publication in the Deutsche Nationalbibliografie; detailed bibliographic data is available in the internet at <http://www.d-nb.de>.

Translators:
Eva Dorn, Mark Franken, Sonja Koroliov
Proof-Reading:
Geoffrey Sammon, Sandra Vathauer, Anne Wegner

ISBN 978-3-631-56067-9

© Peter Lang GmbH
Internationaler Verlag der Wissenschaften
Frankfurt am Main 2009
All rights reserved.

All parts of this publication are protected by copyright. Any utilisation outside the strict limits of the copyright law, without the permission of the publisher, is forbidden and liable to prosecution. This applies in particular to reproductions, translations, microfilming, and storage and processing in electronic retrieval systems.

www.peterlang.de

To my mother

in grateful memory

TABLE OF CONTENTS

INTRODUCTORY REMARKS — 13

1 BASIC INFORMATION AND CURRENT SITUATION — 15

  1.1 Introduction — 15
    1.1.0 Subject and material basis of the study — 15
    1.1.1 The states involved — 17
    1.1.2 The Balkan League — 18
    1.1.3 Working objective — 20

  1.2 Basic information on Macedonia — 21
    1.2.0 History — 21
      1.2.0.1 The ancient Macedonians — 21
      1.2.0.2 The Slavs — 22
      1.2.0.3 The First Bulgarian Empire and the first Macedonian state — 23
      1.2.0.4 The autocephalous Macedonian church — 24
      1.2.0.5 The Ottomans — 26
      1.2.0.6 Early resistance to the Macedonian pursuit of autonomy — 26
      1.2.0.7 The emergence of the Macedonian question — 29
      1.2.0.8 The two short periods of a free Macedonia — 31
    1.2.1 The name "Macedonia" — 32
    1.2.2 The Macedonian language — 35
      1.2.2.0 Language codification in the neighbour states — 39
      1.2.2.1 The Bulgarian language — 39
      1.2.2.2 The Serbian language — 39
      1.2.2.3 The Greek language — 40
      1.2.2.4 The Albanian language — 41
    1.2.3 The Macedonian territory — 42

  1.3 The Republic of Macedonia – in the crossfire of its neighbours — 43
    1.3.1 The Serbs — 43
    1.3.2 The Bulgarians — 44
    1.3.3 The Greeks — 45
    1.3.4 The three neighbouring states — 50
    1.3.5 The Albanians — 51
    1.3.6 The international community — 59
    1.3.7 The problem — 60

2 THE DEVELOPMENT OF THE BALKAN LEAGUE IN THE BALKAN STATES

  2.1 Serbia — 61

2.1.0 Historical Background	
2.1.1 Looking ahead at the Balkan League and Macedonia	64
2.1.2 Serbia between Austria-Hungary and Bulgaria	66
2.1.3 Serbian interest in Macedonia and Russian interest in Serbia as a spearhead against Germany	67
2.1.4 Autonomy for or division of Macedonia	69
2.1.5 The Ilinden uprising	71
2.1.6 The idea of a nation-state	73
2.1.7 A fundamental Serbian document on Macedonia	74
2.1.8 Serbia – Old Serbia (Kosovo) – Macedonia	77
2.1.9 1908 – the annexation of Bosnia	77
2.1.10 Serbia and Bulgaria demarcate their spheres of interest	79
2.1.11 A conference of Slav Social Democrats	82
2.2.12 The status quo	82
2.2 Bulgaria	**84**
2.2.0 Historical review	84
2.2.1 Prince Alexander's plans for "Macedonia"	91
2.2.2 A first treaty draft on the Balkan League	94
2.2.3 False Bulgarians – real Macedonians: the VMRO	95
2.2.4 Foreign influence in favour of the Balkan League against Germany and Austria-Hungary	98
2.2.5 A Bulgarian document of importance for Macedonia	101
2.3 Greece	**104**
2.3.0 Aspects of Greek History	104
2.3.1 Greece, the 8th Russo-Turkish War and the Congress of Berlin	111
2.3.1.1 *Backgroundinformation (1)* *Greece maintains active dynastic connections in Europe (St. Petersburg, London)*	115
2.3.1.2 *Backgroundinformation (2)* *A new dynastic period in the Greek royal house (Berlin)*	119
2.3.2 Greek-Bulgarian exploratory talks on Macedonia	126
2.3.3 The essence of the Greek strategy	128
2.3.4 Greek sueing for Austria-Hungary	129
2.3.5 Bismarck fears disturbances in Macedonia	133
2.3.6 The Greek press demands Macedonia	133
2.3.7 Greek policy on minorities: Romanian cultural policy would hinder the Graecization of Macedonia	135
2.3.8 Greek Ex-Premier sounds out the partitioning of Macedonia	138
2.3.8.1 *Backgroundinformation (3)* *King George's finance and family policies*	139
2.3.9 Crete and the Greek-Turkish War	146
2.3.9.1 *Backgroundinformation (4)* *King George continues working on the international relations of Greece (Rome)*	156

2.3.9.2 *Backgroundinformation (5)*	
George I completes his dynastic network (Paris)	159
2.3.10 The meeting of monarchs in Reval [Tallin] in 1908: A key event for Macedonia - and the Dual Alliance	162
2.3.10.1 *Backgroundinformation (6)*	
George I keeps up his struggle to increase the power of Greece	164
2.3.11 Greece and Turkey haggle over the Balkan League	166
2.3.12 The lead-up to the Greek-Bulgarian Alliance - and to the Balkan War	167
2.3.12.1 *Backgroundinformation (7)*	
The continuity in the solidarity of the European dynasties is preserved	167
2.4 Romania	169
2.4.0 Historical outline	169
2.4.1 Romania vacillating between alliance policy and neutrality	170
2.4.2 Romania's further network of connections with other countries	172
2.5 Albania	174
2.5.0 Excerpts from Albanian History	174
2.5.1 Fragments from reports	180
3 **THE DEVELOPMENT OF THE BALKAN LEAGUE IN THE OTTOMAN EMPIRE**	181
3.0 A look at history	181
3.1 Constantinople and Macedonia as crossroads of foreign interests	188
3.2 The Turkish dilemma in choosing countermeasures	190
3.3 The Young Turks – between a Balkan Alliance and the Dual Alliance	192
3.4 The phalanx against Macedonia takes shape	195
3.5 The ring around Constantinople gets tighter	198
3.6 An observer looks back – and forward	200
3.7 The decision is approaching	201
4 **THE DEVELOPMENT OF THE BALKAN LEAGUE AS SEEN BY THE EUROPEAN GREAT POWERS**	205
4.1 Russia	205
4.1.0 The Balkans in Russian history - an outline	205
4.1.1 Russia promotes the project of a Balkan League	207
4.1.2 Russia intensifies its policy in the Balkans	210
4.1.3 The Russian strategy becomes inscrutable and shows ominous signs	212
4.2 Austria-Hungary	216
4.2.0 The historical role of Austria in the Balkans	216

4.2.1	Austria's thrust towards the Balkans	219
4.2.2	The Dual Alliance	220
4.2.3	Another missed opportunity for Macedonia	221
4.2.4	The Macedonians insist on the fulfilment of the Turkish obligations	223
4.2.5	First signs of negative implications of the Dual Alliance	225
4.2.6	1908 again, - including London's anti German propaganda following the collapse of the Russo-Austrian deal of "Bosnia in exchange fort the Straits"	226

4.3 Great Britain — 233
    4.3.0 Historical impressions on England's Balkan policy — 233
    4.3.1 Macedonia as a piece in the field of the English strategy game — 238
    4.3.2 The English Macedonia policy from the Serbian point of view — 240

4.4 The German Reich, France, Italy — 242
    4.4.1 The German Reich — 242
        4.4.1.1. Germany's unwanted role in the Balkans — 242
        4.4.1.2. A look back at the Congress of Berlin and its consequences — 255
            4.4.1.2.1 *Background information (8) The chain of events around the Balkan League with the cause of the First World War and the question of the war guilt*
    4.4.2 France — 289
    4.4.3 Italy — 291

5 THE BALKAN LEAGUE AND THE BALKAN WARS — 295

5.1 The Formation of the Balkan League — 295
    5.1.1 Russia provides the indispensable prerequisite for the formation of the Balkan League — 295
    5.1.2 The strict secrecy of the plans fort the League conceals further intentions of the Entente — 303
    5.1.3 Elements of the Entente's intrigues — 307
        5.1.3.1 Cheap propaganda the Russian way — 307
        5.1.3.2 The trick of presumably localizing the Balkan War — 313
        5.1.3.3 The alleged refusal of territorial changes after the war — 316
        5.1.3.4 Mobilization(s) — 324
    5.1.4 William II sees through the trap of the Entente — 335
    5.1.5 The German Kaiser, the Greek Crown Prince and Macedonia — 341

5.2 The First Balkan War — 348
    5.2.1 The end of the territorial status quo – and of the Berlin Treaty — 348
    5.2.2 Solun/Saloniki – a Greek city? — 349

	5.2.2.1 Solun as a Germano-Greek source of friction	352
	5.2.2.2 King Georg I and Saloniki	354
5.2.3	The intermezzo between armistice and the Peace Treaty of London	357

5.3 Another sensation: Russia pursues a *new* Balkan League ... 361
    5.3.1 The formation of a new war-coalition in the Balkans ... 366

5.4 On „the brink of disaster" ... 368
    5.4.1 The Russian communiqué of April 1913 ... 368
    5.4.2 A Bulgarian act of revenge brings the truth to light ... 370

5.5 The Second Balkan war ... 377
    5.5.1 The Greek greed for land – a hubris ... 381
    5.5.2 Constantine I continues the Greek expansion policy ... 384

5.6 Bits and pieces ... 385
    5.6.1 An unexpected Turkish proposal speaks volumes ... 385
    5.6.2 A Balkan's expert demonstrates her objective eye for historical coherence ... 385
    5.6.3 The Entente continues to mould a Grand Balkan League ... 386
    5.6.4 Greece continues to work on its increase in power ... 388
        5.6.4.1 Background information (9).
            1. The end of the dynasty in Greece
            2. From Sophie to Sofia ... 390
    5.6.5 Further proof of Macedonia's separate identity ... 390

CONCLUSIONS ... 391

APPENDIX ... 397

Notes ... 397
Bibliography ... 423
Abbreviations ... 428
Technical remarks ... 430
Index of names ... 431
Index of keywords ... 437

Map (with the borders of divided Macedonia after the Balkan Wars 1912/13 according to the Treaties of Paris 1919/20) ... 455
Map (with the borders of the Republic of Macedonia 1991) ... 457

Introductory remarks

1.
In this study, which is based on unpublished documents relating to the Balkan League from the Political Archives of the Auswärtiges Amt, I am presenting proof of the existence of a Macedonian[1] people with its own identity – not a Bulgarian-Macedonian, not a Greek-Macedonian, not a Serbian- or Albanian-Macedonian, but with a separate *Macedonian* identity.
The focus of this investigation will be on the history of Macedonia under Turkish rule in the time span between the Congress of Berlin and the First World War, as it is reflected in reports issued by the Missions of the German Reich in the capitals of the Great Powers and the Balkan States.
After the introduction in chapter 1, the chapters 2 to 4 are devoted to tracing the development leading to the founding of the Balkan League, starting from 1878 and looking at geopolitically separate strands. These are brought together in the comprehensive fifth chapter and then pursued up to the founding of the Balkan League, to the Balkan Wars 1912/13 and partly up to 1914.

The topic of this study is what we can learn from the documents relating to the policy of the neighbouring states as well as the European Powers concerning Macedonia and the Macedonian people's *identity*.
These issues have gained new relevance from the fact that after the historic changes of 1989/90, Macedonia's four neighbours again denied both the Macedonian people and the Macedonian state, i.e. the sovereign Republic of Macedonia established in 1991, their right to exist.

2.
The investigation of the motives and the background of the policy of the Balkan Kingdoms and Great Powers towards Macedonia resulted in an unexpected side-product: it brought out the surprisingly great importance of the Balkan League as an instrument used by the Entente powers in staging the First World War; the Entente had sacrificed Macedonia to the Balkan states in order to prevail upon the latter to join forces with the Entente and thus to participate in the First World War.

3.
In addition to that, a close look at the relations between Germany and Greece in one of their decisive phases sheds some light on the very close connection between the Macedonian question and parts of the history of the German Reich.

4.
The title "The Macedonian Knot" is based on an article published in the evening edition of the Austrian paper "Neue Freie Presse" on November 10th 1902, in which the author "R.L." reproduced a conversation he had had with the president of a Macedonian Liberation Committee, Stojan Mikhailovsky. The latter had embarked on a tour of Europe in order to "inform the continent about the situation in Macedonia". Mikhailovsky quoted a Russian general who had alluded to the well-known expression "Gordian Knot" (ascribed to Alexander the Great on his Asian campaign) in saying of

Macedonia: "The hand that will undo the Macedonian knot will not be found at home, but in Europe." This newspaper cutting was included in a file accompanying report No. 213 of the German Embassy in Vienna issued on 11/11/1902, which can now be found in the Political Archives of the Auswärtiges Amt, the German Ministry of Foreign Affairs, under the registration number R 13623"[2].

In my opinion, this concept provides a good analogy and explanation for the complex nature of the problems affecting the Republic of Macedonia today – and, although it is rooted in a distant, almost mythical, past, it appears to be strikingly modern. Another almost equally apt and justifiable title – an adaptation of the title of Felix Dahn's book "A Battle for Rome" – could have been "A Battle for Macedonia", for that is what it was.

1 Basic Information and Current Situation

1.1 Introduction

1.1.0 Subject and material basis of the study

The present study aims at investigating the motives and background of the policies of the Balkan States and Great Powers towards Macedonia. It is based on the period of history lying between the Congress of Berlin and the First World War that, although 90-125 years ago, still determines the situation in the Balkans, the plight Macedonia is in and the political parameters of Central Europe. Yet the public and the media are not aware of these implications which do not appear to be taken into consideration by national and international political institutions. Knowledge about the *Balkan League* is also largely non-existent, although it played an important role at the time, as the interests of the Balkan states – and of the Entente powers! - were concentrated here like rays of light in a magnifying glass.
Nor is there any more than a vague awareness of the *Congress of Berlin*.
The starting point of my research with regard to the *contents* was precisely this Congress, which took place in 1878 and was the first occasion when the Macedonian Question was raised as a problem. Imanuel Geiss defines the Congress of Berlin as the connecting link between the Congress of Vienna of 1814/15 and the Congress of Versailles in 1919, calling it, with some changes in the points of reference "one of the most important caesurae in the internal and international development of Europe between the French Revolution and the Congress of Vienna on the one hand, the First World War and the 1917/1918 revolutions in Russia, Germany and Austria-Hungary on the other."[3]
The *time* frame of my search for specific references to Macedonian history extends from the events of 1878 to the founding of the Balkan League in 1912, the Balkan Wars in 1912 and 1913 and, in part, the outbreak of the First World War.

As the main source in my attempt to trace developments in Southeast Europe, I used the *original* records of the Political Archives of the Auswärtiges Amt in Bonn (later in Berlin). Some of the material included relates to events in the 1860s and was therefore compiled by the Prussian Ministry of Foreign Affairs of the North German Confederation. The majority of the records analysed reflect the end of the 1878 Congress of Berlin (in the case of Greece some before that), while the latest date back to the Balkan wars, and, in some sections, the First World War.
I have selected and quoted records in so far as they appeared to be relevant to my subject, i.e. Macedonia and the identity of the Macedonians. In a second strand, I look at Greek dynastic politics, as this has had a more conspicuous influence on Macedonia's political fate than in the case of Bulgaria, Serbia and Albania.
On the periphery of this study, yet in close connection with the main subject, there is also some clarification of the effects of Entente policies on staging the First World War.
Only sporadic use could be made of the collection of selected and *printed* political records entitled "Die Große Politik der Europäischen Kabinette: Die diplomatischen Ak-

ten des Auswärtigen Amtes 1871-1914", although this would have saved time and energy. These records were published in more than 50 volumes by a group of scholars (Johannes Lepsius, Albrecht Mendelssohn Bartholdy and Friedrich Thimme) in the 1920s:

Their ambitious goal of correcting the wrong and therefore intolerable accusation that Germany alone was to blame for the outbreak of the First World War as in Art. 231 of the so-called Peace Treaty of Versailles clearly excluded a selection and analysis of records from the complete German Reich material that would have been equally relevant to the chosen topic of this study, i.e. the independent ethnicity of the Macedonian people. It will be shown, however, that the records on the Balkan League and the Balkan Wars would have been well worth looking at in more detail in the context of the aim pursued by the aforementioned scholars pursued at that time. Thus the reports I examined were (with very few exceptions) *unpublished* material.

Any previous doubts as to whether there would be sufficient material on Macedonia from the 19th and early 20th century disappeared during months of research: Of the *2009 large-sized files* kept in the archives of the Auswärtiges Amt on "Matters of the Ottoman Empire", *154 volumes* alone are exclusively devoted to "The Situation in Macedonia" – called by that name as a matter of course. The provisional conclusion must be, therefore, that Macedonia cannot have been so unimportant as its neighbours have been implying for about 100 years.

The main focus during the research work concentrated on groups of files relating to "The Balkan League" and (if falling within the relevant time span) on "The Balkan Wars". In a series of "Background Information" supplements, I also quote details from the records on "The Greek Royal Family" (except No. (8), cf. Section 4.4.1.2.1). In addition to these, numerous records from related fields had to be scanned, in which Macedonia was not in the title but featured in a central role – mostly that of the victim. (All archive volumes are numbered. All numbers are quoted in the footnotes and thus easy to find.)

The files contain reports which were sent by the German Embassies responsible to the Auswärtiges Amt in Berlin and arranged there by date and according to geographical and thematic aspects.[4] Some contain secret papers confiscated from the Serbian Foreign Ministry during the First World War. Furthermore, there are some accounts of reactions in reports and the press resulting from the turbulences following the publication of secret papers by the Trotsky government dating back to Tsarist times.

In order to ensure the greatest possible authenticity, I have quoted the texts in the original.

If any material on this topic is to be considered reliable, it can only be that provided by the reports of the embassies in the Ottoman Empire. In this context, the credibility of German embassies and consulates may even be greater than that of other countries, for, unlike the other powers, the Emperor and the government of the German Reich were then not pursuing any national goals in the Balkans (except in the economic field), so that the reporting ambassadors were less likely to be influenced by political interest and ideology. (For information on the quality and reliability of German diplomatic reports of that time, cf. Hermann Kantorowicz.[5])

1.1.1 The states involved

This approach made it easy to specify those states whose Macedonian policies would have to be examined in terms of their motives and reasons:

1.
The first choice is, of course, the member states of the Balkan League (*Serbia, Bulgaria, Greece* and *Montenegro*) and the participants in the Balkan Wars (i.e. also *Romania*). I have left out Montenegro, as an investigation of its role would not have yielded any new aspects – a fact also mirrored by the relatively small number of reports. The involvement of Macedonia's fourth neighbour, on the other hand, which was not a Balkan League member and did not participate in the Balkan wars, nevertheless had to be at least sketched out, as it has played an increasingly disastrous role in terms of Macedonia's existence in the most recent past and seems to be about to resume doing so in future: *Albania*.

2.
It was also necessary to look at those great powers that had their own interests in the Balkans: Russia, Austria-Hungary and Great Britain. The latter preferred to operate in the background in so far as the Balkans were concerned, but vehemently asserted itself in the area of world politics, including in all matters concerning Constantinople, the Bosporus and Dardanelles – and thus the Ottoman Empire – as well as its traditional balance-of-power policy on the continent. The other three great powers, on the other hand – i.e. Germany, France and Italy – have only been considered briefly, as the German Reich never developed any territorial interest in the Ottoman Empire, while France and Italy only acquired parts of Turkish territory outside Europe.

3.
Central importance is of course to be given to the Ottoman Empire, which played the role of conqueror and colonial power for 300 years, but kept retreating during its last 250 years on the European continent, from the second unsuccessful siege of Vienna in 1683 to the very last years, i.e. the two Balkan Wars in 1912/13. Turkey, with only a shadow of its once imposing command of an enormous empire left, was only kept from complete expulsion from Europe by the great powers' disagreements over their claims with regard to the Straits. Nevertheless, the cruelty of its oppressive and exploitative rule was feared by its Christian subjects to the last.

The preservation of Turkey's independence (and partial territorial integrity) and particularly its continuing presence in Europe – conceived and mostly realized by Great Britain – may have prevented a solution to the Balkan and Middle East question that was, in British eyes, likely to influence the European balance of power, but it did so at a high price:

The Balkan peoples struggling for their national liberation lost invaluable decades in achieving their autonomy or independence. Some were nevertheless able to attain sovereignty, though not until the 20th century. Others became the victim of the Balkan states' territorial greed and the specific interests pursued by Great Britain, France and Russia, as well as to some extent Austria and Germany, and were completely submerged in the torrent of history.

1.1.2 The Balkan League

1). The Balkan League is almost forgotten today, so that the motives behind its establishment are not common knowledge any more. Its objectives and actual consequences were not visibly taken into consideration by European and international political institutions during the last decade, which has been of the utmost importance to the Balkans. This is to be regretted, as knowledge of this background would have provided a more objective basis for the decisions of European cabinets, the EU commission and the United Nations with regard to sovereign Macedonia after 1991 and lifted them out of the murky waters of lobbying and half-truth. An awareness of the past deliberations and actions of Macedonia's neighbours is invaluable in assessing their policies towards Macedonia today and since the disintegration of Yugoslavia, given that, as was mentioned before, the consequences of the Balkan League, particularly the resulting Balkan Wars of 1912 and 1913, have in many ways affected and continue to affect the whole Balkans and especially Macedonia until the present day.

The records also offer some plausible explanations for the interest-governed but unjustified reservations of the neighbouring states towards the Republic of Macedonia when it emerged from the remains of Yugoslavia in 1991.

2). We can read in any standard history book that the Balkan League was established on March 3rd 1912 with a view to *"a division of Macedonia"*.[6] Elsewhere, Herzfeld states that:

> Notwithstanding their many differences, this group of states "again and again joins in a common hope of being able to become Turkey's and Austria-Hungary's heirs in the near future."[7]
>
> One has to look very closely in order to discern the portentous meaning of this statement in its full dimensions: for it becomes clear from this text that the Balkan states were intending to also become *"Austria-Hungary's heirs"*!

Were they going to wage this war - without which there would certainly be no such legacy - against the then Great Power of the Habsburg Dual Monarchy that was at least respected, if not feared even by the other European Great Powers, all alone? This additional aspect gives the Balkan League a dimension which one would not have ascribed to it from its name and its original aim, i.e. that of inheriting Turkey's legacy.

This also clarifies what the "Wiener Sonn- und Montagszeitung" meant by stating five weeks into the First Balkan War, when the military struggle had almost been decided:

> "In the past" the discussion had been about "the Balkan states joining forces in order to protect themselves from external attacks, but at present it seems that the origin of the unrest affecting all of Europe is sought in the Balkan states themselves."[8]

3). At that time, awareness of the Balkan League was so common that the topic was included in various works of reference:

> "The aim of the B[alkan League] was to share out Turkey's European possessions."[9] And: "...the states allied in the Balkan League – Montenegro, Bulgaria, Serbia and Greece – declared war on Turkey, aiming to divide Turkish Macedonia among themselves."[10]

The comparison with the special literature in the field of history (see above: Herzfeld) shows that the encyclopaedia defined the aims of the Balkan League too narrowly with regard to one highly important aspect: i.e. its threat to Austria-Hungary.

4). Several parameters determined the establishment of the Balkan League itself. These were themselves subject to rapid and repeated changes, so that at first we can only see a confusion of many different directions and movements. The complex relations between the Balkan states led to numerous possible combinations of the five

Balkan principalities and kingdoms that were all considered as possible participants. In the planning phase, the choice of participants changed continuously and was not free of surprises, as even the participation of Turkey was discussed, although this could be nothing but a sham regarding the alliance's main objective (at least from the Balkan states' perspective). It was only when the objectives of the Balkan League were extended as part of the *Entente strategy* that the attempt to include Turkey in the phalanx of Balkan states gained its full threatening potential for Germany and Austria.

Things are further complicated as a result of the great powers' interests and policies towards their respective protégés and adversaries, also grouped differently over time, as well mutual relations, whether adversarial or friendly, between the great powers themselves. Among these, the Ottoman Empire was considered of greatest importance – not because it was still regarded and treated as a great power although it had lost that status a long time ago, but because it was the object of the ambitions of all the states involved (except Germany), which were directed at the former European part of Turkey and particularly to that strategically unique point, the Golden Horn of Constantinople.

The establishment of the Balkan League had, in spite of the original clarity of its objectives, been dragging on for decades, but suddenly it was completed surprisingly fast at the beginning of the 20th century. After 1904 and 1907 and particularly after the Anglo-Russian meeting in Reval in 1908, the Balkan League became an instrument of the "global European" interests of the *Entente*, especially Britain (and France), which were directed against the German Reich.

This makes the Balkan League an entity of historic significance.

Finally, the zeitgeist of imperialism exerted its obvious and fateful but clearly inevitable influence. The latter seems to be the basis for the outstanding importance of this historical movement. Theodor Schieder describes imperialism as an "enormous expansion movement of the European powers."[11]

Thus, in the observer's eye the Balkans appear as a side stage on which the small Balkan states - as if infected by the imperial movement of the great powers - pounced like birds of prey on the last Christian peoples remaining under Ottoman rule in order to annex their land (following the example of their great 'models' in Africa, Asia and America).

5). Although the Balkan League was only established in 1912 – initially only between Bulgaria and Serbia, and even then not until Russia gave encouragement and guaranteed support and protection in the event of an Austrian attack – the first reference in the records I checked dates back to 1879, i.e. soon after the Russian-Turkish war of 1877 and after the San Stefano peace and the 1878 Congress of Berlin. Thus, the planning and negotiation phase lasted more than 30 years – in statistical terms, longer than a generation. For an alliance that seemed, in spite of its serious consequences, of limited importance, this is an unusually long time of preparation with an astonishingly short time of realisation. It will have to be demonstrated why.

It could have been expected that the newly emerging states in the Balkans which, like Macedonia, had suffered from Turkish rule for centuries, would direct all their efforts towards enjoying their independence and freedom, consolidating their political structures and maybe increasing the prosperity of their populations. However, the desire for territorial expansion turned out to be the first and foremost motive of all their political efforts. Therefore, it was certainly not the longing for peace that ruled the cabinets of the Balkan states. As soon as they regained their breath after the liberation, the governments of these states immediately turned to plans of expansion. The object of these "great power" dreams were the last Turkish territories with a Christian population on European soil – i.e. precisely those provinces that had been given back to the Ottoman Empire by the Congress of Berlin after the modifications of the preliminary peace of San Stefano. As was mentioned before, these include Thrace, Epirus and, with the greatest territory and thus often mentioned as pars pro toto, Macedonia.

1.1.3 Working Objective

Thus, every step undertaken by any of Macedonia's neighbour states towards establishing the Balkan League needs to be given full attention.

Moreover, it will be necessary to portray and analyse the politics, as shown by the records, of all the states listed above (in 1.1.1) during the relevant time span. Given that the three neighbouring states involved (Serbia, Bulgaria and Greece) have, ever since they first voiced their claims to Macedonia, only allowed subjective versions of Macedonian history which were governed by their interests and have systematically suppressed or denied all facts of *authentic* Macedonian history, and given that the Great Powers then involved did not prevent the continuous falsifications of the past 90 years energetically enough, the world began to become accustomed to the aggressor's version, being distracted by other events of world politics, such as the First and Second World War, the Cold War and the changes of 1989/90. This makes it necessary to thoroughly investigate the policies of each of the states involved, as the records on any of those states might contain information on questions of Macedonian identity.

Anyone denying the facts of history as steadfastly as Macedonia's neighbouring states do even today will certainly continue to defame, evade and reject any conclusions deriving from the description of only one Balkan state, e.g. Bulgaria, or only one great power, e.g. Austria. It is therefore crucial to demonstrate in a comprehensive way that Macedonia was a not just regionally, but internationally known independent territory (albeit still occupied by Turkey), and that the Macedonians were – and still are – an independent people with a discernible identity of their own.

Only an exhaustive description of the motives and background of all the Balkan states and great powers involved, leaving no gaps and representing the information contained in the records, will provide a complete picture – so that the facts, which only historians and the few Balkans specialists have come to regard as certain, finally gain acceptance. Yet, with few exceptions, there are no spectacular revelations at hand. A convincing overall impression can only emerge from the sum of many particular insights, which will seem like by-products at times, but will eventually add up to a mosaic.

Once more it must be stressed that a policy that has thus solidified over decades, even for longer than a century, cannot be moved by means of individual arguments. Instead, it will be necessary to prove by a number of everyday, ordinary indications that Macedonia was ousted from the normality of its regional existence, which had remained undisputed until the Congress of Berlin and the First Balkan War, and that it was

gradually abolished after the Ilinden uprising, especially after the establishment of the Balkan League, and most radically after the end of the Balkan Wars.
Without the continuation of such aggressive power politics on the part of the neighbouring states, the Macedonians would be able to live in a normal, average – even if "delayed" (and diminished) – state at least now, in the 21st century, like all the other residents of the Balkans.

1.2 Basic information on Macedonia

Knowledge about Macedonia in the West has proved to be very fragmentary. Therefore I shall attempt to give a general overview here:

1.2.0 History

1.2.0.1 The ancient Macedonians

The ancient Macedonians are held to be one of the oldest peoples in Southeast Europe. The ancient Greeks considered them to be barbarians because they did not speak Greek, and excluded them from the Olympic Games for a long time (cf. Prof. Rose who mentions 476 BC as the date of their first participation, loc. cit., p.7). Since Philip II came to power in 359 BC, Greece was increasingly forced into submission. After King Philip had inflicted a crushing defeat on the Greeks near Chaironeia in 338, he consolidated "Macedonian hegemony" in the Corinthian Alliance.[12] Then, after Alexander had destroyed Thebes at the start of his Persian campaign, the Macedonian kings increasingly influenced Greece's destiny. (The high repute enjoyed by this commander is more than overshadowed if one also recalls the other, i.e. the Persians' perspective: The latter had given Alexander the epithet "the Accursed".[13] In his book "Mensa Regis", classical historian Konrad Vössing completely does away with any romantic transfiguration of this unrestrained megalomaniac. ...)

Even the film director, Oliver Stone, in his historical epic on Alexander the Great, tells us that the Macedonian philosopher Aristotle "patiently but unsuccessfully attempted ... to teach Alexander the great virtue of moderation", as Dieter Bartetzko wrote in his report made after the excavation of the bust of Aristotle near the Acropolis in Athens (see Frankfurter Allgemeine Zeitung (FAZ), 1.11.2006, p.42)

The Greek attempt at breaking free after Alexander's death in 323 failed in the Lamian war in 323/322: Athens was occupied by Macedonian troops. Freedom was not gained until 100 years later (225), and then only for a short time, as King Antiginos II Gonatas managed to establish another Hellenic alliance under Macedonian hegemony in 224.

There is no doubt that Macedonia was subject to the influence of Hellenism – which was strengthened by the fact of Macedonian hegemony over Greece – and that Alexander the Great spread Hellenism himself. However, the complete Mediterranean, even the whole of Europe and many other countries were influenced by Hellenism, which was spread by the Roman Empire [like Greece, a colonial and slave-owning society]. After the death of Alexander, Alexandria, ruled by the Macedonian Ptolemaeans, also continued to be a cultural centre of the Hellenic era for 300 years, until Egypt, the last big Hellenistic state, was annexed by Rome in 30 BC after the death of

Cleopatra VII. (Thus, the Ptolemaean Cleopatra was the last successor of the Macedonian *diadochoi* on the throne of the Pharaohs.)

But does this mean that Egypt, Persia and Italy were Greek, for example? Or that Egypt, Persia, India and Syria became Macedonian?

Ivan Minev sums up the potential misunderstanding as follows:

> "We should not confuse Hellenism, which had spread across the known world (including Macedonia) after Alexander's campaigns, with Greek ethnicity."[14]

Only the three Roman wars against Macedonia, starting in 215, ended the existence of the Macedonian state, and of its hegemony over Greece, with the battle of Pydna in 168 BC.

After a last uprising against the Romans by Andriskos in 148 BC, Macedonia became a Roman province. "Greece, viewed as an appendage to the province of Macedonia at first, was completely dominated by the Romans."[15] Under Diocletian at the latest (AD 284-305), Macedonia was divided into the administrative districts of Macedonia Prima and Macedonia Secunda.

When the empire fell apart in 395 (and also after the Slavs settled in the area), Macedonia remained part of the Eastern Roman Empire, later Byzantium.

Around 400 AD, the Romans had to end their 600-year exploitation of their colonies and withdraw their occupying forces from Europe, North Africa, Asia Minor and also from the Balkans, in order to return to Italy and defend their own borders against the Germanic tribes.

1.2.0.2 The Slavs

During the migration of peoples, the Slavs moved west along with the (Turkic-speaking) Huns. The latter (and also their Ostrogoth and Gepid allies) were defeated in 451 by a Roman-Frankish-Visigothic army on the Catalaunian fields. Georg Stadtmüller has pointed out that the connection between the Slavs and the Huns must have been a close one, given that the Slav expression "strava" has been historically associated with Attila's funeral. (loc. cit., p.70, 74 and 90).

> "During the 5th century [...] the Slavs moved across the Hungarian plains and Moldova towards the South." (Trautmann, loc. cit., p.23)

In the 6th and 7th centuries, the Slavs overran South-Eastern Europe, where they are still living today. Stadtmüller mentions several times that there were some incursions much earlier, but a continuous intrusion of Slavs in the Balkans

> "is not definitely supported by Byzantine sources for any time earlier than the 6th century; and they arrived there at different times and by different routes."[16]
>
> "Among other things, these circumstances are taken to explain the differences between the modern Slavic languages."[17] (Steinke)

For the Balkan Peninsula

> "the first directly transmitted and undisputed data [...] go back to the beginning of the 6th century. The reports by Procopius (fl. ca. 550), Agathias (died 582) and Jordandes (floruit 550) [...] are good sources of information on the Danubian Slavs in the 6th and 7th centuries."
> "Around 580, after invasions of Greece and Thrace, (this is where) permanent Slavic settlement (began)..." "One of the main streams of Slavic colonisation poured [...] into Macedonia, whose population is mainly Slavic now, [and] turned south towards Greece." (Trautmann, ibid.).

The Slavs also settled on the Peloponnese and advanced as far as Anatolia and Crete. By 650, the complete Balkan peninsula, with the exception of a few stretches of coast and mountain hide-outs, was inhabited by Slavic farmers.[16]

These Slavs had had as little ethnically relevant contacts with the ancient Macedonians as with the Romans and Greeks – naturally, however, these contacts occurred after the migration of peoples. Cf. 2.2.0 and 2.5.0.

The settlement of Slavs in Southeast Europe constitutes a new, separate phase in the history of this region. The migration of peoples caused a complete ethnic renewal in the Balkans, as indeed in all of Europe, but the autochthonous ancient Macedonian population was not wiped out in its course. This did neither happen during Roman or during Turkish rule. The arrival of the Slavs, notwithstanding their many ethnic differences, led to the "emergence of a multiethnic population."[18] Thus it is not an unlikely assumption that the Slavic settlers took over the name "Macedonia" because the Slavs had assimilated the autochthonous Macedonians in the same way as they would later assimilate the Turkic Bulgars in the east of the Balkans – and adopted their names in both cases. However, other Slavic peoples gave their new places of settlement the names of their own tribes – as in the case of the Croats, Slovenes and Serbs.

Names of places and regions were strongly affected by the new language. As in the centuries of Roman domination, almost all the places in Southeast Europe lost their old names as a consequence of the settlement of Slavs during the migration of peoples.

> "Byzantine authors were already lamenting the disappearance of Greek names and their replacement by Slavic ones."[19] (In Greece!)

1.2.0.3 The First Bulgarian Empire and the first Macedonian state

Towards the end of the 10th century there was a period that became very important for Macedonia in spite of its short duration (approximately 40 years) compared with the rest of the Christian era: the Bulgarian Tsar Presjan conquered (Central) Macedonia around 845. After the decline of the First Bulgarian Empire in 971, this western part of Bulgaria, i.e. Macedonia, gained political independence under Prince Samuel after insurrections against the Bulgarians from 969 and against Byzantium from 976 onwards. It is of particular importance that Samuel was crowned by the pope in Rome; at the same time, the Macedonian church was given the status of an archdiocese. During his reign, Samuel temporarily expanded the mediaeval Macedonian state so as to reach the Sava and Danube in the North, the Corinthian Gulf in the South and the Adriatic in the West.[20]

> Following the bad example of its neighbours, Macedonia should lay claim to these regions as a test. It would be interesting to witness the outcry in the countries concerned, the same ones that today refer to similar historical events in the dim and distant past as a matter of course in attempts to substantiate the same kinds of ridiculous claims.

Günter Prinzing, on the other hand, recommends

> "avoiding the basically anachronistic term 'Macedonian Empire' because it too easily obscures its Bulgarian roots", as "Samuel himself, as well as his successors, always saw themselves within the tradition of the Bulgarian state".[21]

Prof. Prinzing has, however, with reference to the standard work "Geschichte des byzantinischen Staates" (Munich 1963), conceded that the opposite view could also be upheld, pointing out that in the book in question

> "there were several mentions of a 'Macedonian empire' or 'Macedonia' in connection with Samuel's reign", although its author, G. Ostrogorsky, had a differentiated view and "initially strongly emphasised the Bulgarian tradition which Samuel had consciously followed, then stating, however: 'In reality, his Macedonian empire was essentially different from the previous Bulgarian one. Both in its components and in its character, it was a new and peculiar con-

struct. Its centre had moved far towards the West and South, and Macedonia, a peripheral area of the old empire of the Bulgars, formed its very nucleus.'"(l. c.)

Macedonian independence ended when the Byzantines defeated Samuel and his successors in 1014. The capital Ohrid did not return to Byzantium until 1018.

"After the reestablishment of Byzantine rule in 1018, the Macedonians rebelled against it a number of times (1040/41, 1072/73)."[22] "For some time (until the Asenid rebellion in 1186), Bulgaria was no more."[21]

Between their emergence in the Balkans in the 7th century and the 9th century, the Turk-Tatar Bulgarians had merged into the Slavic population. (Cf. the historical chapters on Bulgaria and Greece below.) It makes little sense to speculate whether and how much Tatar/Turkic blood Tsar Samuel may have had at the end of the 10th century; what matters is the historically proven fact that he was king over the Macedonians in the "West Bulgarian" or "Macedonian" empire from 969/971 (or 976) to 1014/1018.[22] Consequently, during that time the Macedonians lived in *their own* state, which had all the necessary attributes of a state in accordance with modern international law: *a people, a territory and state authority.*

1.2.0.4 The autocephalous Macedonian church

In addition, the Macedonians also had an institution which was to prove to be of inestimable importance for their future and their survival even down to the present day: their independent Orthodox church.

The Autocephalous Macedonian Church today claims its role as

"a national ecclesiastical variant of the archdiocese Bulgaria/Ohrid as its successor institution." This should raise no objections as the Macedonian Orthodox Church at the very outset had explicitly established (its) sphere of influence ... as covering the territory of the [Republic of] Macedonia and had thus put a stop to any expansionist tendencies that might have arisen from a consideration of the historical borders of the [geographically far more extensive] Ohrid archdiocese."[23]

"After the establishment of Bulgarian rule in the region in 842, Ahrida/Ohrid is first mentioned as an archbishopric in the records of the 8th Ecumenical Council (Constantinople 869/70 and 879/880). ... At the turn of the 10th to the 11th century, Ohrid, where Samuel also had his residence, became the seat of the autocephalous Bulgarian archbishop in the empire of Tsar Samuel."[24] "The truly autocephalous nature of this church is repeatedly supported by the sources and it is an unfailing indication that since 1020, the archbishops of Bulgaria (i.e. of Ohrid) have always been appointed by the tsar and not by the Patriarch of Constantinople, for the same procedure was used in the succession of the equally autocephalous archbishops of Cyprus."[25]

Nevertheless, Prinzing suggests that the Macedonian Orthodox Church should avoid the danger of a prejudiced and false view of history, in order to

"be able to look at events in mediaeval history uninfluenced by the categories of nationalist thought." Prinzing goes on to state that "strictly speaking, there never was an archdiocese Ohrid, but only an archdiocese 'Bulgaria' located in Ohrid."

Yet even here he pragmatically applies the prescriptive law of precedent, continuing:

"It has none the less become customary (even among specialists) to refer to the archbishopric of Ohrid, as the use of the term 'Bulgaria' can easily lead to a confusion with the church in late mediaeval Bulgaria, the Asenid kingdom that had its own Patriarch of Tarnovo from 1235."[26]

As for the fundamental necessity of an independent Macedonian Orthodox Church in the Republic of Macedonia today, this has been shown by Archbishop Michael to be essential from a political point of view, too. Prof. Oschlies quotes the 80-year-old church dignitary as follows:

"In former times, the national churches of Bulgaria, Greece and Serbia were exponents of a Greater Serbia, a Greater Bulgaria and a Greater Greece in Macedonia, and Macedonia needs its own church 'if only to protect us from the megalomania (*megalomanstvo*) and chauvinism of our neighbouring peoples.'"[27]

Starting from 1020, the autocephalous Macedonian church retained its independence for almost 750 years, until the Greeks succeeded in persuading Sultan Mustafa to disband the archbishopric of Ohrid in 1767. Until then, the autocephalous status that had been granted this archbishopric by the Byzantine Emperor Basileios II had, as Prof. Döpmann points out, enabled the Macedonians

"to remain independent to a great extent even while belonging to the 2nd Bulgarian kingdom and the Serbian kingdom under Tsar Dušan.[28] But now "the foreign political rule exercised by the Sultan ... was complemented by a spiritual one exercised by the Greek Patriarch of Constantinople."[29]

On account of this interruption of their tradition on the part of Greek orthodoxy "the Macedonians lost the last space ... in which they ... could cultivate (their) cultural independence." From among the many consequences of this, only one aspect will be mentioned here:

"After the independence of the archbishopric of Ohrid had been abolished by the Sublime Porte and after the subsequent cleansing of the church libraries and archives by the new church leadership, Macedonian traditions could only survive in oral form, handed down as folklore in the form of songs and legends." ... "It is very impressive and the best proof of Macedonian ethnicity that the Macedonians succeeded in preserving an independent identity during these two centuries by cultivating folklore, songs and stories within their families."[30]

It appears that the present Greek government is taking up these old events in its attempt to rid itself of the unloved name of the Republic of Macedonia. Athens is said to be prepared to recognise the autocephalous status of the Macedonian Orthodox Church. In return, Greece allegedly suggests that the name of the Macedonian church be modelled on that of the old archbishopric of Ohrid. The next step would then be the adjustment of the name of the whole republic to that of the historic name of the archbishopric. Thus the name "Macedonia", a feature so crucial to Macedonian identity, would now, after almost 1500 years, be irrevocably lost. This appears precisely to be the goal pursued by Greece, which could then present the southern part of Macedonia it had annexed in 1912/13, and called "North Greece" until ca.1985, as the only successor for ancient 'Makedon' and thus the fiction of an ancient Macedonia that had always been Greek could be sold to the world as reality – a sort of *"réalité à la grecque"*.

Almost exactly 100 years after the abolition of the archbishopric of Ohrid in 1767, a new development initially caused the Macedonians to sigh with relief but turned out to have a disadvantageous effect:

In 1870, the Sultan granted the Bulgarians his permission to establish an autocephalous Bulgarian-Orthodox church, the Exarchate. Later the Sultan boasted about having driven a wedge between Bulgaria and Greece that would have a long-term effect. That was certainly correct; but initially this incriminated exclusively the Macedonians: not only in terms of language and identity, but also almost of the very existence of the whole people.

Initially, the Macedonians were inclined to view the Exarchate as an unhoped-for chance to evade the assimilation pressure of the hated Greek-Orthodox church in Constantinople. Thus they sought the supposedly protective wing of the Bulgarian national church without suspecting that they were jumping out of the frying pan into the fire. The Bulgarians, who so far had had no opportunity of pursuing the same assimilation policies in Macedonia as the Greeks, now presented those who had fled from the Greeks into the Bulgarians' arms with the conclusion that Macedonians who were falling back on the help of the Bulgarian church could really only be *Bulgarians*, for otherwise they would have remained under the "protection" of the Greek patriarchate. (Cf. Ch. 2.2.0, No.6)

In addition to that, the Sultan had accompanied his decree by an insidious order with grievous consequences for the future of Macedonia:

> "At the time when the Bulgarian national church was newly established, he determined that the two Orthodox confessions that would now be competing, i.e. the Greek Patriarchate and the Bulgarian Exarchate, should be allowed to establish new parishes in Macedonia if they succeeded in winning a two-thirds majority."[31]

This means that "the starting signal for the battle for Macedonia" was fired as early as 1870 – and not in 1876 or 1878. This considerably substantiates Prof. Adanir's hypothesis that the *Macedonian question* started with the establishment of the Exarchate.

> Soon "the region was strewn with bands of Greek and Bulgarian mercenaries" who "blackmailed whole villages at a time" into taking sides with one of the nations ... This experience of suffering on account of nationalistically motivated terror against the civilian population has left its mark on Macedonian identity in a way still visible today."[31]

However, as Christian Voss goes on to point out, the Macedonians are resistant to such attempts at changing their national identity. Their consciousness of an identity of their own is

> "nourished by the contradictoriness, ruthlessness and claims to exclusiveness spread by Serbian, Bulgarian, Greek and Romanian propaganda. Their knowledge of the autochthonous character of their people creates enough of an identity, strengthened by collective suffering."[32]

1.2.0.5 The Ottomans

When the Ottoman Turks (who had themselves only just survived the attack of the Mongolians in Anatolia) first set foot on European soil in 1354, their numerous victories brought them as far as Vienna, subjugating all the peoples up to the Ukraine, the Crimea and the Kuban.

Jacob Burckhardt, after discussing the appalling atrocities perpetrated by the Mongols under Tamerlane on their rampage westwards, makes an interesting contribution to this by drawing a "global" conclusion. "Yet, ... [Tamerlane] ... may have saved Europe from the Ottomans. ... The Ottomans ..., however dreadful they may have been for Europe, no longer attained that peak of their strength which Bajazeth I represented before the battle of Ankara". (loc. cit., p. 318) Burckhardt visualised how terrible the fate of Europe would have been without Tamerlane's influence on the Ottomans ...

It was not until the end of the 17th century that the Ottomans were forced to slowly retreat. (For more information on this, cf. ch. 3.)

At that time, Macedonia was part of the Turkish province of Rumelia. All its revolts had failed, e.g. the four-year insurrection beginning 1465 near Dolni Debar or the peasant revolt in Mariovo and Prilep in 1565, or indeed the famous Karpoš rebellion of 1689/90, whose end was equally tragic.

1.2.0.6 Early resistance to the Macedonian pursuit of autonomy

Until the last quarter of the 19th century, the battle lines between the rebellious peoples of the Balkans and the Ottoman occupation were drawn very clearly. The former enjoyed the sympathy, and often the material support, of the Russian Orthodox Church and the Tsar. In the case of the Macedonians, however, their attempts to achieve autonomy were affected by uncertainties and unexplained counter-currents: they experienced resistance without being able to define its origin.

After revolts in the summer of 1875, first in Herzegovina and then in Bosnia, this movement also spread to Bulgaria in 1876. Both Theodor Schieder[33] and Imanuel Geiss[34] point out that the riots spread not only to Bulgaria but also to Macedonia, where a revolt broke out on 7 May 1876 (19 May 1876) near Raslovec (Raslovci).

> [In documents of that time, next to the dates conforming to the Gregorian calendar, there are often the dates (differing by 12 days) of the Julian calendar, which was used in Orthodox countries until the October Revolution – in the calendar of religious festive days, e.g. in Macedonia, it is still used today.]

This revolt is especially noteworthy in that there were unusual events taking place elsewhere which would turn out to be of even greater and more far-reaching importance for the future of Macedonia than the revolt itself:

The Macedonian leader of the revolt, Berovski, who had followed the example of many Slavic/Christian rebels before him and had gone to St.Petersburg to ask for help, was *not even received* !

> In all the recorded material, this is the first sign that Macedonia was treated differently by Russia than all previous Orthodox (and Slavic) petitioners.

From this, we can only conclude, *that already then, Russia had clearly abandoned Macedonia in favour of one of its other protégé countries (Bulgaria or Greece)!*

Thereafter, if Macedonia wanted to gain its independence it thus not only had to fight the Turks but also to overcome this invisible resistance.

This stance of denial taken by the Russian leadership towards an Orthodox Christian and Slavic people that was fighting for its freedom and independence from Turkish rule in the same way as other Balkan peoples - and that thus seemed to be predestined to receive Russian help - was extremely unusual and, falling into a decisive phase of the Macedonian fight for liberation, amounted to a historical caesura in the political development of Macedonia.

Jutta de Jong thinks the following considerations may have been at the root of this strange stance:

> "An autonomous Macedonia could have prevented the Russians in their role as protectors of the Bulgarian claims to Macedonia from gaining access to the Mediterranean."[35]

Hence an autonomous or even independent Macedonia would have been a greater hindrance to Russian plans for the Mediterranean than a Macedonian province as part of the (then) grateful and thus well-disposed Bulgaria.

This is conceivable, but it would have been short-sighted – and this is something the Tsar and Russian governments in general were never accused of. Firstly, such political behaviour would have been incompatible with the Russian religious and pan-Slavic sense of mission during the past centuries. Rather, the Russians could be expected to be explicitly *in favour* of an autonomous Macedonia. For, if St. Petersburg was trusting Bulgaria, it could equally look forward to the gratitude of the Macedonians. At the same time, the Tsar would not be creating a Bulgaria which was too powerful.

However, this combination is shown to be completely improbable by the following argument:

> "The Habsburgs too would have had to renounce their hopes for a land-based access to the Aegean." (loc.cit.) Indeed, they would have!

And would St. Petersburg attempt to stop this Austrian thrust towards Saloniki by denying autonomy to Macedonia? On the contrary: If Russia had really taken this into consideration (and it is a historically proven fact that it actually did), Petersburg should have supported Berovski and the Macedonians most definitely and without hesitation by granting or *even imposing* autonomy, in order to put a stop to Austrian expansion in the Balkans (which was beginning to show on account of the imminent occupation of Bosnia), - and at the same time make a friend of Macedonia.

> However, as Russia did not adhere to its traditional political line, there must have been special reasons for such a radical deviation. These may have been the following:

While the princes of Serbia and Bulgaria were not crowned kings until 1882 and 1908 respectively, Greece had belonged to the illustrious circle of European monarchies since 1832. Otto of Bavaria (1833-62) was succeeded by Prince William of Denmark as George I (1863-1913) on the Greek throne. As democracy can only be spoken of in a very qualified sense with regard to Europe at that time, the influence of the dynasties with their many connections throughout Europe still carried great weight. At the end of the 19th century, it was not only among the great powers that imperialism prevailed; the leaders of the Balkan states were likewise being seduced by visions of becoming Great Powers. In Greece, both the political leadership and the church were following the dream of the Greater Greece of the "Megale Idea". In consequence, it would have been both the ambition and the interest of the princes who had been brought in from foreign lands to prove themselves to be useful and, if possible, even popular kings of the subjects who paid for their allowances. So, what could have been more obvious than striving for the great and commonly approved goal of expansion, i.e. enlargement of power based on enlargement of territory, by using one's own familial connections, which could help effectively but silently in the background to achieve this goal. Thus it was made easy for the aristocratic families, related as they were by marriage or blood, to go on with their centuries-old game of appropriating wholly foreign peoples - and with them their territories - by marriage or by passing them on to each other.

The remaining European Christian lands under Islamic rule appeared to be just the right objects for such dynastic ambitions.

In order to keep its options open with regard to Macedonia, Thrace and Northern Epirus, Greece could have tried to nip the known Macedonian efforts at attaining autonomy in the bud. This could have been easily achieved by way of the Tsar's familial relations to the Greek king.

> *Thus, denial of Russian help to the Macedonian Berovski could have been a consequence of a Greek-Russian agreement.*

It will therefore be important to check the documents for evidence of such an agreement.

> As the ambassadors and foreign envoys were mostly aristocrats themselves, sometimes of high lineage and often from the same countries as the royal families of the Balkan states, their good relations with the courts made it easy for them to report in an unadorned way even about such occurrences in aristocratic circles that would otherwise hardly come to the knowledge of the Auswärtiges Amt unfiltered. (This tradition has proved very advantageous in dealing with this topic.)

1.2.0.7 The emergence of the Macedonian question

The last war Russia waged on the Ottoman Empire (1877-78), which led to the Congress of Berlin, was sparked off by Bulgaria, which Russia had chosen as its protégé as well as its springboard.

During the Congress, Serbian, Romanian and Montenegrin independence was recognised, while Bulgaria at least gained its status of autonomy. Bosnia and Herzegovina fell under Austrian occupation and administration. (Albania and Epirus had remained part of the Ottoman Empire anyway.) Macedonia and Thrace, however, were given back to Turkey at the instigation of the English and the Austrians, although they had been liberated initially.

This eventually led to the *Macedonian* question.

(For the influence of the Bulgarian Exarchate on the Macedonian question in 1870/72, see Section 1.2.0.4.)

However, something else also emerged: Victor Meier points out that the return of Macedonia to Turkey after the Congress of Berlin

> "led to a separate political fate and thus a specific set of interests". This resulted in "a political identity. All the inhabitants of Macedonia, with the exception of the Turks, wanted at least autonomy."[36]

The overall impression this author gains from the records and the literature seems to be that the Macedonians had developed a distinct cultural and ethnic identity even before then; this is the only explanation for the many revolts against the Turks in the preceding centuries. I fully agree with Meier though that the discrimination against Macedonia perpetrated by the Congress of Berlin must have led to a caesura in Macedonian history and thus to a separate development distinct from that of the other Balkan states, which most probably strengthened Macedonian ethnic identification eventually.

As a token of the further development of this identity, another Macedonian revolt, which broke out near Kresna on October $5^{th}/17^{th}$ 1878 can be mentioned, because Turkey, having committed itself to introducing reforms and some steps towards autonomy for Macedonia in Art. 23 of the Treaty of Berlin, was once again failing to meet its obligations. (Giorgi Stojčevski also mentions the revolt near Razlog on 8th November 1878 in the same context.[37]) The insurrection continued until 6th June 1879 but had to be given up as the foreign (i.e. Russian) support hoped for had not been given.

The dice had long been cast against Macedonia.

Here it has to be given an additional explanation of Art. 23 of the Treaty of Berlin: *Section 1* of this article concerns a regulation issued 10 years before for Crete, with the aim of improving the status of this island and its population; it ran as follows:

> "The Sublime Porte undertakes scrupulously to apply in the Island of Crete the Organic Law of 1868..."[38]

This law of 1868 regulated Cretan self-government. The fact that the new text had to repeat an old regulation proves that in the meantime Turkey had – as always – done nothing at all to fulfil the obligation it had once taken on to actually implement the regulation.

Section 2 of Art. 23 then explicitly elaborates on the original law:

> "Similar laws adapted to local requirements ... shall also be introduced into the other parts of Turkey in Europe for which no special organisation has been provided by the present treaty."[38]

The "other parts" included Macedonia and Thrace.

Had the dynastic intrigues in the background already prepared the ground for using the vague [inaccurate] expression "other parts" in order to prevent these two names from even being mentioned, so that no thought of their autonomy could arise?

In Article 15 of the preliminary peace treaty (the antecedent to Article 23), which Russia had negotiated with the Ottoman Empire in San Stefano, two other regions of European Turkey (i.e. two of the "other parts") had been explicitly listed, namely (Southern) Epirus and Thessalia.[39] In the Treaty of Berlin, however, the names were left out because Athens wanted to reserve these regions for itself.

As Richard von Mach, a contemporary observer, wrote at a later stage (his essay was apparently sent to the Auswärtiges Amt directly and not as an attachment of a report), the purpose of the regulation quoted was to arrive at a compromise allowing the Christians in the last Turkish dominions on European soil better conditions of life and development without wholly undermining the Sultan's position of power. This requirement had "theoretically been met by the triple division of Greater Bulgaria", but had sown the seeds of further complications:

1) The establishment of the new and independent but still tributary Bulgarian Principality had been placed "under European guarantee". Thus it was a natural development that Bulgaria should seek full sovereignty and strive to shake off its tribute obligations. On the basis of its previous experience, this was quite clear to the Sublime Porte without it being able to do very much to prevent it.

2) The autonomous province of East Rumelia was also controlled by "European Commissions"; "their troops were commanded by Russians."(!) Thus "the incorporation of this province into Bulgaria ... in 1885 took place without permanently impairing relations with the Porte"[40]

3) The future of the third part of this Greater Bulgaria which had been liberated by Russia, established officially on 3rd March 1878 in San Stefano and now divided in Berlin in June/July, i.e. the future of Thrace and Macedonia, both restored to Turkey, was organised quite differently.

"Here, no European commission was delegated to work out all the details of the new order, as in East Rumelia. This is a remarkable, and, considering the Turkish character, an incomprehensible flaw of the Peace of Berlin not to have placed this new order in the semi-autonomous regions under European supervision."

Given the concentrated competence of the statesmen of Christian Europe convened in Berlin at that time, it is indeed beyond comprehension how such a grave mistake could have been made, leading to tragic consequences in the development of Macedonia and Thrace.

Or was it not a mistake at all? Had a dynastic directorship far-sightedly and purposefully revised the text even then?

If this assumption is true, then the Greek intrigues against Macedonia today would be continuing a long tradition, and the imposition of the preliminary name for the Republic of Macedonia in 1992, a kind of endless thumbscrew, would have been ominously modelled on the other, more distant event.

As von Mach has pointed out, Section 3 of Article 23 did in fact mention that the Sublime Porte would appoint special commissions, but the well-meaning addition

> "in which the native element is to be well represented in great number ..., so that these new regulations can be elaborated in detail in each province" (loc. cit.)

was of no use, as the implementation of this prescription was entirely the responsibility of the Turks, for whom, in practice, it was null and void.

Von Mach rightly concludes that the commission had been provided as a control organ only

> "but not as an administrative unit meant to take the initiative in elaborating and implementing the details of the agreement."[41]

The consequences are described by von Mach as follows:

> "The Porte, then, did nothing to fulfil its obligations. It even tightened the reins on the rajah. Despite much talk about reforms nothing happened. The recognisable principle underlying all this was the Porte's fear that in allowing a semi-autonomous country they would only be creating a transitional form, a kind of caterpillar that would soon develop into an autonomous chrysalis and finally into an independent butterfly that would not even pay tribute any more."[42]

This also explains the fact that the Macedonians' disappointment and bitterness that, as in Crete, the promise of "the solemnly decreed equal rights for the Christian population" was once more left unfulfilled, was immediately vented in the form of another revolt.

- The decision against Berovski in St.Petersburg
- and against Macedonia at the Congress of Berlin

seriously hampered Macedonia's development at that time but also during the Ilinden uprising in 1903, the Balkan Wars in 1912/13, and it even affected its status as a recognised part of the Federal Republic of Yugoslavia in 1944 and its full independence in 1991.

> *The fate of some other peoples was even more tragic. It was sealed. Thrace and Epirus are no more. The former was divided between Greece and Turkey, the latter between Greece and Albania.*

The author of this book at least could not find out anything about the Thracians after the political changes of 1990, when the large Macedonian minorities in Greece and Bulgaria made themselves heard. This was clearly not so at the end of the 19th century, for J. de Jong also mentions "the Thracian efforts at liberation".[43]

> *The world must not allow the injustices of the imperialist age to be continued even in the 21st century!*

1.2.0.8 The two short periods of a free Macedonia

As was set out, Macedonia - like all other Balkan states before their liberation - was part of the Ottoman Empire for centuries. However, there were two exceptions:

1.

After the last Russo-Turkish war in 1877/78, Russia handed over Macedonia and Western Thrace to the newly emerged, or in fact re-emerged, state of Bulgaria (then only of autonomous status) in the Peace of San Stefano on 3rd March 1878. As the Great Powers, most of all Great Britain and Austria-Hungary, were not under any circumstances willing to accept the results of the Peace of San Stefano, in so far as it strategically favoured Russia with regard to the Straits, the San Stefano Treaty was annulled at the Congress of Berlin (June 13th – July 13th 1878) which had been brought about by exerting pressure on Russia. This resulted in Macedonia and Thrace, both of which had enjoyed three and half months of - relative - freedom, at least as far as the Turkish occupational regime was concerned, being given back to the Ottoman Empire.

It is very much to be doubted whether the Macedonians would have succeeded in pursuing autonomy and ultimately achieving independent statehood from their position under Bulgarian rule, especially considering the plight of the Macedonians in Aegean Macedonia that was occupied by Greece in 1913, and Bulgaria's continued chauvinist endeavours to achieve a Greater Bulgaria.

Stojčevski is therefore right to conclude that:

> "From today's point of view, this revision can be seen as a correct decision setting the stage for Macedonia's future."[44]

2.

During the last Macedonian revolt against the Ottoman Empire – the famous *Ilinden Uprising on August 2nd 1903* – the Macedonian people had succeeded in freeing the city and region of Kruševo from the Turkish yoke and declaring a *"Republic of Kruševo"*, once again without the benefit of international support. They even managed to elect a local council.[45] Ten days later, however, this revolt was crushed with much bloodshed by Turkish superior military power.

> In view of this, what are we to make of Greek protests against the fact that the Macedonians have included this undeniably national experience in the preamble of their republic's constitution!?

For reasons set out above, the strategy so often successful in the past, i.e. to prolong the revolt and publicize the high toll of Christian victims, aimed at inducing the Great Powers, especially Russia, to interfere, had failed on this occasion.[45]

Subsequently Macedonia, exhausted and defenceless as it was, constituted a power vacuum and thus an especially attractive target for its expansionist neighbours.

1.2.1 The name "Macedonia"

Dependent as Macedonia may have been in the times of Turkish rule, all records, from the beginning of the described period to its very end, show that the name "Macedonia" was applied continuously to the region in question and as a matter of course by all statesmen of all Balkan states (including Greece!), as well as of all the great powers.

This trivial matter deserves particular attention because the Greek foreign secretary Papakonstantinou issued an official briefing in 1992 with the purpose of persuading the "friendly" member states of the (then) EC that the name Macedonia had been randomly and unlawfully attributed to the Yugoslav sub-republic of Macedonia by Tito as late as 1944 and had nothing to do with this republic's own past. As it became clear from a well-informed source, Papakonstantinou's briefing had not included a single piece of factual information, nor had he advanced any single historical, ethnic, religious or political reason, but only emotional appeals, Byzantine incantations and reproaches levelled at the new Republic of Macedonia.

This fiction is still upheld by Greece today, undisturbed by the EU, NATO, UN, OSCE or the Council of Europe.

It is therefore important, when reviewing passages from old reports, to always keep in mind that *"Macedonia"* is a *traditional* name for the Slavic areas of settlement, so that this fraudulent misrepresentation of facts perpetrated by the Greeks may be exposed and the anachronism of the present name "FYROM" shown to be absurd.

This tradition is supported by positive evidence, for there are examples showing that the name Macedonia had been in use throughout many centuries:

1.2.1.1 First and foremost, in the Auswärtiges Amt itself. Among roughly two thousand files comprising reports from the Ottoman Empire, there are – as I have already pointed out under 1.1.0 – 154 files dealing exclusively with the situation in "Macedonia", as is indicated on the title page of each file. This collection of files was started in the year 1867 by the Prussian Ministry of Foreign Affairs of the North German Confederation. It would be absurd to suggest that the German authorities of that time invented this name themselves, without referring to reality and usage by other European powers.

1.2.1.2 The sources of the other powers whose relations with, and interest in, the Balkans was closer than that of Prussia or the German Reich, are even older:
The Austrian emperor Leopold I, for example, issued a declaration of protection for Macedonia on the occasion of the tragic Karpoš uprising. I cannot, however, furnish conclusive proof, for my request for the relevant document was answered by Prof. Auer of the 'Wiener Haus-, Hof- und Staatsarchiv' on January 2nd 2001 in the following manner:
> "An assurance of safety for the Macedonian people issued by Emperor Leopold I in 1690 has indeed been mentioned in literature several times; however, the material kept in our house yields no evidence for its existence."

(He then refers to other Austrian archives; the author means to follow this up on another occasion.)
In fact, the existence of these decrees has been confirmed by an eminent British historian. Arnold Toynbee writes that the decrees of Emperor Leopold constituted "a great step forward ... in the interest of religious freedom and administrative autonomy of ethnic minorities in south-east Europe ..." (loc. cit., p. 458)
One of the reasons for the "tragic" end of the Karpoš insurrection was General Piccolomini's plan for a safe withdrawal of the Austrian army, which, in 1697, involved burning down Skopje, which in his opinion was the most beautiful town in the Balkans at that time, so as to be able to lead his army, exhausted from numerous battles and territorial conquests and decimated by cholera, safely out of Macedonia under the cover of the burning city. In vain ...

1.2.1.3 Around 250 to 300 years before, the Turks were in the process of organizing the European territories they had conquered, and although they called their new acquisition in the south-east of the Balkans Rumelia as a whole, one of the five districts of this province bore the name Macedonia even then.[46] Later, the Sultans were eager to refer to the region exclusively by the Turkish name Rumelia in communications with foreign representatives. When the Sultan registered a growing interest of the European powers in the plight of the Christians under the Turkish yoke after the peace treaties of Kütschük-Kainardschi in 1774 and Adrianopolis in 1829/30, he reacted so strongly as to expunge the name "Macedonia" occurring in the Acts of the Apostles from the Turkish translations of the Bible existing in his empire - a fact to be commended - (although these passages can only have referred to ancient Macedonia under Roman occupation). (Acts ch. 16. 9, 10, 12; ch. 18. 5 and ch. 19. 22, 29)
It must have escaped the zealots that the name Macedonia can also be found in the First Epistle of Paul to the Thessalonians (three times), in the Second Epistle to the Colossians (five times) as well as in the Epistles to the Romans and Timothy (once each), also in the First Book of Maccabees, ch. 1. 1. (Konkordanz zur Lutherbibel. Loc. cit., p. 992)

1.2.1.4 Finally, to go back even further into the past, this is what Bojić/Oschlies wrote about the appearance of the Slavs in the Byzantine Empire:

> "In the official language of Byzantium, the term 'Macedonian Slavs' referred to those Slavs who had come into its territory during the sixth century A.D."[47]

There is a report from the same period in the "Miraculi Sancti Demetrii" concerning the history of Thessalonica which was besieged by the Slavs in Macedonia at the end of the 6th century, quoted by Michael Weithmann:

> John of Thessalonica, "who apparently took part in the defence himself", is said to have written that "the Avars had taken over the initiative of the attack in 585... Part of the Slavic army driven out of Thrace ... joined the great expedition of the Khagan against the capital of the Diocese Macedonia."[48]

Thus, there is every reason to assume that Byzantium had adopted the term "Macedonia" for that region in the wake of the Romans and had handed it down to the Slavs, who retained it through the centuries and still do so today.

Therefore, one can appropriately speak of a continuous tradition of using the name Macedonia, starting from pre-Christian times and continuing throughout the Roman and Byzantine eras, the Slavic settlements and the Turkish conquests, and still upheld when the idea of the nation-state emerged in the 19th century and even until the Federal Republic of Yugoslavia was established in 1944 and later on the Republic of Macedonia in 1991.

> Consequently, the untrue argumentation of the Greek government in 1992 regarding the supposedly random interpretation of the name of the Republic of Macedonia were tantamount to a deliberate attempt to mislead the official representatives of the EC countries in Athens.

Thus, the Greek strategy of belittling every reference made by the Macedonians to Macedonia as a historical name, pointed out by Jutta de Jong, as "a revival of the name Macedonia no earlier than the 19th century" can be exposed as an unjustified attempt to deny the Slavs inhabiting the territory of ancient Macedonia for 1400 to 1500 years the right to this name. As part of the same coup, Greece has also made the dubious attempt to declare the ancient Macedonians to be Greeks and the Greeks themselves to be the sole heirs to the name Macedonia.[49]

In their attempts to falsify historical events in the pre-Christian era, i.e. in the dim and distant past, it is conspicuous that the figure of Alexander the Great (and maybe also of his father Philip II, judging by the way the latter is glorified in the excellent museum of Thessalonica) had a magnetic attraction for the Greeks; this may be due to the hope that the aura of grandeur surrounding that people's famous descendant might also lend some splendour to modern Greece.

However, this is only the external, glamorous aspect of the matter. The ultimate goal of this strategy seems to reach far beyond that: As soon as this false account had been sufficiently spread around and world opinion had accepted the historical misrepresentation of ancient Macedonia as already being Greek, Athens would have been able to deal the final blow:

If ancient Macedonia was Greek, then the territory of ancient Macedonia was also Greek. It follows that the territory of modern Macedonia must also be Greek. Thus it would have been consistent for the Greeks, who already owned the southern part of Macedonia annexed after the Balkan wars, to demand the "return" of the (once Ser-

bian) "Vardar Macedonia", i.e. the present Republic of Macedonia, to Greece. Even if this did not succeed, the "Republic of Skopje" would not be allowed under any circumstances to adorn itself with the "Greek" name Macedonia.
The casual appearance of this description should not obscure the fact that Athens has already taken two steps in that direction:
1).
On the international level, Greece already denied the Republic of Macedonia its rightful state name in 1992 and 1993 by infiltrating the provisional name "Former Yugoslav Republic of Macedonia" (abbreviated as: "FYROM") into the (misinformed) international organizations, in particular the EU and the UN.
2).
When the United States officially recognized the Republic of Macedonia in February 1994, Athens arbitrarily imposed an economic blockade on Macedonia. (It seems that Athens had not dared to do this on the occasion of the recognition of Macedonia by the EU member states a few weeks earlier on December 16th 1993.) In the subsequent negotiations conducted by the former US Secretary of State Cyrus Vance Macedonia was blackmailed into giving up the symbol on the Macedonian national flag, i.e. the star (or the *sun*) of Vergina, in return for the Greeks lifting the blockade.
Was the former minister Vance informed of the fact that Greek archaeologists had found this symbol of the sun on a gold-plated *ossuary* supposedly containing the mortal remains of Philip II during excavations in Vergina around 1987 and that the place where this receptacle was discovered was precisely in the region forcibly annexed by Greece in 1912/13? *The sun will bring it to light.*
This means that, in this grotesque, Greece claimed the exclusive right to use a symbol that even Greek archaeologists, for instance Prof. Manolis Andronicos[50], have clearly ascribed to Macedonia and that was found in a place that, in the many thousand years of Greek-Macedonian contiguity, only became Greek as a consequence of the annexation 90 years ago! The matter is even worse: Considering the well-known American concern for justice towards small countries in need of protection, it must be assumed that it could only have been a falsification of history that made the United States insist on Macedonia giving up this symbol during the negotiations that led to the interim agreement of September 13th 1995.

> *This event is not the result of a historically proven claim but a show of strength behind the back of a state whose friendship was abused.*

Now that the Republic of Macedonia has modified the flag accordingly, the question of the flag is done with, but I do think that the Macedonian Slavs who have traditionally settled in the region of ancient Macedonia for 1400 years certainly have a more established claim to the pre-Christian Macedonians' star/sun of Vergina than the Greeks with their 90 years – especially considering that this symbol is not Greek and not even Hellenistic, but purely *Macedonian*.

1.2.2 The Macedonian language

The language is the primary aspect used by the Bulgarians in support of their claims on Macedonia which amount to an attempt at persuading the world that language is the appropriate lever for remodelling the Macedonians into Bulgarians. These attempts are accompanied by repeated insinuations to the effect that Macedonians are "really" Bulgarians and speak Bulgarian. (Cf. 1.3.0.1) Therefore, this question is too important to only be touched on briefly.

Not all peoples have had the historical luck of their language manifesting itself at an early stage. The Macedonians did.

The Byzantine emperor Michael III (842-867) entrusted his fellow-believers Cyril and Methodius with an orthodox mission to the Great Moravian kingdom of Prince Rastislav.[51] (Their work there is documented from 863.) What the emperor Michael said to the two brothers has come down to us:

- "You two are people from Saloniki, and the people of Saloniki all speak Slavic." (Trautmann, loc. cit. p.39)
- "The works of the two brothers brought great enlightenment, to Russia, Bulgaria, Serbia and Croatia, also to Bohemia and Moravia, and even to Romania where the language is different." (Trautmann, p.36)

Who would not want to share in the glory – or even have it all to himself – of having been the native land of these two missionaries! And so this is what the Bulgarians, and of course the Greeks, claim for themselves.

The Bulgarian Tsar Boris himself, however, adopted the Christian faith no earlier than 865, as did his people. And the two missionary brothers were not from Varna or Tarnovo or Serdika, but from the environs of Thessalonica, being sons of a Macedonian mother and a Greek father. There is no evidence of that region being conquered by the Bulgarians then, for the historical texts are explicit about the Bulgarians marching on "Central" Macedonia (and not the Aegean) between 840 and 850 – not to mention the fact that the Turk-Tatar proto-Bulgarians no longer existed but had merged into the autochthonous Slavic population and also adopted the Slavic idiom.

Orthodox Constantinople was competing with Catholic Rome early on. Both centres of Christendom were striving to win over the immigrant settlers in the Balkans as new believers.

Cyril and Methodius

> "seemed to have swayed the situation in favour of Constantinople. Ultimately, the result was a division of power ... in south-east Europe. ... Since 1054, the time of the great schism, at the latest, these two spheres and the people belonging to them have developed very different cultures."[52]

In order to facilitate their missionary work, the "teachers of the Slavs" Cyril and Methodius created "their own so-called Glagolitic script".

> "During later measures for reintroducing Greek culture, the Cyrillic alphabet ..., half of which consisted of Greek characters, was established as a standard."[53]

And again: The dialects forming the basis on which the Slav apostles translated the Gospels, did not have their origin in Bulgaria (neither on the Bulgarian Black Sea coast nor the Rhodope Mountains), but, like the brothers themselves, in the environs of Thessalonica, i.e. in Macedonia.

Prof. Weithmann states more precisely that Cyril and Methodius preached and wrote in the language

> "spoken in the environs of Thessalonica, i.e. by the Rychines, Segudates, and Drugubites." Weithmann also adds: "Congruities with other South Slavic languages such as Serbian or Croatian are either non-existent or of later origin"[54]

(Any non-specialist reading and hearing the languages might, however, gain a different impression.)

The achievements of the apostles were of lasting value in so far as

> "by introducing the Slavonic liturgical and written languages... they broadened the range of European cultural languages to include three. Until the establishment of modern standard languages, Old Church Slavonic had the same role throughout Slavia Orthodoxa as Latin in the Catholic regions, i.e. it was both the liturgical and the official language. One should not, however, stretch this parallel too far, as Latin differed from Old Church Slavonic in that it not only passed on cultural values, but also incorporated them."[55]

Thus, some of the lustre of this cultural achievement also falls on the originally Turk-Tatar Bulgarians, as they were not only assimilated by the Slavs, but also adopted the Slavic language, i.e. Church Slavonic, and the Cyrillic alphabet. (For more details cf. the chapters on Bulgaria and Greece.)

In the modern era, the following development can be traced:

> "When the French Revolution had replaced the old states by the modern nation-state, language gained a new importance so far unknown. ... It now became a supporting pillar in establishing group solidarity within the nation. The demand for liberty, equality and fraternity, these foundations of the modern nation-state, was soon complemented by that for a common unified language. Since then, the term "nation" has often been understood to mean a uniform "linguistic nation", which has served to justify homogenization efforts aiming at unifying a language region in order to support and consolidate the nationstate."[56]

This development did not start affecting the Macedonians until Macedonian was first put down in writing. According to Torsten Szobries, this process began at the start of the 19th century when clergymen first used the Macedonian language for popular sermons and devotional texts which had been printed in Macedonia itself since 1838.[57] When Slavic intellectuals started rebelling against *Greek cultural hegemony* in the middle of the 19th century, this also led to a growing number of publications on the folklore, language and history of the Macedonian Slavs; these culminated in the demand that "the Macedonian dialects be chosen as the basis for the 'common written language'."[58]

For the Macedonians, fighting for their language - and thus also for their national identity - 1870 was the fateful year that brought the Sultan's permission of the *Exarchate*, the autocephalous Bulgarian-Orthodox church (cf. 1.2.0.4). The Bulgarians played this trump card in advancing the Bulgarization of Macedonia (which had had hardly any Bulgarian population until then).

The following example illustrates the underhand tactics applied by Bulgaria: Bulgarian newspapers accused a Macedonian teacher of "betraying Bulgaria" because he had published schoolbooks based on the Macedonian dialects.[59]

This case also shows (in the same way as the events involving the League of Nations, cf. Section 1.3.0.3) that the Macedonians had a language and identity different from the Bulgarian and that the Bulgarians saw this difference then – even if they do not want to admit it to this day.

For the same reason, the famous book "On Macedonian Matters" by Krste Misirkov in which he had written about ethnic and political unity for Macedonia, was banned in Bulgaria in 1900 and all available copies destroyed.[60] Even at this early stage, Misirkov had warned against unification with Bulgaria, Serbia or Greece!

The tactics described became common practice. Later, they were also (and with particular insistence) applied to *Goce Delćev*, the famous Macedonian co-founder of the VMRO and co-organizer of the Ilinden Uprising, who was confronted with the statement that he had used the Bulgarian language in his correspondence – therefore he himself must be Bulgarian! Leaving aside the fact that at the time of the transition from the 19th to the 20th century there was no codified standard Macedonian language yet (although it was already being called for by Macedonian student associations, at home and abroad, even in Bulgaria, who demanded that foreign elements be minimized and Macedonian be based on Central Macedonian dialects[61]), the unsoundness of this reproach can be demonstrated by the convincing example set out by Mito Miovski during the II. German-Macedonian Conference in Jena in November 2001:

The Slovak author Ján Kollar had written in Czech around 1830. Do we have to conclude, asked Professor Miovski, that

1. Kollar was Czech and
2. that there was no Slovak language at all?

Nobody, either at that time or today, would support such an absurd idea. Such a policy could only be adopted against Macedonia, which was defenceless at the time.

Similarly, the allegations that Delčev had even referred to himself as Bulgarian can be invalidated by resorting to the following fundamental line of reasoning:

As was pointed out by Torsten Szobries who quotes a 1906 study by Jovan Cvijić, an internationally recognized Serbian geographer, entitled "Remarks of the Macedo-Slavs", the term 'Bulgarian' must be understood in the context of the historical situation:

> "The fact that they" [the Macedonians] "referred to themselves as (Bulgarians), is simply a consequence of this term's being used synonymously to denote *raja* (i.e. non-Muslim subject)."[62]

This is another example supporting Adanir's claim that the set of problems constituting the Macedonian Question really started with the Bulgarian Exarchate's decree of 1870/72 favouring religious over ethnic affiliation, and not with the Congress of Berlin in 1878.

Besides, the Bulgarian allegations against Goce Delčev fully suppress the fact that he not only fought for Macedonian autonomy personally, but also lost his life in that fight for Macedonia.

There are exceptions from this general rule of Bulgarian behaviour: Szobries quotes a rather reasonable editor of the newspaper "Makedonija" who evinces some understanding "for the "Macedonists'" fear ... of an Eastern Bulgarian cultural and economic hegemony". Szobries describes the relevant article of 1871 as "the first testimony to Macedonian separatism."[63]

Thus, even at that time, there was Macedonian linguistic and ethnic separatism. Jutta de Jong also supports this by her research, proving in her study that the Macedonian language already differed from Bulgarian in the 19th century and did not need to be manoeuvred into that position by Blaže Koneski on Tito's instructions:

> On the contrary, "between 1891 and 1903, Macedonian student initiatives in Bulgaria, Serbia and Russia were clearly starting attempts to shape the Macedonian Slavic dialects into a standard language which was different from the Bulgarian literary language spread by the Exarchate's schools in minor but normative ways."[64]

To this day, Bulgarians and Greeks deny this for pragmatic reasons in pursuit of their expansionist politics. They are not content with derisively pointing to the year 1944, but even declare this date to be the beginning of the existence of a Macedonian language as such. This approach is completely unjustified.

As for the matter in question, we simply have to take note of the fact that the establishment of a "standard written language" was a parallel development with respect to the "declared belief in Macedonian ethnic independence".[65]
It should be added that the Macedonian Georgi Pulevski published the first Macedonian four-language dictionary in 1873 and a textbook in three languages in 1875, followed by a collection of Macedonian folk songs in 1879 and a Macedonian grammar in 1880.[66]

1.2.2.0 Language codification in the neighbouring states

1.2.2.1 The Bulgarian language
Reinhold Trautmann (loc. cit., p.29, §10) already set out the basic elements of the "Bulgarian" language in 1948:
> "The Bulgarian language, i.e. the Slav Bulgarian language in our understanding..."

In Bulgaria, as throughout the entire Slavia Orthodoxa, old Church Slavonic was the liturgical language in use. Educated Bulgarians, however, often "wrote and spoke" Greek, as Greece was putting a massive effort into "hellenizing the Slavic believers."[67] In 1762, therefore, the Bulgarian educator Paisij Chilandarski exhorted his countrymen to start using their own language.
> "In the discussion about the basis for the modern Bulgarian standard language, two opposing positions can be distinguished: The first group, the 'Church Slavonic' school, was trying to modernize written Church Slavonic and to adapt it to contemporary needs, while the other group, the 'New Bulgarian' school, wanted to develop a new standard language based on the people's vernacular. Finally, a compromise was reached as the 'Slav Bulgarian' school won the day, which included elements of both movements and spread the new language by means of new schools and literature."[67]

The Bulgarian language was codified when Bulgaria gained autonomy in the years 1878-80. It was based on the East Bulgarian (Varna) dialect, "but, in the 20th century, West Bulgarian gained a stronger influence."[68]
Does this kind of language history justify looking down on Macedonia?

1.2.2.2 The Serbian language
As for the language question in Serbia, "the dignity of Church Slavonic and the Old Serbian language derived from it" was undisputed "on account of its early cultural benefits, but the latter was increasingly being displaced by the imported Russian form of Church Slavonic during the 18th century, which then became a starting point for the development of a new composite language called "Slavo-Serbian". This new artificial language, however, was not highly regarded and little use was made of it, so that it soon met with serious competition from the people's vernacular."[69] It was not until the beginning of the 19th century that language reformer Vuk Karadzič succeeded to raise the latter to the level of a written language. In the Vienna agreement of 1850, Serbs and Croats agreed on the dialect of East Herzegovina as the common Serbo-Croatian standard language, which nevertheless took a long time to become popular. Starting with the agreement of Novi Sad in 1954 (!), the prevailing arrangement was to talk of a bi-centred standard language divided between Belgrade and Zagreb. Only the new constitution of the Federal Republic of Yugoslavia, set up after Croatia had gone its own way, establishes the official language as Serbian.

This said, these two languages have much more in common than Macedonian and Bulgarian. Nevertheless, both states insisted on separate languages for political reasons concerned with their people's identity. This is not reprehensible, but why is the same right denied to the Macedonians?

1.2.2.3 The Greek language

> "Greek is the oldest language of European civilisation, a fact impressively testified to by names such as Homer, Plato and Aristotle. The Greeks founded the first advanced civilization in Europe and can be seen as the European bridge which allowed the transmission of the written cultures of the Middle East."[70] (Prinzig)

But is there a unified Greek language today? This is not merely an academic question, for

> "shaping and standardizing a language or language variant was ... of major importance in 'shaping the nation' in the 19th century."[71]

What do the language historians say?

In Ancient Greece, the *koine*, i.e. the general vernacular, was to some extent held to be vulgar, so that learned men were trying to keep to the more classical Attic dialect.

> "At the time of the Roman Empire and during the Byzantine period, there were still, in a way, two languages ... the people's vernacular and the Atticizing 'high' language."[72]

Should this cause any humanist effusiveness, it is curbed here by realism from an authoritative source:

> "The real Greeks who took up arms" and fought the Ottomans on the Peloponnese "in their battle for that which was to become a new, independent national state, spoke as little Ancient Greek as the Italians spoke Latin."[73]

After Greece was liberated from the Turks, the language question was still unresolved. Two languages were competing: the literary (written) language *Katharevousa* and the spoken vernacular *Demotike*.[74]

> "In due time, the difference between the language spoken by the people and the one spoken by scholars became so great that understanding the written language presupposed a high level of education, accessible only to Greece's upper classes. So, as the use of a particular language depended on social standing, language turned into a status symbol." This led to "linguistic anarchy".[75]

In 1850 (*AD*), the philologist, translator, reformer and doctor Adamantios Korais developed an official educational and national language based on Ancient Greek[76], incurring the enmity of the *Greek* Orthodox Church on account of his "brotherly teaching" which conflicted with the patriarch's "fatherly teaching" that "theologically justified the Ottoman imperial power structures".[77]

Among the people, however, Korais' patriotism had won him an almost legendary reputation, although he lived in France. This is exemplified by some remarks by von Bülow, then envoy at Athens, who – in the face of the tense situation in the Balkans, with only four days to go before Russia declared war on Turkey in 1877 – showed surprise at the "indifference of the majority of the Greek people ... as to current events":

> "How little excited the general mood is could be seen again today, when the dead body of the great patriot Korais was brought here from Paris and interred under the eyes of all Athens. Among the egregious persons who spoke at the burial of this 'spiritual father of new Hellenism', no one said only a word on the imminent danger of war on the Danube."[78]

Katharevousa remained the language of the newspapers, laws and academia. It was specified as the official language in the constitution as late as 1911. Only in 1917, did Venizelos introduce Demotike in elementary schools. (Adrados, p. 288)

In 1964, the Centre Union party considered both languages to be equally important. Under the Greek Junta, Katharevousa was yet again declared the official language in 1967, while the use of Demotike was to be limited to the first four years of elementary school. This language dualism remained in place until 1976 (!): Demotike then became the official language in education and administration. However, for a long time, Katharevousa was still the language of the courts, the church and the army (p. 288).
Yet Demotike prevailed, though not without difficulty:

> "Of course there are various types of Dimotiki Greek. ...Thus what we tend to call Modern Greek is not entirely homogenous, as it preserves ... numerous elements of the old standard language."[79]

Is everything clear?

1.2.2.4 The Albanian language

> "Albanian raises many difficulties, as it is not based on any of the older cultural languages. Illyrian, which is often mentioned in this context, does not provide a secure basis, as it is mostly unknown and can certainly only be called a cultural language in a limited sense. ... The Illyrian origin of Albanian has by no means been proved and is often questioned outside Albania, so that a lack of appropriate sources makes it impossible to produce direct proof of the early presence of Albanians in south-east Europe."[80]

(Just like the Greeks and Bulgarians, the Albanians also prefer to make up their history to suit their requirements.)

- "The attempt has also been made, although it is controversial even in Albania, to claim the Pelasgians, an even less well known prehistoric Balkan people, as the true forefathers of modern Albania. According to this theory, the Pelasgians are the true founders of Western culture and have handed it down to Greece."[81]

- "Such hypotheses were, however, useless in setting up an Albanian standard language, as these ancient languages are merely attested in small remnants and cannot contribute to any solution of the current problems faced by Albanian. The discussion of language standards could therefore not have recourse to an old cultural language, but rather had to weigh up different, fairly young vernacular forms against each other. The differences between these reflect the disparate Albanian religious and cultural traditions. Externally, this shows in the use of different alphabets – Latin in Catholic contexts, Greek in Orthodox and, occasionally, Arabic in Muslim contexts. In addition to that, there have been further, partly independent attempts to solve the question of orthography. But the present use of the Latin alphabet was only established in 1908 at the congress of Monastir, today the Macedonian town of Bitola. Furthermore, several divergent written language approaches developed from the two great dialect forms, Gheg in the North and Tosk in the South. Until the end of World War II, the common Gheg official language of Elbasan was mainly used, but there was also a Northwest Gheg and a common Tosk written form."[81]

- "Under communist rule, the development of a unified national language was promoted and the parallel existence of several written languages ended. At the orthography congress of 1972, the new standard language was introduced and recognized both inside and – even more importantly – outside Albania as binding. This meant that Kosovo Albanians abstained from developing the Kosovar dialect into a separate standard language and thus distancing themselves from Albania which would certainly have met with approval in Tito's Yugoslavia."[82]

1.2.3 The Macedonian territory

Up to its division after the two Balkan wars in 1912/1913, the Macedonian territory obviously consisted of the sum of the three regions that were allotted to Serbia, Bulgaria and Greece, i.e. of: Vardar Macedonia, Pirin Macedonia and Aegean Macedonia (or North Greece, as it was called until 1985). It also comprised the stretch of land to the south-west of the Lakes Ohrid and Prespa that was given to Albania (or in any case not conquered). (Albania did not take part in the Balkan wars, as it was not yet established as a state.)

These were the borders of said territory:

(The places named here are not border towns, rather the author has chosen to list some of the better known places in order to make himself understood also to non-geographers, even though these may not be directly adjacent to the border. The list starts in the north-east and proceeds anticlockwise.)

North: north of the Razlog line, via Kriva Palanka and Skopje to Tetovo;

West: west of the Tetovo and Debar line, then to the west of the Lakes Ohrid and Prespa and Kostur, as far as Grevena:

South: south of Grevena, towards Katerini, including Thessalonica, the Chalkidiki peninsula and the island of Thassos; and

East: east of Kavala, via Drama, then east of Nevrokor and reaching the area to the east of Razlog.

These borders are based on the real situation at the beginning of the 20th century. They are not taken from any Macedonian maps, by which the author might have incurred reproach on the Greek side. They are indicated on a Bulgarian map issued by the "Institut Scientifique Macédonien" in Sofia – and certainly, after Greece itself, Bulgaria would be the last state to be expected to print a map favourable to Macedonia.

It is a well-known fact that in the first years after Macedonia had declared independence in 1991, governments in Athens protested loudly and energetically, trying to prevent such maps from being shown and discussed in the media – as if the past would disappear if no one was allowed to talk about it. This was done in spite of the fact that this map merely reflects the borders established by the *Treaties of Paris* (Neuilly and Sèvres), in which the European powers endorsed the previous division of Macedonia in 1919. (Cf. the technical notes in the appendix.)

Did I write "in the first years after ... independence in 1991"? Then I must correct myself: As late as February 2007 some Ambassadors of EU member states, following the initiative of the Ambassador of the EU commission in Skopje, intervened according to press reports in Skopje on behalf of the Greek Government and suggested they should stop an exhibition of historical maps and remove the exhibits. (The maps showed the territory of Macedonia since the Slav settlement in antique Macedonia, including, of course, the border lines before the outbreak of the Balkan Wars 1912/13, i. e. before the annexation of Macedonian ground by Serbia, Bulgaria and Greece.) Although being in principle under the protection of the European Union the Macedonians definitely had no other choice than to follow this "friendly advice"; nevertheless, they can regard this event as a moral victory of their historical position, since the affair proves that the greatest, practically almighty power in the Balkans shows signs of a guilty conscience.

With reference to international cartography, let me add that the aforementioned Serbian geographer J. Cvijić for the first time referred to the Slavic population of Macedonia as "Macedo-Slavs" in 1908.

> "After the Balkan wars, Cvijić published another ethnographic map of the Balkan Peninsula, which ... divided the Slavic population into Serbocroatians, Makedoslavs and Bulgarians. This map was published in "Petermanns Mittheilungen" and was widely acknowledged."[83]

This estimation was strongly opposed by Gustav Weigand's "Ethnograpy of Macedonia" in 1924. Nevertheless, this cannot change the Macedonians' consciousness of their own ethnic and linguistic identity, as that is after all a question of their right to self-determination.

1.3 The Republic of Macedonia – in the cross fire of its neighbours

Before we look at the archive material, let us reconstruct the historical situation of Macedonia as it presented itself after the declaration of independence.
After the Republic of Macedonia was founded on September 8th 1991, its neighbours conspicuously failed to greet it as a new, finally free and independent member of the family of peoples – unlike in the case of Slovenia and Croatia. On the contrary, they protested, made claims and imposed conditions. They denied the Macedonians their history and culture, their ethnicity and language, and even their rightful name, i.e. their complete identity.

1.3.1 The Serbs

The Serbs did not accept the Macedonians as a people in their own right. Up until the fall of Milošević on the October 5th 2000, they always referred to Macedonia as "South Serbia", and there was a permanent danger of the Federal Republic of Yugoslavia, or in fact the sub-republic of Serbia, retaking the Republic of Macedonia by force on account of its status as a former Yugoslav republic.[84] In the Balkan wars of 1912 and 1913, Serbia had annexed part of Macedonia, i.e. 38% of the former Macedonian territory under Turkish rule.[85] This territory, i.e. "Vardar" Macedonia, was included as "Serbian" in the Kingdom of Serbs, Croats and Slovenes which was established in Versailles after World War I and retained without any changes after the country was renamed "Kingdom of Yugoslavia" in 1929.
After World War II, Tito granted the Macedonians the status of a nation and a sub-republic within the framework of the Federal Republic of Yugoslavia. Its territory is exactly that of today's Republic of Macedonia. This means that, in the imperialist perspective and language of the 19th century, Serbia was the only Balkan War participant to lose its "territorial gains" after the political changes of 1989/90. Thus Milošević declared Tito to be a "traitor to the Serbian people" on account of Kosovo and Macedonia, for, as Prof Weithmann quotes further, for Serbian nationalists, Macedonia is "a 'perfidious Titoist invention', an artificial state and nation construct"...[86]
However, it is to be hoped that the new Serbia will not jeopardize its return into the circle of modern states by any adventures such as attempting to "annex" Macedonia. Only the manoeuvres of the Serbian Orthodox Church in 2006 are not very encouraging.

1.3.2 The Bulgarians

The Bulgarians claimed, and continue to do so, that there is a Macedonian state, which they even recognized in 1992, but no Macedonian nation and no Macedonian language, rather that the Macedonians were really Bulgarians and spoke Bulgarian. One would have thought that this presumptuous position taken by Bulgaria ever since the Congress of Berlin and its annexation of part of Macedonia, the area of Pirin Macedonia at the beginning of the 20th century, could not seriously affect the existence of the Republic of Macedonia, in view of the fact that Bulgaria has applied for EU and NATO membership and that the present situation forbids such extravagance. However, even in recent years, unmistakeably chauvinist sounds are to be heard from Sofia.

First, the Bulgarians surprised the Western world by demonstrating a readiness to adjust to European political and human rights standards: When, on February 9th 1999, the city court of Sofia recognized a party representing the Macedonian minority in Pirin Macedonia called "OMO-Ilinden"[87], this nourished Western and especially Macedonian hopes of the Bulgarians' ability to understand and accept historical and political facts.

The EU then granted Bulgaria the status of a pre-accession country; the Republic of Macedonia, on the other hand, immediately allowed itself to be tricked into a "false compromise regarding the already completely clear language question" in a joint declaration made on the 21st and 22nd of February 1999, according to which "there is only a Macedonian language 'according to the constitution' while the rest of the Macedonian language is thus considered by Bulgaria to be a Bulgarian dialect".[88] The "previous practice ... of formulating contracts in English or in both national languages" was thus eliminated by Bulgaria. This compromise was so inadequate and unsatisfactory that Klaus Schrameyer called it "painting over the difference of opinions". Gerhard Seewann, on the other hand, sees a positive aspect in the success of the "promise of not making any territorial claims" and also in the "recognition of Macedonian as an official language contained in the agreement of February 1999".[89]

One year later, however, Bulgaria's contractual partners faced a rude awakening: On February 29th 2000, the Bulgarian constitutional court declared admitting the party of the Macedonian minority in Bulgaria to be unconstitutional![90] As to the EU, Schrameyer thinks that the European Court of Human Rights will probably not accept this ruling, as it also decided to "lift the ban on the Greek-Macedonian organization Vinožito (Rainbow) in North Greece". Interestingly enough, even the Bulgarian magazine "Kapital" saw this ruling as a "totally nonsensical and absolutely emotional act" based on "nationalist conviction".

Furthermore: in the first days of July 2001, a remark made in the cabinet in Sofia started making the round in the Bulgarian press, to the effect that one should stop talking about the integrity of Macedonia's borders. (Before the political turnaround in 1989 similar remarks would have been seen as warmongering.)

In view of the fact that in the course of the 20th century alone, *Bulgaria participated in four wars in order to seize Macedonia* and even started one of these wars – the second Balkan war (but cf. Sec. 5.5) – some understanding for the Macedonians' alarm in the face of a clearly still existent expansionism on the part of Bulgaria will be necessary.

The short phase of Macedonian-Bulgarian unanimity between February 1999 and February 2000 is reminiscent of the Yugoslav-Bulgarian agreement between Tito and

Dimitrov after 1944. As Balkans expert Viktor Meier sets out in his brief recapitulation of the events, communist solidarity went so far that both

> "... seriously considered a Balkan federation, which they proposed to pursue in principle and 'step by step' in August 1947 in Bled. This plan envisaged a unified 'Greater Macedonia' as part of the alliance."[91]

This is not meant to promote any revisionism. The important point is that

> "Dimitrov's Bulgaria ... was easily moved to accept this concept of a unified Macedonia within the Balkan Federation and ... (allowed) corresponding activities in the Pirin region."[91]

Yugoslavia's participation in the Greek civil war on the side of the Communists in 1946-49 even opened up the possibility to win back the Macedonian territory annexed by Greece in 1913 and incorporate it into the sub-republic of Macedonia founded in 1944 as part of the Federal Republic of Yugoslavia, until Stalin (probably on account of the "percentage" agreement with the West, i.e. primarily with Churchill) vetoed any further pursuit of this project.

Incidentally, the Macedonian minority in "North Greece" had also participated in the civil war on the side of the Greek Communists on account of the latter's promise to grant autonomy to the Macedonian province in Greece at a later date. (They paid a high price for this after the defeat.) Thus Mark Mazower was able to write that

> "...the Greek civil war ... became in part a war between the Athens government and the members of the Slavic-speaking minority in the north, who hoped to win some form of autonomy..." "The Greek communists...were only defeated after a long civil war, which ... left more people dead, imprisoned and uprooted than German occupation itself had done." (loc. cit., pp.124-5 and 131)

The most elaborate, exhaustive analysis of the four-year Yugoslav-Bulgarian episode has been offered by the German Balkan's expert Magarditsch Hatschikjan in a voluminous study which includes a detailed consideration of Macedonia. In the past – when Bulgaria had no need to operate with wrong figures – a census carried out by the Bulgarians under realistic conditions in 1946 ascertained the Macedonian proportion of the overall population in Bulgaria to be 2.4% (169,544 persons). In the Pirin region alone, "approximately 70% of the population had specified their nationality as Macedonian."[92] After Stalin's veto, it was not only the aforementioned decree that Dimitrov "promptly revoked after 1948."[93]

In the next census, the statistical figure for the Macedonian population in Bulgaria was only 0.01%, a figure invented by the communists.

The whole procedure was even more shameful and could be called ridiculous if it had not been so serious: During the official census that followed the first one after the usual interval of ten years, the new party directive had not yet wholly penetrated the Bulgarian communist bureaucracy, so that even in 1956, the Macedonian proportion of the overall population was still specified as 2.5% (187,800 persons). Only the next census produced the desired result.

From that time, Sofia used every crisis to "renew its historical revisionist claims upon Macedonia", namely – besides 1948 – during the Soviet intervention in Hungary in 1956 and the invasion of Czechoslovakia by the Warsaw Pact states in 1968.[94]

1.3.3 The Greeks

Finally, also the Greeks deny the Macedonians the right to call themselves Macedonian and their country Macedonia. In order to give the world the impression that their anti-Macedonian policy had a legal basis, they claimed that Macedonia had stolen the cultural heritage of Greece, e.g. by adopting the name Macedonia, and was presuming to use an old Greek symbol, the *Star of Vergina*, for its flag. They claim that Greece has the exclusive right to use the name Macedonia and this ancient Macedonian symbol, as even the ancient Macedonians had been Greeks. Only this – false – argument can have enabled the Greeks to foist the anachronistic and destructive name "Former Yugoslav Republic of Macedonia" on the EU and UN member states.

> "The refusal of the Greek government and public to use the name "Macedonia" for the new state ... is an instance of Greek language nationalism in its most elementary sense."[95]

Christian Voss starts his article on "Slavophone Greece – remarks on the end of a taboo" with the sentence:

> "Our idea of Greek political culture is still shaped by the wave of hysterical nationalism experienced in 1991-1995, after the Republic of Macedonia had declared independence."[96]

One of the most spectacular reactions by the Greek government was the so-called "pasta boycott" against the Netherlands. But there were not only ridiculous measures: the Greek synod was even on the verge of breaking off relations with the Vatican.

As early as in 1984, a few years after Tito's death (previously, Athens had probably not dared to pick an argument with this statesman of international standing), the Greek parliament passed a law implausibly stopping the recognition of diplomas issued by Skopje University, thus making it impossible for hundreds of "Greek" students from North Greece to study in Skopje in their Macedonian mother tongue and trying – if they really had to study abroad and in the communist neighbour state of Yugoslavia of all places – to at least divert them to Serbia or Croatia.[97] This form of harassment is a clear sign of the existence of a - still unrecognized - Macedonian minority in Greece.

In 1955, when the Macedonians who had fled or been expelled from "North Greece" after 1912/13 and after the Greek civil war and who had been separated from their children and scattered across all the communist states as far as Kazakhstan, were permitted by Tito to return to the sub-republic of Macedonia, Greece officially declared this measure to be "a hostile act".[98]

According to Michael Weithmann, the Greeks make the following claim:

> "The usurpation of the Hellenic name and thus the Hellenistic tradition by the Macedonian Slavs is a sign of their claims on the whole Macedonian territory."[99]

This claim may be a Greek pretext meant to put the Macedonians in the wrong; however, it completely ignores the facts. For the Macedonians do not even dream of usurping the 'Hellenic name' and the 'Hellenistic tradition'. What they do claim, however, is the right to use the name of the geographic region called Macedonia which they settled in during the migration of peoples in the 6th and 7th century AD and have been inhabiting ever since.

In addition to that, it is pointless to underpin current political claims by quoting the history of the pre-Christian era, especially in view of the fact that in Central Europe, people hardly dare to go back even a hundred years where border conflicts are concerned. Viktor Meier points out, not without reason:

> "All the states involved took recurrence ... to historical myths that are often ludicrous and completely ignore reality." Concerning the Greeks in particular, he quotes a well-known text by Demosthenes, adding the following advice: "... the Greeks would be well-advised not to rely too strongly on antiquity in their exclusive claim to the Macedonian name."[100]

If we looked at the Greek claim to Macedonia as supported by international law, Italy would stand a good chance of being allowed to reclaim Augsburg, Trier, Bonn, all of

Spain, "Gaul" and England as far as Hadrian's Wall, as well as many other countries - among them: Greece.

In order to reinforce this factitious claim, Greece obstructs Macedonia diplomatically in all international political institutions, wherever possible, and has also caused this country great economic damage – the most obvious example being the arbitrary economic embargo of 1993, that was only lifted two and a half years later as a result of an intervention by the USA. Not the EU, as might have been expected. (The EU even quashed the proceedings in an international dispute where Greece was on the verge of being defeated on precisely this question.) Another example is the way Greece brought the Macedonian petrol market to a standstill in the summer of 2001.

This was not all: on August 29th 2001, the Greek government's press office issued a threat that had been voiced by the Greek defence minister Tsochatzopoulos in addressing the parliamentary committee for foreign affairs and defence, which contained the following sentence, which can hardly be believed to stem from a member of the EU and NATO in the 21st century:

„Greece's national goal is the respect of international borders and the status quo in the Balkan region, but the country will not be apathetic in case of revisory policies aim at changing the existing borders."

Yet this Greek attitude towards Macedonia is in fact nothing new: Even in 1992, the international press speculated about secret plans by the then Greek Prime Minister Mitsotakis and the Serbian President Milošević to divide Macedonia up between their two states.[101] In yet another case, the Greek press reported on a US study which claimed that in the case of a spill-over of the Serbian-Albanian conflict into Macedonia, the government in Athens was planning a military occupation of an area measuring 30 km in width along the border, but *within Macedonian territory* – allegedly in order to fend off the impending flood of Albanian refugees.

What else is this, if not a case of imperialism in Europe at the end of the 20th century! (However, it seems that a certain Great Power prevented such nonsense when the contingency actually arose.)

As early as in the summer of 2002, Rainer Hermann wrote:

"In the nineties, Greece was the only member of NATO and EU to support the regime of Slobodan Milošević." "Unlike German and American companies, Greek companies did not adhere to the" [UN-] "embargo against the residual Yugoslavia."

But also:

"Greece's uncritical solidarity with Milošević's regime, especially during the premiership of Papandreou, has given way to a more constructive policy under his successor Simitis."[102]

Greece seems to fear that the existence of the Republic of Macedonia "could stimulate the national consciousness of the Macedonian minority in Northern Greece."[103] In their view, Macedonia might possibly claim rights for this minority or even the return of Macedonian territory annexed by Greece in the Balkan wars 90 years ago, then amounting to 51% of the total territory of Macedonia.[104]

On this topic, Prof. Höpken writes:

"Above all, Athens took offence at Skopje's constitutional claim to represent the Macedonians living outside the country, fearing that it might derive territorial claims from this right."[105]

For, as Marie-Jeanne Calic points out, Art. 49 of the Macedonian constitution of November 17th 1991 "postulated the protection of minorities and the cultural advancement of Macedonians living abroad."[106]

Prof. Calic does not fail, however, to add
> "that Art.108 of the Greek Constitution also claims Athens' responsibility for the Greek diaspora." (loc.cit.)

Greece is evidently applying double standards.
> "Even the fact that Skopje had explicitly renounced all territorial claims in the constitution was not able to dispel Greek reservations in this matter."[107]

The amendment to the constitution in 1992 was based on a recommendation of the Badinter commission in Brussels, of which the former German President Herzog was a member, as the then President of the Federal Constitutional Court; according to this commission, of all the Yugoslav successor states, only the Macedonian and Slovenian constitutions met West European standards.

Greece's alleged fear of small Macedonia appears to be a pretext meant to cover up for, and ensure the continuation of, and its aggressive policy towards Macedonia.

This shows that NATO member Greece is not concerned with its safety from an attack by the "Great Power" Macedonia, but only with disturbing and ultimately preventing the normalization of relations between the Republic of Macedonia and the other member countries of the UN, especially of the EU and NATO.

At an Easter reception for the diplomatic corps held in Skopje in 1994, the "Archbishop of Ohrid and Macedonia" Michael made a small speech in which he put the Greek pretext of "fear" in relation to a moral category, saying that the Greeks were suffering from a guilty conscience rather than from fear on account of Macedonia. However, it is hardly possible to apply such high standards of ethics and morals when dealing with the unscrupulous and powerful Southern neighbour, particularly in international relations dictated by hard interests.

Since the annexation of the total Macedonian territory in 1912/13, there has, inevitably, been a Macedonian minority in Greece. International support for this minority is long overdue and sorely needed, especially as Greece does not acknowledge any of its minorities under its state doctrine.

Among others, Christian Voss points out
> "that the EU member state Greece does not recognize the ... Slavic minority, and that important human rights (such as the free use of its mother tongue) have been trampled underfoot for decades."[108]

In addition to that, some states are handled with kid gloves even when they have signed minority resolutions without reservations. Thus, Gerhard Seewann points out that, according to the Helsinki document of the 4th CSCE follow-up meeting of July 1992, the High Commissioner for National Minorities, former Dutch Foreign Minister Max van der Stoel
> "has so far not addressed the legally and politically precarious situation of the Turkish, Pomak, Macedonian, Albanian, Aromanian and other national minorities in Greece ", although his mandate would allow him to do so.[109]

If, for comparison, you then look at the fact that in 2001, the Republic of Macedonia was forced by the Europeans under the leadership of the United States not only to explicitly guarantee the rights of the Albanian minority in the constitution – which was acceptable as it remedied an omission in the constitution of 1989 – but also to grant an amnesty to Albanian UÇK terrorists – which is not acceptable at all – it becomes clear to all the world that, once again, a double standard was being applied. This was proved convincingly by Seewann:

> "All Southeast European governments without exception consider minority rights to be a kind of act of mercy on the part of the state, and not at all a guaranteed object enjoying legal protection. In this, they act in conformity with the majority of governments in other parts of Europe." To cite only two of the examples listed: "In this regard, Bulgaria and Romania are pronounced by their constitutions (both of 1991) to be national states in which minorities are only tolerated. Here, Romania declares itself to be a 'unified and indivisible national state' based on 'the unity of the Romanian people', in which 'national sovereignty belongs to the Romanian people'. Bulgaria has chosen a similar approach."[110]

Will these states be made to change their constitution before they join the EU? It seems so.

Greece has not always denied the existence of a Macedonian minority in Northern Greece. Whenever it was important for Greece to appear in a positive light in international organisations, the Greeks very flexibly adjusted to international expectations:

When, at the End of World War I, Athens had signed the contract of Sèvres on August 10th 1920, the Greek government met its obligations by presenting the League of Nations with a school primer for Macedonian children living in Southern Macedonia which had been annexed by Greece in 1912/13; this was the famous ABeCeDar book based on the dialects of Lerin and Bitola (En Athinaiz, Typoiz P.D. Sakellarioy, 1925). It appears that the background for this primer, i.e. a corresponding need of the children of the Macedonian minority in the area annexed by Greece, was quite clear to the League of Nations. Its Secretary-General, Sir J. Erik Drummond, accepted the primer in its original form. (To understand and approve of this acceptance, it suffices to look at the facsimile reprint of 1985 in Makedonska Revija, Skopje, which the author was able to consult.) Discussions within the League of Nations led to the irony of history that the Greek representative, Vasilis Dendramis, defended the primer against the Bulgarians, who claimed the ABeCeDar to be incomprehensible, by arguing that the Macedonian language was neither Bulgarian nor Serbian but an independent language of its own!

> *The Macedonians could not have wished for a more effective advocate of the independence of their language than Greece.*

On the other hand, these past events do not provide much support for the Bulgarian case. For how can Bulgaria proclaim to the world that Macedonians speak Bulgarian if they do not even understand a Macedonian elementary school primer!

However, Macedonian schoolchildren in northern Greece never even caught sight of that primer. After the session of the League of Nations, the existing copies were destroyed. Instead, the use of the Macedonian language was prohibited and offences led to severe fines and corporal punishment; even children in schools were beaten if they spoke Macedonian among themselves. In churches, using the Macedonian language was declared from the pulpit to be the "greatest sin". Also, orthodox services held in Old Church Slavonic were banned; Slavic inscriptions on Macedonian icons and gravestones as well as on frescoes were destroyed or painted over. Slavic family names had to be changed to Greek ones. At village festivities, gangs of thugs made sure that the Greek national order was maintained by stopping Macedonian music and Macedonian dances in particular. (This was not only restricted to the period of the notorious Premier Metaxas who came into office in 1936.)

But, nobody at the League of Nations did anything about it ...

There have always been similar situations of conflict in history. In former times, these were solved by force. Today, better methods are available. If the Greeks have any reason to complain, they should consult the appropriate bodies instead of using diplomatic tricks behind the backs of great powers and international organizations to gain advantages that will put a weaker neighbour into a hopeless situation. The Greek tendency to stop all discussion of these questions only leads to the suspicion that there might by something wrong with the Greek claims. Or, to put it in the words of ex-Chancellor Helmut Schmidt: "If you take criticism amiss, you have something to hide."[111]

1.3.4 The three neighbouring states

Prof. Weithmann reminds us that these three neighbouring states of Macedonia held bilateral talks in spring 1991 which resulted in "joint statements" to the effect "that there were only 'Serbs, Bulgarians and Greeks living in Macedonia', so that there was 'no Macedonian nation'."[112]
Nota bene: This was not in 1891, but in 1991.
As late as 1998, the renowned historian Stefan Troebst has had to deal with the claims these states still are making with regard to Macedonia because they refuse to come to terms with the political reality of the democratically legitimated Republic of Macedonia, and the following description of their national historiographies certainly casts doubts on the state of democracy in these countries, as well as their respect for human rights:

> "Institutionalization and a professional status have not necessarily led to greater maturity in the national historiographies of the neighbouring countries; quite the contrary, these are often anachronistic. ... They rarely exhibit an ability to react flexibly to the occurrence of glaring discrepancies between myth and reality."[113]

Four pages later, Troebst adds:

> "Even if the Hellenic hysteria of 1992-1995 concerning Macedonia is currently subsiding, Greek historiography still plays the part of a collective propagandist in macedonicis."

In another publication, he points out:

> "The exploitation of the past for day-to-day political purposes, as it is practised everywhere from Greece to Slovenia, and the resulting merging of the political sphere with institutionalized historiography have, in the socialist period, brought forth the hybrid type of the historian-politician who easily switches from one area to the other".[114]

Generations of historians in Bulgaria, Greece and Serbia have tried hard since the last third of the 19th century to rewrite the history of Slavic Macedonia on the basis of "entirely different ethnographical premises", governed by ideology and national interest. "Historical knowledge ... is taken out of its context and converted into political statements."[115] This reduces their scientific value, but the governments in question seem to be hoping that the world public will get used to, and bored, with all this.
Finally, another comment by Christian Voss:

> "In the epoch of national 'rebirth' in the 18th and 19th centuries, the national movements in Greece, Serbia and Bulgaria ... develop a discourse of unbroken continuity with their extensive dynastic kingdoms of the Middle Ages" ... "with the ultimate aim of regaining the territories ... that ... belonged to the respective countries for a short time."[116]

1.3.5 Albanians

In the period this study is concerned with (i.e. from the Congress of Berlin to the First World War), Macedonia's fourth neighbour Albania was only of minor importance. In the Republic of Macedonia today, however, the Albanians play a more important role than any of the other neighbouring peoples. This is due to the fact that the Albanians do not only live in neighbouring Albania and in the Serbian province of Kosovo (as well as in Greece and Montenegro), but also as a minority in Macedonia itself. This means that the Albanian ethnic group - unlike the Bulgarians, Serbs and Greeks - is itself a part of Macedonian society rather than just a factor of foreign politics.

1.)
As early as 1991, when Macedonia declared its independence, it was clear that Albanian action was not aimed at a peaceful future of living together within the borders of Macedonia. On the contrary, their single-minded measures had a very different purpose:
The Albanians refused to participate in the census. This gave the impression that they were trying to prevent any attempts to substantiate the extrapolated value of 22,9 % of the total population of Macedonia. The ulterior motive may have been the desire to obtain a disproportionately large share both of the Macedonian territory and its social and state institutions. They would still need several years to reach the proportion of 40% which they were already claiming, and in the meantime no census was to be held. In addition to that, they were supporting the naturalization of those Albanians who had immigrated from Albania or Kosovo to Macedonia illegally, as well as of the refugees who had streamed into Macedonia after the first instances of unrest in Kosovo in 1981, and especially during the Kosovo war of 1993. Due to their high fertility rate, they would probably be able to reach a proportion of 40% after a certain period and would then be willing to take part in a census. Macedonian reactions expressed misgivings concerning this development and a feeling that Macedonians were under pressure from a growing minority in their own country.
This fear led to a formula from the Yugoslav constitution of 1974 being introduced into the Macedonian constitution of 1991, defining Macedonia as the "nation-state of the Macedonian people" rather than e.g. ' the state of the Macedonian people and the Albanian and Turkish minorities.'[117]
Christian Voss comments as follows:
> "By introducing this passage ... Macedonia repeated the mistake of the other Balkan states who had declared themselves ... monoethnic nation-states in the 19th and 20th century and especially after the Balkan wars in 1912/13."[118]

Gerhard Seewann, on the other hand, points out that, after all, the preamble of the Macedonian constitution
> "... has guaranteed equal rights to the – explicitly listed – minorities of Albanians, Turks, Vlachs or Aromanians and Roma, along with 'other national groups', so that these groups are all formally acknowledged by the constitution."[119]

Regarding this crucial aspect, the Albanians seem to have succeeded in making the western powers accept their own biased view.

At least the ethnic Albanians did take part in Macedonian parliamentary elections, after they had at first boycotted presidential elections. Surprisingly, the number of representatives elected by the Albanian minority in Macedonia did not even reach the proportion of the total population specified in the official statistics, i.e. 22,9% (not to mention the claimed 40%). The first free elections in Macedonia in 1990 produced 23 Albanian representatives in a parliament of 120, a proportion of 19.2%. Then, in 1994, there were 19 representatives, i.e.15.8%, whereas in 1998 there were 21 (+1) = 22, i.e. 18.3% of the total number of representatives. So quite a lot less than 22,9 %.

These figures are not compatible with the alleged 40% of Albanian population in Macedonia – especially since no Albanian, or only a marginal, not to say infinitesimal number, would have voted for a non-Albanian party. The ominous figure of 40% of Albanians in Macedonia thus seems to the author to be nothing else but the result of political strategy.

Prof. Oschlies lists a number of irritations on both sides, among them the Albanians' "unilateral proclamation of an Albanian 'Republic of Ilirida'" in western Macedonia after their illegal internal referendum (on January 11th and 12th 1992).[120] To the author's knowledge, none of the usually vigilant international organizations nor any of the dedicated Western arbitrators have ever encouraged the Albanians to remove this stumbling block from the path towards interethnic understanding.

The crux of the problem lies in the fact that nobody can prove to, let alone guarantee, the Macedonians that the Albanians would have abstained from proclaiming their own republic within the Republic of Macedonia or dropped secessionist plans if the Macedonian constitution of 1991 had contained a modern text in the first place.

Experts in this matter actually claim the opposite: had the Albanians been recognized as an official minority (or even constitutive part) of the Macedonian state, they would have used this status to claim autonomy and seen it as a first step towards separating their territory from Macedonia and a subsequent unification with Kosovo (or even Albania). Seewann pointed out that the Albanians in Macedonia (as if in preparation thereof) "are demanding a federalization based on the Belgian model."[121] As if *one* "Belgian solution" in Europe was not enough! Seen against the background of the tragic consequences of ethnic polarization since Belgian independence in 1830, such a suggestion cannot but arouse concern.

Similarly, the highly significant but hardly comprehensible, insistence of the Albanian ethnic group in Macedonia on hoisting a *foreign* flag, the Albanian flag, (if possible not accompanied by the Macedonian national flag) points in a direction that is conspicuous as well as unacceptable both for the Macedonian titular nation and for all foreign countries: towards Great Albania!

During a meeting of members of the European Parliament with Macedonian and Albanian members of the parliament of the Republic of Macedonia, the Sobranie, which was held in the house of the author of this book, a member of the Danish delegation tried to explain to an Albanian colleague that such an absurd plan would be completely unthinkable in Denmark, his home country. However, he met with insensibility and a complete lack of understanding on the part of his interlocutor.

The Macedonians made it clear that behind this separatist behaviour, they feared a tendency towards cutting off western Macedonia. They quoted radical Albanian leaders who had publicly supported the unification of all Albanians.

Voss comments on this quite correctly:
> Against the historical background, "current division scenarios relating to the separation of the ... territories inhabited by Albanians ... are regarded by the Macedonian population ... as a

compulsive repetition ... of the division of the Macedonian region endorsed by Western Europe after the Balkan wars of 1912/13."[122]

He also takes account of the burden borne by both peoples:

> He says it is fatal for the Macedonian-Albanian conflict that both peoples see themselves "as victims of the development throughout the 20th century: due to a belated nationalism which was borne out of a defensive position, a considerable part of the ethnic group ... remained outside the new state structure when the state was first founded."[122]

Any kind of Albanian unification would be equivalent to the destruction of the Macedonian state. In so far, there seems to be a coincidence of interests between the Albanian minority and the three other neighbouring states, in which, however, the Macedonians cannot acquiesce.

Another look at some historical processes will make this even clearer: Macedonia's chance to free itself from the Turkish yoke at the beginning of the 20th century was thwarted by the military intervention of its neighbours Bulgaria, Greece and Serbia. The Macedonians could only escape their clutches that might have proved fatal for their identity, by obtaining recognition as a nation in the Serbian part of their former territory and - a certain degree of - independence within the Yugoslav federation of 1944, albeit on part of their territory. In addition to that, they had to put up with considerable delays compared with their neighbouring states, i.e. they were freed

31 years after Albania
36 years after Bulgaria
66 years after Serbia, Romania and Montenegro and
115 years after Greece.

Only the turn taken by world history in 1989/90 finally brought them full political sovereignty in 1991.

Thus, the above-mentioned omission in the constitution is not only to be attributed to the Macedonians' relief and joy about an aim achieved happily even if belatedly, but also to their unbelievably bad experience with the neighbouring peoples in the past and the ensuing mistrust they feel in the present. (A quite justified mistrust – as the reader will be prepared to admit after reading this book.)

2.)

Nobody can seriously claim that the Albanians have suffered or been victimized in Macedonia in the past 50 years, unlike in Serbia – or in Albania itself. This did not stop Albanian extremists from acting as malefactors in Macedonia. Since the beginning of the year 2001, Albanian radicals have made every effort to truly "enforce" the creation of a second state for their compatriots within Macedonia. Unimpressed by the complete lack of any justification by international law, they began, in a first step, by making Western Macedonia "free of Slavs".

However fundamental the Albanian minority in Macedonia may have considered the aforementioned constitutional fault to be – it was certainly not irreparable. It in no way justified the deployment of ethnic Albanian and even foreign, i.e. Albanian or Kosovar, terrorists, so that in order to save the Macedonian state and to avoid an outburst that would have been a danger for the whole Balkan area and thus for Europe itself, international institutions had to intervene to prevent a civil war. The brutal UÇK action was so excessive that it gave rise to the suspicion that its aim was not to achieve a constitutional reform long overdue but to use it as a pretext to disproportionately extend

Albanian territory within the Macedonian state at the expense of the Macedonian titular nation.

The Albanian political programme left no doubts as to the objective of the terrorist actions. In the FAZ of June 19th 2001, Prof. Troebst quoted UÇK leader Salihu as follows:
> "Bitola" [in Macedonia] "is the most southern city of Great Kosovo and Bar" [in Montenegro] the most northern."

At roughly the same time, Jakup Krasniqi, spokesperson of the party of Menduh Thaci ("The Snake") was quoted in the bulletin of the Südosteuropa-Gesellschaft with the following remark:
> "We want more than independence. Our aim is the unification of all Albanians in the Balkans."

Thus the German Member of Parliament Willy Wimmer who spoke on March 17th 2001 on Deutschlandfunk radio could only sum up:
> "The Albanians' aim is Great Albania."

The accompanying propaganda vividly illustrates the Albanian method: When the first gunshots were fired by Albanian terrorists in Tetovo in February 2001, one of the UÇK leaders appeared in the MONITOR program on German TV on April 5th, saying:
> "We were returning the fire."

(Only a specification of the time was missing to make this comparable with a propaganda trick used at the end of the thirties which the older among us still remember very well.)

One of the elements of Albanian strategy is the systematic vilification of their adversaries, the Macedonians. Once, when some Albanians were demonstrating in Macedonia (and why should they not), you could read the reason given by one of them in the FAZ of April 7th 2001:
> "This is a demonstration against Macedonian state terrorism."

Clearly, the international accusation of terrorism levelled at the UÇK Albanians was perceived to be so objectionable on account of its potential to damage their reputation that it was immediately converted into a groundless counter-accusation in order to redirect international attention from the beam in one's own eye to the splinter in the Macedonian eye – an age-old method.

To give the Macedonians and the world a foretaste of the dimensions of their political and territorial pretensions, some radical Albanians have, with unique aggressiveness, gone as far as to call the Slavic Macedonians "occupiers".
In their own country!
Obviously, they are following the example of the Greeks and Bulgarians, insinuating that Macedonia is original Albanian territory. It is their bad luck that the Greeks have already claimed it as Greek and the Bulgarians as Bulgarian territory. (And the Serbs used to see it as Serbian.)
Also in summer 2001, the chief editor of an Albanian newspaper based in Switzerland voiced the following abuse on German television:
> "The Macedonians are barbarians, they are a brainless people."

Is this the ideal procedure: to raise one's children in the spirit of disintegration in a country where all ethnic groups have no choice but to live together in peace?

3.)
One of the most popular arguments used by Albanians both in Kosovo and in (western) Macedonia is, as already shown, a claim that recalls the Bulgarian, Greek and Serbian method, namely the claim that the Macedonian region has "always" been inhabited by Albanians.

Therefore, they do everything they can to ethnically cleanse western Macedonia. Given that in summer 2001 Albanian representatives did not even refrain from using German media to declare the Macedonian capital Skopje their own for allegedly "historical" reasons, I would like to take this occasion to correct this shameless falsehood by citing a literary example. As for the "literary" example, it is worth mentioning how highly internationally recognized historians rate their "writing" colleagues; Barabara Tuchman ("Der stolze Turm", (A portrait of the world before the First World War, 1890-1914)) draws on some of the authors of novels as "social historians of priceless value". In the opinion of this author, this is also true for Luan Starova (and for Rhea Galanaki, cf. chapter 2.3.0).

The award-winning Albanian author Luan Starova has related his childhood experiences in one of his books: His father, whose "reasons for such a sudden departure" from the Albanian homeland were incomprehensible to the young boy, had asked a good friend to take him and his family in an old boat "like in Noah's ark" to the other side of Lake Ohrid, where the "uprooted people" then lived "in this city so severely tried by history" [he is referring to the capital Skopje]:[123]

> "For a long time, our family history remained a great secret for all who lived in the shepherds' quarter. Newcomers that we were, with a foreign language and a strange religion ... we were ... like an inaccessible island for a long time." (Starova: loc. cit., p. 59) "The breakers of war had cast many arks with rescued families upon this land, from all parts of the Balkans and from even further abroad. There were a few Sephardic families, a family of Armenian musicians, there were ... a few Turkish families, a few families from Greek Macedonia, and here, too, was our Albanian family, amid the large Macedonian population in this little shepherds' republic." (p. 83 et sq.)

Moreover, the reader finds out about the political and ideological background:

> "The party had promised all these people a dazzling future, if only they left the mountains and became a new class – the strong, steely, stormy, exemplary, fearless, invincible working class..." (p.51)

It can be assumed from these slogans that this is no eyewitness account of 1690 (about the Karpoš insurrection) or 1878 (about the Congress of Berlin), nor of 1903 (about the Ilinden Uprising) or 1913 (about the Balkan wars), nor does it even stem from World War I – it is simply a literarily idealized description of events in the first years of Yugoslav (and Albanian!) communism after 1945.

> *One may assume that the author would not have hesitated to write about a large community of Albanian families in Skopje if it had existed. But it simply did not exist – contrary to the claims of the "new class" of Albanian extremists in Macedonia.*

This is also supported by plain facts, even though they are not as impressive as a story which is lyrical despite the hardness of the times; for instance Christian Voss, who writes:

> "In 1946, the Albanian share of the population of the Republic of Macedonia was not more than 8% (89,000)". He therefore concluded: "There was no Albanian problem in the nineteen-fifties and nineteen-sixties."[124]

Besides the Macedonian themselves, all Balkan experts know that the next batch of Albanian immigrants only came to Skopje after the earthquake in 1963 at Tito's invitation, who was then pursuing a population strategy similar to the policies of the Great Powers France and England since the end of the Second World War. After the internal student revolt in Kosovo in 1981 there was a further immigration of approx. 150,000 Kosovo Albanians who were legally recognized as Yugoslavs but not as citizens of the Macedonian sub-republic.

In the recent past, radical Albanians have used the desperate plight of the refugees from Kosovo who fled to Macedonia for fear of Serbian massacres etc. for their political aims: It became known from reports in the press that in order to bolster their claims to Macedonian territory and increase moral pressure both on Macedonia and abroad, they strove to keep as many of the 335,000 Albanian refugees (a UNHCR figure[125]) from Kosovo as possible in Macedonia.

(For them, this was the only way of approaching the figure of 40% for the ethnic Albanian population of Macedonia, as opposed to the 22.9% established by the census.) Following the Bulgarian-Greek-Serbian example, the Albanians have construed a claim to Macedonian territory that is allegedly based on historical rights. At the time Starova's book was written, the Albanians had common values; at the time, the exemplary part of the Albanian *canon leca duqadini* was still applicable (as was pointed out by the Albanian politician and journalist Adelina Marku at the second German-Macedonian conference at the beginning of December 2001 in Jena).

Thus, the book also contains the following passage:

> "My father (was) not only a newcomer to this town ...but also an immigrant, a person who had crossed a border to come into this land. So he had to ... behave loyally if he wanted to gain the citizenship he aspired to for himself and his family."[126]

At that time, the hospitality for which the Albanians were renowned was still a highly respected value. Today, things are different. Today, the world is confronted with the down side of the "canon", under which everything is allowed and even imperative that will serve Albanian interests: demands, threats, insults and violence.

> In this way, the extremists among the Albanians are trying to drive the Macedonians out of their own country in order to come closer to the aim defined above.
>
> *In doing this, they seem to remain indifferent to the fact that their peaceful country-men, too, are suffering from the general loss of reputation.*

4.)

Although the Albanians had to acknowledge that neither the USA nor the EU were prepared to break international law on their account and arbitrarily alter borders, which would have incalculable consequences for the whole world (especially for the successor states of former colonies, but also for 'neuralgic' regions in Europe), they are doing everything they can to turn the 'Field of the Blackbirds' (Kosovo) into an independent state.

The international public, on the other hand, cannot understand why the Albanians should be the only people in Europe with two states. Voss reminds us of the argument of the English social historian Eric Hobsbawm:

Even in the Yugoslav constitution of 1974, the Albanians "were not recognized as a constitutive people ... even though they were more numerous than smaller but constitutive peoples such as the Slovenes, Macedonians and Montenegrins", because they had a national state of their own, namely neighbouring Albania.[127] This is still the case.

Hobsbawm may not have developed the underlying theory all on his own, but he certainly expressed it most concisely:
To each nation a state, but only one state to each nation.

Quite consistently, neither the USA nor the EU or any of its member states have supported the Albanians in their open pursuit of independence. And if this is true of Kosovo, which did not even have the status of a sub-republic in the Federal Republic of Yugoslavia, but only that of an autonomous province within the sub-republic of Serbia (similar to that of the Vojvodina), then it is true a fortiori for the western part of the Republic of Macedonia, where the Albanians never had any other status but that of a minority.

The Albanians have understood how to use their lobby to present themselves as victims (which they actually were – in Serbia and Kosovo, but not at all in Macedonia) and to secure international support against the Macedonian government, the parliament and the whole people.

How many international politicians and other well-meaning decision-makers had sworn to themselves: The 20th century ended with terrible ethnic cleansings – and the 21st must not repeat this! This sounded good. But in western Macedonia, the very first stroke of the bell that announced the 21st century and the third millennium brought *ethnic cleansing*. We can still hear the echo of the words of NATO Secretary General George Robertson and the EU High Representative Javier Solana: There will be no negotiations with (UÇK) terrorists. (After the official abolishment of the old UÇK, they can hardly have overlooked the prompt founding of a new UÇK under the name AKSh that wants to "continue the armed conflict" und openly pursues "Great Albanian objectives."[128]) However that may be, radical Albanians in Macedonia and in the rest of Europe are now allowed to take the microphone and naïvely confess to the world:

"We'd rather live amongst ourselves."

What if the Dutch were to express this opinion in the Netherlands or the Danes in Denmark?

Macedonian Albanians not only express their desire for segregation, for active *apartheid*, they also act accordingly. At the time in question, the press was full of reports about houses set on fire and churches exploding. It was reported that Christian Slavs were being driven out, kidnapped, forced by violence to leave their neighbourhoods or even murdered. Not on a massive scale or spectacularly, only in individual actions, - but systematically and consistently. This can be compared with the events of 2004 in Kosovo, which a renowned historian has called "tailor-made unrest".

This procedure suggests that for the unspeakable suffering they had to endure at the hands of the Serbs, the Albanians are taking bloody revenge on the Macedonians who are innocent and present no danger to them.

5.)
Let us not be mistaken.
The ethnic Albanians in Macedonia have already come a long way: With the help of the West, which has been behaving both naïvely and thoughtlessly, the Macedonian government and parliament have been pressured in to accepting a right of veto for the Albanian minority in parliamentary legislative processes – allegedly, this was "only" to apply to laws that affect minorities. But, as the retired Ambassador Schrameyer rightly pointed out at a conference in summer 2002: "Which law doesn't?"

Already the Albanians in Macedonia can do as they please, since the Albanian minority can overrule the Macedonian majority. This means that, as a result of international action, the Macedonians have been legally incapacitated in their own state in an unparalleled and degrading process.

Further goals are clearly discernible: As in western Macedonia, it is also reported from the north of the capital Skopje that the Macedonian inhabitants are systematically being driven out with the aim of staking out the Albanian claims according to plan.

In view of Albanian violence, Europeans and especially Americans should show more understanding for the Macedonians' hesitation in the face of the increasing danger to their political - and possibly even individual - existence. Instead, the West made the Macedonian government amnesty terrorists. Some of these now occupy high political posts in Macedonia. Will they remain as peaceful as they pretend to be? It does not take great intelligence to imagine what would otherwise be in store for the Macedonian population - and for Europe - in the years to come.

If you judge the Albanians by the potential for criminal energy they ostentatiously display and you are not lulled into believing their words and lamentations, the prospects for their living peacefully with the Macedonians are extremely unfavourable.

SPIEGEL correspondent Walter Mayr summarized his impressions in the edition of March 26th 2001:

> "There may be reasons for improving the Albanians' situation in Macedonia even further. But it is a clan-based organized culture of ritualized lamentation, of disguise, of deception..." "It is the shadows of the oriental heritage that separate the Albanian people from its neighbours and even more from the rest of Europe."

When there were Albanian acts of violence against Serbs and Roma in Kosovo in March 2004, even the most famous Albanian writer Ismail Kadaré criticized this "racist" outbreak, as Beqë Cufaj reported in the FAZ of April 18th 2004: In his essay "Humiliation in the Balkans" he "also tackled the problem presented by the fact that the Albanians tended to posture as victims not only in Kosovo but also in Macedonia."

Thus, with a view to finally dismantling some psychological barriers, it is to be welcomed that "Forensic scientists of the International Criminal Tribunal for the former Yugoslavia in Den Haag" have started exhuming alleged ethnic Albanian victims of a Macedonian police action dating back to August 2001.[129]

Still one wonders how the Albanians succeeded in having Albanian victims of the Macedonian police exhumed while having been able to prevent the exhumation of Macedonian victims of the Albanian UÇK.

This seems to fit in with the fact that the Albanian murderers of Macedonian policemen are classed as "criminals" by the Europeans and Americans, not as terrorists as international usage would suggest. Is there a bias involved?

Prof. Höpken points out that solving the Macedonian-Albanian conflict "will largely depend on further developments in Kosovo":

> "Especially if Kosovo moves towards independence, there would be noticeable consequences in Macedonia, whereupon the demand that areas with Albanian inhabitants in western Macedonia be united with an independent "Republic of Kosova" might be voiced."[130]

This potential threat cannot but increase the Macedonians' mistrust of the ethnic Albanian minority in their republic.

Quite appropriately in this context, the voice of the Yugoslav president Vojislav Koštunica coming from the background of the residual Yugoslavia can be heard, who points out in an interview with FAZ correspondent Michael Martens with regards to the relations between Serbia and Montenegro:

> "We should understand that a bigger state can contribute more to stability in the Balkans than several smaller ones. During his stays in Macedonia, he had been under the impression that the Slav Macedonians shared this opinion and were convinced that they would be safer within the framework of a larger federation, without desiring the reestablishment of Yugoslavia, said Koštunica."[131]

We can gather from an essay by Wim van Meurs (Südosteuropa-Mitteilungen 04/2002) that *Albanian terrorism* has long gone beyond the borders of little Macedonia and even Kosovo and Albania. However, reports on connections with Islamic fundamentalism in other countries, such as the Al Qaida network, are still only hearsay. We hope they remain so.

Finally, it may be helpful to quote former Foreign Minister Genscher who wrote in his "Memoirs":

> "No aggression can ever be justified, just as victims and aggressors should never be put on the same level and ethnic cleansings never be accepted. Whoever undertakes them – he should never count on later approval."[132]

The hope remains that the day may not come on which we will be in the embarrassing situation of having to call to mind the incontestable principles thus laid down by Foreign Minister Genscher.

1.3.6 The international community

The international community did respect the legal consequences of the free elections in Macedonia in November/December 1990 and the referendum of September 8th 1991. However, it left the reservations of the neighbouring states unresolved. Even worse: without objecting - and clearly even without checking the justification - it fulfilled the Greek request of imposing the provisional name "Former Yugoslav Republic of Macedonia" ("FYROM"): first in the EU, with the European council deciding in Lisbon on June 26th 1992 (Prof. Troebst has called the resulting Macedonian declaration an anti-Macedonian declaration[133]), then at the UN on April 8th 1993.

This name degrades the Republic of Macedonia and reduces its political integrity to a temporary arrangement in the eyes of the world. Unlike Bulgaria and Serbia, Athens can afford to push the EU and NATO candidate Macedonia about as it pleases, because Greece, being a full member, need not fear any pressure, let alone exclusion, from these organizations – at the worst, it would receive a half-hearted warning.

The population, parliament and government of Macedonia have to live with the fact that, after finally gaining independence, they are dependent on the good or bad will of their neighbours. If it is to follow the principles arising from the European values, the EU must not allow one of its members to bar the access of a recognized sovereign European state to European and international institutions under its rightful name for no established reason.

> *This gives rise to the suspicion that this denial of its rightful name is meant to deprive the Macedonian state of the basis of its existence so as to leave it to destruction. As I have already hinted, Greece need not be the sole cause of such*

destruction. As the end of the 19th and the early 20th century have shown, and as can again be seen at the beginning of the 21st century, there are enough interested parties seeking to profit from the extinction of Macedonia.

Such relapses in particular, which recall bad memories of the period of imperialistic expansionism prove time and again that any hopes that Macedonia might dispense with a rectification of its provisional name in order that international relations may continue undisturbed, are misfounded.

For, as Claudia Hopf has summed up as one of the results of her study:

> "... Language and language-based designations (represent) an eminently important means of exemplifying and promoting nationalist goals."[134]

1.3.7 The problem

The stance adopted by Macedonia's neighbouring states raises a number of questions:

- What induces seemingly respectable states like Bulgaria, Serbia and Greece, as well as the Albanian minority in Macedonia, to deny a sovereign state its right to exist?

- What are the reasons for this denial and resentment?

- Did this Macedonia which they lay claim to not exist as a region inhabited by a people with its own identity?

- Do the neighbouring states really have a historical right to Macedonia?

- What are their claims based on?

- And were the Macedonians really Bulgarians, Serbs or Greeks after all?

Quod esset demonstrandum.

2 THE DEVELOPMENT OF THE BALKAN LEAGUE IN THE BALKAN STATES

2.1 Serbia

If this analysis starts with reports about Serbia, this is not just due to geographical reasons such as the fact that the liberation of the European and Christian peoples from Turkish and Islamic rule took place in a relatively organic development from North to South, i.e. contrary to the original sequence in which these countries were conquered.[135] It is also a consequence of chronology. At the beginning of the 19th century, the Serbs were the first Balkan people to start rebelling which did, in spite of serious setbacks, ultimately lead to their separation from the Ottoman Empire, even if they were not the first state to do so.

2.1.0 Historical background

1.
"The Serbian tribal community had" migrated to the Balkans "around the year 626".
> "The individual tribes succeeded only gradually to form tribal states on small territories, which could then be unified in the second half of the 12th century."[136]

Unlike the more agile cultures of the Eurasian horsemen whose activities, including those of an economic kind, were wider-ranging, the agricultural peasant cultures of the Slavic settlers were only based on subsistence farming, but were also less prone to crisis. Thus, a rapid and long-term expansion of their territories was not a matter of political existence for them.
> On the contrary, "establishing lasting kingdoms ... could well take centuries: More than 500 years passed between the settling of the Serbian tribes and the establishment of the medieval kingdom."[137]

The first "comparatively favourable basis for the political unification of the Serbian tribes offered itself in the 11th century, first in Duklja on the Adriatic coast (Dioclea, the later Montenegro)", when a number of local princes started resisting Byzantine suzerainty.
> "However, the attempt to maintain and extend independence failed because of internal disputes."[138]

The later state of the Nemanjic´ dynasty first took shape in the 12th century in the old Serbian town of Raszein (Raška). The two sons of Stefan Nemanja succeeded in putting themselves at the head of both the state *and* the church and manoeuvred skilfully between powers, so as to finally make Serbia the "leading power in the central Balkans".
> "The weak period of the Byzantine Empire after the conquest of Constantinople by a "Latin" crusading army under Venetian leadership in 1204 made it easier for Nemanja's successors to continue their work of unification unhindered. The unexpected influx of Mongol Tatars into the Danube area in 1241/42 protected them from further ambitions of the Hungarian kings and gave them an irreversible lead over their Bulgarian competitor."[138]

"Under the youthful king Stefan Dušan Uroš IV (1331-1355), a large Serbian kingdom emerged, which reached from the Dalmatian coast and Epirus to the Morava-Vardar line and included parts of central Greece." [After his coronation in Skopje] in 1346, Stefan Dušan proudly assumed the title of Emperor of the Serbs and Greeks. After his death, however, the Serbian-Greek kingdom disintegrated into a large number of smaller units run by powerful dynasties."[139]

These included, among many others, the kingdom of Prilep under Volkašin since 1365 and of his son Marko. (This kingdom was independent from 1371 to 1385, then became a Turkish satellite and fell entirely under Turkish rule after Marko's death in 1395.)

Even before then, the Byzantines had felt pressured by the Serbs into calling the Ottomans in from the other side of the Bosporus – a fatal decision, as the Turks not only crushed the Serbs (on June 28th 1389 on Kosovo Polje) but also conquered Byzantium in 1453.

When the Holy League, under Austrian leadership, had to call off their campaign for liberating the Christian Balkan peoples and withdrew from the central Balkans in 1690, the fear of reprisals at the hands of the returning Turks was great among the Serbs.

> "... in 1691 and 1740, many Serbs went north, seeking the protection of the Habsburg Empire, and the Albanians moved up from the West."[140]

These new settlements on the "Field of the Blackbirds", which the Albanians later called Kosova, have been the cause of bloody territorial conflicts unto the present day. Viktor Meier quotes a relevant passage:

> "Even in 1939, the ratio of Serbs to Albanians in Kosovo was only approx. 40:60. Then, after the census of 1981, 77.5% of the inhabitants of the Kosovo region – or 1.23 million – were Albanians."[141]

The Serbs (about 300,000 families) were moved behind the Save-Danube line "in a deliberate rescue operation during the withdrawal of the emperor's troops" in 1690.

> "By imperial privilege, which granted them religious freedom and autonomy, they were allowed to settle on South Hungarian territory" [recaptured by Habsburg], "in Slavonia, and on the military border between Slavonia and Croatia."[142]

As we know, the ethnic mixture in these regions did not lead to the "melting pot" effect hoped for, but to the most appalling military conflicts and ethnic cleansings even at the end of the 20th century.

In their "phase of national awakening", the Serbs - like the Bulgarians, Greeks Macedonians and Albanians - based their competing territorial claims on their extensive power structures of the Middle Ages[143]; for, in the 19th century, the Serbs were still seen as one of the peoples of Southeast Europe without history who still had to find a suitable point of reference for their historical projections."[144]

2.

It was not the ideals of the French Revolution[145] that set off revolutionary groups in the Balkans and, from 1804, encouraged the Serbs under Hajduk leader Karadjordje (Black George) to revolt. First hopes were kindled as early as 1768, after the 3rd Russo-Turkish war[146] and the peace of Küçük-Kaynarca in 1774, when the sultan, after withdrawing from further territories, was still recognized as caliph but had to guarantee protection for the Christian religion.

Besides the cultural influence of the Venetians and their "political education", Stadtmüller also mentions the following factor:

> "The powerful progression of the Serbian national consciousness ... would not have been possible without constant and close contact with the neighbouring Habsburg Empire. It was on Habsburg ground that his national consciousness first stirred, namely on the Austrian 'military border'."[147]

For Serbia's future, the Russian intervention on Serbia's side in the 5th Russo-Turkish war from 1806 onwards was also of eminent importance. However, in 1812 Russia had to make peace with the Ottoman Empire (in Bucharest) so as to be able to react to Napoleon's invasion and protect its Balkan flank. The autonomy Serbia had gained earlier was immediately annulled by the Sultan in view of Serbia's military weakness, and in the following year Turkey reconquered Serbia.

After the second uprising under the peasant leader Miloš Obrenović in 1815, Serbia became a Turkish tributary state. "On this occasion", writes Mark Mazower, "the Serbs' timing was better: Napoleon's defeat at Waterloo allowed the Russians to attend to their Balkan clients (p. 90)."[148] Miloš bought his hereditary title from the Turks by murdering "Black George" and sending the Sultan his head – to the Serbs and Slavs in general, this was a particularly abominable crime, Karadjordje being his godfather.[148] But it was not until the next, 6th Russo-Turkish war, which started in 1828, that Serbia gained full autonomy as a result of the peace of Adrianople in 1829/30. Ottoman supremacy, however, remained in place, and the Turks "had no intention of putting up with the fact that the Serbs they despised were now bearing arms."[149] (On the other hand, many Muslims also disliked the fact that - at a later stage - their Sultan travelled by train; their reaction was crushing: "The Padishah has become a *giaour* [Christian]." Mazower, loc. cit., p.106)

After Miloš's son Michael Obrenović (1860-1868), his 14-year-old nephew (and adopted son) Milan succeeded to the Serbian throne. He received his official title when he came of age in 1872. The Tsar's court arranged a marriage for him with the daughter of a Romanian colonel in the Russian army, Natalya Keshko – although he had hoped for a nobler present from St. Petersburg. A year earlier, the regent (Ristić) had introduced the young Milan to the Tsar; politically, this circumspect step was to pay off:
Following the threat of a war against the Turks in Montenegro in 1874, the uprisings that had been going on in Bosnia and Herzegovina in 1875 spread to Macedonia and Bulgaria in the subsequent year. In June 1876, the Serbs, who had previously conspicuously demonstrated their disobedience by withholding tribute payments, declared war on the Ottoman Empire, thereby coming to the aid of the Bosnians. The Montenegrins followed suit in July, helping the Herzegovinians. The Bosnians declared their allegiance to the Serbian prince – on the legendary 28th of June of all days[150]. According to the Russian-Austrian Reichstädt agreement of July 8th, Bosnia and Herzegovina were either to be given autonomy or divided between Austria and Serbia.[151] However, the Serbs were defeated again and suffered a complete military collapse in October, so that the Turks could have reinvaded Belgrade as in 1813. Serbia was spared by a Russian ultimatum to the Sublime Porte, so that in February 1877, Belgrade could once more make peace with the Porte.[152]
The failure of the conference of Constantinople and the Turkish rejection of the London protocol intended to clarify the situation concerning Bulgaria led to the outbreak of the 8th and last Russo-Turkish war. In mid-December 1877, Serbia jumped on the bandwagon and once more declared war on Turkey. "After initial military up-and-downs, the Ottoman Empire collapsed in January 1878."[153]
The Congress of Berlin not only brought the Serbs full independence and religious freedom, but also new territories in south Serbia, including Niš, Vranje and Pirot. Nevertheless, Belgrade saw the approval of the Austrian occupation of Bosnia and Herzegovina by the Congress of Berlin as a serious setback for their aim of unifying the Serbs with their Bosnian brothers – and later never stopped pursuing that objective.

However, since the Serbian minister of the interior Garašanin had drafted a plan for a large South Slavic state under Serbian hegemony as early as 1844, the multiracial state Austria-Hungary felt compelled, if only by an instinct of self-preservation, to prevent such a solution, as the mass appeal for the Slavic ethnic groups in their own empire would have been almost uncontrollable.

However, it seems to be more than doubtful whether the Austrian occupation of Bosnia had to be the desirable course of action. Less megalomaniac solutions would certainly have done better service to the alleged goal ("order, safety, peace").

Serbia's long struggle to win back old Serbian - as well as additional foreign (in this case: Macedonian) - territory started as soon as Serbia gained independence.

This is approximately the time, German embassies abroad started to issue reports from which we hope to gain information on the Balkan League and the Serbian will to conquer, - but especially about the history and identity of Macedonia.

2.1.1 Looking ahead at the Balkan League and Macedonia

Every embassy or legation abroad - in the past as well as today - is not only responsible for maintaining bilateral relations and looking after fellow-citizens in the host country, but also for keeping the home country informed by means of reports. It is the ambition of all these missions - in the past as well as today - to venture a look into the future of the host country or region by extrapolation and to foresee future developments. For the period we are looking at, we have an impressive instance of this during the term of office of one German ambassador. In 1880, i.e. no later than two years after the Congress of Berlin, the Imperial Ministerial Residency in Belgrade sent a report to the Imperial Chancellor and Foreign Minister Prince Bismarck. *It was shown later that this report anticipated the established historical events of the following decades.*

Mr. von Bray briefly sketches one of the main problems of Balkan politics after the 8th Russo-Turkish war in 1877/78 seen from the Serbian perspective:

> "A majority of the leading statesmen in Serbia are ... convinced that the oriental question has not found its final solution yet and that sooner or later Turkey will be forced to withdraw ever more from the Balkan Peninsula."[154]

This statement demonstrates a good overview and detailed knowledge, not least because the Great Powers had by no means intended to see the results they achieved in Berlin as a short-lived patchwork solution, but had hoped to be able to draw the line under centuries of discord over the Straits and Constantinople. Neither did Turkey have the least intention of considering the resolutions of the Congress to be a final judgement on its presence in Europe; instead, it continued to keep an eye on the chance of a return, even by way of conquest, as e.g. Serbia had found out in 1813.

The ambassador went even further: Although based in Serbia, he defines Bulgaria as one of the mainstays of antagonism towards Turkey and here, too, he looks forward across a period of 30 years:

> "In this case, we think above all that a powerful Bulgaria will be an element which, encouraged by Russian and Panslavist support, will certainly extend its expansionist endeavours to include those provinces which Serbia has never stopped claiming on historical grounds."[154]

It is interesting to note that regarding European Turkish territories the ambassador does not speak of reunification or reconquest, but of "expansionism" – which, after all, it was.

The term "those provinces" defined as the object of such expansion clearly refers to the provinces that had been given back to the Ottoman Empire after the Berlin Congress: Thrace and Macedonia.
As to the "historical grounds", the Great Serbian mania is here based on a few years of supremacy over the Bulgarians, Montenegrins and Macedonians in the reign of Tsar Stefan Dušan the Powerful. As he had also conquered large parts of Greece, he put forward his claim to succeed the Byzantine emperor. A short dream – for after his death, the Great Serbian kingdom between the Danube and the Gulf of Patras fell apart. After 1389, he was succeeded by the Ottoman Turk-Tatars who had streamed in from Asia Minor.[155]

> *These less than 50 years of Serbian rule over Macedonia in the 14th century are the Serbs' justification for the annexation of North Macedonia ("Vardar Macedonia") at the beginning of the 20th century, with which they try to give their present claims at least the appearance of continuity – a preposterous argumentation.*

The report contains further interesting statements:

> "The relations between Serbs and Bulgarians provide such a slight basis for the pursuit of common interests, that there is no question of a rapprochement, let alone an alliance between these two neighbouring peoples."[156]

This evaluation, too, remained valid for more than 30 years – until the adversaries found themselves compelled after great efforts and setbacks to look for a common solution if they were to attain at least a partial goal. Nor would they have succeeded without external help (i.e. from the Tsar, or rather the Entente).
Clearly none of the Balkan states could simply enforce its alleged claim to the entire Turkish legacy on European ground without assistance.

In the following context in particular, the report quite hits the nail on the head: Russia's preferential treatment of the newly created principality of Bulgaria

> "...seems to have stirred pretensions extending not only to territories inhabited by the Bulgarian nation, but also to foreign territories, as is made clear by the projected neutralization law."[156]

It is easy to understand where the unusual explosiveness of the quotation lies. Unlike in the previous text, the report here refers not to "those" territories but to "*foreign*" territories. This shows that the inhabitants of said foreign territories were not Serbs or Bulgarians. Instead, this refers to the population of Thrace, i.e. the Thracians, and to the population of Macedonia, i.e. the Macedonians.
The envoy thus plainly calls attention to a state of affairs which - with the exception of the aggressors themselves - is only known today to historians and Balkan experts.

In the past 120 years, Serbs, Bulgarians and Greeks have grown accustomed to systematically warding off any discussion of a Macedonian identity in its own right. In the past, they used this distortion of history to pursue their imperialistic goals, and today they do not want to be reminded of their annexations that took place following the Balkan wars.

> Any references to history in this context are brushed off on the grounds that they would disturb the peaceful coexistence of the Balkan peoples – a procedure strongly smacking of decades of arguments with the ideological opponents in the Communist bloc during the Cold War.

2.1.2 Serbia between Austria-Hungary and Bulgaria

After the Congress of Berlin, Serbia had every reason to be bitter on account of the Austrian occupation of Bosnia. The allegedly temporary occupation postponed Serbian hopes of a closer connection with its Bosnian brothers indefinitely – until these turned out to be wholly illusory 30 years later. This Austrian move has poisoned the political atmosphere in the region even to the present day.

I have already explained the Austrian dilemma in this matter; but the other Balkan states may also have been relieved that a unification of Serbia and Bosnia had not taken place. For a Great Serbia would certainly have had a magnetic attraction for the neighbouring territories outside its borders – as Slobodan Milošević proved almost exactly 100 years later with his programme of expansionism. (Today, Bosnia has become so independent that the Deutsche Welle radio station even broadcasts programmes in Bosnian!)

Serbia, on the other hand, was not pleased either to see power concentrated in other hands and did not hesitate to react accordingly. In this way, a constellation developed in 1886 (the year of the next relevant reports) which caused Serbia to even be indebted to Austria in spite of the bitterness it felt towards this country: In 1882, Serbia had been made a kingdom; Milan, then 28 years old, was the youngest king in Europe. When Bulgaria violated the Berlin treaty in 1885 and proceeded with the unification with East Rumelia, which although autonomous was still Turkish province, the Serbian king Milan decided this was sufficient reason to attack Bulgaria and annex East Rumelia himself, although he could not establish any historical, ethnic or legal claims. This aggression triggered the *Serbo-Bulgarian* war. After a crushing defeat, esp. near Slivnica (near Sofia), only an Austrian intervention saved Serbia from the usual loss of territory to Bulgaria – this practice was then referred to as "compensations". This gesture naturally led Serbia to adopt a pro-Austrian stance – at least for a time.

The Austrian readiness to intervene stemmed indirectly from a rivalry between Vienna and St. Petersburg about who commanded the greater influence in the Balkans; Austria expected that Bulgaria, hopefully defeated in Serbia's "proxy war", would easily be drawn into the Austrian sphere of influence.[157] More directly, this Austrian assistance was a consequence of a secret treaty of friendship which Belgrade and Vienna had concluded in 1881. But when Bulgaria won the war and the Austrian plan thus failed, there was nothing left for Vienna but to openly take side with Serbia.

A further consequence was that towards the end of 1886 Austria (with the support of England) was able to suggest to the Serbian king to seek closer relations with Romania, with a view to creating a Balkan League and with the well-founded prospect of positive reactions, on the grounds that

> "...the situation in the East, especially regarding Russia's proceedings, would suggest such a recommendation."[158]

The recommendation probably matched similar fears on King Milan's part, for it is reported that regarding his south-eastern neighbour, he hoped that Bulgaria might be able to maintain its independence.

> "However, should the Russian influence wholly prevail there, that would also be the beginning of fatal days for Serbia."[159]

A follow-up report from the mission (now legation) in Belgrade comments on this perpetual nightmare of all small countries:

"The king believes that to conclude "an alliance" while demonstrating a general submissiveness towards Russia is the only way to avoid being absorbed by Russia and Panslavism."[160]

The Serbian king seems to have been so impressed by the intimidating setting created by Russia that he pretended to be prepared to agree to "establishing such an alliance even with Turkey at its head",[160] – but knowing the wily fox, this declaration was certainly only part of a political gamble.

Still, the Russians seem to have had a similar view of the situation. At least we know that the Serbian king informed the German ambassador

"...that the Russian Ministerial Resident ... had approached him directly on account of the rumours circulating concerning the creation of a Balkan League and had added that Russia would not tolerate the establishment of such an alliance as it ran counter to its interests."[161]

This constellation, however, was only an episode, as both the Russian and the Austrian attitudes towards the Balkan League were to change very soon.

2.1.3 Serbian interest in Macedonia and Russian interest in Serbia as a spearhead against Germany

1.)

Only five years later, the coalitions, and with them the attitudes, seem to have changed. It is conspicuous that, once more, the central issue of the whole Balkan conflict, not only of the Balkan League, came to the fore: Macedonia.

The legation reported to the imperial chancellor - now the infantry general v. Caprivi - that the Serbian envoy in Sofia had occasionally allowed himself to remark

"...how strongly all Serbs still felt the need of a 'revenge for Slivnica' in their bones, and how popular a new war against Bulgaria would be."[162]

The Envoy von Wangenheim immediately and concisely provided the real point of the argument:

"The most sensitive point is, of course, the Macedonian question: 'Even if there is no formal alliance between Serbia, Montenegro and Greece, these three states would not tolerate an expansion of Bulgaria to include Macedonia, but would answer any step in that direction with a prompt declaration of war.'"[163]

In plain words, this means that all four countries named above were first of all bent on annexing left-over Turkish territory exclusively for themselves; but their second preference was to avoid an imbalance in the Balkans by not letting any of the other states have the full inheritance.

For obvious reasons, there is no mention of historical, political or ethnic claims – because they did not exist. Why should the interested parties worry about legal questions if they were intending to capture the foreign territory by force anyway?

One thing was clear to all potential participants: To set up a Balkan League with the aim of conquering Macedonia would not be possible without or even against Bulgaria. Therefore the project was shelved. They had to wait for a more favourable opportunity.

During the years of forced quiet, the Balkan states were by no means idle. Revolutionary committees and their leaders, called Komitadjis, worked hard to prepare the provinces which were still Turkish for their future rule by influencing the population through Serbification, Bulgarification and Graecization – a pitiful contrivance meant to obscure the fact that the population of the territories to be annexed still had to be made into Serbs, Bulgarians and Greeks, because it had been nothing else but Macedonian until then.

Of course, there were Macedonian committees, too, but in order to avoid persecution by the Turks, they were based in Romania, Bulgaria or Serbia – just as the Bulgarian committees had been based in Romania and Serbia before the liberation of their own country and had been unable to recruit actively in Bulgaria itself. Nonetheless, the location of their committees in Bulgaria was repeatedly used against the Macedonians later, with the claim that all Macedonians in Bulgaria were really Bulgarians; why else would they have come to Sofia, when they could equally well have gone to Greece.
Especially after it had lost the war about East Rumelia against Bulgaria in 1885, Serbia tried

> "...to pursue its goals in Macedonia in the same way as Greece and Bulgaria did, i.e. by relying strongly on cultural, education and church politics."[164]

The official permission of the Porte to open Serbian schools in Macedonia was only issued in 1893.

> "In addition to that, the Serbs awarded scholarships to Macedonian schoolchildren enabling them to go to school or study in Serbia, so that they could indoctrinate them with Serbian nationalism there."

They also promoted the establishment of Serbian-Macedonian societies for the purpose of agitation and - interestingly enough - the collection of historical and ethnographical evidence "meant to prove the non-Bulgarian character of the population."[165]
That was no doubt a success – just as any Bulgarian-Macedonian society could easily have proved the *non-Serbian character of the Macedonian population.*

The Serbs must have thought it so besides the point to also try to prove the *non-Greek* character of the Macedonian population, though this could have been done with little additional effort, that they obviously did not even consider such an absurd plan.
Instead, they took additional administrative measures: as early as 1887, the Serbian government set up a special section for Serbian schools and churches "outside Serbia" (sic!). Another special department with the same purpose was established in 1889 within the foreign ministry – not the ministries of the interior or of cultural affairs!
2.)
In 1889, King Milan abdicated in favour of his 13-year-old son Alexander who continued his father's pro-Austrian policy. As Milan had been striving to obtain a divorce from Natalie for some years now, the Russians lost the stronghold they had been sure of in Belgrade. Queen Natalie emigrated and had to experience all the harshness of political and diplomatic business during her visit to Vienna; for, according to A. H. Kober, she received the following notification from the Russian envoy there:

> "After King Milan had at first accepted and exploited Russia's powerful assistance both in war and in peace, he threw himself into Austria's arms, concluding agreements and trade contracts with them. The Tsar had thought that Your Majesty ... would be able to counteract these endeavours and reassert Russia's influence in Serbia. This hope, however, has not been fulfilled."
> "We can see that you have no influence in Serbia anymore."[166]

In 1890, the pro-Russian regent Ristić had the occasion during a visit to introduce the young Prince Alexander - like his father Milan twenty years before - to the Tsar (now Alexander III). A year later, the pretender to the crown had the regent poisoned. The young man's tenacity was quite breathtaking: In 1893, when he was 16 years old, he carried out a coup d'état. It was successful. Against all resistance and objections, he also insisted on a morganatic marriage with Draga Mashin, a former chanteuse from Hungary.[167]

When a conspiracy of officers murdered King Alexander and his wife on the night of June 10th 1903 (this was the ultimate extinction of the Obrenović family), the world public had proceeded from a continuation of the cruel feud between this family and the Karadjordjević clan.
The real situation was different:
Not until years later did it emerge that Alexander's pro-Austrian policy had been the real motive for that nocturnal carnage in Belgrade in June 1903: during the First World War the Dutch Foreign Minister told the Imperial Envoy Mr. von Rosen in The Hague what the latter then telegraphed to the Auswärtiges Amt, that

"The murder of the Serbian king in 1903 ... was *also* perpetrated on behalf of the Entente."[168]
(The italics do not belong to the original text.)

So, King Alexander had to be put to death in order to enable, or rather force Serbia to return to Russia's side, and at the same time, even more importantly, to detach it from Austria.
This was nothing less than a regicide and it happened in *1903*! Let nobody say that Russia, or the Entente, did not plan the First World War well in advance.

(It is known that the Entente was not officially established until a year later. However, joint activities need not have started the moment the papers were signed. On the contrary: The public announcement of the alliance could have served as a seal on activities that had been planned or even carried out long before – not to mention the fact that Russia could easily have instigated the conspiracy without previous agreement with the Entente.)

As for the word "also" used in the report: The Dutch Foreign Minister had used this word in his conversation with the German Envoy with reference to the situation in Greece, because according to his information the deposition of the Greek king Konstantin (who was married to a sister of Emperor Wilhelm II) a few days before (i.e. in this case: in June 1917) had *also* been "brought about on behalf of the Entente."
Long-term planning! (I shall come back to this point later.)
In any case Alexander's successor, Peter Karadjordje, gradually returned to a pro-Russian, i.e. anti-Austrian policy (but also to the old idea of a Great Serbia: Omladina). However, the situation in the Balkans only changed fundamentally "when Serbia finally freed itself from Austrian paternalism in 1906."[169]

2.1.4 Autonomy for or division of Macedonia

The journalist Franklin Bouillon of the Parisian paper "Figaro" had conducted a series of interviews with Serbian and Bulgarian statesmen in October 1897, which were also printed in the "Pester Lloyd".[170] Almost 20 years had passed since the Congress of Berlin – enough time in which to clarify one's opinions. In the interviews, two concepts were referred to, which were considered to be very important even then (the following quotations are all from the same report):
The majority of the Bulgarian interviewees had committed themselves to the idea of a kind of *autonomy* for Macedonia; the Serbs, on the other hand, believed that this step was only designed to postpone solving the question of the Turkish possessions in Europe in order to give Bulgaria time to develop its economy and to arm. Moreover, the Serbs suspected the Bulgarians of expecting that an autonomous Macedonia would one day fall into their lap the way autonomous East Rumelia had done in 1885. The Serbian Prime Minister Simić summed up his impression of Bulgaria's intentions as follows: "Autonomy is always fraught with annexation." Given that it was also useless

to await the result of reforms (which had been imposed on the Ottoman Empire at all conferences and in all agreements, but had never been undertaken), as these were "an impossibility in view of the Turkish lethargy in the Orient", one had to "already contemplate the necessary *division* today."

The Bulgarians countered this (in 1897) by the argument that they could not form an alliance with the Serbs because

> "...the Serbs are laying claims to Bulgarian Macedonia which they can by no means justify." Therefore "it would be impossible to delineate spheres of influence." "A division of what we consider to be rightfully ours" was out of the question.

Former Serbian Prime Minister Novaković could allow himself to realistically admit to the Figaro:

> "To tell the truth, whether Bulgarians, Serbs or Greeks, none of us is as yet sufficiently prepared to start the fight that will ultimately seal the fate of the Orient."

The Serbian-Bulgarian dispute illustrates vividly that

> 1. the Macedonian territory belonged to neither and
> 2. that it was only Russia's support that enabled the four Balkan states to wage war on Turkey.

In view of the pure power politics behind the Serbian plans of division, the serious and circumspect comment on this plan made by the German consul general in Sofia about a year later would seem almost unworldly:

> "A Serbian-Bulgarian agreement about delineating their respective spheres of interest in Macedonia, which would in fact mean nothing but an anticipated division of this Turkish province and which does not recommend itself either by feasibility or by the achievement of order and quiet in the region, cannot expect any approval or support on the part of the Imperial Government..."[171]

As if the Serbs and Bulgarians (or Greeks) had been concerned with "ensuring order and quiet" in Macedonia!

Yet the consulate general's statement correctly expressed the position of the German government and especially of Emperor Wilhelm II at that time. However, even such seemingly steady parameters can one day be subject to changes, as we shall see below.

How strongly the Austrian occupation of Bosnia still influenced inner-Balkan relations and that it even had an effect on the Macedonian question is also shown by the words of former Bulgarian Prime Minister Dragan Zankov (who, ten years earlier, had been partly responsible for the overthrow of the first Bulgarian leader, Prince Alexander of Battenberg):

> "Ever since taking the two Serbian provinces Bosnia and Herzegovina, Austria has been trying to erase this annexation from memory by promising the Belgrade government compensation in the South."

Macedonia lay in the South.

Although it was legally an *occupation* according to the wording of Art. 25 of the Berlin Treaty of 1878, Zankov actually referred to it as an *annexation*, as if he had already guessed in 1897 what the adventurous Austrian policy would lead to about ten years later (1908). Directly on the subject of Macedonia, he added:

> "Outside the Kosovo plain, there is no Serbian Macedonia, for the excellent reason that there are no Serbians in Macedonia."

In saying this, the Bulgarian Prime Minister had described the situation perfectly correctly. (Of course, he had not mentioned that the same was true of Bulgaria.) Regrettably, this fact was repeatedly contested and suppressed by both Serbs and Bulgarians in the following 100 years.

But since a division of Macedonia was accomplished in 1913 after all, it has become clear that the political behaviour accompanying the Balkan haggle over the trading object Macedonia revealed the real situation:
If these two governments had really been convinced that Macedonia was part of their national territory, they would never even have commenced negotiations about it with the neighbouring government.
Bulgaria would never have advocated Macedonian autonomy - to Serbia (and later Greece) of all countries - if it had really been convinced that Macedonia was Bulgarian. Consequently, Belgrade had promptly exposed Bulgaria's true intentions.
The Serbian side was even more inconsistent: If Macedonia had really been Serbian territory at any time no Serbian government would have been prepared to tolerate a division of its ancestral property.

> In spite of their Orthodox belief, the Serbs do not seem to have been particularly familiar with the Bible; otherwise they could not have so shamefully ignored the Solomonic judgement about dividing the child in order to ascertain its real mother: if Serbia agreed to divide "the child Macedonia" it never can have been a true "mother".

Therefore, this was only a question of two robbers arguing about who was to obtain the greater part of a booty to which neither had the least inner relation.
In his accompanying report, Envoy von Waecker-Gotter went into detail on two points.

1.) "As for the project of an autonomous Macedonia which has been launched by the Bulgarian government and - as I gather from the remarks of the local Bulgarian agent[172] - is still part of the government's programme, the Serbian side still views it as an impracticable and disastrous experiment. Only Novakovich, with that typical idealism of an enthusiastic history professor and archaeologist, took kindly to this Trojan horse by which Bulgarian hegemony was to be smuggled into Macedonia."

The envoy could not have described the real circumstances more clearly.
Ex-king Milan, on the other hand, had a different view of the matter. Though far less educated than the professor, yet he sensed the Bulgarian trap and persuaded his son Alexander to reject this suggestion: No "Trojan horse" for Skopje (or Saloniki or Ohrid...)!

2.) "I have always been convinced that the "Balkan League" is a chimera, today more than ever, and if it ever came into being it would only lead to an outbreak of war between the small Balkan states."

He was to be proved right! To Macedonia's disadvantage.

2.1.5 The Ilinden Uprising

The author had the opportunity to convince himself that the unsuccessful Ilinden uprising of 1903, which led to the temporary establishment of the *Republic of Kruševo* has found ample coverage in the files of the Political Archives, namely in the hundreds of volumes on Turkey, and that the documentation covers a significantly longer period and a considerably larger geographic dimension than the short designations "Ilinden" (the 2nd of August) and "Kruševo" would suggest.
In those files, however, that have been grouped under the heading "Balkan League", there is only one report concerning this uprising.
The German legation in Belgrade quotes from the newspaper „Ustavna Srbija", the semi-official organ of the moderate radicals, which had borrowed an article from the

paper "Zastava" in Novi Sad (which was then called Neusatz), referring to some passages on the desperate situation in Macedonia and the urgent need for a Balkan or at least Slavic alliance. The reporting official pays his due respects to the victims and denounces the neighbouring states with unusual frankness:

> "In Macedonia and Old Serbia, numerous burnt-down villages are still smoking and many thousands of people have fled into the mountains."[173]

He points out that Bulgaria had had the biggest hand in propagating the uprising but had also made the biggest mistake: planning to do everything single-handed, it had ultimately not got involved in the war. In his opinion, if the next winter is not used

> "...to come to an understanding between the Balkan states, there will be no liberation anymore for Old Serbia and Macedonia..."

He suggests that if an alliance is not feasible, these states should abstain from undertakings they are unable to carry through and that will only cause further damage to their brothers. In the name of the "many thousands of helpless human beings ... wandering about in the desolate and cold mountains of Turkey"

> "...we have to call out to those concerned: Your actions so far are not the way to liberate one's brothers!"[173]

The way the journalist wrote his report suggests that he believed the neighbours to be sincerely willing to help their Macedonian fellow-Christians and that he took their absence for a mistaken policy, a simple blunder or, at the best, a misunderstanding. Indeed, it must have appeared logical to him that those peoples who had received assistance from the Great Powers for their liberation from Turkey would in their turn help the adjacent countries in their struggle for freedom, especially seeing that the Great Powers had withdrawn their support.

For if there had been Serbs, Bulgarians and Greeks living in Macedonia as always claimed, the neighbouring states in question would definitely have helped their countrymen, just as the Bulgarians had helped their fellow-Bulgarians in East Rumelia and the Greeks had helped theirs in Thessaly. But given that this was a "foreign" people, i.e. Macedonians (who had an identity of their own but no state of their own as yet), their fellow-Slavs restricted themselves to cheering the Macedonians on and then letting them run into the fire on their own.

There was another circumstance reported by Edith Durham, the experienced Balkan expert, based on the impressions she gained during her extensive travels:

> "In the rebelling towns it appeared that the unhappy population was being stirred up in the faith that Russia would hurry to their liberation as in 1877!"[174]

The barely concealed reproach expressed by the journalist raises the suspicion that the attitude adopted by the Serbs and Bulgarians was not a result of sloppiness or failure, but of cold deliberation: A decimation of the courageous Macedonian population would fit perfectly into the calculations of such neighbours who were in any case intending to conquer the territory in question for themselves in the near future; and if there were fewer forces able to resist the aggressors in a future conflict, because they had already been worn down, this could only profit the attackers.

This is not an over-subtle speculation. Edith Durham, who has already been quoted, wrote elsewhere in her memoirs:

> "In Macedonia I discovered ... the strange fact that ...the Balkan Christian churches actually kept the Turks in power. The Greeks and Serbs organized Komitadji bands and sent them to Macedonia, not to "free their Christian brothers" – they wanted nothing of the sort – but to help the Turks to suppress their "Christian brothers"."[175]

On the following page, she sums up:
> "These were the Christian believers for whom people were praying in the European churches then."

One further aspect needs to be mentioned here:

Texts that were printed as early as five years after the uprising and can therefore be considered contemporary (and, after this phase of reflection, have been included in an encyclopaedia) show that after the Macedonian uprising had flared up in spring 1903, which led to the *Ilinden uprising* in August, Russia and Austria (each for their own good reasons) had issued an urgent warning to Macedonia's neighbours, enjoining on them for the sake of peace (sic) not to intervene or get involved in Macedonia: i.e., they were not to help the Macedonians (even if that had been their intention)![176]

This is mysterious – for almost ten years later, in 1912, when the neighbours Serbia, Bulgaria and Greece got even more involved and were by no means only offering assistance to the insurgents but were rather breaking the peace previously invoked and directly attacking the Turkish provinces of Macedonia and Thrace in order to conquer them, there was no warning from the Great Powers about maintaining that peace!

It emerged later that Russia and the two other members of the Entente not only knew all about the plan for a Balkan League but had even promoted it – even before the Entente was officially founded in 1904.

> We can conclude that there must have been an understanding between the Great Powers and the aggressors concerning the latter's annexation plans. And that in turn allows the conclusion that **the Entente powers sacrificed Macedonia** to the Serbs, Bulgarians and Greeks quite deliberately. Why?

This was no accident, but dynastic support from the Great Powers for the Balkan monarchies, especially in Greece – in conjunction with the Entente's strategy over against the German-Austrian Dual Alliance.

2.1.6 The idea of a nation-state

After describing the festivities for the coronation of Prince Peter Karadjordje as Serbian king in 1904, the German envoy in Belgrade made a few general remarks on the development of a self-reliant national feeling.[177] He said:

> "The conspicuous appearance of the representatives of Montenegro and Bulgaria at the Serbian coronation ceremony gave this political idea an embodiment that must have impressed itself on the imagination of the Slavs from Dalmatia, Croatia, Slavonia, Bosnia and Bulgaria who had poured into Belgrade in crowds. For the first time in Serbia's recent history, the related Slav nations were able to look upon the royal throne erected in Serbia with respect and a feeling of national pride, and they saw it surrounded by the gestures of friendship of the other two Balkan states."

This is followed by a list of the dynastic persons grouped around the ancient throne in the crowded Serbian-Orthodox Cathedral of Belgrade. Then Mr. von Heyking continues:

> "When the whole congregation kneeled together with the king before the blessings, and the male and female voices, unaccompanied by any instruments, were singing "Kyrie eleison", the well-known melancholy prayer of the Greek church, from the choir above, the king who was receiving the sacred rites of kingship may also have begged mercy with his people for all the misery of which they may or may not have been guilty."[178]

Although Serbia was already a kingdom in 1217 under the son of the Great Župan Stefan Nemanja and remained so until the battle of Kosovo Polje on June 28th 1389, the envoy rightly points out that a new national consciousness still had to develop after centuries of suppression by the Turks. By stating that the making of the Serbian nation had not yet been completed at that stage, the report does not detract from the worth of the Serbian people. In addition to the joint experience of rebellions for the sake of the noble goals of freedom and independence, additional symbolic actions were necessary to create an awareness of unity, which was felt all the more strongly because for centuries the Orthodox Church had been the only haven where cultural characteristics could be preserved and thus the survival of an independent sense of community ensured. (According to Prof. Adanir, the Bulgarians were also a different people in the 19th century than during the Middle Ages.[179])

The Slavic people living in Macedonia must also be granted the chance to have gone through the same processes. There has always been an awareness of a shared culture and history, but political identity in Macedonia could not assert itself under Turkish rule without foreign military help (even worse: against the resistance of its neighbours and against the will of the dynastic clique of the Great European Powers).

> "After the Congress of Berlin (1878) and the emergence of the Macedonian question, however, a M(acedonian) national identity began to develop."[180]

The author would like to add: "At the latest." For the numerous Macedonian uprisings before 1876/78 are also unthinkable without presupposing an underlying sense of togetherness. Prof. Weithmann extends the possibility for a further development of this feeling into the 20th century:

> "Supported by Tito's political idea, the Slavic inhabitants of Macedonia have developed a consciousness of their language, history and nation that is equally independent both of Serbia and of Bulgaria and has led to a sense of national identity."[181]

Just because, for reasons outside the inhabitants' responsibility, a Macedonian state was established at a late point in history, they are not less worthy of self-determination, freedom and independence than any of the other Balkan peoples.

Therefore the Macedonians' unrestricted identity, statehood and independence must not be curtailed by its neighbours.

Georg Stadtmüller gives a non-specific definition of the idea of a nation-state for all South-East European nations, seeing the intrusion of the Western idea as triggering the rise of national consciousness:

> "In its wake, the concept of a "nation" completely changed in the Ottoman sphere of influence as well. Until then, the "nation" had been equated with the religious community there. The denomination had been the distinguishing characteristic. Even in the Greek War of Independence, Orthodox Greeks and Orthodox Albanians had fought together against Muslim Turks and Muslim Albanians. With the arrival of the Western concept of nationality, denomination was replaced by language as the main characteristic of national affiliation. This in the first place created the conceptual basis for the formation of modern nation-states in the Balkans."[182]

2.1.7 A fundamental Serbian document on Macedonia

In the Political Archives of the Auswärtiges Amt there is a document from 1904 which is very illuminating with regard to Macedonia.

In a report addressed to the Imperial Chancellor and Foreign Minister (Count von Bülow as of 1897), the envoy in Belgrade relates the contents of an article published by a certain Mr. Balugdjić in 1886 in a Berlin paper. Previously, Balugdjić had been chief press officer to the Serbian Prince Peter (Karadjordjević) during the latter's exile in Geneva, Switzerland, where he had already enjoyed his confidence. In 1904, he de-

cided - possibly under the impression of the unsuccessful Ilinden uprising in Macedonia in autumn 1903 - to republish his article in his own country, namely in "Slovenski Jug", the organ of the Young Serbs of whom he was considered to be a member. Balugdjić was still chief press officer, but now of *King* Peter, and arranged the publication a few weeks before the coronation ceremony which took place on September 21st 1904.
In this article, *"all claims to Macedonia are described as a great aberration."*
A sensation!
> "Before Bosnia was occupied by Austria, nobody in Serbia would have thought of laying national claims to Macedonia." "... while Serbia was seeking a coastline on the Adriatic, it had never been claimed that there was any Serbian population in Thessalonica." "Only after Serbia's expansion to the Adriatic coast, naturally Serbian by virtue of history and language borders, had been cut off by an act of violence perpetrated by the Congress of Berlin, Serbia's political ambitions had been wrongly directed towards Macedonia due to artificial agitation."[183]

This admission must sound like a revelation to Macedonian ears still today.
I have two remarks to make in this context:
- 1). It is obvious how strongly Austria influenced the fate of Macedonia by its carefully planned yet crazy attack on Bosnia.
- 2). Balugdjić and the Young Serbs, evidently supported by the king himself, were striving for a real reconciliation with Bulgaria for the sake of peace in the Balkans and in order to strengthen the individually weak forces of self-defence against attacks from the outside. The key statement of this text shows how serious and moderate these efforts were:
> "As soon as Serbia renounced its unfounded claims to Macedonian territory, the only obstacle on the path towards sincere fraternization with Bulgaria would be removed."[183]

Besides this extremely frank admission of the truth, it is conspicuous that the Serbian wounds caused by the Austrian occupation of Bosnia had not healed even a quarter of a century after the event.
This insult had tragic consequences both for Austria and for Germany:
Like the Russians after the Congress of Berlin, the Serbs did not mainly blame the Austrians or the English (who had put forward the motion in favour of Austria) for the fact that they had done so badly, but the Germans: The Russians felt cheated of their legitimate reward after the 8th Russo-Turkish war in which they had suffered heavy losses; the Serbs, on the other hand, resented the fact that the Austrians - backed by the German Reich - had forestalled them in Bosnia. The Serbian grudge against Austria (and Germany) had also grown continuously because the Serbians had initially believed the Austrian promises of a speedy retreat from Bosnia – a belief that was disappointed again and again every year. When the subsequent annexation (1908) brought the Austrian breach of faith into the open, Serbia's reaction - then supported by Russia, France and England - was all the more one of hatred. This hatred caused further speculations to run wild about a possible Austrian march on Thessalonica, and even Constantinople.

It hardly requires mentioning that Balugdjić's article set off a vehement polemic in the rest of the Serbian press. An opposition paper called his idea "a betrayal of our country". The (maybe well-timed) news from Macedonia about "the barbaric treatment of Serbian inhabitants of Macedonia by Bulgarian Comité bands" did not in the least motivate the Serbian press and public to keep quiet.

Some of the "younger Serbian politicians who had been educated in Europe", however,

> "...were so keen on setting up a Balkan League consisting of the three Slavic states that they were even prepared, for the sake of this higher goal, to forego the national hopes concerning Old Serbia." According to Envoy von Heyking, on the other hand "these young people were nurturing the strange misapprehension that the Balkan League would enable them to drive the hated Austrians out of Bosnia."[183]

However, this variant of expectations connected with the Balkan League was only an episode in the years of development leading up to its establishment in 1912. In any case,

> the growing "Serbian aspirations to unification with their Bosnian brothers now languishing under foreign rule" caused a "bad mood" in Vienna.[183]

Nota bene: "foreign rule" referred to the Habsburg, not the Ottoman Empire.

In the end it has to be pointed out that Balugdjić's attempt at objectivity was soon choked by Serbian nationalist interest. Yet with regard to our topic and the present Republic of Macedonia, we have to state that Serbia does not qualify as a serious contestant for Macedonian territory, as it has been shown conclusively that Serbia cannot lay any claims to Macedonia.

> *Thus its repeated attempts none the less to wrench Macedonian land from the Ottoman Empire and to annex it – which actually happened in 1912/13 – were evidently nothing but acts of violence in the imperialist manner and must in no way be considered a "liberation" of "Serbian" citizens and territories in Macedonia.*

It was mentioned at the start of this section that Balugdjić had already published his article in 1886 in Berlin. The fact that it had not raised a storm abroad at that time the way it did in 1904 at home, i.e. in a Serbia roused by nationalism, was due to the fact that the information, which was treated in Belgrade either as a revelation or maligned as treason in 1904, had not led yet to that general, resigned rejection of the Macedonians' independence 20 years earlier in Berlin, - although the neighbouring states had already confidentially been planning to sell their own claims to Macedonia to the world as historically indisputable. Balugdjić's article had rather simply described the real situation – why should there have been any surprise or protest in Germany?

The Serbs, on the contrary, did not want to hear the truth at all; instead, they made continuous efforts to disguise and suppress it. This also affects their historiography. Jutta de Jong tells of historians' efforts in neighbouring countries to use their allegedly scientifically founded arguments in the struggle for Macedonia, reporting

> ...that "Karl Hron set the Slav Macedonians apart in ethnic terms as early as 1890. Two decades later, this is even confirmed by a Serb, the geographer Jovan Cvijić, by his 'Macedoslav' compromise." [Cf. the introductory section 1.2.3] "The small number of modern treatments – e.g. by Dakin, Owings, and, with a few exceptions, Fischer-Galati – do not deny the existence of an independent Macedonian movement either."[184] In footnote 34, she adds: "A special interpretation has been provided by Stavrianos ... who classifies the population in central Macedonia as "being distinctively Macedonian."

Hron too must have sensed the resistance the chauvinist neighbours would put up against the Macedonians' right to exist. He must have had good reasons to express the conviction, quoted by de Jong in another footnote (No. 32),

> "that a Macedonian nationality is being proved ever more clearly by advanced research."

2.1.8 Serbia – Old Serbia (Kosovo) – Macedonia

Still, chief press officer Balugdjić's unusual advice to limit Serbia to territories that had really belonged to it was no exception; there were other moderate politicians.
Thus Milovanovich, the Serbian envoy in Rome, is quoted to have seen no obstacle to a close alliance between Belgrade and Sofia in spite of Serbian and Bulgarian ambitions concerning Macedonia or to a moderation in Serbian geopolitics:

> "Serbia (could) not expand towards the sea, as its true interests would dictate... Austria had cut it off from its natural coastline on the Adriatic. Similarly, it would have to renounce the thought of expanding towards Thessalonica. If Macedonia was to be divided, Serbia had to be content with Old Serbia and only make absolutely sure that it would always find its export route via Thessalonica open."[185]

He still upheld the demand that "Macedonia be divided", but restricted himself to Old Serbia, i.e. Kosovo, to which a Serbian history and population could be ascribed with full justification.
The most conspicuous feature in the remarks of the Serbian envoy is his circumspect commitment to the foreign trade interests of landlocked Serbia. Despite all willingness to practise political and military moderation, even then it would have been crucial to keep open the transport routes from Belgrade to the Aegean, i.e. along the age-old routes in the Morava-Vardar dip.
This is a complex which is also of existential importance to the Republic of Macedonia today, as e.g. was shown by the arbitrary Greek economic blockade against Macedonia in 1992.

Some interesting points on the Albanian question in Old Serbia, i.e. Kosovo, can be found in a report by the legation in Belgrade, which is still of such relevance that it deserves to be quoted in detail. At the same time, it is a vivid illustration of what we can read in history books or – more in keeping with the current trend –see on television today. The ambassador in Ratibor comments on a conversation he had with the Serbian Prime Minister Pašić:

> It could not have escaped the latter "that in Old Serbia the Serbians are increasingly giving ground to the Albanese. This is no new development but is known to have started as early as the end of the 17th century, when 500,000 Serbians migrated to Hungary under the leadership of Metropolitan Ipek and were replaced by Albanese. Gradually, the Serbian community was so strongly infiltrated by Albanian elements that complete towns that used to be Serbian are now Albanese. Hard pressed by an alien tribe, the Serbians find themselves in a deplorable position. In the event of an autonomy for Albania, even one that was within the geographical limits suggested by Mr. Pashich, " [he had referred to the provinces of Janina and Skutari] "would certainly mean further suppression of the Serbian element by the Albanians in Old Serbia."[187]

2.1.9 1908 – The annexation of Bosnia

Then came the turbulent year of 1908, and with it the Young Turk revolution (in July). This influenced and sped up important decisions in Southeast Europe. But the Young Turkish revolutionaries had also been driven by external influences. Imperial Chancellor v. Bülow gives us the following interesting indication in his "Denkwürdigkeiten": The Turkish revolution which he describes as cutting through the oppressive atmosphere in Europe in the high summer of 1908 "like a thunderstorm that cleared the air" "had been partly motivated by the reform plans for Macedonia announced in Reval by Russia and England."[188]

For in the view of the "Turkish patriots", Sultan Abdul Hamid had "not shown enough opposition" to the European reform plans.

(The fact that the cautious Imperial Chancellor had been taken in by an Anglo-Russian ploy is discussed in detail in Chapter 5.)

What followed was the well-known chain reaction:

In Sofia, Prince Ferdinand had declared Bulgarian independence most precipitously. According to the words of the then Imperial Chancellor, Emperor Wilhelm II, who had already been irritated by the overthrow of his "special friend" Abdul Hamid, was even more annoyed that, on top of everything else, Ferdinand had dared to have himself crowned as king without first asking for Wilhelm's permission.

> All this was complicated enough. But what was it in comparison with the role played in world history by the Austrian annexation of Bosnia and Herzegovina!
> *That could only end in disaster.*

At first, all remained calm in the Balkans, not least because Russia had managed to calm down the embittered Serbs, although it pretended to be shocked itself by this breach of the Treaty of Berlin and the (allegedly!) different interpretation of the agreements of Reichstadt and Buchlau. But after Reval, there was a long-term perspective that was much more important to Russia and the other Entente members than Bosnia (or Serbia) so that despite a lot of noisy propaganda they preferred not to let things boil over. The reason is easily explained: *In the eyes of the Entente, the moment for a great confrontation with Austria and Germany had not yet arrived; moreover, armament in Russia and France had not yet reached the required level.*

Thus it is no surprise that even in the explosive situation created by the Austrian provocation, the German embassy in Belgrade noted that, according to Serbian press reports, the Russian Foreign Minister Izvolskij had recommended Serbia "to patiently await diplomatic talks". From the Serbian point of view, however, "such talks had rarely resulted in any benefit to Serbia so far."

What a cheek! Where did Serbia get the courage for such effrontery?

The legation notes that

> "the true, disheartening impression" made on leading circles was not reflected in the press. In any case, it would be wrong to conclude from Serbia's despondency "that Serbia would permanently renounce its 'rights' and refrain from further efforts to attain them. It is possible that Serbia will stay calm for a while..."[189]

It did not stay calm.

Serbia was unable to put up a fight alone, so it entered into a military convention with Montenegro in the same month, i.e. in October 1908. This is remarkable, seeing that it had been in severe conflict with it for years. Both mobilized their armies and would have been prepared to march against Austria but were hindered from doing so by Russia and Great Britain. For the time being!

> For both British and Russian strategists, this would have meant an untimely and unnecessary waste of energies they meant to reserve for a more suitable moment – and not just for an enemy such as Austria-Hungary!
>
> *For all signs indicate that during the Wilhelmian era London had come to the conclusion that the Continental balance of power was in need of being redressed by England.*

An overhasty unilateral move by two subaltern - albeit much needed - marginal countries could have spoiled everything with regard to this long-term strategic goal. To achieve this, other situations were certainly thinkable – and could be provoked if necessary.
In military terms, the Serbian-Montenegrin convention may not have made a great difference. But the speed with which the participants found themselves prepared to put Balkan disputes aside when it was necessary to defend shared interests against a common, external foe was to become exemplary in the not too distant future. And one thing was evident both to those involved and to the onlookers:
The annexation would not remain unavenged. Clear words.
Only on Ballhausplatz did nobody seem to have been willing to hear them. This led to the devastating result that the Habsburg diplomats overestimated themselves while underestimating the consequences of their imperialist act.
But what about the German Emperor? The files seem to suggest that he read all the reports carefully. He was known to react rather impetuously on occasion but took an extremely great interest in politics and used to advocate high ethical values. Moreover, he knew all the persons involved by name, and presumably most of them also personally. Should this report in particular have escaped him? And in case this report was really not presented to him for some sound reason (his being out riding, taking the waters, or even illness), where was Imperial Chancellor von Bülow? What did the members of the cabinet and the high officials of the civil service think when they were compelled to read:

"It" [Serbia] "will go on arming for better times."[189]

"Arming"! "Better times"? This sarcasm can only have been caused by some evil coincidence. The hidden meaning of this word-play would only have been revealed in retrospect. (I shall return to this point later.)

2.1.10 Serbia and Bulgaria demarcate their spheres of interest

The story is approaching a juncture: the final establishment of the Balkan League, the exact date of which was not foreseeable for the participants then, although they had occupied themselves with it and worked towards it for decades. Starting with the revolutionary year of 1908, the current of historical development which often enough flows along quietly, even sluggishly, gained speed and swelled to new dimensions.
The supreme principle of all Serbian governments as regards the Balkan League was a catchy slogan meant to convince all the other Balkan states of the absolute necessity of such an alliance:

"The Balkans for the Balkan peoples - may we be able to repel any foreign invasion together and in solidarity."[190]

This at least was the tenor of a confidential note sent by the Serbian government to its representative in Sofia. This caution was no doubt well-founded. Austria had just shown the world public how dangerous its expansionist politics could be; moderation was evidently not part of the Habsburg vocabulary. This inevitably made Austria-Hungary the target of the Balkan states, especially of Serbia. Besides, a further greedy and vengeful great power was also still lying in wait south of the Serbian border – the Ottoman Empire. Therefore any Balkan politics that were to make sense had to aim at concentrating all forces.

Bulgaria repeatedly offered itself as the first potential partner. Consequently, the Serbian foreign minister provided his envoy in Sofia with the following official version as a guiding principle in his dealings with the host government:

> "Serbia was prepared not only to establish a customs union with Bulgaria for that purpose, but even a military convention, which should, in his opinion, be kept open for a potential accession of the Principality of Montenegro. As for both countries' national spheres of influence in Macedonia, Serbia was ready to discuss that with Bulgaria at any time."[190]

As I have set out before, this idea was not at all new. But now it was transformed from an idea into a project.

Certainly, Serbia was not always frank in its dealings with Bulgaria, but in this case it was a matter of a very real fear of Austria and the revival of the old plan of extending its own basis of power at the expense of Macedonia (and, as soon as possible: of Austria). So a certain measure of openness was advisable.

Turkey, on the other hand, met with a totally different Serbian response which resembled the biased, two-faced behaviour by which the Turkish Muslims themselves had deceived the Christians for centuries, following the principle of religiously legitimated concealment and misrepresentation (*takiye* in Turkish, *taqqija* in Arabic). In this sense, the Serbians proved to be quick learners.

The Envoy von Reichenau sent the Imperial Chancellor (now Dr. von Bethmann Hollweg) a report on two leading articles in the Serbian government organ "Samouprava" which referred to an article in the Turkish paper "Tanin".

There, the option of a Balkan League

> "was recognized as a means of preserving the freedom and independence of the Balkan peoples, but at the same time, the fear (was) voiced ... that this alliance could be directed against Turkey."[191]

What it undoubtedly was – at least as far as the Balkan states' primary goal was concerned. The Entente, on the other hand, sought to redirect the activities of the Balkan states from Turkey towards Austria and Germany in the long term. Turkey (still a large country) was, if possible, to be integrated into a complete chain of Balkan states and closely associated with the Entente in its hostility towards the Dual (or Triple) Alliance.

> *It will be shown that this ideal construction would not work because the preferences of the Balkan states could simply not be harmonized with Entente policies.*

In this situation, the Belgrade government paper concentrated on pointing out to Turkey the harmlessness of the planned alliance: We Serbs owe it to ourselves to express clearly

> "how little foundation there is ... for the afore mentioned fears. The situation ... is so serious that it is worth every effort to remove every doubt and every misunderstanding."

The hypocrisy went even further: The goal and task of the Balkan League had been

> "dictated by Serbia's continuous friendship and loyalty towards Turkey."

Pledges of allegiance to absolute rulers have always - right down through the ages - been the order of the day. But "Samouprava" connects the appeasement with a particularly devious form of homage, writing that

> "a potential Balkan League would be inconceivable without Turkey if it were to count on success."[192]

That made the deceit complete. The only question is whether the Sultan, who took up this idea later, was only out-roguing the rogue or had really been taken in.

The tactics of misrepresentation were upheld throughout. A report by the embassy in Constantinople demonstrates that the Serbian envoy there had clearly read his instruc-

tions carefully, for the German ambassador reported from a conversation with his Serbian colleague Nenadovich that Serbia could only participate in this Balkan League that was being promoted by Russia (!) on the condition that
> "it was not directed against Turkey but Turkey actually took part in it."[193]

The Serbian envoy did not conceal from Baron von Marschall that the Bulgarians were putting all their cards on the table. Their motto was: Balkan League yes, but only if it was to exclude Turkey and be directed against it. Nenadovich gave the reason that the Serbians had always been compelled to harbour suspicions against Sofia:
> "Serbia was ... only going to be used as a backup lest Bulgaria should be prevented from putting its plans for a Great Bulgaria into action." Therefore "the status quo ... was to be preferred to the creation of a Great Bulgaria" as Serbia might otherwise be in danger of being squashed between two powerful neighbours and only serve as a provider of territorial compensation.[193]

Nevertheless, the German Ambassador in Vienna thought he could descry a gradual rapprochement of the Serbian and Bulgarian standpoints, as was suggested by Russian sources. In his opinion the crux in the relationship of these two countries still lay in the Macedonian question. So far, all attempts to *delimit national spheres* in Macedonia had failed "on account of the chauvinist intransigence exhibited by both sides". But then, Mr. von Tschirschky pointed out, there was some progress in the search
> "for an agreement on the demarcation line that had been sought in vain for so long." The condition for adopting it was "that each side should withdraw its national propaganda from the sphere that was not declared its own."[194]

This made it perfectly clear that the negotiation was not about territories that belonged or had once belonged to the Serbs or Bulgarians but about such territories that still needed to be "declared" theirs.

In these zones, the two sides agreed to stop their "national propaganda" – without which the Macedonians would not have known that they were really Serbs or Bulgarians.

The agreement on the Serbian-Bulgarian demarcation line mentioned in the last report from Vienna actually seems to have been a success, for only a few days later the Belgrade legation announced that the Serbian government had decided
> "to stop Serbian propaganda in Serbian schools in South Macedonia – a decision that, according to the Imperial Consul in Thessalonica, has already partly been put into practice in the *vilayet* there."[195]

The Serbian cabinet would never have made such a decision if the territory in question had ever been part of Old Serbia.

In view of what history has to offer on this subject, the arbitrariness and impudence of even starting a process of Serbification in an area that had simply been defined as Serbian can only be understood as one of the fatal consequences of the imperialist zeitgeist.

Once the agreement had suddenly materialized, both countries felt obliged as a precautionary measure to send the High Porte a "note of reassurance" (this is the term really used in the report), which affirmed
> "that this rapprochement involved no hostility towards any third power, least of all against Turkey, whose noble friendship both governments were sincerely eager to retain."[195]

It probably made the Sultan cry with emotion. Wilhelm II, however, kept his realism and wrote in the margin of this passage – maybe slightly drastically but with a refreshing aptness: *Nonsense!*

Wilhelm may have foreseen that the Serbs and the Entente would treat Germany in the same way. Unfortunately it had escaped him that they were *already* doing so – especially since he would never have believed his English relatives to be capable of such malice.

2.1.11 A conference of Slav Social Democrats

The communists of the 20th century often took an objective stance on the question of Macedonian national independence. This attitude also made itself felt during the Greek civil war in 1946-49, when the Greeks promised autonomy to the Macedonians in North Greece (this is what Athens called the province of Aegean Macedonia since its annexation in 1912/13 until approx. 1987), if they helped them in the civil war. This attitude has also persisted into present times. Even during the term of office of Prime Minister Mitsotakis, the Greek communists never took part in the witch-hunt organized by the government and the Greek Orthodox Church against the Republic of Macedonia.

A report from Belgrade gives us the opportunity to look at some activities, if not of communists, at least of Social Democrats at the time:

At the end of 1909, a conference of the delegates of the Social Democrat parties of the Slav Balkan states took place in Belgrade. The list of participants contains a surprising feature which the Serbian government, in view of its plans of annexation, would probably never have admitted in this form at an official gathering: the list transmitted by the embassy includes, next to Social Democrats from Serbia (12 participants), Bulgaria (11 participants) and Croatia (2 participants) and some participants form Bosnia and Herzegovina and from Montenegro (1 participant), 4 participants from "Macedonia".[196]

These could not have been Serbian or Bulgarian Macedonians, as they would have insisted on their nationality being registered accordingly, nor Greek ones, as the Greeks, being non-Slavs, were not even participating, but only autochthonous *Macedonian* Social Democrats.

2.1.12 The status quo

A permanent topic that was discussed again and again in the period between the Congress of Berlin and the Balkan wars because it had left its mark on the political concepts of all parties involved was the question of the *status quo* in the Balkans. As I have mentioned repeatedly, the Great Powers, lacking any better alternatives, had decided in Berlin against the Christian peoples of the Balkans who were not yet free, and in favour of preserving the status quo, i.e. in favour of allowing Turkey to stay on European soil. For the governments of the small Balkan countries, this concept became a challenge to their skilfulness in defending their diametrically opposed interests in this international gamble, for *only a change of the status quo* could bring them closer to the acquisition of the additional land they desired. Yet they were not allowed to speak of their resistance to this concept openly. Outwardly, they had to grin and bear it.

This resulted in a permanent game of confusion which was only resolved when it was clear after the Balkan war that Russia and the other two Entente powers had not only

encouraged the Balkan states to set up the Balkan League over many years and in ever-changing new variants, but that in the background they had done everything to upset precisely that status quo except for a little remnant – East Thrace and Constantinople.[197] (In principle, the status quo had in any case been opposed to the policy Russia had followed for centuries, namely to drive Islamic Turkey out of Europe.)
But why had the renunciation of the original Russian goal of 'liberating the Christian and Slavic peoples from the Islamic crescent' been kept a secret with such effort and indeed so successfully?

For Russia's initial goal had been replaced by a new goal of a higher order that was shared by the Entente. This meant that, *in principle*, Balkan states were no longer to be assisted in taking possession of formerly Turkish land on European ground. Instead, the Entente powers were now more interested in integrating Turkey as firmly as possible into their "global European" concept directed against Germany and Austria.
This had to lead to conflicts of interest, as the Balkan states may have been willing to support the Entente strategy against the (still Triple-) Alliance [Germany-Austria/Hungary-Italy], but would certainly not be persuaded to abstain from attacking Turkey.

Chapter 5 will deal with the outcome of this rather complicated tug-of-war between the two opposed groups of interests.

Back to Serbia and the status quo:
The Serbs developed a remarkable mastery in the strategy of confusion. The aforementioned Foreign Minister Milovanović was quoted by the German embassy in Constantinople as saying:

> "For Serbia, the preservation of the status quo is better than any other state of affairs."[198]

A whopping lie! But it was Milovanović's task not to prematurely attract the attention of the Great Western Powers, more precisely the Western non-members of the Entente, i.e. Germany and Austria, to the impending solution for the Balkan League or, even more importantly, to its objectives. Instead, the press was allowed to play a major role in this performance. The Serbian trade journal "Trgovinski Glasnik" at least criticized status quo politics:

> "Simply holding on to the status quo in the Balkans is not enough. The status quo can only benefit Serbia's enemies who have seized whatever they could and now want to use this formula to secure their spoils."[199]

With this description, the paper had quite correctly exposed Austria's trick of securing annexed Bosnia for itself behind the protective barrier provided by the status quo.
"Opposition papers", the ambassador adds, "are mounting an even fiercer attack." Unlike the Coburg, King Ferdinand of Bulgaria, the Serbian king had no obligations to the Tsar.

> "We were released from such obligations by the [Russo-Austrian] agreements of Reichstädt and Buchlau, the Treaty of San Stefano and the Berlin Congress. Faith in Russia, which used to be strong in Serbia, has completely vanished on account of the annexation crisis."[199]

As a matter of fact, the pendulum of Russian favour was gradually swinging from Bulgaria to Serbia. For in spite of the Russo-Bulgarian reconciliation in 1896 it was becoming increasingly evident that Bulgaria would not be pushed in the direction favoured by the "new" Balkan League (i.e. against the Triple Alliance rather than Turkey) either by Russia or by the Entente, certainly not as easily as its Serbian neighbour who had "deserved" a certain measure of Russian good-will, considering how often it had been disadvantaged by Russia in the past.

Besides, Serbia held an unbeatable trump which made it much more attractive for the Russian strategy than Bulgaria: its border with Austria-Hungary. In any case, Milovanović's plan was working out.

A visit by the Serbian King Peter in St. Petersburg from March 22nd to 26th 1910 showed that the general political climate was changing in Serbia's favour and the tense relations with Russia were improving. Even the leading article of the Russian paper "Novoe Vremya" saw the *friendly, brotherly and cordial* relations confirmed by the fact that, for the first time, toasts at the table were not proposed in French as usual, but in Russian and Serbian.[200] Outwardly, however, calculated deceptions were continued, now clearly following an agreement with the Russians, seeing that in an interview with the aforementioned paper, Foreign Minister Milovanović described the idea of the Balkan League as a *beautiful utopia and a naïve dream*.[201] Why?

In order to lull the world public, especially Turkey and Germany/Austria into a false sense of security, Foreign Minister Izvolskij, who had arranged everything, was not satisfied with an "appeasement note" this time. In order to disguise the true purpose of the Balkan League as promoted by Russia, England and France, King Peter (and subsequently also King Ferdinand, cf. the chapter on Bulgaria) was sent to kowtow to the Sultan in Constantinople on April 3rd 1910.

2.2 Bulgaria

2.2.0 Historical review

The Eurasian nomad horsemen were of crucial importance to the whole migration of peoples. Most of them spoke Turkish. The area the "Turkish migration of peoples" originated from was Inner Asia, the starting point for Huns, Avars, Magyars, Tatars, Seljuqs (the later Ottomans), the Pechenegs and, in fact, the Proto-Bulgars. The Turkic peoples first entered into European history with the great Hun attack on the Gothic kingdom of King Ermanarich.[202]

> "This advance ... had opened a path right into the Danube area for the (Eurasian) steppe peoples."[203]

(Only two of the political foundations of that time have survived up to the present day: Hungary and Turkey.)

1.
Some territories of later Bulgaria that had been inhabited by Slavs since the 6th century
> "were conquered by a group of Bulgarian Turkic tribes (coming from the north) in the second half of the seventh century; these were not part of the Indo-European language group."[204]

(By way of explanation: the equally Turkic Ottomans came from Anatolia in the South and did not reach the Balkans before 1354.)

Unlike the Slavs, the Bulgarians under Chan Asparukh succeeded in founding a state North of the Lower Danube as early as 679 – the *First Bulgarian Kingdom*, which was recognized by Byzantium in 681. In doing so, Asparukh had created "the conditions for a Turkic-Slavic symbiosis that would have far-reaching consequences."[205]

> "Like all political foundations of the Eurasian nomad peoples ... this Proto-Bulgarian kingdom was a typical "layered society": A large class of Slav peasants were ruled by a far less

numerous class of proto-Bulgarian conquerors. Then the two peoples gradually merged. By the 9th century the ruling class had merged into the Slavic mass. ... All that is left of the former ruling class is the name "Bulgarians" which now refers to the new Slavic-speaking mixed population."[206]

This process started in 681 and took over 200 years, until 893, when Tsar Simeon made "Slavic the official language of the state and the church." (Loc. cit., p. 32)

Thus the *name* of the proto-Bulgarian state has survived in history, but *not* the proto-Bulgarian, i.e. Turkic people, and not the proto-Bulgarian, i.e. Turkic *language*. (Mazower points out the conspicuous similarities with the ruling class in England and in Normandy and the role of the Varangians in Russia. Loc. cit. p. 99)

The fact that the Slavic language now spoken in Slavic Bulgaria is also referred to as "Bulgarian" has led the Bulgarians to entertain misconceptions about possible political claims as regards the Slavs in Macedonia. These, however, had nothing to do with the Bulgarians except that they belonged to the First Bulgarian Kingdom in the Early Middle Ages, probably between 845 and 971, and to the Second Bulgarian Kingdom in the High Middle Ages, more precisely between 1185 and 1393.

(So what? Who would dare tell the Dutch that they are really Spaniards or Austrians – although their occupation by Spain and their dynastic connections with Austria are far more recent.)

2.

In 803, the Bulgarians conquered the territory of present-day East Hungary and Romania from the Avars, and in 809, (under Chan Krum) Serdika, present-day Sofia.

"That also gave the Bulgarians access to Macedonia."[207] They "merged the Slavic tribes in the north-eastern part of the Balkan peninsula with the remaining Thracian and Greek-Roman substratum into one kingdom."[208]

Between 840 and 850, Tsar Presyan conquered (Central) Macedonia.

Michael Weithmann explains:

The Slavs in Greece speak "a language most closely related to that of the Slavs in Moesia and Thrace, i.e. of the Slavic population which formed the ethnic substratum of the First Bulgarian Kingdom as early as 681 and later, after assimilating the Turkic ruling class, assumed their name of "Bulgarians"."[209]

At this point I would like to add the following consideration:

If there is conclusive proof that when the Bulgarians settled they encountered some population that was ethnically Thracian and assimilated it, then it is even more probable that the Slavs who had settled in Ancient Macedonia around 150 years earlier (that would make five generations) were even more certain to have found autochthonous "Macedonian" population and also assimilate it.

While recognition of these historical processes is considered normal in the case of Bulgaria (and in the case of Romania with regard to the Dacians), the Greeks vehemently deny this recognition to the Republic of Macedonia, simply because it does not fit into their own project of taking possession of the ethnos of Ancient Macedonia in order to justify their annexation of Macedonian territory at the beginning of the 20th century and does not serve as an argument for Athens' claim to the Macedonian name today.

As a matter of fact, we have to argue by analogy: If the Turkic Bulgarians can refer to their predecessors, the Thracians, and the Walachian Romanians to their predecessors, the ancient Dacians, without being attacked by the world – or rather by Greece –

for that reason, then the Slavic Macedonians are even more entitled to refer to their predecessors, the ancient Macedonians.

3.

Since Tsar Boris converted to Christianity in 865, and even more since the reign of Tsar Simeon (893-927), we speak of the first Slavic Christian Orthodox kingdom in the Balkans.[210] (It was a *Slavic* Christian kingdom. The Turk-Tatar, proto-Bulgarian element had long since lost its importance for the political and cultural life of that kingdom.)

4.

Like Khan Krum before him, Tsar Simeon (893-927) was aiming at conquering Constantinople[211] and acquiring the title of Byzantine Emperor in order to establish a Great Bulgarian kingdom.

> "During its largest territorial extension in the 9th and 10th century, the kingdom of the Bulgarian khans presented a serious danger to the imperial power on the Bosporus. Only Russian military assistance enabled" [the Byzantine] "emperor Basileios II (976-1025) to finally break the Bulgarians' military power at the end of the 10th century."[212]

The offer of Russian assistance at such an early stage may be surprising. The background:

The Varangians were already involved in lively trade relations with Constantinople. The Kievan princes concluded treaties with the Byzantine emperor Basileios. Svyatoslav, the first Kievan prince with a Russian name, whose mother Olga actively conducted government business for him from 945 until 969, undertook military campaigns not only to the Caucasus and the Crimea, but also to the Balkans where he helped the Byzantine emperor to defeat the First Bulgarian Kingdom. Saint Vladimir (978-1015) who made Christianity the official religion in Kiev, was given Anna, the sister of Basileois II, in marriage.[213]

So: The Bulgarians were defeated by the Byzantine Empire in 971 (972). The victor Basileios took cruel revenge on the Bulgarians, for which East Roman historians later gave him the "celebratory" byname of "Bulgaroktonos", killer of Bulgarians.

> "Thus, after a stretch of glorious history, the First Bulgarian Kingdom was submerged in a river of blood and tears. The gloomy memories of the Greek-Bulgarian internecine war stayed in the political consciousness of both peoples as bloody shadows of the past which stood and still stand between them and separate them."[214]

Imperial Byzantine rule over the inner Balkan Slavic territories was thus restored for more than one and a half centuries.

However, the tide of history turned again.

> "In 1185, the brothers Petar and Ivan Asen" had successfully "raised a revolt against the emperor ... with Cuman and Walachian help." The Bulgarians were well on their way towards becoming the successors of the Byzantine emperors and establishing themselves as the rulers of the Balkan Peninsula." Only a few decades later, Ivan Asen II (1218-1241), the most important king of this so-called Second Bulgarian Kingdom of the Asenides, ushered in the last significant period of Bulgarian great power politics."[215]

For some time, Serbia, Macedonia and parts of Greece also belonged to the Second Bulgarian Kingdom, which thus grew to be the largest Southeast European state of that time.

> "The Tatar attack of 1241 abruptly ended this ascent. The Bulgarian kingdom was never to recover from this serious calamity. In 1257, the last of the Asenides died; in 1330, the Shishmanides had to finally clear the way for the victorious Serbs. The Bulgarian rump kingdoms in Tarnovo and Vidin became victims of the Ottomans in 1393 and 1396."[215]

5.
The Ottoman Empire had divided its province Rumelia into five Sanjaks: Vidin, Nikopol, Silistra, Macedonia and Thrace; the population had to pay high taxes and was encouraged to convert, "partly even by force".[216]

As with the other Balkan peoples, all Bulgarian peasant uprisings against the Turks failed, e.g. in 1598 in Tarnovo, in 1686 in Tarnovo and Gabrovo and in 1757 in Chiprovec. The same was true of the revolts in the 19th century, i.e. in 1835, 1841 and 1850. Historiography offers a plausible explanation, saying that

> "the Bulgarians in the East of the Balkan Peninsula ... were more isolated from the West, where the new national ideas had originated, than the rest of the Balkan peoples. ... On the other hand, they were located in close proximity to the centre of Ottoman power, the capital Constantinople, so that a national revolt had little chance of success from the very start."[217]

6.
Besides the awakening desire for freedom and national awareness, the Bulgarian Orthodox Church played a crucial role in the liberation of Bulgaria. This had the following background:

After the Turkish conquest of Constantinople in 1453, the Sultan had acknowledged the Greek ecumenical patriarch as the religious head of all Orthodox Christians. Thus the Hellenization of the Bulgarian high clergy, that had begun long before the fall of Constantinople, was officially confirmed by the Ottoman Empire.

> "Though the Greeks had lost their former political importance under Turkish rule, they had succeeded in inheriting the legacy of Byzantine high culture and thereby securing their cultural, clerical and economic pre-eminence among all Christian peoples."[218]

Stadtmüller continues in his standard work:

> "Thus the Greek Orthodox Church ... became the Christian state church of the Ottoman Empire, whose spiritual dominance pushed aside the old autocephalous national churches of the Bulgarians, Serbians and Romanians which were forced into a marginal spiritual existence. The official churches of the Serbs, Bulgarians and Romanians were hellenized ... the intellectual life of these peoples in general was swamped by the Greek influence." "Only the monasteries in remote mountainous areas remained places of refuge for independent thinking. Thus, they gained immense importance for the preservation of national consciousness among the Balkan Slavs and the Romanians."[219]

It may have struck the reader that *Macedonia* is not mentioned in Stadtmüller's list of affected autocephalous churches. This is correct: for

> "the Macedonian national church was still existent in the form of the "archbishopric of Ohrid."[220]

The archbishopric of Ohrid was only given up in 1767 at the Greeks' instigation, which led to a low point in Macedonian history.

> "Nevertheless the monasteries remained strongholds of Macedonian writing culture" and even strengthened "the awareness of cultural independence."[221]

Next to the significant income from church tax, ousting the Slavic churches had the invaluable benefit for Greece that the Slavic orthodox believers now had to go to Greek Orthodox churches and institutions for want of their own autocephalous churches, as in order to observe certain rites they had to go to some orthodox church, even if it meant going to a Greek one. This had weighty long-term consequences: in censuses, Slavic believers were regularly registered as Greek. Thus, an inappropriately high proportion of Greek population always appears in the statistics. Because of this

> "excessive way of determining nationality ... all believers of the Greek Orthodox patriarchate – without regard to their ethnicity – were to be considered Greeks. This also applied to the Macedonian population."[222]

In the case of the Serbs, Bulgarians and Romanians, the same procedure started (depending on the source) soon after the fall of Constantinople in 1453 and lasted until their churches became independent of the Greek patriarchate:

For Serbia, until 1832, i. e. approx. 380 years,

for Bulgaria, until 1870/72, i. e. approx. 420 years, and

for Romania, until 1885, i. e. approx. 435 years.

In contrast, the Macedonians only needed 200 years to restore the independence of their church, as it had been independent for almost 750 years *before* 1767. The new autocephalous *Macedonian Orthodox Church* was already proclaimed in 1958, - i.e. in Tito's Communist Yugoslavia! The patriarch of Moscow was prepared to recognize it in 1967[223]; under pressure from the Serbian Orthodox Church, however, the MOC had to be content with a lower status. Nonetheless, the Macedonian Orthodox Church declared its independence anew in 1967 (i.e. exactly two hundred years after its forced liquidation in 1767), after the Serbian-Macedonian interim solution of 1958 had proved not viable.

7.

Thus there were good reasons why the Bulgarian and Romanian national struggle for freedom

> "was not only directed against Turkish domination, but equally bitterly against 'Hellenization', i.e. the overwhelming Greek influence ..."[224] "Bulgaria was largely swamped with Greek and Turkish influences. The Greeks controlled the Official church, literature, trade and the economy. ... Literary and cultural life in Bulgaria was wholly conducted in Greek at the time. The Bulgarian language was not considered socially acceptable. ... Members of the educated classes ... were ashamed to bear the name of Bulgaria and called themselves ‚Bulgarophonoi hellenes' ... The Greek influence in Bulgaria caused a decline of Bulgaria's own culture and national consciousness as was the case in Romania." [225]

Therefore literature often speaks of the "double yoke":

> "Ottoman dominance in political life" and "Greek authority in matters of the church."[226]

Edith Durham has written about the consequences of this merciless Hellenization after her decades of travels in the Balkans at the beginning of the 20th century:

> "No Western European who has not lived in the country himself can comprehend the depth of hatred between the Greek and the Bulgarian church."[227]

At that time, Bulgaria made a decision fundamentally different from all the other Balkan states which were fighting to end their suffering under the Turks: It began its struggle for freedom not by fighting against the Ottoman Empire, but within the Orthodox Church. The result was that in 1870, the Sultan gave in to Russian pressure – a request from Bulgaria alone would hardly have been sufficient – and approved an *exarchate* that was independent of the Greek Orthodox patriarchate: "a historically unique event."[228]

The Serbian Ambassador in St. Petersburg D. Popović referred to the consequences of this "unique event" in his confidential report of December 8th 1913 (R 20728-2, page 116), i.e. shortly after the armistice of the First Balkan War, paraphrasing a conversational remark by the Bulgarian general Dimitriyev:

> "Bulgaria had ... put down roots in (parts of Macedonia) by creating political situations (exarchate etc.)." (The brackets are part of the original text.)

It was rather frank of the general to admit that Bulgaria still had to put down roots in Macedonia by means of the "exarchate etc."

Why? *Because previously Macedonia was inhabited by Macedonians only!*

> "A period of 40 years and more helped the Bulgarians not a little to exert their influence on the feelings of the population..."

It is sheer mockery to describe Bulgarization euphemistically as "an influence"; but at least in this there seems to have been a full consensus with a representative of Serbification (which one French historian once described as "serbisation brutale").

The loss of considerable tax revenue for the Greek patriarchate due to the creation of an exarchate probably was much greater than the significant reduction in the number of believers. Two years later, when the written order (firman) of the Sultan had finally been issued, the ensuing tension between the two churches led to the patriarch's far-reaching decision to declare the Bulgarian exarchate shismatic. The Sultan as the rejoicing third party was only too pleased with this internal power struggle; for such arguments always started anew, whenever the Sultan decided to grant the Bulgarians another bishop's seat. Years later in Constantinople, Ambassador von Saurma recounted a revealing remark of the Sultan's:

> "The Sultan said ... that the Greek patriarchate did not want to forego the pecuniary benefits which it was losing as result of the foundation of Bulgarian bishoprics."[229]

An episode that happened as much as seven years later, when Turkey found itself so hard pressed by Russian troops during the Russo-Turkish war of 1877 that it even had to look for allies in Athens shows that the Sultan clearly recognized the consequences of the religious restructuring and the ways he could use it to blackmail both Greece and Bulgaria politically. The Sultan had ordered his "Greek private banker, Mr. Sarafi" to ask the Greek FM Conduriotti

> "what the Porte could do to win Greece's friendship and whether maybe the abolition of the Bulgarian Exarch might meet with approval there."[230]

And behold: Athens gave an evasive answer! Conduriotti may have seen the Sultan's predicament and speculated on why Greece should be satisfied with the removal of the obstructive exarchate as the bird in the hand when it might be able to obtain the two in the bush at the end of the war: i.e. maybe the elimination of all Bulgaria or at least very large territorial gains.

8.

To start their national liberation in 1876, Bulgaria and Macedonia used the the rebellions which had begun in Herzegovina and Bosnia in 1875. The Bulgarian revolt of April 1876 was crushed with a degree of cruelty that was unusual even given the brutality for which the Turks were notorious. The massacre perpetrated by the Adyghe troops, the so-called "*Bulgarian Horrors*", appalled all Europe and led to solidarity with Bulgaria – though not with the same enthusiasm with which the Greek revolts against Turkey had been cheered and supported about 50 years before.

It cannot be held against the Greeks that they opposed the settlement of Adyghe troops by the Porte near the border of (still Turkish) Thessaly in the 80ies of the 19th century – that would have meant that during the conquest campaigns they were planning in the long term, they would also have had to deal with such notoriously wild customers.

It was a stroke of luck for Bulgaria that in 1876, unlike two years later at the Congress of Berlin, the Great Powers had not yet proclaimed their status quo policy. For at that time, Russia was still feeling inspired by the need to protect Orthodox believers in the Balkans and was still pursuing its Pan-Slavist ideas – and of course, it had never given up its longing for the warm water of the Mediterranean.

The Bulgarian atrocities provided a suitable, generally accepted opportunity for a political intervention by Russia. However, the conference of the ambassadors of the

Great Powers convened in Constantinople to settle the conflict failed because of the disaccord between Russia and England. When Turkey had rejected the next step, i.e. the London paper containing the proposals of the Great Powers, the 8th Russo-Turkish war broke out. Following the victory - which was by no means gained without effort - Count Ignatieff, head of the Asian department at the Russian Foreign Ministry and former Russian ambassador in Constantinople, imposed "a one-sided agreement ... on the Turks, namely the unsuccessful Treaty of San Stefano."[231]

> Speaking of Ignatieff: He boasted of having won the byname "Father of Lies" for his dubious negotiating methods during his time as ambassador, a predicate which his two successors in the office of Foreign Minister, Izvolskij and Sasonov, could certainly have appropriated without effort – as we shall see below.

In the preliminary peace of San Stefano of March 3rd 1878, Bulgaria was given Macedonia and Western Thrace. The dream of a Great Bulgaria as it had existed in the dim and distant past seemed to be approaching fulfilment. (The Romanian king saw things quite differently. The Serbian ambassador in Bucharest, Ristić, quoted King Carol in his secret report No. 29 of March 6th 1909 to the Foreign Minister Dr. Milovan Milovanović (R 20727-3, page 207 f.) as having said that "the Treaty of San Stefano ... has created a greater Bulgaria than ever existed in the Middle Ages.") But as the existence of a large country in the Balkans was something that neither England nor Austria wanted, and Russia's new proximity to the Straits was even more unacceptable in their opinion (especially because Russia could have used its "satellite state" Bulgaria to simply circumvent the Straits[232]) and since the Peace of San Stefano was a breach of the Treaty of Paris of 1856 (after the Crimean war) anyway, they practically threatened Russia with war.[233]

By convening a conference in Berlin, this war was averted for the time being. During the Congress of Berlin from June 13th until July 13th 1878, Bulgaria was the first topic on the agenda, because the conference chairman Bismarck wanted "to deal with the most difficult question first".[234] However, a different historical analysis of this situation has come down to posterity: Imanuel Geiss wrote in his book on the 100th anniversary of the Treaty of Berlin:

> In retrospect, it turned out "that a different set of problems was to have a more explosive effect on further developments: Bosnia-Herzegovina..."[234]

Bulgaria was on the agenda in the second session on June 17th 1878 and in the fourth to sixth sessions; in the seventh session on June 26th, the discussions were concluded. Although England had reached agreements with Russia, Austria and the Ottoman Empire in the run-up to the congress in order to pave the way for negotiations, contrary to expectations the Congress did not run smoothly, seeing that the Russian chancellor Prince Gorchakov even threatened to depart. Nevertheless, the Russians did not blame England and Austria as the actual wire-pullers for the fact that the outcome of the Congress was not in their favour, but the German Reich and Bismarck – this version was the one promoted by the anti-German, Pan-Slavist and chauvinist press, and also by part of the officers' corps and the Russian Orthodox Church.

This (unfounded) feeling of resentment was something which France and later England did their utmost to nurture during the following decades.

Art. 1 of the Treaty of Berlin reads:

> "Bulgaria is constituted an autonomous and tributary Principality under the suzerainty of His Imperial Majesty the Sultan. It will have a Christian government and a national militia."[235]

The practical consequences looked less noble than this wording. Said Bulgaria under the suzerainty of the Sultan only comprised the northern part of the country, consisting of Moesia and the Sanjak. East Rumelia which lay south of the Balkan mountains was to remain under Turkish rule, i.e. to be governed directly by the Sublime Porte, though with administrative autonomy and a Christian governor.[236]

This had practically annulled the preliminary Peace of San Stefano – and that after all had been the goal of the Congress of Berlin. A further practical consequence was that after three months and 23 days (cf. 1.2.0.8) Bulgaria had to withdraw from its new provinces Macedonia and Thrace, as these reverted to the Ottoman Empire.

> *In view of all this, it seems provocative that in 1988, the modern Republic of Bulgaria chose the 3rd of March, i.e. the day of the – annulled – Peace of San Stefano, for its new national holiday.*

125 years after this long by gone event, Bulgaria solemnly commemorated this day March 3rd 2003 (in the presence of the Russian president Putin). There is surely no clearer way of articulating *revisionism* in politics. It is hard to imagine that the EU and NATO will put up with such a provoking anachronism before Bulgaria's planned accession.

It is very probable that shortly after the Congress of Berlin there were considerations in Bulgaria about overcoming the division, i.e. about unification with East Rumelia. Moreover, it is to be assumed that the parliamentarians, the government and the head of state (in spring 1879, Alexander von Battenberg, the son of Prince Alexander von Hessen was elected Prince of Bulgaria at the suggestion of Russia) immediately hatched plans about how after all Bulgaria could get hold of the two provinces that had been given back to Turkey, i.e. Macedonia and Thrace. The execution of that plan, however, took more than 30 years. The outcome of these endeavours remained unclear until the very last moment. The result did not come anywhere near of fulfilling Bulgaria's hopes.

Such hopes, considerations and plans must have found expression in the reports of the German embassies – which we shall have to explore.

2.2.1 Prince Alexander's plans for "Macedonia"

It seems to confirm the report quoted at the beginning of the chapter on Serbia that we can now quote a report of the German embassy in Vienna which comes to the same results concerning Bulgaria: An Austrian agent from the consulate in Plovdiv (formerly Philippopolis) had reported to the Austrian Foreign Ministry in Vienna on the visit of the Bulgarian prince to Belgrade and commented upon the Bulgarian attitude towards the "Balkan League" project:

> "The interests of the individual Balkan states, obsessed with expansionist ideas, are so contradictory that a political unity of these states can only be brought about by an exceptional political situation and even then it will only last for a limited period of time."[237]

It is very telling that the Austrian consul did not describe the Balkan states as 'in need of expansion' or 'worthy of expansion', nor as 'entitled to expansion', but simply as "obsessed with expansion". The "exceptional political situation" which would make a Balkan League possible was going to occur about 30 years later and would indeed only last for a limited period of time as he had already foreseen in 1880.

The year 1885 was a milestone in the history of the young Bulgarian state: A secret revolutionary committee had pressured the Bulgarian government into bringing about a full union with East Rumelia. On this subject, the American ex-ambassador George F. Kennan writes that Prime Minister Karavelov must have

> "convinced Prince Battenberg that it could cost him the throne if he did not show sympathy with the unification movement" ... "So he risked being put down by the Powers if he supported the revolt" [because he would thereby be breaking the Berlin Treaty] "or by his own people if he opposed the revolt." Kennan adds a few pages later: "The action was carried out in September 1885 ... by a group comprising a number of Macedonians."[238]

Kennan does not explain the background to this information but we can assume that once again the Macedonians had trusted the promise that after the unification of East Rumelia and Bulgaria was completed successfully with their assistance they would also be helped to gain autonomy for themselves – another fatal miscalculation; the result of another deception.

In explanation, Torsten Szobries quotes Fikret Adanir:

> "The ease with which Ottoman administrative structures had been removed in East Rumelia suggested that in order to annex Macedonia as well, the right way forward would be to grant Macedonia a provisional status of autonomy."[239]

Although this measure had been under consideration in Bulgaria since the Congress of Berlin, it had promptly elicited demands for compensation[240] from the Serbs and Greeks who were full of envy although they had no claims to this territory at all. But, as we know, at that time this did not deter anyone from desiring somebody else's land. Serbia even considered itself entitled to start a war against Bulgaria on account of East Rumelia but was defeated by Battenberg (who had won his spurs in the Russo-Turkish war of 1877/78) near Slivnica – and only Austria which had concluded a secret agreement with Serbia spared it from having to give up very large stretches of land to Bulgaria. Such activity by Battenberg, who being a German was not very popular at the Tsar's court anyway, met with disapproval in Russia, especially as it would have preferred Prince Alexander to have been a "devoted vassal".[241]

Literature often puts down the Tsar's aversion to the Bulgarian prince to the described unification. Prof. Adanir, however, argues convincingly that even in the document of the "League of the Three Emperors" of June 18th 1881, "the unification of East Rumelia with Bulgaria" was accepted "in principle".[242] This agreement does not exclude the possibility that the Tsar regarded the date of the unification as too early and used every opportunity to find fault with Battenberg's occasional naiveté and recalcitrance (not to mention the risk of a German-Bulgarian dynastic connection), but in principle unification had mainly been promoted by Russia.

This success may have gone to the young prince's head. During a visit to Bucharest, he had allowed himself to make some compromising remarks to the Romanian King Carol and his Prime Minister Bratiano. As Dr. Busch heard from the latter, Alexander was determined

> "to extend the unionist movement to Macedonia, too." Moreover, Alexander had suggested that King Carol should become the president of "a confederation of Balkan and Danube states still to be formed." "If expansion to Macedonia succeeded"["if"!] "the Prince would compensate Romania by enlarging Dobruja.[243]

The Auswärtiges Amt in Berlin might have been able to put up with this behaviour, which the Romanian Prime Minister described to the German ambassador as one of "boasting" and "carelessness"; but according to Bratiano, Battenberg had also intimated that Germany regarded his plans favourably. After Bismarck had promptly issued instructions to Sofia, Envoy von Saldern was able to report after an audience with the prince that Alexander had denied everything. But even his toned-down statement on Macedonia ("He was going to leave his hands off Macedonia for as long as possible..."[244]!) was reason enough for Bismarck to issue another instruction to the embassy in St. Petersburg, lest the Tsar should wrongly harbour suspicions against Germany (something Bismarck was always very concerned to prevent):

> "Since the prince had suggested that his plans ... for ... an annexation of Macedonia ... were known to us ... I do not have to state expressly that ... the ways of German politics can never lead ... to the approval of such nonsensical and revolutionary combinations."[245]

Bismarck's alarm was to prove only too justified. He knew the Tsar and knew of the strong antipathy felt by the Tsar's wife Dagmar (daughter of the Danish king Christian IX) against Germany – which may have rubbed off on to Tsar Alexander III in the long years of their marriage.

The Romanian king and his Prime Minister feared

> "that Russia would not go on watching the Bulgarian prince's behaviour with indifference for much longer and that there would be an armed intervention in Bulgaria, which was always undesirable for Romania as a bordering and transit country."[244]

That was a definite understatement, for Romania had already repeatedly suffered from Russian troops marching through the country during their campaigns in the Balkans, most recently during the 8th Russo-Turkish War over Bulgaria in 1877.

In an instruction, Prince Alexander is also quoted as saying that he must declare Bulgaria's independence from Turkey.[246] This goal, however, was something he was not able to attain personally:

Alexander's and Bulgaria's relations with Russia were so uneasy that pro-Russian officers forced Battenberg to abdicate on August 9th 1886. Parliamentary president Stambolov then succeeded in persuading him to return to the throne once more, but a month later he gave up because of long-term reservations voiced by Tsar Alexander III.

We know from George F. Kennan and Paul Sethe that this everyday story was given additional flavour by a budding romance. The Bulgarian prince Alexander v. Battenberg and the seventeen-year-old granddaughter of Wilhelm I, Viktoria (daughter of Crown Princess "Vicky", thus granddaughter of the latter's mother Queen Victoria and therefore sister to Wilhelm II) secretly considered themselves engaged and could even count on motherly support (by the later Empress Friedrich). A Hohenzollern princess on the Bulgarian throne? In the country, moreover, that Russia had freed from Ottoman rule (which was quite rightly referred to as the "Turkish yoke") only a few years before with a high death toll and had primarily chosen as a playground for itself? Out of the question!

Consequently, in a conversation with the Iron Chancellor, Prince Alexander had to listen to some iron principles of German political reasoning:

> "Germany is not interested in Bulgaria, but in peace with Russia. This includes convincing Russia that we are not pursuing any interests in the Orient." "On the day the German princess becomes the Princess of Bulgaria, Russia will become suspicious and not believe this assurance. And I cannot let that happen..." And elsewhere: "Your Highness has all the sympathy of the influential circles in Germany, and I myself respect you highly; but I am chancellor of 45 million Germans whose interests I cannot sacrifice to the interests of one German." (The last half-sentence is spaced in the original.)[247]

This was an irreversible verdict against the marriage of love the prince had hoped for. Bismarck had also added that Bulgaria would once become an object of compensation in the negotiations of the Powers. Here, he was wrong.

(We are left with an insight into the typical way in which the Balkan countries were treated: i. e. as if they were colonies.)

Ultimately, the poetic search of "two royal children" for private happiness was crushed by the laws of high politics in the interest of avoiding international entanglements. According to Sethe, in the "Battenberg affair" "the Tsar's wrath" had "cost the young prince the throne of Bulgaria"[248]

Kennan proves that Bismarck's prudence and determination (he had even threatened to resign) turned out to be futile. Despite Bismarck's prohibition, the Tsar's distrust of Germany was so strong due to *French intrigues* that he continued to suspect that Germany was still backing Battenberg despite all statements to the contrary.

It is a historical fact that 40 years later Victoria, now a widow and bitter, in her "unquenched thirst for happiness" married the young adventurer Alexander Zubkoff in Bonn, as if "in belated revenge" (once more against the advice of her brother who was now living in Doorn), while the former Bulgarian prince Alexander, having assumed the name of Count of Hartenau, enjoyed a happy marriage [if also of short duration] with a former actress at the court theatre in Darmstadt, a Madame Loisinger.[249]

To return to Bulgaria and Sofia:

Almost a year after Prince Alexander had resigned, on July 7th 1887, Ferdinand I of the House of Wettin and the House of Sachsen-Coburg-Gotha, was elected to be Alexander's successor. The Tsar was still disgruntled. Nor did the Sublime Porte officially recognize Ferdinand straightaway, but only "tolerated" him. Only in March 1896 did the Sultan issue two imperial firmans recognizing Ferdinand as Prince of Bulgaria and Governor-General of East Rumelia. (Three years before, in 1893, Prince Ferdinand had married the Bourbon princess Maria-Louise of Parma and thereby considerably polished up his international reputation. The conversion of his son Boris to the Orthodox faith in 1896 had also contributed to that – at least in Russia and in the Balkans.)

The final reconciliation with the Russian court also took place in 1896, under Tsar Nicolaus II.

The "Coburger" did not declare independence for another 20 years and only dared to do it - in connection with assuming a king's title himself - after the Young Turk revolution in 1908, hoping his step would lose significance in the turmoil to come. In this expectation he was correct.

2.2.2 A first treaty draft on the Balkan League

After the reconciliation with Russia and the resulting recognition of the united Bulgarian kingdom by the Great Powers and the Ottoman Empire, the old spirit of cooperation returned to newly inspire Bulgarian-Russian relations.

In the aforementioned interviews with Bulgarian (and Serbian) politicians appearing in the "Figaro", which were reprinted in the Lloyd in Budapest on October 14th 1897, Prime Minister Dragan Zankov went as far as to say:

"Bulgaria has to rely on Russia alone, to which it owes its existence and without which it cannot live." Foreign Minister Grekov added: "We will never forget what Russia has done for us...", and went on: "but we cannot ... subordinate our own interests to Russia's."[250]

These "interests" were, of course, directed at gaining land in Macedonia. With the Russians' help, one day (this remark stems from Karavelov) the Sultan would grant the Bulgarians "autonomy for Macedonia".

The prince's adviser voiced a similar opinion:

"We have demanded autonomy for Macedonia and we will insist that it be granted to us." "The Greeks and Serbs would be wrong if they interpreted our efforts concerning autonomy for Macedonia unfavourably." (Foreign Minister Grekov)

The fact that their partners - or rather adversaries - were not wrong in that matter has been sufficiently dealt with in the chapter on Serbia.

It was the Figaro's intention to find out why the Balkan states had not assisted Greece in its struggle for Crete and Thessaly which had ended in defeat (on account of English objection) and which Athens had started against the advice of the Powers. The interviewees answered these questions candidly: The Great Powers had prevented them from doing so; among other reasons, because, according to the prince's adviser, all Bulgaria would have been prepared "to continue the work of liberating Great Bulgaria". Precisely that would not have fitted into the plan of the Great Powers. Realistically, the adviser also indicated his scepticism concerning the consequences such action would certainly have had:

"What would have been the result? The Bulgarian army would have occupied Macedonia, and the Romanian army Bulgaria."[250]

Thus, the adviser had summed up the problem of Macedonia's neighbouring states aptly and vividly: The goal, i.e. to take possession of Macedonian territory, was clear; the way to attaining this goal without risking one's own political existence was not.

Was this a chance of survival for Macedonia?

The editor of the Figaro, Monsieur Bouillon, made some derogatory and derisive remarks on the frankness and naivety of the Bulgarian and Serbian politicians in his comment on the interviews. This was very unfair, after he had profited from their readiness to give interviews.

At the same time, his revelations concerning the Balkan League and Macedonia were by no means sensational. The "Münchener Neuesten Nachrichten" had already printed the wording of a first draft of a treaty for an alliance between the Kingdom of Serbia and the principalities of Bulgaria and Montenegro a year before (copied from the Bulgarian "pro-Russian opposition paper "Svetlina", Zankov's mouthpiece").[251]

It is a clumsy text, as if it had been pieced together by a few imaginative journalists – but it could equally have been "dashed off" by professionals on purpose. Besides, Art.1 starts with a lie, in that it specifies "the defence of the integrity and independence" of the partners as the alliance's goal.

Art. 4, on the other hand, is revealing, almost sensational, and can speak for itself:

"Given that the states concluding this contract also have brothers in Turkey and in Bosnia and Herzegovina under Austro-Hungarian rule that have not yet been freed, they assume the responsibility of taking action to ease the lot of these brothers."[251]

The aims of the Balkan League, i.e. its being directed not only against Turkey but also against Austria-Hungary, were rarely expressed with such unabashed openness at that time, (i. e. before the turn of the century – and long before the annexation of Bosnia).

Leaving that aside, it is a stroke of intolerable cynicism to refer to the Balkan war against the Ottoman Empire over the territory of Macedonia and Thrace, which is anticipated in this draft, as "easing the lot of these brothers."

2.2.3 False Bulgarians – real Macedonians: the VMRO

In spite of this publication which was said to have been arranged by the Bulgarian government itself, the Bulgarian prince Ferdinand was very intent during his visit to the Montenegrin prince Nikola in Cettinje in 1898 on quashing rumours that he was seeking an alliance with Montenegro. On this difficult mission in Cettinje he was accompanied by a close friend, the Bulgarian envoy in Serbia, Georgiev, whose subsequent task would be to confidentially persuade Serbia to accede to the dual alliance allegedly already concluded against Turkey between Bulgaria and Montenegro. The same man endeavoured to dispel such rumours in talks with his German colleague, the chargé d'affaires in Belgrade, and to present the prince's visit as a pure courtesy visit. Count Schwerin, however, seems to have put his questions so skilfully that Georgiev was induced to reveal some information that was of interest from the Macedonian point of view:

> Georgiev did not deny "that several Serbian teachers in Macedonia have been murdered recently and that an opposition paper here" [a Serbian paper] "is attributing the murders to a Bulgarian secret association bent on destroying Serbian agitators." But he also stressed "that many individuals in Macedonia were passing themselves off as Bulgarian although they were not."[252]

Individuals in Macedonia who were claiming to be Bulgarians when murdering Serbian teachers, i.e. who were not really Bulgarians, could - obviously - not have been Serbs. Had they been Greeks, Georgiev would not have hesitated in the least to reveal the evildoers' names and nationality. And we can hardly imagine what other groups would have been prepared to relieve the Macedonians of the task of protecting themselves from too much foreign influence – in this case from Serbification. Besides, as we know from the chapter about Serbia, the activities of the Serbian committees were called off "on orders from above" following the Serbian-Bulgarian agreement on spheres of interest. Consequently, these individuals could only have been *"real" Macedonians*. Such cases may not reflect any credit on the Macedonians, but they do the Macedonians honour as actions of self-defence taken to prove their own identity.

And another point: *As a matter of course, the Bulgarian envoy referred to the area which his state considered a Bulgarian region as "Macedonia".*

As an isolated detail, such events may appear to be meaningless; but for the history of Macedonia and the Macedonians' identity, they are of crucial importance:

For at the time, such assassinations and guerrilla acts on the Macedonian side were perpetrated by the IMRO, the *Internal Macedonian Revolutionary Organisation* (VMRO in Macedonian).[253] Founded in 1893 in Thessalonica as the MRO, it was renamed IMRO in 1896 in order to distinguish it clearly form the External Macedonian Revolutionary Organization which had been founded in Sofia.[254] Once again, the Bulgarians used the fact that it was founded in Sofia for their dialectical contortions, trying to prove that "therefore" the Macedonians must have been Bulgarians.

According to this logic, the former Bulgarian "komitadji", e.g. Karavelov and Levski, who also operated from areas not under Turkish rule, namely Walachia, would have had to be defined as *Romanian*, and others, such as Rakovski in Belgrade, where the first Bulgarian legion was founded, as *Serbs*.

Of course nobody did that – for good reason; but in the case of the Macedonians, the Bulgarians thought they could confront them with this insinuation.

> "This was intended as a Macedonian organization, which did not want to be dependent on any of the neighbouring states. Its goal was to achieve autonomy for the whole region referred to as Macedonia that was still under Turkish rule. Its motto was: 'Macedonia to the Macedonians.'"[255]

Its two most famous founders and leader personalities were Goce Delćev and Dame Gruev.

J. de Jong mentions that besides the VMRO, there were also "Macedonian student initiatives in Bulgaria, Serbia and Russia" supporting "the demands for national independence".[256]

Again, it was the VMRO that had planned the *Ilinden uprising*, which had, however, broken out too early as a result of several misfortunes. Edith Durham points out another fatal detail:

> "Instead of starting a simultaneous, general revolt, one village (rose up) after the other..."[257]

(Significantly, even after the Balkan wars and after 1918, VMRO was still fighting for the separation of Macedonia from the Kingdom of Yugoslavia.[258])

In order to be in a better position to counteract the Macedonian VMRO activities, the Bulgarian government founded the "Macedonian committee" that was later made the "Supreme Committee" and, in that quality, betrayed numerous VMRO members to the Turks.

For that reason, Jutta de Jong's study correctly qualifies the "Supreme Committee of Macedonia and Adrianople" (VMK/VMOK) as a "competitor" of the VMRO, especially since

> "to combat the VMRO" ... (is) explicitly defined "as the main task of the VMK/VMOK."[259]

In this context, de Jong's study provides useful information as to the professions of the members of the two "competing" organizations:

> "The comparatively high proportion of officers in" the [Bulgarian] "VMK/VMOK and, in contrast, of teachers in the supporting structure of the [Macedonian] "VMRO" documented the different objectives on both sides, namely, on the Bulgarian side, the plan of "swiftly provoking an intervention by the Great Powers" and, on the Macedonian side, the "long-term programme of self-liberation through independent nation-building."

Even Alan Palmer, the specialist for Ottoman Balkan history, is, unfortunately, not able to clearly differentiate between the *Macedonian* IMRO (VMRO) – which, for obvious reasons, was mainly in exile, including in Bulgaria, and which he (therefore?) wrongly calls "Bulgarian" – and the truly *Bulgarian* EMRO of the "fanatic nationalistic Bulgarian <Suprematists>". (loc. cit., p. 271)

The fact that this nation-building failed nonetheless, is attributed both to the "strong Bulgarizing influence of the ... VMK/VMOK" and to the fact that (unlike the Macedonians who sought to integrate and preserve the different groups in a polyethnic state) the

> "other ethnic groups of any significant quantity (Greeks, Albanians and Aromanians), on whose behalf the Slavic activists were also claiming freedom" [!] "largely limited themselves to demands of autonomy for their own ethnic group without extending them to any others."[260]

The Macedonians' politically circumspect, generous and fair plan went even further: Although the movement was a Slavic one and did wish to

> "include everybody who lived in this region under the regionally determined name of 'Macedonian', it had no intention of forcing Slavicism on any of the other ethnic groups."[261]

The Macedonians received no thanks for this generosity, as all representatives of the neighbouring states proceeded to pursue expansionist and nationalist policies:

> "In Macedonia, the Greek patriarchate, the Bulgarian exarchate as of 1872 and the Serbian school institutions as of 1896 all competed for pre-eminence in shaping the Christian Macedonian ethnic group."[262]

The fact that the Macedonians react less generously today and are more likely to be distrustful is more than understandable after their bad experience with all their neighbours in the last 125 years and unto the present day.

De Jong continues: It was a Slavic movement and

> "it remained a Slavic movement. It drew its integration patterns mainly from ambivalent processes of differentiation. At first these were based on accepting the numerous offers of Bulgarification pressed upon it since the exarchate was founded and extended in 1870-71, and directed against the Hellenizing pressure of the established Greek Orthodox patriarchate. Then the Serbian nationalizing efforts at the end of the 19th century created a competitive constellation which was generated externally"[263] making further efforts at differentiation necessary.

In other words: In order to avoid he greater pressure from Greece, part of the Macedonians accepted the shelter of the Bulgarian church as an intermediate solution. This choice, however, ended in a precarious position between Scylla and Charybdis; the Bulgarians used the fact that some Macedonians had declared themselves Bulgarians pro forma by their allegiance to the Bulgarian Orthodox Church as a means to summarily declare even those Macedonians who were steadfastly insisting on their Macedonian ethnicity to be Bulgarians - and to demand their territory as Bulgarian. Such behaviour was probably further promoted by the overall scale of preferences favoured by the Macedonians, as described by de Jong:

> "...The beginnings of the Macedonian national movement (developed from) a two-phased ... oppositional disposition: The main impetus was directed against the Turkish dominance which was socially oppressive but not nationally assimilating – and only in second place against the nationalizing pressure of the competing neighbouring states, who used their newly established or planned autocephalous churches and the mono-poly on education institutionalized by these churches to make full use of the benefits of the Ottoman millet system which was based on religious denomination categories and partial autonomy, and go beyond the limits."[264]

2.2.4 Foreign influence in favour of the Balkan League against Germany and Austria-Hungary

The Young Turk revolution in July 1908 brought about great changes not only internally, by the downfall of the autocratic sultan Abdul Hamid II, but also outside Turkey itself. The Young Turk programme with its motto of "Freedom, Equality, Justice" seemed to be announcing a new departure along the lines of the French revolution.
The consequences were probably not quite intended:
For a start, Austria announced it was going to annex Bosnia. Bulgaria reacted promptly to this signal on the following day, i.e. on October 5th 1908, declaring its independence and proclaiming Bulgaria a kingdom. Only then did Vienna act: it occupied Sarajevo – but against unexpectedly vehement resistance.
The potential members of the Balkan League also became active. They rushed into action in a way that made "The Times" remark that the Young Turk revolution had had the effect of a "deus ex machina" on the plans for founding a Balkan League.[265] The main reason for this unseemly haste was the fear that somehow the Young Turks could succeed once more in consolidating the moribund Ottoman Empire; for in that case the realization of their own plans, which were primarily bent on expansion, would have had to be postponed ad calendas graecas.
That was one reason for the Balkan States to quickly create an alliance with the aim of waging war with Turkey over Macedonia. But the wish alone would not have been sufficient for putting the idea into practice – which will be proved below. (See also section 5.1.1.)
Foreign countries also exerted their influence on the Balkan League – at the start quite unashamedly and therefore quite openly! Ambassador v. Romberg reported from

Sofia, a certain Mr. Buxton of the English Balkan Committee had tried in Sofia – with Russian help –

> "to win the Bulgarians over for the idea of an alliance between the Balkan peoples and Turkey, with an edge against Germany/Austria."[266] (!)

Did nobody in Germany or Austria hear the alarm bells? An alliance structure that was directed against the two German states so unequivocally could surely not fail to elicit a reaction from their two governments!

This plan and the coalition behind it (i.e. the "Entente") mirrored the new front lines in Central Europe: here, too, a true revolution had broken out. After the major historical turning point marked by the establishment of the Entente Cordiale in 1904 between England and France, the year 1907 had brought the fateful Triple Entente with Russia. (Bismarck must have turned in his grave.)

This was not all. Subsequently, the Entente tried to use the Balkan League which was known to have its very special objectives concerning Turkey, to strengthen its strategic coalition around the Triple Alliance i.e. the Central Powers.

The good old "Times", however, never wrote anything about this explosive aspect. It was probably in league with the British government (or had at least been asked to maintain confidentiality). In so far, its aforementioned article has to be seen as a contribution to the Entente's manoeuvres to obscure the situation and play down the evidence rather than to provide information or clarification.

> *Secure in knowledge of the complete ignorance of their adversaries, the Entente could continue with its long-term planning: the procedure of taking influence on the Balkan states was repeated.*

The next time, it was a Russian emissary, a Mr. Shcheglovitev, who – surely with English help – was to "win the Bulgarians over to the idea of an alliance of Balkan states under Russia's aegis."[267] Unlike Mr. Buxton, Gospodin Shcheglovitev had brought an almost irresistible present:

> "His bait was that Bulgaria could hope for Russian assistance in its Macedonian aspirations." (loc.cit.)
>
> *A key scene for the Entente's strategy before 1914 – and further proof of the complicated structure of the "Macedonian knot".*

Bulgaria's prospects - unlike those of Macedonia - were not bad. Yet things were to turn out differently. England and Russia used every means at their disposal to integrate the Balkan states in their alliance plans against Germany and Austria.

In Serbia, they met with a certain response. Bulgaria, however, resisted the lure despite the attractive offer. Perhaps it did not consider it desirable to be all too dependent on Russia – past experiences with Russian dominance had not been forgotten that quickly. Besides, Bulgaria did have an interest in Macedonia – but not at the cost of a forced enmity towards Austria and Germany. Thus, ultimately Sofia decided differently because it thought it could expect more from the German Reich.

Later, when Bulgaria actually entered the First World War on the side of the Central Powers in 1915, its prospects of having made the right decision did not look too bad until shortly before the end of the war.

In spite of the relatively unambiguous constellation of interests, we know from the Envoy v. Romberg that Bulgaria refrained from expressing any opinion and only gave voice to its hope that peace might be preserved.

The Bulgarian press, on the other hand, was able to rant and rave all the more openly, trying to divert Serbia's attention from Macedonia:

> "For the present critical situation provides an occasion to prove to the Serbs, who are Bulgaria's most bitter enemies in Macedonia,
> 1.) that Serbia's legitimate interests are in Bosnia and Herzegovina,
> 2.) that, as soon as these interests are threatened by the enemy of all Slavs, the Bulgarians as blood brothers who can expect the same fate, will come to Serbia's aid."[268]

The Bulgarian ambassador in Belgrade Toshev, however, was not satisfied with a siren's singing. In order to bring Serbia to the negotiating table, he sounded the death knell for them. Thus, he said to his German colleague von Reichenau:

> "But the thought that Bulgaria, Old Serbia and Uesküb" [today's Skopje] "would be left to Serbia was one of the figments of Serbian imagination." This meant that Bulgaria "would persistently adhere to its old policy of preserving Macedonia's unity and achieving autonomy for the whole of Macedonia. The ... goal of this consistent policy is the future incorporation of Macedonia with Thessalonica into the Bulgarian state. A southward extension of Serbia does not fit into this political plan." ... Concerning the more remote future of Serbia, Mr. Toshev held that Serbia as an independent state already bore the mark of death. If, one day, the Austro-Hungarian monarchy turned into a triad by virtue of natural evolution, the law that a smaller body is attracted by a larger one would lead to Serbia's being absorbed into that triad."[269]

(Whether in addition to the many explosive multiethnic forces already existing, the Habsburg Dual Monarchy actually entertained the megalomaniac vision of a triple monarchy with Bosnia would have to be checked up in the Austrian documents.)

The fact that a Bulgarian-Serbian rapprochement did ensue after all cannot be attributed to any Bulgarian efforts. It happened quite surprisingly, as we shall see in Chapter 5. The sudden reversal could not have been the result of now exactly thirty years of plans (and hopes) for an alliance of all Balkan kingdoms. That would be very improbable, even incredible. *There must have been more powerful negotiation partners with more attractive offers hovering in the background*:

When King Ferdinand of Bulgaria made two short consecutive visits to the Serbian king in Belgrade in 1909, both sides were in such a hurry to convince the political environment of the harmlessness of these meetings that

> "it almost looks as if both sides were feeling guilty."[270]

When the Tsar's court invited the Bulgarian royal couple for a visit to St. Petersburg from the end of February until the beginning of March 1910 in order to urgently recommend the conclusion of the Balkan League to Ferdinand (and shortly before to the Serbian king Milan), Foreign Minister Izvolskij made the Bulgarian king pay a visit to Constantinople (carried out on March 20th),

> "in order to allay Turkey's suspicions concerning the Balkan group and ... divert them from Austria-Hungary and Germany."[271]

At this point, Wilhelm II wrote "correct" in the margin, which means that he was not unaware of the Russian (and English) manipulations. Or did he see the tug-of-war about Turkey as normal everyday political life? Then he must have clearly seen the consequences of the meeting of the English and Russian monarchs in June 1908 off Reval. (Cf. ch. 2.3.10 and ch. 5.)

Did he and other leading men in Berlin and Vienna at that point fully recognize all the potentially dangerous implications of the aforementioned Entente strategy of isolation which was, once again, explicitly directed against "Austria-Hungary and Germany"? (This is something we shall have to explore.)

The devastating impression made by the last quote is not mitigated by the fact that Foreign Minister Izvolskij – intent on demonstrating that the visits of the two Balkan kings in St. Petersburg were harmless – even ordered the Russian ambassador in Berlin

Shebeko to explain to the Auswärtiges Amt that "the journies of the two Balkan rulers ... were only pursuing peaceful aims."
On the contrary: this conspicuously revealing step of heavy-handed diplomacy, at the latest, should have opened the emperor's eyes and those of his government.

Only when England and Russia attempted to close the southern flank of the ring around the Dual Alliance (Germany/Austria-Hungary) and to also draw Turkey into the anti-German coalition did the Balkan League become dangerous not only to Macedonia, which was the short-term goal of the Balkan states, but also to the two German states – which was the long-term goal of the Entente powers.

In the context of the visit paid by the Bulgarian king to Russia, there is a further point of interest to be noted:

"The military representative at the Russian court Captain von Hintze reported on March 7th 1910 that King Ferdinand ... had suggested a joint military campaign against Turkey, with the aim of winning Constantinople for Russia and Macedonia and Thessalonica for Bulgaria."[272]

Ferdinand may have correctly discerned Russia's secret wishes, but in the meantime Russia had set its preferences quite differently: in the Entente against Germany.

2.2.5 A Bulgarian document of importance for Macedonia

The Imperial Ambassador in Serbia used a report in December 1909 as an opportunity to send the Auswärtiges Amt a copy of the wording of instructions

"which the Bulgarian government had sent to its representative in Belgrade in 1900, concerning Serbia's suggestion to allocate spheres of interest in Macedonia, and" as Mr von Reichenau continues, "of which I was able to get a copy at the time."[273]

(The specified years "1909" and "1900" are not typing errors.)

In obtaining this set of instructions, the ambassador had saved a document so fundamental for the annals of the Republic of Macedonia that it seems justified to quote the relevant part of the report in some detail – especially since in the whole material I have looked at, this is one of the rare cases in which the Macedonian people, though still occupied by the Ottoman Empire, does not, as usually, appear in the role of a victim of aggressive neighbours, but can be perceived as an active subject.

In this document of the Bulgarian government sent to its representative in Belgrade, it says:

"We have incontrovertible proof, and the events of recent years have also shown clearly, that the greatest part of the Christian population of Macedonia is absolutely against any partition into spheres of interest. Their only wish is to be guaranteed their personal safety and possessions and granted the freedom to develop quietly and peacefully and enjoy all the rights of equal Ottoman subjects according to international treaties and the laws of the Ottoman Empire. Any attempt at division would lead to the greatest dissatisfaction among the Macedonian population and bring about such conflict and discordance in this our sister nation that there could be a damaging influence not only on the population there, but also on peace and quiet in Bulgaria and Serbia. When the question of "spheres of influence" was touched on for the first time a few years ago, we received the strongest protests ever heard at the time from the population of Macedonia. It resisted such a division with all its strength and declared that it did not want to put itself under the aegis of either Bulgaria or Serbia. The idea of separatism and independent development became so popular in the shortest time that in many places in Macedonia, people even started denying the existence of any kinship or other ties between the population there and other Balkan states."[273] *Another sensation!*

In principle, it suffices to let the overall impression of the document sink in to make you realize the tragic nature of history, whose constellation at the time allowed the

Macedonian people to become the object of the greed for power of its Christian neighbours, although it could have been freed from Turkish dominance just like the other Balkan peoples. 78 years after the dismemberment of Macedonia it needed another great moment of history at the end of the 20th century before Macedonia – or at least part of it – could re-emerge from historical oblivion.

As each sentence of this text is so meaningful that it can speak for itself, I do not have to comment on every single one:

- So Macedonia's hostility to any plans of division and its tendency towards national independence had become manifest well before 1900, and under the name of Macedonia;
- Attempts at division would have led to dissatisfaction and conflict in Macedonia, so that this could also have damaged peace and order in Bulgaria and Serbia.
- Above all, the Macedonians had denied all kinship with the peoples of other Balkan states!

Documents of self-determination that will stand any comparison!

Besides, it is conspicuous that the Bulgarian instructions only mention Serbs and Bulgarians. That Greece could also have been tempted to incorporate Slavic territories must have appeared quite absurd to the Bulgarian government in 1900.

Still, a few side comments seem appropriate:

1.

Although all the inhabitants of the Balkans were demonstrably aware of the fact that the Macedonians were a people in their own right, the Bulgarians, Serbs and Greeks did not hesitate to attack their brothers in Christo before the First World War and to lead them from one form of servitude to the next. They had planned and prepared that for decades. Even worse: although there is no excuse for such behaviour, we can ascribe it to the zeitgeist of that time; but in 1990/91, we were not living in the age of imperialism any more, but in the age of self-determination, minority and human rights. But even then, the same states did not hesitate - as if still acting according to the "takiye" rules they had learned from the Turks - to use misrepresentation and deception to feign to their "friends", the European governments, and the world public that the Macedonians unlawfully possessed their state, the name and the symbol of their state and even their language! And that is not enough: Even in the 21st century, even today, the same agents (except Serbia until recently) are using the same untruths to keep the whole international community in the mistaken belief that they are lodging their reservations, restrictions and claims against Macedonia on legitimate grounds.

> They continue to do so unchallenged, and our "system of states" does not call them to order or put an end to this deplorable state of affairs!

All democratic forces in the West and at the United Nations are presented with a miserable show of weakness in the defence of our values – even, and especially, within the European Union.

It is the duty of the international institutions to bring this arbitrariness to an end.

2.

Especially at such junctions of history, we can see the tragedy of the powerlessness of those affected – as if history were not made by acting persons but as if it simply rolled over the guilty and the innocent. In this context, may I be allowed an otherwise impermissible excursion into historical speculation:

If the envoy who already held office in Belgrade in 1900 (such terms of office were not unusual then) had already sent the Bulgarian instructions to Berlin in the year they were issued, namely in 1900 and not in 1909, or if his European colleagues who had certainly also received this document, had sent it to their respective capitals, and if the real crux of the matter, i.e. the *independence of Macedonia* and the Macedonians' desire for freedom and independence had met with the same understanding in Western Europe and Russia as had been the case earlier with Serbia, Greece and Bulgaria: then, subsequently, the last Macedonian revolt in 1903 would have been supported and successful. Macedonia could have been resurrected in its old borders, like Greece, Serbia, Romania (or Moldova and Walachia), like Montenegro and Bulgaria (and later Albania). The *effect* on Balkan affairs would have been a *peaceful* one: the injustice of the Balkan wars in 1912 and 1913 need not have happened and entailed further injustice and the Macedonians would not have had to wait until the historical turning point in 1989/90 to gain independence in at least part of their former country which they have, after all, inhabited for 1300 to 1400 years.

> But that is not how history works. It does not follow the principles of right, law and appropriateness, let alone justice.

But neither must it follow the path the Bulgarians, Greeks and Albanians want to prescribe in pursuit of their own nationalist and egoistic interests. In this case, the controlling powers of the political world system must change the course history is taking, particularly since it is a falsified history, in order to act in the interest of the weak and those deprived of their rights.

3.
There is one sentence in the context of the Bulgarian instructions which are otherwise so dramatic for Macedonia of today that is easily overlooked in its inconspicuousness:

> The only wish of the Christian population in Macedonia is "to be guaranteed their personal safety and possessions and granted the freedom to develop quietly and peacefully and enjoy all the rights ... according to international treaties and the laws ... "[273]

What a commendably moderate maxim! How much wisdom lies in this self-restriction of the Macedonians of that time to have no other ambition than to lead their life in the circle of their family in peace and quiet. – An engaging feature is equally valid in Macedonia today, as the author knows from experience. These were the only people to learn the right lessons from centuries of subjugation – not the imperialists with their greed for power who even in the 20th century were not prepared to relinquish the bad habits of the 19th century and are still assuming the same attitudes even in the 21st century...

I would like to add to this positive assessment that Balkan experts attest the Macedonians high human and moral qualities even today. In the context of writing about the hatred felt against Muslims in the Balkans after 500 years of Turkish rule, a hatred the devastating power of which was demonstrated once more by the war in Bosnia, Christian Voss writes that as far as he can see

> "due to a long tradition of ethnic tolerance and an 'ecumenical identity', this hatred was much less pronounced in Macedonia than in its Orthodox neighbouring states Serbia, Greece and Bulgaria, which were founded as a direct consequence of their liberation from the Ottoman Empire."[274]

Macedonian tolerance was abused then and is being abused now, in the 21st century – both inside the Republic of Macedonia and by forces outside.

2.3 Greece

2.3.0 Aspects of Greek history

Historians for ancient history describe the origins of the Greeks as follows:

> "Some of the ethnic groups coming from Asia and staying permanently in South-eastern Europe came as equestrian peoples. This probably applies to the Greeks, Illyrians and Thracians, and similarly later on to the Turkic-Tatar Bulgarians and the Finno-Ugric Magyars." [276]

This historically based opinion gives an understanding what Stefan Weidner thought when he wrote in his review of the book, "The Life of Ismail Ferik Pascha" by the Greek author, Rhea Galanaki:

> "The strange identity of modern-day Greeks, who first had to have their being explained to them by the Northern Europeans, and thereby totally repressed their oriental traditions," could not be more vividly shown than in Galanaki's book. "The Greeks...are not so much the inventors of Europe but more a European invention. ... If one wants to understand the Greeks in any and every case as Europeans, one is not being fair to them." One has to try to see them "as if their ancestors were indeed not the founders of Europe, but rather as much strangers to us as the Turks and Albanians, their neighbours ..." [277]

But voices of those who hold the traditional point of view about antiquity should also be heard:

> "The Greeks founded the first advanced culture in Europe and formed, so to speak, the bridge-head for the spread of the writing-culture taken over from the Near East. Also their ancientness or autochthonism is ... not doubted, as they were, in any case, at home there earlier than the Romans or the Slavs." [278]

1.
The *Romanization* of Greece during the approx. 600 years of Roman colonial rule must have been extremely profound. This is evident in the fact that even at the beginning of the 19th century at the start of their war of independence against the Turks - thus approx. 1500 years after the Roman troops withdrew from the Balkans - the Greeks still referred to themselves as Romaioi (Romans) and their country as Roman Land, even though in the meantime there had been permanent Slavic settlement from the 6th to the 9th century and, starting at the end of the 14th century, more or less 500 years of occupation of Greece by the Ottoman Empire. (The effect of the Romanization of the Greeks was only surpassed by that of the Romanians and the Aromanians (Vlachs), making its way into their language and national names.)

2.
As already mentioned, the *Slavs* inundated all of South-eastern Europe in the course of the "Migration Period" [*"Völkerwanderung"*]. After they had lived for a long time in the kingdom of the Goths, including in the Ukraine, they moved westwards in the tow of the Huns. After the Huns had been defeated by the Avars (also Turkish-speaking), the Slavs moved on with the winners, among other places to Dalmatia.

Through their immigration and settlement over hundreds of years, the Slavs made their imprint on the population structure of the Balkans so that it became approximately as we find it today.

Curious as it may be, there seems to be a certain distance to this part of Greek history in Greece. Since it is, however, of particular significance for the chosen subject, the advice of the scholars of the history of South-eastern Europe should be sought again:

In contrast to the Germanic migration in the 4th and 5th centuries, that

"like a violent storm wind ... shook the Roman rule on the Balkan Peninsula to its foundations", the whole area of South-eastern Europe, through the mighty migration movement of the Slavic tribes, became ... a homeland for the Slavs."[280] "To be sure, the Slavic swarms had threatened the Eastern Roman Empire again and again during the lifetimes of two generations and overrun the border provinces. From then on a permanent Slavic settlement began." (Stadtmüller: p. 91)

Hans-Wilhelm Haussig writes:
- Already in the second half of the 6th century, the Avars had "brought the world of the Slavic peoples into motion. These Slavs ... crossed the border of the Empire then under the protection of the Avars. Macedonia became Slavic at that time ..." "Further advances were aimed at Greece and here they even reached the Peloponnese. It can be said that since the end of the 6th century a stronger and stronger Slavic occupation took place, especially of the Peloponnese."[281] "Even Herakleios acknowledged the Slavic occupation of the Balkan Peninsula." (Haussig: p. 183)
- The Slavist Max Vasmer quotes from the chronicle of the Bishop Isidor of Seville, in which it is ascertained, "that the Slavs, during the rule of Emperor Heraclius, robbed Greece from the Romans." ("Sclavi Graeciam Romanis tulerunt"). (Loc.cit., p. 14) Despite all historic evidence, "Greek scholars had always tried to deny the presence of Slavs in Medieval Greece." (L.c., p. 313)
- "... in 585 (they undertook) a major plundering raid through Thrace up to Constantinople."... "In the year 591, the Slavs dared their first attack on the strongly fortified Thessaloniki (Salonika). After these temporary pillages, they went on at the end of the 6th century to take permanent control of the open country." (Stadtmüller, p. 92)
- Trautman (l.c. p. 34) writes as follows: "In the 7th century the Slavs' control of Greece far down into the Peloponnese seems to have been completed, at least the land around Monemvassia was referred to about 725 as <Slavinia>."
- "The Roman and Greek population fled to the fortified coastal towns and to the islands.... Five Slavic tribes with wives and children appeared before Salonika." Since the city withstood, despite an army put together of Avars, Slavs and Bulgarians, "the five Slavic tribes settled in the surroundings of Salonika." "In the year 611 ... a Slavic advance pushed into the southern parts of Greece for the first time." (P. 93)
- "Already around the middle of the 7th century, the Slavic land seizure was basically finished off. The whole of the Balkan Peninsula, except for the coastal areas and individual fortified places in the interior, was settled by Slavic peasants..." From Silesia and Bohemia up to the southern tip of Greece, everything was occupied by Slavic farmers. ... At that time, the Slavs had also taken by far the biggest part of present-day Albanian and Greek homeland. In the 8th century Slavs lived not far from antique Athens and Sparta. The Greek mainland was largely Slavic settling-territory and stayed that way over centuries, as numerous and still preserved place-names testify." (p. 95)

Michael Weithmann says in connection with this:

"The abundance of Slavic place-names in Greece ... is to be assigned to different times of origin."
"...the place-names of Slavic provenance (are) the only still 'living' testimonials of the Slavic past of Greece."[282]

This is not entirely correct, as Weithmann himself also mentions the influence of Slavic languages on Modern Greek vocabulary.

"There are about five-hundred Slavic roots of words in modern Greek, of which the majority are only used regionally. Merely about sixty loan-words are found in common Greek ..."[283]

Once again, Haussig:
- "In Greece the development proceeded similarly to that in Bulgaria and Macedonia. Here, too, the major part of the peasant population, especially on the Peloponnese, headed towards the mountains. They too gave up their previous form of life and lived henceforth as nomads. ... Using ships another part of the Greek population had cleared out to southern Italy and provided here, together with the refugees arriving from Syria and Palestine, a further strengthening of Greek ethnicity in the lower part of Italy."[284]
- Still differently as Jakob Philipp Fallmerayer concluded, according to Vasmer, there could not be "...talk at all about the destruction of Hellenism" (p. 325). Rather, the Greek "retrieval of the old homeland", as R. Trautmann describes it on page 34, started from the coastal areas "approximately

around the area of Arcadia, Methoni, Kotroni" as well as "Monemvassia in the south up to Corinth in the north" where a strong Hellenic population was situated. And on page 35: "In the 10th century, Slavism reached its peak, then the supremacy passes over to the Greeks – at the turn of the millennium <the development of the unitarily Greek-speaking people of the medieval Peloponnese fulfilled itself from the fusion of Slavism and Hellenism, whereby the part with Slavic blood must have been relatively high. (Stadtmüller).>"

- "The Slavic immigrants met the strongest resistance in the Greek homeland; there they were also most completely absorbed in the course of the following centuries through Hellenization in connection with Christianization." (Stadtmüller, p. 99)
- "Slavs were still living in Morea in the 13th century, and William II (1245-78) fought against the Slavic tribe of the Melengi in northern Taygetos; in the 14th century there was still talk about Slavs in the Maina.... For us, Slavism in Greece vanished at the beginning of the 15th century." (Trautmann, p. 35)

In this connection, Weithmann quotes a Slavic historian (Petur Boev), who wrote about his Greek colleague Poulianos, that he

"conspicuously avoids accepting the fair-pigmented racial type as of Slavic origin that was added to the ethno-genesis of the Greek people."[285]

When, in another place, Weithmann repeats the Greek claim that the inhabitants of Macedonia "...are, in accordance with the Greek understanding, partially Slavicized Greeks,"[286] then on the other hand, with much more justification from the opinions of academic authorities, the author must come to the conclusion that a majority of the inhabitants of Greece are Hellenized Slavs.

The Greeks do not like to hear such comments. When the Italian envoy to Athens, Silvestrelli, remarked at the beginning of the 20th century that the Greeks were a mixture of Slavs, Turks and Venetians, the entire Greek press attacked him:

"His cockiness goes beyond the limit of madness. It transverses the terrain of brutality." "Unscrupulously he is touching the virginity of Greece with his dirty hands, and, in an outrageous manner disrespectful and cowardly, he does not allow himself to be moved by the most magnificent historical splendor."[287]

The press did not miss the chance to immediately stake the claim for the Greek plans for expansion, whereby an interesting formulation slipped in on them (1904 and not 1944 !). The newspaper "Astrapi" found that

"from Sivestrelli's side-remarks the intentions that official Italy has on Greek territory became apparent. Instead of writing that Greece borders in the north on Macedonia and Epirus, he wrote that it borders on Macedonia and Albania. So, he totally suppressed Epirus and/or identified it with Albania ..."[287]

Moreover already at the beginning of the 19th century, scholars had contradicted

"the unbroken ethnic continuity" of the Greeks, by pointing out "the immense consequences of the Slavic land occupation and the later settlement extension of the Albanians". (Compare ch. 2.5.) "The direct descendents of the ancient Greeks are not to be recognized in the contemporary folk-mixture of Scythian Slavs, Illyrian Arnauts, Serbs and Bulgarians, Dalmatians and Muskovites."[288]

In addition, Klaus Steinke writes:

"Recently the British historian Eric J. Hobsbawm took up this criticism again and was harshly reprimanded by the Greek side. It continues to be a sacrilege to undertake a critical analysis of the picture of the Greek nation that was formed in the last century, as the present quarrelling with the neighbour to the north about the name *Macedonia* as well as the language harassment of the Slavic and Albanian inhabitants of northern Greece show."[289]

Such a harsh rebuke would naturally be more difficult for official Greece in the case of the above-mentioned Greek author, Galanaki.

3.
When the *Turks* overran South-eastern Europe, such differences lost their importance. On the surface at least, the conquerors did not care if they were ruling over Orthodox Greeks or Catholic Hungarians, as long as they were undisturbed in wielding their power, not to say their despotism, in collecting taxes. In other words all they wanted to do was accumulate riches and be able to dispose over cheap labour.

Those knowledgeable in the material have written that this indifference of the Moslem Ottomans towards Christianity (which is often erroneously mistaken for tolerance) was the beginning of their later downfall in Europe. (This experience seems to have taught the Moslems a lesson, as it is known that contemporary radical Moslem groups strive to push a speedy Islamization of the Christians in the European states, among others in Germany. Consequently, the director of the Egyptian Al-Jeel-Center for Social Studies in Cairo, Ahmed Abdallah, called upon the Muslims who live in the European states in 2006: "Islamize Europe!")

Is the argument with the "cheap labour" exaggerated? Not at all. Lorenz Jäger quotes from a report of an Ottoman traveller, Evliya Celebi, who, when he came to Vienna in 1665, was also supposed to worry about the question,

> "whether the inhabitants of Vienna could then one day become good subjects of the Sultan."[290]

As long as the subjects preferred to convert to Islam, the Bosnians and the Albanians taking the lead in this aspect, it brought them exemption from taxes and opened the ladder of hierarchy to them.

Five years after the famous battle on the Amselfeld [Battle of Kosovo] in 1389, the Attica and the Peloponnese were also conquered by the Turks; approx. 50 years later, the Ottoman Empire occupied all of Greece. Only Corfu and Zakynthos were never Turkish, and Kephallenia was Turkish only for 20 years.

4.
As everywhere on the Balkans, the *revolts* of the Greeks proceeded at first in an uncoordinated way and remained unsuccessful because they were bloodily put down again and again. The first Greek revolt worth mentioning took place not in Greece but in the Danube principality of Moldavia at the beginning of 1821.

This, at first glance, not very plausible connection can be immediately understood when one considers this quotation from Francisco R. Adrados:

> "The Phanariotes of Constantinople took over important administrative und political offices and ruled Walachia and Moldavia for the Sultan."[291]

Georg Stadtmüller contributes an informative detail to this background:

> "The great Greek merchant families dominated the trade of the Empire ... and ... acquired ... huge fortunes. Thus, a certain Michael Kantakuzenos to whom the lease for the collection of imperial customs and the extortion of the Romanian Danube principalities, which became more and more an economic colony of the Greek merchants, brought in so much that he could pay the Sultan 160 000 Taler annually. For him, like for some other representatives of the Greek plutocracy, his richness became his undoing. He was strangled on command of the Sultan, and his fortune was confiscated (1576)."[292]

By the way, the Greek revolt in the principality of Moldavia failed, because the Russians did not come to their assistance as the Greeks had hoped. At that time Greece was not yet the pampered child of the Tsars and the other European monarchies.

It was not until March that the revolts in Greece itself broke out and it was during the course of these that the Peloponnese and Athens were liberated. Rainer Hermann points out that on the 22th of April, Easter Sunday of the year 1821, Patriarch Grigorios

V and three Metropolites were hanged for high treason in front of the great door of the Church of Saint George in Istanbul (which has never been opened again since that tragic day), although, as Mazower adds (l.c., p. 140), Gregor had issued a letter "in which he excommunicated the Greek revolutionaries":
> "At the beginning of the Greek struggle for independence, they were alleged to have supported the Greeks' endeavours to win their freedom."

> "The Turks named the street that the patriarchate is on after the grand vizier ... who had given the order for them to be hanged."

This atrocity still fills every Greek Orthodox heart with sadness today – not only on Easter Sunday. Thus, one is not astonished about his final statement:
> "And with that, the fruitful co-existence between the Turks and the Greeks came to an irrevocable end."[293]

5.

The proclamation of the independence of Greece in Epidauros on the 1st of January, 1822, came too early, since the Turkish governor in Egypt subdued the Peloponnese again later. (By the way, the reformer of the Greek language, A. Korais, criticized the Constitution of Epidauros,
> "as he saw the continuation of the feudalistic structures and the phanariote-regime of the Ottoman era in it."[294])

In two civil wars in 1823/24, the rebels annihilated each other, which proved, according to C. Hopf, that despite some positive aspects this people
> "did not constitute a 'nation' yet, which could organize itself into an independent 'national state'."[295]

Theodor Schieder also ascertained that,
> "the new Greece, that was born as a national state with the sympathy of the educated world of Europe, without having a nation at its disposal at first," was for him "the classical example (for a) 'national state' which" had "neither a national standard language, spoken and written, nor a national society".[296]

A new revolt broke out in 1827.
> Already at "the beginning of the ... rebellion ... Russia attempted, through diplomatic pressure, to achieve improvements for the situation of the Christian peoples in the Balkans."[297]

But only when Russia, England and France decided, in the London Agreement of July 6th, 1827, to intervene in favour of Greece and destroyed the Turkish-Egyptian fleet in the sea battle near *Navarino* on the 20th of October and in addition Russia officially declared (the 6th) war on Turkey in April (the naval war had not been declared), Turkey was really defeated. Thereupon followed
> "the first fundamental retreat of the Ottoman Empire before the national consciousness of the Rajah" (the non-Moslem population).[297]

Through the Treaty of Adrianople in 1829, and in accordance with the Protocol of London in 1830, Greece became an autonomous republic and two years later a sovereign kingdom. In 1833, the Great Powers installed Otto von Wittelsbach of Bavaria as King of Greece. About this, Theodor Schieder wrote:
> The Greeks were ruled by "monarchs of a foreign nationality, foreign religion, and foreign language." Serbia alone of the Balkan countries in the 19th century possessed its own "old, native dynasty".[298]

Schieder was mistaken here. Edgar Hösch points out that the Montenegrins could also safeguard their "chance to fill the regent's position with representatives of native dynasties".[299]

On the other hand, the heads of state from abroad set up by the Great Powers paid off positively in the decades to come – first and foremost for the political expansion-objectives that Greece would have, as will be shown later.

The border of the independent sovereign Greece of that time ran only just north of Corinth, which means that big regions like Thessaly, the Ionian Islands and Crete did not yet belong to the new state.

6.

From this moment on, if not before, the foreign policy model of the Greeks, the *Megale Idea*, took effect: the dream of a great Greek Empire with Constantinople as its capital, its borders being those of the Byzantine Empire. Even though by no means all of the territories of this aspired-for great empire were of Greek origin, this idea determined henceforth the political acts of the state *and* the church. Greece continued single-mindedly with this policy, first as a reunification policy, later as an expansion policy in the Balkans (after the First World War also in Anatolia).

The practical implementation began when Athens took advantage of the confusion during the Crimean War in 1853-56 to annex parts of South Epirus. This attempt failed of course because England and France (due to a Greek violation of the treaty) forced the Greeks to retreat by occupying the Piraeus. But a start had been made.

The revolt on Crete in 1866 (declaration of the union with Greece = Enosis) also came to nothing since in the further course of the crisis, the Great Powers prevented the Greeks from annexing the island, and at the Conference of Paris in January of 1869, they mediated between Greece and the Ottoman Empire: Crete remained Turkish.

7.

For the "Great Idea" of Greece it was a bitter setback when in 1870, with Russian help, Bulgaria, before its independence, even before its autonomy, achieved the *Exarchate*, meaning the independent Bulgarian Orthodox Church. Through the redirecting of the church taxes of the Bulgarian faithful into the Bulgarian church treasury, the Greek Ecumenical Patriarchy in Constantinople suffered severe financial losses, along with the curtailment of its cultural scope of influence.

A report from the year 1868 by the chargé d'affaires to Constantinople, Mr. von Uebel, to the Royal Prussian Minister President who was at the same time Federal Chancellor, as well as Foreign Minister of the North German Confederation, (at that time Count) Otto von Bismarck, recalls the background history of Greek-Bulgarian relations: The Greek Patriarchy in Constantinople and its dignitaries - named "Phanariotes" after their residential area - had been "the indispensable advisors and interpreters of the Porte for centuries" and had

> "used their influence and the ignorance of their Turkish masters to drive the national Bulgarian element out of the church."[300] "A Greek clergy, Greek schools and religious services in the Greek language ... (were) ... gradually imposed on the Bulgarian nation and the mass of the people were abandoned to ignorance and to the extortions of the Greek clergy."

Only after the Crimean War did the idea of the principle of nationality begin to exert its influence

> "and the question of the Bulgarian church increasingly gained political significance. The first impetus ... came from Russia.", as "the attitude of the Greek clergy, as well as that of the whole Greek population of the Turkish Empire in general during the Crimean War, had not met up to the expectations that Russian politics had placed in them."[300]

After the Russians, with force and at the cost of great sacrifices, had supported Greece between 1827 and 1829 in attaining its independence, the restraint of the Greeks in the

Crimean War, when Russia itself needed help, was obviously felt as ingratitude. For this reason, St. Petersburg showed favour henceforth to the Bulgarians, who were also Orthodox – and at the same time Slavs within the "oriental church" up to the Exarchy in 1870/72.

Russia learned its lesson from these experiences later. Thus, Tsar Alexander II did not hesitate in 1877, a few days after the declaration of war on Turkey, to have his brother the Grand Prince Constantine write his son-in-law, the husband of the Grand Princess Olga, the Greek King George, that Russia hoped "to hear good news from Greece soon". Also the Russian envoy to Athens, von Sabourow, told George I again and again, "that Russia would only be able (one day) to show its gratitude for real services."[301] At the same time, St. Petersburg did not even expect Athens, in contrast to Sofia, to instigate a general revolt, but only to incite the Greeks living in the Turkish regions.

> These events convey not only the certainty that dynastic assistance was no one-way street, but rather they allow the assumption that Russia would never have placed such expectations in Greece if it had not thought to receive certain favours in return – as actually happened in the run-up to the Congress of Berlin and during the negotiations.

After years of negotiating about the Bulgarian Exarchate, the Porte, for its part, could not put off making a decision without giving rise to another "Bulgarian insurrection". The Grand Vizier, Aali Pascha, also feared that otherwise "the Bulgarians, who had been so docile up to now" ... would be driven ... "into the arms of the Russians". For all intents and purposes, he was encouraged in this assumption, by the cunning Bulgarians.

> Only the granting of church autonomy could ... "protect the loyal Bulgarian inhabitants from the revolutionary provocations coming from outside and keep them in their old submissiveness."[302]

8.

During the Herzegovinian uprising in 1875 (with Montenegrin help) and the Bosnian revolt in 1876 (with Serbian support), Greece tried to stay neutral, although

> "in the press ... voices became loud, which held the passive spectator role of the Hellenes during the fight that had begun for incompatible with the 'dignity of the nation' (and) with the 'holy interests of Hellenism'."[303]

However, after the debacle in which Greece found itself in 1868, when it - unsuccessfully - actively supported the uprising in Crete, Athens preferred, in view of its small army, inadequate military equipment and miserable financial situation, instead of getting involved in a war to hope that

> "Greece would gain a real advantage from the peaceful behaviour it displayed."[304]

Thus, the Greek government aroused the impression as if the wish of the population to really take part in the war could only be suppressed by absolute willpower and abstinence. This policy brought a double advantage: Greece spared itself from going to war and at the same time, by not doing so, expected that the Great Powers would not let it "end up empty-handed". The latter was the greatest nightmare of the Greeks, because

> "the jealousy towards the Slavic element on the Balkan peninsula (is) here decidedly stronger ... than the animosity against the old arch enemy, Turkey."[304]

What the German Consul, Graf Beust, reports from Salonika fits here, namely that

> "the Greek priests stir up the Turks against the Bulgarians, because they hope in this way, with the help of an uprising or with support from Europe, to drive first these and then the Turks out of the territories that they claim for their nation."[305]

Here too, a meaningful formulation catches one's eye (as in the entire reporting): there is, appropriately, talk again and again of "regions claimed", but never of the "Greek

regions" or "the regions belonging to Greece" and just as little about "former Greek regions".
Since these areas had never belonged to the Greeks in the past, it was not important to them in the present to take possession of any certain region, but rather,

> "that Greece was predestined to obtain an appropriate share of European Turkey if the territorial circumstances were changed."[306]

Legally speaking, a totally irrelevant basis for a claim – it showed that for the Greeks it was more a question of the desire for recognition, a lust for power and their national vanity.
This strategy seems to have been followed continually:

> "The majority of the so-called politicians who cannot get over the fact that Greece does not play any bigger role at the present, would like ... to see a war break out between Russia and Turkey. Indeed with the definite intention of not taking part actively in such a war but in the expectation that it would eventually be possible that something would be left over for Greece if both sides were weakened in the fight."[307]

The competitive relationship with the other Balkan states with the same, parallel aims led to the observation by the German envoy that it

> "fills the hearts of the Greeks with genuine satisfaction ... that that Slavic tribe" [the Serbians], "who felt called upon to play a leading role on the Balkan peninsula, emerged from ... the struggle with great sacrifices in possessions and blood and without further acquisitions [in the Separate Peace of Feb. 28th, 1877]."[308]

2.3.1 Greece, the 8th Russo-Turkish War and the Congress of Berlin

By the end of January the intermediation conference of Constantinople had already broken down. When the Turkish assembly of notables (also in January) opposed the reforms and Turkey even rejected, on the 9th of April 1877, the London Protocol of the 31st of March 1877, all means of mediation were at an end. On the 24th of April, 1877, Russia declared war on the Ottoman Empire.
Still in April, two days before the Russian declaration of war, the Russian envoy to Athens, von Sabourow, had summarized to his German colleague the Russian policy towards Greece like this:

> "He surely believes to assume that under no circumstances his government will grant Greece any kind of territorial enlargement."[309]

In accordance with the just cited report, the Greeks too had feared this outcome.[310]
The estimation also coincided with the judgement which the State Minister of the Foreign Ministry, von Bülow (sen.), had given in his report for Kaiser Wilhelm I. There it quoted with reference to the relevant reporting that Greece had pushed St. Petersburg and Vienna in London:

> "to reward it for its loyal neutrality in the present crisis" otherwise "it would have to take over the Turkish bordering provinces by means of a rebellion of the Greek population there." An expansion of the Greek boundaries was essential for the future of the country and its dynasty, "without, however, finding a reasonable reception for its wishes. St. Petersburg actually seems to have more interest for the Slavs than for the Greeks and refers to the nicest dream of the latter, a Greek Empire in Constantinople, as in no way acceptable; in Vienna and London it was simply pointed out that Greece had to thank its existence to the European treaties and that this existence could only be secured through loyalty to the treaties."[311]

A good year later, such a striking turn-about occurred in the development that the Messieurs von Sabourow and von Bülow must have been astonished at how much the

Russian attitude towards Greece had changed and with which considerable territorial enlargement the Greeks could return to Athens from the Congress of Berlin.
An explanation for this has still to be found.

Not only the Russian, but also the English attitude had changed. Already during the war, England had, in consideration of the risks in view of an uncontrollable spread of the war, taken action against Athens with all imperative consequences. Greece had tried, against all good advice, to occupy Thessaly on the lee side of the war (like Epirus roughly 20 years before) – but had not counted on London's alertness. Even the relatives in Buckingham Palace could not cover such a breach of law: Athens was ordered to call off the occupation, for the sake of avoiding unforeseeable complications and in consideration of the integrity of the Ottoman Empire.

> Even among the dynasties, one was more willing to intervene on behalf of a relative at a conference for his - previously agreed upon - interests than to accept military engagements for him. Nevertheless, the matter ended well for Athens. For that, however, another Greek "coup de theatre" was needed....

It is hardly necessary to mention that the Turks did not hesitate to dig in their bag of tricks in order to come up with the propaganda that seemed suitable to them. A couple of days before the Russian troops crossed the Danube River, Bernhard E. von Bülow, henceforth envoy to Athens, reported that his Turkish colleague Photiades Bey had handed over to the Greek Foreign Minister Trikupis a dispatch from the Turkish Foreign Minister Safvet Pascha, in which Sultan Abdul Hamid, after the cabinet shuffle in Athens (Admiral Kanaris had replaced the "Ministry" Kumunduros),

> "expressed the hope that the new cabinet would support the Sublime Porte in its fatherly efforts dedicated to the benefit of the Orient".[312]

So much for the Turkish policy of glossing over and blandishment.

The envoy came up with other information in his report about the talk:

> "Feeling obliged by the "fatherly efforts" of the Porte, the Minister got to talking about "the conditions in the Greek provinces of Turkey of which he painted a quite dark picture. In Candia the desecration and looting of churches, notably in the villages situated on the inland, is on the agenda; in Thessaly, the Turkish troops were hardly behaving less terribly."

The Greek strategy during the war was, of course, also known to the Turks. The German Ambassador to Constantinople, Prince Heinrich VII Reuß[313,] summarized his insights as follows:

> "(In Athens) one would like to initially insurge only the Greek provinces in Turkey and try to twist the matter so that no war would break out from this."[314]

This is understandable and more than smart.

At the beginning, the war proceeded for the Greeks just as they wished. Russia did prevail but only under heavy sacrifices. The hoped-for "mutual weakening" had, thus, occurred. Even when the tide started to turn in favour of Russia, the Greek foreign minister subscribed further to the opinion,

> "that the official Greece does well to keep out of the fight as long as this fight might still be connected to perils."[315]

This reasonable maxim also dictated the further tactics of the Greeks. It was not until October that the decisive turn in favour of Russia took place – at first in the Asiatic theatre of war. In December then, the Turkish fortress Plewna surrendered under pressure from Romanian and Russian troops after a strong and, for a long time, successful defence. And, in January 1878, after the Russians had crossed "the Balkans", the

Turks capitulated at the famous Shipka Pass. On January the 27th the Ottoman Empire agreed to the armistice.
In this moment, a striking opportunity arose for Greece to prove to the world the willingness for self-sacrifice of its heroes and the exalted greatness of the Hellenes:
Four days later, on the 1st of February, Greece declared war on Turkey![316]

At the beginning, it did not do any good: Thessaly had to be cleared out first (on the 8th of February 1878).
On top of that, there was an abrupt awakening on the 3rd of March in Athens: in the Preliminary Peace of *San Stefano*, Russia had granted, of all things, the whole of Macedonia and a major part of Thrace to the hated Bulgarians.
But this time, the English-Austrian vigilance worked for Greece. The Congress of Berlin was summoned in order to annul the peace treaty. And Greece was allowed - in its pose as a victorious power - to bring its demands over defeated Turkey to a hearing.[316]
Now, finally, the protection from London and the fact that the government in Paris was looking for allies paid off.
In the 9th meeting on the 29th of June and in the 13th meeting on the 5th of July, 1878, both delegations, supported by the representative from Italy, endorsed an expansion of Greek territory towards the north – (of course) for the preservation of peace on the Balkans: "Greece could not prosper within its present boundaries".[317]
The Turkish delegation still tried to act against this with the argument that Greece "had not even tried to back its advance with any kind of legal principle."[317]
A remarkable argument – but when were the Turks ever concerned about legal principles while on their conquests? Furthermore:

> "The easy opportunity to acquire provinces of a neighbouring state is no satisfactory legal justification. The opinion is intolerable that Greece does not have sufficient land for its population."[318]

This objection too was, in fact, completely justified; however, after the war was lost, Turkish arguments did not help any more – just like countless sultans in the past centuries had also not accepted any arguments against their victorious troops.

> The famous and worldwide respected, even admired, Sultan Suleyman the Magnificent himself preferred in case of doubt the "off with his head" argument, as, among others, Venetian legates who had been sent to him had to witness when they were forced to hold their noses because of the scent of decomposing flesh of the impaled heads on the long walls on the way to the palace.

Vae victis....

> And from a more recent past, Norman Stone writes about the exhibition of the Royal Academy, "The Turks" (FAZ newspaper of the 10th of March, 2005): With pyramids of skulls the Turks made clear "what would happen to people who had different opinions than they themselves. In front of the Topkapi Palace lay such a pyramid ..., until Kaiser Wilhelm II on his visit in 1899 convinced Abdul Hamid II that this was tasteless."

In this context, it is of interest that the above-stated argument of the British delegation at the Congress of Berlin is after all reminiscent of the text of a report from London which the ambassador, Fürst zu Münster, had sent two years before to the foreign ministry which began as follows:

> "The presence of the King of Greece in London was less a visit to relatives, but had more the purpose ... to possibly attain the support of England for his plans in relation to Greece."[319]

In his talks with Lord Derby and Lord Salisbury (as well as with the commentator himself), the King had explained that Greece "in its present form is too small and poor ... to really develop and make progress without an enlargement towards the north." It would depend upon "obtaining the enlargement of Greece through Thessaly and Epirus ... and possibly even more" at the peace agreement after the battle against Turkey or at the partitioning.

This argumentation must have fallen on fertile ground in St. Petersburg, more exactly: in the Peterhof, and in London, more precisely: in Buckingham Palace, for there, the changed attitudes of both governments towards the Greek demands were shaped. This is how at the Congress of Berlin Greece actually got what it had desired for such a long time: Thessaly; more precisely: Thessaly south of the Salamvria River; moreover, South Epirus, rather the district of Epiros south of Arta.[320]

For reasons having to do with the lack of time at the Congress of Berlin, Greece and Turkey were assigned to negotiate the final borderlines autonomously. That is why the relevant provision was not incorporated into the Treaty of Berlin, but rather recorded in the minutes. This small shortcoming was enough for Turkey to delay the surrender again and again with flimsy arguments. After the negotiations were abandoned without any success, a separate (follow-up) conference had to be summoned in Berlin, on the 16th of June, 1880. Only on the basis of the Greek-Turkish convention agreed upon at this conference did Turkey withdraw from Thessaly in 1881 and (not until) 1884 from Epirus. Only Crete still remained Turkish – and, in fact, for about another 30 years.

Consequently, Greece had pushed through an enormous shifting of the borders in its favour within the foregoing 50 to 55 years.

Nevertheless: the Greeks understood something completely different under the *Megale Idea*, something a lot more far-reaching, although the Greek Foreign Minister Delyannis had assured at the 9th meeting that if Greece received Thessaly and South Epirus,

"the realisation of the solid and unshakable will of the population in these provinces ... (would give) the Kingdom peace and a permanent existence."[321]

At that time the Greeks did not mention a single word about *Macedonia!*
This is more than astonishing. In consideration of the almost unique opportunity of the personal presence of a Greek delegation at two international conferences of the European Great Powers about the Balkans, this would have been unthinkable if Greece had even the slightest of reasons for a claim to Macedonian territory.

Nevertheless: for the moment, the Greeks could be content with the result of their blockade policy. Macedonian representatives were not admitted to represent their interests at the Congress of Berlin, so decisive for the fate of Macedonia, although they surely had also sent their petitions like several other petitioners via the consulates and embassies to Berlin and although delegates from other regions such as Romania, Persia and particularly from Greece were listened to.

Why actually not from Macedonia? Had a foresighted management prevented such a distracting admittance from the start?

Indeed the presumption that King George, as the driving force, stood behind this exclusion as a family favour on the part of the British Empire and of the gigantic Russian Empire for the tiny little Greece is not unlikely. The behaviour of Greece during the Crimean War, that at the time had embittered Russia so much, lay over 20 years back then. Besides, George's predecessor, Otto from Bavaria, could be blamed, if necessary, for that ingratitude. But since 1863, he, the son of the Danish King Christian IX, had been sitting on the Greek throne. In the same year, his sister, Princess Alexandra of Denmark, married Crown Prince Edward VII of England, so that George, already at his assumption of office, was the brother of a daughter-in-law of Queen Victoria, who on the 1st of January, 1877, was even crowned Empress of India. Not enough with that: another one of George's sisters, Princess Dagmar, became, as Maria Fjodorowna, the wife of Alexander (who in 1881 as Alexander III should become the successor of his father Alexander II, after the latter had been killed in an assassination). Over and above that, only one year later in 1867 George himself had also married a niece of Alexander II, in the person of the Grand Princess Olga.[322] The King of Greece and the Emperor of Russia, both born in 1845, were consequently family-linked, and he was even related by marriage with the Tsarevitch.

How easy must it have been for the sisters-in-law Olga and Maria, at the Russian court, and Alexandra, at the English court, to forward certain Greek ideas of a reorganization of the Balkans to the "right address"!

For even a Tsar is subject to a certain degree of influence within the bounds of his family ties – maybe just insinuations. And the dynastic ties of the courts across Europe were close, especially since it has to be taken into account that the crowned heads were often "aliens" in those countries by which they were "chosen", or, more precisely, to which they were "suggested" by the Great Powers without their being granted any right of refusal. (On the other hand, Mark Mazower cites the example of Romania: "... the local upper-classes did not (accept) a native head of state and a royal family had to be imported from abroad. (L. c., p. 161) (Similar things happened on the throne of the Tsar.)

The feeling of "alienation" applied all the more for the wives. The tendency to maintain the close ties with the old family must have been, therefore, especially great. In this way, some wishes and recommendations must have reached the decision-makers.

As a practical example, a case from Paul Sethe can be cited, which actually does not come from the life of the above-mentioned Tsar Alexander III and his wife the Danish Princess Dagmar, but rather from the next generation, namely his son Tsar Nicholas II and the Tsarina Alexandra (Princess Alice from the House of Hessen-Darmstadt) but can be taken for the intended demonstration as characteristic:

> "Often Nicholas asks her for advice, and, since she always answers in a clear and resolute way and Nicholas adores her, things in Russia often happen the way the Tsarina wants them to happen."[322]

In this way, the Greek king might possibly have been favoured.

As a clear proof of the hypothesis of dynastic - i.e. predominantly the Russian and English - support for the Greek expansionist aspirations in the direction of attaining Macedonian and Thracian territory (without wanting to underestimate the underlying French revenge plans in the slightest way), relevant excerpts from reports in the existing records about the Greek royal family will be inserted from this point on at irregular intervals but, if possible, integrated chronologically as *background information* (exception no. 8), in as far as they are suitable to document the argumentation of a "monarchist cooperation" on the European level against Macedonia.

2.3.1.1 Background information (1):
   Greece maintains active dynastic connections in Europe (St. Petersburg, London)

Did King George - or did his family members - even have the opportunity to make use of the family relationships? This will have to be investigated.

Telephones did not exist yet. In letters, the exchange of which in those days was extremely cultivated, some inflections of the human voice, meant to appeal to the emotions, get lost. Thus, only face-to-face talking remained. For that, the potential conversational partner had to undertake the often arduous journey himself. It is a lucky coincidence that the Greek King, who came from Denmark, and Queen Olga, who originated from Russia, both loved their home countries. So, regular journeys were on the agenda. Regular means every year if unusual circumstances did not force a delay.

1.

Even the first available report from the extensive collection of records about the royal family in Greece includes information about this topic. Accordingly, George, as mentioned before, used a "journey home" in 1876 for side-trips to London, St. Petersburg, Berlin and Vienna. And since he always went first from Athens to take the baths at Aix-les-Bains, Paris was included (not in 1876, but otherwise regularly) in his itinerary. What Ambassador zu Munster reported about this visit has already been mentioned above. That the brother-in-law of the heir to the throne had easy - even if *a priori* non-binding - access to the members of government goes without saying.

Also, there is a report at hand from St. Petersburg by Ambassador von Schweinitz, who had inquired dutifully in August about the purpose and outcome of George's visit. His report throws a characteristic light on the persistence of the King:

> "Also now, with almost the same words as nine years ago, at the time of the Candiot Uprising, His Majesty the Emperor Alexander expressed himself to me on the issue of Greece; this time, he repeated the old axiom to the young King that Russia could not tolerate a Greek Kingdom in Byzantium."[323]

With all respect!

George, therefore, had not lost any time and had conveyed to Tsar Alexander II, the uncle of his wife Olga, the not exactly modest wishes of the Greeks for the first time "nine years" before, i.e. virtually directly after (if not even during) his wedding to the Grand Princess. Anyhow, he should have known as King (and at that time he had already held this honour for four years) that not only Russia itself, but other quite renowned states in Europe were striving for the possession of Constantinople, e. g. Great Britain, Austria-Hungary, and - as successor to Venice - surely also Italy, furthermore the unloved Slavic states from the Balkans, Serbia and Bulgaria. (Exactly this competetion was the reason why they all had been forced to be content with leaving the Sultan and his Ottomans at the Golden Horn – even beyond the First World War.)

But George acted obviously on the principle of: one only has to demand more than enough to receive at least something in the end.

And in the following decades, it was a question of this "something" – which in the end became way too much.

2.

Despite missing family ties to the Imperial and Royal Court of Austria-Hungary, George paid again a visit to Vienna in October of the same year - and not only out of courtesy. (As a result of an unusual Habsburg deviation from the proverbial tradition "tu, felix Austria, nube" and the possibility that the royal Danish family may have run out of further beautiful daughters, the Greek king of Danish origin must have missed those family ties in Vienna he normally found in practically each European capital.)

The year in question was the restless year of 1876, when the uprisings in Herzegovina and in Montenegro had already spilled over to Bulgaria and Macedonia, and Serbia had suffered the previously mentioned military breakdown. In that situation, all possi-

ble combinations on the Balkans were imaginable. Despite the financial and military limitations of Greece King George wanted to have a say in it all – at least verbally.
The German Ambassador to Vienna, Carl Count von Dönhoff, reports that George had constructed the following constellation:

"If the Romanian troops occupy Bulgaria ... (one) would demand an entry of Greek troops into the Greek provinces of Turkey and the government" [in Athens] "would not be able to oppose this demand." [324]

From the further text it can be seen that the King understood under "one" the patriotic Greek population, which was used as a pretext for actions like these – for which, however, it had at first to be stirred up in advance by the government, though.
It is clear: after being rebuffed in St. Petersburg, George actually did refrain from his maximum claim – but he did, by no means, let loose.

3.
It can be assumed, that George himself did not leave the country during the Russo-Turkish War of 1877-78, or during the Congress of Berlin, when it mattered to Greece to get a hold of "compensation" for the autonomy granted to the Bulgarians (undoubtedly as a compensation for Macedonia that had been taken away from them again). With success – as seen before. (Instead of his journey, a visit of the Princess of Wales to her brother, the Greek King in Athens, is documented.[325])
But already for 1879, there are again signs in the records at hand for George's trips abroad. For 1880, he even had planned to continue his beloved travelling diplomacy over a period of five whole months, between the middle of May and the middle of October[326.] There was reason enough for political talks and complaints in Paris, London and St. Petersburg, as the Porte habitually tried, as stated, to hinder its obligations from the Treaty of Berlin, concerning the cession of Thessaly and the South of Epirus that had been wrested away from it – or at least to put them off. To emphasize the Greek concerns, Athens had even mobilized and had unmistakably threatened to occupy the two provinces (once again). The English military attaché to Constantinople, Captain Swaine, who was to make a

"journey to Macedonia, Thessaly and Greece in order to collect information about the state of the military preparations on the Greek and Turkish sides," had, however, not noticed in Greece "any enthusiasm whatsoever regarding the national increase in power to be expected from the extension of the borders." [327]

Consequently, George's blackmail manoeuvre with the help of mobilisation failed. In the end, South-Epirus and Thessaly actually did become a part of Greece, as mentioned above, but, even years later, George was so upset about the missing English support for Greek affairs that he still avoided London in 1886 on his return from his annual holiday in Denmark.[328]

From which is to be learned, that he as a minor King was also well versed in putting major monarchs in the wrong, or at least in giving them a guilty conscience.

4.
In 1887, however, the King travelled, after his displeasure with England had evaporated - in the end, he was and remained a realist - with the whole Greek royal court (via Paris) again to London. There it was imperative to celebrate the 50th Jubilee of Queen Victoria.[329] The Greek King, of course, could not miss this opportunity. The guests at the celebration could almost have also celebrated the Silver Anniversary of Crown Prince Edward at the same time, as it was due the following year. [Certain parallels with the present are obvious.]

117

Afterwards, the entire crowd made its way (via Germany) to Copenhagen for the 70th birthday of the Danish Queen Louise, George's mother. From there, George accompanied his wife Olga "home", i.e. to "Mummy Russia". And on his return to Athens, George stopped off again in Vienna. A full programme.

Under such circumstances, nobody should have dared to say that the King was not looking after Greek affairs! But strangely enough that is what a lot of people said in Athens.

Like in 1883 the Greek Ambassador to Vienna, Count Ypsilanti, had done (see ch. 2.3.3), in 1887, now the King himself eloquently complained to the Austrian foreign minister. Ambassador Montgelas quoted him:

> "The neighbours on the Balkan Peninsula – Serbs, Bulgarians and Romanians – were on the whole hostile and all were attacking the Greek issue with the same animosity."

Thereby, he intimated once again "ambitious aspirations" (about the) future enlargement of the Hellenic Empire up to the Hellespontus, etc."[330]

But, at that time, most Europeans were still in agreement in refusing such adventurous impulses. Hence, the Austrian Foreign Minister, Count Kálnoky, suggested to George,

> "that he should direct his full attention to the settlement of his finances and the introduction of an orderly administration ... as well as the inner-development of the state." However, to the German Ambassador, von den Brincken, the Austrian foreign minister said that the "ideas brought forth were often (lacking) the necessary logic and clarity..." "The overall impression that Count Kálnoky has gained from the Greek Sovereign has not been an especially advantageous one."[330]

As usual, George did not let himself be discouraged by rejections of that kind. In the subsequent year, 1888, the King was in Vienna again with the Austrian foreign minister. This time, the German ambassador, in the meantime it was Prince Reuß, heard that Count Kálnoky had had to tell some truths to the Greek King, for example:

> "that the Greeks could not possibly demand from the Vienna Cabinet to make propaganda for them in Macedonia."[331]

This says a lot about the Austrian attitude concerning Macedonia and says everything about the long-term planning and persistence of the Greek King. These qualities he needed indeed: If the Greek sovereign had to beg abroad for PR work for the Greek interests in Macedonia, the so-called Greek population in Macedonia must have been quite a long way from the truth.

He himself did not experience the indisputable fruits of these preliminary works; not until 25 years later did they ripen – against the will of Vienna.

After George had been snubbed in such a way, he started to act out a drama for the Austrian statesman. Since he was - this time in reverse order - in Vienna passing through to St. Petersburg, he seized the opportunity to pull the wool over the foreign minister's eyes by assuring him,

> "that he was (going) very reluctantly to St. Petersburg." "He was wrongly claimed to have sympathies for Russia."[331]

In consideration of the fact that the Russians had done everything for Greece and that he had been married - in the meantime - for 20 years to a Russian grand princess, a cousin of Tsar Alexander III who had been reigning since 1881 and for whom he was even the brother-in-law through his sister Dagmar/Maria F., such cheap remarks should have been below his dignity - even if they had been correct. But a certain aristocratic sensibility was not inherent to him, as emerges from countless evidence. (On the other hand George was said to have, indeed, harboured certain reservations against the Russians – and certainly (like almost the entire Danish tribe) against the Germans, primarily: the Prussians.)

5.
One month later in August of 1888 (that is one month after the death of Kaiser Friedrich III), Graf von Berchem made a note in the foreign ministry that the Greek King, who was passing through Berlin from St. Petersburg, had complained,
> that the "Austrian officials in Macedonia ... were encouraging Kutsovallachian" [or Aromanian, therefore Romanian] "efforts against the Greeks."[332]

The constant dripping of water wears away the stone...

2.3.1.2 Background information (2)
A new dynastic period in the Greek royal house (Berlin)

Even good dynastic relations would be exposed to natural decay if they did not receive fresh supplies from time to time. In this aspect, George was certainly equal to the classic Austrian marriage-policy. Consequently, he made sure that the family bonds did not wither away, but rather that they multiplied, even exponentiated if possible.

1888 was, as is generally known, the year Germany had the most Kaisers. In the German-Greek relations it should also prove to be loaded with fate.

At the end of April, the oldest son of the Greek royal couple, the twenty-year old Crown Prince Constantine was staying in Berlin on a visit. There he met Princess Sophie of Prussia.[333] Not only was she graceful, well educated and beautiful, she was also the third daughter of Kaiser Friedrich III; therefore, she was a grand-daughter of Wilhelm I as well as a grand-daughter of Queen Victoria, since her father had married a daughter of the English Queen. Apart from this, however, she was, which for Greece should attain a lot higher importance, the *sister of Wilhelm II*, and consequently of the later, better said soon-to-be, German Kaiser. It must have been love at first sight, for they celebrated their engagement already on the 3rd of September.[334] (At the time of these festivities, Sophie's brother, Wilhelm, had already been on the Prussian and German throne for three months.)

It is no surprise that already four days later the British "Standard" described the Greek King George, the father-in-law of Kaiser Wilhelm's II sister, as "an intimate friend and relative of the German Imperial Family."[335] What was of decisive significance for this union: the Kaiser was content with the engagement of his beloved sister.[336]

At least higher politics exercised caution also in the case in question. The Iron Chancellor from Friedrichsruh, how could it be otherwise, cleared his throat. Count Bismarck again made the universally valid analysis. He had been asked if the German squadron of training ships could not drop anchor at the Piraeus to celebrate the wedding ceremony the following year. This he regarded to be completely unobjectionable – but only because the fleet would be crossing the Mediterranean Sea at that time of the year anyway, and its appearing before the coasts of Greece and Turkey would not cause any misinterpretations in Europe. (!) Nonetheless, in the text which the stenographer (probably, as usual, his son Herbert Count Bismarck) had taken down, His Highness requested the Auswärtiges Amt, to draw the Kaiser's attention in the oral report to the fact,
> "that the marriage ... as pleasant as it might be from the personal point of view could not be accentuated without political repercussions. The Greek policy is known to be ambitious, stirred-up and unpredictable and would naturally collide first and foremost with the Turkish. ... But then the Greek policy, depending on which fluctuations it might be exposed to, would soon collide with

the Russian, soon with the English, sometimes because of the mixing ratio in Macedonia also with the Bulgarian and Rumanian agitations and with Austrian and Italian plans. An obvious approximation of Germany to the Greek policy would worry all the Great Powers, especially our present allies Austria and Italy."[337]

Who would have thought that to disprove the cheeky statement of the Greek foreign minister, mentioned in the introduction of this work, that Macedonia as a name was first introduced in 1944 by Tito, one might be able to refer to, of all things, the authentic language of Bismarck in an instruction to the Auswärtiges Amt for an oral report to the German Kaiser in 1888 !?

If further proof had been needed for how much "Macedonia" was of general interest, i.e., how tangled "the Macedonian knot" in reality was it was brought forward here by an authoritative source!

The text continues:

"Besides, the power of the King would not be totally effective in Athens, with the Ministers alternating, insincere and unpredictable. It would be, therefore, not without consideration to emphasize outwardly the ties which would be created through the marriage to Greece, than would be necessary for the dignity of our royal house and the interests of Her Royal Highness the Princess."

Then a passage follows which, regarding the German-Greek relationship especially during the First World War, can be seen as almost clairvoyant:

"The Greek Royal Family, in accordance with its European relationships, would outrank in reputation and trustworthiness the Greek nation and its policy. It would not be possible for the German Empire to follow the latter on the uncertain paths which might still lie ahead of them, ... and the German Empire would be exposed to the most manifold interpretations by the other Great Powers with regard to the plans and future of our policy. The Imperial Chancellor should most humbly advise His Majesty to avoid having the family-ties to the Greek Royal House receive a political importance through which the German policy towards the other Great Powers could be prejudiced."[337]

So much for Otto von Bismarck – virtually a prophet, as still will be seen! If only Wilhelm II had stuck to Bismarck's recommendation.

The German press was, in comparison to Bismarck, depressed by a worry which, as was later seen, also burdened the Kaiser: the possible conversion of Princess Sophie to the Orthodox Church. That is why the *"Politische Correspondenz"* inserted, probably with relief, on the 15th of September, 1888, the following news in its columns: in the question of the change of faith, the regulations in the Greek constitution have been brought to the attention of the newspaper,

"which only in consideration of the children of a particular royal couple contains the regulation that they have to be raised in accordance with the Orthodox faith. But no regulation whatsoever exists, which would stipulate anything to the Royal Family concerning the faith of the new members by marriage." [338]

This information might have pacified simple minds – but not the Kaiser. And Sophie knew better anyhow....

The fastest reaction of the international press, even faster than from London, came - for obvious reasons - from Athens. Already two days after the announcement of this engagement, the Greek press spoke in this connection of

"being able to view a proof for the sympathies which the Greek Dynasty and Greece in general enjoy in Germany". [339]

Here the self-adulation was already starting!

Only the French press was fretting and fuming and poured out tirades of hatred. The German legate to Athens, Le Maistre, forwarded an example:

> "The 'Messager d'Athènes', a paper published here, ultra-French and full of Germanophobia, insinuates maliciously that the rumour" [of the abdication of King George] "was launched by Berlin, where they were impatient to see her Royal Highness Princess Sophie ascending the Greek Throne." [340]

Of course, a further reaction came from the Danish parents of the father-in-law. The event was "welcomed at the Danish Court with upright satisfaction and hearty delight." King and Queen "repeatedly spoke to Ambassador von den Brincken with distinctive satisfaction about the honouring and gratifying connection for their beloved grandson".[341]

This was not to be taken for granted, because, since the marriage of their daughter Dagmar with the Tsarevitch Alexander in 1866, the former never got over her antipathy - realistically the term "hatred" should be used - for the Germans resulting from the Danish defeat in 1864, not even by the wedding of her own son Nicholas with a German (1894), and she tried to transfer it onto him throughout her life.[342]

The same sympathy was shown to the German ambassador in Copenhagen by the rest of the court, the Danish cabinet and by "here accredited foreign representatives" – with one exception. Only the French colleague Monsieur Thomson

> "expressed himself by name, therefore, in a derogative manner about the engagement which had already taken place ..., because it is henceforth obvious, that Greece, which has so much to thank France for, wants to break with the latter and is willing to turn towards Germany." And since the world is really small in the diplomatic service, he added: "Also, I hear that both the appointed French legate to Athens, Count Montholon, and Admiral Lejeune, the long-time friends of the Greek Royal Family, did not feel obliged to even take notice of the engagement of the Crown Prince, let alone to congratulate His Royal Highness. ...Even the well-educated and rational-thinking French (can be) so blinded by their Germanophobia..., that their further feeling for tact and manners almost seems to have gotten lost".[343] "Almost"? "Seems"?

In the course of the following weeks, the German legate in Athens, Le Maistre, was so impressed by the "most delightful excitation" which the news of the engagement had evoked all over Greece, that he, in addition to the above-quoted report, made an attachment-report on top of that. Therein, he reflects, among other things, about the Greek policy of interest connected to this matter:

> "That the flattered national vanity has its part in this joy cannot be denied. ...Likewise, the opinion has been formed in the public that these family ties will also procure Greece material support in case of need, and will bring it the fulfilment of its national aspirations with the said territorial expansions." [344]

Bismarck had foreseen this future burden! It did not come at a high price for Germany alone - but also for Macedonia.

In the meantime, the legate tried to be just to the Greeks despite their perhaps unseemly, however not really unusual, expectations, for he wrote:

> "Yet one would be mistaken to believe, that only egoistic considerations and calculations determine the feelings with which the selection of the heir to the throne has been welcomed here. Germany, whose interests do not collide with the Greek wishes and ambitions, therefore enjoys a greater popularity here than various other powers." [345]

Then, he even reported about a certain nostalgia that was to be noted with the Greeks about George's predecessor, King Otto from Bavaria, whom they had driven out in

1861, although (according to Hannes Hintermaier in FAZ of 11. 3. 2005) Otto during his reign had developed Greece up to the West European level:

> "The thirty years of a German Kingdom have left behind some thankful memories and some closer relationships to Germany. German industriousness, German devotion to duty, competence and education are regarded here still more than anywhere else with recognition and appreciation. The German education of children is often preferred in the wealthier classes of the population, and knowledge of the German language is in those circles of society strikingly common. Thus, the German Princess is already welcomed because she is a German." ... "Due to this, the prospective marriage is becoming ... even more favoured by the Greeks; the native royal dynasty, which brings the country such consideration of the most powerful states, is gaining popularity"[345]

As a further example for King Otto's beneficial effects, the following detail can be added:

> "The newly arisen Hellas took over the statute books from Bavaria, which the legal scholar Georg Ludwig Maurer had worked out as a member of the Ottonian regency council."[346]

The nostalgic "wistfulness" was definitely a more recent development. For as late as the year before, 1887, the Greek request for a military-training for the second son of the Greek royal couple, Prince George, was, in fact, *positively* decided upon by the Saxonian King in favour of "a regiment of the Leipzig garrison in the common arts of warfare like strategy, tactics, fortification and the like", but had nonetheless been labelled with the following justification,

> that to be exact "the King of Greece was a Danish prince and the Queen a Russian princess, that furthermore the country would sympathize with France, and French officers had been called upon as instructors for the Greek troops, hence the court and the country could not be counted to the German-friendly ones."[347]

Already a couple of months before the wedding celebration and the arrival of Princess Sophie in Athens, it had become known that "she is already busy learning the Greek language", which caused common delight.

> "The picture of Her Highness is all over on display in the shop windows, finds the most advantageous appraisal and sells like hotcakes."[348]

Exactly this Greek sympathy for Sophie and, therefore, for Germany, was, however, an unbearable thorn in the side of the French in Athens. Not only the King but also parliament was made to feel this. In his speech for the opening of the chamber session in November, 1888, George had also dared to mention "the ties with a glorious and powerful dynasty" ("ce lien avec une dynastie glorieuse et puissante"). Despite its pure character of protocol, this comment had provoked the envy of the French colony of Athens – so desperate for admiration. "Local French influences and malicious agitations" had, as the legation reported, convinced an opposition politician "to interpellate the government in the debate of address about the meaning of this passage".[349] Prime Minister Trikupis had no other choice but to explain the position of the Greek government in a long statement. He said,

> "that the engagement of the heir to the throne, being first of all a consequence of affection, surely did not lack political significance." This alliance did not "mean a hostile position towards any other power." "He bore friendly convictions for Germany but not any less for France. ... In ... the [King's] speech ... on this occasion there had been no cause to talk about the feelings of Greece for France. But that does not exclude their existence."[349]

This shows how slippery the diplomatic-political-dynastic dance-floor can be.

The representative Kosakis Typaldo [as you see, not only a literary figure from Verona] was content. Not so the French. The time up to the marriage a year later was used intensively for anti-German propaganda. There was one exception. In the summer of 1889 the "Messager d'Athènes" showed its satisfaction and gave "the King a good grade this time":

> "By making his way to Paris, he demonstrated tact and political wisdom." [350]

To the background: George was travelling again in that year. Since his planned tour to London went via Paris, George received a positive French response in doing so. The Greek papers on the other hand emphasized the independence of their country, because their King

> "met with the same friendly reception from all the powers of Europe and hoped that the good relationships which the Greek Dynasty maintained with the leaders of all states would prove effective in case of a future European involvement for the fulfilment of the just Greek wishes." [350]

There again it appears that the sword of Damocles, which was not only held by Serbia and Bulgaria but also in particular by Greece, hung permanently threatening over Macedonia – in fact (since Greece had finally gotten Thessaly and a part of Epirus) with the sharpness of the blade increasing while the thread was getting thinner.

When a suspicion came up in the press that Queen Olga would, as always, want to await the birth of her latest child (the eighth!) in St. Petersburg and, before the marriage of her son, would hardly be able to part from the sickbed of her father, the Grand Prince Constantine, it was insinuated by the French - this time, in fact, also by the Russian press

> "that the actual reason for the noble woman's staying away was that deep down in her heart she did not approve of the marriage ... with a German and Protestant Princess." [351]

Not only the embassy could invalidate this interpretation immediately through a personal statement of the Queen; also Sophie herself disproved this maliciousness later – very much to the distress of her brother.

Something similar was unreeled by the French colony in Athens, when the Crown Prince after the marriage to the Prussian princess sent a personal letter of thanks to the "Municipality of Berlin",

> because "the all too strong Germanophile tone of the questionable paper evoked an unpleasant impression in Paris."

This time the Prime Minister apparently was prepared, for he answered that the letter did not contain "anything offending for France".

> "In the case that it had occurred, the Crown Prince would have answered exactly the same to the congratulations of a French city."

The government-friendly press also struck back this time:

> "To what extent was Greece so greatly indebted to contemporary France anyhow? – asked the semi-official "Acropolis". It is solely the fault of France that Greece does not possess Ioannina...." [352]

In this case one has to back France, though, for the area in question was Albanian territory. This did not keep Greece from annexing exactly this territory later during the Balkan Wars.

The German Kaiser's readiness to participate himself in the festivities for the marriage of his sister in Athens did provoke an especially "bad mood" among the French.

> "Today (the French press) is trying on the one hand to cast suspicion on the genuine joy" of the population, "and on the other hand to ridicule it. The article in the 'Figaro' from the 10th of this month does this in a very significant way" and neither does it spare the King himself. [353]

The French legate was awarded a special accreditation as ambassador in order to, as was joked in Athens, "secure" him "the precedence before all other authorized representatives, but in particular, however, His Excellency the State Secretary, Count von Bismarck [jun.] and to document with this, that France still plays the most important role in Greece."[353]

As a result of the French insinuations, the new Ambassador to Athens, von Tschirschky, evaluated

"the sudden dismissal of the long-time German tutor of the Crown Prince, Dr. Lüders."[354] This measure was taken in consideration that "one has to spare the feelings of other powers;" since the 'Journal des Débats' had "'carried on' vehemently against the prevalence of the Germanic influence at the Greek Court". At the same time, with the removal of Dr. Lüders through the interested circles at court, "the inadmissible circumstance of a German's remaining longer at the court" was regulated by the "Greek national feelings that had been hurt by this".[355]

The same Greek national feelings, however, were not hurt in the slightest way when the Greeks noticed

that "the surely most pleasant consequence of the alteration of the German nation's feelings" for the Greek [nation] was "the complaisance of the Germans in the financial area", as the newspaper "Ephimeris" stated enthusiastically under the title "German Feelings".[356]

The agitation received new fuel when Lüders appeared again 18 months later in Greece as General Consul in Piraeus by proposal of Bismarck. Lüders replied to the doubts of the King ("all diplomats came running and explained that this was a very unjustified influence on the Crown Prince which Germany would thus gain and keep") and of the Minister President Trikupis ("one would point at you as the originator for every action the Crown Prince would undertake in the future" [this reproach was actually raised at that time in connection with Constantine's letter to the Berlin Municipality[357]]),

that he "considered himself very lucky, to be incorporated again by the grace of His Majesty, the Kaiser, into His Majesty's service after 14 years of interruption" and "that he would naturally never go to his Royal Highness, the Crown Prince, uncalled", after all, he knew how "upset the French legate … was about his return". In this situation, the King himself could only answer: "…but all this is only jealousy."[358]

Unaffected by this, the impression of the ambassador remained that King George, despite the "marriage of the Crown Prince with the daughter of a German Kaiser" which he felt as an honour, had "a deep-rooted mistrust of everything German".[359]

Indeed, why should he have reacted differently than his sisters in London and St. Petersburg?!

All's well that ends well. The marriage took place and the monarchs of half of Europe were present: "Kaiserin Friedrich" ["Vicky", Victoria, the wife of the deceased Kaiser Friedrich III, the mother of the bride], as well as Kaiser Wilhelm II, her brother; the Danish royal couple as the grandparents of the husband-to-be, and their grandson from St. Petersburg, the Tsarevitch Nicholas, son of their daughter Dagmar/Maria F., the latter appearing as the aunt of the husband-to-be; finally, Edward the Prince of Wales, with his wife, a further daughter of Christian IX and Louise, therefore aunt of the husband-to-be as well, together with their family.[360]

What could not have been talked about at the table or while having the mocha or during a match of crocket! And everything to its disadvantage – as far as Macedonia was concerned.

In connection with the union of the Greek Crown Prince Constantine with Princess Sophie of Prussia, it has already been stated that the Greek constitution did not demand Sophie's conversion to the Orthodox faith. Also, the Greek (Protestant) King would never have envisaged (probably differently than his Russian-Orthodox wife Olga) stating a wish like that. It was Sophie herself, who (like 15 years later Alice of Battenberg out of love for the Greek Prince Andrew) wanted to be completely taken up by the people and the language of her beloved husband. Brother Wilhelm did not leave her in the dark with his disappointed, even sad reaction. When the "Kölnische Zeitung" published the announcement of the conversion in 1891:

> "Crown Princess Sophie will, catechized by the Metropolitan, convert to the Greek Church ... on the Greek Easter Saturday," [361]

the Kaiser noted on the corresponding report of Envoy von Wesdehlen, with which the official message of the conversion was announced:

> "My poor father would turn around in his grave!! As soon as the conversion is carried out, von Wesdehlen has to signal to Her Royal Highness that she has to temporarily avoid the Prussian boundaries until further notification; conform to the warning I gave the Princess last December." [362]

Maybe a hard reaction – but, after all, Wilhelm's generosity also had its limits somewhere. Incidentally, under the brash, maybe even awkward, language of the monarch was a much too soft core of the brother, as if even the most remote parallel could be drawn to the Prussian case of "Katte" almost 160 years ago.

An anecdote about the Austrian-Bulgarian relationship might show that Wilhelm's reaction was not just an individual quirk of an eccentric nationalist, but was quite current at that time: when the (German) Grand Prince of Bulgaria, Ferdinand of the House of Saxe-Coburg-Gotha, decided, as mentioned above, to let Prince Boris convert to the Orthodox faith (which was the *law* in Greece with reference to children of the monarch), he was boycotted by the Austrian court. [363]

One of the more harmless consequences of Wilhelm's being the hurt-brother resulted in ill-feelings with King George himself, because the German Kaiser had not personally received George's son, the Crown Prince, in Berlin. But, he apparently did not really know Kaiser Wilhelm, who wrote in the margin of the corresponding report from Athens:

> "1. I categorically only receive Sovereigns themselves or Crown Princes of the three Empires, when they come on a special mission, otherwise not them either.
> 2. Unbelievable! This blasé attitude." [364]

In search of understanding for King George's displeasure, the Italian envoy to Bucharest, who was passing through Athens, speculated that George might have felt criticized by Sophie, because he himself had not converted. But there again, the Roman apparently did not really know the Danish-Greek King, who was totally unsusceptible for something so absurd – and was, therefore, pleasantly insensitive.

In the end, it only took a couple of years until the wrath and bitterness of the Kaiser had vanished, and he again embraced his beloved sister. This reconciliation must have occurred around the end of May of 1898, since, from a report of the embassy, it follows that:

> "the gracious and hearty welcome, which ... was given to the Crown Prince and his wife, the Crown Princess, in Berlin" had aroused great joy to the public in Athens. [365]

When the Greek Prime Minister, however, in the exuberance of his relief ordered the Greek ambassador in Berlin, Rhangabe, telegraphically, "to convey to the Imperial Government the gratitude of the Greek Government" for this reception, Wilhelm again reacted very fussily and wrote in the margin of the report:

> "That does not concern our Government, since this is a family matter. The gratitude is tactless beyond all measures."³⁶⁵

(Well, well – the degree of tactlessness would definitely not have been intended that strongly in Athens. By the way, the Kaiser, who often enough knew how to make himself unpopular with his ranting and boasting tactlessness, might have enjoyed taking the opportunity to reproach others for their misbehaviour – at least by way of a note in the files.)

After Wilhelm had cooled down his temper in such a Wilheminian way, he surely went back to his role as a faithful, caring patriarch. At the latest, this was evident the following year, when the Greek King himself was welcomed in Berlin, after the two monarchs had not seen each other for ten years. This event led to the usual reaction in Athens:

> "All over, there is delight about the visit of the King, and one is willing to attach all kinds of expectations and hopes to this."³⁶⁶

This time, even the Francophone newspaper in Athens "Levant Herald" of the 25th of October, 1899, remained with polite, noncommittal remarks and added to their article the discreet explanation:

> "L'entrevue du roi avec l'empereur est due aux efforts personnels du prince Constantine, beau frère de Guillaume II."³⁶⁶

Complete peace had seemingly returned when Wilhelm again a year later (on the 8th of June 1903, from volume R 7482 of the files) had approved of admitting the Crown Prince's brother, Prince Andrew, Lieutenant of the Greek Cavalry, to the service with the 1st Grand Ducal Hessian Dragoon Regiment No. 23.

A veritable tradition was to develop from this over the generations: in this way Crown Princess Sophie did not miss the chance later, after the *Abitur* (school-leaving exams at grammar schools) of her oldest son George, immediately after his swearing-in "as Lieutenant … (of the) First Greek Infantry Regiment", of accompanying him herself to the legation, to introduce him to Envoy von Wangenheim as an officer and thereby redeem the promise of her brother, the German Kaiser, to admit the Prince for two years "to a Prussian regiment, preferably the First Guards Regiment."³⁶⁷ Moreover, a younger brother of the Crown Prince, Sophie's brother-in-law Prince Christopher, already had

> "the hope that his entry into a Prussian regiment could be made possible at the same time as that of the future heir to the throne."

Wilhelm's note in the margin, short and sweet: "Yes." ³⁶⁸

At the beginning of this section, the further expanding network of Danish-Greek marriage diplomacy was referred to. Therefore, it should be indicated at this point that, three months after the Greek-German betrothal, the third child of the Greek royal couple, their oldest daughter, Princess Alexandra, also celebrated her engagement – with Grand Prince Paul, the youngest brother of the Russian Tsar. ³⁶⁹

> Now back to the end of the Congress of Berlin and to the development of the Balkan League from the Greek point of view.

2.3.2 Greek-Bulgarian exploratory talks on Macedonia

Greece got additional competitors with the independent states of Serbia, Romania and Montenegro, which had been newly created at the Congress of Berlin in 1878, as well as the autonomous Bulgaria in the struggle for the remaining Turkish provinces in

Europe, first and foremost, of course, for Macedonia. For the Bulgarians, the Serbs and the Greeks any means was justified in achieving an own great empire.

Five years after the Congress of Berlin, in 1883, and during a visit to Greece, the Bulgarian Prince Alexander - on the initiative of the Greek Prime Minister, Tricoupis, - made the first attempt to sound out the terrain in Athens for common action. The German envoy to Athens reported about an improvement in the atmosphere of their bilateral relations.

> Mr. Von Brincken doubted, "however, whether the idea of a grand Balkan Federation, that was as powerful as possible and with a territory that was extensive as possible," was feasible," if it was led by Greece, - especially considering the entanglements occurring in the Orient.[370]

The reason for this doubt was less to be sought in the Greek wish for supremacy within the alliance but more in Greece's wish for extensive territorial expansion – for this actually Alexander had already envisaged for Bulgaria.

The Greek envoy to Constantinople, Condouriottis, paraphrased the words, "entanglements occurring", to the German ambassador as follows:

> the "future events putting the present balance of things on the Balkan peninsula in question."[371]

That was ornate diplomatic language, but, even in 1883, it pointed directly at the things that were to come exactly 30 years later. At that time, the Greeks restrained themselves since they suspected, as Mr. von Radowitz continued to report, that an alliance with Bulgaria would "only lead to an exploitation of Greek forces for Pan-Slavic purposes". The Greeks' real fear, however, went in another direction:

> "If a new and bigger clash should take place on the Balkan Peninsula, then the Austro-Hungarian and the Russian monarchies would stand face to face as the main combatants."[371]

This sounds like an unusual way of seeing things, perhaps as if Greece wanted to deflect suspicion away from itself and onto other states. Considering the fact, though, that the Russians, in their last war against the Ottoman Empire, had pushed the Turks again a little bit out of Europe in favour of the Bulgarians, and Austria had been allowed to occupy Bosnia thanks to the decisions of the Congress of Berlin, the Greek concern that these two Great Powers could take advantage of what was left of European Turkey was not at all unfounded.

All the Balkan states, whose aims were territorial acquisition, had to take this uncertainty factor into account for the whole thirty years leading up to the actual outbreak of the First Balkan War (in the end without any Great Powers, at least not as participants, but only operating in the background).

Finally, a comment in the press will round off the impressions that the visit of the Bulgarian count had left in Athens. In contrast to what might have been expected, the principles of Greek foreign policy were not only the insider-knowledge of experts, being also known to the public, as an article in the "Kölnische Zeitung" shows:

> "The rumour has spread that the Bulgarian visit to the Greek Court had the purpose of establishing an agreement between Greece and Bulgaria with regard to their mutual claims on the Balkan Peninsula."[372]

Even at this early stage, *partition procedures* were becoming apparent, although these would not become concrete until shortly before the founding of the Balkan League, or, strictly speaking, not until during the Balkan Wars themselves.

> "The idea of the restoration of the Byzantine Empire with its seat in Constantinople is still alive in the hearts of the Greek patriots, an ideal which has its natural rival in a Greater Bulgaria; that is why Hellenism and Bulgarianism are struggling in every village and every school for supremacy."

The Greeks had been living with the illusion that the historic glory of their culture seemed to promise them in advance superiority over the Bulgarians. The bitter experience of the ecclesiastical dispute since 1869, which ended with the Bulgarian Exarchate (1870), had taught the Greeks

> "that the Bulgarians are aspiring to the eradication of their nationality, which is why they should prefer the Turkish yoke, under which, of course, neither their church nor their language would be in danger."[372]

All of this could be read in the newspaper in Köln (Cologne) on 23rd May in 1883.

2.3.3 The essence of the Greek strategy

What little success the Bulgarian count had with his overtures to Greece can be read in the report of the German envoy to Athens about a conversation he had with the Greek Foreign Minister Contostavlos:
He said that he directed all of his efforts at preserving the peace and initiating good relationships with the Porte,

> "not necessarily out of a special fondness for Turkey, but rather ... because he deemed a good relationship to be definitely in the well-understood interest of both states."[373]

The first impression is that these words seem patronizing, almost presumptuous, but it was probably more a kind of tactless familiarity, since Contostavlos continued:

> "The enemy against which both Turkey and also Greece would have to make a stand is the Slavism which is expanding across the Balkan Peninsula, since it threatens the authority of the Sultan and also Hellenism in the same manner."

What if Prince Alexander and his Bulgarians had heard that!
What was behind it?
In principle, the main thrust of Greece in gaining the remainder of the Turkish territories in Europe was aimed at the Ottoman Empire. This would have required, though, cooperating with at least one of the competitors as a Greek partner, since none of the Balkan states could march alone against Turkey. Logically, such an alliance would have inevitably brought with it the obligation of *sharing* the Turkish spoils. Fortunately, the Megale Idea left room for flexible and generous interpretations: namely, if Greece turned the tables and went together with Turkey against the other Balkan states, then a larger part of the territory that was regained for Turkey would fall to Greece than if Greece had to share the territory with one or even more alliance members. Such a procedure, even if treacherous, would be insofar advisable since Turkey seemed to be getting stronger again, as experience had proved, even in the case of Greece.[374]

This strategy reveals the fundamental attitude of Greece towards the question of extension of power through expansion, as well as the question of on which territory the expansion should preferably take place. It turns out that the Greeks had not developed a scale of preference for this. What was important to them was the expansion of power as such. That is why the Macedonians had not played a prominent role as a target of Greek imperialism originally (with perhaps the exception of Salonica). Rather, Athens regarded *all of the Slavic (and Albanian)* territories as potentially of the same value to be incorporated into Greek national territory. A reason for this was not at all necessary – in the 19th century. If necessary, Greece would have pleaded that before the downfall of Byzantium each of these regions had after all once been at some time a part of the Eastern Roman Empire and/or (after the division of the Empire in 395) of the Byzan-

tine Empire. Reason enough for Athens to see all of the peoples, who as a consequence of the Age of Migrations had settled on the Balkan peninsula and in the Ottoman Era, like Greece itself, had been reduced to vassals by the Turks, as equally eligible to be conquered and assimilated. And, moreover, they would also profit from contact with Hellenic culture. That Macedonia, of all places, should become the target for Greece was simply because it was located so conveniently just "in front of the Greek door" and that it was also in such a state that it posed only a relatively minor risk for the Greeks from the military point of view. This, of course, did not exclude the other regions of the Balkans from the plan that they would also be Hellenized, as, among others, the Bulgarians knew from painful experience.
(Compare also ch. 2.3.7. on Greek strategy)
Nevertheless, in order to keep both options, Foreign Minister Contostavlos followed up with threat which was couched diplomatically, but still clear:

> "Of course, a rapprochement between Constantinople and Athens would only be conceivable if the Turkish side were to break, once and for all, with the policy that up to now has so frequently hurt Greek national feelings and done damage to Greek interests ... If the Porte persists in its present hostile attitude towards Hellenism, there would be nothing left for Greece to do, ... in the event of possible new complications in the Orient, ... but to take a stand on the side of the enemies of Turkey, in order not to come out empty-handed in the end in the event of a catastrophe."[375]

Who else but the Greek foreign minister would be able to so precisely define the Greek path for achieving its aim! There was *not a word at all, of course, about possible legitimacy. It was only about the extension of imperial power.*

With regard to the "expanding Slavism" from the quotation of the Greek foreign minister, given on the previous page, please refer to the historical introduction to this chapter. Contostavlos' words seem to be expressing deeper feelings than could be expected from mere antipathy towards annoying competitors. Did the intensive fusion of the Greeks with the Slavic immigrants have anything to do with the Greek aversion to Slavism? Since it could not have been ignorance in the case of a foreign minister, then one has rather to assume mechanism of repression.
(Compare also the Albanian immigration into Greece in ch. 2.5 in connection with this.)

2.3.4 Greek sueing for Austria-Hungary

In that year, 1883, the Foreign Ministry in Athens undertook the attempt to also test the quality of Greek relations to Austria – a venture that King George personally consolidated four years later. (Compare ch. 2.3.1, Nr. 4)
The German embassy in Vienna reported what the Greek envoy, Count Ypsilanti (apparently a descendant of the famous leader of the First Greek Revolt in 1821) had lamented to Austrian Foreign Minister Count Kálnoky:

> "Greece feels isolated; not one of the Powers bothers itself any more about Greek affairs, and this has given rise to the strong feeling in Athens, which the King shares, that in the event of possible complications on the Balkan Peninsula where Greece might be endangered, no one whatsoever would look after this kingdom."[376]

Remorse on the part of the Count followed this mild accusation, as if a little Greek would be aware that his country had irritated the adult powers of Europe:

> "It is being said that the Greeks themselves are to blame for this situation and that the insatiability of the Greek patriots has lost them the sympathies of Europe. That is why people see the necessity

of ... giving up the dream about things that are totally unrealizable at the present and the pursuit of which has robbed the Greeks of the trust of the Great Powers."³⁷⁶

It was apparently already customary at that time to shift the blame for the "insatiability" for land acquisition from the king and from the government to the *patriots*. What can the cabinet do about it if the people crave a bigger territory? His following argument was cleverer, since the casually interwoven "dream about things", that are "totally unrealizable at the present" leaves all doors open for the future. Who knows today what tomorrow will bring?

It continued in this tone, whereby the Count with his eloquence knowing how to elegantly insinuate the actual Greek aims of gains with the following flattering remarks, where he once again played the anti-Slavic card:

> "Greece turns at this point first to Austria-Hungary to find support here. It is well known in Athens that Austria will not allow the Greeks any more benefits at the expense of Turkey; it is also being said there that Austrian interests would not be served if Greece wanted to expand its sphere of power up to Salonika," [Oh, really?] "but it is expected that, in the struggle of Slavism with Hellenism on the Balkan Peninsula, the Austrian sympathies would be found more on the side of the latter. For this reason, in Athens one seems to view an alliance with Austria as an anti-Slavic one and is, therefore, principally in favour of the same."³⁷⁶

Amazingly honest! It is completely obvious: Greece itself also regarded the previous, as well as the envisaged, territorial acquisitions as "benefits" and not as legitimate acquisition (not to mention the re-acquisition) of territories – which is how the theft from 1913 up to the present day is depicted.

Incidentally, Ypsilanti's behaviour is reminiscent of Lafontaine's fable of the raven and the fox: "Tout flatteur vit aux dépens de celui qui l'écoute. " [*Every flatterer lives at the expense of whoever listens to him.*]The intended result: the good Count Kálnoky told Ambassador Prince Reuß that he did not mind,

> "shaking the hand that the Greeks offer, of course, but only ... on the basis of the status quo and the Treaty of Berlin."

One can't believe one's eyes: "... the Treaty!" And that from a minister of the Austro-Hungarian monarchy that was to break this very same treaty one day!

Be that as it may – it still took 25 years until the *annexation of Bosnia*....

But as regards the *status quo*: should the foreign minister of the Habsburg Empire of all people have been the only personality of that era who did not know the true aims of Greece? Was it true that Kálnoky really did not know that the status quo constituted more or less the last state of affairs in the Balkans which Greece (like both Bulgaria and Serbia) was prepared to accept as given? Or did he perhaps amuse himself royally by leaving the Greek count in the belief that he [the minister] did not see through his [the count's] intrigues? That would be an example of the haute école of diplomacy.

It did not look like that, however, because a few paragraphs later the ambassador writes that the count had said about the topic of a *Balkan League*,

> "such an alliance ... would naturally not be in the interests of the Austro-Hungarian Monarchy as long as the continued existence of the present state of the Ottoman Empire is considered necessary."

The count actually said "as long as" – and that after he had shortly before insisted on the necessity of maintaining the status quo and had spoken about preserving the peace!

It's clear: one sly fox met another sly fox. The one, Count Ypsilanti, could be satisfied with himself: a policy clearly directed at expansion, the aggressive motivation behind was concealed by his seductive courteousness – a diplomatic master stroke. The other was hiding behind his righteousness the fact that Austrian deviousness and lust for power probably surpassed that of the Greeks. Vienna did not have the intention either of doing without an even more extensive and, as a result, even more complicated multi-ethnic state. Unbelievable.

And now, back to Ypsilanti's bait of a "common" Greek-Austrian anti-Slavism. Should the Greek envoy to the imperial and royal double monarchy really not have been informed about one of the biggest problems, if not *the* problem of Austria? The man would be beyond all hope.
It fits well that the above-mentioned [*Cologne Newspaper*] "Kölnische Zeitung" wrote the following about Austria-Hungary at that time:
> A ruthless nationality policy (like the Russian one) would contradict the guiding principle of a state "which is composed of different peoples like a kaleidoscope."[377]

Correct – except that the Slavs, whom the Greek count was alluding to in his démarche, made up a larger part of the Habsburg Empire than he and his interlocutor were prepared to admit. The statistics below proves this:
According to statistics from 1900, only 11.3 million of the 28 million inhabitants of Austria were Germans, whereas *17.8 million were Slavs* (Poles, Ruthenians, Czechs, Slovenes, Serbs and Croats). The number of Slavs in Hungary with 5 million from approx. 20 million inhabitants improves the overall result for the German population a little. But in 1907, when, under the impression of revolutionary developments in Russia, universal franchise was introduced in Austria, there were 259 Slavic representatives compared with 233 German representatives.[378]
Fragments?
The "Anti-Slavism" was thrown into the debate by, of all people, a Greek diplomat who was sitting in the glas-house himself, considering the numerous minorities that his country houses up to the present day. Prof. Troebst enumerates the following minorities in Greece:
> "Southeast-Slavs, Turks, Aromanians, Albanians, Pomaks (Moslem Bulgarians), Roma, Meglenites, Sarakatchans, Sephards, Yifti, Yürüks, etc., etc."[379]

Even more names can be added to the list (here are some from an essay by Prof. Türkkaya Ataöv): Gagavus (Christian Turks), Circassians (Moslem Cherkess) and Armenians. Since he apparently wanted to have the Ashkenazi included besides the Sephards, he listed this group under the general name "Jews". The minorities which Troebst summarized as "Southeast-Slavs" were more precisely described as "*Macedonians*".
The significance of the latter should not be underestimated, inasmuch as the Turks had 500 years' time to thoroughly study the ethnic origins of their subjects.
Bismarck, who, after the meeting between Kálnoky and Ypsilanti at the Ballhausplatz, was asked for his opinion about the Greek intention of getting Austrian support, had agreed not to reject the Greek hand of friendship. (This event took place five years before the marriage of the Greek Crown Prince to Princess Sophie von Hohenzollern), but he had warned about making formal agreements with Athens,
> since the "pretentious extravagance that is typical ... of the chauvinists there," the danger of "unwanted complications" due to their unfeasible national policy cannot be ruled out.[380]

A smart man, that Bismarck.
His subsequent decree to the embassy in Vienna probably left the Greek count pretty cold, in as far as its contents were reported to him (as can be assumed considering the lively exchange of ideas among diplomats). When, though, the "Journal d'Athènes" a couple of days later double-crossed the count's efforts to improve the relations with

Austria and, moreover, to at least coax a hint of agreement to further Greek expansions from the double monarchy with a recommendation, whereby it

> challenged "all the peoples of the Balkan Peninsula to unite as one against Austria, whose 'push towards the East' threatens both Slavs and Greeks equally and against whose steady advance only a common alliance can serve as an effective barrier,"[381] ...
> ... Count Ypsilanti could not have been very amused about that.

The tentative Greek experiments in Vienna had their repercussions, as were discernible from reactions in Constantinople: the Greek envoy, Conduriotis, (in the report at hand the spelling has been altered) allowed the German ambassador to once again have access to the information of his brother-in-law, the Greek Foreign Minister Contostavlos, (which was, first and foremost, apparently intended for Turkish ears), that

> "the Greek government would not become involved in any agreements" which would result in "a disturbance of the peace" ... "and that now it is only interested in sincerely maintaining good relations with Turkey."[382]

In this passage of the report (*which is the height of hypocrisy*), one frankly misses the Kaiser's typical, characteristic note in the margin: *Donnerwetter!* ['My goodness!'] Brilliant - that the little word "now" was so inconspicuously smuggled into the text. In this way, Athens would have been able, and then honestly, to claim later that this assurance was really sincerely expressed at the time. What was honest at the time the report was made at least was the continually repeated comment that Greece still had important desires for reciprocity with Turkey as regards the "Cretan conditions". What Athens itself intended to introduce, in turn, as its part in the "reciprocity" was probably just a question of semantics.

There was not a single word said about regions like *Thrace and Macedonia* (except for a vague mention of Salonika). If Macedonia had ever been Greek in earlier times, Athens certainly would not have hesitated to list this region (these regions) in particular, since Greece was approaching the moment when it would have a part of Epirus (1884) passed over into its hands after Thessaly (1881). But even the Hellenes were not quite so daring that they would publicly claim more foreign territories at this time. Or were they?

Foreign Minister Contostavlos expressed his satisfaction about the consequence of the démarche of Count Ypsilanti to his brother-in-law with the comment:

> "It was especially gratifying for the Greek government to hear" the Austrian statesman "expressing, of his own free will, the explicit assurance that Austrian policy is not thinking about blazing a trail to Salonika and that all such insinuations have been dismissed as arbitrary fiction."[382]

Donnerwetter! (Please, excuse my presumption.)
One could have almost bet that all the talk in the files about Austria's push to the Aegean Sea was only malicious insinuations – and now one has to, albeit only indirectly, realize that in reality there was fire where merely smoke was seen.
This disarmingly generous renunciation on the part of Austria, which understandably "made a huge impression" on the Greek Prime Minister Tricupis, raised the Greek chances of expanding in the direction of Macedonian Salonika.

The reference to the name *Salonika* needs clarification at this point: during the last eight or nine decades, the Europeans have become used to the Greek claim that Salonika already belonged to Greece earlier. In reality, though, *Salonika was never Greek before 1913*. Even if Greek merchants, seamen and monks, maybe even artisans and teachers, had already lived there for a long time, as on a lot of other coasts, the city belonged to Macedonia under international law. Viktor Meier writes:

"At that time, Salonika was a Slavic - Turkish - Jewish city rather than a Greek one."[383]

(For more, compare the remarks about Salonika at ch. 5.2.2)

2.3.5 Bismarck fears disturbances in Macedonia

Three years later, in 1886, the throne of the Greek king seemed to have been getting shaky. A few weeks after the Bulgarian revolutionaries had achieved the unification of East Rumelia with the Principality of Bulgaria, "the whole Greek coastline ... was blocked by the united ships of all the European Great Powers" to keep the Greeks from starting a war with Turkey over Crete. Bismarck informed the embassy in St. Petersburg about a discussion with Count Shuvalov, the Russian ambassador in Berlin. The decisive passage reads:

"If the Great Powers had not stepped in in favour of peace and the dynasty in Greece, it would have been very probable that the latter would have become fugitives and that, as a result, a Hellenic republic would have been proclaimed, which could not have missed passing on the contagious poison to Macedonia as well as the radicalized Bulgarian and Serbian tribes...."[384]

Bismarck did, therefore, worry about Greece and was in favour of preserving it as a state. In fact, the Greeks, including their royal family, were a little bit dubious in his eyes, but to see republicans on the Acropolis would have been even more disagreeable for him. Moreover, for Bismarck it was apparently a matter of course to also equally mention Macedonia along with Serbia and Bulgaria – and, as neighbour of Greece, in fact, in first place. As a consequence, Bismarck perceived the Macedonians as a separate people. (Also, compare ch. 2.3.1.1 above.) But, as a convinced monarchist, in accordance with the zeitgeist, he regarded the Macedonian people - since they were a folk without a state - exactly as ruthlessly as disposable as did the neighbours, who were eager for booty.

A sympathy for freedom, independence or the right of self-determination - even in its rudimentary form of that time - or even for the peace-disturbing activities of the Komitadjis, the revolutionaries, was absolutely not to be expected of Bismarck; even less so since he also supported the well-known line of the Kaiser once again in the above-mentioned decree that "Germany was in no way whatsoever interested."

As far as his Kaiser was concerned, this was to change considerably later.

2.3.6 The Greek press demands Macedonia

One cannot say that the Greek plans for expansion were not consistent. Their planning for the long-term is remarkable.

After the Greek territorial gains in Thessaly and a part of South Epirus had been achieved, Greece immediately turned its eyes towards the next object of its desire, despite the declarations of the Greek delegation in Berlin. As a result, the discussion in Athens about the question of the usefulness of Greece's joining a possible Balkan League continued.

As the Envoy, Count Leyden, reported in 1886, the Athens newspapers wrote,

"with a certain amount of satisfaction that the conviction of an independent political development of the Balkan countries is beginning to catch on." As regards the possibility of Greece's becoming a member: "Greece, which represents Hellenism, cannot be expected to enter into contractual commitments on the basis of its present territorial possessions."[385]

The newspaper "Acropolis" went even further:

"Greece could only be represented in a Balkan League, in a manner corresponding with its national dignity, if Crete, the islands, Epirus, and Macedonia were united with the motherland."[385]

So, the name appeared here! What the government did not dare to do, and/or what it was not foolish enough to do, the press could allow itself to do. At any rate: it made the news, so no one can claim that this expansionist megalomania, totally in the sense of the Megale Idea, was not common knowledge.

Even at that time, the newspaper was so presumptuous as to write about a "unification" of (Albanian North) "Epirus" and (Macedonian) "Macedonia" with the Greek motherland. However, in 1886, it did not foresee either that Greece would one day reach out for Thrace and even East Thrace and the Asiatic mainland, for Anatolia – although Greeks had lived there long before the appearance of the Seljuks and even in pre-Byzantine and pre-Roman times, in contrast to Macedonia, so that there a claim would certainly have been more convincing.

(One has only to think of the famous Greek city of Miletus, which was only destroyed after the failure of the Ionian revolt in the Persian Wars and later finally wiped out by Alexander the Great, or of Ephesus, which was only turned to ruins by the Goths in the third century A.D. as well as by earthquakes in the fourth and seventh centuries.)

It was not long before the new demands of the Megale Press influenced the King, who, after completing the first tasks, now made them into his own goal.

As far as the number of Greeks living in Macedonia is concerned – and this information was considered a fundamental criterion at that time as well as after 1991 – the Greek cause suffered a severe setback a few years later in the form of a realistic disclosure. On one of his regular visits to Vienna, King George not only carried on talks with Kaiser Franz-Josef but also again with Foreign Minister Count Kálnoky. Ambassador Prince Reuß heard from the latter that he had not detected any more of the "high-flying Greater Greece ideas" in what the king said; George had not even spoken about Crete.

"His complaints had been, namely, in reference to the church situation in Macedonia, where the Greek element got a raw deal, and Bulgarian interference was encouraged by the Turkish government. Finally, His Majesty had to admit to the Minister that there were actually very few Greeks in Macedonia."[386]

An unexpected confession by the Greek king about the real situation in Macedonia, which still has its validity up to the present day. (Background: the Greeks used to count all Slavs who had to go to Greek churches as "Greeks", i. e. as Greek tax payers!)

From the well informed level of Count Kálnoky, it follows that - other than could have been feared - the brain-washing with the constantly repeated false claims about the supposed ethnic and historical rights of Greece or the other Balkan kingdoms to Macedonia at that time (twelve years after the Congress of Berlin) had dulled the mind of the Austrian foreign minister just as little as it had that of Bismarck; in other words, they had not believed the Greek historical misrepresentation.

On the other hand, this case gives the opportunity once more to point out the persistency - or rather the pushiness - of the king in particular, as well as the Greeks in general in their aspirations to be a great power. George did not allow himself to be swayed this time either. Exactly a year later, he popped up in Vienna again. And what does Prince Reuß report from his inquiries at the Austrian foreign minister's?

> "He ... had never heard the King speaking so sensibly and calmly. He was not satisfied with the state of affairs on Crete, and he was happy that things seemed to be beginning to calm down there. His main worries concerned Macedonia, where the Greek element was increasingly being driven out by the Bulgarian element."[387]

Persistence leads to success.

Only six weeks later, the king attracted attention with a meaningful gesture, which stood in close connection with the next intermediate goal for Greece. For the celebration of the coming of age - and of the traditional oath of allegiance - of Crown Prince Constantine in December of 1886,

> "the King" sent "rather significant greetings" to "Crete, Epirus and Macedonia at the court dinner which took place to honour the deputations that came ... from outside the kingdom."[388]

Two years after the celebration of the coming of age, an *artificial cause* was made up due to a lack of a suitable memorial day in order to be able to continue the psychological warfare with statements full of symbolism. King George declared namely,

> "He would abdicate if his brother, Prince Waldemar of Denmark, were chosen to be the Prince of Bulgaria,"[389]

although according to a report of the Envoy, Le Maistre,

> "as far as I know, nobody has been talking recently about a renewed candidacy of the prince in question for the throne of the Bulgarian Principality." ... "There's no doubt any more that any justification" [for a candidacy by his brother] "is completely unfounded."[389]

Nevertheless, the king took the opportunity of his own manipulation of the facts as the occasion to proclaim his patriotic stance in this matter:

> "Since conflicts with him" [Waldemar in Sofia] "about Macedonia would be inevitable then."

(Waldemar often had to be the scapegoat in such little games.) This willingness for self-sacrifice in the interest of the new national concern of the Greeks demands proper respect. Thus, it is hardly any surprise that the report continues with:

> This remark by the king sufficed for "a crowd of Greek Macedonians ... to gather who wanted to show their gratitude by cheering for the pan-Hellenic ethos which was brought to light again on this occasion."[389]

The envoy commented about that part of the press reports which "was blown up as much as possible" with the remark that Prince Waldemar's candidacy was only invented "anyway for the purpose of this demonstration". The commentator did not allow himself to be fooled by the press as to the size of the demonstration:

> "As an eye-witness and ear-witness of the same, I can, however, assure you that it turned out to be extremely weak and of no importance whatsoever."[389]

This Greek policy of deception has been continued in more or less increasing or decreasing waves up to the present day.

2.3.7 Greek policy on minorities: Romanian cultural policy would hinder the Graecization of Macedonia.

There is a report from Bucharest from those years which allows interesting insights into the long-term Greek plans in connection with Macedonia.

In the report, it is confirmed that Romanian committees were attempting to encourage the national feelings of their fellow tribesmen in Macedonia, the Macedonian Wallachians [Vlachs], by donations for cultural matters. The Romanian government denies, namely, that it was looking for political influence with the Vlachs in Macedonia, but they were, nonetheless, sympathetic towards the cultural endeavours of the committees. Even this attitude, though, was

> "felt" [in Athens] "as an especially hostile one, since it was perceived that it would hinder a later Hellenization of Macedonia."[390]

There, this term appears again. Greece did not even bother to claim that Macedonia was inhabited by Greeks and that, for this reason, it had the right to this region. Rather, Athens acted completely soberly on the basis of the actual situation that the Macedonians were not Greeks and did not speak Greek, so that they would simply have to be Hellenized one day when Greece would had conquered the country.

> *This inhumane policy by the mother of European democracy has been violently pursued in northern Greece for the last 90 years and not only towards the Macedonian minority but also towards the Albanian and Turkish ones, as well as some dozen other minorities. (Compare ch. 1.3.3)*

Weithmann says about this:

> "The Slavs are described as 'Slavophone Greeks' by Athens, and so, without the status of being a minority, they have been exposed to rigorous pressure to become Hellenized up to the present day."[391]

One would have expected that the Council of Europe and human rights organizations would look into the "rigid assimilation policy" and the situation of the minorities in Greece in a publicly discernible and sustained manner.

Allegedly around the year 2000, a noticeably more objective attitude by the Greek government on minority issues[392] emerged. There has been very little of this to be noticed in the media and in the European public. Christian Voss places great hopes in the "Athenian journalist Tasos Kostopoulos"; not only because the latter wrote a very factual monograph "The Forbidden Language – State Suppression of Slavic Dialects in Greek Macedonia" (Athens: Mavri Lista 2000). His hopes are based, moreover, on the fact that this book "has ranked in the Greek bestseller list for months". For him that seems

> "to be an indication for the momentary process of reappraisal that Greek society is going through."[392]

Voss also mentioned the political formation of the Slavic minority in northern Greece after 1989 in the "Macedonian Organization for Balkan Prosperity" (MAKIVE) and the "RAINBOW" Party (Greek: "Ouranio toxo").

This author would more than like to join Voss in his hopes, but remains for the most part sceptical until proven wrong regarding an approval by the Greek government for "the setting-up of a Slavic-language radio station" and "Slavic-language schools", and more still about the hoped-for "solution to the tiresome dispute with the Republic of Macedonia about its name ("FYROM") 2002". He feels confirmed in his scepticism by the Greek reaction to "the USA refraining from the use of the term FYROM in the ICC Agreement" [International Court of Justice] with Macedonia in the summer of 2003. (Compare the Neue Züricher Zeitung of 4th July, 2003, p. 3)

The author's scepticism requires an explanation:
He has set himself the task in this book of seeking signs of the separate identity of the Macedonians. The book has shown which fundamental goal was planned long before

the actual conquest of Macedonia in Greece, Bulgaria and Serbia for the time after the annexation – and which was implemented exactly as planned:
While the Ottomans strove to exercise their power freely, to accumulate looted riches, and to exploit the people as beasts of burden, and carried this concept through with force and draconian punishments but otherwise allowed their slaves to maintain their own language, religion, and the customs of their tradition (which, as was already mentioned, has been wrongly considered as tolerance by interested persons even today) from the very beginning the intention of the Greeks, Bulgarians and Serbs went far beyond this "primitive" level of taking possession through conquest. As was already described elsewhere, the Greeks did not only want to take the Macedonian land and people "into their possession", striving by all possible means to convert both, the Slavic people and their territory, into their permanent property! To accomplish that, they had to – unlike the Turk who were much too indifferent towards the despised Christians – also take possession of the souls of these people. In order to achieve this difficult goal, their identity first had to be destroyed.

Such an ambitious goal can only be attained after years, decades of systematic work at oppressing. The rights of minorities and human rights hinder such a process considerably. That is why in the 20th century Greece met all international efforts in this direction with the greatest possible, but still practicable resistance in order to avoid such obligations and not to drag out the forced assimilation of the Macedonians in northern Greece any longer, the end of which was already foreseeable. Then, only at the end of this process would the world have to accept the Hellenic claim that Macedonia had not become Greek only in 1913 - rather, *was forced to* become - but instead, had also always been Greek *before* 1913. Who could refute this assertion then, and above all, who would profit then from any right that was gained?
A *"Republic of Macedonia"* though, *even if* it or exactly *because* it only covers a part of the old Macedonian territory, disturbs the process of the absolute claim for the Greeks' exercise of power over an alien people, not only marginally or on the surface but *fundamentally!* The Greek concept, whereby there is one and only one Macedonia - a Greek one - is most strongly affected (and this is obvious to all nations of the UN) by the existence of the *Name "Macedonia"* in connection with another state, the Slavic state Macedonia, which is not Greek. What does "affected" mean! "Affected" is not an adequate term for the effect that the existence of a Republic of Macedonia has on the Greek claim for a single Macedonia which is Greek: the Greek concept is not only affected by the existence of the state of the Republic of Macedonia, more precisely it is cancelled, it is shattered – it is totally ruined!

That is why Greece, even if it can no longer overrun the Macedonian people and their state with war in our time, will do its utmost to fight against the name of this neighbour with all means and to extinguish it. Only then would the Greek plan for the *destruction of the identity of the Macedonian people* have prospects of succeeding. It does not seem to bother anyone in Athens that Greece would first have to make the despised Slavs into Greeks to achieve this goal.
> It is imperative for the international community to prevent this crime! In the first place, the European states of the EU, the European Council and the OSCE are obligated to defend the historic truth and the Western system of values.

2.3.8 A Greek Ex-Premier sounds out the partitioning of Macedonia

After the Greek Prime Minister Trikupis had set up the visit of the Bulgarian Prince Alexander to Greece in 1883 (which, by the way, was used by Athens to ingratiate itself with the Turks by passing on to them the Bulgarian expansion plans that were learned on this occasion), he undertook as Ex-Premier in 1891 a personal initiative in Serbia and Bulgaria.

General-Consul Baron von Wangenheim reports,

> Prime Minister Stambulow "refused both to participate in the common action suggested and to agree to the delimitation question."[393]

Apparently he hoped, as was already explained above, to achieve the longed-for Bulgarian goal via autonomy for Macedonia, namely, to be able to reserve the whole province for Bulgaria which Sofia had already possessed for three months in 1878. That's why Stambulow's assumption that,

> "Serbs and Greeks apparently had the feeling that they were losing terrain in Macedonia step by step," sounds quite conclusive.

He did not hesitate either to accuse the Greeks of having inhumane feelings:

> "Trikupis did not show any interest whatsoever in the lot of the Macedonian population as such, and did not want to know anything about the suggestion of pursuing an improvement in their situation in the sense of Article XXIII of the Treaty of Berlin."[393]

Beginning in 1878, the famous Article XXIII was the lever of the Cretans, Macedonians and Thracians to keep reminding the Sultan and the Porte about the promised reforms, regarding the equality of the Christians with the Moslems and about the elimination of numerous discriminations in the judicial system and in the administration – which were never implemented by the Turks or only in homoeopathic doses.

Ambassador von Radowitz in Constantinople also reported about the event of the visit of Mr. Trikupis to Sofia on the basis of a talk with the Bulgarian Envoy Natschewitsch:

> "Unfortunately, Mr. Trikupis did not disclose a more exact plan about the proposed partitioning of Macedonia among the various inhabitants. The knowledge about this ethnographic feat would have been especially interesting."[394]

A fine irony.

The Greek Ex-Premier surely possessed the knowledge about the ethnic make-up of the population of Macedonia (at least from the Greek Orthodox Church), but he could not have been interested in announcing how small the number of Greeks in Macedonia actually was. Finally, the German ambassador repeats a further remark of his Bulgarian colleague, who had declared in Constantinople,

> "that the Bulgarian government had refused all unreasonable demands of the Greek Ex-Premier and had referred to its common bond with Turkey."

One infamy is worth another one. (The Bulgarians had not forgotten the earlier Greek betrayal so quickly.)

In addition, a report from London is cited. The chargé d'affaires, von Metternich, quoted what the correspondent of the "Standard" had to report about the Macedonian question from Vienna:

> "Mr. Trikoupis was supposed to have sounded out a possible partitioning of Macedonia in Sofia and Belgrade."[395]

Would Greece ever have dreamed of publicly discussing the question of the partitioning of Macedonia, or even have consulted with other (Slavic) governments about it, if

even just a tiny piece of that region had ever belonged to Greece? Completely out of the question.
The rest of the quotation confirms what is already known:
> "Belgrade most willingly agrees with this thought and has declared itself satisfied with it as long as the region known as 'Old Serbia' falls to Serbia." (!) "In contrast, the Ex-Minister did not have any success in Sofia."[395]

A report from Belgrade is quoted as the last source on the Trikupis trip, in which Envoy von Bray succeeded in making a fitting formulation:
Of all people, the Greek Ex-PM should have known,
> "how absolutely unthinkable a peaceful settlement among all the small politically and ethnographically heterogeneous Balkan states appears as each one of them lays claim to more or less the whole European part of Turkey, and much more, as its legitimate possession."[396]

Despite the brilliant formulation, it becomes clear that even at that time those responsible in Europe were completely aware of the injustice which was becoming apparent with the preparations for the Balkan League and the Balkan Wars as well as the partitioning of Macedonia. But no emperor, no king, no government, and no statesman were to be found who would put an end to the impending injustice against Macedonia, Thrace, and Epirus.
On the contrary: at the insistence of Greece, the monarchs even joined in the sell-off of the Macedonian people and their territory to the three Balkan states.

2.3.8.1 Background information (3)
King George's finance und family policies

After the hypothesis was set up at the beginning about a Greek influence on the European monarchs as to the fate of Macedonia, this train of thought must be pursued further and substantiated at intervals as an instrument of this policy – parallel to the development of the Balkan League. That is why an overview of several years will be fitted in here again as a continuation of the sections *"Background information (1) and (2)"* about the travels of King George and about the intensification of the dynastic family ties of the Greek royal house to successfully obtain support for the Greek policy of expansion. Even if it seems to interrupt the chronological flow of the stages of the Balkan League, it constitutes an integral part of the evaluation of Greek policy in connection with Macedonia.

In contrast to what the people believed and also in contrast to what many parliamentarians thought, the Greek king had not (only) carried out his numerous trips abroad as pleasure-trips (with the exception of his stays at the health resort, Aix-les-Bains; the amorous goings-on there were food for gossip at many a European court – apparently the price he had to pay for being so well-known, which from all appearances he calmly paid). In fact, George was constantly endeavouring to represent the interests of Greece, i.e., in the first place, to bring the desires for a Greater Greece closer to their realization.
As was already mentioned, George had made a stopover on his way back from his annual holiday in 1890[397], and also in 1891, for talks in Austria-Hungary among other places. On his last visit there, he only returned to Athens at the end of November.[398] Even though comments can be gathered from numerous texts that the king went on holiday every year, there are no records available for the year 1892. However, in the

summer of 1893, he was drawn to his native country, Denmark, again. Who was also lingering there in summer retreat? His sister Dagmar/Maria F. with her husband, Tsar Alexander III.[399] Well, quite ideal conditions for setting up at least moral and political if not military support for the Greek expansion plans.

But even the ideal conditions of a Danish summer retreat were valid only with reservations. For, as can be remembered, certain Russian expectations had already been placed in King George and his Greeks; and only two years before in 1891, the "exalted relative" from St. Petersburg had brought up the subject of "Greece becoming a member of the Russian-French Alliance". George pulled back though, since entering into obligations that might possibly cost something was not a Greek thing.[400]

>Nevertheless, it is remarkable how far the planning went so soon after the Franco-Russian Convention of 1892 and which obvious tendency it showed from the start – against Austria-Hungary, and, thus, also against Germany.

That's why it was necessary for George to manoeuvre carefully, even while on his summer holiday.

In the autumn of 1895, George visited not only Aix-les-Bains but also Paris for the first time not only incognito, as Ambassador zu Münster expressedly emphasized. At the official reception and at the state dinner given for him by the President of the Republic in the Elysée, he promptly attempted to do justice to the matter that concerned him and "to sway France ... in favour of Greece."[401] Incidentally it was also a matter of money. George was at pains to assure the French government that Greece's creditors would get their money back through the repayment of a loan – a position which by no means found undivided approval at home in Athens. Taking the Greek parliamentarians into account, that maybe does not sound too kosher – but the king himself was also not always an aristocratic man-of-honour in his personal business practices.

Thus for example, a report from the Envoy von Waecker-Gotter arrived in Berlin from Belgrade in March of 1897, the two short sentences of which should be quoted:

> "From financial circles, I hear that the King of Greece, who is known to be a successful administrator of his private fortune, had gone into very considerable speculations on a slump before the outbreak of the current confusion." [It is known to have been about Crete again.] "As it probably concerned Greek and Turkish funds, it can perhaps be determined on another occasion if this claim is based on the truth or not."[402]

Could George have speculated against "his" Greece?

Well, he would certainly do it again, or wouldn't he...? Yes, of course! One recognizes very clearly in the margin of the handwritten report the familiar *"Donnerwetter"* in the straight script of Wilhelm II., and in fact in view of the seriousness of the misconduct with the still careful but, nonetheless, hardly flattering addition: "That would be more than vile!"[402]

The information system of the Foreign Ministry worked smoothly. A confirmation for the still uncertain information from Belgrade did not take long in coming: Ambassador von Eulenburg was able to contribute a remark of the Viennese head of the House of Rothschild:

> "Baron Albert Rothschild said it was a fact that King George had worked hard in speculations on a slump on the Parisian Market shortly before the outbreak of the Crete crisis and earned very well."[403]

When any everyday annoyances occurred, the Kaiser liked to rant and carry on; this time, though, a short but scathing "Yuck!" written in the margin was enough for him.

Considering all the malicious things that were said about Wilhelm II after the First World War, the fact should be recognized that for the German Kaiser and Prussian King, with his upright and principled nature, who was conscientious, hard-working, God-fearing, even pious, and, yes, also punctual, just like each one of his reliable, guaranteed incorruptible and loyal public servants, a roguish trick against the interests of one's own state like the speculation described above would have been totally unthinkable.
Exactly this quality seems to be one of the reasons for the insatiable yearning of those less steadfast characters who have to belittle the high and for them unattainable Prussian virtues of the Kaiser.

George went into detail with regard to politics with the German ambassador in Paris:
> "The agitation between Moslems and Christians is taking on a very disturbing character, especially in Macedonia and on the island of Crete. There, the whole population demanded the same concessions as those granted to the Armenians..."[401] ("Macedonia"!)

Also in that year, it was still the year 1895, George together with Queen Olga only returned to Athens after an absence of three-and-a-half months.[404]

Another generation-determined consolidation of the Greek-Russian dynastic ties was added in the spring of 1896: Princess Marie, the fifth child and the second, and at this point the only, daughter of the Greek royal couple (after the early death of their older daughter Alexandra, who was married to the Russian Grand Prince Paul [she was murdered in St. Petersburg in 1891]) became engaged to Grand Prince George Michailovich[406]. The wedding did not take place until April of 1900 for various reasons [that especially today would find their enthusiastic readers via the appropriate popular press but which would deviate too far from the topic of his book].[407] The author will simply mention here that King George was soon supposed to have pursued a cancellation of the engagement,
> "after the Russian government had followed a policy which did not conform with the wishes of King George."[408]

Well, look – our little king! He did not shy away from exerting moral pressure, as a little partner, on the gigantic Russian Empire with the help of his dynastic ties. This time, though, he failed. There are sometimes also disadvantages with family ties, which one cannot choose, in contrast to friendships.
At the beginning of the year 1900, the engagement which had been broken off in the meantime was again renewed and the marriage was carried out in such a "fabulous hurry", that it caused Envoy von Plessen to characterize King George in this way:
> "His nature generally tends towards deciding very fast, without bothering very much about other considerations, and towards having his decisions carried out immediately. It was characteristic of him to rush into this event in such a conspicuous way."[410]

So now, two children and a granddaughter of the Danish royal house had – if the Austrian royal and imperial expression is permitted here – got hitched together with the Russian royal family. And, that was not the last one yet.
> But, there was still a lot to do: Greece's path to the annexation of Macedonia and western Thrace was definitely not easy – on the contrary, it was long, steep, and rocky.

A part of the Greek press was *against* this additional connection of the Greek royal house with the Peterhof. A marriage of Princess Marie with the Serbian king would

have been preferred because of the geographical proximity, the usefulness and the manageability. That was probably not such an unfounded idea. That Greece would ever come into question as the heir to the throne of the Tsars was surely pretty unlikely. Anyway, entirely different arguments were being dealt with in the background: (1) there was a Russian Slavic-association that agitated against the Greek interests in the Balkans, and (2) the Russian Tsar had supposedly prevented Crete from being united with Greece.
Yet, the real reason was that the Greek government wanted to save the dowry of 400000 drachmas (approx. 100 000 euros).[411] Cherchez l' .... argent !

A human, all too human story can be inferred from the same report that moves the affectations of aristocratic behaviour at court pleasantly into the background: when in this summer of 1896, just shortly before the afore-mentioned Crete crisis, another big family reunion took place in Copenhagen, where were not enough suites of rooms even in the Danish palace for all the guests. No problem: the Russian Empress Dowager Maria Fjodorovna, whose husband Alexander III had died about one and a half years before, and Princess Alexandra of Wales, whose husband Edward, who was then 59, would still have to wait another five years to ascend the throne, slept in one room: after all, as children of the Danish royal couple, they were sisters.[411]
Over and above the charming local colour, this little anecdote is a convincing sign of what a deep insight into the life and the doings at the courts the (German) diplomats had.

Before George went on his summer holiday in 1896, there was another of those tiresome parliamentary debates about his long absences and "the conduct of the King was ... once again subject to sharp criticism".[412] The representative, Petropoulakis, pointed out,
> "that in former times His Majesty King Otto only returned once in the course of his thirty-year reign to his old homeland, while King George is absent for many months every year. ... One ... often cited reason as an explanation, that the king serves the Greek state interest considerably through maintaining close and family ties to other courts is invalid, since, as is well-known, the interests of nations in this day and age are not served by such bonds."

This bureaucratic and short-sighted way of thinking was not only unfair, but also incorrect. Over and above that, the representative disqualified himself with the example he gave as an explanation:
> "When the German Kaiser came to Athens a few years ago, it was generally thought that this event would turn out to be an advantage for Greece." ... "But after he made a visit to the Sultan from here, this hope was immediately destroyed."[412]

National vanity as a guide-line of political views! It's as if Wilhelm (assuming for once the case that he might - even at that time - have wanted to arrange something in some way for the Greeks) should not, then at all times have gone to see the Sultan!
Parliamentary debates about King George's travel activities were - unjustly - regularly on the agenda.
One must ask why the king had hidden his light so much under a bushel in reference to his international pressure attempts solely *in the interests of Greece,* even though he could have aroused such a big impression among his subjects with only a few other arguments, as with his efforts to achieve the enlargement of Greece. He must have known, however, that he was walking on very thin ice. The possible attempt to receive

praise from the government and in parliament for his efforts, and in fact for achievements whose results were not yet foreseeable and, as far as Macedonia was concerned, even pretty improbable, could have brought him into discredit with his relatives in the European dynasties. That is why he apparently rather preferred to profit from his thick skin when, at regular intervals, Parliament kept a close eye on his long "working holidays". A couple of years later the *casus* was embarrassingly dragged out into the open (by Representative Pop):

> "For 45 years now, the Crown has been orbiting around in Europe every year with the punctuality of an astronomical phenomenon. Since 1870, the King has been travelling every year on an average of 3 ½ months, so that he has spent 11 years and 11 ½ months of his entire reign in travelling. ... The King goes only once at Easter to the barracks to amuse himself and asks the soldiers: "when will your sufferings come to an end?" By that he is implying that the service under the flag of the fatherland means suffering. Only once in 40 years did the King make his way to the arsenal. In order to see if the steam-pipes on his yacht "Amphitrite" were properly installed. (Applause in the auditorium and in the visitor's galleries ...)" "While the Greek people were in fear, the King of the Hellenes functioned, with the consent of the government, as the President of the Committee for the Flower Carnival in Aix-les-Bains and attended the dog-show there...."[413]

Did the representatives Pop, Patsurakos und Michaleas offer their apologies to their sovereign later (1912/13), after the - totally unjustified - annexation?
The last parliamentary debate took place (as far as is clear from the records) a good year before George's - violent - death.[413]

There is a report from the year 1897 which shows that the insinuation that the dynastic relationships had been used for political power games was not only a hypothesis. Ambassador von Kiderlen reported from Copenhagen:

> "How very much one is accustomed here at court to consider the representation of Danish family interests to be a duty of Russia is proven by some remarks which His Royal Highness the Crown Prince of Denmark ... made. 'My sister', i.e., the Empress Dowager of Russia, writes that she is not able to do anything for my brother George, because the interests of big politics are always given as a pretext. Her son, i.e., His Majesty the Tsar of Russia, also suffers very much from the fact that he took action against Greece like that, but he allowed himself to be ensnared by [the Russian foreign minister] Count Muravieff.' His Royal Highness also added: 'Who would have thought that of Muravieff! We have always treated him so well here.' "[414]!

This is another confirmation that providing each other with political advantages was one of the habits of the monarchs. Absolute power was even at that time in the process of disappearing - especially in affairs that needed international agreement - less spectacular actions could still be pursued (and still can today even without monarchs).

It should also be mentioned in this connection that an uncle of the Greek king actually judged the crisis about Crete at that time to be so critical that he even regarded George as a "king in exile". Ambassador von Kiderlen describes the "activities" of Prince Hans von Glücksburg as follows:

> He "was busy not only with questions of residence ..., but also told, with a wretched expression on his face, how his nephew, if he left his present post, vis-à-vis de rien (*face to face with nothing*) would simply be dependent on the pension that the Tsar of Russia gives to Queen Olga."

Ambassador v. Kiderlen comments very soberly on this lament:

> "This is contradicted by the fact that King George has bought a house in Copenhagen whose interest would provide revenue. He also has an estate on Zealand. His savings in Greece are generally considered quite high."[414]

The agreement that Ambassador v. Metternich recalled in a later report from London was also important here:

> "Russia, France and England had promised him, on his accession to the throne, an annual pension of 12000 pounds, but only in the event that he would be removed from office, not ... if he voluntarily abdicated."[415]

The protecting powers would most reluctantly have liked to have seen the latter because they

> "had had certain difficulties already after the banishment of King Otto to find a suitable successor."[416]

A follow-up report from v. Kiderlen tells us where the actual fears of the Danish royal clan lay:

> "Above all, it is feared here that King George, forced by the Great Powers to retreat, could abdicate and then pitch his tents here, ... meddle in politics here and spread 'parliamentarian' ideas. ... This fear of interference ... contributes considerably to the loving attention that is given to making sure that he keeps his present throne."[417]

This "worry" was not completely unfounded. After an audience in Athens, Consul General Klehmet had repeated, in fact, the intelligent and pragmatic remark King George had made about the subject of the - half-hearted - Prussian reform of voting rights at the beginning of the 20th century:

> "In the end, there will be no alternative to granting universal suffrage."[418]

As for *"the parliamentarian ideas"*, King George must be given a lot of credit for broadening his knowledge on this topic during his reign (in contrast to the other family members in Copenhagen, Petersburg, Berlin und London). A few years before, a minor occurrence had taken place at his court which showed the (no: all) monarchy's dislike for parliamentary system. Amused, some might have passed it on to others as a bon mot. In the end, many a state has paid a price for the deep-rooted stance behind it:

For the baptism of the first son of the Crown Prince, i. e. George's grandchild, Constantine's mother-in-law and, consequently, the grandmamma of his son, the "Empress Dowager Friedrich" (III) [Victoria], Sophie's (and Wilhelm's) mother, came to Athens.

> "On this occasion ... the so often recently mentioned Dr. Hatsiskos was introduced to Her Majesty. Her Royal Highness, if I may say this confidentially, greeted her daughter's obstetrician with the question: "Are you a deputy?" and dismissed him after a few moments."[419]

This anecdote derives its real piquancy from the fact that Victoria was, after all, English and not only that but the daughter of Queen Victoria. Aside from this, she had continually harried her son Wilhelm (II) and (in an insistent, un-English way) proudly praised the tradition of democratic parliamentarianism in the constitutional monarchy in her home country in contrast to backward Prussia....

As a contribution to avoiding George's all too early surfacing in Copenhagen

> "the philhellenism" ... in Denmark ... "that is promoted from above bears more and more opulent blossoms, which remind one of the 20s of this century. For several days now, an appeal is being published in the local papers which calls for contributions for the suffering Cretans as a sign of the admiration for Denmark's royal son and his heroic nation."

The Envoy von Plessen in Athens did not allow himself to be fooled as regards the chronicle of an announced *abdication*. Instead he recalled that even during the time of his first stay in Athens "18 years ago" rumours about the abdication of the king ... "even for the slightest reason ... were repeatedly spread" and, consequently, "could not generally be taken seriously".[419] He admitted, though, that this time there was a more urgent reason, and both the King and the Prime Minister Rhallis "definitely had to avoid" a new war with Turkey now.

"The government ... does not have the backing of the assurance of support from any other side, even if repeated and encouraging promises seem ... to have reached here, namely, from the noble relatives of the Royal Family in London and Petersburg."[420]

It has already been pointed out that not only King George attached great importance to his regular holidays, and that he constantly made use of them – also in the interests of the country whose crown he wore. Queen Olga also travelled to her beloved Russian homeland with the same reliable regularity, where she, likewise, did not remain inactive. It can surely be taken as proof of her good standing and her popularity at the Tsar's court that, at the command of Tsar Alexander III, her cousin, her photo had to hang next to that of the Russian Tsar and Tsarina, in the dining-rooms of all the Russian ships cruising both the Black Sea and the Sea of Azov.[421]

Well, if that's not a sign of Russia's good relations to the Greek court! The Greek king knew how to dutifully return this gesture: On the occasion of his imperial Russian brother-in-law's birthday (after all, Alexander was married to George's sister Dagmar/Maria F.), he gave a banquet in Athens to which, for the first time, the complete Russian legation as well as the consulate, the officers of the Russian ships lying at anchor off Piraeus and the representatives of the Orthodox Church as well as the royal household were invited.[422]

Here the envoy in Athens, von Chirshky, should have his turn in making a few remarks about *Queen Olga*. He began his report with: "the Greek Queen ... has really remained a Russian Grand Princess."[423] (To properly appreciate the value of this assessment, one must consider that the report was written 22 years after her marriage to King George and her move to Athens!) She wears

"her heart on her sleeve for Russia ... and (turns) her favour to everything that is Russian with little consideration for her duties as Queen and Greek ... Last spring and winter, this Russian cult was increased even more by the presence of Princess Alexandra and her fiancé of that time, Grand Prince Paul, as well as the Russian war-ships that appeared in his entourage. Almost every day, some of the naval officers dined at court; and the Queen never failed to appear at the parties that were organized on board the ships. The presence there of members of other foreign diplomatic missions was not desired, and not even the Greek Minister of Naval Affairs received an invitation."[424]

At the Greek New Year's celebration, Queen Olga exchanged New Year's greetings with each sailor on the Russian ships, but "not one single member of the court" took part in the Greek Orthodox New Year's celebration "that was celebrated annually with great pomp in the Metropolitan Cathedral of Athens". At the departure of the princess, the doyenne and the ladies of the diplomatic corps, at their wish, were invited to a reception, but the Russian ladies were received especially with "a pointed disregard for any diplomatic tradition or for the politeness that was due to other countries".

"The King is personally no friend of the Muscovites; he allows his wife, though, a completely free hand in this direction. Even if the Greeks find it painful that their Queen has shown no interest whatsoever in the country, it cannot be said that she is unpopular. Some value her resolution, a quality in which she is far superior to her royal husband; the others praise her kind-heartedness."[424, 425]

The disregard of the Danish-Russian court for the Greek Orthodox New Year's celebration was no exception. Years later the Greek press complained about "the absence of the Royal Prince at the official festive church service on the national holiday" as an "unpardonable contempt for the most holy moment of the nation." In another paper, the princesses also became a target of the critics:

> "Unfortunately, the Princesses have not got to know the Greek women yet." ... "None of our Princesses has become Greek. They speak French, think German, behave British, walk American, dress Austrian, and despise everything Greek."[426]

2.3.9 Crete and the Greek-Turkish War

The island of Crete - in Italian, or more precisely in Venetian times: Candia - had developed into one of the trouble spots of the history of Greece since its independence. To make matters worse, it was also blown up into a central problem of the bilateral relations on the part of the Turks and even by the Young Turks. (It was conquered by the Ottomans only in the 6th Turkish-Venetian War, which, after all, lasted from 1645 to 1669.) The Greek claims to Crete were made definitely clear to the Sultan, the Porte, and the Great Powers from the very beginning, so that no one could remain in the dark about the long-term goals of Athens in connection with Crete.

After the bad experiences Greece had had with the Great Powers due to its unseemly haste up to then in connection with Crete, the warnings from competent - and friendly - mouths should have actually sufficed. Or should one imply that the Sphakiots (the restless inhabitants of the Cretan high plateau Sphakia) actually found themselves constantly (and of their own accord) prepared to revolt without the influence of the Greek mainland? Hard to imagine.

A comparison of the Greek approach towards Macedonia shows clear differences: at the beginning, Macedonia played no role whatsoever in the Greek strategy and was only gradually mentioned when southern Epirus and Thessaly began to move within reach.

Unlike in the case of Crete, Greece had no ethnic or historically legal right to Macedonia.

A new revolt broke out on Crete in 1896 with a further proclamation of Enosis with Greece. The Austro-Hungarian envoy in Athens, Baron Kosjak, returned from his holiday in Vienna with instructions to make it clear to the Greek leaders that Vienna saw the proposed (renewed!) international blockade as the only means "to loosen the Cretan entanglements and to obtain the necessary reforms for the Christians." The Greek cabinet would have to bear the responsibility for the consequences all by itself,

> if it "is too weak to stop the constant support for the insurgents on Crete with weapons and ammunition."[427]

The German envoy, von Plessen, was able to further supplement this argumentation in his relevant report: in connection with the hypocritical way in which King George and Prime Minister Delyannis "branded" and described the desertion of Greek officers and their crossing over to Crete as "a grave criminal act", he assessed this course of events with the words:

> "The remarks ... definitely do not rule out, in my humble opinion, the possibility that the officers in question and perhaps also others who might follow their example, will (one day) be highly acclaimed as national heroes and return to the Greek army."[427]

The rare unanimity of the Europeans was only broken by the conduct of the Russian representative in Athens. Mr. Bakmetieff, who in this respect consistently represented the traditional political line of Russia,

> "loves to describe the whole blockade as an absurdity and to make fun of the plan which would only lead to watching the slaughter on the island from the ships with binoculars."

Actually, the patience of the Great Powers with the Ottoman Empire and its atrocities against the, as always, oppressed Christian population is aggravatingly inconsistent. As was already emphasized several times, it can only be put down to the reciprocal envy and ill-will - also in part to caution and mistrust - of the Europeans among themselves. Otherwise, they could, in fact, have put a swift end to Turkish atrocities on European soil and with very little effort. (Constantinople could have been under the joint administration of all the Great Powers then, as the Russians had suggested several times.) That is why one cannot simply dismiss it when the Greek king stated "that the ambassadors in Constantinople bore the guilt for the delay in settling the Cretan question."[427]

George varied the Russian idea of an international administration of Constantinople in a few years later, as he himself explained to the German ambassador in Vienna, Count Wedel, during another visit to Austria in 1903:

"Constantinople with the bordering regions (i.e., "straits") should be declared a free city." "As I interjected at that point that as experience shows such small state-entities tended to usually become the spoils of a powerful neighbour if there is some upheaval, His Majesty came out with the somewhat amazing remark that one could in fact entrust America with its protection, whereupon I replied that it seemed more than doubtful to me if it were in the interest of Europe to smooth the way as it were by force for transatlantics who were so keen on going into action anyway to meddle in affairs this side of the Atlantic."[428,429]

How prescient !

It is worthwhile taking a look at the fusion of interests of the European monarchies in the new Crete crisis. The Danish-Greek dynastic network, which had spread itself through Europe, based on Danish, English, Russian and German marriages, should not be linked to the benefit of Greece for nothing. Ambassador von Kiderlen reported from Copenhagen:

"Directly after Russia seemed to want to put itself at the forefront of the anti-Greek campaign for a moment, King George sent two urgent letters to his sisters, the widowed Russian Empress" [Dagmar] "and the Princess of Wales" [Alexandra], "with the latter of whom he is especially intimate. ... That the Russian ideas, proposed in Vienna, of co-operation of the continental powers" [against Greece] "were dropped, can be traced back here to those two letters."[430] !

This event proves, to all intents and purposes, that – apart from the author's above implied limits to the scope of monarchical interventions in official foreign policy – even important international decisions of big-time politics, including military ones, were still being made on the basis of family considerations.

A prime example of *dynastic wheelings and dealings*!

That may be true but: the love - or the capacity - of Tsar Nicholas, who had only been on the throne for two years at the outbreak of the new conflict, did not go so far as the Greeks chose to interpret from the Russian gestures that they thought they could consider using this love as the thin end of the wedge wherewith to enlist greater Russian support. It was important to be economical with one's requests for 'friendship' service even towards kindred courts. The Tsar could not foresee - and, therefore, could not avert the consequences either - that the Greeks would soon rush into another military adventure, which would violate agreements under international law.

In the end, it was not "only" a question of the above-mentioned "branded" Greek "deserters". In fact, an official Greek expedition corps landed on Crete in February of 1897. As great as the joy of the Danish public was about the landing ("here one feels sort of related with the 'Hellenes' through the royal family"), "the disappointment about the aftermath was so much the greater."[430]

In v. Kiderlen's report it goes on:
> "Since energetic efforts were made from here in St. Petersburg in favour of Greece, I would gather that His Majesty King Christian, as I have learned from reliable sources, has expressed in very intimate circles that he cannot understand why the Russian Tsar is also letting King George and his family down. After all, King George is a close relative of the Russian Tsar" [indeed, he was the uncle of Tsar Nicholas, since the Danish mother of the Tsar, Maria F. (Dagmar) was George's sister], "and Prince George had even saved his life."[430]

But, which emperor likes to be reminded of such things!
The last remark refers to an adventure in 1891 that the Tsarevitch luckily survived thanks to the commitment of his cousin, Prince George of Greece, the second son of King George and Queen Olga, on a journey together through Asia which also took the two of them to Japan.[431] The journey of the then twenty-three-year-old Nicholas took place three years before the death of his father, Tsar Alexander III. The news that his cousin George had rescued the Tsarevitch from an assassination attempt in Kyoto was at first celebrated in Europe and especially in Greece as a heroic deed,[432] "a new bond which Providence has tied around the two related and intimate dynasties",[433] (and, unfortunately, also published in Athens).
Wilhelm II heard later from his relatives in London that the two young men only got into that critical situation through the "stupid boyish pranks" of George "Hellenicos" (as the Kaiser called the brother-in-law of his sister Sophie in a note in the margin).[434] For that reason, the Russian adjutant had the heir to the Tsar's throne return alone from Vladivostok to Petersburg, while Prince George was brought to Yokohama with a Russian cruiser and from there he was sent home with the post-ship by way of America.[435]
All the same though – George did save his Russian cousin (who, in the end, had to undergo an operation of 1½ hours because of the wound on his head). And for that, he was made "Commander of the Battalion for Mobile Defence" when he returned to Athens after one-year's absence.[436]
Back to Crete.
When the attempt at mediation by the Great Powers, disappointed with Greek stubbornness, failed after the landing on Crete because they could not agree on a common line to take, the Greeks got a little too light-headed and they overreached themselves marching across the border on the continent at the beginning of April of 1897 and invading the Turkish part of Thessaly. Ten days later, the Porte declared war on Greece. Several victorious battles for the Turks led also to their conquering Greek Thessaly. The Turks were already marching towards Athens – so, Greece had to beg for peace in May.
Only then, after the war was as good as over, did the protective hand of the European relatives over the Greek royal dynasty finally become noticeable.

In the meantime in Athens, criticism was pouring in from all sides, most of which came to rest upon the king because he had approved of the invasion – although, as everyone knew, his power over the government was even at that time restricted. Critical remarks about the monarchy in Athens even came from Munich[437]. (For a better understanding of the background for this antipathy, it is helpful to remember that after the overthrow of the Wittelsbach Otto, as King of the Greeks in 1862, i.e. after thirty years' reign, many merchants returned to Germany and Austria, and also many Greek wives of German civil servants or officers came to Germany and stayed there.) Their derogative judgement of George (and they were not alone in their sentiments) culminated, as Envoy von Montgelas reported, in the assessment that George "only thought about making money", for him "only his personal interests were decisive and not the interests of the country".[438]

That was once again only half the truth.

On the other hand, the king had not hesitated to profess to "the man in the street" after the lost war that he had been against the war and that he - unlike the Greeks - would have preferred to accept autonomy for the island.[439]

To make matters worse, the army of Crown Prince Constantine was also defeated by the Turks in Thessaly. Consequently, at the end of April, the Greek royal family was already contemplating evacuation plans, which, however, were not realized.[440] When the truce had to be accepted on 20th May, an invitation to the jubilee celebrations in London came just at the right moment for the royal family, so that Constantine did not have to return to Athens directly from the battlefield with the hope that things would have calmed down in the capital by the time they would return from London.[441] In spite of the despondency and resignation of the inhabitants, they would have no choice but to remember that on appropriate occasions before the war they had shouted huzzas for the war instead of the usual ones for the king: "Long live the war (lenos)"![442]

The envoy, v. Plessen, wrote in a report that the conduct of the crown prince and his brother, Prince Nicholas, was especially disappointing. They

> "did not show the right degree of military courage, energy and initiative, and in decisive moments allowed themselves to be guided by personal considerations rather than by those of military duty and honour."

He added that, "all the same, leading personalities and even the press tried to gloss over this image and to make the entourage and others around the Prince out to be responsible."[443] Insofar, it remains to be hoped that "this impression will soon fade with the fickleness of the general mood". The envoy reported further that the refugees from Crete, Thessaly and Epirus made the Greek residents of Athens clearly aware of the misery of war.

> "Reports multiplied about terrible atrocities, supposedly committed by regular Turkish soldiers on Christian inhabitants of Epirus and Thessaly."[443]

However, when an assassination attempt was made on the King and Princess Marie on February 26th, 1898 [444], and George proved to be quite brave in that critical situation, the war was actually as good as forgotten by the Athenians; the government, the people and the press were full of praise for their king:

> "The King can be thanked for the granting of the war loans, the coming appointment of Prince George as Governor General of Crete, the withdrawal from Thessaly" [by the Turks] "and the sympathy of Europe for Greece, which is beginning anew, and these facts prove what influence he has on the country's fortune."[445]

This praise for the king was by no means undeserved.

Further proof of the protective forces of the pro-Greek dynasties in the background is revealed in the conditions of the Peace Treaty of Constantinople, which was signed on 4th December, 1897. They turned out to be downright mild for Athens. The winner of the war, the Ottoman Empire, had to evacuate Greek Thessaly again! Greece had to pay reparations, so to speak as a fig leaf, and had to accept some adjustments to the borders in Thessaly in favour of Turkey. Fikret Adanir quotes the statement of a baffled English historian:

"Rarely has a victorious power been put off with so little of the fruits of victory; even more rarely has a state so completely defeated as Greece emerged from a war of aggression so lightly penalized."[446]

Nonetheless, the self-confidence of the Turks, as a result of their series of victories, grew so much that they pretended to be especially stubborn in the Crete question.

"Only after there was a terrible outbreak of Moslem fanaticism in Candia on September 6th, 1898, where hundreds of Chrisians were massacred, did the Sultan finally give his consent for a withdrawal from the island and, on 29th November, appointed Prince George of Greece as Lord High Commissioner of Crete, which after that advanced to a vassal state of the Porte, albeit being obliged to pay tribute."[447]

This further triumph of the "family ties" also deserves to be mentioned because the preliminary decision to, one day, appoint Prince George as Governor of Macedonia too would become important. "At any rate", so reported Ambassador v. Kiderlen from Copenhagen in the preliminary stages of the appointment of the prince,

"from here it is being ... worked towards again at full speed in Petersburg".[448]

Meanwhile, this planning was not without controversy in the private circle of the Danish court:

"The young Princes in the family circle have raised the objection ... that Prince George surely could not sincerely swear an oath of loyalty to the Sultan. The young Princes were gravely admonished for this heretical opinion."

On the other hand, their uncle, Prince Hans von Glücksburg, opined,

"that, in the end, political situations sometimes would just necessarily entail a certain 'dishonesty'."[448]

Prince George's father, King George I, hardly had any qualms in regard to Crete, three years before, father George had still reacted sensitively when a discussion took place in the press, after a rumour about the possible abdication of the Bulgarian Prince Ferdinand, whether Prince George should not be considered as a possible successor. Other papers had held this idea to be an insult to the Greek royal family,

"since a Greek Prince cannot be a vassal to Turkey, and they recalled that, before the selection of Prince Ferdinand, there had been talk of nominating Prince Waldemar of Denmark. His Majesty King George had spoken out against this candidacy of his brother, which was impossible considering the different Greek and Bulgarian interests."[449]

That such decisions should be well thought out is clear from the fear of the Russian ambassador, Muravieff, that Prince George, "as the Russian candidate" could provoke the Sultan's ill-will.[450] How very much Tsar Nicholas struggled with this decision is apparent from a further move by the relative camp: "the Grand Princess Xenia, sister of the reigning Tsar of Russia" and Grand Prince Alexander Mikhailovich had come to Copenhagen in the preliminary stages of the deliberations, so that the potential Governor of Crete

could "join the royal couple and could make ... his entrance to the Russian court under their auspices". "When the Prince betakes himself now to Petersburg, Her Majesty, the widowed Tsarina of Russia" [the - Danish - mother of the Tsar and aunt of the 'aspiring Governor', Prince George] "apparently considers the terrain to be well enough prepared for her to play her last trump card, that his 'rescuer' should make a personal appearance to His Majesty Tsar Nicholas."[451]

That the mother of the Grand Princess and Greek Queen Olga, and, consequently, the grandmother of the Crete Pretender, was against his candidacy, as, in general, "definitely not in agreement ... with Greek policy"[452], did not make the decision for Tsar Nicholas easier. This shows, though, how extensive the family interests were and how they sought to make themselves heard in political affairs.

And, thus, the decision was drawn out until the end of the year. Prince George could only take up residence in Candia from February of 1899 as Lord High Commissioner for the Great Powers and execute his regency over Crete. However, later, on the occasion of a visit by the prince to Rome, his adjutant gave the German ambassador, Count Wedel, "a rather dreary description of their existence in Candia."[453] In answer to the ambassador's natural question "why the Prince did not get married", the adjutant said fairly enough that "it was not possible to find a suitable princess for him because of his denomination." (It is clear from a later text, however, that: "it was assumed that George would never marry because of certain tendencies."[454])

People do talk a lot about all kinds of things! Later, in 1907, George belied these rumours and did marry after all – although it was more or less a morganatic marriage. (Some side effects will confirm the rumour, though. See ch. 2.3.9.2)

As Russian "mummies" are, Queen Olga naturally wanted to visit her son in his new position – which was, of course, also the result of her efforts.[455] The meeting was originally supposed to take place on another island, therefore on Greek soil, out of consideration for the Sultan. Her courage (or foolishness?) to go to Crete anyway was rewarded with enthusiastic cheers from the inhabitants there: "Long live our Queen; long live our Mother."[456] (Underlined in the original.)

The Envoy, von Winckler, suspected in private diplomatic correspondence to the state minister in the foreign ministry that the aspirations of Prince George and the Cretans were directed at the

> "creation of an independent Principality of Crete ... and not for an incorporation ... into Greece" because, as he thought, the Cretans, "considering the miserable financial status of Greece, scarcely have any desire to share in the blessings of the Greek government and administration systems."[457] The envoy conceded that "Prince George is certainly too loyal to intrigue against his brother and to drive him from the throne",

but the Cretans and the British (his information was from a certain Sir Edward Law) would simply appoint him. It had apparently been the British who did not want Crown Prince Constantine in Crete, because he

> "did not seem to be such an obedient tool as ... the present king actually is, and as they hope Prince George will be."[457] Prince George is "deep down like a Russian Grand Prince with the patina of an Englishman".

Thus, he had always understood how to make himself popular with his Russian as well as with his English relatives and "sometimes played the English card and sometimes the Russian one ..., depending on which seemed opportune at the moment." (Private diplomatic correspondence to ministry, p. 8.) Then, von Winckler drew the comparison to the "completely characterless ... King", who is "always only thinking about his own advantage and his personal convenience." (Pp. 5 and 6)

Crown Prince Constantine in contrast

> "is German in his whole nature and his intellect; in the time of hardships ... he has become an earnest man, filled with the best intentions and sincerely endeavours to utilize his strengths even now for the common good." (P. 6) He shows "the greatest interest in military matters" and also in "all other branches of state affairs, and is, based on his German educational background, constantly busy with his further education. It is obviously very clear to his practical mind that public life in general is nowhere better than in Germany". "One (notices) on every occasion ... how determined he is to bring his personality to bear as sovereign one day. Yet this is exactly what makes him disagreeable to English politicians." (P. 7) "..... above all because [they] see, like a vision, the figure of the German Kaiser taking shape behind him." (P. 8)

This eulogy may seem too enthusiastic for some, especially since Crown Prince Constantine was Sophie of Prussia's husband, not her son. However, his mother was Olga, the daughter of Grand Prince Constantine, who for his part, like his brother Alexander II, was also a son of Tsar Nicholas; and, as is well known, Nicholas I was married to Charlotte, a Princess of Prussia. Consequently, Olga had a Prussian grandmother and, therefore, her son (her sons) a Prussian great-grandmother. (Note: ever since Catherine the Great, all the subsequent tsars were married to Germans - Tsar Paul even twice -, with the sole exception of being Tsar Alexander III, who was married to the Danish Princess Dagmar.)

It should still be added in connection with the Greek-Turkish War over Crete and Thessaly in 1896 and 1897 that Greece had cherished hopes that Serbia and Bulgaria would also rush in to help by attacking the Turks from the rear.[458] But the Great Powers had prevented this, as was already pointed out in the relevant sections before.

With regard to that, Minister President Delyannis wrote in his party organ "Praia":

> "Turkey is so cocky after the success it has scored over Greece, so that both Bulgaria and Serbia" would soon see how hard it would be to obtain something from Turkey. How frustrated the Greeks were is shown by the call Delyannis makes in his paper for "the strongest bond for the Christian Balkan states, at least for Greece, Bulgaria and Serbia."[459]

The crisis must have been exceptionally great if the Greeks, aware that they were the trustees of Hellenism and that they belonged to the only true church offering salvation, even demeaned themselves once to invoke the common bonds of Christianity with the despised Slavs. The well-known English expert on the Balkans, M. Edith Durham, who was consulted by the British Foreign Ministry and other governments, gathered her own experience in connection with the so-called Christian common bond on countless journeys during many years at the beginning of the 20th century, which she summarizes as follows:

> "Not one single Balkan people ever wanted to free his 'Christian brothers', if there were no prospect of annexing them."[460]

The devastating judgment of a Christian about the Christian Balkan peoples.

It has already been mentioned that the Figaro had carried out an interview with Serbian and Bulgarian politicians in 1897. The Serbian Prime Minister Simić had confirmed that the Serbs felt true and honest grief "about the defeat of the Greeks". Likewise, it has already been shown that Serbia and Bulgaria could not offer any help because they had to bow to "formal orders". Simić: "One must, no doubt, obey if one is not strong enough to be able to be disobedient". Simić did not rule out, however, a joint action with Greece for the future.

> "Of course, Greece must give up that arrogant and clumsy policy which only results in uniting all the Slavs against the Greeks."[461]

Over and above that, if Greece would renounce its pretensions (towards Macedonia), the ridiculousness of which is obvious (among other things, because of the clear lack of any language similarity at all), an understanding would be possible. "We are, admittedly, still very far away from an alliance."

Indeed, 15 years still. But, the moment was approaching, and since the alliance did materialize, there must have been good reasons for forging it despite all the discord.

In continuation of his father's travelling diplomacy the Governor of Crete, Prince George, betook himself in the summer of 1903 to Copenhagen, to London (to "come to an understanding" with the husband of his Aunt Alexandra, who had been, as Edward VII, the King of Great Britain for two years then), and to St. Petersburg, to "come to an understanding"[462] with his cousin, Tsar Nicholas II. The consequences could be promptly read in one Copenhagen newspaper. Two weeks later, Ambassador Prince Reuß quoted the "Politiken", which had

> "given the activities of the General Commissioner of the Great Powers on Crete an especially commendatory critique".[463]

His loyal interaction with Greeks, Christian Cretans and Turks was praised, although his mission was only temporary, and "nothing would stand in the way of the approaching annexation of the island by Greece." He considered his task to be finished. Now, the prince intended to travel to Darmstadt for the wedding of his brother Andrew with Princess Victoria Alice of Battenberg[464] (a new example of a balanced marriage policy after his older brother Nicholas had married Grand Princess Helena Vladimirnova the year before[465]), where he "(would) meet with the powerful rulers of Germany and Russia". A small drop of bitterness wells out of Wilhelm's marginal note: "no, not of course with me" – but maybe that was only an impulsive fit of pique because the announcement was already in the newspaper, even though he had not been asked at all.

Then, the decisive concluding sentence of the article follows, and even today, after almost exactly 100 years, one's eyes are opened:

> "Who knows if Macedonia won't need a competent General Commissioner soon, just like Crete did earlier."

At that, the Kaiser became seriously angry and wrote in the margin:

> "No, I won't allow that. That would be highway robbery."[466]

The Kaiser had immediately seen through this Greek-Danish-Russian-English trick and he described it appropriately as well as precisely from a legal and moral standpoint. Insofar he would have possessed the political instinct to prevent standards from being set – but wasn't Wilhelm too good-natured (a quality which the picture of his distorted personality in the witch-hunt against him did not allow to be granted him) to also really stick to his totally justified and negative attitude, if his beloved sister Sophie would beseech him in the interests of her brother-in-law?

One day, the *fate of Macedonia* would depend exactly on this *crucial question*! More about that later. (See ch. 5)

For the Macedonians of today, the bitter realization remains that, while their ancestors striving for independence in that famous Ilinden Uprising in August of the year 1903 died fighting against the Turkish troops as well as against the Bulgarian, Serbian and Greek bands, their fate was at the same time being haggled over and decided at wedding banquets.

In continuation of the dynastic consultations, the following theatre farce was acted out for the general public only a month later:

> "The English government (was supposed to have) inquired of the King of Greece ... if he would be favourably disposed to a candidacy of Prince George as Governor General of Macedonia."

And now follows the ingenious dramaturgy of experienced actors and directors:

> "Both the King and Prince George", so quoted the Athens newspapers from the Brussels "Petit Observateur", "had declined."(!)

This was the second prank, but the third one came right on its heels:

> "His Majesty explained, though, that he might accept it for Prince Nicholas, who as a consequence of his marriage was persona grata for the Tsar of Russia."

And finally, during a flattering kowtow of little Greece to the Powerful of the Western World, the sound of horns ring out – and in fact as loudly as possible so that the Powerful cannot hear how the little king laughs up his sleeve about his own chutzpa:

> "However, Russia, Austria and Turkey would have to declare their approval for such a project in advance." !

Who was still concerned that "the Bulgarians were strongly opposed to the candidacy of Prince Nicholas"? [467]

> *And the Macedonians did not have any time anyway to protest – they were fighting for their freedom and for their lives.*

When in the same year King George I took up his round of visits again, he also automatically included Vienna in his tour. During his talk with Ambassador Count Wedel in November of 1903, he complained that Bulgaria could occupy (Eastern) Rumelia in 1885 without being chastised at all and could also annex it; "in the Crete question, however, the European intervention set in immediately." Interestingly enough, a kind of confession slipped out in the Greek king's following remarks:
As far as *Macedonia* is concerned, the Bulgarians pretended, "as if only they were entitled to have a claim to Macedonia"; and, although it was often said that all of Macedonia was inhabited by Greeks, he continued,

> "whereas the Greek element is by far the more prevalent one in the coastal areas and in individual cities of the interior such as Monastir." [468]

In saying that, George came at least more or less in proximity to the real situation.
With regard to Macedonia, the propaganda-machine was running at full speed in the Greece of those times, since there had still not been unification of Greece with Crete after such a long time and so much bloodshed. Envoy von Ratibor vividly demonstrates this in the following example:
At the beginning of January in 1904, the Greek royal family gathered together in full force for the Orthodox Christmas festivities in Athens, including daughter Marie with the Russian Grand Prince George Mikhailovich and son Andrew with the German Princess Victoria Alice of Battenberg, whom he had married in October of 1903. (In the coming years, between 1905 and 1911, the two would have four children; the fifth child - and the only one living today – was not born until 1921 and, thus, a sort of latecomer, was Prince Philip, who, through his marriage with the British heir to the throne in 1947, received the title of the Duke of Edinburgh when his wife became Elizabeth II, Queen of the United Kingdom in 1953.) The clearly moderate participation of the population in the festive reception for Prince Andrew and his wife (a Te Deum in the cathedral) was explained by v. Ratibor as being due to a "dangerous competitor":

> "Because on the same day Professor Kasasia returned to Athens from his tour diplomacy. The enthusiastic Hellenes flocked in great crowds to meet him, waving flags and cheering. The horses of his carriage were unharnessed and replaced by students and a priest ... The celebrated professor naturally gave a speech from (his) balcony, which ended with more or less the words: 'Words have been exchanged enough! Nothing practical can be achieved for Macedonia with quill and ink. Action is necessary, serious, successful action!'" [469]

Not only on the Greek mainland, but also on the island of Crete, the national hysteria was being stoked up more and more. That had unexpected consequences – at any rate, for the regency on Crete. Since the agitation for the unification of Crete with the motherland did not ease off (and if, in retrospect, one looks at the main agitator Venizelos, it is no wonder), because the liberation committee in contrast to the Great Powers and

(necessarily also) official Greece, did not want to wait until the time was ripe, Prince George resigned from his position as Governor. The English must have regretted this step, since for them the prince seemed the most suited to serve as an instrument for the realization of their old plan with which they had been toying for such a long time – namely, to also include Crete with its ideal harbour into their sea-based empire. The British chances of annexing Crete sank, though, with George's successor, Zaimis.
According to a report of the envoy, von Below, their supposed puppet, Prince George, just managed, in the meantime, to

> "escape like a refugee through the backdoor of his house in Halepa and to embark on a ship for Piraeus. It can probably be said that the Prince set off for Crete with one thousand masts at that time only to return to the harbour of his home country now after an eight-year virtually unsuccessful job disappointed and bitter, albeit on a Greek armoured gunship. This is certainly tragic, especially when one knows that the Prince already had the programme lying in waiting in his drawer, in accordance with which he proposed to march into Athens one day crowned with glory after the joyful unification of the island with Greece and to lay the Cretan flag at the feet of his royal father."[470]

Actually, Prince George, just like his father, did not fail in Crete because of any incorrect conduct or because of the Cretans, but rather, as the king said in the "most intimate circles of the royal family", because of the "attitude of the Crete Powers". The four Powers had duped him. England and Russia (he also listed Italy), "each one for itself, aspired to have Suda Bay" on Crete.[471] Neither he nor Greece could assert himself/itself against these over-powering interests.

> Indeed: even family connections are worthless when the relatives raise the same claims of ownership and are concocting the same annexation plans as their protégé. Then, only the law of the jungle is valid when representing one's interests, survival of the fittest.

A last bon mot:
In the spring of 1903, the Sultan surprised the Greeks by conferring high awards on the Greek King, the Crown Prince and to Prime Minister Delyannis. This gesture, too, had indirectly something to do with Macedonia.
In those days of reignited revolts, the feeling was spreading in Greece that there could be "complications in Macedonia and ... (a) conflict with Turkey".

> "One feels that with a liquidation of Turkish rule in Europe, which is appearing in the background with the storms breaking out in Macedonia, Greece with a state of military inferiority and financial weakness like the present one would not have anything to say and fears a solution that does not fulfil the wishes and dreams of the people. This fear alone makes the Greeks behave calmly and act as correctly as possible with Turkey."[472]

This incident shows with what irony history likes to mark its emphases. The Sultan wanted to reward the Greeks for their good behaviour "with the awarding of medals", although the Greeks were only staying quiet out of necessity and had not backed away from their plan in the slightest

> "to not only seize control of the provinces of the Turkish Empire in the future ..., but also to build up the Byzantine Empire anew."[472]

For the Greeks, merely the timing of the new unrest in Macedonia was extremely inconvenient for an attack on Turkey, since they would still need some years for their arms build-up.
Eighteen months later, the good Turkish-Greek relations had even risen to such undreamed-of heights that a rumour about a possible "Turkish-Greek Alliance" was making the rounds. The envoy in Athens, von Below, did not allow himself to be confused by it, suspecting

> "that that rumour had been launched from Constantinople by Mr. Gryparis to scare Bulgaria and maybe also Romania."

He did not wish, however, to totally rule out

> "that here, with the usual overestimation of one's own strengths, one had approached the Porte with an offer for an alliance; but Constantinople should be too well informed about the military impotence of Greece at sea and on land not to judge such an offer by its true value, ... with the motivation that one could not seriously think about joining forces with a people whose unreliability has been sufficiently well known for a long time."[473]

2.3.9.1 Background information (4)
George continues working on the international relations of Greece (Rome)

Some details should back up this heading.

In the last year of the 19th century, George once again did not return from his summer holiday until autumn.[474]

His plans for 1903 were already mentioned above; they did not prevent Queen Olga from visiting her own home country.[475]

In 1905, they were expecting important company. After the reconciliation with Sister Sophie and after the visit of the Greek king in Berlin, Wilhelm II travelled once again to Corfu (where he had bought the famous Achilleion as a holiday residence that Empress "Sissi" had once had built), a visit that he was very taken with.[476] This time. For there is a note in a margin from 1891 in which he complained "about the bad reception that we received two years ago".[477] The Kaiser apparently did not bear a grudge – but he did not let it go unmentioned either.

> Didn't Wilhelm II notice at all that he was on the verge of allowing himself to be dragged into the Balkan and especially Greek affairs and not only personal or family affairs, since he was doing exactly what Bismarck, with good reason, had warned about? But, blood is thicker than water.

The Greek royal family did not remain one-sided in their tour diplomacy; and it goes without saying that the other family members were also included in the Greek touring activities.

-- In the summer of 1905, Crown Prince Constantine, with his wife Sophie, was staying in London, about which Ambassador v. Metternich reported.[478]

-- In the autumn, Prince Nicholas and Grand Princess Helene also stopped off in Constantinople on their way to St. Petersburg as well as to Germany, France and England. This did not happen without an underlying motive, for they were received there by the Sultan.[479] Also for the Grand Vizier it was clear, as he told the German envoy,

> "that the Greek press would capitalize on this in order to demonstrate that Turkish-Greek relations were currently especially intimate despite the agitations of the Greek gangs directed against the Bulgarians and the Wallachians in Macedonia."[480]

One surely has to admire how the king managed things: in the autumn of 1905, he was once again received by the Kaiser in Potsdam and by the Imperial Chancellor (v. Bülow) in Berlin before he travelled on to France and Great Britain.[481] The "Messager d'Athènes" reported relatively cautiously in its Bulletin about the satisfaction of the Greek people in view of this new show of favour by the Kaiser. However, the paper immediately stuck its finger in the wound once again by

> "pointing out the rights and aspirations of Hellenism", "which are represented by sovereign Greece".[482]

Bismarck ...., always Bismarck ! – He was missing for an emotional Wilhelm, and he was missing for an emotional Germany. Obviously, he would have been the only one who could have anticipated the effects of the Greek intrigues and could have limited them.

Before he returned home, George made - but that's no surprise - a detour to Vienna again, where he spoke to both Emperor Franz Josef and Foreign Minister Count Goluchowski. From his subsequent tour d'horizon with Ambassador Count Wedel, two remarks of the king about *Macedonia* were captured in a relevant report. George could hardly have assumed then that one day, one hundred years later, they would find an important place in a documentation about the Republic of Macedonia and its history:

1). George complained,

> "Romania ... is sacrificing large sums in Macedonia for schools and churches and won't achieve very much with it anyway, while the Hellenization work there is only being sponsored through private funds."[483]

Apart from the fact that Count Wedel could hardly have taken his claim at face value, alone because of the "private funds", the confession from the royal mouth about the "Hellenization work" in Macedonia has value as a rarity.

But, not enough with that: we already had the comment by Edith Durham above, who was filled with indignation about how the Christians of the different neighbouring countries "stabbed each other in the back" for chauvinist reasons. Whoever is not satisfied with the judgment of that Balkan expert will find here a royal confirmation for those outrageous occurrences.

2). The ambassador went on:

> "In the course of the conversation, the tendency of the different gangs in Macedonia was touched upon ..., where I pointed out that the Christians were massacring each other there. Up to now it was always claimed that the fighting was directed against the Turks and, when they were driven out one day, absolute joy and harmony would rule among the liberated Christian peoples. But now it is apparent that the Christians are attacking each other and that the Turkish element represents the order and provides the anchor of stability."[483]

At last a refreshingly clear word from an experienced mouth.

The King of the Hellenes reacted:

> "... unfortunately, it's only too true, and, as a Christian, one must be ashamed of the events in Macedonia."

This justified shame did not prevent George from forcefully and systematically continuing with the Greek expansion plans in Macedonia after having shed the obligatory crocodile tears.

In the next year, 1906, George already started off from Athens in the spring and, on the way to Copenhagen, stayed once again in Vienna, where he continued his traditional talks with the Austrian statesmen.[484] The reason for his unusually early start in his summer vacation reveals itself immediately when one learns with whom George was to meet in his parents' home: with Wilhelm II.

For him, an encounter with the German Kaiser was worth the strenuous journey from the southern edge of Europe to the north. George surely had his reasons. It is no problem for the observer to imagine exactly what they were.

A rebuttal for the insinuation that George's spring trip was an early start to his summer holiday can be found in the press coverage in autumn of 1906, when George set off on his actual annual holiday trip. It is clear from that that he, in fact, "only" went to Copenhagen because of Kaiser Wilhelm!

The Greek king knew how to set the tone and use his influence. In autumn, his journey led him to France and Italy. A report from the embassy in Paris, where George I met with the French Prime Minister Clemenceau, shows an interesting detail about the close relations of the Prime Minister with Greece:

> "Clemenceau (is) very popular in Greece ... As the editor-in-chief of "Aurore", he spent his holidays in Greece and on Crete on repeated occasions and published a large number of enthusiastic philhellenic articles about these trips."[485]

Personal connections can facilitate political negotiations considerably, as is well known.

As far as George's trip to Rome is concerned, there was first of all the question of protocol matters in advance of the visit.

> "The restless politics of the little country were disagreeable ... to Italy. Furthermore, the omission of a visit by the Greek king (up to then) was considered a lack of courtesy. His Majesty, King Victor Emanuel, had called on the Greek court several times as Crown Prince, but King George has never undertaken the effort on his regular autumn homecomings to make the small detour from Trieste to Rome."

The political position of Rome was of a more serious nature:

> "In Rome one wishes autonomy for Albania, with an enlargement at the same time to include areas that Greece claims."[486]

This was, of course, totally unacceptable for Athens, especially since the Greeks suspected that for the Italians it was really a question of their own expansion plans on the other side of the Adriatic Sea. And in Greece, too, the remark of the Italian envoy about the ethnic make-up of the Greek people had not yet been forgotten. (See ch. 2.3.0) Nonetheless, the tone in the Italian press was friendly. Turin's "La Stampa" alone fell out of line:

> "In their welcoming article before the arrival of the guest in Rome, the Italian prophet of the national newspaper, Cirmeni, reproaches the King for having visited Vienna before Rome."

Apparently an unbearable snub to the dignity and honour of the Italian nation.
Ambassador v. Monts quotes Signor Cirmeni further:

> "That's why he should have better refrained from visiting Italy altogether."[487]

Rude manners in the business of politics. But as always, such attacks bounced off of George without leaving a trace, like water off of a duck's back.

It goes without saying that Topic Nr. 1 was once again on the agenda. However, since even before the visit

> "in political circles ... it (was) manifoldly assumed that King George would want to stir up opinion in favour of ... the annexation of Crete or would ask for it directly",

Foreign Minister Tittoni preferred to define the whole visit as an 'act of courtesy' only. In the meanwhile, the "representatives of the small Balkan states" did not fall in line with this "courtesy":

> "The Serbian Envoy is on a business trip in Vienna. The Romanian is feigning a journey, but showed himself the day before yesterday in an open coach on the Pincio. The very robust Bulgarian became suddenly ill. ..."[487]

The interests of all of these states were identical: directed at Macedonia. Consequently, the Greek activities were a constant thorn in their flesh. They discovered their common ground inevitably just before the Balkan Wars: in the Balkan League – but also only with foreign help! In the meantime, there were only about five years left up to that point....

About the king, the embassy report says:

> "His Majesty, King George, behaves very simply and naturally. Of course, people say here that the noble gentleman is not Greek."

Nonetheless, George's behaviour must have left such a big impression in Rome that Ambassador v. Monts also quoted Minister Tittoni in his follow-up report:
> "His modest manner is extraordinarily advantageous in contrast to that of all other Greeks known here."[488]

The ambassador learned from the minister in a confidential conversation that George had actually broached the subject of the Greek desire for a "speedy annexation of the island". The answer to the Greek king, though, was that this question not only
> "depended on the so-called four protecting powers but on all the signatories of the Treaty of Berlin. In the lap of the powers, though, people bear in mind the overall picture of the oriental things. It isn't possible to single out Crete alone. To satisfy the Greek wishes would awaken so many other claims and desires that the most serious Balkan complications would be the result."[488]

Since these details were not known to the public, the Roman press, as the "Tägliche Rundschau" reported, concentrated instead on the question of whether the Greek king would also visit the *Vatican*. George was ready and willing to do the Italian government a favour, so that the Vatican could not accuse the Quirinal "of having thwarted" such a visit. Besides, George had already met the Pope once in Venice. The latter, however, attached a lot of importance to the king's appearing not in a tailcoat and certainly not in a frock coat, which George would have preferred the most, but in a uniform, exactly like he had arrived in Rome to be able to stay at the *Quirinal* with the king.

On the other hand, George did not want to
> "hurt ... the religious feelings of his by no means Pope-friendly subjects ... and for that reason to also emphasize the p r i v a t e character outwardly in a suit."

For similar reasons, he had, as the "Corriere della Sera" assured,
> "refused as the o n l y g r a n d p r i n c e to c o n g r a t u l a t e L e o XIII on his Jubilee!"[489]

"The visit" ... almost seemed ... "to be going to fail because of a 'question of tailoring'." The newspaper did describe this position of the Vatican as "vanity ... and daydreaming about sovereignty", the Vatican for its part reminded them, though, that even King Edward had driven up in a general's uniform. But on the other hand, since it knew all about the Greek king's steadfastness, it could not do anything but give in.
> "He wouldn't like ... to miss a king. So he accepted him, then, in his f r o c k c o a t."[489]

By the way, King Victor Emanuel returned this visit already six months later with his visit to Athens[490] – a former colony of his ancestors (after his mother country and Sicily had been colonized by the Greeks long before that).

(It is hardly necessary to add that Crown Prince Constantine and Crown Princess Sophie also undertook the obligatory tour to France, Britain and Germany in the summer of 1906.[491])

2.3.9.2 Background information (5)
The Greek king completes his dynastic network (Paris)

It's a good thing that there was once the often (admittedly also by the author) vilified "court circular". By this means, the news about travel activities of the Greek royal family developed in the summer of 1907 has been maintained for posterity.[492]

George took up his usual tours. Olga went with her - Russian - daughter-in-law, Helene, (by way of Vienna: because of a medical consultation) naturally to St. Petersburg. Constantine and family travelled by way of England - just as naturally - to Germany.

Prince Andrew made his way with his Alice von Battenberg to Darmstadt. This author quotes a report about this couple (with a slight chronological delay) – not only because the envoy, von Ratibor, wrote such a touching text about this young couple, but because it also provides insights (not to mention, showing human idiosyncrasies) into the land of the Greeks, which, in the end, portray the topic of the background information. V. Ratibor writes:

> "If a female being that follows her beloved husband to a foreign country, sets herself the task of belonging to the nation of her husband with all her soul, then this is certainly understandable. For Princess Alice of Greece, it was so much easier to render homage to this principle since she had never seen Greece up to the point of her festive entrance with her husband into Athens and surely never had the opportunity before either to get to know the Greeks well. From the moment of her engagement, Her Royal Highness devoted herself to the study of the Greek language, and it can be attributed to her influence that Prince Andrew did not return again to Germany" [to the Hessian Dragoon Regiment]. "For Princess Alice, it can be wished that she, who came here with ideal notions of the splendours of this classical land and the excellent qualities of its inhabitants, will not be disappointed. Even their daily life won't be the ideal existence of a young married couple. For the Prince and Princess will not have their own household but instead will live in a few rooms in the palace and will be dependent on His Majesty the King, who is, above all, a tyrant in the family."[493]

The text arouses additional attention because it is obvious from a marginal note by Wilhelm II that, despite having long since made up with his sister Sophie, there was still the thorn of bitter experience sticking in his side, as he wrote next to the spot "belonging to the nation of her husband with her whole soul" the remark:

> "Only German princesses do that, and, in addition, usually also to the detriment of their original fatherland." (We will come back to this remark in Chapter 5.)

In the list above from the "court circular", one journey is missing and, above all, the result of the journey, which in the interest of balance had been an urgent matter of concern to the Greek royal family and to the whole Greek people.

There was, namely, a relationship between Prince George and the French princess, Marie Bonaparte, in the offing, and with it Athens could finally close a long gap - which was felt as a sensitive wound, also by France - in the dynastic network of Europe. After Prince George departed from Paris for Copenhagen in June of 1907, his potential father-in-law did have a notice released to the press "that for now this marriage is out of the question," although he was the one who was "pursuing" the marriage project "with great enthusiasm".[494] Then again, there were "powerful influences" working against this idea: "The Queen of England is named in this respect."[494]

Well I never! That was, of course, the wife of Edward VII (English king since 1901), i. e. Alexandra, King George's sister, an aunt of Prince George, moreover, even his favourite aunt! (Could that have been the reason for her visit to Athens in May of that year? [495]) And, why this resistance?

The explanation is extremely easy: the bride was the only child of Prince Roland from his morganatic marriage with the "daughter of the gambling licensee Blanc".

At the Greek court "one would ... surely disregard the drawbacks of such a union." There is a relatively plausible explanation for this in the report:

> "The young lady is supposed to have her own peculium of 15-20 million francs, apart from the fortune of her father."[496]

So, the engagement took place in September of the same year.

However, one future sister-in-law, the wife of George's brother, Nicholas, the Grand Princess Helene, is supposed to have refused to acknowledge Princess Marie Bonaparte.
> "Prince Nicholas is supposed to be considering moving to Russia and joining the Russian military service."[497]

The rest of the Greek royal family generously disregarded such aristocratic scruples: the marriage to the Catholic bride took place on the 29th November and the 12th December, 1907. As Envoy von Arco reported in conclusion, it was originally supposed to have been celebrated in Paris.
> "However, since the Holy See demanded a written promise that the children of the marriage would be raised as Catholics, the idea was dropped. The wedding will only be carried out in accordance with the Greek Orthodox ritual. A civil wedding is unknown in Greece."[498]

One year later, the new Greek princess presented the happy grandparents with their fifteenth grandchild, Prince Peter.[499]

Onto which of the last sentences could one attach the French motto which has tradition in England: Honi soit, qui mal y pense?
Or would the considerably older saying "pecunia non olet" be more suitable?
Perhaps the money held its promise – the matrimonial bliss did not.

A couple of years later (during the First World War), Prince George, whose brother Constantine had been King of Greece since 1913, hit the news by turning out to be "an unconditional supporter of the Entente"[500], while the King - despite full sympathy for Germany - with all the power that the unscrupulous Venizelos allowed him, tried to maintain the Greek neutrality and, consequently, to keep Greece out of the war.
About a year later, this information was enriched with the rumour that Prince George was "an intimate friend of Briand's", and that he was playing "Venizelos' game against the King".[501]

The affair became quite delicate, as the Military Attaché reported from Madrid,
> the "Princess ... of Greece, Marie Bonaparte, is using her intimate relations with Briand to push ahead the succession of her husband to the throne by using French policy in Greece."[502]

Astonishing enough – but, in all fairness, one has to make allowances for Ms Bonaparte's efforts when one remembers that earlier speculations, described above, about "certain tendencies" of George's were apparently not unfounded. Looked at it in this way, Marie was searching for a fair compensation and found it, since the relationship just described with Briand as "intimate" is to be taken completely literally. The envoy, Bethmann Hollweg (jun.), had transmitted a remark by the Legation Counsellor von Brüning from Berne at the end of 1916 with the unambiguous observation that
> "Princess Bonaparte" ... (is regarded) "in the general opinion as ... the mistress" of the "French Prime Minister Briand".[503]

The above-mentioned passion of the Danish-Greek royal family for calculations and financial operations was no coincidence, no slip-up and no exception. It must have run in the family or been part of the "social" environment. In 1913, rumours circulated in Bucharest,
> "that the engagement of Princess Elizabeth of Romania to the Crown Prince of Greece is intended."

The Envoy, von Waldburg, heard from the Romanian Prime Minister Take Jonescu,
> "His Majesty the King is sympathetic to such a union. ... In Greece, one would first like to have some clarity about the financial side of this alliance."[504]

In the end, there was another morganatic marriage in the Greek royal family. The news got through from the Berne exile to Berlin,

> "that the wedding of Prince Christopher of Greece to the American, Mrs. Leeds, is approaching." (In the end, it did not take place until 1920.) "The fortune of" [the widowed] "Mrs. Leeds" [née Stewart] "is estimated at around 30 million dollars."[505]

The affair received an unpleasant touch through the message in a report from Copenhagen by Envoy v. Brockdorff-Rantzau,

> "according to which the marriage of Prince Christophorus of Greece to an American is being encouraged by King Constantine, because the King hopes to obtain financial resources for his fight to recover the Greek throne through the marriage of his brother to the rich Mrs. Leeds."[506]

(King Constantine was forced into exile by Venizelos with the help of the Entente in 1917. See chapter 5.6.4)

2.3.10 The meeting of monarchs in Reval in 1908: a crucial event for Macedonia and the Dual Alliance

As emerges from a discussion between the chargé d'affaires in Athens, Mr. von Arco, and the Greek king in June of 1908, an English-Russian meeting had taken place in *Reval* [Tallinn] at the beginning of the month with the presence of an unusual entourage for a supposedly private visit, viz. the leading generals, admirals and ministers of both sides.

Edward travelled to this meeting with the Tsar even though British members of parliament were speaking of Nicholas II as a "common murderer" and a "blood-thirsty monster"[507] – perhaps another result

- of the appalling Bloody Sunday in St. Petersburg in January of 1905, (which, according to Paul Sethe, would not have occurred if the Tsar himself had had his way[508]),
- or the Dogger Bank Incident, when the Russian fleet sank a couple of (allegedly) harmless English fishing boats on the way to Japan,
- or the rigorous Russification policy in Latvia.

Since the English travelled there anyway, there must have been an even bigger *"monster"* for the English interests! It subsequently transpired that this monster was Kaiser Wilhelm II.

The Greek king divulged some extraordinary information about this meeting:

> *"He didn't know himself exactly what had been agreed upon in Reval about Macedonia. He had only heard that the two sovereigns had come to an agreement."*[507]

Wait a moment - slow down. - First, take a deep breath....

So: in June of 1908, *Russia and England* negotiated with each other about *Macedonia*!

> Let us think back a moment and repeat: the British King Edward VII was the husband of the Danish Princess Alexandra, the sister of the Greek King, and George was, thus, Edward's brother-in-law; and the Russian Tsar was the son of another sister of King George, the Danish Princess Dagmar, and was, thus, George's nephew. And, in case there should be any further doubts that the decisions about the *future of Macedonia* were solely dynastic-related, I will additionally cite the remark of the Greek king that "the Queen of Greece was also present"[509] at the Russian-English get-together in Reval, thus, George's wife Olga, the Russian Grand Princess, the wife of the English King Edward's brother-in-law and the cousin of the father of Tsar Nicholas - but first and foremost the mother of the potential Governor General of Macedonia - of Prince George!

The meeting in Reval is a key historical scenario for the fate of Macedonia – which was to be divided up in just a few years.

> Here and only here, the decades-old doctrine of the status quo in the Balkans, in connection with the preservation of the Ottoman Empire on European soil can have been knocked over while the (in principle) continuance of Turkey on the Golden Horn has been reduced to a minimal leftover crumb of its former territory.

(Thus, in exactly the form that the shrewdness of the cunning Serbian King Milan had already foreseen many years before.)

And here, the reason can also be found for the puzzling behaviour of the Great Powers during the coming phase that led to the founding of the Balkan League as well as to the triggering of the Balkan Wars: in all the military campaigns against Turkey up to then, and even in smaller skirmishes, the whole phalanx of the big European powers had intervened in an almost incredible unanimity (a model even for present-day European institutions) in order to establish their political philosophy of the status quo – but when it really became serious, when the Balkan War broke out, they did not lift a finger!

Quite the reverse: they became the driving force behind it!

With that, George's strategy began to bear fruit. Over the course of the years, his patience had changed to persistence, his persistence had grown into stubbornness and this to obsession. He, who was certainly often enough considered as a nuisance, had finally achieved the consent of his relatives in St. Petersburg, London and Paris for the Greek territorial cravings in the forthcoming realization of the Greek expansion plans.

> *The Greeks would have every reason to erect a monument to George* if they have not long since done so.
>
> *The Macedonians can only curse the Greek king* – like the Persians once cursed Alexander the Great (see ch. 1.2.0.1).

The irony of history has no limits, like this circular reasoning: she raises her favourites to Olympian heights – she strangles her victims. With the same indifference.

But still, with all respect due to history – she is not subject to any automatic mechanism: Politics (and consequently also history) is made by people. In this case: *by the Danish Greek King George I.*

Only the immediate effects on Macedonia are thereby outlined. The far-reaching, portentous significance of the meeting in Reval has not been exhausted. It compels us to ask further questions:

> *Is it plausible that two such powerful men as the Russian tsar and the English king come together for a meeting on the roadstead of Reval to discuss nothing other than a little Turkish province like Macedonia and how it should be divided up among its neighbouring states – even if it involved a favour for a relative?*

That would be absurd.

And the not less closely related Germans, who were supposed to believe that the meeting in Reval was devoted to a reform programme for Macedonia, should they buy that tale from the two monarchs? Ridiculous!

The truth was dreadful. Not only for Macedonia! (Compare: Chapter 5)

2.3.10.1 Background information (6)
  George keeps up his struggle to increase the power of Greece

In spite of the good news from Reval, King George unwaveringly adhered to his tour diplomacy. He knew the ups and downs and the whims of politics and of his relatives – you never could know.... One had to be constantly on one's guard. Alexander von Battenberg on the Bulgarian throne had to learn in a very unpleasant way that the beloved relatives are not always a guarantee of untarnished goodwill, even though he was also a nephew of Tsar Alexander II. The Greek king did not need this shining example. Greece had found itself often enough in a desolate situation – he only had to think about (South and North) Epirus, Thessaly and Crete. It should work out better for him with Macedonia.
But precisely this triumph is something that he did not live to see.

On the 17th and 18th November 1908, George was (once again!) a guest of Kaiser Wilhelm II in Berlin on his way from Copenhagen to Paris.^{510}
In the autumn, Queen Olga was still passing her time in Russia and only pressed for an early and speedy return to Greece after Bulgaria had (in the shadow of Austria's annexation of Bosnia) declared its independence at the beginning of October and had dared to put itself on the same rung of the ladder as Greece [as well as Serbia and Montenegro] and to also proclaim itself a kingdom.
The German ambassador in St. Petersburg, von Miquel, reported that Olga
  "had expressed her indignation about the action of the Prince of Bulgaria in her sharpest form."^{511}
A very resolute lady.
Even worse than the Greek envy and jealousy at the surprising progress of the upstart and rival Bulgaria in the competition (or rather, in the fight) for the Turkish legacy on European soil, were the disappointment and the anger in Athens about the missed chance of pursuing their own aims at the same time as Austria and Bulgaria, i.e., of having moved against the Turks on Crete and perhaps in Epirus – or even in Salonika. In this respect, one cannot spare the shrewd Greek Rex the reproach of a remnant of naiveté when he complained in retrospect that the two governments had not informed him about their planned steps^{511} – as if they should have had the greatest interest in drawing the attention of their biggest enemy in the Balkans, Greece, to a convenient opportunity to attack Turkey, so that Athens might possibly have been able to beat them in breaking off one piece or another of the territory of the Ottoman Empire, for which they themselves were also most hungry.

What was happening in Constantinople in the meantime?
Just as the Young Turks were initially friendly towards minorities and tolerant towards other religions, they also seemed to be Greek-friendly. The reactions of the Greek population to the revolution in Constantinople were correspondingly enthusiastic. The envoy, von Arco, even reported about "glowing speeches avowing friendship". The fact that, on the other hand, the Sultan demoted his Vizier, Munir Pascha, who was known to be pro-Greek, and was not able to receive the two Greek princes, Christopher and Andrew, the latter with his wife Alice, on the occasion of their visit to Constantinople due to urgent affairs of state (which should be understandable during a

revolution – especially since his overthrow was the result), was received with disappointment in Athens and left a bitter aftertaste.

On the other hand, the Sultan for his part was supposed to have been upset "about the tremendous ovations given to the princes and about the somewhat sentimentally laid out visit to the Hagia Sophia".[512]

The Ecumenical Patriarchy, which "sees the new turn of events somewhat sceptically and fears for the rights of the Greek Church (under) the assaults of the Christian 'sister nations', reacted once again in a solely power-conscious manner".

Nota bene: "the Christian ones"!

In October of 1908, the Cretan National Assembly proclaimed Enosis for the umpteenth time. In the face of the offence against international agreements and because of their own military weakness, the Greek government did not dare a new war against Turkey, as they could not be sure that the powers would help them – and that even in spite of the meeting in Reval ! There remains only one conclusion:

> It must have been clear to George that the two potentates had not undertaken the journey to the roadstead in Reval (only) for him!

It is possible that Queen Olga knew more, as George confided to the German envoy.

As a counterpart to the Young Turks, a movement of rebellious officers had formed to a military league on the Greek side, a successor organization to the *Philike Hetairia*. Originally, the people were sympathetic towards this group of officers, but when the league misused its power, i.e., muzzled Parliament, forced new taxation laws and reproved the royal family, disillusionment returned. "An almost hopeless anarchy" held sway in the army.

Envoy v. Wangenheim reported (p. 6):

> "Yet, the King and Parliament are talking about the supposed successes of the new regime in order to morally justify their own forced submission." ... "Outside this charmed circle, no one dares to express an opinion." "The King has repeatedly stated that he would abdicate in the event that a dictatorship is proclaimed. Actually ... a dictatorship of the supreme Zorba ... is already ruling here, while dynasty, government and parliament are excluded or condemned to walk-on roles."[513]
> "Moreover, the muddled situation within the country is made even more complicated by the Crete question ..."

The practical solution arose from the decision of the league to summon the political leader of the Cretans, E. Venizelos, to Athens.[514] This led to the actual struggle against the dynasty breaking out. With varying degrees of success – until King George was completely politically isolated by "Dictator" Venizelos within one year.[516]

Then again, the Prime Minister did not want to rule either without the king in the background. There is a document in the files that can illustrate his train of thought.

Chargé d'affaires von Riepenhausen reported from Athens:

> "The Greek generally has a fine feeling for what is of benefit to him. It wouldn't be difficult to make it clear to him what significance the family relationships of his royal family have had for the development of the present external crisis. Neither of the two powerful factors of the Crete Concern which were obliged to intervene – England and Russia – would have supported a republican Greece, as happened recently in Constantinople."[517]

The "Daily Graphic" of London as the mouthpiece of the British government and the King may also have given Mr. Venizelos meaningful ideas for his decision during "the recent unrest in Greece" after the "mutiny of the fleet":

"Greece ... would not win anything through the deposition or abdication of King George but it would, to the contrary, alienate itself from the sympathies of all Europe. It is on the brink of disaster and, if it proceeds further in its blindness, it could forfeit its independence which it has so abused."[518]

Two fundamental observations that had universal validity for the existence of the state of Greece.

The question of the possible deposition of the king was, nevertheless, not only of a hypothetical nature. A German newspaper reminds one that Parliament, "completely under the influence of the military league" ... had taken over "all the demands of the military party without debate":

"One of their first actions was to depose the Greek Princes from their military posts. The latter, among them also the Greek Crown Prince, the Commander-in-Chief of the Greek Army, had already relinquished their positions and had left the country."[519]

Thus, the dictator had the Greek royal family still at work for him and for the reputation and the power of Greece as long as he considered it useful.

For Greece itself, Venizelos' half-rabid, half-flexible politics paid off, since the lasting continuation of the string of successes of Greek imperialism began at that time.

2.3.11 Greece and Turkey haggle over the Balkan League

The idea of a Balkan League underwent a special variant after 1908 through the attempt of the Young Turks to bring Turkey once again into this alliance as a member. Since Athens signalled its willingness, such an alliance could only function as an object of demonstration for the reasons known. Envoy von Riepenhausen wrote in this connection:

"Almost every Hellene carries ideas of a Greater Greece more or less locked away in his heart and sees contemporary Greece as only an incomplete torso. Every open or concealed increase in the power of Bulgaria in Macedonia crosses in the process the path of his hopes for the future. For that reason, Bulgaria is the arch enemy in his eyes; that's why Turkey must be preserved in as far as it limits the power of Bulgaria. For, where the Turk rules there is still hope for Greece, where the Bulgar has set his foot there is none. Greece is too aware of Slavic doggedness, the high Bulgarian fighting virtues." For that reason, it can be assumed that "despite all the guarantees they have given to each other" "the national passions would clash again and again."[520]

In the further course of time, the Turks had apparently constructed a realistic analysis, since the representative of Turkey in Athens confessed to his German colleague at the end of 1909 that the Sultan and the Porte "were set in no little state of excitement by the news about a Balkan League".[521] A late reaction!

Even if all the rumours, announcements and threats of thirty long years proved repeatedly to be in the end unfounded (and the information was false this time too), the Turks had had enough time and experience to prepare themselves for the casus belli.

In addition, they were also startled by the rebellion of the Albanians that had flared up again. (They played a major role in the fall of the Young Turks). In this connection, an article of the "Times" will be referred to which reported that the Albanian Revolt in the spring of 1910 was put down with merciless cruelty by the Turks. And then, this procedure continued in Macedonia, too, even though no revolt had taken place there; a general disarming of the population was carried through with the same methods as were used in Albania:

"The full history of the horrors which then took place has never been disclosed; the Great Powers, which had withdrawn their military officers from the country without obtaining any guarantee for its future good government, refrained from publishing the reports from their Consuls, and a conspiracy of silence prevailed in the greater part of the European Press."[522]

It would be worth doing an investigation of the details to find out why the Turks committed these totally unprovoked atrocities in Macedonia of all places and to whose influence it could be traced that the Great Powers pulled back their military checkpoints at exactly the same time when the Macedonians needed international help urgently! !

The author dares to assume that even in this case the Greek king was behind it, since it is not without reason to suspect that the Greek strategists also played a role here again in order to have the Macedonian enemy, whom they increasingly and clearly had an eye on, disarmed in time before the forthcoming struggle. .

Back to the Balkan League:
The Greek Foreign Minister Mavromikhali (probably the descendant of a further member of the first provisional government after the revolt of 1821) tried very hard to give the Turkish envoy a false sense of security:

"The Greek antipathy to Bulgaria (is) much too strong ... for an alliance with that country to be a realistic proposition at all."

It was exactly this alliance that was entered into one and a half years later!
The foreign minister informed the envoy, Naby Bey, that, between Serbia and Bulgaria,

"the bilateral spheres of interest in Macedonia have (already been) defined".[521]

In his report, Baron von Wangenheim announced his doubts about the credibility of the foreign minister:

"I can't completely share Naby Bey's belief in the honesty of Mavromikhali. It is in the interest of Greece, through warnings about Bulgaria, to influence Turkey to reach a rapprochement with Greece and to concessions concerning Crete."[521]

In conclusion, another quotation from the Auswärtiges Amt:
the Under Secretary, Freiherr von Rotenhan, recorded in a note that the Austrian foreign minister had

"earnestly admonished Athens, to prevent all instigations to enter a conflict in Macedonia. Otherwise, Europe will not be able to concern itself with possible Turkish atrocities."[523]

This note throws a telling light on the subversive activities of Greece in Macedonia, which the Great Powers saw as illegal, as well as on the atrocities of Turkish retaliation, which they took as normal for the Turks.
This reputation of the Turks was formed over long centuries of the worst of experiences of the oppressed Christian peoples: the reality of the Turkish regime was in no way so tolerable and tolerant as the appeasing representatives of some interest-groups like to claim today.

2.3.12 The lead-up to the Greek-Bulgarian Alliance – and to the Balkan War

With the assumption of office of the Cretan, Venizelos, as Prime Minister at the end of 1910, Greek politics gained even clearer contours, in accordance with the principle of the sacro egoismo, subdued only by gestures of Byzantine protocol and pretty but empty words. Manoeuvring with or against Turkey and the Balkan states was also a part of this. The German envoy reported in May of 1911, i. e. a year before the conclusion of the Greek-Bulgarian *Balkan League*, about the visit of a Bulgarian student delegation to Athens which was loudly acclaimed by their Greek fellow students. The speeches about a "political get-together against the common enemy, Turkey", were, of course, condemned by the government-influenced press, but, nonetheless, the sympathy and jubilation of those Greeks who approved of co-operation with Bulgaria were symptomatic.

Baron von Wangenheim reported:

"Even if there is hardly any Greek who does not see the Bulgarian as his arch enemy, most of them still expect their government to achieve an alliance with Bulgaria, so that the latter fights on the side of Greece against the Turks when the issue of Crete is dealt with one day. The thought of an alliance of the Balkan states, in which the rights and duties are evenly divided among the signatories of the agreement, is, in contrast, completely beyond the Greeks. The Hellene would never accept the Bulgarians, Romanians or Serbians as equals or to have the same rights as they themselves. In his opinion, the future in European Turkey and in the Levant belongs only to Hellenism."[524]

There were also objective Greeks. Von Wangenheim quotes the former prime minister, Theotokis, who looked at such cases as the Greek-Bulgarian student alliance as "coquetries". Theotokis commented this scene with:

"Greece shouldn't ever join a Balkan League. A defence alliance is unnecessary, since recapturing the Christian states by Turkey would not be allowed. So, it can only be a question of an offensive alliance. But, let us assume that the allied states totally defeated Turkey; then a war would break out immediately between the victors for the spoils. Such a war could become the grave of Hellenic hopes."[524]

And it happened exactly like that in 1912 and 1913 – however, with the difference that the war between the victors did not become the grave of Hellenic hopes. In that, the former prime minister was mistaken because the two Balkan Wars brought Greece (thanks to the Entente) an enormous increase in foreign territory.

The Hellenic hopes, the Megale Idea, were carried to the grave that Theotokis anticipated only ten years later, in 1922, in the battle near Ankara – by the Turks.

2.3.12.1 Background information (7)
The continuity in the solidarity of the European dynasties is preserved

Finally, the author will quote a report from Copenhagen by Envoy v. Waldthausen to confirm the persistence of King George in pursuing imperialistic aims with the help of his dynastic connections. While the Italian government was starting a war against Turkey for Libya and the Italian envoy in Copenhagen was fulfilling his duties to notify the Danish government about Rome's declaration of war against Tripoli (in the place of Turkey), the Greek king was once again passing his time in his native country. The embassy dutifully covered this in their report to the court:

"Besides the Danish royal family, at the present there are the following relatives of the King of Greece here: Their Majesties the Dowager Tsarina of Russia [Dagmar/Maria F.] and the Dowager Queen of England [Alexandra] [King George's sisters], Prince George [the oldest son of the Greek Crown Prince Constantine] and the Princess [Marie Bonaparte] of Greece, Grand Princess Xenia Georgiewna of Russia [the sister of the Tsar], Princess Victoria of England [Edward's and Alexandra's daughter] and Prince Christopher of Greece [Constantine's youngest brother]."[525] [The brackets are additions of the author.]

As the old "sung", so chirp the young. (Corresponding to: "Like father, like son.")

2.4 Romania

2.4.0 Historical outline

The strategic location of the principalities of Moldavia and Wallachia on the lower reaches of the Danube and the curve of the Carpathian Mountains offered considerable advantages but also made them into coveted objects. As both were situated in the north of the Balkans, Wallachia had to pay tribute to the Ottoman Empire only at the beginning and Moldavia at the end of the 15th century; at the beginning of the 16th century they were annexed.

Russia pushed through autonomy for the Danube principalities in the Peace of Adrianople in 1829 after the 6th Russian-Turkish War, and at the same time it took over the protectorship which resulted in their immediate occupation. This was the cause of the 7th Russian-Turkish War starting in 1853, the Crimean War. As is well known, England and France entered the war on the side of Turkey. Austria of all countries which had remained - formally - neutral, played a historical role for Romania through its concentration of troops forcing Russia to withdraw from the principalities. (Austria had reason enough to often regret this role later.) According to Stadtmüller, the most important result of the Crimean War was "the liberation of the two Danube principalities" in the Peace of Paris in 1856.[526] (This, however, was only the local consequence; as for the severe and long range consequences see the chapters on Russia and the UK.)

Romania shook off the remainder of Turkish dominion with the cessation of paying tribute to the Sultan and with the unification of the two principalities in 1859 under the name of Romania even though this violated the Peace Treaty of Paris.[526] International recognition followed in 1861; in the plebiscite five years later, Karl von Hohenzollern-Sigmaringen was elected Prince Carol I. (He married Princess Elisabeth zu Wied.)

During the preparations for the 8th Russian-Turkish War in 1877, Romania had to grant Russia free passage for its troops in accordance with the Convention of the 4th of April, 1877, i. e. only eight days before the Russian declaration of war against the Ottoman Empire. In return, Romania received the guarantee for its territorial integrity. After Turkey, as a reaction, had declared war on Romania, on 8th May, 1877, the latter reacted with the proclamation of its independence on the 21st of May.[527]

After the initial defeat of the Russian army at the Turkish fortress of Plewna at the end of July, Russia demanded active support from Romania in the Military Convention of the 21st of August, 1877. With success: just four months later, the turning point of the war took place with the Turkish capitulation before the Russian-Romanian armies in Plewna (December 12, 1877). After the "detour" over the Preliminary Peace of San Stefano, the Congress of Berlin recognized the independence of Romania (as well as that of Serbia and Montenegro). However, it also yielded to Russia's insistence and awarded it Romanian Bessarabia again, which had been taken from Russia after the Crimean War, despite Russia's violating its guarantees according to the Convention of the 16th of April (and despite the Romanian protests).[528]

Romania "considered the surrender of Bessarabia to Russia as painful, while Southern Dobruja as compensation only created a new source of friction with Bulgaria."[529]

2.4.1 Romania, vacillating between alliance-policy and neutrality

In the time leading up to the Balkan League, Romania took on a special role. To be sure, in the course of the decades after the independence of 1878, there were governments in Bucharest, , who declared themselves in favour of participating in an alliance – of course in a leading position. Thus, only one year after the Congress of Berlin, Count Gregory Sturdza recommended an alliance of the Balkan states in the Romanian senate.[530] The tendency to approve of the project of a Balkan League including its aggressive programme in regard to Macedonia continued to catch on, (although Romania had no common border with Macedonia), but it would not have ever come to Romania being a member. Instead of that, Romanian politics concentrated on supporting the Wallachians or Aromanians (in Macedonia they are called Vlachs) in their cultural individuality through schools, books, etc., since they are regarded as belonging to the same original tribe as the Romanians themselves because they also speak Aromanian, or Macedo-Romanian, etc.[531]

Even years later, Bratianu, Minister President of Romania, which had been a kingdom since 1881, hesitated to get involved in an alliance with Serbia and Bulgaria, as territorial disputes existed with both of them. "Neutrality and reserve" were "the right policy" for Romania.[532]

Bucharest countered rumours to the contrary so clearly and plainly that the Auswärtiges Amt required a report from its envoy in Bucharest, von Berchem, when it learned from the German chargé d'affaires in Athens in 1886 that the Greek foreign minister had mentioned a Romanian alliance initiative.[533]

Von Berchem shed light on the background of the rumour. It does not come as a surprise that it is along the same line as that which has already appeared in the chapter on Greece. His Greek colleague "confessed" immediately that the Romanian leaders had actually given no sign at all in that direction.

> "Alone the efforts of the Romanian Comités to raise the national awareness among the Romanians of Macedonia by setting up schools were considered suspicious in Greece, and made it seem possible that, 'at some point later' the Romanian government would join forces with the Bulgarians against the Greeks in Macedonia. That is why Athens is observing the relationship between Romania and Bulgaria with suspicion; they cannot imagine that Romanian comités would spend considerable sums in Macedonia and in Epirus for school purposes without political ulterior motives."[534]

An old word of wisdom: he, who constantly harbours malicious ulterior motives, presumes that everyone else also does the same.

The envoy commented:

> "These tendencies displease the Greeks because it would make the Hellenization of Macedonia more difficult, and, if one even wants to get involved in speculations about the distant future of Macedonia, then it must certainly be correct that the Romanian government sooner expects that the Bulgarians would spare the nationality of their fellow-tribesmen than the Greeks would."[534]

The perfidious term "Hellenization" also appears here once more, which exposes the necessity of having to first Hellenize the population of Macedonia after its annexation, because, like it or not, they were not Greeks.

The Romanians were aware of this imperialistic plan of Greece with regard to Macedonia; so they at least tried to save their own ethnic group there.

Then one year later in 1888, the new envoy, von Bülow, also reported:

"Even if the Romanians, despite their ambitious plans for the future, aren't earnestly thinking about an annexation of Macedonia, then they do not want to allow the Kutso-Wallachians [Koutsovlachs] ... to be turned into Greeks."[535]

Bulgaria, on the other hand, had made advances to the Romanians again and again in the hope of being able to move them to an alliance of some nature. For Sofia, it would have been optimal to win Romania as a comrade-in-arms, or at least as a neutral neighbour, since Romania was trying as far as possible to keep on the side of both the Great Powers and Turkey. The Romanians, for their part, lived constantly with the nightmare of an agreement or even of an alliance between Russia and the Ottoman Empire. As they saw it, the worst situation would be if Bulgaria were also to join this alliance.

Inasmuch, they must have welcomed the following offer:

The Bulgarian Prime Minister Stambulow brought forward the question to the Romanian consul general in Sofia in 1888 whether King Carol would not be willing to have himself elected also as the Prince of Bulgaria in order to establish a personal union.[536] The German envoy reports that the king declined this offer with the following explanation:

"His rank as King of Romania was too high to be able to wear beside this crown the one of a Bulgarian prince as an equivalent."

And after "He" had let off "His" steam about the widespread Romanian dialect in northern Bulgaria, he added:

"The sonorous and well-developed Romanian language is too superior to the still underdeveloped and rough Bulgarian idioms, so that the Romanization of the Bulgarians could offer insurmountable difficulties."[536]

Contrary to the wise old saying, this pride did not come before the fall.

In the opinion of the Austrian foreign minister, in 1891 it looked like the Russians had

"raised false hopes for the King of Romania with the tempting project of a Balkan League that would be independent of Austria."

The vanity of the Romanians was apparently taken sufficiently into account with the offer, as this alliance was supposed to be under Romanian command. That this alliance, in the meantime, should "naturally (be) under Russian patronage" was, however, an all too obvious obstacle[537], because "Romania's situation would have suffered a substantial endangerment" through this.[538] After all, it had not even been fifteen years since the Russians had demanded the right to march through Romania so that they could carry out their military operations against Turkey (at that time because of Bulgaria).

Even if King Carol described the "brotherhood south of the Danube" as a farce, he did feel himself obliged to avoid the risk of isolation. In 1896, the German envoy believed he recognized an increasing tendency,

"to use the renewed establishment of diplomatic relations with Greece for agreements about a common reaction towards Serbian-Bulgarian subversive activities in Macedonia."[539]

Despite the dilemma of having to seek support, the Romanian government went on

"sticking to the principle that the Porte had to continue to be Romania's best friend in the Balkans."

Romania went so far as to offer Turkey its army in the case of a war against Bulgaria breaking out. Bulgaria and Serbia had wanted to come to the aid of the Greeks in their war against Turkey in 1897 but were prevented from doing so by Russia and Austria. Against this background, the Romanian offer to Turkey (as well as a Romanian-Austrian convention) understandably worried Bulgaria and Greece. That is why both of them tried very hard to display a peaceful conduct towards Turkey. Athens was looking for additional protection and, in 1901 in Austrian Abbazia (now Opatija), agreed to an entente with Romania, in fact one that was staged by Vienna against Bulgaria. This phoney friendship was not to hold for long, though, since Romania in 1906 was to break up its diplomatic relations with Greece again this time due to

> "maltreatment of Romanians in Macedonia by Greek gangs".[540, 541]

For the time being, though, in 1896, Romania was still keen for peace on the Balkans. The Romanian minister president, Count Grégoire Sturdza, would even have been prepared to encourage Russian hegemony through bilaterally safeguarded agreements of all Balkan states with St. Petersburg,

> "until the psychological moment for the partitioning" [of Macedonia] "had come, in which the Ottoman Empire fell to pieces and the great Slavic protecting power came to chair the meeting for dividing the spoils."[542]

The contradiction to the newly declared friendship with Turkey did not seem to bother anyone: Why shouldn't Romania long for the disintegration of Turkey and up to that point be on good terms with it – like all the other countries too?

Not to be overseen and even in those years, long before the beginning of the First World War, Romania's break with the German states and its defection to the Entente was looming.

(The following example may serve for the continuous observation of the *dynastic networking* in Europe: in the year of 1893, the heir to the Romanian throne, Carol's nephew Ferdinand, married the Princess Marie of Saxe-Coburg and Gotha. In 1921, their daughter Elisabeth married the later Greek King (from 1922), George II, the oldest son of Constantine I and grandson of George I.)

Years later, in 1911, when, after a three-year term in office, the Romanian Prime Minister Bratianu, the son of the earlier minister president, fell from power the danger that came from Romania for the Bulgarians seemed to diminish – and "the defensive forces in Bulgaria grew weary."[543]

The Bulgarians should not have allowed themselves to do so because 18 months later in the Second Balkan War, not only Serbia and Greece but also Romania and even Turkey would go against Bulgaria, giving grounds enough for the disintegration of the Balkan League (*this* Balkan League), which was mainly pushed by Bulgaria and so often predicted by diplomatic observers.

2.4.2 Romania's further network of connections with other countries

Russia was so very interested in the creation of a Balkan League (!), that it would have taken the detour of a customs union, if necessary, to get closer to this goal. From the very beginning of the alliance process, economic considerations had also repeatedly a part to play in the reasoning behind the establishment of an alliance. The core of the customs union was supposed to be Serbia and Bulgaria. Romania was always being pressured by Russia, as Envoy v. Kiderlen heard from Minister President Sturdza, to come to an understanding with these two states. After that Russia would

> "bind" all of them "to itself by granting them trade policy advantages." Russia "probably had in mind the role the customs union had played for the unification of the German Reich."[544]

The Russians might have exerted less (or more?) pressure if they had known about the secret agreement that the Romanians had already concluded with the Middle Powers in 1883[545], when they had been pressured by Petersburg in a similar way. This support was what made the Romanians' policy of neutrality towards their neighbours considerably easier in those years.

The times (and interests) changed, however. That is why Romania's partisanship for Germany and Austria (as well as Italy) lasted a while, but did not survive the First World War, as is known.

For the time being, however, the Romanian antipathy towards Bulgaria was not beneficial for an agreement between Bucharest and Sofia/Belgrade. The Serbian envoy was hardly welcomed with open arms when he came with a corresponding proposal in 1906:

> "The hatred towards the Bulgarians, which is based for the most part on envy about a possible future expansion on their part, does not allow such thoughts to emerge here at the present time."[546]

Encouragement for a Balkan League reached the Romanians from an unexpected direction, even though the good advice contained in it remained only a marginal event of history. Thus, in 1908, the German embassy in Vienna learned about a circular letter from Ricciotti Garibaldi, the son of the famous Italian revolutionary, to the Romanian League of Culture. In this letter, Garibaldi full of disgust for the Austrian annexation of Bosnia and Herzegovina which had just taken place two months before, advised the Romanians "to join the other Balkan peoples" under a complete dissociation from Austria.[547]

> "We Italians have always regretted Romania's Austrophile-policy. ... An alliance between Romania and Italy, based on deep and mutual sympathies, cannot come into its own as long as the oppressive, reactionary and freedom-killing Austrian influence is in the way."

Then, Garibaldi reaches beyond the Balkans and dares a prophecy about the withdrawal from the Triple Alliance – which actually did happen in the First World War. (That is how, after entering the war against Germany in 1915, Italy could pocket the traitor's reward of South Tyrol on the basis of the secret Treaty of London.)

- One may surely insinuate that the Italian exit in World War II, also for the sacro egoismo, can be looked at as exemplary, when Italy, under the pressure of its defeat by the USA also left the alliance with Germany, allowing it once again to count itself among the victorious powers – an apparently very popular procedure not only in the Balkans.

From remarks made by the Romanian Foreign Minister Djuvara to the German Envoy von Bray in the year 1909, it emerged that Russian and Turkish efforts - Djuvara spoke of "insinuations" and "kindnesses" - to pull Romania over to their respective sides were always evaded by Bucharest.

> "However when recently the Turkish envoy here, Séfa Bey, pressed for a committal answer, it turned into a not-to-be-misunderstood rejection. And that's what would ... happen to anybody who would come to the Romanian government with such nonsense as the Balkan League or with proposals that were aimed at loosening the old ties of friendship and trust which link Romania with Germany."[548]

Were the Romanians already trying to give the German government a (false) sense of security in 1909, even though they knew at that time where they were going to hang up their coats?

If one keeps all the broken promises in mind that Romania or the other Balkan states made to Turkey or to each other, then the German Empire should have actually been warned in advance about what could be thought of such assurances.

King Carol's last remarks before the establishment of the Balkan League, passed on by Envoy von Rosen in 1911, are not without a certain irony and can be understood as a clear indication:

> "The gossip about the Balkan League worried His Majesty King Carol just as little as the Macedonian question. He is convinced that such an alliance is not capable of action without and against Romania, and he is not willing ... to deviate ... from his present calm and maintaining policy in favour of the adventurous plans of Greece and the Balkan states."[549]

A king can also be a fool - or rather, fool others. The Balkan League was established less than a year later, in March of 1912 - perhaps not against but certainly without Romania. In October of 1912, the First Balkan War broke out. Romania itself took part in the Second Balkan War (from June of 1913) – under King Carol.

There were two prerequisites for this other special constellation: first, the Revolution of the Young Turks in 1908, with its speedy return to nationalistic goals (e.g., the Turkinization), reinforced by the Austrian annexation of Bosnia and Bulgaria's declaration of independence, virtually forced the willingness of the Balkan states, including Greece, to a minimal reconciliation, so that the "TIMES", as already mentioned farther above, described the Revolution of the Young Turks in its function for the founding of the Balkan League as deus ex machina.[550]

And second: without the intensive effort of Russia in the name of the Entente, the Balkan League would never have materialized.

To come back to the Romanian-Greek relations: in 1911, the now indispensable diplomatic relations of Romania to Greece were rapidly restored, for which Athens had also long since been pushing. The Greek Minister President Venizelos seems to have hastily filled the vacant post in Bucharest; at any rate, the German embassy showed a certain professional sympathy in its relevant report for the newly appointed Greek colleague in Bucharest, who would discover "thousands of unanswered complaints there" (Romanian victims of the Greek cruelties in Macedonia), "each single one of which contained a cause for conflict."[551] But - experienced enough - the embassy continued its report:

> "Perhaps exactly for that reason, Mr. Venizelos sent an inexperienced outsider to Bucharest ...[who has] never been in the civil service and who, as an amateur, [has] in fact dealt with economic questions but never with politics. He will leave the running of the embassy to his bureau in Bucharest, in order to be able to apply himself all the more to his social duties. He is ... married to a well-to-do and charming Greek lady from Marseilles. He is a favourite of the King and, for a Greek, curiously civilized and unprejudiced."[551]

2.5 Albania

2.5.0 Excerpts from Albanian history

In order not to have to copy the tendencies of all other Balkan states and follow a one-sided interpretation of history limited by interests, it is advisable in this case to go back to objective scholarship. The following paragraph is based mainly on the renowned expertise of Georg Stadtmüller in the history of South-eastern Europe. The author considers it not only justifiable but also helpful if the quotations turn out to be somewhat more detailed because the text is not only relevant for Albania but also for all of the Balkan states and for the subject under study.

- "In the myths of the Balkan peoples, sagas about their beginnings and origins live on. They point to a prehistory that reaches far back into the past and that allows them to claim an unbroken ethnic homogeneity and continuity in their ancestral areas. In the historical remembrance, an immediate inner interrelation is postulated between the ephemeral establishment of dominions in the early and high Middle Ages and the national states of the 19th and 20th centuries. The ideologists of the aggressive ethno-nationalism felt themselves logically as the executors of a historical mission. They sought justification and legitimacy in the stereotypes of a national historical tradition, which does not know any breaks in continuity. The Albanians continue to refer to their Illyrian origins ..., the Romanians recall their Dacian prehistory, the Bulgarians think of themselves as the heirs of the Thracians as well as of the Turkish-speaking Proto-Bulgarians and the Slavic immigrants."[552]

Only the modern-day Macedonians are not allowed to refer to the ancient Macedonians, even though they, along with the Greeks, are the only people who still carry the name of their antecessors in the region.

Karl Kaser is restrictive in regard to the Albanians:
- "Many Albanian researchers, who deal with this subject (archaeologists, historians and linguists), defend the theory of a continuity from the Illyrian to the Albanian ethnos which is questioned by many non-Albanian scholars."[553]
- "The homeland of the prehistoric and of the early Albanian people was in the mountainous regions of northern Albanian in pre-Slavic and post-Slavic times." "In the course of the Roman Empire, the general Romanization had included and altered the complete inner areas of the Balkans. ... In their mountains the tribes of nomadic shepherds had evaded the Romanization the longest. The prehistoric Albanian shepherds could maintain their ancestral language in the Mat District in northern Albania, protected from the disintegrating contact with the culture of the Roman Empire and the imperial language, Latin, by mountainous walls that were difficult to surmount. But with time, the idiom of the prehistoric Albanians would have also succumbed to the over-powerful influence of the Romanization. Step by step, Latin elements penetrate the prehistoric Albanian language. ... If this development had gone on for another century, then the prehistoric Albanians would have also turned into Balkan-Romans. ... The prehistoric Albanian idiom ... froze at the level of development which it had reached under the influence of the Romanization at the time of the Slavic land seizure. (Loan-words from Latin still make up about one-quarter of the modern-day Albanian vocabulary.) After the Slavic acquisition of land, the Albanians and the related Romanians ("Vlachs") led an almost ahistorical life for nearly a millennium."[554]

It has already been cited above that inhabitants of the Greek interior only survived the great Slavic onslaught on scattered coastal strips – and on the islands.

- "A further part of the pre-Slavic Balkan population fled before the attacking Slavs not to the coasts, but rather into the mountains and there changed from farmers or half-farmers to shepherds once again, the ancestors of the modern-day Albanians and Romanians, under the pressure of the new economic environmental conditions."[555] "Albanians and Romanians ... lived as wandering stock farmers in the mountains from the 7th to the 11th century without an external state history. It was only after the turn of the millennium that were they mentioned at all by the Byzantine historians."[556] "This course of events ... is only discernible in the mirror of etymological facts. The Slavic words, which came into the Albanian and Romanian language along with loan objects, give important indications about the social and cultural neighbourhood relations."
- "... The completely or partially Romanized original population of the northern Balkan Peninsula (suffered) a serious cultural setback after its retreat to the mountainous regions. When then, after some generations, a peaceful neighbourly relationship with the Slavic intruders developed, nomadic "Valachian" shepherds learned farming and the settled way of life again ... in the course of the centuries ... from the Slavs. The "prehistoric Albanians" and the "prehistoric Romanians" owe

> a great part of their material culture to their borrowing from the Slavs, as can be seen through the loan-words from Slavic languages." (Stadtmüller: page 97)

- "Most of the expressions for house and farm and their parts as well as many expressions for household goods and for making bread were taken over from the Slavs, as were quite a few expressions for the plough and its parts. Through the Slavs, the Vlachs and the Albanians also got to know: clear-cutting (of woods), irrigation, threshing, meadow-management and the measurements for grains, furthermore crafts and trade, especially weaving, making pottery, carpentry, the craft of forging and making weapons, the art of braiding, building walls and houses, the mill and the walk-mill." (Page 97) "Especially numerous are also the Slavic loan-words in the area of civil and state law. Thus, the Albanians used the Slavic loan-words: for their expressions for established rights, compurgator (character witness), nobility, tax collector, serfs and metayers (sharecroppers) and numerous titles for civil servants (governor, village headman, commander, etc.). The numerous taxes, levies and duties have Slavic names without exception, as do the following occupations: watchman, field ranger, coachman, blacksmith, woodcutter, gravedigger, restaurant (also: pub or inn) owner, cellermaster. A Slavic word is also used for the "family farm". It is obvious from these borrowings how deeply the Slavic cultural influence affected the Albanians." (Page 98) In regard to farming there were also (Slavic) expressions for field, woods, garden, pomiculture and viniculture.

Under the dominion of the First Bulgarian Empire, the rapacious Albanians and Romanians had to

> "stay calm, whether they liked it or not. When, however, the Great Bulgarian Empire fell apart at the end of the 10th century under the blows of the Byzantine armies, the historical hour of the two pastoral peoples had come."

In the 11th century, the Albanians appeared in the reports of contemporary historians – and "after that almost continuously" – as mercenaries serving foreign masters. Edgar Hösch mentions some examples in this connection:

> "The Serbian ruler, Stefan Dušan, used Albanian auxiliary troops in his military campaigns and assigned them new settlement sites in the conquered territories. After the end of the 14th century, Albanians were settled by the Byzantine Emperors, the Venetians and the Catalans as soldiers and as settlers to compensate for the loss of population on the Peloponnese, on Euboea and some Aegean islands. The Turks followed this tradition."[557]

They soon started spreading.

> "In 11th and 12th centuries, the coastal areas of lower Albania were settled, in the 13th century ... southern Albania." (Page 206) When the Great Serbian Empire fell apart after the death of Tsar Dušan, "the Albanians also began a tremendous push to the south. First, Epirus was settled, of which the northern and western part (southern Albania and Camerija) is still traditional Albanian homeland today. Then, the Albanian expansion went further towards Akarnania, Aitolia and from there on the one side over the Golf of Corinth to Morea" [Italian for Peloponnese] "and on the other side to Boeotia und Attica. ... Approximately half of the Greek homeland was occupied by the Albanians at that time. ... In the course of the centuries then, Hellenism won back the lost territory step by step through its cultural superiority and, above all, through the cultural effectiveness of the Orthodox Church. Under the influence of the church, the Orthodox Albanians adopted the Greek language and soon began to feel like Greeks themselves." (Pages 206/207)

In the *15th century* the Albanians were

- "obliged by the broaching Turkish rule to take on a new settlement expansion. The new emigration took place in different forms: first, greater masses of Albanians left their homes in Albania and Morea as refugees and settled in Italy (Sicily, Calabria, Basilicata, Apulia and Rosciano)". (Page. 207)
- "At the end of the 16th century ... the Islamization of Albania (began). For the Albanians, the declared profession to Christianity was always only of an outward appearance, which only superficially concealed their old heathen beliefs. That's why it was so easy for Islam to gain ground

there. ... The progressive expansion ... was ... due exclusively to political and economic conditions. Islam was adopted in order to escape paying the capitation tax." (Page 274)

Here is Hösch once again on this topic:
- "Large numbers of conversions to the Islamic faith made the integration in the multi-ethnic Ottoman Empire easier for the Albanians and opened various career chances for them in the civil service. Their predominance in numbers led to a gradual Albanization in Kosovo during the time of Turkish rule."[557]
- "The Albanian mountain tribes were favoured from the time of their being 'Turkicized' by the Ottoman government and could, thus, continue their settlement expansion ... without interference. First, they plundered the neighbouring areas with constant raids; then, they occupied western Macedonia and the territories of 'Old Serbia' (Raška). The Albanians (Arnauts) also made up a considerable part of the Ottoman army and, in the imperial administration, the leading 'renegade class'. Gradually, the majority of the Albanians became Moslems under Turkish rule ... and then played an important role in the Ottoman Empire. Numerous statesmen ... and high-ranking civil servants in the administration were Albanians." (Page 277)

Of the 47 grand viziers in the 170 years after 1453, only five were Turks, but eleven were Albanians, eleven Slavs, six Greeks, one a Cherkess (Adyg), one an Armenian, one a Georgian, one an Italian and ten of unknown origin.[558]
- "In the 17th century, the Serbian population was slowly pushed out of the old Serbian basin-landscape (Raška, Dardania) by this advance of the 'Turkicized' Albanians. Albanian immigrants took their place. This unstoppable advancing of the Albanian peoples into the old Serbian territories only seems to have come to a standstill at the end of the 19th century." (Page 278)

Besides the often mentioned flight of the Serbs around 1690 from the revenge of the returning Turks after the withdrawal of the Imperial Habsburg troops to the north, Karl Kaser enumerates additionally simple, almost technical geographical reasons:

"Independent of the eternal dispute about who had settled this region first - Serbs or Albanians - the fact must be emphasized that the distance from the northern Albanian tribal lands down to the Kosovo plains is small; apart from the fact that there was also no border there to cross until 1913. And so, it happened that in the 18th and 19th centuries thousands of Albanian mountain families wandered down to the plains, searching for better living conditions, and mingled among the Serbian inhabitants."[556]

As one sees in this example, the "borderless" Ottoman Empire had characteristic consequences for the occupied and exploited peoples. Karl Kaser writes further:

"Due to the circumstance that the Ottoman Empire also spread over the Near East and North Africa, no boundaries were set for immigration to and emigration from Asia and Africa from or to Europe."[560]

In connection with the depiction of the "spread of agrarian feudalism" in the Ottoman Empire as well as the "striving for autonomy of the big provincial governors, who, far from the imperial capital, claimed their actual independence", ("The most important... - Ali Pascha of Janina and Mehmed Ali Pascha of Egypt - ... were both Albanians. ... In Skutari the family Buschatlija, also Albanian upstarts, occupied the position of Pascha for almost a full century, 1752-1832.") Stadtmüller says further:

- "Another fatal mistake which played a part in the progressing internal disintegration of the Empire was the unleashing of the belligerent mountain tribes on the borders of the Empire – in the west the Albanians, in the east the Kurds. Through centuries, a strong central government had subdued the inherent pugnacity of these tribes. With the increasing inner anarchy in the provinces, the chance came for these predacious tribes to attack the surrounding areas with constant plundering raids and to expand their own territory through terrorism. That is how the Albanians occupied western Macedonia and the Old Serbian basin landscapes in the 17th and 18th centuries. In Armenia, the big Kurdish chiefs wielded an almost unbounded despotic rule." (Pages 346-347)
- "Out of this inner anarchy, the revolts of the Balkan peoples, their success and their state formation are understandable. ....the subjugated Balkan peoples continually (gained strength). ....the Balkan

peasantry (was) already advancing at the end of the 18th century; the Turkish peasantry, which had forced its way into the region colonizing in the older Ottoman era, now began to retreat. At the same time, the self-confidence of the Balkan peoples increased through the reflection on their own history ... and through contact with new ideas that found their way to them from the West. That is how these peoples prepared themselves for their fight for freedom, supported by the great foreign powers: Habsburg – Venice – Russia." (Page 347)

The goal of the first reformer on the Sultan Throne, Selim III, was,
> "to make the Ottoman Empire into a modern state by adopting progressive Western institutions (military reform, finance reform, administration reform). His attempts failed because of the resistance of the Janissaries"[561] [*Die ich rief, die Geister, werd' ich nun nicht los!* (Translator's version: I cannot rid myself of those that I summoned, the spirits.) From: Goethe's "The Sorcerer's Apprentice"], "of the reactionary Moslem clergy and the reactionary courtiers. The Sultan was ... decried as a religious reformer and as a heretic. ... An uprising forced him to revoke the reform laws. ... A fatwa of Sheikh-ül-Islam declared that, as a heretic, he should forfeit the throne (1807). Soon thereafter, he was strangled (1808). However, the necessary course of development ... was not to be stopped."

Mahmud II continued his work.
> "The big feudal lords ... in Anatolia and in the western Balkans ... were overthrown. They submitted or their heads arrived in Constantinople one after another. ... When the Janissaries revolted once again against the reforms ... they were declared heretics" – once again with the "support of the Moslem clergy." "The holy religious war was called out against them. The Janissary troops were literally wiped out in a massacre (1826)." (Page 348)

[*In die Ecke, Besen! Besen!* (Back now, broom, into the closet.) Also from Goethe's "The Sorcerer's Apprentice".]

After comments about the fundamental victory of the idea of the nation-state, as it was manifested in the Peace of Adrianople (modern-day Edirne) – to confirm the Greek independence, Stadtmüller only shortly touches here the development of the other Balkan states and ends then with:
> "Throughout the 19th century, there were only two provinces of European Turkey where no national independence movement rooted in the population arose: in Bosnia and in Albania." (With this Stadtmüller does not deny the revolts to attain more rights.) "....the Islamization had also reshaped the political consciousness of the population. In place of a national consciousness of the people, the supranational imperial consciousness of the Ottoman Empire had grown deep roots there." (Page 376)

This development is also responsible for the Albanians' constituting a special case in that they did not have a state of their own earlier, unlike the other Macedonian neighbours and Macedonia itself. The Albanian nationality was considered as non-existent, even as late as at the Congress of Berlin.[562]

However, the continuance of Albania in the Ottoman Empire foiled the Serbian and Montenegrin hopes of obtaining the opening of the access to the Adriatic Sea at the Congress of Berlin. As compensation, Serbia got back Old Serbia (Kosovo) with Niš und Sjenica; the Turks had to hand over to Montenegro a 37 km-wide strip of the northern and eastern Albanian mountainous regions. But since the Albanians did not want to accept these cessions, unrest broke out – and in fact on the part of all Albanians, the Moslems as well as the Christians (i.e., the Catholic and the Orthodox Christians). To be sure, this revolt was also put down by the Turks, but it went on breaking out again at intervals, e.g., in 1881 and 1883. In 1879, the Albanians even invaded Serbia.

This was last but not least "the consequence of the 'delay', which the Albanian national movement shows in contrast to those of the Greeks and the Slavs."

Viktor Meier reminds us that the Albanians tried first in 1878
> "to counter the, at that time already threatening, partitioning of their territory by the newly developing Christian national states through a Pan-Albanian representation, the 'League of Prizren'."[563]

The text in Article 1 of the *"Convention of the Albanian League"* talks about the "decisive repulsion of any annexation of our land by a foreign realm"; whereas it says further that "our convictions and our dignity ... are focused on the defence of the rights of His Majesty the S u l t a n". (Art. 2) Consistently, according to Article 3, the names of the participating districts are listed in a book with the title "The Loyal of the Empire and of the Fatherland". It is astonishing to read that the participants commit themselves to protect, in accordance with "the Chéri [Sharia], ... the life, the honour and the fortune of the non-Moslem subjects like we protect our own honour and our own fortune." (Art. 4) On the other hand, this generous, modern regulation becomes relative again in the final article, no. 16, where it says: those, "who are not in favour of this alliance, and in so doing are offending the Chéri, will be considered as N o n – M o s l e m s ..." Also their own members, who do not fulfil their duty or who even "withdraw from our League", are threatened with strong punishments.[564]

After the Balkan Wars, Albania was separated from the Ottoman Empire in 1913 through the ruling of the European Great Powers. The Conference of Ambassadors in London established a constitution for Albania on the 29th of July, 1913. At the same time it was declared to be an independent state. Alternatively, as a result of the surrounding independent states, it would have become a "small leftover area of European Turkey", a Turkish enclave geographically separated from Constantinople.[565]

In conclusion, another quotation from Viktor Meier:
> "The Albanian declaration of independence of 1912 came at a time when the territorial cards had already been dealt out to a great extent. That is the reason why large parts of the Albanian settlement area as well as approximately one-third of all Albanians remained outside of the 1913 internationally acknowledged Principality of Albania. This was true for the Çameria region in the Epirus Mountains that went to Greece, for Kosovo as well as for the north-western Macedonian areas around Debar, Gostivar, Tetovo and Kumanovo that went to Serbia, and for the southern and northern coastal areas of the Scutari Lake that became Montenegrin. Only in the period of 1941-44 were all of the Albanian settlement areas ruled from Tirana, but this happened under the regime of Fascist Italy, which had annexed Albania in 1939, and under the German occupation of 1943-44. In 1944 the Kosovo and north-western Macedonia went once again to Yugoslavia, and the Çameria went back to Greece."[563]

For its part, Albania was "compensated" by the dividing powers, whereby they took an additional area southwest of Ohrid and Lake Prespa from, as it was, defenceless and carved up Macedonia and gave it to the new state of the old Shqiptars.[567]

2.5.1 Fragments from reports

In the Political Archive there is an abundance of material on Albania. In contrast, the yield on reports on the selected subject area for this book is extremely meagre in the file series named in the introduction. However, the few that there are go very far back:

thus, the royal ambassador in Vienna, Freiherr. von Werther, had already forwarded a report of the Consul von Lichtenberg from Ragusa, modern-day Dubrovnik, in 1865 to the Prussian Ministry for Foreign Affairs, in which the latter reported about "conditions of criminality in Albania that the Porte can hardly keep under control".[568]

Then again, the Consul had also gone on in great detail about the legal system of the mountain tribes around Scutari. Of these, he particularly emphasizes the following famous names (among others): Hotti, Clementi [here one recognizes the obvious trace of the Romanization], Skreli und Castrati [ditto].[569] The natives did not seem to completely trust their own legal rules, though, because when the ruler of the Miriditi – "a middle-Albanian tribe who speak Gheg dialect" – died, the French consul from Ragusa was appointed to be the executor.[570] Shortly afterwards, the royal Prussian consul had to forward a report with the following announcement:

"In the night of the 20th of August, the grave of the Prince of the Miriditi, Bib Dada, in Scutari, who died on the 31st of July, was opened, the corpse was pulled out to a distance of ten steps, and the cross standing on the grave was smashed." "Apparently, robbery was not the motive for this crime, since not a bit of the suit in which the corpse was dressed, that was richly embroidered with gold, was stolen at all. ...The hardly dormant fanaticism of the Moslems in Upper Albania raises its head defiantly again."

Von Lichtenberg's conclusion:

"Events that could be of a very serious significance and have very sad consequences."[571]

Another quotation should be brought in here, which shows that the quintessence of such developments was already reflected early on, even in reference books:

"They are brave and bold, but also fanatic, vengeful and thieving. The vendetta is strictly practiced."[572]

And, that is the keyword that is suited to irritate the other Europeans down to our days; but modern television can, by all means, enlighten:

"The vendetta was the only chance to make up for the authority of the state that was missing."[573]

To be sure, the vendetta was described as a "cancerous growth" in Albania on the same programme, but on the other hand, it conceded that the regime of Enver Hoxha was even worse. The rigid communist methods did lead to the old scores not being settled at that time, they were not cleared, though, only set aside. That is why, up to today, there is no alternative to the law of the jungle.

Or is there?

KFOR (in Kosovo) may be the substitute for the missing legal system.[573]

3 THE DEVELOPMENT OF THE BALKAN LEAGUE IN THE OTTOMAN EMPIRE

3.0 A look at history

After the Ottomans (Osmanlis) had first set foot on European soil in 1345 following their crossing of the Dardanelles at Gallipoli, a rapid series of victories began in which large parts of south-eastern Europe were conquered and subjugated. Seven years later, they had already degraded the Byzantine Emperor to a tributary vassal. In 1389, the Serbs with their Hungarian and Bosnian allies suffered a devastating defeat at the Battle of Amselfeld (later called Kosovo). But *Byzantium* fell only in 1453. In 1529 the Turks even appeared in front of the city gates of Vienna. They conquered Hungary and the Crimea. All of Europe was trembling with fear of the Moslems – except for France which had been allied with the Sultan since 1536 under Francis I (of the House of Valois) and which, in the lee side of the Turkish threat, continually pushed its eastern border practically unhindered into the German Empire. The successors of Francis, the Bourbon kings, systematically continued this strategy – as Napoleon also adamantly did.[574]

Pushing back the Ottomans turned out to be lengthy and with great losses in human lives. Exactly 500 years after the first triumphal victory of the Turkic Tatars (who then still called themselves (Rum-)Seljuks) over the Byzantines on the Armenian border near Manzikert (Malasguir) in 1071, the Turks, under their leader Ali Pasha (the conqueror of Cyprus), suffered a devastating defeat in the naval battle near *Lepanto* on October 7th of 1571. The defeat did not, however, determine everything yet, even though Pope Pius V was of a different opinion. After the battle with an estimated 50 000 dead victims, he decorated the commander-in-chief, Juan de Austria, and the other admirals and confirmed to them that they had saved Western Civilization.[575]

How low Europe's fortress had sunk and how high the Ottomans had already set their claim to power emerges obviously a generation later from the humiliation that the Sultan must have felt in 1606 when he had to acknowledge the Austrian Emperor as equal, after a war that had lasted thirteen years.

The actual turning-point is generally considered to be the year 1683 when the Moslems laid siege to *Vienna* for the second time. Europe had the choice of either to be destroyed or to defend itself. Despite this explosive situation, the French king declined to give Emperor Leopold the help that he had requested. This was because just two years before, in 1681, in the midst of peace, Louis XIV had annexed Straßburg for France in a totally ungrounded invasion, and so he was not interested in strengthening his opponents with the possible risk that they could take the stolen Straßburg away from him again at the end of the war with Turkey. As a result, the Europeans had to combine their forces without France. This took place in the Holy League, a pooling of the German-Austrian, Russian-Polish (under King Jan Sobieski) and Venetian armies. They succeeded in keeping Vienna and afterwards in even pushing back the Turks in a series of victorious battles (e. g. Zeta, Belgrade, Petarwardein), whereby, among others, Prince Eugene of Savoy, actually a vassal of Louis XIV, distinguished himself as a bold commander. Nonetheless, bitter setbacks and great losses had to be accepted time after time.

Thus, the Ottomans reconquered Bulgaria, Serbia, Belgrade and Transylvania in a counteroffensive in 1690. And with that, the hopes of the Macedonians for freedom were also shattered. The famous Karpoš Revolt broke out. However, since Emperor Leopold I was not able to stick to his declaration of protection, this uprising was also destined to fail. Nevertheless, the Peace of Karlowitz [Karlovci] of 1699 after the second Russian-Turkish War, which limited the Turkish Empire in Europe to the Balkan Peninsula, is considered the real beginning of the decline of the Ottoman power. The Porte was forced to hand over huge territories again: among others, Asov and the Ukraine, Dalmatia and Slavonia, the Peloponnese and Transylvania as well as all of Hungary.[576] Further progress was brought by the Treaty of Passarowitz of 1718.

In any case, the epoch of the Turkish conquests had ended, and with it, the time in which the Turkish armies could plunder, murder and burn as they liked. The fact, though, that soldiers and officers were no longer able to enrich themselves on the goods of the Occident had unforeseeable consequences for the population of the remainder of Turkey. After the immense spoils from the plundering raids of his bands of soldiers had also stopped for the Sultan, additional heavy taxes were imposed on Christian subjects in the Ottoman Empire to cover the enormous costs of the exorbitant lifestyle of the imperial system. This was yet another reason for the coming unrest, - after the humiliating oppression of the European peoples and the drastic cruelties of the Turks ("who treated their subject infidels like dogs", wrote André Maurois in his biography of Benjamin Disraeli, Berlin, 1929, pp. 305 and 307).

Also continuing in the 18th century were the series of wars against the Ottoman Empire of which not all were won, e.g. not the one that Russia and Austria carried out together against the Empire from 1735 to 1739. Nonetheless, in the second half of the 18th century the initiative to push the Turks out of Europe fell principally to Russia. Only when Russia demanded further cessions of territory and also rights of religious protection for the Christian subjects of the Sultan, e.g. in 1774 in the Treaty of Kuçuk Kainarji and in 1792 in the Treaty of Iaşi, was the power of the Ottoman Empire in Europe really coming to its end.

The two sultans, Selim III (1789-1807) and Mahmud II (1808-1839), still tried to comply with the hopes of the Christian peoples and the European powers through their reform projects, but it turned out that

> "the demands of the Great Powers for the equal status of the Christians in the Ottoman Empire were inconsistent with the basic principle of the Islamic-Ottoman concept of empire and power, and the internal structural reforms petered out in the jumble of a social order that had become unpliant and unreformable."[577]

The Moslem citizens were not willing to acknowledge the Christians as equal and having the same rights. In connection with this, we may refer again to one of the countless examples from a report from Ragusa that was mentioned further above:

> "Gatherings in which the equal status of the Christians was agitated against and murders in broad daylight were common occurrences in Scutari."[578]

Is there equality for Christians in "modern" Turkey today like there is for Moslems in Europe?[579]

The first endeavours of the Russians for the equal status of their fellow Christian Orthodox brothers began more than 250 years ago. From a realistic point of view, one cannot help but wonder how many more centuries the European Union will continue to put up with the situation without reciprocity.

The strange principle of the "Islamic-Ottoman concept of empire and power" led to - perhaps unexpected - conclusions. At the end of the 19th century, Richard von Mach, a contemporary observer, ascertained that:

> "At first despised and ignored, the Christian religion became ... a dangerous power by keeping through the centuries the conquered in an inner state of contrast to the victors and by directing their view to the world outside. Thus, we are presented with the picture of the Balkan Peninsula today where the conquerors, who marched in there earlier than the Spaniards did into Mexico and Peru, are faced with the conquered who are - after more than four centuries - just as alien to them in language, religion and customs as they were then. ... If we add the Moslem Albanians, Slavs and Greeks of the Balkan Peninsula together, the sum only results in a small part of the total population that changed its religion in the course of the centuries: but even so, they did not become Turks because they all stayed true to their own language."[580]

This observation can also be supplemented with the example of the islamization of Persia: the old Persians took over not only the new religion but also the Arabic alphabet – but since they preserved their language, they did not lose their Persian identity and, consequently, did not become Arabs.

In connection with the Balkan peoples, Karl Kaser points out the far-reaching effect that, despite the Islamic-Ottoman system,

> "the ethnic and religious identities were preserved" which formed "a basis for the national liberation movements in the 19th and early 20th centuries".[581]

The first practical realization of the new parameter became manifest in the *Peace Treaty of Adrianople* of 1829, when, after a further war in which the defeat of the Turkish-Egyptian fleet at *Navarino* in *1827* played a very important role, Greece became the first Balkan country to be liberated completely from Turkish rule (even though the last uprisings there had started more than 15 years later than those of the Serbs).

Up to this time, Russia had been able to chalk up considerable territorial gains. One of the consequences was that France, for its part, felt encouraged and entitled to feather its nest at the expense of declining Turkey - although still being allies - by annexing the Ottoman Algeria after an arduous 40-year struggle that had started in 1830. In order to prevent future imbalances in the distribution of the Turkish estate, Great Britain and Austria-Hungary proclaimed the territorial integrity of (the remaining) Turkey. Not that their policy arose from a feeling of sympathy with the hard-pressed and increasingly ousted Turks. When it had been the other way around in bygone centuries, the Turks themselves had not shown the slightest scruples in their conquests and subjugations; on the contrary, they viewed the European territories as if they were their rightful property. England and Austria were extremely worried, though, about the continually expanding Russian Empire on the south-eastern edge of Europe.

Both represented their own imperial interests. Britain was concerned that the strategically invaluable Straits might possibly come under the control of someone else other than the English. Already in 1838, London had arranged a trade agreement with Turkey, supposedly for the consolidation of the Ottoman Empire, which later proved to be the staking out of a "chasse gardée". For the protection of its shipping routes to East

India, England had brought about an alliance in 1840 which not only put an end to the series of victories of the Egyptian Mehmed Ali over parts of the Ottoman Empire in the Near East (Egypt was forced to withdraw from Syria) but also included an agreement for the protection of Turkey. Over and above that, England secured its interests with the London Treaty of the Dardanelles.

The characteristic English continental policy of the balance of power was simultaneously and systematically promoted by these measures, but precedence was given to the pursuit of British interests. Ludwig Dehio writes about this:

> "For two centuries, England (had) no doubt (been) the silver-tongued protector of the balance of power on the continent – at the same time, though, the quiet advocate of its own predominance in the world."[582]

The price was high, for on the other side the Balkan peoples, fighting for their liberation and independence, were left in only half-sovereign or even in total dependence on Turkey. But who in London was interested?

As a result of this policy of interests, the Ottoman Empire was saved from being totally expelled from Europe – if not from its complete extermination. This is one of the explanations for the different development of the Islamic movement into and out of south-western Europe [Spain] and south-eastern Europe [the Balkans].

When the Ottomans appeared in the Balkans in 1354, the *Reconquista* had long since started in Spain. As is generally known, the Moors (Saracens) had already crossed over to the European continent from Africa at Jabal Tāriq (Gibraltar) in 711 under General Tariq ibn-Ziyad, that means over 600 years earlier; and although they stayed considerably longer in Spain (in the end approx. 780 years) than the Turks did in the Balkans, they were pushed to totally abandon Spain as a result of the unanimity of the Spanish Christian liberators. This unanimity was missing in south-eastern Europe, and actually not because of the autochthonous Orthodox Christian Balkan peoples - with all their differences, covetousness and petty jealousies - for instance that they were divided in their goal of liberating the remaining European territories from the Turkish yoke, but rather because the humanely, religiously and historically justified liberation of the Christian peoples did not matter to the *European Great Powers in their imperialistic presumptuousness.* With the exception of Russia! What mattered to them was getting advantages and displaying their power (especially in the case of England and Austria).

These motives led to the Great Powers dictating the guidelines to the new Balkan states:

> "The European statesmen negotiated directly with the Sultan about the fate of the Balkan peoples and normally without giving the affected a hearing. They dictated the borderlines and determined the monarchical form of government. The ethnographical principle and the right of self-determination played only a minor role." [That is why they so thoughtlessly disregarded the fate of the Macedonians.] "The newly created royal thrones were occupied for the most part by strangers from other countries who neither possessed detailed knowledge about the countries nor were they fluent in the languages of their subjects and, moreover, did not share the religious beliefs of the latter."[583] (The exceptions - Serbia and Montenegro - were already mentioned. Also compare Mazower's comment on the reverse attitude of the Romanians in ch. 2.3.1)

For the concession that Turks should be able to remain in the Balkans, the Porte would have to make efforts to abolish the oppression of its Christian subjects and make their lives more bearable through the introduction of *reforms.* Sultan Medschid fulfilled this request in 1839 with a new reform-programme, in which he accepted the political rights of the Christians. It was also important for him not to give the Tsar any pretext for constantly browbeating him. It's true though that, as before, the Moslems considered equal status between them and the Christians as totally unjust.

Approximately ten years later, Petersburg made another attempt to push through a protectorship of Russia for the Christians in the Ottoman Empire. In 1853, the extraordinary and plenipotentiary Russian ambassador in Constantinople, Prince Menschikow, demanded on behalf of Russia the right to protect the Christians. When the Sultan refused this demand and Russia marched into the Danube principalities, Turkey declared war on the Russians (the *Crimean War*); a war Turkey won with the help of England and France (Sevastopol). After the Sultan had introduced "total religious freedom" in February of 1856, the Europeans even allowed the Ottoman Empire to join the "European Concert" of the Powers one month later in the (3rd) Treaty of Paris.[584] On this occasion, the Black Sea was demilitarized again at the insistence of England (Pontus Clause).
The Turkish promises with regard to the equality of the Christians remained once again unfulfilled because the devout Moslems saw this concession as a violation of the rules of the Koran and fiercely opposed it. In summer 1860, especially bloody persecutions of the Christians took place once again, particularly at the other end of the Ottoman Empire in Damascus and in Lebanon. In 1861, France felt obliged to intervene militarily to protect the Christians in Beirut.

Under the Khedive Ismael Pasha Egypt declared its independence in 1866, and starting in 1873, the centrifugal forces also became more and more evident in the European vassal states.
In 1874, a war was imminent for the Turks with Montenegro; in addition a revolt broke out in Herzegovina in 1875 (not without some assistance from Russia). Mark Mazower cites from different sources that the revolt was triggered "by harvest failures and the resulting maltreatment of the peasants by the soldiers who were accompanying the tax leaseholders." (Loc cit, p. 84) The Bosnian Christians also rose up. Despite the reforms (better said: reform attempts), a war with Serbia was also threatening. To make matters even worse, the German and the French consuls in Salonika were murdered by an angry Moslem mob at the beginning of 1876.[585]
In the meantime, the revolt had long since spread to Macedonia and Bulgaria. In the Serbian-Montenegrin uprising against the Ottoman Empire, the Turks were driven completely out of Montenegro in 1876, but in Serbia, in comparison, the Serbs were thrown back once again to Belgrade.
In this critical situation, Tsar Alexander II threatened the Sultan with breaking diplomatic relations. The Conference of Constantinople that was convened as a result failed after two months of negotiations. When the Porte also rejected the suggestions of the London Protocol of March 31st, 1877, Russia declared war on the Ottoman Empire on 24th of April. After its victory, St. Petersburg aspired for a solution in favour of Bulgaria in the preliminary peace treaty of March 3rd, 1878, in *San Stefano* (close to Constantinople, where the Russian army was encamped). This was, however, not consistent with England's or Austria's aims in the Balkans, especially concerning the Golden Horn. "England is loudly arming for war", as it says in the volumes of 1908, and is sailing to protect Constantinople with an ironclad fleet into the Sea of Marmara.[586]

This argument was convincing. Exhausted from the costly war with heavy losses, Russia had to obey and place the Peace Treaty of San Stefano at the disposition of the *Congress of Berlin*. As signatory powers of the 1856 Treaty of Paris six European Great Powers and the Ottoman Empire convened in Berlin from the 13th of June to the 13th of July 1878. Despite its victory over Turkey, Russia had to bury its hopes for a Greater Bulgaria and a convenient access to the Mediterranean Sea, a loss that it - thanks to English and French intriguing - chalked up to Bismarck and the German Empire.

The real loser, though, at the Congress of Berlin was the loser of the war: the Ottoman Empire which was "to a great extent only an object for the real European Great Powers".[587] Anyway ...

"The Great Powers in Berlin ... were not able to give a conclusive answer to the Oriental Question." The *Conflict about Macedonia*, "the heart of 'European Turkey' ", was only glossed over and postponed. The tensions continued to ensure "a permanent state of emergency."[588]

The public finances in the Ottoman Empire were in bad shape even before the Congress of Berlin; starting with the Crimean War the military costs had become unbearable. The wastefulness of the Sultan and his entourage had always been so exorbitant that in the above-cited reference book of 1908, when one felt the vicinity of the "Orient" more closely, it says: "But everything disappeared in the financial abyss of mismanagement."[589] Turkey was insolvent in 1875 and had to declare national bankruptcy – not a helpful reputation after another lost war for its appearance at the European Congress of Berlin.

What a catastrophic effect the financial situation had on the Turkish capability to carry on war is clearly demonstrated in a report by Envoy von Bülow from Athens which he had written just a few days before the outbreak of the war. There it says that the Greek government intended

"to buy 60 000 Henry Martini rifles from an American agent who is presently in Athens. The rifles were ordered by the Porte which was unable to pay for them, though."[590]

The realization of the rulings of the *Treaty of Berlin* turned out to be a downright blood-letting for Turkey:

- Serbia, Romania and Montenegro had to be given their independence,
- Bulgaria was obliged to continue paying tribute, but became an autonomous principality,
- Eastern Rumelia, i.e., Southern Bulgaria, remained under Turkish authority but obtained a Christian governor,
- Austria received the "mandate" to occupy and govern Bosnia and Herzegovina,
- England had reserved Cyprus for itself in a bilateral agreement that was opportunely concluded *before* the Congress, (Already years before, London had bought the usufruct for the Cypriot domains of the crown estates from the Porte.)
- Greece was granted large territories; however, it had to wait until 1881 for Thessaly and until 1884 for southern Epirus,
- Russia, the victor, received some areas in eastern Anatolia and also Bessarabia from Romania as a consolation.

With the exception of small Algeria, France did not have anything yet. So, after the Austrians and English had helped themselves to their share, it occupied Tunisia in 1881. This step made it easier for England that now felt discriminated, to finally oc-

cupy the Suez Canal in 1882 and (by taking advantage of the occasion) directly afterwards also whole Egypt.
In addition, there were disturbances and unrest in Albania, on Crete, in Armenia, in Syria, in Yemen, etc. The internal political difficulties must also be mentioned which, starting after the so-called Young Turks founded the Turkish Reform Party in 1876, gradually worked up to a revolution (1908) and must have given the Sultan many a sleepless night. Although the Turks have been aware of their key role at the Straits within the framework of the constellation of the European powers, there was no guarantee that they would not be swept off from the European continent after all when the next war came (and it had to come – and it did come). Even the existence of the whole Ottoman Empire could be at stake. Nonetheless, there was no talk of any particular ner-vousness or of special defence or precautionary measures of the Sultan.

Perhaps, one had to be the Sultan of an enormous empire in a long row of Sultans to be able to take a stance like Romulus the Great in Durrenmatt's comedy of the same name, who calmly fed his chickens while the Roman Empire fell to pieces around him. It must surely have been "hüzün" (melancholy, tristesse)....

The Moslems also showed indifference towards the Christians; Richard von Mach speaks about "the contempt of the Moslem for the Rajah." [591] To declare this attitude as tolerance would be a complete misinterpretation. The Ottoman Moslems felt superior to Christians in religious and ideological questions in such a way that it would not have occurred to them to convince the Christians to the Islamic faith.
Von Mach comments in this connection:
"The proud Turks do not care if the Rajah" [the Christians] "believe in this or that god ... as long as they remain submissive and till the land. The Moslem is even reluctant ... to see the infidels convert to the faith of the Prophet."[591]
Nevertheless, initially there were forced conversions, especially among the important Orthodox dignitaries, - although nobody wants to admit this today. Moreover, the constant kidnapping of underage sons of non-Moslem families to train for the army and administration (Janissaries), that went down in history under the harmless sounding name of "Devshirme" [collection, gathering], was combined with *forced conversion*.[592] (In a touching book, the Greek author, Rhea Galanaki, traces the life-long psychological burdens of these children (in the figure of Ismail Ferik Pasha), who were kidnapped and forced to convert to Islam.[593])
Later, the Moslems preferred to rely on their own strategy for converting: the exemption from paying taxes and the opening of the way up the hierarchy of the army and the civil service - and the right to purchase land as well - that had otherwise been closed to Christians. These possibilities were clearly recognized by all the Christians of that time – and for that reason rejected by the vast majority, so that they would not have to disown their Christian faith (exceptions: Bosnians and Albanians).
That is also why the awareness about the historical development between the two religions was so strongly pronounced. No one, not even Moslems, was so badly informed that they would have, for example, overlooked the fact that the Crusades were the effect caused by the *previous* violent spreading of Islam. No one at that time would have fallen for the ideological trick of defining that the spread of Islam with fire and sword was not a war because it was not allowed to call the Jihad a war. That is why the attitude that one runs across frequently among Western leaders - including academics - to admit the guilt of the Christians on the Crusades without taking the Jihad into con-

sideration, would have been looked upon at that time not as a sign of humble conviction or noble willingness to compromise but rather as a knowledge gap and a false understanding of the order of events in history.

While the Scottish specialist in Arabic studies, W. Montgomery Watt, characterizes the European reaction to the Islamic challenge as an "answer" (l.c. p. 65, et.al.), the U.S. historian, Will Durant, describes the connections as follows:

> "For three long centuries, Christianity experienced the encroachment of Islam and had to watch as it conquered and devoured one Christian land and people after another" ... until "the two rivalling civilizations ... (clashed) against each other in the Crusades." (L.c. p. 602)

3.1 Constantinople and Macedonia as crossroads of foreign interests

The very first relevant document in the files offers a surprise. An offensive-alliance of the Balkan states Greece, Bulgaria, Serbia and Montenegro (feared by the Porte) that was aimed at the Ottoman Empire, is indicated in a confidential aide-mémoire which the Imperial Turkish Ambassador in Berlin, Said Pasha, brought for a démarche to the Auswärtiges Amt in 1883 due to a directive from Constantinople.[594]

In the previous chapters on the different countries, this author has already referred to various documents which proved that in the course of a development of over thirty years, from the Congress of Berlin up to the Balkan Wars, it became apparent that the "conspiracy" of the Balkan states against the Ottoman Empire to annex its last Christian possessions in Europe had not remained concealed from the Sultan and his government, the Sublime Porte.

It is all the more surprising that the news of an offensive alliance against Turkey had already gotten to Constantinople *five years* after the Congress of Berlin which means, at a time when such plans were in fact actually being hatched but when the Balkan League itself was still a long way off. Accordingly, it can be mentioned that the Ottoman Empire was in no way unsuspecting, but rather that it could have reacted early enough with retaliatory measures. On the other hand, remembering the steady retreat of the Turks out of Europe in the last centuries, the Sultan and his cabinet were probably aware of the force of liberation movements and the importance of the powers standing behind them, while the Turks in their fatalistic passivity were looking on helplessly at their own downfall. Because of this awareness, they probably reacted just as unrealistically to the signs of the time as other imperial and imperialistic powers before and after them: with stalling tactics, denial and similar mechanisms.

A report from the embassy in Constantinople bears testimony to this. It implies that the Porte simply ignored the threatening facts:

> "The ... rumours about a political agreement concluded between Greece, Bulgaria and Montenegro, which should also extend to a mutual reaction in the case of a war in which Turkey were involved, won't have made such an impression here where one does not want to believe in even a temporary merging of Bulgarian and Greek interests."[595]

The Turks must have clung to the hope that the Great Powers, as was proven so often before, would not let them fall totally – which turned out to be true in the end (at least up to a certain - territorial - extent).

It can also be assumed that the *Macedonians* had a similar attitude. They, as well, could not imagine that Europe would really abandon them in their just struggle for liberation.

There is an informative article which the "Norddeutsche Allgemeine Zeitung" had taken over from the Sofian newspaper "Balkan", in which it was stressed that:

> "Already for years now, the existence of Turkey is a question for which the solution is prevented solely by the powers that have interests in the matter. Turkey is aware of its situation and, for that reason, does not consider it necessary to worry about the inner-organization of the country. It is convinced that its continued existence depends only on luck and that the interests of the Great Powers meet there."[596]

With that the newspaper accurately summarized in a nutshell the essence of the survival of the Ottoman Empire on European soil.

Interestingly enough, the paper continues its observation by transferring the relations between the Great Powers and Turkey to the relations between the small Balkan states and the remainder of Turkey, i.e. Macedonia. (It goes without saying that the Bulgarian newspaper depicts the circumstances in such a way that neither Serbia nor Greece but only Bulgaria itself could lay claim to Macedonia.) Aside from this mantra-like repetition, it remains remarkable that the newspaper acknowledges the fact that the paths of these three Balkan states would *"cross in Macedonia"*.

It cannot be ruled out that the Macedonians – insofar as they were informed at all about the wheelings and dealings of their neighbours, which can at least be assumed on account of the activities of the gangs from the bordering states – had already cherished the hope at the end of the 19th century that the antagonistic interests of its neighbours would not only cross paths in their country but also be neutralized in the process.

This means that, as the cravings of the European Great Powers for Constantinople (and the Straits) neutralized each other, maintaining the Ottoman Empire, Macedonia could have similarly survived in the quiet eye of the whirlwind that its neighbours were causing.

If the Macedonians had come to such conclusions after the Congress of Berlin, their hopes did not deceive them for thirty long years – until 1912.

The calculation of the Macedonians might have also endured later if the Entente Powers had not chained the Balkan states more closely to them by way of alliances, at the expense of the victim Macedonia. Might have....

To draw a parallel between the Macedonia of the 19th century and the Republic of Macedonia since 1991, it can be proven that the considerations of the newly independent state really went in this direction. In numerous political discussions with foreign politicians, the Macedonian president, *Kiro Gligorow,* pointed out the advantage of Macedonia being in an *equilibrium between the wishes of its neighbours.*

If, in the eyes of the world at large, just one of the four neighbouring states disgraced itself by attacking the defenceless Republic of Macedonia (as in 1912) in order to carve it up (as in 1913), the other neighbours would immediately join in once again, of course. On the other hand, the international organizations would have to guarantee the protection of Macedonia in accordance with international law. Initially, the radicalization of Serbian politics under Milošević gave the European states and America reason for such fears, because:

> "The Serbian 'megali idea' did not differ at all in its basic structure from the Greek, Bulgarian and Croatian 'megali idea', and that, more or less, is how it still is today. Depending on what

seems more advantageous, the nationalists invoke the historical-territorial rights, or on another occasion the ethnic-cultural ones."[597]

Because of this constellation, the pictures by Michael Weithmann of the "four fires around Macedonia"[598] and the comparison with the "four wolves" by Stefan Troebst became common metaphors in the first years of Macedonian independence.

It has worked out all right for approximately ten years. In the meantime, though, it seems that the hope of survival of Macedonia in the eye of the typhoon will be ruined by an unexpected source. In representing the other three neighbours, the *Albanian minority* seems to have gained so much support from the Western side - American as well as European - that there are grave doubts about maintaining the equilibrium described above. Despite a small shortcoming in the creation of the constitution, the Albanians do not have any legal right at all to be permitted to push through their expansive territorial and secession plans in the direction of a Great Kosovo (or Great Albania). Since they know this themselves, they are trying to push through their territorial concepts *with violence and ethnic cleansing.*

3.2 The Turkish dilemma in choosing countermeasures

In 1886, Milan, who had become Serbian king in 1882, considered a peaceful solution to the Oriental Question quite possible – he said. The *Balkan League*, the idea of which "is still in its early infancy", "does not endanger anyone."

> "The essential precondition, though, for such an alliance, the head of which would necessarily be the Porte, is that the latter would have to decide to satisfy the national aspirations of the individual states and to be content with Constantinople and an appropriate territory." [599]

Was it Milan's fault then that the Sultan simply did not realize that he could keep the peace: if only he would forego his European possessions aside from Constantinople and a small patch of territory? (This small patch of territory to which, in fact, the solution later amounted was *Eastern Thrace.*)

Despite all the apathy and all the resignation of the people of the Middle East – what King Milan developed with this concept for Envoy von Bray was not only an underestimation and a false estimation of the Turkish willingness and preparedness for defence, but was, frankly said, an impudence (and consequently also perhaps another symptom for the general decline of the Ottoman Empire). The main idea of the Turkish leaders was the assessment that the Balkan League would inevitably be directed against the Ottoman Empire. Consequently, a Turkish participation in the league would serve the purpose of bending the tip of the spear that this alliance was pointing at Constantinople long before the outbreak of hostilities – if not breaking this tip off. The other Balkan states were increasingly signalling their approval; of course, as already explained several times above, they were only putting on a show for the Great Powers as well as for Turkey.

In the meantime, an additional motive had come up. As a stalling tactic, they could have established any old alliance with Turkey in order to gain time, since the programme of the secret society of the Young Turks of 1889 "Unity and Progress" gave new hope to many of the oppressed. It is true that the latter were disappointed in 1892 when an assassination attempt of the Young Turks to kill Sultan Abdul Hamid failed and the members of the secret society had to emigrate (to Paris) to escape being prosecuted. But, the flame of the revolution never went out entirely.

For a while, even the Sultan himself belonged to the advocates of a Turkish participation in the Balkan League. The German legation in Bucharest in this connection reports about an incident they had heard from the former Romanian Foreign Minister, Alexander Lahovary: the Sultan had happened to meet the Serbian (at that time, ex-) King Milan in Paris and had approved of an alliance made up of Serbia, Bulgaria and Romania, which

> "would find Turkey as a true protector and which, for its part, could contribute a lot to keeping up the integrity of the Ottoman Empire."[600]

(This probably concerns the fast one that the Sultan was trying to pull on the Serbian king, as mentioned above; otherwise, one would have to consider his suggestion terribly naive: as if Serbia would ever have been interested in the integrity of the Ottoman Empire!) At any rate, Milan found himself between the devil and the deep blue sea: as ex-king, he could not simply accept the offer for his successor, even if this was his own son, but he wanted to speak frankly so he tried to

> "make it plausible to the Sultan that Serbia would have to receive a compensation for this ... service."[600]

Thereupon, the Sultan immediately dropped the subject.

Well, not naive at all.

Milan did not need to be so "considerate" towards the German Envoy in Belgrade, Freiherr von Waecker-Gotter. Instead, he could speak freely, what he in fact did when he said:

> "No one would want to deny that, sooner or later, the Turkish rule has to disappear out of Europe."... "The Turkish population of the Balkan provinces feels this instinctively itself, as it is constantly decreasing through emigration."[600]

The monarch was also informative in his remarks about the idea of the *partitioning of Macedonia*: the powers were faced with the necessity of "establishing an approximate equilibrium among the small Balkan states". Very remarkable!

Milan was totally indifferent to the question of which part of Macedonia would fall to Serbia as long as it was not less than "our competitors" would get. Since there were anyway mainly Macedonians who he would have to integrate in Serbia – like the Bulgarians would have to do with the Macedonians in Bulgaria and the Greeks in Greece – only the absolute size of the Serbian share of Macedonia would be important.

Very revealing!

Milan considered the Great Powers, as the highest authority, responsible; which means that he was pretty close to the truth:

> "The Balkan states ... are in the last place the creations, the children of the Great Powers. The latter, therfore, have certain fatherly duties...."[601]

The Macedonians had, no doubt, also set their hopes in these duties....

Milan, for his part, had probably meant his remark more as an appeal to the protective function of the powers and less as a gesture of subordination, since the Great Powers were actually indispensible for the act of the final dissociation of the individual Balkan states from the Ottoman Empire; while the Balkan peoples remained responsible for the inner solidarity of the tribes, meaning also for their integrity.

3.3 The Young Turks – between a Balkan Alliance and the Dual Alliance

One could say that, beside the decisive year of 1878 and the First Balkan War in 1912 with their far-reaching consequences, all other dates between these two fade in their importance. Since history never begins anew at a fixed point, however, but is always embedded in a past history, other events in-between necessarily also have their importance and their effects. Think only of the years, e.g.:

-- 1885 with the Bulgarian Unification and the Serbian-Bulgarian War,
-- 1891, 1894 (in Bitlis) and 1895 (in Trapezunt, now Trabzon) with the massacres of the Armenians, as well as another climax in August of 1896 in Constantinople, (a great crisis that Turkey only survived because the powers could once again not agree about reform plans).
-- 1894 and 1896 with the new disturbances on Crete, also 1897 with the Greek landing there,
-- 1895 and 1896 with further revolts in Macedonia, which were suppressed again and again but which also constantly reminded the Great Powers of the failure of the Turks to realize the promised reforms,
-- 1897 with the Greek-Turkish War in Thessaly,
-- 1898 with the butchering of hundreds of Christians by fanatic Moslems on Crete and starting in
-- 1902 once again disturbances in Macedonia (as well as in Albania), and once again linked with dreadful atrocities.

When the Great Powers compelled Turkey in December of 1902 to finally start initiating realistic measures and the latter was willing to engage a competent inspector, Husni Hilmi Pasha, it was too late, because the revolt in Macedonia had flared up again in the spring of 1903, and it escalated until the 2nd of August, Elias Day (Ilinden Upising), in Kruševo.

As already mentioned in the introduction, this event had a fateful significance for Macedonia. In extension, it also had international repercussions: since Turkey took up repression measures again after the Ilinden Uprising, Austria and Russia believed that they had to intervene to help the Macedonians. For that reason, they passed the so-called *Mürzsteger Punktation* [Mürzsteg Programme of Reforms] on the 3rd of October of 1903 in the hope that they could finally get the Turkish reforms in Macedonia going since no substantial progress had been made in an equal status of the religions or in the administration, especially in the judicial system. And this in spite of the reform plans of the Sultans Selim and Mahmud and the written commitments of the Turks in the peace agreements of Küçük-Kaynarca in 1774, of Paris in 1856 and the Treaty of Berlin in 1878.

Incidentally, "Mürzsteg" did not prevent Russia from prohibiting Macedonia's neighbours to intervene for assistance in the Macedonian uprising, as said above. *Why did Russia do that ...?*

Stefan Troebst writes about the Mürzsteg Programme:
"In the years from 1904 to 1909, the Great Powers tried in vain to stabilize the trouble spot of Macedonia, which was shaken by the uprising." For example, "the Great Powers decreed a reform of the Gendarmerie in the restless Ottoman region of Macedonia, which was actually implemented by police officers from Italy, Russia, Germany, France and Austria-Hungary in the period from 1904 to 1909. Who would not be reminded of the international deployment of police under

the aegis of the Western European Union in Mostar in Bosnia and Hercegovina in 1994-1995 as well as in Albania since 1997?"[602]

On the other hand, the events of the Revolution of the Young Turks of the year 1908 had a special quality for all of the Balkan states and also for all of Europe. This becomes clear considering the development before the background of the "revolutionary" change in the power constellation in central Europe due to the British-French *Entente Cordiale* of 1904 and, on the basis of it, Russia's being pulled into the *Triple-Entente* of 1907.

The consequences for all of Europe are not conceivable without the knots that were tied in the course of those years.

The revolution had the effect of a catalyst in the Balkans. For their part, the Young Turks had let themselves be pushed to speed up their plans for their coup because the Sultan announced parliamentary elections on the 24th of July, 1908, which might have possibly stabilized his power. Such a stabilization would have been detrimental for the goals of the Young Turks' revolution as well as for those of the Balkan states. There is even the hypothesis that the Young Turks had felt encouraged to speed up their plans for a revolution as a result of their misinterpretations of the decisions made at the meeting of the English and Russian monarchs in Reval [now Talinn] at the beginning of June of 1908 (with the alleged aim of intensifying the reforms in Macedonia).

After that, actions and reactions of some states stumbled over each other:
The independence of Bulgaria followed as well as the Austrian annexation of Bosnia and Hercegovina. There were also further attempts to proclaim the union of Crete with Greece – but at one point enough was enough: the (Young) Turks stubbornly sank their teeth into exactly this object in order not to lose after so many setbacks the island, too.

Ambassador von Wangenheim later summarized his impressions of the events as follows. The reasons for the Turkish hostility probably arose from the mood that

"was gaining ground among the Young Turks when they were unable to prevent the well-known pruning of the Turkish national territory shortly after they took over power. The Turkish chauvinism that was aroused through the loss of Bosnia and Eastern Rumelia was looking for a way out and naturally turned to the question of Crete. Crete could just be saved for Turkey...."[603]

That the Young Turks should continue to march on the well-trodden paths of the Sultan was an unexpected surprise – and a disappointment. Many Turks also had hoped for modernization, constitutionalism and perhaps even democratization from them, especially after their reform programme of Paris (1907) had become known. Above all, the still Turkish (Christian) territories in Europe would have expected concessions and even assistance with the liberation from the old feudal system. This also applied to the Macedonians that had set their special hopes on the later "Father of Turkey", *Kemal Atatürk*, who was born in their midst in Salonika and who had lived for long years in the Turkish garrison in Bitola and who had also discussed the revolution with them there. Not only that:

"The Young Turk Revolution broke out ... in Macedonia." "The Macedonian population was also involved in the events of the Young Turk Revolution. Thus, various Macedonian revolutionary groups under the leadership of Jane Sandanski fought on the side of the Young Turks for the goals of the latter as well as for the autonomy of Macedonia within the framework of the Turkish State. However, when the Young Turks actually did take over power, the promises that had been made to Sandanski were not kept."[604]

Mark Mazower assigns the Macedonians an even much more active role. Referring to the "British Documents on Foreign Affairs", he writes (loc.cit. p. 172):
> "Reformist officers, who were angry about the Ottoman weaknesses and the continual intervention of the West, led the Macedonian army in a revolt against the Sublime Porte in 1908. When Sultan Abdul Hamid announced that he would reinstate the Constitution of 1876, a wave of enthusiasm spilled through the whole province and it looked as if the Empire under the revolutionaries would change into a multi-ethnic state with equality in religion and civil rights. There was a short moment of jubilation in Macedonia."

It must have been a very short moment....

Sandanski, the leader of the (leftist) Seres Group, had become well-known through his efforts to improve the chances for Macedonian autonomy by trying to embed it in Balkan federation plans "in order to be able to absorb the conflicting interests of the competing Balkan states." Because, in the decades since the Congress of Berlin, he could not overlook the growing currents against the
> Macedonian "efforts to prove the non-Bulgarian, non-Serbian and non-Greek i*dentity of the Macedonians*".[604]

Even though in 1909, the Macedonians could be sure of the support of the "Macedonian Emigration", first and foremost from Switzerland, and even of some Young Turks, the *resistance of the neighbouring states* was not to be overcome. Since they were pursuing their imperialistic goals with iron determination and had in the meantime long since gained the *approval of the Entente*!

Torsten Szobries cites a comment by Fikret Adanir on this topic:
> The approach of the Sandanski group for a "modern political nation-building process in Macedonia" ... was ... "condemned to failure due to the political development among the powers at that time...."[605]

It's getting clearer and clearer why....

In an interview for the Reuters News Agency, the leader of the Young Turks Party, Ahmed Riza Bey, on behalf of the Committee for Unity and Progress (as Ambassador von Metternich reported from London) had remarked on the topic of the Balkan League: that such an alliance between the Balkan states and Turkey would be "possible and desirable on a political and economic basis".[606] But already a week later, this wishful thinking gave way to a realistic view of things. It was the semi-official Turkish newspaper "Tanin", which set a counter-balance to Ahmed Riza's optimism:
> "In principle, the idea is very humane and noteworthy, but its implementation will have to remain a pipe dream under the present conditions; since the actual prerequisites for it are missing. Turkey could only join such an alliance under the condition that it would have the "hegemony", more or less like Prussia practices it in Germany. Turkey would be willing to take over this role ... But, considering the newest events", [here: the annexation of Bosnia] "one would have to doubt very much that the small states would want to confer that kind of hegemony on Turkey. Bulgaria is not capable of turning its gaze from Salonika und Tsarigrad [Constantinople], Serbia is pursuing its Panslavonic ideas, and Greece is pursuing its utopian Great Hellenic plans. Thus, far away from accepting the hegemony of Turkey, these states are striving to establish their own hegemony. That is why Turkey is not considering an alliance and does not dare to even think about an Entente."[607]

This insight should not actually have been new at the Porte, since by 1883 the Turkish Foreign Minister of that time, Aarify Pasha, had already ironically answered the question of Ambassador von Radowitz about a possible Turkish membership in a Balkan League with,
> "J'espère au moins que personne ne nous jugera assez bêtes...."[608]

Out of necessity, Turkey was forced to seek the support of *European alliances*. Ambassador von Marschall gathered from the Greek newspaper "Tachydromos" that the tendency in Constantinople was towards the German-Austrian Dual Alliance; and this all the more because the Young Turks were convinced "that a Balkan League would be established under the patronage of Russia and Italy. This alliance would fight for the principle of 'The Balkans for the Balkan Peoples'".[609] The Young Turks saw this very clearly.
Consequently, the Turkish decision with regard to Germany, which really only came into effect during World War I, was already initiated quite early.

An almost identical assessment reached the Auswärtiges Amt from Athens. Envoy von Wangenheim reported on a conversation with his Turkish colleague, who said,

"The purpose of the alliance could only be an enlargement of other countries at the expense of Turkey."[610]

As it turned out later, this was only the ostensible aspect for the Balkan League, because the Entente followed totally different goals.
Since it was universally known that Petersburg - as the spearhead of the Entente - stood behind this alliance, Naby Bey predicted,

"that Iswolsky's [the Russian foreign minister's] wheelings and dealings would drive Turkey into the arms of the Triple Alliance."[610] (Germany, Austria and Italy)

As indeed happened later.
The reaction of the Turkish Foreign Minister, Rifaat Pasha, to a question of the German ambassador concerning an article in the "Tanin" about the Balkan League was correspondingly cool. One would consider possible suggestions of the small Balkan states without taking the initiative oneself, but

"our only real interest lies in a confident relationship with Romania, which builds a natural counterweight to the Great Bulgarian endeavours."[612]

This grouping was actually confirmed by the later development – at least as Turkey's and Romania's joint declaration of war against Bulgaria in the 2nd Balkan War is concerned. In contrast, in World War I the two followed separate paths: Turkey entered the war on the side of the Central Powers on November 1, 1914, and Romania through its declaration of war against Austria on August 27th, 1916, on the other side.

3.4 The phalanx against Macedonia takes shape

Among Turkish politicians, the ranks of the realists were by no means united; as always (also in 1910) there were enough of them who "longed for a Slavic Balkan alliance under the aegis of Turkey" – apparently in the eternal wishful thinking "that (through it) Turkey could force Serbia and Bulgaria to maintain the status quo in the Balkans."[613] An illusion, of course.
Envoy von Kiderlen reported from a conversation with Romanian PM Bratiano that neither was Russia letting up in its attempt "to reconcile ... Bulgaria and Serbia". Both states should "commit themselves to a mutual désintéressement with regard to Macedonia even" if the status quo should not continue to exist. *Interesting!*
The sharp-eared Serbs and Bulgarians must have concluded immediately that a territorial change was about to take place, which would exclude them; the reason for this could have been that Greece alone was to be favoured. Russia had the following consolation ready for Serbia and Bulgaria: in case the status quo should change once,

"Serbia ... would get the Sandžak." However – "what Bulgaria should get", the Russians themselves "had perhaps not found yet...."[614]

How come? Could Russia not find a small area of land that it could have promised to the Bulgarian government "as compensation" in a region which the Bulgarians constantly claimed belonged to them because it had been inhabited earlier by people who had spoken Bulgarian and who actually were Bulgarians? There is only one explanation for this:

It goes without saying that Russia, like all the Great Powers, was exactly informed about the ethnic relations in the Balkans. If some area in Macedonia had been inhabited by even a small *Bulgarian minority*, Petersburg would not have hesitated for a moment to promise the Bulgarians this area, like it had promised the Sandžak to Serbia – and like it had let the Bulgarians have (nolens volens) Eastern Rumelia in 1885. But there just wasn't such an area. How could even powerful Russia make a halfway plausible commitment? As PM Bratiano said, the Russians had "simply not found" this area yet.

Speaking of a "Bulgarian minority"; actually there was not even a small Bulgarian minority in Macedonia. The following can be gathered from statistics of the "East European Handbook, Yugoslavia" as well as the "East European and Soviet Data Handbook" by Paul S. Shoup for the years 1921 and 1948 – (both tables are subdivided in accordance with the six regions within Yugoslavia):[615]

1). For 1921 under Macedonia, there was *no* Bulgarian minority indicated, even though minorities down to a size of 100 persons were recorded among the seven ethnic groups and an accumulative column named "Others".

For obvious reasons, there were also no Greeks. Where should they have come from? After all, the Macedonians did not annex Bulgarian and Greek territories in the Balkan Wars, but rather these two countries had taken over Macedonian territory for which reason they both - up to today - have Macedonian minorities even though their numbers are played down, coyly renamed ("Slavophone Greeks") or completely disclaimed.

2). For 1948, there were actually 900 Bulgarians recorded (share of the total population: 0.0%) among eleven ethnic groups and under the accumulative column named "Others", – but no Greeks either.

That did not keep Greece from pulling the wool over the eyes of the general public after the Macedonian independence in 1991 and claiming that an - oppressed (!) - minority of 300,000 Greeks were living in the Republic of Macedonia. Since from this propagandistic magic number it was not possible to construe even by any stretch of imagination the tiniest basis for a claim to Macedonian territory, Athens later made the attempt of an excuse that this number referred to the [Macedonian !] refugees and emigrants (during the Balkan Wars in 1912/13 and the Greek Civil War 1946-48) – who, after all, had once lived in northern Greece!

What a big mess the Greeks got themselves in for this wilful deceit! Being too obvious, it had to fail.

But since the world is pretty ignorant and forgot this scandal, dust settled on this provocation soon – much too soon.

If it had been the other way around, the Greeks for their part would not have missed the chance to use such a matter against the Macedonians for years....

There is even another explanation for the above-mentioned Russian order to Serbia and Bulgaria to practise restraint in regard to possible violent conflicts in and about European Turkey.
It is really strange: Russia made efforts to oblige (!) Bulgaria and Serbia to avoid being entangled in case there were a change in the status quo one day - or more clearly than PM Bratiano might have liked to express it to Envoy von Kiderlen - if there was a war over Macedonia: they would, somehow, receive some other compensation.
Wait a minute! Did Russia want to reserve Macedonia for itself after all?
By no means. It catches one's eye, though, that no one was talking about how to compensate a third neighbouring state of Macedonia, which was also yearning for acquiring some additional territory: *Greece*. At that time, Greece was actually exempted from the Russian exhortations about restraint in case it should come to a change in the status quo. And that day was only one and a half years away.

> *Can one still speak of hair-splitting when it is implied that the European dynasties under the direction of the Tsar believed that they had come to an agreement to entrust the Greek monarchy with the Turkish-Macedonian territory as a present?*

After Reval, this conclusion can count as certain. Or, why should Greece of all countries have been allowed to annex the lion's share of Macedonia in the Balkan Wars? Athens, however, had to struggle by itself to get its share – without Russia's intervening militarily (and above all without England).
Christian Voss describes the situation after the war as follows:

> "Greece and Serbia – seeing themselves since then as the two heroic peoples who liberated the Balkans – are the big-time winners and receive 51% and 38 % respectively of the bankrupt Ottoman estate of Macedonia."[616]

As it turned out later, Russia, or better said the Entente, had not reckoned with the two disadvantaged countries. From the viewpoint of Serbia and Bulgaria, the "deal" looked originally like this:
The Great Entente Powers put force before justice – as long as it was ensured that at least the impression of the principle of the status quo was maintained. Since Russia and England would not intervene in order not to get involved in a war in Europe *prematurely* and through that to possibly provoke military reactions from the Dual Alliance (while Austria had already annexed its booty, and France had no other interest since 1871 than revenge against the German Empire), *Serbia* did not need at all to be fobbed off with the Sandžak but would rather annex another piece of land in addition, - which later proved to be Vardar Macedonia. *Bulgaria*, for its part, would not allow either to be distracted with a vague promise from its dreams of a Greater Bulgaria, but plunged into the long planned adventure for Macedonia with vehemence.
This means, however, that Serbia and Bulgaria would in no way let Greece alone take over Macedonia, as the Entente seemed to wish.
This is getting ahead of the events, though.

Another informative aspect can be taken from the report of the envoy in Bucharest: PM Bratiano replied to a Russian diplomat's question about how Romania assessed the problems of a Balkan League with the statement that Turkey would certainly demand guarantees "that Bulgaria and Serbia refrain from any meddling whatsoever in the inner-affairs of Macedonia."[617]

That is an astonishing statement: Bratiano is not speaking about the Turkish province but rather about "Macedonia" – as about a country. Moreover, he is speaking - and that, too, is not exactly a common habit in connection with dependent territories - about the *non-interference "in the inner affairs of Macedonia"*.
Macedonia was not yet able to claim this international law for itself at that time. Much time was to pass before that would happen: it took about 35 years until its status as a (constituent) republic within the Federation of Yugoslavia was recognized; ... (If, under Tito, the head of a constituent republic had dared to speak about 'non-intervention in the inner affairs' of his republic, he would have at best found himself later on the island of Goli Otok, the Yugoslavian concentration camp.) ... and until its full sovereignty about 80 years.

3.5 The ring around Constantinople gets tighter

It has already been depicted in the chapters on Serbia and Bulgaria how the two governments (on the recommendation of Russia) had sent "appeasement notes" to the Porte to cover up their real plans with regard to the Balkan League, meaning with regard to Macedonia. In their endeavours, after the founding of the Triple *Entente*, to supplement the French and English efforts to enlarge the *anti-Austrian and anti-German coalition*, the Russians even went a step further with their manoeuvres to deceive the Sultan: the two kings, Peter and Ferdinand, were supposed to scatter the obvious - and justified - doubts of the Turks by formal courtesy calls to the Sultan.[618]

The first reactions in the Turkish press to the visit of the Serbian King Peter in 1910 turned out as planned:

"Any attempt to secure the peace and calm in the Balkans (fills) the Ottomans with satisfaction."[619]

In his follow-up report on the next day, Ambassador von Miquel offers his own assessment of the situation. On the occasion of visits by two Slavic kings to Constantinople, he concludes:

If "the Slavic rulers make up their minds to pay the Sultan a visit despite the little sympathy that the Christian Balkan peoples have for the Moslems," then there must be definite preparations for the creation of an alliance of the southern Slavic states with Turkey on the agenda.[620] Russia, supported by France and Italy, is trying "to convince the Turks of the necessity of an alliance."[621]

The ambassador had clearly recognized that the Entente was attempting to pull the Ottoman Empire into a large Balkan alliance against Germany and Austria-Hungary. He, nonetheless, had his doubts about their success:

"Turkey is cautiously withholding its decision; it finds all the courting uncanny because it has already had its bad experiences with Russia."[622] There was only "one consideration that could make the Sublime Porte more inclined to the idea of an alliance, namely the fear of the Balkan states joining together without Turkey."

This fear was justified; that's exactly what happened later.
Moreover, the embassy mentioned that the French press in Constantinople had, "without being shy," referred to Austria *"as the enemy to fight against"*:

"All Balkan people must enter into a protective and defensive alliance against the common enemy in V i e n n a. The assurances of Count Aehrenthal after the annexation of Bosnia and Hercegovina are not to be trusted; ever since the Defeat of Sadová[623], the Habsburg Dual Monarchy has been pushing towards the southeast and is being supported in this by Germany."[624]

It is evident from this French attack on Austria (and indirectly also on Germany) that Russia was very serious in its efforts to draw the Turks into the Balkan League. What Petersburg did not succeed in, though, was reconciling the Balkan states' greed for land, which could naturally only be satisfied at the expense of Turkey, with the wish of the Entente to integrate exactly this Turkey into their anti-German coalition.
(More about this in ch. 5.)

On both sides there were reasons for constant mistrust which, it is true, was calmed down time after time but was just as often fired up again. One has to admit that; after the Congress of Berlin and even stronger after 1908, Turkey's mistrust of Austria because of Bosnia was not unjustified. It remains, nevertheless, irritating that, as the embassy in Belgrade reports on announcements in the "Politika", the Turkish War Minister, Mahmud Schefket Pasha, was looking for the driving forces which "were blowing up the Macedonian issue" not among Balkan states but rather on a completely different, third side. Since he expresses in the same breath his trust of the Russians, of whom he was convinced that they felt "no need for conquests" (sic!), only the Austrians were eligible to be the target of his fears. They were accustomed to "seeing Turkey as the sick man who is already lying on his deathbed and whose possessions should be divided up as soon as he dies". "That's why they give so much attention to Macedonia and the Albanians."[625]

In as far as the Turkish Pasha meant the imperialistic excessiveness of Austria-Hungary, one must unfortunately agree with him – however, he did not recognize the real aspirants to the remainder of European Turkey and especially to the Straits and the Golden Horn.

In any case it seems absurd for him to accuse that "third side" of "having created our inner-issues"! No sign at all of recognizing one's own shortcomings! Over and above that, there was a total underestimation of the character of the popular movements for the liberation of the Balkan peoples from the alien Turkish rule as well as the longing of the Christians for freedom and independence from the Islamic yoke. One can perhaps take the war minister's expression of his determination, "not to give away an inch more of land and even if we get into armed conflict with the whole world about it", as a typical ritual of conquerors: but when, after the violent amassing - and the loss - of one of the biggest empires of history, the Ottoman minister makes the point that the Turks have no craving for foreign land and moreover even describes this "foreign" land on which he is standing as his own property,
(c. f. Envoy von Reichenau's report:
"we have no craving for foreign land, but we don't give ours away either"[626]),
then this amounts to pure mockery of the millions and millions of victims during the 500 years of Ottoman military campaigns, the occupation, enslavement and exploitation of "foreign" peoples as well as complete misjudgement of European humanistic values.

That the European peoples obtained their liberation in the end not from the remorse and understanding of the former conqueror but solely from their willingness for resistance with disregard for their own lives may perhaps be felt as a blind spot on the Christian scale of values, but in reality it is only the dark side of the actually shining medal of freedom. *Also, the "freedom of a Christian subject".* (M. Luther)

3.6 An observer looks back - and forward

In the spring of 1910, Ambassador Marschall von Bieberstein gave his assessment of the situation of the Ottoman Empire and its relationships to the Great Powers in an over 20-page long report [typed on a typewriter, at that time already]. It was his intention to justify to the Imperial Chancellor why he was convinced that the Young Turks, like the Sultans before them, would try to find support from Austria and Germany despite all the enticement attempts of the Triple Entente. For Constantinople had discerned that the Russian efforts were directed at using the Balkan League to turn "the European Turkey and the Slavic Balkan states into a Russian protectorate."[627]

What Freiherr v. Marschall unfortunately did not comment on (or did not recognize?) was that the coalition efforts of Russia and England in the Balkan League already represented the groundwork for the European military conflict that broke out four years later. His view on Russia also seems (in retrospect) perhaps a bit stereotyped.

In the meantime, his assessment with regard to the politics of his host country was to be fulfilled 100% – manifested in the secret military agreement of Turkey with the German Empire of August 2, 1914 and finally the Ottoman Empire's entry into the war in October 1914.

> "I do not see any prospects of success for the attempts that Russia is presently carrying out in order to sow mistrust against Austria-Hungary and against us. Whoever wants to make someone else mistrustful has to hold the trust of that person whom he is trying to influence. This precondition is missing in this case." (P. 6) "The thought that Russia is the arch enemy, from whom also in the future only the worst can be expected, is deeply rooted in the soul of the Turkish people. And the radical change in politics has not altered this either." (P. 7)

Then, the ambassador continues:

> "In the last century, the Turkish Empire was not preserved through its own strength but rather through the conflicting interests of the European Great Powers. The competing heirs of the "sick man" were so numerous and powerful that not one of them could dare to accelerate opening up the inheritance through an act of violence. The English-Russian antagonism was the most conspicuous in every respect. It led to the Crimean War and became effective last time after the Treaty of San Stefano. The fact that England was determined then to draw the sword in order to force Russia to alleviate the peace terms that had been imposed on the Turks and that all of Prince Bismarck's skills in statesmanship were needed to prevent this further war belongs to more modern history." (P. 8)

Did von Marschall not notice that Bismarck had made a professional mistake?

Furthermore, the ambassador considered a membership of Turkey in the Balkan League to be out of question:

> "For that ... there is a decisive reason: the Porte would demand as a conditio sine qua non <u>that the Balkan states abstain in the strictest legal form from any territorial expansion at the expense of the Turkish Empire.</u>" [Underlined in the original.] "Neither Bulgaria nor Serbia nor Montenegro would ever accept this condition. Russia cannot take sides with Turkey either in this matter without breaking with its traditional policy. That's so clear that I must earnestly doubt if Russia is really already striving now for the Balkan League to take form or only temporarily encouraging the idea as a means to an end...." (P. 6)

This doubt is admirable since we, the descendants, have all the possibilities to get at least an approximate picture of the plans and motives of all the small states and big powers, all the governments and political parties through studying the extensive sources. The ambassador, however, did not have them at that time. He only had his education and experience as well as his political instinct to draw up his analyses from the information he had before him - and then to synthesize his conclusions.

Nevertheless!
Nevertheless, admiration for this far-sighted man is mixed with the regret that he did not take more closely into account the devastating consequences of the Entente Cordiale of 1904 and of the Triple Entente of 1907 for Germany. (Reval should be left out of consideration for once here). Otherwise, the AA in Berlin could have been aware of the warnings of this top diplomat and taken them more thoroughly into account.

One last example on the matter of the *status quo*:
> "Austria-Hungary wants the status quo which serves their interests. On the other hand, the 'status quo' only forms a sort of decorative phrase for Russia. One allows it into a first sentence in order to reserve the possibility to knock the status quo over then in some twisted editorial."

As far as Russia is concerned, history proved the ambassador to be completely right – but didn't he judge Habsburg too positively? And further:
> "Usually one speaks about the consolidation and the free or national development of the Balkan states, although they are not endangered at all but form the danger for the status quo themselves."

The aggressive policy of war that Serbia, Bulgaria and Greece executed against their Orthodox Christian Macedonian neighbours - while being originally considered endangered states themselves - could not have been described more accurately.

3.7 The decision is approaching

Approaching the founding of the Balkan League that for decades had been so much aspired (now, only four months remained) one has to state that the tone of the statements of the potential participating states became tougher, while that of Constantinople became more worried.

It can be taken from the files that the powers - on the basis of the Treaty of Berlin - made an appeal to Turkey and called upon the Turks to conduct themselves peacefully. The Porte agreed but rightly expected that the same appeal be also directed at Bulgaria so that it would refrain from making any attack whatsoever on Turkey.[628]

Turkish Foreign Minister Assim Bey expressed himself to the German ambassador with great bitterness about the Russian attitude towards the Balkan League,
> "about which every Turkish politician knows that it will be the beginning of the end for the European possessions of Turkey."[629]

This statement by an important Turkish dignitary in the last hour must be described as remarkable due to its realistic content: already the fact that Assim Bey spoke about 'European possessions' and not about 'Turkish property' shows the standpoint of an educated man with a clear overview.

Indeed, the coming development did - almost - bring the end of European Turkey. But it was not, as Assim Bey formulated it, the "beginning of the end". That lay much deeper and much farther back, as the author has tried to explain in this chapter.

The always newly igniting revolts belonged to the group of problems that the Young Turks had taken over from their predecessors, the autocratic governments. It cannot be assumed the Young Turks were aware that the renewed outbreaks of the Albanian revolt in 1909 and 1910 represented a first step to their general collapse.[630] They lost their power in 1912 and could regain it for another five years through a coup d'état only in 1913 until their resignation in 1918 and their subsequent emigration.

Italy, which had been tormented with resentment for years about possibly not being able to lop off a single colony from the Turkish estate for itself, set a new ball rolling with its attack on Tripoli and the Cyrenaica in September 1911. Among other things, the Greek-Bulgarian rapprochement in April of 1912 (demonstrated in the above-mentioned farce of the Bulgarian students being enthusiastically greeted in Athens) had contributed to the Italian nervousness. In view of this reconciliation, Sultan Abdul Hamid in his exile in Salonika, who had managed to fuel the Greek-Bulgarian enmity for decades, is said to have not refrained from being satisfied with a certain malicious joy about this failure of the Young Turks. ("The Times" actually used the German word ["Schadenfreude"] in their report).[631]

Should Italy not have known that its overhasty activities would work like a trigger? At any rate; that which had been long expected, or better said feared, followed in the lee of the Italian-Turkish war in Libya when the military forces of Turkey were focussed on North Africa:

Macedonia's three neighbouring states united to form the Balkan League.
(As far as Montenegro is concerned see below.)

One cannot say that they had "joined forces" despite all of their mutually exclusive interests - because they were all focussed in the same direction. It only looked that way from the outside.

But one argument has to be repeated again and again:

Without the interest of the Entente powers in having additional accomplices in the Balkans for their big plan of a war against Germany and Austria-Hungary, the Balkan states would never have been able to find a common denominator nor would they have dared to carry on a war of aggression against the Ottoman Empire. But since the Entente Cordial in 1904, the Triple Entente in 1907 and Reval in 1908, there was more at stake.

This "stake" of the Entente powers was *Macedonia – and behind Macedonia: the Dual Alliance.*

The Macedonian land and its people were now "fair game". The Entente had opened the "hunting season" in order to bind the Balkan states to the Entente over the detour of their greed for land with the goal to close the southern ring around the two German states in this way.

At the beginning, the Entente might still have believed that with vague promises they could induce Serbia and Bulgaria to give Greece the right of way to serve itself in Macedonia. The two Slavic states, however, would not have dreamed of doing that, as depicted above. Since this concept could not work out, a phase followed in which Russia, on behalf of the Entente, gave contractual *security guarantees* to Bulgaria and Serbia (see below, ch. 5.1.1), so that they would not have to be afraid of any intervention of the (German) great powers. Exactly this risk had kept the Balkan kingdoms for decades from invading Macedonia which they coveted – and the same risk would have *prevented them* (without the Entente) *from doing so forever.*

Greece did not need any guarantee agreement, since it had received the signal that it would have the consent and backing for its course of action (without military support though).

(At least a Russian-Greek agreement was not mentioned in the files the author combed through.)

The treaty between Bulgaria and Serbia to found the Balkan League was signed on March 13, 1912. Montenegro joined the following October. *The Greeks* signed a similar agreement with *Bulgaria* in May 1912.

All of the great powers - all, with the exception of Germany - would have surely liked to have profited from this situation if only they had been able to reach an agreement about how to share the spoils – at least with regard to Constantinople and the Straits. That proved to be impossible (although there was no lack of - Russian - suggestions for a compromise), so that in the end the makeshift solution of a minimal status quo had to be continued.

In this respect, the *circle of the Great Powers* around Germany (and Austria) bore a strong resemblance to the small *circle of the Balkan states* positioned around Macedonia that were getting ready to annex the latter. At the same time, the "little ones" had the invaluable advantage over the big ones that they were allowed to pursue their imperialistic goals (henceforth!) scot-free and, after the talks in Reval, even with the approval of the Entente powers.
In the lee of the meticulously planned and already looming catastrophe "on a global scale" the *fall guy Macedonia* was a negligible price if the involved Balkan states could be kept from a coalition with Austria and the German Empire in this way. During the preparatory period the Entente aimed to seal off the southern flank of Europe by separating Turkey from the Dual Alliance through League partners of the Entente (in case it should not prove possible to pull Turkey into the Balkan League itself).
A perfect cleverly thought-out plan.
Only, as far as Bulgaria was concerned - due to its revisionist aspirations – this plan did not work.

And then there was also the political experience, the watchful eye and the warning voice of Kaiser Wilhelms II, even if he could not turn back the tide – i. e. the catastrophe of 1914. We will go into this in detail later.

Without the protective hand of the dynasties of the Peterhof and Buckingham Palace and of the Elysée over the Acropolis, this historical turn of events would not have been conceivable – that is, *not without the war plans of the Entente itself*:
In decades-long, patient but systematic intrigues, *France* had developed the basic initiatives for forging an alliance against the German Empire to finally satisfy its thirst for revenge for Prussia's "robbery" of the Alsace. Because of the forced "exclusive war guilt of Germany" it can never again be placed on the scales of justice by the German side despite the historical truthfulness that France, for its part, had once robbed the Alsace territory, including Straßburg, from Germany.

These activities were superposed by the *Russian* efforts to finally bring the cheeky cockalorum and oppressor of the Slavic and Orthodox peoples in Vienna to reason by letting him fall into his own trap of greed for additional Turkish land in the Balkans. As well, Russia never had forgotten Austria's anti-Russian stance in the Crimean War – just as little as the alleged anti-Russian policy of the German Empire towards the tsardom during and after the Congress of Berlin in 1878, - thanks to French-English intrigues in St. Petersburg.

And finally, as always in the background (in the most decisive spot): *England*, pulling the threads of its old balance of power policy (which, if looked at closely, had always been a policy of English predominance) against a too cheeky and much too strong and successful German people on the continent, if only, as a result of the English self-righteousness and self-content, its own power, its own wealth and the British Empire could be preserved or, if possible, even enlarged.

A *fateful moment* – not only for Balkan but also for European history.

4 THE DEVELOPMENT OF THE BALKAN LEAGUE AS SEEN BY THE EUROPEAN GREAT POWERS

4.1 Russia
4.1.0 The Balkans in Russian history - an outline

About a century after the fall of Constantinople, the so-called second Rome, the Russian-Orthodox church under Ivan IV (the Terrible) developed the idea of *'Moscow as the third Rome'*. Thus the Tsar became responsible for all Orthodox Christendom. Even though this idea had anti-Islamic tendencies, it was initially seen as purely religious and apolitical. Elements of expansionism developed much later. Primarily in the 19th century it had a strong influence on the Russians' sense of mission, in particular regarding their responsibility for the Orthodox Balkan Slavs.

A hundred years later, the suppression of the Cossack rebellion with the conquest of Kiev in 1654 together with the "Eternal Peace" of Moscow in 1686 paved the way for Russia's membership in the *"Holy League"*[632], an anti-Turkish alliance concluded between the Holy Roman Empire of the German Nation, Poland and Venice [633]. It was this alliance that fought the great Turkish War against the Ottoman Empire from the second unsuccessful siege of Vienna in 1683 until the Treaty of Karlowitz in 1699. The Pruth campaign of Peter the Great against the Turks from 1710 to 1711 got lost, as was the aforementioned war fought by Austria and Russia against Turkey from 1735 to 1738.

With the crucial victory over *Sweden* in 1721 after 20 years of war Russia had cleared its northern front (Prussia had already succeeded in doing so at Fehrbellin in 1675) and became the main opponent of the Ottoman Empire in the second half of the 18th century. (It was also in 1721 that the Tsar decided to change his traditional title to the central European one of "Emperor".) In the following century Russia fought more than half a dozen wars against the Turks, - not only for unselfish reasons, but almost always for the advantage of one people or the other until then oppressed by the Ottomans, and above all to the benefit of the enslaved Christians.

Thus Russia developed three main lines of expansion:
- to the west across the Ukraine, the Crimea and the Balkan Peninsula,
- to the east across the Caucasus, Georgia and Armenia and
- in the centre (across the Black Sea) towards Constantinople and the Straits.[634]

The outcome of the third Russo-Turkish war of 1768-74, that ended with the aforementioned Peace of Kutschuk-K. (in the Dobruja), had lasting effects: Russia moved its borders further southwest and gained free passage for all ships in the Black Sea as well as for trading vessels through the Straits. In the Peace of Jassy in 1792 (Potjomkin!) the Sultan had to guarantee protection of the Christian religion.

At the same time the nationalist movements of the oppressed peoples were strengthened, not least by the ideas of the French Revolution.[635] This development found its visible expression in the Serbian rebellions of 1804 and 1815. However, with the Turkish retreat, rivalry among the Great Powers became much fiercer than it had ever been at the time of the Ottoman Empire, which was generally considered to be a Great Power with equal rights.[636]

Peter the Great succeeded in expanding the Russian Empire as far as the Black Sea. And in 1783 Catherine II conquered the Crimea:

> "The Black Sea was no longer an inland sea controlled by the Ottomans, but was hitherto subject to Russian supremacy."[637]

Some of the Great Powers, England and Austria in particular, reacted to this fast expansion with resentment and apprehension.

After the fifth Russo-Turkish War of 1806-1812 Russia gained Bessarabia under the Treaty of Bucharest. At the same time Russia supported the Greek War of Independence and in the Peace Treaty of Adrianople of 1829 achieved autonomy for the Danube principalities of Moldavia and Walachia.

As mentioned above (ch. 2.1), in 1812 Tsar Alexander I was forced to seek peace with the Ottomans in Bucharest, because Napoleon's Russian campaign required the concentration of all Russian forces. Four years previously Napoleon had tried to repay the Tsar's restraint during French hostilities against England by making an "offer". With the sweeping gesture of the great Corsican, Napoleon had painted a tableau of the partition of the Ottoman Empire in 1808:

> "The Balkans were to become Russian, Serbia and Bosnia Austrian, and Egypt and Syria French."[638]

It was clear, however, that even Napoleon, great strategist as he was, would fail in one point just as the Europeans did much later:

> "The crucial question between France and Russia remained unanswered: the future of Constantinople and the Straits."[638]

Subsequent to the progress made by Russia in liberating the Orthodox religion in the Ottoman Empire, Nicholas I went so far as to demand a Russian protectorate over the Christians under Turkish rule. The prospect of Russian intervention in religious questions with possible effects on Constantinople as well as the Straits, convinced England and France, however, that the *continued existence of the Ottoman Empire* was necessary to protect their own colonial interests as well as their trade routes. In order to put Petersburg in its place, in 1854 they sided with the Turks in the Russo-Turkish (Crimean) War (since 1853) and inflicted a crushing defeat on Russia (i.a. at Sevastopol). The Treaty of Paris of 1856 ended Russian hegemony in southeast Europe, and at the same time Turkish dependency on Russia was terminated. Furthermore, London once more demilitarised the Black Sea by enforcing the application of the Pontus-clauses.

From the point of view of the Tsar, the role of Austria was particularly infamous: although, at the request of Austria, Russia had crushed the Hungarian rebellion in 1849, Vienna had clearly sided with England, France and Turkey in the Crimean War. It is true that Austria had not exactly taken part in the war, however, by moving its troops to the border it had bound a considerable number of Russian forces there, so that they could not be deployed on the front and thus contributed to the heavy Russian losses in the war.

St. Petersburg took revenge by remaining neutral in the Austro-Prussian War in 1866; and accordingly in the Franco-German War in 1870/71. In the shadow of this war Russia finally succeeded to rid itself of the discriminating Pontus clauses with the help of Bismarck. This, on the other hand, almost led to another Anglo-Russian war.

If only Bismarck had realized what fatal consequences this mediation was to have for his alliance policy and the peaceful role of Germany in Europe!

If only ...

As a consequence of the Crimean War, the Russian urge to expand was temporarily
> "diverted to the Far East and Central Asia, which made Russia, directly or indirectly, collide again with the interests of the British Empire."[639]

After the plans of Russia in East Asia had failed, Russian interest was redirected towards the Balkans following rebellions on the Balkans in 1875/76; all this was motivated by the old long-term Russian goal, i.e. to control "Constantinople and the Straits". The idea of religious solidarity with the Orthodox Christians was increasingly supplemented by the ideological motive of *Pan-Slavism* with the South Slavs, who were of the same ethnic and linguistic origin.[639]

Theodor Schieder describes the situation as follows:
> "...Following the Balkan rebellions in Herzegovina and Macedonia, Russia intervened in the Serbo-Turkish War. The third Russo-Turkish War in that century ended in a complete Russian victory and the Preliminary Treaty of San Stefano in March 1878, according to which Russia together with Serbia, Montenegro, Romania and Great Bulgaria (extended to the Aegean) created a system of protégé states on the Balkans."[640]

According to section 15 of the Preliminary Treaty of San Stefano, Epirus, Thessaly, and "the other parts of the Turkish territory in Europe" (thus also including *Macedonia*) were also to become satellites. In those states the Sublime Porte was committed to a "precise" application of the law of 1868 that was passed to achieve autonomy on the isle of Crete.[641]

The approach of Russia advancing as a "spearhead" to the Golden Horn and the Bosporus via (Great) Bulgaria was strictly objected by England and Austria-Hungary. They both forced Russia to attend the *Congress of Berlin*, unless it wanted to risk another war on the scale of the Crimean War with possibly the same outcome. In Berlin, Russia was obliged to agree to the preservation of what remained of Turkey in Europe. This change in direction also required St. Petersburg to "surrender the protectorate over the Christians in the Ottoman Empire".[642]

When the provision of section 15 of the Treaty of San Stefano (promotion of autonomy) – that was almost literally adopted as section 23 of the Treaty of Berlin – was again disregarded by Turkey, another rebellion broke out in Macedonia (at Kresna) on 17th October 1878, ending in a bloody suppression by the Turks on 6th June 1879.

4.1.1 Russia promotes the project of a Balkan League

For obvious reasons Russia was disappointed about the outcome of the Congress of Berlin: the creation of a (Great) Bulgarian gateway to the Aegean had failed. Instead, despite having won the war, St. Petersburg had to accept the *Austrian occupation of Bosnia* as well as Herzegovina. The fact that England had reserved Cyprus for itself also clearly showed the direction of this strategic move. Even if Russia did not intend to start another war, and actually began to identify with the idea of a status quo on the Balkans, there were enough reasons to distrust the other powers, which were pursuing their own interests on the Balkans. Being itself the cause of the Austro-German Dual Alliance of 1879, St. Petersburg used this alliance as an opportunity to present it as exemplary for the development on the Balkans. The initial doubts of Russia about a Balkan League had since long given way to the idea of supporting an alliance of the rather weak individual Balkan states. The main motivation for this was *alleged to be* Russian anxiety about, and the prevention of, further Austrian expansionist adventures.

This line was also taken up by the Russian press:

> "If the Great Powers are free to ally for certain reasons..., it is the duty of the smaller states to ally as well, in order to protect their independence of the Great Powers."[643] "Do the South Slavs want to wait," a Russian newspaper asks, "until the German and Hungarian knights cross the Danube and set up an alliance, and in doing so swallow one Slavic principality after another? Austria-Hungary has already crossed the Danube and has reached the Balkans."[644]

In section 25 of the Treaty of Berlin Russia had most unwillingly agreed to the Austrian occupation of Bosnia. (See also chapter 4.1.2 and esp. chapter 4.2.6 as well as 4.4.1.2.1, no. 4) Now Russia at least tried to remind Austria of its promises to withdraw. In the "Neue Zeit" St. Petersburg was at first presented as a shining example:

> "Bulgaria and Eastern Rumelia have each in their own way received a national government and an independent administration." "The Austro-Hungarian occupation has lasted much too long..." Then the paper appeals to the Austrian "duty" to copy Russia: Just like the Russians "the Austrian and Hungarian officials should leave the territory they are administering temporarily." "The people of Bosnia and Herzegovina should be able to breathe freely again."[645]

It is true that Russia fulfilled its obligations under the Treaty of Berlin on time, however, it should not be forgotten that St. Petersburg was the one who virtually unleashed the war with the Ottoman Empire in the first place; with the consent of the Great Powers, but also in its own interest.

It has already been mentioned that Serbia, too, had relied on the temporary character of the Bosnian occupation and its sole purpose of establishing a representation of the people as well as a proper jurisdiction and a functioning administration. In vain.

Initially the Russian government seems to have had a rather unlucky touch in the way it chose to improve its influence on the small Balkan states. News had already reached the German press that Russia was losing all the sympathies it had doubtlessly won by supporting practically every liberated people.

> "In Bulgaria public opinion is now vehemently turning against the clumsy attempts to Russianize... The massive intrusions of Russian elements into public offices is bitterly resented by the Bulgarians."[646]

Fifteen years later the Consul-General von Reichenau reported from Sofia that Austria had gained ground in Bulgaria and was even exerting crucial influence:

> "From the liberation of Bulgaria onwards, Russia has not stopped treating this country like an underage child that needs controlling in every step it takes and ... letting it feel that it is not concerned with the independence of Bulgaria, but only with the extension of its own influence."[647]

Bismarck was convinced that Russia had only earned ungratefulness for its support of the South Slavs, - a thought that keeps on reappearing in the files, not only in Bismarck's remarks. Seven years after the establishment of the autonomous principality of Bulgaria by the Congress of Berlin, Bismarck informed the German Embassy in St. Petersburg about a conversation he had had with the Russian Ambassador in Berlin, Peter Graf Shuvaloff. Bismarck told him that Germany felt "no need to be opposed" to the Russian interest in expanding Bulgaria [Eastern Rumelia!], nor did he want to hold back his opinion

> "that Bulgaria would develop more anti-Russian tendencies, the bigger and stronger it got." ...
> "These vain small nations no longer want to remain planets of the Russian sun, but want to shine themselves. Russia has played the same role as liberator first for Greece, then for the Danube principalities (Moldavia and Walachia), then Serbia, and finally Bulgaria, and in each single case the outcome was the same: the liberated people expressed its gratitude by attempting to emancipate itself from the influence of its liberator."[648]

The Russian Ambassador was so honest as to express his expectation that a great Balkan League" (would) become a natural enemy of Austria and a friend of Russia."[648] This assessment was initially only true to a certain extent.

About a year later the Embassy in St. Petersburg came up with an evaluation confirming Bismarck's view, - still under the impression of the Bulgarian unification with Eastern Rumelia in 1885. According to the Embassy, the Bulgarians had worried the Russians immensely by taking this step. The "unfortunate dilemma" that the Russians found themselves in, was the fact that the Balkan peoples were not only to an increasing extent

> "seeking to emancipate themselves from Russia, but also putting themselves in direct opposition to "Holy Russia" in their tendencies and institutions."[649] The Russian leaders do not mean to exercise any form of coercion - least of all the Tsar -, but "casting off the hundred-year-old traditions of Russian oriental policy, however, is a difficult matter."

(This is to say that the Bulgarians would be wise not to provoke the Russians too much. Otherwise a Russian intervention in Bulgaria could not be ruled out.) Even though this did not actually happen, the Russian Court continued to harbour feelings of bitterness towards the Bulgarians for a long time.[650] (See also the discussion of the "Battenberg Affair" in chapter 2.2)

It was not necessary to draw the attention of future Russian politicians to Russia's real position on the Balkans. Thus, the German Chancellor v. Bülow noted from a talk with the Russian Prime Minister Witte that the latter had expressed disapproval of the Slavophile enthusiasm for the Balkan peoples,

> "which had all repaid Russia's sacrifices of blood and money without exception with shabby ungratefulness, first the Serbs, then the Bulgarians, and the Greeks and the Romanians had taken every opportunity to do so."[651]

The files had confirmed the assumption more than once that because of their identical goals it would be impossible for the Balkan states to agree upon an alliance. According to the German Ambassador in Rome, Graf Solms, the Italian Prime Minister Crispi shared this view:

> "Mr. Crispi told me that he did not believe in an alliance between Greece, Serbia and Montenegro. The main obstacle to such Balkan Leagues was Macedonia, that is considered equally by Serbia, Bulgaria and Greece to be their heritage."[652]

It is always rather infuriating to read that all the high-ranking politicians of the great European powers at that time showed how constructed they considered the neighbouring states' claims to Macedonia to be, but that they lacked the courage to go against the stream of the zeitgeist and prevent a major injustice.

As far as Prime Minister Crispi was concerned, he, however, supported the plan to build a wall against Russian expansion tendencies by establishing a "confederacy of all Balkan states". Ambassador Solms, on the other hand, feared that in view of the growing Russian influence such a confederacy might result in a dangerous threat to Austria. (Later Italy was more worried about the risk of Austrian expansion than about the danger of a possible threat to Austria.)

Both reports quoted date from *1890*. It is impossible to let this date pass without commemorating the Russo-German Treaty of 1887 which guaranteed a "benevolent neutrality" negotiated by the two statesmen v. Bismarck and v. Giers. Not only due to the tragic consequences the termination of this Treaty by Bismarck's successor Chancellor von Caprivi had (How could he have made this mistake!), but also because the *Rein-*

surance Treaty was closely connected with the Balkans and the Ottoman Empire, a fact which seems to have been long since forgotten.

> The German Reich had not only acknowledged Russian influence in Bulgaria, but in a secret amendment had also accepted the *Bosporus as a Russian sphere of interest*. This concession would never have been made to St. Petersburg by London or Paris - except in promises!

Unfortunately, Germany did not benefit from this in the long run, as Russia soon succumbed to French and English insinuations - and benefited from the German mistakes.

4.1.2 Russia intensifies its policy in the Balkans

The subject of Russian oriental policy (then: Balkan policy) was given repeated coverage by the press. Ambassador v. Metternich, for example, commented on a correspondent's report from Bulgaria in the London "Standard", according to which Russia was striving

> "to extend its territory southwards under the guise of pan-Slavism and the foundation of a gigantic Slavic Empire. The danger of Russification was greatest for Romania and Bulgaria..."[653]

All in all, the "Standard" did not express much hope for the success of the Balkan League, as it needed a Great Power to lean on. But which one would that be? Not Russia – with its national egotism; Austria perhaps – but then Austria would have to withdraw from Bosnia, which it would never be prepared to do; Turkey was out of the question because of Macedonia, which "Greece, Serbia and Bulgaria unmistakably coveted."[653]

> It seems that even the press shared the same imperialistic ideas as the governments and crowned heads of state, as here, too, there was no talk of any claims of these countries to foreign territories. Such digressions were deemed unnecessary. On the contrary, the press, too, decided arbitrarily in public on the fate of whole nationalities, because it considered the "greed" of the neighbouring states to be sufficient basis for their claims.
>
> *The same still applies today: although Macedonia enjoys the status of a legitimate, democratic, independent republic and is a member of the UN, the neighbouring states still shamelessly boast about their alleged claims and spread doubts as to the status of Macedonia under international law. Reasonable Great Powers or vigilant organisations do not intervene decisively, nor do they refrain from being part of this policy.*

The fact that the *Russian* press at the time supported the attempts of the Russian Government to establish a Balkan League seems almost inevitable, because the "common interests of the South Slavs" predominated and it was assumed that these interests "were diametrically opposed to those of Austria". Therefore, the League, that Vienna was trying to prevent, should

> "seek support from Russia, that would guarantee its independence, whereas Austria was only trying to violate the Balkan states as it had Bosnia and Herzegovina before."[654]

The propaganda was directed more against Austria than in favour of Bosnia, as Serbia did not want to free Bosnia from Austrian occupation for its own sake, as had been the case with the Turkish occupation; quite the reverse, Belgrade intended to simply swallow Bosnia, just as it planned together with Bulgaria and Greece to annex Macedonia. Russia would (initially) have no objections to a Serbian Bosnia as long as it stopped being an Austrian Bosnia.

Russia's traditional Balkan policy created an *ideological dilemma*, though: As is characteristic for times of political change, different trends in Europe conflicted with one another. As a tribute to the ideas of democracy since the French Revolution, monarchy as a form of government was becoming less popular; this was especially true of France and Italy. Absurdly enough, the republican form of government in those countries did not stop them enforcing their imperialistic greed with the same ruthlessness and violence as in the monarchic Empires of the Sachsen-Coburg-Gothas in Great Britain, the Habsburgs in Austria-Hungary and the Romanows in Russia. (It is known that the German Reich gave in to the urge to colonize rather late and, as a consequence of the First World War, only for a very short period of time.)

Nevertheless, all the Great Powers from Petersburg to Paris and from London to Rome were united in vehement sympathy for the Greek War of Independence from the Turkish yoke.

Hence, many more forces must have influenced the course of history. Maybe the following:

Despite the respectful way the Royal and Imperial rulers treated the Sultan, the *Mohammedan Occupation Regime* had for centuries been considered to be an *intruder on European territory*. Thus, relief at the liberation of the Christian peoples was felt by all monarchies and republics alike. At the same time the Turks had to continuously withdraw towards the Asian continent of their origin, - although the threat of a possible Turkish attempt to re-expand remained lurking in the background.

Inevitably, the Russian liberation doctrine was overlapped by other - conventional - structures and even partly conflicted with them. Gotthold Rhode concludes from these contradictions:

> "The enforcement of the nationality principle could in no way be desirable for Russia, as Russia itself ruled over many non-Russian nationalities. Driven by pan-Slavic ideas, Russia could only accept it in some cases, but by no means as a general principle."[655]

Therefore, the Russian Monarchy cannot have had any difficulty in *not* helping the Macedonians on their way to becoming a state – although they were Christians and at the same time Slavs. This decision might have been influenced and reinforced by the left-wing Seres-Group of Jane Sandanski, who was in contact with Russian revolutionaries and was most probably aiming at setting up a *"republic"*. (See ch. 3.3)

Two years before the end of the 19th century, statesmen from Russia and other countries had probably foreseen what Austria actually dared to do later in 1908. It is understandable that Russia for this reason had repeatedly propagated the idea of a Balkan conference.

The newspaper "Nowosti" even drew up an agenda:
- "Bosnia and Herzegovina should ... become neutral,
- Bulgaria should gain independence,
- in the question of Macedonia it is necessary to determine the rights of the individual nationalities, and
- a Balkan League shall be established."[657]

This agenda could have secured peace on the Balkans and given Macedonia a chance for the future. This, however, was neither in the interest of the neighbouring states, - nor was it, soon afterwards, in the interest of the Great Powers.

The proposed conference was never held - despite intensive pressure from Russia and the ensuing frustration felt in St. Petersburg - not even when Item 1 on the agenda became highly relevant, i.e. when Austria annexed Bosnia.

Russia reacted with consternation, because "Austria had alienated pieces of the Turkish inheritance on its own account" and had thus done what Petersburg had tried to prevent; after all, this was what Russia was denied in 1878.[658] The fact that the conference was never held caused Russia to energetically support the Balkan League.

It will emerge that in contrast to the way this case is presented in history books, the intensive efforts undertaken by Russia were in the interest and on behalf of the Entente. (See chapter 5)

After the annexation, Russia tried to induce Vienna by means of proposals and threats to make concessions, as was reported from St. Petersburg, where Ambassador v. Pourtalès quoted from the newspaper "Slowo",

-- that Russia had suggested autonomy for Bosnia and Herzegovina under the supremacy of the Sultan,

-- that Russia had "spoken of the oppressed situation that both provinces found themselves in under Austrian administration",

-- that furthermore, "the Bosnians' hostile attitude towards Austria was brought into play and a plebiscite demanded",

-- that Russia had demanded "territorial compensation for Serbia and Montenegro at Austria's expense" and had also conjured up the danger of Germanization; and finally

-- that Russia had sought to bring about an alliance of the Balkan states.

"But all that had only been academic discussions." Russia had to try "to accept the Austro-Turkish understanding concerning Bosnia."[660]

The so-called master piece of Austrian diplomacy, i.e. to have negotiated with the Young Turkish regime that the Habsburg monarchy did not need to justify itself at an international conference, was soon to be reversed. Vienna did not reckon with the price it would have to pay later on, when Russia settled accounts with Austria. It was only able to enjoy its spoils for barely six years, - until 28th June 1914.

4.1.3 The Russian strategy becomes inscrutable and shows ominous signs

In 1909 Ambassador v. Pourtalès reported from St. Petersburg that Russia's constant attempts to establish a Slavic Balkan League in the interest of all Slavic nations indicated that Russia

"was more than unsympathetic towards the regeneration of the Turkish Empire."[661]

This spoke for itself.

Any other strategy could have hardly been considered compatible with the centuries-old Russian policy towards the Ottoman Empire, i.e. to drive Islam out of Christian Europe and at the same time to restore the Orthodox cross to the originally Christian *Hagia Sophia*.

This ascent to the heights of combined politics and ideals might be found in the emotional instinct for power of the Greeks and Bulgarians, - however, it did not apply to the English or the Austrians. The British Empire was all that ever counted in London. As long as the British Imperial accounts were in order, the Turkish flag with its crescent could forever flutter on the Christian-Orthodox church. (Could Napoleon have been right in his characterization of the English "shop-keeper mentality"?[662])

Meanwhile Russia continued its efforts to establish a Balkan League, in order to "build a natural frontier on the Balkan Peninsula against the advance of any foreign power". At the same time the Russian Ambassador von Charykow, as his German colleague von Brockdorff-Rantzau reported from Constantinople, had instructed the Balkan states to refrain from "any provocation of Austria".[663]

This announcement is rather surprising and does not quite fit into the actual picture, i.e. the competitive situation between Russia and Austria, in particular in view of the aggressive policy pursued by Vienna. One would have expected a vehement reaction from Russia rather than an appeasement.

Consequently, the Central Powers should have regarded this tactfulness "on command" as conspicuous and as a forerunner of the new concealment strategy, which was to become more and more obvious.

The relevant documents of the time, of course, do not reveal whether this unusual order goes back to the Anglo-Russian agreement reached in *Reval* the year before. It showed, though, that Russia obviously had more in mind than just containing Austrian expansionism.

It was rather an early sign of the Entente plans for a great European conflict.

V. Tscharykow's instructions went on to say that a careful diplomatic procedure by the Serbian government would "result in the strongest support of Russia and all its allies". Serbia acted accordingly and proceeded as carefully as recommended by the Russians: at first until the day the Balkan League was founded on 13 March 1912 - and later until 28 June 1914!

As promised, Serbia was able to rely on the support of "Russia and all its allies" against Austria and the German Reich, which became manifest in the unconditional backing by Russia when Serbia rejected the foolish Austrian ultimatum of of 23 July 1914. More about that later.

> (The outbreak of the war might have been prevented at the time, had Vienna weighed up the odds reasonably and shown more willingness to consider the German warnings instead of focussing on its self-importance as a Great Power. But the Imperial Hofburg Palace of Vienna, aware of being able to rely on the support of Germany, remained trapped in its excessiveness.)

But pride will have a fall.

In addition, Russia spread a smoke screen concerning the *Balkan League*. In December 1909 v. Tscharykow told his German colleague that the so-called Balkan League was simply meant as an "Entente" (and not as an alliance). Bulgaria, Serbia and Greece had to

"agree to refrain from any "politique annexioniste" towards Turkey and not to interfere in Turkey's internal affairs."[663]

At that point the concealment strategy starts to become more obvious.

This lie was the beginning of many years of deceiving of the Germans that was to end in the (first) catastrophe of the 20th century.

Did this not arouse anybody's suspicions in Vienna or Berlin or make them sit up and notice? Yes, it did:

V. Tscharykow further stated that the basis for the Entente policy was the "maintenance of the territorial status quo". To a simple mind this sounded convincing, even promising. But there were a few personalities who remained level-headed: the Kaiser's rather apt marginal comment on this naïve statement of the Russian Ambassador: Rubbish (with an exclamation mark).

> There was no need to be informed about "Reval" to see through such a cheap, if not primitive smoke screen. Nevertheless, it would be interesting to know whether William at the end of 1909 knew about the agreement in *Reval* of 1908. This question will be discussed later.

Evidence suggests that the members of the Entente kept strict secrecy towards Austria and Germany: definitely not in order to protect the Balkan states, so that they had time to proceed with their expansion plans against Turkey! Such a trifle would not have been worth the effort.

A conclusion by analogy suggests that this was not the case: after a meeting with the Tsar in late summer 1912 William expressed his disappointment in his journal that Nicholas II had not informed him about the *Balkan League* although it had been established six months previously"![664]

> Why did Nicholas keep this information from his cousin although it was said to have been so harmless? Because the Balkan League only related to the Balkan kingdoms? Impossible, for otherwise the Tsar could have talked about it unreservedly.

If, on the other hand, two years before the outbreak of the First World War Kaiser William saw through this Russian feint and most likely drew the conclusion that a great storm was gathering over the alliance with Austria, over Germany in particular, the question emerges, why he did not warn Vienna more urgently, and why he did not withdraw his promise of assistance or at least modify it. After all, Nicholas II withdrew from the alliance agreement reached with William II in 1905 at Björko (on the Finnish coast), after the Russian cabinet, mainly its chancellor, Count Lambsdorf, had insistently reminded him of the existing obligations towards France.[665] The conclusion is easy to be drawn:

> Like many German politicians, William had set his hopes on England (which deliberately stayed in the background – probably in order to create precisely this expectation). He simply could not imagine that his relatives would thus maliciously stab him in the back. And the risk of an attack by Russia or France alone did not seem to alarm the Emperor as long as England did not intervene!!
>
> *The English must have seen right through him, as this was exactly what they made him believe.*

But where were the Habsburgs? Were they less alert than our notorious Kaiser? Had they forgotten how many wars Russia had fought against the Ottoman Empire so that, after Bosnia, it would not let Austria also grab Serbia with impunity? That was unthinkable.

> So Vienna chanced it – and relied on the Germans. This turned out to be criminal negligence. On both sides.

A postscript concerning "Björko":
This name is connected with the understandable and necessary attempt of William II (which may perhaps have been undertaken too vehemently) to loosen the grip around Germany that was already building up in 1905.
Although this strategy has gone down in history very aptly as *"the encirclement"* of the German Reich by the Entente, Hermann Kantorowicz, many years later, saw this process as a German tactic to isolate England; however to do so, he had to perform a dialectic somersault in favour of England and completely disregard the historical facts. (See below)

It continued in the same fashion. The Austrian Embassy in Petersburg reported that the Russian Foreign Minister Izvolsky had complained about the Austrian press, which was accusing Russia of pursuing a "policy of intrigues on the Balkan Peninsula" (which was absolutely true):

> "Russia wants nothing but peace. ... If one wishes to represent the advice given to the Balkan states to keep the peace as an instigation to form a Balkan League aimed against a third power, this can only be called frivolous incitement."[666]

This tone sounds familiar to the 20th century contemporary. The rise of the revolutionaries is beginning to have its effect on the choice of words used. The era of polite manners (with the knife behind one's back) seems to have passed; the knife is no longer hidden.[667]

> By the way: asked by the ambassador about the current situation, the minister referred "to Macedonia where unrest was being created by the Turkish government's disciplining of the national committees."[666]

Obviously, it was natural for the foreign minister to speak of '*Macedonia*' when he actually meant Macedonia, rather than Bulgaria, or Southern Serbia and certainly not Greece or even Turkey. And he was objective enough to use the term 'national committees', and being familiar with the situation he can only have meant the national "Macedonian" committees.

The last report on Russian affairs that Ambassador von Tschirschky in Vienna addressed to the Auswärtiges Amt before the foundation of the Balkan League, was based on information from the Russian Embassy and clearly revealed why the Macedonian path to independence (compared with other Balkan states) had failed.

In its Balkan policy at the beginning of the 20th century, St. Petersburg advocated two principles – at least as a pretext that served to conceal dynastic interests:

> "In the face of all these allegations and conclusions concerning the Balkan League, we must firmly adhere to the principle that we desire neither the formation of new states nor any great agglomerations on the Balkan Peninsula."[668]

The Russian policy against a Balkan state which was too large and much stronger than its neighbours was convincing and made sense (even from today's point of view); the reasons for this have already been mentioned in previous chapters. On the other hand, it is incomprehensible why Russia should have been opposed to the formation of new states, which would actually have meant the re-establishment of former states – as was the case with the other Balkan states. It is obvious that this guide-line was only a construct, a pretext; otherwise St. Petersburg could never have accepted the formation of the state of Albania.

> (St. Petersburg indeed intended to *prevent the creation* of an Albanian state, as will be proved below).

Dynastic arrangements must have had their effect in the background which were supposed to prevent any further formations of states - in Macedonia, Thrace, and Epirus - in order to enable the neighbouring kingdoms, above all Greece, to achieve the imperialistic "consolidation" of their territories.

However, even the family relationships between the European monarchies would not have been of much use to the Balkan states if the Tsar, the King of England and the French Republic had not needed the neighbouring states of Macedonia in order to further their own interests in their war plans within the Triple Entente against the two German states.

4.2 Austria-Hungary

4.2.0 The historical role of Austria in the Balkans

> "Up to our times, the destiny of Southern Europe was mainly determined by two multinational empires, the Ottoman Empire and the Habsburg Empire. Both were multilingual and multiethnic and besides having one dominant religious faith, Islam or Catholicism, they each at least tolerated a number of other religions. What held these empires together, were the dynasty and the state religion, while language and nationality for a long time played only a minor role or no role at all. This situation changed completely with the emergence of the national 'renaissance movements'" when it was exactly those aspects which gained importance.[669]

Austro-Turkish relations determined the destiny of the whole Balkans and of Europe.

> "The threat of Turkish aggression gave Austria a new historical role as bulwark and defender of Christian Europe against Islam. For one and a half centuries the Habsburgs and the Sultan alike waged wars with each other that continued to flare up."[670]

As a result, the Ottoman conqueror and the Emperor in Vienna shared the possession of the Balkan Peninsula along a demarcation line which had long been the subject of bitter warfare.

The rise of Austria was made possible following the successful repulse of the second Turkish *siege of Vienna* in 1683, above all, however, after the great Turkish War that ended with the Treaty of Karlowitz in 1699 when Austria acquired Hungary. This treaty finally put into effect what had not been achieved previously despite the inheritance of Hungary in 1526 (the last Jagiellon king, Louis II of Bohemia and Hungary, had fallen in the battle of Mohács against the advancing Turks), as large parts of Hungarian territory had been lost notwithstanding the failure of the first Turkish siege of Vienna in 1529.

> "After the relief of Vienna in 1683 the leaders of the imperial troops, Prince Eugene of Savoy, Margrave Louis William I of Baden, the "Turk-Louis", and the Bavarian Elector Max Emanuel, ushered in the heroic age of the Occidental Turkish Wars with the recapturing of Hungary. For the first time after centuries of foreign rule, the fall of the Sultan's regime enabled the Balkan nations to decide their own destiny."[671]

In the Treaty of Passarowitz after the Turkish War of 1716-18 Austria gained (amongst other territories) northern Bosnia and northern Serbia with Belgrade, but suffered a setback by losing the Turkish War of 1739, when almost all the territories gained under the last peace treaty were lost again. The acquisition of Bukovina in 1775 as well as the Turkish War of 1788-91 which had practically no consequences were no more than episodes.[672]

According to Andreas Hillgruber, Bismarck, as early as 1862, the year of his appointment as Prime Minister (and Foreign Minister) of Prussia, had intended to focus Austria's interests on Hungary and southeast Europe, in view of his own plans to unite the Empire.[673]

(It seems impossible that at that time even the great Bismarck himself could have foreseen the catastrophic consequences, Austrian Balkan policy would have later on "his" German Reich.)

The Austro-Prussian War of 1866, the so-called German War, that had revived the old conflict between Hohenzollern and Habsburg, enforced the inevitable compromise ("Ausgleich") with Hungary (dual monarchy 1867). Furthermore, Hillgruber states that the territorial loss in northern Italy after the Italian War of 1859-61 was of more importance for Austria than the loss of Holstein and Lauenburg, since Austria in any case intended to claim compensation in Germany south of the Main! (See also: Hillgruber, p. 33). In contrast to that, the separation of Germany from Habsburg after the foundation of the German Reich (i.e. after the loss of Austrian supremacy in Germany) probably hurt the Austrians more in their self-esteem than in terms of territorial losses. The Preliminary Peace Treaty of Nikolsburg made it very clear that the Prussian reorganization of Germany also affected European interests (Stürmer, p. 150). To uphold French hegemony Napoleon III did not hesitate to offer his services as mediator immediately after the battle of Königgrätz ("revenge for Sadova"), - not without threatening to march against Prussia should the offer be declined, in order to enforce the separation of Germany from Austria. Therefore, Bismarck broke off the German War; despite the lively support for unification of the Reich shown by the Liberals in northern and southern Germany, it proving to be too soon to pursue of the German national aim (Stürmer, pp. 144, 150, and 154).

Due to the disputes with Prussia, the Austrian interests might to a certain extent have indeed taken a turn towards southeast Europe. A glance at history, though, shows that this trend of the Habsburgs is not exactly a new one. The opposition to Russia had already emerged when in the (7th) Russo-Turkish War of 1853-56, the Crimean War, Austria which was formally neutral forced the Russians by means of unambiguous troop movements to leave the occupied Danube principalities Moldavia and Wallachia. It was *then* – and not after the formation of the German Reich – that Austria launched out on its disastrous expansion policy, that in the end led Austria to compete against Russian pan-Slavism on the Balkans and thus hurled itself, Germany and Europe into the catastrophe of the First World War.

As early as 1875, the year of the Orient Crisis at the great state conference, the Austrian Foreign Minister, Count Andrassy, mentioned the "coming annexation of Bosnia". In the same year the Bosnian rebels nominated the Serbian sovereign as their head of state, - rather than the Austrian Emperor! (It should be added that in 1872/73 Austria had agreed to seek a rapprochement with the Russian Tsar and the German Kaiser which eventually resulted in the Three Emperors League.)

Before Austria was granted the right to occupy the Turkish provinces of Bosnia and Herzegovina at the Congress of Berlin, Austria had made the same determined preparations as England had regarding Cyprus and Egypt. The first Russo-Austrian talks in Buchlau (the Bohemian country house of Count Berchtold, the future foreign minister), were followed by the (oral) Russo-Austrian agreement of Reichstadt in 1876, in which the autonomy or the possible partition of Bosnia between Austria and Serbia was arranged. It must have been easy for Vienna to repeat its commitment to stay neutral towards Russia in the Treaty of Budapest on 15 January 1877, as it was now even put down in writing that Russia had permission to annex Bessarabia, and Austria to annex Bosnia. Better to be safe than sorry: two months after the Anglo-Russian convention for the prevention of a Great Bulgarian state the Treaty of Vienna once more confirmed the Russo-Austrian agreement regarding Bosnia and Bessarabia.

Now the stage was set for the next Russo-Turkish War. And there it was. A week later, on 24 March 1877 the Russians declared war.

Everything would have run smoothly perhaps, had not St. Petersburg so openly promoted Bulgaria's expansion up to the Aegean and almost as far as the Adriatic Sea in the Preliminary Peace Treaty of *San Stefano*. This procedure did not only violate some recently made agreements but also breached the Treaty of Paris concluded after the Crimean War.[674] England had been anxious to prevent the formation of a Great Bulgaria, just as Austria had opposed the formation of a southern Slavic state of Serbia, Montenegro and Bosnia,

> "because otherwise it would not be able to trust the South Slavs in its own country."[675] A great southern Slavic state would "sooner or later attract the remaining South Slavs of the Danube monarchy ... so that its decline would only be a question of time and modalities."[676]

Apart from that, San Stefano provided for

> "such a vast increase of Russian power on the Balkans ... that England and Austria intervened in order to avert Russian supremacy on the Balkans and in the Straits."[677]

By indirectly threatening to go to war they forced Russia to attend the Congress of Berlin in summer 1878.

How far Austria's delusion regarding Bosnia actually went at the international Conference in Berlin, is illustrated by Foreign Minister Count Andrassy, who believed to be able to justify the Austrian expansion policy with the help of a far-fetched historic relict. In addition to a lot of diplomatic babble, he actually went so far as to defend the Bosnian occupation by referring to "Wallenstein's advance into Bosnia in 1626."[678]

(This procedure can only be disregarded if one takes into account that the traditional colonial powers – from west to east – Portugal, Spain, France, Great-Britain, Belgium, the Netherlands, and Russia did not justify their imperialistic acts at all.)

The Austrian occupation of Bosnia was sanctioned on the 8th day of the Congress of Berlin in 1878, on 28 June (of all days),

> "in the manner of old-cabinet style policy to disregard the national right of self-determination which was already being applied and repeatedly demanded."[679]

The *occupation* itself was carried out according to the same pattern. Even the announcement or rather publication led to protests and riots. The majority of the population was not inclined "to accept the Austro-Hungarian occupation in replacement of the Turkish one." Resistance became so strong that

> "the Austrians had to raise almost 200,000 men to enforce the occupation of the two provinces. The climax of the regular campaign was the seizure of Sarajevo, the capital of Bosnia, after many days of bloody fight in the streets."[679]

Another riot broke out in 1882. This resistance was now directed against the new occupation power Austria-Hungary instead of against the Ottoman Empire:

> "30 years later the new generation of resistance" gave birth to the "assassins of Sarajevo."[679]

As already mentioned above, these processes are closely connected with the question of *Macedonia* as well as the future development on the Balkans. The direct consequence of the decision taken at the Congress of Berlin regarding Macedonia lies politically closer, as described by Imanuel Geiss:

> "By returning Macedonia to Turkey the Congress of Berlin once again adjourned the great Balkan conflict concerning this region, maybe ignorant of the abyss that Europe was heading towards in this question. Because later Macedonia turned out to be the major cause for conflict ..."[680]

There is no better way of describing the *failure of the Congress of Berlin* concerning its disregard of the longing for freedom and independence also of those nations whose territories were returned to the Turks. In imperialistic fashion, considerations of dynas-

tic favours outweighed the wish of four nations to make use of their right of self-determination:
> The Albanians were the only people to gain independence after the Balkan Wars of 1913. Macedonia was re-established in freedom on part of its original territory as late as 1991, after an interim solution in communist Yugoslavia in 1944, whereas the two peoples of Thrace and Epirus ceased to exist.

Austria as well had to face a difficult future. In the year of the Congress of Berlin a south German newspaper issued an almost prophetic warning:
> "Count Andrassy, too, will soon learn that forbidden fruits are not always sweet, and that extending the borders does not always mean strengthening the Empire."[681]

And looking back, Geiss adds 100 years later quoting Vladimir Dedijer:
> "Indeed Austria-Hungary swallowed ... this critical mass of conflict material and brought about its own downfall via Sarajevo and the First World War."[681]

4.2.1 Austria's thrust towards the Balkans

The first relevant report on this topic that is available in the files leads right to the heart of the problem of Bosnia and the *Balkan League*. Ambassador von Hatzfeldt in Constantinople quotes his departing Austrian colleague as saying that Austria had to direct its whole attention towards Bosnia and "the possibility of an alliance between Serbia and Montenegro, which Austria could never permit."[682] Why not? In order to prevent the Serbian neighbour from becoming too large and its own pursuit of expansion from being inhibited? It is safe to assume that all this was based on the logical consideration that it would be much easier to annex a small Serbia than a big one.
Consequently, the Austrian Foreign Minister Baron Haymerle informed the German Ambassador in Vienna about his intention of warning the Bulgarian Prince Alexander against a possible alliance with Serbia, because "the majority of the powers would very likely oppose this and it would not be of benefit to his country."[683] As regards the lack of benefit, the minister was right in his prediction, - at least regarding the small extent of the territory seized by Bulgaria in the Balkan Wars. His assessment of the Serbo-Bulgarian alliance, however, was not confirmed by historical developments. In contrast to the Russians who only initially misread the aim of the Balkan League as directed against their country, and in contrast to the Turks who until the bitter end refused to believe that the Balkan League could only be directed against their interests, Austria utterly distrusted the plans for an alliance – with good reason.

With regard to Serbia, Austria itself had contributed for centuries to the cohabitation of Serbians and Bosnians by settling Serbian "peasant soldiers" along the Bosnian-Turkish military frontier to protect the country from Turkish attacks. In spite of the Serbian disappointment at the Austrian occupation of Bosnia, the Consulate-General of Belgrade reported in 1880, i.e. two years after the Congress of Berlin, about renewed attempts by Serbia to achieve a rapprochement with Austria. Serbia's belief in Austrian assurances that the occupation of Bosnia was nothing but a temporary measure to develop a well-functioning administration and to guarantee safety and order was initially so great that Belgrade was convinced
> "that in case of further oriental complications ([one] could) only rely on Austria to take account of the national requirements of Serbia ..., as their fiercest enemy would be a great Bulgaria."[684]

It is characteristic of the complex relations on the Balkans that Serbia considered its neighbour Bulgaria to be an opponent (in the fight for Macedonia) and at the same time an ally (against the Ottoman Empire and Austria!) with which it kept secret contacts. The same goes for Bulgaria. In Vienna this constellation led to the long upheld misinterpretation that there was an unbridgeable gulf between these two principalities. Soon after Bulgaria became autonomous, the aspirations of Sofia in the direction of a Great Bulgaria and its pan-Slavic efforts became apparent – obviously in Russia's wake. This meant a further antagonist for Austria.

4.2.2 The Dual Alliance

Two of the aforementioned reports date from 1879, a year which seemed harmless enough but which later proved to have grave consequences for the future of Austria and Germany. The stage was set and could evidently no longer be altered, although it would seem that there had been enough time to do so. The reports seem to reflect Austria's readiness for adventure that can hardly have originated from Austrian self-confidence owing to its former strength. Even Bismarck, the brilliant foreign policy strategist of international renown, could obviously not provide for all eventualities, nor could he foresee such dangerous high-handed acts.

It is well known that after its foundation, the German Reich was the only great European power without any ambitions abroad – except for the pursuit of peace, economic and industrial progress and inner stability. Thus, Germany was able to convene the Congress of Berlin, the other states not being suitable in view of their interests in the Balkans and the ensuing mutual distrust between them.[685] Consequently, Bismarck had to play the (famous) part of "the honest mediator", which he performed with excellence, - if not at times with too much Prussian fervour.[686]

He was, however, poorly rewarded for taking on this role, particularly by the country that was the object of his greatest care and prudence: St. Petersburg unjustifiably blamed the Germans for the bad outcome of the Congress from the Russian point of view.

Therefore, in 1879 the German Reich reacted by concluding the *Dual Alliance* with Austria-Hungary, sacrificing the traditional League of the Three Emperors. This, however, was done in the face of fierce opposition by William I, who did not want to be forced into the Dual Alliance with the Habsburgs, not even after the Tsar's harsh reaction to the result of the Congress of Berlin.[687] (See also ch. 4.4, esp. 4.4.1.2)

> "This ended the alliance-free period among the Great Powers,"[688] – at least with regard to military alliances. "The actual aim of the Austro-German 'Dual Alliance' of 1879 was his (Bismarck's) attempt to curb Austria's ambitions on the Balkans and achieve a balance between Austria and Russia."[689]

Tragically, both sides started out from two completely different interpretations:

> "Germany saw the alliance as a means of stopping Austria's expansionist aims on the Balkans, whereas Austria took it to mean a support of its Balkan policy." ..."The basic difficulty lay in the fact that despite all the precautionary measures taken by Bismarck the 'Dual Alliance' bound Germany to Austria. If the preservation of Austria was essential for Germany, Bismarck would eventually have to save Austria-Hungary, no matter how aggressive its action was. Bismarck's diplomacy after 1879 was a constant fight against this inevitable fact."[690] ...
> "The Triple Alliance Treaty of 1882" [with Italy] , "the Serbo-Austrian Alliance of 1881 and the alliance that Bismarck concluded with Romania in 1883[691] all led to a further involvement of Germany on the Balkans and the Mediterranean regions, where, according to Bismarck, it

held no interests..." (This is followed by a quotation of his most famous remark about the Balkans concerning the bones of a Pommeranian rifleman.)[692]

These European alliance activities had serious consequences. The steps taken by the other side accordingly prove that after years of endeavour *France* finally drew nearer to its aim of obtaining revenge for the annexation of (German, French) Alsace:

> "With the Dual Alliance ... Germany had ... ended the alliance-free situation among the Great European Powers that had existed since the Crimean War and the Franco-Prussian War. For France this in the medium-term meant a way out of its isolation."[693]

Thus, one year after renewal of the Reinsurance Treaty of 1887 became due but was never effected, i.e. 1891, the *Franco-Russian Consultation Agreement* was concluded. This was followed two years later by the Franco-Russian Dual Alliance and in 1894 by "the *Franco-Russian Alliance* ..., one of the main elements in the development of the fateful situation of 1914."[694]

After the rapprochement between England and France in the unexpected *Entente Cordiale* in 1904, - and after England and Russia had agreed upon the delimitation of their spheres of interests in Persia, Afghanistan and Tibet - the year 1907 culminated in the Treaty of St. Petersburg and the *Triple Entente*: a masterpiece of French and English diplomacy, although in the Russo-Japanese War of 1905 London sided with Japan in accordance with the Anglo-Japanese Alliance of 1902 which was aimed at keeping imperialistic Russia in check. (It was England's first step out of its "splendid isolation").[695]

> *(It seems as if only the Anglo-French [insincere] promise to Tsar Nikolaus II of getting "Konstantinople" brought the latter to betray his relative Emperor William II.)*

The way to the Franco-British Entente was paved by the French Foreign Minister Delcassé during the Faschoda Crisis by giving up the Sudan[696], - just as England had started its rapprochement with America by withdrawing from the Caribbean.[697]

As if the serious consequences for the foreign relations within Bismarck's system of alliances were not enough to contend with; in the internal affairs of the alliance the third candidate turned out to be unreliable and rash:

> "The Dual Alliance" [with Austria] "was followed in 1882 by the Triple Alliance with the German Reich and Italy, an alliance that due to Italian irredentism had been rather dubious from the start."[698]

One of the reasons for the Italian readiness to join the alliance was the anger that Rome felt about the failure of its own aspirations regarding Turkish "colonial territory", after the French had gained Tunis in 1881.[699] But frustration and defiance are not particularly appropriate recommendations for an alliance.

Thus, disaster took its course.

4.2.3 Another missed opportunity for Macedonia

Looking back at the years 1883/86, it is impressive to read in the files about the constant wish of the German Reich to win the trust of Russia despite several setbacks and to offer the same trust in return.

Therefore, it is not surprising that the German Ambassador in Vienna, Prince Heinrich VII Reuß, still defended the Russians many years later, when he tried to convince the Austrian government that "there was no evidence of Russia's intention", never to leave Bulgaria "once they had occupied it for some reason or other."[700] (As mentioned above in connection with Bulgaria's insubordinate attitude towards Russia, in particular after the untimely, arbitrary unification of Bulgaria with Eastern Rumelia, this risk really existed; and one should not forget that the actual reason for the resentment felt in St. Petersburg was to be found in the person of the Bulgarian sovereign, and in particular in the "Battenberg Affair"). The Austrian Foreign Minister, however, reminded him of the Vienna's maxim,

> "that the Russians' permanent presence on the Balkans cannot be tolerated, whereas the formation of independent states must be supported." ... "Austrian interests require a system of independent states, which should prevent the permanent establishment of an exclusive Russian supremacy."[700]

Very soon, however, Vienna abandoned this seemingly modern political line of policy. Disregarding the Italian suspicion that this proclaimed Austrian policy of supporting smaller Balkan states was actually designed to create a reservoir for its own future expansion plans according to the principle of "divide et impera", this policy could have helped to find a solution to the *Macedonian problem*, that had recently been postponed at the Congress of Berlin.

The reason, or rather one of the reasons why this modern policy was never put into effect is to be found in a broader political context. This emerges from a directive of the Auswärtiges Amt, in which Baron von Marschall, Secretary of State at the time, reminded the Ambassador in Vienna of a proposal that the Bulgarian Prime Minister Stoilov had put to the Austrian government in the past:

> "...but Count Kálnoky was strongly against a European conference about Macedonia." Marshal von Bieberstein provides the reason for this rejection: "Once the Macedonian problem is placed on the agenda of a conference, we can be sure that the Straits, and the Armenian and Egyptian question will also be presented to the forum of this conference."[701]

But no one was willing to go near this "powder keg". The future of whole nations depended on the lack of readiness to deal with such inconvenient matters. In addition to this, the complexity of the Balkan issues was actually due to the existence of various divergent international interests on the Balkans. Ambassador zu Eulenburg reported a month later, at the beginning of August, - this time after talking to the Austrian Chancellor, Count Goluchowski, - that the latter had told him

> "the Macedonian problem (would be) completely extinct ... once the Russians relinquished their interest in the country."[702]

And that is what Russia had already done following the urgent request of Greece at the Congress of Berlin at the latest, but even before that: over against Berovski.

Furthermore, he reports in a second telegram that the Austrian Chancellor had established two basic principles for Austrian policy regarding Macedonia: Austria would never

> "relinquish the basis of the agreement of all Great Powers." [Really?] "Secondly, he would never tolerate a repetition of the Armenian cruelties in Macedonia."[703]

His intentions sounded reasonable. Unfortunately, he did not abide by them. The losses and the cruelties that Macedonia had to suffer again after the Ilinden Uprising evidently were still not bad enough. Gulochowski himself had foreseen such a situation, because the Ambassador closed his report stating:

> "The Count is convinced that a massacre in Macedonia would inevitably lead to an acute state of the Macedonian problem."[703]

But it didn't ...

Due to foreign interests the counter-forces were more effective. Obviously there were agreements between the courts of Athens, Petersburg, and London. Even the Royal Family in Copenhagen seems to have collaborated, - especially the female part of the family. This is not a claim lightly made; it can actually be proved. Many years before, the Ambassador in Copenhagen, who had previously been posted in Athens as well, reports:

> "it is undoubtedly true that the Queen of Denmark is an intelligent and prudent lady, who not only exercises great influence on her Royal Consort and her children, but also on her sons-in-law including the Russian Emperor."[704]

4.2.4 The Macedonians insist on the fulfilment of the Turkish obligations

The relative lack of information contained in the files relating to Austria in connection with the Balkan League in those years leaves room for a study of the chronological reports – for once not taken from the original volumes of the Political Archives, but from reports selected and published after the First World War in the collection of more than fifty volumes entitled "Die Große Politik der Europäischen Kabinette", which dealt with a much wider range of topics (under section 231 of the Treaty of Versailles) than the relatively small complex of the Balkan League.

However, in retrospect it appears that a more thorough consideration of files relating to the Balkan League and the Balkan wars would certainly have been worthwhile when reviewing the question of Germany's sole responsibility for the war.

The reports quoted help to complete the picture; for instance the German Chargé d'Affaires in Constantinople reported that his Austrian colleague had confided that

> "the efforts made by Macedonians to achieve political autonomy for their country were developing into a threat for the Porte".[705]

It is important to emphasize that the Austrian Ambassador did not refer to the Bulgarian, Serbian or Greek Macedonians, he simply spoke of the *Macedonians*, - those Macedonians who were striving to obtain their political autonomy. Despite the different claims made by present-day neighbouring states, at that time this was the term "normally" used.

As described in the introduction,

> "the Macedonians based their demands on Turkey on Section 23 of the Treaty of Berlin, according to which the Porte was to introduce self-administration statutes in its European provinces with the help of commissions consisting of local people."[706]

It is remarkable how close the Macedonians and with them the other Turkish provinces had once again got to the status of autonomy, which for all the other Balkan states had constituted the first step towards independence. In order to be successful, however, two indispensable requirements would have been necessary:

1. The Ottoman Empire would have had to fulfil its international obligations that had been agreed upon in writing.
2. The Great Powers would have had to be on the alert at all times, as well as insist on, and supervise, their fulfilment.

In fact, none of this happened. With regard to the repeated breach of the Treaty by Turkey, the reason for this Turkish/Islamic conduct has often been mentioned. Once again, the only explanation for the strange reluctance of the Great Powers to react is that the royal dynasties must have intervened. The anger at this insulting disregard

forced the Macedonians once again to consider alternative - violent - ways of achieving autonomy. This movement was strengthened by the spreading of information that England, supported by Russia and France, had approached the Sultan on behalf of the Armenians in Asia Minor. That was a legitimate, understandable and welcome encouragement for the tormented Armenian people.
But why did this not apply to the Macedonians?
It was this disappointment that motivated the plans which a few years later, in 1903, led to the Ilinden Uprising.

This report contains further informative aspects, in that it states:
> "This Macedonian agitation meets with support in Bulgaria, and even the reprimanding words of Prince Ferdinand cannot change the situation."[707]

The "reprimanding words of Prince Ferdinand" are explained in a footnote:
> "On 22 April [1895] in his answer to a petition presented to him by a Macedonian deputation, Prince Ferdinand rejected and condemned the agitation of the Bulgaro-Macedonian committee."

In other words: a "*Macedonian*" deputation appeared before the Bulgarian sovereign – and not just any deputation "from" Macedonia. The reason for the rejection of their request by the Bulgarian head of state has already been examined in this work in various remarks and explanations: It was to be expected that Ferdinand would condemn the agitation of the "Bulgaro-Macedonian" committee, because he knew that the *committees* (including the Bulgarian one!) supported *Macedonian autonomy* rather than a Bulgarian expansion policy. The Bulgarian leaders tried to bring influence to bear on the Macedonian committees both politically and ethnically as the latter were located in Sofia.

> (The same strategy was insidiously applied at the Ilinden Uprising. Bulgarian flags were hoisted and Bulgarian songs sung in *Krusevo* with the intention of converting the Macedonian uprising into a Bulgarian one. This was successful to some extent, part of the European press being taken in by this ruse.)[708]

The report further states:
> "Hundreds of thousands of people of Bulgarian origin are living in Macedonia and about 60,000 Macedonians are resident in Bulgaria."[709]

Regardless of these numbers, it is worth noting how the Austrian representative – whose home country for centuries had not only been the enemy but also the neighbour of the Ottoman Empire and thus was able to obtain first-hand information about the situation in Turkey – as a matter of course clearly distinguishes between Macedonia and Bulgaria, i.e. between Macedonians and Bulgarians, as being different countries and peoples.

Interestingly enough, the text reveals that the Bulgarian people – in contrast to their government with its hunger for power – actually felt sympathy for the Macedonian autonomy movement, and expressed this through common activities.

The final remark of the Austrian Ambassador ("It is understandable that under these circumstances [i.e. "the Macedonian agitation"] the Ottoman officials in Macedonia are not treating the politically rebellious population leniently.") again throws light on the inhuman conditions in Turkey at that time.
Woe betide those who claimed their internationally guaranteed rights!

4.2.5 First signs of negative implications of the Dual Alliance

Soon after the Congress of Berlin, plans took shape for the formation of a Balkan League as the linch-pin of the next military confrontation with the Ottoman Empire. This confrontation was intended to change the situation on the Balkans, i.e. to drive the Turks further out of Europe. It was a moot question, whether the neighbouring states of Macedonia would be the only ones to try to annex the territory or whether or not other "Balkan countries" would also take the opportunity to fish in troubled waters. Ambassador von Romberg evidently did not think the Austrian government capable of any evil deed and thus tried to see the positive side of the formation of the Balkan League, after it had been prematurely announced in a Russian newspaper ("Wjedmosti") in summer 1904, by referring to the Russo-Austrian Agreement of Mürzsteg in the previous year and wrote:

> "If the Austrian diplomats want to remain correct and are not pursuing any aggressive plans, the formation of this league is bound to cause them nothing but pleasure, as it will definitely benefit to the implementation of reforms in Macedonia."[710]

Both Hofburg and Ballhausplatz must actually have felt unmasked. The fact that the German leaders still firmly trusted the Austrian motives is illustrated by the instructions sent by Chancellor von Bülow to the Embassy in Belgrade:

> The Chancellor has attempted to dispel as unjustified "the suspicion of some Italian politicians as regards alleged Austrian expansion plans on the western half of the Balkan Peninsula."[711]

Is it possible that Prince von Bülow reread his instructions four years later, after the Austrian annexation of Bosnia? And could this have led to a rescue operation, had he reread them on time? Probably not. But this was not all:

> "The assumption ... that Austria is systematically aiming at an aggravation of the situation on the Balkan Peninsula and that it is intellectually the driving force behind the attacks by Bulgarian gangs on the Serbian population is only conceivable if Austria-Hungary is actually planning to extend its borders towards Saloniki."[711]

This eventuality does not seem to have scared the German Chancellor at all. He therefore did not even bother to ventilate this possible outrage and put it up for debate. On the contrary, he retreated to the typical (pardon!) legal-bureaucratic way of reasoning: "There is absolutely no proof of this."

Von Bülow at least offers a political reason:

> "It would be difficult to explain such a procedure on the part of the Habsburg monarchy that has already got so many disparities to contend with."

One can only agree with the Chancellor. If only Vienna had seen these facts as clearly as that!

Finally, von Bülow's directive contains another doubtful credo:

> "We, who do not show any direct interest either in one direction or the other, would be well advised to practice a policy of utmost reserve with regard to the aims of both Empires."

Pardon? The German Reich had not shown "any direct interest" in either Austria or Russia? This was most certainly not Bismarck's aim in his German foreign policy, - and Chancellor von Bülow had always admired the Iron Chancellor (for good reasons). If the author were not familiar with many examples of Chancellor von Bülow's political prudence, he would have to ask himself - on the strength of this mistake alone: should one not expect the Chancellor and Head of German foreign policy to have a clearer understanding of the situation at the time? Such a head-in-the-sand policy could only be misleading.

In the course of this work it has been remarked that a crucial motive for the formation of the Balkan League might have been of an economic nature, e.g. a customs union. One of the counter-arguments regularly put forward was the fact that those considerations were only suitable for serious projects, such as those pursued in central Europe since the Second World War – and nowadays even on the Balkans - , whereas in the past the neighbouring states of Macedonia were in reality driven by different, namely imperialistic motives. Only in order to conceal this fact, the responsible politicians did apparently resort to the harmless idea of a "customs union". In contrast to the Russian Chancellor Count Lamsdorff, who gave this project his support, his Austrian colleague, Baron Aehrenthal, watched this development with great concern, because he realized that the economic aspects

> "were a cover-up for a purely political action", as its "final aim (was) nothing but a dismembering of Turkey ..., which meant a serious danger to peace on the Balkans."[712]

Knowing Austria's greed for territorial expansion, this alleged concern for peace on the Balkans can only be defined as pure hypocrisy. Without his imperial delusions, Aehrenthal might have succeeded in seeing through Russia's plans and attempts to mislead the public. In doing so he could have done his country (and Germany) a good service.

When Austria was allowed to occupy Bosnia in 1878, it did not have any such scruples; even less so, two years after this statement by the Baron, when Austria confronted the Ottoman Empire, Russia and above all Germany (as well as the rest of Europe) with the annexation. At the Ballhausplatz they announced that the breach of the Treaty of Berlin was committed for the sake of preserving peace. History did not follow this dialectic line of reasoning.

4.2.6 1908 again, - including London's anti-German propaganda following the collapse of the Russo-Austrian deal of "Bosnia in exchange for the Straits"

It cannot be emphasized too often that the Serbo-Austrian relationship had been badly shaken by the occupation of Bosnia in 1878 – it remained strained despite a temporary improvement. At the turn of the year 1906/1907, the Envoy von Ratibor reported from Belgrade that Prime Minister Pasic fully agreed with the Serbian people,

> "calling the occupation of Bosnia a constant obstacle to the establishment of sincere and friendly relations between Serbia and Austria-Hungary."[713]

Pasic was referring to an event that at that time had occurred 29 years previously, - and in contrast to the Austrians themselves, he was not able to foresee the dramatic development of the coming year!

Nor could anyone know that the Sultan would announce elections for the Ottoman Imperial Parliament and thus reinstate "the constitution of 1876 (that had been suspended in 1878)" that would now also apply to Bosnia.[714]

> Vienna was bound to see this barbarian act as a violation of Austrian interests in the *Turkish* part of Bosnia, which deserved punishment by annexation in order to preserve peace. Surely it would be mischievous to think otherwise.

Consequently on 19 August 1908 Austria decided to *convert the occupation into an annexation.*

The way Austria acted in relation to the German Kaiser and his government was particularly provoking and insulting (the Chancellor described it as a "thunderbolt"):

> "at the beginning of October Aehrenthal (proclaimed) the annexation off his own bat."[715]

This quickly revealed the long-term disadvantages of Bismarck's wrong decision to enter into a Dual Alliance with Austria-Hungary against the will of Kaiser William I, who would have preferred to maintain good relations with Russia. What an enviable instinct for long-term strategies the old Kaiser had!

Henry Cord Meyer describes the inevitable consequences of Aehrenthal's risky policy as follows:

> "It is true that Germany had not been informed about the annexation plans, but nevertheless it was forced to give its backing."[716]

It was only afterwards, on 16 September, on his estate in Buchlau, that Aehrental attempted to obtain the consent of his Russian colleague. And Izvolski in fact agreed to the annexation! As Izvolsky, in return, did not succeed in getting Vienna's agreement to the international support of a Russian access to the Straits the meeting proved to be highly embarrassing for him.

This failure opened the door for the English diplomacy; it succeeded - with more and more arguments - to tempt the Tsar slowly into war against Germany.

According to Herzfeld, the encounter "remained ambiguous" because of the uncertain situation for the other Great Powers.[716]

In order to cover up this public disgrace, the Russian Foreign Minister, who was thought to have been duped, complained about the outright disloyalty of Austria in general and Baron Aehrenthal in particular. As usual (and it is no exaggeration to say so) Izvolsky had lied and concealed the important detail that he had actually consented on behalf of Russia to the annexation. This way he presented the Austrian Foreign Minister in such an unfavourable light on the international stage that Aehrenthal had to defend himself against this damage to his reputation. Thus, von Bülow writes:

> "On 14 March 1909 the Russian Ambassador, Count Osten-Sacken paid me a visit. ... (He) appealed to us for support, in rescuing the Russian Foreign Minister from a situation that was both personally and politically embarrassing for him. The Austrian Foreign Minister had threatened to prove his integrity (that had been called in question by the Russians) by publishing a number of secret documents that not only revealed Izvolsky's acquiescence to the annexation of Bosnia ... but proved that he had actually encouraged the minister to take this step..."[717]

It hardly requires mentioning that this appeal to decency, helpfulness and human kindness made an impression on the German Chancellor. At any rate he expected a diplomatic "service in return" for his help [Obviously - a typical German penny pincher!], in that Russia should put "the Serbs on the leash", - a highly justified suggestion which was truly in the interest of peace. At least ostensibly - this was temporarily complied with.

But did the concession made by the German Chancellor improve Russo-German relations or make peace more secure any way? Absolutely not, quite the contrary! Despite many years of intriguing against Germany, Izvolsky was not ashamed to whimper for help in Berlin of all places (instead of Vienna) to redeem his tarnished reputation (worse still: he asked others to whimper for him!). After this successful kowtow, by means of lies and deception Izvolsky took even more vigorous action against Germany on behalf of the Entente, - last but not least to repair the damage to his reputation.

Consequently, the generosity of the German and Austrian governments was not worth the effort. On the contrary, they soon had to pay the price for it, even if it happened in a roundabout way, as is usual in diplomacy:

The Russians had assured the Chancellor - who was well informed about the influential position of the English Ambassador in St. Petersburg, Arthur Nicolson, - that they would not involve this wily anti-German diplomat in the "deal". When Nicolson, however, learned of the official "unconditional consent given by Russia to the annexation", he

> "expressed his anger and disappointment by spreading the lie that Germany had compelled Russia to yield by means of threats and pressure 'with its armoured fist'." (l.c.)

Von Bülow suggested to his Russian colleague, Chancellor v. Tsharykow, to issue a joint press statement in order to clarify this untruth; this suggestion was treated by the Russians so dilatorily on the pretext of small technical changes that the Chancellor finally refrained from the publication altogether

> "so that the whole Bosnian problem does not leave any feeling of resentment between us and Russia." (l.c.)

The Germans did not want to be regarded as "trouble makers", - but the polite restraint shown by the Chancellor and the government was a major mistake!

Far from conforming to their polished image of being fair and noble, if it was in their interest to further damage Germany's reputation, – the English (A. Nicolson!) as well as the Russians preferred to exploit the case by disseminating propaganda.

Therefore, despite the German attempts to relieve the strain on their relations with Russia, the "malicious suspicions spread" by England remained in the air and heavily burdened Germany's reputation in the world – even in America!

This falsification even found its way into history books, where it says that by means of a "barely concealed ultimatum" Germany forced the Russians to give in and to cause the Serbs to retreat. The inevitable consequence of this was renewed hatred and bitter feelings among the English and Russian population. As it was intended.

> The "unconditional siding of Germany with Austria" fitted perfectly into the image of the evil Prussian as drawn by propaganda. And it was this version that influenced the readers' view of history to the detriment of Germany.

As a consequence, Fritz Fischer of course also "confirms" in his so-called "expertise" that Aehrenthal had "outrageously betrayed" the Russian Foreign Minister in Buchlau (p. 376). In "Weltmacht und Niedergang" he writes (p. 41) that Germany „enforced the changes of power on the Balkans against a Russia that was still weakened ". Even as late as 1977 (!) Fischer believed in the fairy story of Germany having brought pressure to bear on Russia with regard to the annexation of Bosnia. ("Der Erste Weltkrieg..., l.c. p. 277) And still in 1978 („Krieg der Illusionen", p. 105) he disregarded important details that would have served to correct the common cliché against Germany. Robert K. Massie, too, argues mistakenly that Izvolsky had been "duped". (l.c., p. 505) And still recently in 2002, Mark Mazower repeated the mistake by showing sympathy for the fact that

> in 1914 the Russians "could not afford to lose their face a second time after the events of the Bosnian crisis in 1908."

Thus, by means of tricks and lies a report was spread around the world, found its way into historiography and was passed on from generation to generation without further questioning; it all fitted perfectly into the propagandistically caricatured image of the evil Germans.

> Another success in England's psychological warfare in decades – I repeat decades – of propaganda campaigns against Germany.

Such a short time after Reval, things could not have been more favourable as far as the long-term aims of the Entente against the two German states were concerned. And until March 1909 this conflict conjured up the danger of a great war on more than one occasion. Therefore, this should have been an urgent warning to both Austria *and* Germany. A policy of prudence and restraint would have been highly advisable at that time. But what do we read about Austria's reaction? The German Embassy in Vienna reports that Foreign Minister von Aehrenthal even mentioned the idea of *occupying Belgrade!*[718] This occupation was meant as a "temporary" measure only, but who could possibly have relied on this promise?

Even the Ambassador in Stuttgart reported that on a farewell visit to the King of Württemberg (also a William, William II to be precise) and the Prime Minister (W. Blos), his colleague, the British Ambassador in Berlin, Cartwright, complained vehemently about the "intransigent attitude" adopted by Austria, that "(was aggravating) the situation from day to day", and he explicitly mentioned Foreign Minister Baron von Aehrenthal.

> "If Vienna continues to move troops to the border, ... there will be war with Serbia this winter. Although all powers, with the exception of Italy, ... support the peace, under the pressure of the atmosphere in the Duma and in the army, that has been stirred up by the press, the Tsar will be forced to stand by the Serbs in spring at the latest... Furthermore, all Balkan states including Romania will unite ... against Austria."[719]

Nor did Cartwright miss the opportunity to hint at the serious assessment of the situation made by Prime Minister Georges Clemenceau!

Cartwright's justified and concerned reference to France's agreement with England cannot have come as a surprise either to Vienna or Berlin. But it is hard to tell whether anyone had suspected that Romania or Italy had secretly gone over to the Entente.

This constitutes a further proof of Fritz Fischer's thesis that William II sadly overrated the significance of his family relations with the "non-native dynasties" in Romania, Greece (and Bulgaria?) as well as their influences on the respective governments (and parliaments). ("Der Erste Weltkrieg ..." l.c., p. 270 and 280)

What Sir F. L. Cartwright did not know, was the fact that the "much dreaded war against Serbia ... this winter" *was part of the plan of the Entente,* since he probably was not informed about top secret issues, but was motivated by a feeling of personal responsibility based on his political analysis.

Chancellor Prince von Bülow, alarmed by a report from the Envoy von Below foretelling disaster, sent instructions to the Embassy in Vienna on the following day. [A perusal of the files leads one to expect that] the Austrian government would at last be called upon to be conciliatory and compliant. But nothing of the sort happened!

The annexation was not questioned at all; on the contrary von Bülow wrote:

> "I am not inclined to view the situation pessimistically, but I believe that it is advisable for Baron Aehrenthal to communicate with Turkey and to secure Bulgaria's good will as soon as possible and if possible also Romania's. The only real danger for Austria-Hungary in the event of a conflagration lies only on the Russian side." ["Only"! *Only?*] "By the way, I am convinced that the adversaries of Austria-Hungary do not really want the war, but are determined to play a game of bluff and intimidation and in diplomatic terms humiliate Austria-Hungary and consequently our country at the same time."[720]

The only possible reaction for subsequent observers can be a painful sigh. (Obviously, the Chancellor had not the slightest idea of England's intrigues behind the scenes.)

Herzfeld's work shows the degree of consideration with which the Germans excused one of von Aehrenthal's least acceptable characteristics, and thus reveals the extent of the disastrous error:

> "Only in February 1909 did the German mediation with its calming effect succeed in persuading Aehrenthal, who was *rather sensitive in questions of prestige*, to make financial concessions to Turkey, which made them acknowledge the annexation."[721]

Being sure of German backing, the Austrian Foreign Minister could face the German Ambassador v. Chirschky-Bögendorff when he carried out his instructions with composure so that his report (of December 1908) reads as follows:

> "The Minister does not wish to take seriously for the time being the nightmare conjured up by Sir F.L. Cartwright in the shape of a Balkan League (that would also include Romania) directed against Austria-Hungary."[722]

"Not to take (it) seriously for the time being..." sounds as if there was still a lot of time left until the formation of the Balkan League on 13 March 1912 with all its inevitable consequences. How thoughtless!

Should Cartwright have issued a threat rather than a warning?

> *Two years later a league was formed against Austria, which included Romania (but excluded Bulgaria)! That was to be expected.*

At any rate, v. Aehrenthal endeavoured to pacify the members of the Triple Alliance by making an agreement with Italy guaranteeing it a certain influence on the Balkans. Although this bait was tailor-made to suit Italian interests, it was obviously not tempting enough to keep Italy in the Triple Alliance longer than three years, before it succumbed to the enticements of the Entente.

In another set of instructions his German colleague interpreted the "English and Russian warnings" simply as "attempts to intimidate",[723] no serious statesman in St. Petersburg would think of war. V. Bülow explained this by economic considerations, that would not allow Russia to wage a war, the same also applying to France that had every interest in obtaining the repayment of the thousand million loan it had made to Russia. *A fateful error!*

The Prussian statesman did not recognize the psychological power of the thirst for revenge and of hatred which could not be explained and certainly not be quenched or extinguished by economic criteria. With parameters such as national honour and chauvinism, reason plays only a marginal role even in the country of Descartes. Furthermore, how was the Chancellor to know that France would later make Germany pay many times the amount of the Russian debts! Thus: if it was not a question of "reason", at least it was a question of calculation.

Only once, almost two weeks later, did the Chancellor seem to have had second thoughts. In one of the many sets of instructions he drew up at the time, he developed a scenario that must have made his blood run cold, when he wrote:

> "Should Russia really succeed in bringing about such a Balkan League, the situation for Austria-Hungary and thus for our country would become very difficult and truly serious."[724]

And Russia had indeed succeeded, - with the help of England and France. Therefore, von Bülow's realization came too late.

But Austria's unspeakable use of diplomatic trickery went much further: a Serbian newspaper reported that "Austria (was) spreading the news that Russia had allegedly already consented to the annexation". Basically this was true (see above), - but it was contrasted by excerpts from a categorical Russian note by the Belgrade press, according to which "the basic principle of international law concerning the immunity of international treaties was upheld, and the Balkan issues were to be discussed on this one and only correct basis."[725]

This was followed by an addition from Belgrade that was in many ways threatening, because

"the Russian views were identical with those of England, France, and Italy."
"Having ears, hear ye not?" (Mark. 8, 18)

Around the same time, von Schön wrote a memorandum in Berlin concerning a diplomatic move made by the Austrian Ambassador von Szögyény. According to this memorandum, the Austrian Foreign Minister v. Aehrenthal was "rather worried by a passage" from a Russian circular note, which contained a request for the amendment of section 25 of the 1878 Treaty of Berlin concerning the occupation of Bosnia. The Russians had intended in this way to "smuggle" the "idea of autonomy" for the Balkan states into the treaty.[726]

At long last a constructive proposal from St. Petersburg! This was, however, quashed right away by reactionary Vienna.

In Berlin no one thought of the obvious idea of supporting this excellent plan in relation to Vienna. Nor did anyone summon up a minimum of irony, as Ambassador v. Rombach had done shortly before, who had remarked to the Austrians that such a plan must surely have been fully in keeping with Austrian intentions. But the former lip-service to the principle of autonomy of Austria was not to be revealed so clearly as such!

(Or was the Russian proposal simply a ruse, another diversionary tactic?)

At any rate the Macedonians and their fellow-sufferers would have welcomed this step towards the freedom they longed for.

The aforementioned report by Ambassador von Ratibor from Belgrade ends with the remark that Serbia was expecting *"European complications"*. As the ongoing crisis had been defused in time by Emperor William II and the next one would probably not develop as soon as hoped for by Serbia (and France), the Serbs following instructions by the Entente took the initiative on 28 June 1914, in order to produce "European complications" their way.

No one - especially not in Vienna - could claim that this had not been foreseeable. It was inevitable that the Bosnian crisis would have much wider repercussions. Thus, the German Ambassador in Rome, von Jagow, repeated remarks that his Bulgarian colleague Rizoff had made in an interview given to the Italian socialist newspaper "Avanti":

"The independence of the individual Balkan states without a confederation ... was a rather precarious issue and was being threatened daily by the increasing gravitation of German [i.e. more precisely: Austrian] interests[727] towards the Mediterranean. The annexation of Bosnia made this threat even more immediate. Austria might say now that Bosnia was sufficient ... With the same degree of sincerity with which it now declares that it is no longer considering marching to Saloniki, it has always declared in the past that it is not interested in the annexation of Bosnia." ... "Whoever wants to invade Macedonia and advance to Saloniki must inevitably pass through Serbia."[728]

Such was also the reasoning of the other Balkan states. Therefore, Vienna and Berlin should not simply have taken note of it but actually should have anticipated it.

These concerns about the Austrian expansion policy were shared by Turkey. Baron von Marshall, who was at that time Ambassador in Constantinople, described the view of the Turks,

> "who do not regard Austria–Hungary as a friend, but as an enemy, who is constantly trying to damage Turkish territory for its own benefit."[729] The annexation of Bosnia had confirmed Turkish suspicions. "At that time the grudge borne by Turkey against Austria-Hungary was much stronger than it was against Russia, as the former has taken possession of Turkish provinces in times of peace while the latter had diminished Turkish territory after successful wars." "The position of the Cabinet of Vienna on the question of Macedonian reforms had also caused a feeling of deep-seated resentment among the Turks." [Mürzsteg].[729]

Yet, in view of its own interests, Turkey decided to support the German, i.e. "Germanic", side in the First World War – (ironically, so did Bulgaria, but for the opposite reasons).

Beside the seemingly endless chain of devastating mistakes made by Austria and Germany, some praiseworthy facts need mentioning. According to Paul Sethe, the Austrian heir to the throne Franz Ferdinand left Vienna after the annexation of Bosnia and went to Lucerne for a cure, in order to demonstrate by this reaction – which at the time was unusual and courageous – his heart-felt protest against the irresponsible act of Emperor Franz Josef and his cabinet.

Paul Sethe mentions two remarks by Franz Ferdinand, who, in view of the Kaiser's age of more than 90 years and the apparent imminence of his own reign, had already developed some conciliatory ideas for reform:

> "A state should not pursue a pretentious policy if the conditions within the state are not in good order." ... "Von Aehrenthal and his friends might believe recklessness to be the best policy – but I intend to keep the army clean."[730]

It was this policy of restraint and his idea to "secure a share of power" for the Slavic population that was to prove his doom. K. R. Massie quotes the assassin Gavrilo Princip, a Bosnian Serb and thus Austrian subject, as saying that "certain ideas and reforms .... (which) stood in our way."[731] (That is: the way to Great Serbia!) According to Brigitte Hamann, Crown Prince Rudolf, too, would have been in favour of a gradual democratisation, had he not precluded his succession to the throne by taking his own life.

One would have expected that all the catastrophes the Austrian monarch had to suffer (such as the assassination of his wife ("Sissi"), the mysterious suicide of his only son at Mayerling Castle, two lost wars and the execution of his brother in Mexico), would have led the old man to the height of wisdom. Quite the contrary: narrow-mindedness, overrating of the rules of protocol, megalomaniac moods, and amorous adventures characterized this senile man. Thus, he saw in the assassination of Sarajevo the restoration of world order: after all, his nephew Franz Ferdinand had entered into a morganatic marriage, as instead of a princess he had "only" married a countess. Massie quotes the Austrian Emperor, who - in total misjudgement of reality and priorities - had commented on Ferdinand's death as follows:

> "As far as I am concerned, it is one great worry less."[731]

History can be so merciless.

4.3 Great Britain

4.3.0 Historical impressions on England's Balkan policy

For centuries England has been known as the country exercising a *balance policy*. But this old doctrine cannot remain without additional interpretation because only the powers on the European continent were supposed to be in balance. England itself did not intend to be on a level with the rest of Europe. The only role that England considered appropriate was that of hegemony – not just within Europe but in relation to the whole world. As soon as another state on the mainland threatened to become more powerful than the other continental powers, or had already become so, London presided over a counter coalition against the respective great power by means of a "mainland force" until the continental powers were again below the English level. Ludwig Dehio writes:

> "England was used to ... overpowering continental supremacy, restoring balance in Europe and consolidating its own predominance beyond the oceans."[732]

Only then could England safely pursue its original aim of using a rigorous colonial policy under the guise of these hegemonial battles to forge an empire which would allow England a level of power that it would never have conceded to any other state in the world. The famous balancing strategy therefore was nothing but the means to an end, namely to expand and strengthen England to truly imperial heights. According to Dehio, Robert Seeley, e.g., had

> "the Anglo-Saxon world leadership in mind, rather than a system of individual states competing against one another."[733]

André Maurois made a similar comment about the English Prime Minister Disraeli. (l.c., p. 296)

The provision of safety for the *sea routes* leading to parts of this empire was indispensable and strongly connected to this maxim. The chain of protection posts to the Middle East and above all to India as well as the waterways became corner stones in England's power game for wealth and strength. This way the Ottoman Empire, too, moved into England's calculation for political supremacy in the world. However, at that time London was as disinterested in the future of the Balkan nations, as in the future of the peoples of Africa, Asia and America; let alone in their liberation (for fear of riots and instability). All that ever counted was permanent and safe exploitation of the colonies.[734]

After Russia had been strengthened under Peter the Great,

> "England – having just disposed of the concern for French hegemony – saw a new enemy rising out of the depths of the mainland..."[735]

England had watched with sympathy, or at least leniency, several Russian wars against the Ottoman Empire that had brought an enormous loss of power and territory to the Sultan. But gradually the Tsar came too close to the English spheres of interest so that the question arose,

> "whether a Russian victory in another Turkish War would really comply with English interests. So far each of Catherine's victories against the Ottoman Empire were regarded as blows against the French enemy. But could England approve of a Russian invasion into the Mediterranean?"[736]

This would also mean a disturbance of its enormous Asian colonies. Consequently, England required clear and, if possible, unchallenged conditions in *Constantinople and at the Straits. (And this move proved to be the true essence of English strategy.)* That way Turkey and the Balkans - and with that Macedonia - became another focus of London's attention.

But Russia was not the only country potentially disturbing the peace of the English hegemony. After the victory of the Egyptian Mehmed Ali over the Ottomans in the Near East, England began to be concerned about East India. Therefore, as a preliminary preventive measure, London concluded a trade agreement with the Porte in 1838. Nevertheless, England's greatest antagonist in the world remained Russia. Together with Russia and France in the naval battle of Navarino in 1827, England had won a victory over the united Turkish-Egyptian fleet. This constellation determined the English position towards the Straits and the rest of Turkey. Assessing the situation at the Golden Horn realistically, England knew that it could not claim Constantinople for itself, having already established military bases all around the globe to protect its colonial empire. The second best solution for London was thus to prevent any other Great Power from seizing this precious treasure. The logical consequence was a policy of maintaining the "sick man on the Bosporus" as an appropriate keeper of England's interests at the Straits.

This was the maxim that determined the undeserved future of Macedonia, Thrace and Epirus as well as - temporarily - Albania.

> "In order to secure its sea route to India across the Mediterranean, the newly built Suez-Canal and the Red Sea, England's predominant aim was to prevent at all costs Russia's emergence from the Black Sea through the Straits and into the Mediterranean."[737]

In 1840 the Great Powers had concluded a mutual agreement for the protection of Turkey. Then Russia tried to effect a permanent right to intervention in favour of the Orthodox christians in Turkey. This was, however, rejected by the Sultan and, in turn, Russia occupied the Danube Principalities causing England to take this as an opportunity to stand by the Ottoman Empire, together with France, and put Russia back in its place in the *Crimean War* of 1853-56. Mark Mazower offers a rather simple explanation: "in order to protect the Turks from the Russians" (l.c., p. 39). The real reasons, however, were England's own interests. (It should be recorded that England alone had fought the notorious Opium War in China from 1840 to 1842 before leading a war against China lasting five years until 1860, not to speak of the massacre during the Indian mutiny in 1857.) The British Empire was used to continuously fighting wars against insubordinate peoples who were not as prepared to take its right to power as given: wars were the sanctified means to the end as far as imposing British interest policies was concerned.

England had obviously studied the politics of the Roman Empire very closely.
Rule Britannia, - Britannia rule the waves ...

In a report from London, Ambassador Baron zu Münster gives a vivid example of the English principle of operating a double standard in order to justify the preservation and expansion of its power. When the Greek King George I on his visit to London in 1876 announced the wishes of Greece to move its borders into the Turkish Empire, he also complained about the Greek constitution that left little room to manoeuvre and was only "exploited by individual political intriguers for their own selfish aims". The Ambassador also stated that the English ministers had to

> "be careful with regard to their own country as well as Parliament and cannot admit that a constitutional government is not necessarily the best one. In India the English are not true to

their constitution; they govern absolutely and would laugh at or declare mad anyone who wanted to try to introduce the constitutional government in India."[738]

The German ambassador has apparently viewed this correctly. According to B. Tuchman, still 25 years later the famous British PM and Foreign Secretary, Lord Salisbury, (to give only one of Tuchman's numerous examples) had expressed the concern "the democracy will lead to ... the political vilification of the people". Of course, one can presume that the entire English press and society – in complete opposition to the case of the German Kaiser – wanted this honest conviction to be considered more as an ingenious, yes, witty aphorism, as an incentive to the British aristocrats to show even more English democratic attitudes.

In 1877, St. Petersburg seemed to have attempted another grasp at the Byzantine "Zarigrade" (Constantinople), by taking the riots in Herzegovina and Bosnia of 1875 and Macedonia and Bulgaria of 1876 - stirred by St. Petersburg - as a pretext to wage war against the Ottoman Empire for the eighth time. After initial disastrous defeats Russia won the war.

Before the war began, English diplomacy performed a series of showpieces:

On 18 March, London enforced a convention with Russia, according to which there should be no Great State on the Balkans.

A few weeks after the Turkish rejection of the compromise that had been reached with much difficulty in the protocol of London on 31 March 1877, Russia declared war on the Ottoman Empire on 24 April. It did not take Prime Minister Disraeli long to dictate to St. Petersburg the English conditions for the Russian procedures on the Balkans on 6 May 1877 and thus clearly mark out its spheres of interest:

-- no Russian conquering of the Straits and Constantinople
-- no blockade of the Suez-Canal
-- no occupation of Egypt and the Persian Gulf.

In spite of the cool-headedness of the English, this list must have been sewn up in too much haste because, when Russia seemed victorious, London added another condition:

-- no destruction of the Ottoman Empire.

The latter one in particular was a basic decision to the detriment of (a. o.) Macedonia.

In addition to this, Europe is still dealing with the long term effects of the vast and immeasurable consequences of this hegemonial policy which was purely in English interest.

This note was written precisely when the Russian troops reached the coast of the Marmara Sea and Russian soldiers bathed their feet in the *"warm water"* of the Mediterranean. Was the old Russian dream about to come true? – Not quite this time.

England and Austria unequivocally threatened Russia with the repetition of the Crimean War. When Russia was bold enough to announce on 10 February 1878 its march into Constantinople from San Stefano, the English fleet anchored at the Golden Horn.[739] (See also Maurois, p. 324 ff.) Bismarck's famous "agent"-speech once more relaxed the Anglo-Russian relations.

If only Bismarck had foreseen what this would mean for him and the German Reich. All the states around Germany struggled to sow disputes against Germany – and Bismarck prevented an Anglo-Russian war! Was this German decency or naivety?

On 3 March 1878 Russia concluded the Preliminary Peace Treaty of San Stefano with Turkey (mostly to the benefit of Bulgaria). How much time passed this time until London showed a reaction? Not even 24 hours. On the same day the Earl of Beaconsfield (Dis.) demanded a review of the treaty, but St. Petersburg declined. In this situation England again proved its cold-bloodedness coupled with diplomatic mastery. In no way insulted by the Russian representation of its own interests and unimpressed by a further possible war, England negotiated an agreement with Russia for the specification of the present treaty, which had proscribed the formation of a Great State on the Balkans, and demanded the territorial limitation of Bulgaria. (Signed on 30 June 1878).

A similar agreement was made a week later between England and Austria.

This tightened a number of principles before the peace negotiations in Berlin began. Nevertheless, this congress almost resulted in a breach between London and Petersburg. Again it was Bismarck who played a major role in the prevention of this breach, - but the laurel wreaths that the "honest agent" had been awarded for the success of the Congress of Berlin would not have been possible without groundwork by England. Bismarck cannot be blamed for this, as it was simply in the interests of England to act like this.

London's policy of the expansion of power according to exclusively British interests is illustrated even clearer by its further course of action. On 4 June 1878, and thus shortly before the Congress began on 13 July, England had made a secret agreement with the Ottoman Empire about the "right" *to occupy Cyprus* – so to say as a "down payment" on the future negotiations when London promised to support the Turks at the congress in the representation of their interests. This did not prevent the British delegation from also favouring decisions against Turkey, e.g. pro-Greek, pro-Austrian and pro-Christian, i.e. pro-reforming decisions. On other occasions, however, England decided in favour of Turkey – in order to guarantee the presence of the Ottoman Empire at the Golden Horn, even if this meant on a piece of ground that is only a foot wide (this description seems justified if one compares East Thrace to the former gigantic Ottoman Empire). Imanuel Geiss has phrased the English doctrine for the Congress of Berlin as follows:

> "After the Turkish defeat the only important question was to which extent the Ottoman Empire should be weakened."[740]

Furthermore, England guaranteed Turkey the possession of Asia Minor, Syria and Mesopotamia. But this assistance, too, was not really worth great thanks from the Sultan because this, again, was only granted in England's own interests: to prevent Russia from marching further south, - until England was capable of expanding its own power in that direction! And this is what actually happened later.

Rule Britannia ...

It is important to mention that British troops landed with haste (very un-English) on Cyprus on 12 July, one day before the conclusion of the Congress of Berlin. This step was bound to cause a chain reaction:

> "The occupation of Cyprus ... proved to be another step towards the coming "scramble for Africa", the colonial division of Africa and towards the completion of European colonial imperialism."[741]

Now France felt entitled to annex Tunis (1881). And after this threat in memory of Napoleon's Egyptian Campaign, who would blame England for the precautionary occupation of the *Suez-Canal*, that the French (Lesseps) had erected after ten years of construction work? After all, this was just a formality, after London had already given friendly support to the bankrupt Khedive in 1875, and taken over the Egyptian share of 44% of the canal project and, together with France, given the Egyptians ruinous credit. Descriptions stating that Disraeli had snatched the shares from the French, disregarding their option of purchase, are opposed by Maurois who explained:

> "The French government does not obstruct him, on the contrary, the Duc Décazèz actually encourages Disraeli's support against Bismarck and calls off the French banks."

This was an example of how France makes an art of profiting from sacrifices: long-term planning in order to obtain British support against Germany (until Sarajevo and Versailles).

The fact that, in 1882, England not only occupied the Suez-Canal but also the whole of Egypt, might perhaps be regarded as a tribute to the English inclination of realigning their colonial territories properly. Thus Stürmer writes (p. 230):

> "That is when a new era of colonial dream worlds began…"

Rule …

Part of this kind of "rule" was mocking at the native population (in this case the Egyptians). The Serbian agent in Cairo, Tscholak-Antitsch wrote in his report no. 220 of 20 June 1911 (i.e. 30 years after the English annexation of Egypt), that became known after the seizing of the Serbian file material (R 20727-2, sheet 119), that

> "the main cause for the nationalist unrest (of the indigenous population) originates in the declarations of the British government that the occupation of Egypt was only maintained in the interest of the Egyptians."

And this, although they had agreed after the battle at El Kebir to retire as soon as the country was peaceful and a functioning administration had been implemented. After all, this method paid off until 1956.

However, this was not enough to satisfy the British ambition for power and wealth. There was another interesting island project in this region with an ideal natural harbour: Crete.

In view of Britain's own interests, that London attempted to fulfil in the longer term, it becomes obvious why – as Ambassador zu Münster reported from London – in 1876 the English government

> "had advised" the Greek King George on his visit to St. James's Court when discussing a further riot on Crete "not to participate too rashly, [but] to hold Greece back."[742]

What the Ambassador additionally reported to the Auswärtiges Amt as ordinary information, must have worried both the Greek King and the Greek population:

> "England wants Candia [Crete], and therefore it generously grants Greece Thessaly and Epirus."[743][744]

As for the population of Crete itself, England had not expected to receive so little respect. Of course, this did not bother the English at all. For, in contrast to other nations that are driven by the constant need to be loved, the British seem to be foreign to this feeling. As good businessmen, however, they must have known that such a degree of antipathy towards England could have pushed the price for gaining and keeping the island higher than its actual value even before the troops had set a foot on it. For what did Ambassador Prince Reuß report about his Greek colleague Conduriotti's remarks concerning this issue about a year later? (It must not be forgotten that Greece was busy enticing riots in Thessaly, Epirus and Crete – at the same time concealing them.):

> "The population of Crete was determined to rise on an agreed signal; the people there preferred to remain under Turkish rule rather than fall into the hands of the English. … A Greek

newspaper had declared that if Crete was meant to be under foreign rule, it would be better to surrender to the German Reich than to England."[745]

After this report, Germany must have appeared to the English as the devil incarnate. In this case it would be better to leave Crete to the Greeks!

Nevertheless, it took decades until London got used to the idea that it could not occupy Crete for the English Crown. Around the turn of the century, Ambassador von Winckler wrote to the Chancellor:

> "Crete with its Suda Bay would mean valuable property for both England and Russia. As the only way of gaining this for either party would be a world war, both of them will probably come to a tacit agreement for the time being to neutralize the island under the rule of a regent they both feel comfortable with, and that both of them are therefore kindly disposed towards Prince George's efforts."[745]

This is the last piece in the mosaic that had remained open in the chapter of events around Greece.

4.3.1 Macedonia as a piece in the field of the English strategy game

The German Embassy in London had sent papers proving that despite the unsuccessful and disastrous riot of 1903, Macedonia remained a sufficiently valuable object for a role in the strategic field of power in the Balkans – even if it would initially serve only as a chess-piece in England's global politics. This function of Macedonia is also connected with the interests of the German Reich, which since its formation had only been described as economic ones, - even regarding the large project of the *Baghdad Railway*, the construction of which had begun in 1903 (with a German share of two-thirds). In this case the German government grossly underrated the British interests and their sensibilities, because London saw the trans-Anatolian railway from a totally different perspective.

In a report the Ambassador quoted from a fundamental essay of the *"Fortnightly Review"* of 1906, which is indispensable for the understanding of the English policy towards Germany in the years to come. The essay deals with the British defence against the "danger of the pan-Islamist movement".

> "The movement ... could only become seriously dangerous for countries with a Mohammedan population, especially for England and France, because it was supported by Germany."[746]

(It may be permitted to remind the reader that the article was written 100 years ago.)

> "The recent report by Professor Delbrück, being spokesman for His Majesty, proved that Germany saw pan-Islam as a fundamental pillar of its policy, according to which Germany's main aim is to spread its influence around the whole world of Islam."

To create this impression of Germany as a new power in the so-called "European Concert" was almost as bad as wanting to put this illusion into practice, which was definitely not the case. German and foreign critics alike treated Professor Delbrück with the same rigour as Court Chaplain Stöcker, in order to present them in a distorted picture and provide evidence for an anti-semitic attitude of the German monarch. Of course, nobody mentioned Eduard Lasker, for example. In this context it is interesting to quote an excerpt from the letter the renowned half Jew historian Golo Mann wrote to his colleague Joachim Fest on 25 November 1986: "Hitler's anti-semitism has very little to do with the anti-semitism of the Germans, that was in no way stronger than that of the French; in France the Dreyfus-affair occurred in the same era in which German jews could actually be promoted to Prussian ministers or imperial state secretaries, but, of course, they got baptised and were awarded a peerage."[746a] Consequently, according to Tuchman, Theodor Herzl did not write his famous Zionist book "The Jew State" from experiences in Germany or, as would have been plausible (following Brigitte Hamann in her books: "Hitlers Wien" and "Rudolf") in his Austrian Vienna, but after he had heard the screaming of the hysterical mob at the public degradation of the Jew Dreyfus in Paris (after the process with false proof): "Death to the jews!" (loc. cit., p. 223 f)

This means that one preferred to keep out the fact that there had always been honest scientists, philosophers and poets among the counsellors of the German Emperors, like the Prussian Kings before them. *Where else should the enormous success of the Wilhelmine Age then have come from?*

> "The greatest threat for England from the spreading Islamist movement was less in Egypt than in Sudan, India ... Afghanistan and finally Arabia. In the latter areas the problems were the greatest but they were totally underestimated by the English. Furthermore, the "Arabic issue" was closely connected with the problem of where the Baghdad Railway ends."[746]

This assessment of the situation challenged the English balance policy (rather: policy of their own supremacy); possibly with the aim of one day seizing the Baghdad Railway, - as the Suez-Canal, Cyprus and other strategically important objects before.

> "Soon steps must be taken to fight the danger and expansion of the pan-Islamist movement. Above all, the connection between Berlin and Constantinople must be interrupted. Pan-Islam was a problem that needed to be solved with others together with Germany. It was no use claiming that the relations between Germany and England were good, as long as Berlin did not experience a complete change of attitude." "As long as England did not succeed in building a barrier between Germany and Turkey, pan-Islamism would expand even further, and the pressure of Germany to advance towards the East would become increasingly dangerous. The real danger of the Baghdad Railway was the fact that through this railway there would be a connection between Asia Minor and the European possessions of Germany."[746]

The term "European possessions of Germany" sounds obscure (this was surely not intended to insult the Austrians?), but: in addition to the intent to polemicize against Germany, the main task of the essay was to analyse the way of thinking of the English colonial empire at that time as well as to present in unsurpassably clear words the leitmotif for the future conduct of Great Britain towards the German Reich.

This is when Macedonia re-enters English calculations:

> "The barrier ... shall be achieved by seeking an agreement of the English government with the three Danube states of Serbia, Romania and Bulgaria."

This is a key phrase in the programme of the future British policy, not only in order to sacrifice Macedonia to achieve "an understanding with the three Danube states", but mainly against the German Reich.

> "The agreement between these states, whose only hope is the possibility of a peaceful development," [This is not the only hypocritical and misleading point in this long article.] "would be achieved if Serbia was granted access to the Adriatic Sea with Skutari, and Bulgaria was granted access to the Aegean Sea with Kavala. The Vilayets Saloniki and Monastir shall become autonomous under international control."

Just imagine! England, the best-informed world power, assumed a *Macedonian Saloniki*, whereas since 1913 Greece had tried to make the world believe that Thessaloniki had always been Greek. And so on:

> "Greece shall regain the territory lost in the last war" [Thessalia, 1897] "and in addition to that, regardless of Crete" [certainly, as Crete was meant to become English one day], "a further piece of coastline up to Corfu". [Thus Albanian territory.] "Turkey shall keep the possessions of Adrianople and Constantinople and shall receive a certain amount of damages. Under

Italian or international control, Albania shall form a separate state. Uesküb [Skopje] will be the only bone of contention and will thus have to fall to Serbia or Macedonia." Surely, "England will be able to achieve an agreement with the Balkan States and thus solve the problem of Macedonia."[746]

Interesting indeed. Nobody can deny that this was an objective and neutral view of the real situation on the Balkans at that time. The neighbouring states of Macedonia later distorted these facts, because they did not correspond with their own ambitions concerning the annexed Macedonian territory.

The "solution to the Macedonian issue" was finally so catastrophic that from 1912 to the present day Macedonia has suffered from it. Great Britain and France do not even consider it necessary to recognize the Republic of Macedonia under its official name.

The Macedonians today must realize once more, how close their nation had moved towards the much desired status of autonomy and thus towards independence, - if the sacrifice of Macedonia had not achieved first priority in the interest of the Entente's aims.

The importance of this analysis lies in the fact that these were the considerations of the leading Great Powers of Europe. Despite the missed opportunity at the Congress of Berlin and the unsuccessful Ilinden Uprising, history again left the door to freedom slightly ajar for Macedonia, - until it could be half opened in 1944 and completely opened in 1991.

Needless to say that London did not act for Macedonia out of sympathy or the struggle for justice and equality. Nevertheless, the significance of the essay in the "Fortnightly Review" should not be underestimated. It revealed the basic principles of English policy, which in the years to come were going to constitute a crucial guideline in their attitude towards the German Reich. As a principle aim of its political considerations, England - even in 1906 - pursued closing a hermetical ring of allies around Austria and Germany. This is by no means speculation: At that time, it was two years since the formation of the Entente Cordiale, and the preparation for the Triple-Entente of 1907 must have been in full progress. The Reval convention in 1908 was to be the final step.

Over time, this was part of the program of teaching the Germans a lesson!

4.3.2 The English Macedonia policy from the Serbian point of view

Interestingly enough, four and a half months *before*, in May of the same year (1906), the popular Serbian newspaper "Politika" had commented on the English attempts *to isolate Germany* and Austria and noted "that England's struggle is directed towards the formation of an autonomous Macedonia under a Christian governor."[747]

The German Embassy reported:

> "The author gives ... an overview of the development of the political constellation in Europe since the Japanese-Russian War. The common fear of Germany has united England and France. In the expectation of being able to pursue its aims on the Balkans more effectively, Italy has joined both Powers and finally France has negotiated the approach of Russia towards England." [This ascertainment was thus made before the concretisation of the new alliance of the Triple-Entente in 1907!] "The tendency of this group of Powers headed by England, is the isolation of Germany as well as of Germany's ally Austria-Hungary, whose plans on the Balkans are supposed to be thwarted. The latter will be achieved by including Italy into the affairs of the Balkans as well as by the formation of a Balkan League: thus, England's interest in the

> issue of Macedonia. Both Romania and Bulgaria have tried to get into contact with this new power constellation and therefore both profit more from the solution to the Macedonian problem than Serbia would (which is constantly concerned with internal affairs)."[747]

In this article the strategy of England, respectively the Entente, is clearly outlined until 1914. Was there more need for clarity?
The only question is, why the target of the aims, Germans and the Austrians, who could not have failed to notice the danger of the strategy described in "Politika", did not react appropriately!
Again and again: worthiness and gullibility, delusion, short-sightedness, naivety and illusions...

A few years later, in 1909 (ergo after Reval), a report from Belgrade revealed that Macedonia was still a piece on the English chessboard, but the aim reached far beyond small Macedonia and would one day crush the country. Beside Russia, England had continued its efforts of promoting the thought of a Balkan League between Serbia and Bulgaria,

> "certainly with the intention and the aim of not only creating difficulties for Austria-Hungary, but above all counteracting the inner consolidation and strengthening of Turkey. After all, despite all Turkophile phrases, neither Russia nor England wanted a strong Turkey. Russia must try (as long as it is too weak for the realization of the so-called legacy of Peter the Great) to protect Turkey from decline but at the same time to prevent it from becoming strong. In addition, England needs Turkey to permanently be kept in check and busy, in order to prevent it from concentrating its interests and strength on Africa and Asia Minor. Therefore, it is traditional for English politics to support a status quo in the Balkans, but at the same time to incite Macedonia against Turkey."[748]

In view of this obvious description any comment is futile. Ambassador Marshall von Bieberstein had - once more - developed a plausible explanation for this striking change in the English policy towards Turkey: Almost a year later (1910) he stated:

> Soon after the "historic events" of the revolution of Young Turks, "English policies became anti-Turkish. The Young Turks explain this with hatred against the despotism of Abdul Hamid. This is nonsense. The English have never practiced sentimental politics. The turning point lies in a historical process: in the occupation of Egypt. With the possession of this country, the policy of the Crimean War and the Congress of Berlin became incompatible for England. The future may bring change to the one or the other territorial possession of England. Great Britain will remain an Empire as long as it rules over India, South Africa and Egypt." ...
> "Being in possession of Egypt, in contrast to its former policy, England is interested in making Turkey a politically and militarily powerless state. This meant the collapse of the Anglo-Russian differences. On its ruins the Anglo-Russian community of interests is rising."[749]

Brilliant! And yet (like in ch. 3.6), this author can still find no clear hint from the European component of this community of interests as a cause of the "turning point" in the Anglo-Russian policy towards Germany. For it was not Turkey that made London change its attitude, - nor was it Egypt. It was Germany, -
the Wilhelmine German Reich.

The Anglo-Russian community of interests was said to have been supported by the Turko-German project of the Baghdad Railway, which made both Petersburg and London feel restricted in their plans against the Ottoman Empire in the Balkans. It may very well be that this project played a certain role in British considerations, but it can have only been marginal.

It is sufficient to remind oneself of the traditional English patterns that have not yet been discarded to the historic waste by the British aristocracy. The historical awareness of the English would never have allowed such modern thoughtlessness. On the contrary: as far as the continent was concerned, they continued to act steadfastly, even stubbornly, as if they were following a manual, - and indeed, it was again Macchiavelli's compendium.

Consequently, the matter of priority was this:

Since the unification of the Reich in 1871, a power had grown on the European continent that challenged the English balance policy to reduce it to a size convenient for England and not too risky. But this required a long-term as well as perfect *encircling strategy*. London approached the problem with such a high security margin that not even the Giant Empire of the Tsar or the Empire Francais including France Outre-Mer sufficed as allies. In order to finally close the circle of a coalition of states around Austria-Hungary and the German Reich (as presented in 1906 in the "Fortnightly Review", see ch. 4.3.1), no country on the "English-global" chessboard, at least theoretically, was too insignificant for England as a mosaic piece in this ring, - not even Macedonia, albeit as a bait, or pawn sacrifice, to inescapably bind the Balkan states to the system of the Entente in order to encircle Germany.

The long-term categories in which England planned its policies and diplomacy can be found in the files of the Serbian foreign office that had been seized in 1917. In the directive of 7 April 1909 (R 20727-1, sheet 62) the Prime Minister and Foreign Minister Dr. Milowanowitsch informs the Serbian Chargé d'Affaires in London, Gruitsch

> "that already in April 1909 the English government has officially taken steps against Austria-Hungary and thus against Germany in Sofia, that would prepare the future Balkan League."

This means that England had acted promptly in the year after Reval, i.e. two years after the formation of the Triple-Entente and long before the Russian Secret Treaty (on behalf of the Entente) with Serbia and Bulgaria in 1911.

4.4 The German Reich, France, Italy

4.4.1 The German Reich
4.4.1.1 Germany's unwanted role in the Balkans

Bearing in mind that "since the High Middle Ages there had, on the whole, been a vacuum of power"[750] in Germany, and the German states had been toyed with by other powers (first Spain intervened under Charles V, later France: from Francis I and Richelieu to Napoleon III), it becomes apparent how essential the unification of the Reich was for the survival of the Germans. Even Paul Kennedy recognizes right in the beginning of his famous book the

> "power vacuum in the heart of Europe, ... vulnerable to the military incursions of ambitious neighbours." (Loc. cit., p. 4)

Justification can be found by glancing at the well known French map which was recently still on display in French book stores – and almost certainly viewed in a positive light by all the French. It shows the broad band of French "acquisitions" at the east border in the centuries before 1800. Astonishing: German (or Dutch, or Italian) acquisitions of French territory cannot be found. And yet, the Germans are not even allowed to regret their losses because this would be objectionable revisionism and revanchism and would not serve the peaceful understanding between good neighbours.

For obvious reasons, the neighbours would have preferred the continuation of a conglomeration of *insignificant* states in the heart of Europe: as a permanent source of supply for increasing their own territory at the cost of the Germans.

After 1871, the European neighbours may have called the German Empire a troublemaker, because for the first time there was a German (and this was not Bismarck, by the way) who dared to express his wish: 'I want my country back.' [In 1812-1815 all European states wanted their country back from France.]

But the Reich could hardly be called a newcomer (although even German historians of the younger generation repeat this cliché, for example Peter Zolling, l. c., p. 13 ff). Before the Congress of Vienna, the Holy Roman Empire of the German Nation had already existed for almost 850 years until 1806. Until 1763, the end of the Prussian Seven-years-war, for English politicians "empire" was not yet the British one but still the "...Empire of the German Nation" which they regarded, so Brendan Simms (Cambridge), as their main land force against France.[750a] But (lacking comparable institutions), some of the European Great Powers tried to erase this from the memory of the European peoples. After the two World Wars, even many Germans themselves were ready to suppress all memory of this immortal legacy.

So basically, the neighbours had had enough time to get accustomed to the existence of a German nation:

The German monarchies, dukedoms, earldoms and the free cities in the East Franconian Empire had born the name "Regnum Teutonium" since 925, and *within* the Holy Roman Empire (962), the addition "Nationis Germanicae" had been known as early as 1442. This name was first mentioned in an imperial statute in 1486.

Only Napoleon on his own authority simply abolished the Holy Roman Empire of the German Nation under the threat of violence. (Only two years before, he had crowned himself Emperor – as if the French, and particularly the democrats under the revolutionaries of 1789, had wished for nothing but to be able to serve under a new Emperor immediately after they had abolished monarchy. The reason for the French people's enthusiasm about Napoleon might have been the fact that he had managed, in the name of France, to subjugate in a relatively short time the whole of Europe, - which then appeared to be the natural and well deserved property 'de la grande nation'.

It was, therefore, not without reason that in 1806 Prussia consequently justified its - thoughtless and irresponsible - declaration of war on Napoleon because of his illegal dissolution of the Empire. The Prussians, however, were shamefully beaten at Jena and Auerstedt, after Napoleon had already defeated Austria-Hungary and Russia at Austerlitz before.

It cannot be ignored, on the other hand, that even the partial "reunification" of the German Empire in 1871 meant an unusually deep break for the whole of Europe. The European Great Powers, above all England, regarded the founding of the German Reich as a disturbance of the "balance of power" in Europe. England would not rest until this balance was restored with unshakeable and merciless rigour in accordance with its own interests.

The proclamation of the Kaiser after the Franco-Prussian War is known to have been made on 18 January 1871. (By the way, Herr von Bismarck, was it necessary to do so in Versailles of all places? Is it not true that this psychological mortgage had been too much of a burden for the German Reich from the start?) Already in February, in a speech in the House of Commons, the Conservative opposition leader Benjamin Disraeli called the *unification of the German Reich "a greater occurrence than the French Revolution* a century before."[751] (Similarly, too, P. Zolling, loc. cit., p. 11) In choosing the following quotation, Michael Stürmer (p. 187) gets even closer to the core of the British argumentation:

> "In the House of Commons in 1871, Disraeli mentioned the <German Revolution> as being even more detrimental to the interests of Britain than the French Revolution a lifetime ago."

Furthermore (p. 14), he repeats another central phrase of the English policy of 1871:

> "The balance of power is destroyed." (Rather than: disturbed.)

The vehemence of this argumentation and the long-term consequences for the British hegemonical policy in the following 43 years should not be underestimated in their historical significance for Germany.

This might be the reason for Gordon Craig (allegedly a "friend of the Germans", for which this author was unfortunately unable to find much evidence in Craig's standard work) *not* to quote Disraeli's fateful remark, although he dedicates a whole paragraph to the - negative - reactions to the proclamation of the German Reich. (l.c., p. 52 ff)

Refreshing, and almost ruthlessly English and - in theory - almost as radically as Disraeli and other politicians in practice, Stürmer comments (p. 198) on Bismarck (but only regarding the situation in 1878):

> "Had he not better escalate the cold war between Russia on the one hand and England and Austria on the other hand to a hot one?"

But Bismarck did not represent the sort of hegemony driven exclusively by political power as did his English colleagues. Just as little was he cast in the same mould as Frederick the Great, who, after the Kaunitz Coalition, that had been formed according to the famous "reversal of the coalitions" under the motto "destruction totale de la Prusse", disturbed the war plans of Austria, France, Russia and Sweden by "initiating a preventive war." (p. 190)

It did *not require the unification of the Reich*, however, to declare plans to attack and divide Germany. In 1863, still in Prussian times, Disraeli stated:

> "Prussia without nationality, the principal of the day, is clearly the subject for partition." (Stürmer, p. 13)
>
> *Imagine a German in a similar position uttering a similar comment or threat against a friendly state in the midst of peace: the whole of Europe, starting with England, would have cried out and would have remonstrated against the Germans for generations.*

Reverting to British threat against Germany, it is revealed that, in 1871, Disraeli's 1863 statement only represented the final touch, because the stage had already been set a long time ago, - long before 1914, 1878 and even 1871.

Disraeli's attitude towards Prussia may partly have been influenced "by the refusal of Prussia to side against Russia with the allies in the Crimean War" (in 1854/55), which cooled off the relationship between Berlin and London considerably.[751a] But was this a reason for such a far-reaching reaction?

Hillgruber provides a reminder of the fact (l.c., p. 15) that even at the first attempt of founding a German national state in 1848, all the Great Powers were opposed to the German efforts. Thus, England moved its naval force against Germany – because of the "impending" *democratic* unification (imagine the uproar in Britain in case of a Prussian/German corresponding action the other way round!); and Russia unequivocally threatened with intervention. This refutes the common thesis that this opposition originated in "the particular style of Bismarckian foundation of the Reich".

The German ambitions not only indirectly disturbed the traditional balance in central Europe, but also directly influenced "the interests of many ... states." Above all, those states that, for centuries, had been used to annex other states' land, i.e. in this case German territories. It was therefore understandable that those states took action against the unnatural and ruthless wishes of those upstart Germans, who all of a sudden wanted to live in a national state as all the other great European nations. In 1848, France e. g., had taken the issue of Schleswig-Holstein as a pretext to enforce its resistance against the German unification efforts. On another blatant occasion in 1850, when Austria was in alliance with Russia, it took action against the Prusso-(minor)German unification with the Punctation of Olmütz. After the Polish Uprising of January 1863, England, on the other hand, had not hesitated to intervene in the resulting Russo-Prussian strategy debate about the future of Poland after the Convention of Alvensleben and immediately raise serious doubts, according to which "Europe ... (would) never tolerate ... a ... conquest policy." Likewise before the foundation of the Reich, albeit after the Danish-Prussian and the Prusso-Austrian Wars, the English Foreign Minister Clarendon had issued in 1868 the unmistakable warning in the Liberal Gladstone Cabinet that "a Prussian policy of pressure to cross the Speyer line was unacceptable." (Hillgruber, l. c., p. 100) (This was clearly a German domestic affair!) Although even Disraeli admitted that an evolutionary unification of the northern and southern German states would have to be accepted, his statement remained a long-term effective threat.

If only Bismarck had accepted the offer of Tsar Alexander II to enter into a Russo-Prussian alliance! "If only..."

This represents another case of historic irony: Bismarck hesitated because he wanted to prevent the risk of letting the German Reich be drawn into some bargain of Russia and Austria about the Balkans. The Balkans of all places! (How often must the poor man, the so-called "Iron Chancellor", have turned in his grave when this actually happened.)

If the skilful and popular Regimental Adjutant von Hintze had already served at the Court of the Tsar at that time, Bismarck would most likely have been informed about the Tsar's words to the French Ambassador in 1849, as quoted by Stürmer (p. 13) according to George F. Kennan:

"Should the unification of Germany be achieved, ... this mass of weapons would be rather problematic, and this would then be your problem and ours."

Instead, after the Russian termination of the Pontus-Clause on 31 October 1870 (that is, during the Franco-Prussian War), Bismarck contributed considerably to the negotiations between England and Russia on the Black Sea Conference in London from January to March 1871 in truly German naivety. This was nobly done in order to prevent an impending war, - but wasn't it also short-sighted? Whereas England had, for centuries, repeatedly incited the continental powers against one another, worthy Bismarck, as an "honest agent", tried to prevent an Anglo-Russian war. According to Hillgruber, consequently the Anglo-Russian arrangement reduced the "difference between the two wing powers back to <normal>".

> "England and Russia could no longer be counted on as being opposed to each other, (as they had been since the Crimean War) which the Prusso-German side had always regarded as a fact." (l. c., p. 128)

This constituted a serious change in the structure of the European Powers that many German politicians (among them von Holstein and von Bethmann Hollweg, but also the Kaiser himself) did not want to admit until the last days of July 1914, - and some even until 4 August!

In view of this constellation, Bismarck had reason enough to pursue a policy of reluctance on the basis of a

> "realistic modesty for a better consolidation of previous gains in political power, which had recently changed the balance in Europe so enduringly."[752]

This positive description of some of the principles of Bismarck's policies really does not fit easily into the almost continuously negative picture that foreign countries and the German left-wing drew of the first Reich's Chancellor. He is almost always portrayed as a power-hungry, a warmonger, and as a Chancellor of blood and iron. All the more reason to take a short look at the circumstances behind the three wars which are constantly laid at his feet. Even more so because the internationally renowned historian Paul M. Kennedy also seems to have a false impression of this part of Prussian-German history (opt. cit., p. 466)

Information on the obvious reason for the Prussian-Danish war in 1864 is provided in another chapter (see 4.4.1.2.1, number 4).

The so-called "German War" in 1866 has also been wrongly portrayed by many national and international historians. It is a fact that, after the First World War 1914-1918, the Austrian National Assembly voted unanimously to remain in the German Reich, - a request which was strictly refused by the victorious powers. The same situation had already happened in the mid-19th century. All commentators who condemned Bismarck for the war against Austria seem to ignore the old Austro-Prussian "dualism" and the simple interdependency that any sort of unification of the German Reich *together* with Austria would have led to a war against Germany even then. Consequently, instead of going for the Greater German solution in the sense of the Holy Roman Empire of the German Nation as desired by Austria (and which Habsburg hoped would have implied a continuation of its supremacy over the Germans), Bismarck was forced to opt for the lesser German solution. This meant that Austria had to be "kept outside" *against its wishes*. This led to the battle at Königgrätz, - and thus to the (French!) "revenge for Sadova".

Bismarck certainly did not want to make Germany as strong and powerful as the other big European states. Otherwise he could easily have saved the war against Austria and could have gone, together with Austria, for the Greater German solution. This does not prevent Paul Kennedy from making reproaches to Bismarck and the Germans "to seek a solution in overseas expansion after its failure to gain 'a place in the sun'." Kennedy's addendum: "to repeat the Bismarckian tactic of solving domestic questions by a foreign war", is equivalent to a misjudgement of Bismarck's policies and, in addition to that, to the use of stale clichés in doing so.

As for the Franco-German War of 1870/71: In spite of Napoleon's defeat in the battles at Leipzig in 1813 and Waterloo in 1815, France continued to consider it to be its natural right to indiscriminately exert a sort of practical hegemony over Germany (until the founding of the Reich). There are enough indications that France would never have voluntarily given its agreement to the unification of Germany, especially since, for centuries, France had been the greatest territorial beneficiary of the weakness of the Holy Roman Empire of the German Nation, which was only strong on ideals. Paris furnished proof of this strategy when Napoleon III declared war on Germany in July 1870.

By the way: after the Franco-German War and the ensuing (official) proclamation of the Reich, England seamlessly took over the French attitude towards the right to decide on Germany's fate – until 1914.

The first touchstone for the new Reich was revealed as early as 1875 in the "war-in-sight-crisis" with France, which asked the Great Powers of Russia and England for assistance; this was granted in the form of an intervention in Berlin and caused Bismarck to withdraw.

At least this is the version prevailing in conventional history books. For decades German pupils, students and citizens have been (and still are) fed with this politically and ideologically influenced indoctrination.

As far as the author is informed, George F. Kennan was among the first to uncover the so-called crisis of their propaganda potential and to refute the eagerly cultivated version of the "war-in-sight-crisis" with detailed evidence. It is true that Tsar Alexander II had been in Berlin in 1874 with his Chancellor, Prince Gortschakow, - but there is no evidence whatsoever that the Tsar warned his uncle (Emperor William I) to the benefit of France. Nor does Kennan deny that "in the public opinion in Europe and after that in historiography"[753] this impression had eagerly been created, but these were "grave and fundamental errors", - if not *intents to mislead*. (Unfortunately, Michael Stürmer follows the common version detrimental to Germany. P. 189 ff. as well as 183 and 193; also Gordon Craig, p. 126 ff., and of course André Maurois, p. 299)

In this respect, Fritz Fischer may have been right in his assessment stating that England already then seemed to "take sides with the two continental neighbours of Germany." ("Krieg der Illusionen", p. 85) This distinct anti-German policy four years after 1871 would also provide a plausible explanation for England's rejection of Bismarck's alliance offers in 1877, 1887 and 1889. (l. c., p. 86-90)

(England's clear attitude, on the other hand, must be called realistic, because bearing in mind all antipathy against Germany it still did not go as far as pretending a willingness to enter into an alliance with Germany.)

Kennan proves beyond doubt that France showed great interest in making the world believe in Russia's function as protector of France, in order to turn this illusion into fact as soon as possible – that is, long before the actual bilateral agreements between Paris and St. Petersburg in 1891, '92 and '94. In this respect, Kennan writes, the newspaper article in the "Post" of 8 April 1875 "Ist Krieg in Sicht?" described an intended atmosphere, - but went back to errors and intrigues. He continues:

> "French diplomacy had easily defeated the Germans' sleepy complacency with passion, determination, dynamism, ingenuity and skill and thus not only created an astonishing political legend, but also anchored this achievement in the historical documents of the decades to come."[754]

One of Kennan's *practical* counter-arguments reads: if Bismarck had really intended to wage another war against France, which was often insinuated, he could easily have taken the (8th) Russo-Turkish War of 1877/78 as an opportunity, because France would have been completely without support. Bismarck, however, did not wage this war, thus he did not intend it.[755]

Another example of the French inclination to intrigue is elaborated on by Kennan under the question:

> "Why did the French Foreign Minister in 1887 under the seal of utmost secrecy pass into the hands of the Tsar false documents, which were intended to convince him of Bismarck's disloyalty?"[756]

Lies and treason as instruments of French anti-German coalition policy!

In the "Orient Crisis" of 1875-78 Bismarck was very careful not to
> "be dragged into a war of all the Great Powers over questions of the Balkans, because this war could put the existence of the newly founded German Reich at stake."[757] There was no active Balkan policy of the German Reich to speak of, as it had "very few direct economic or political interests on the Balkans."[758]

On the other hand, Germany was very interested in keeping the new balance of power in Europe, and like Austria (and England), did not want Russia to fill the vacuum of power on the Balkans that had been caused by the decline of the Ottoman Empire.
> "The new industry in Germany (in addition to that) still concentrated on the home market only..." Furthermore, despite the defeat at Königgrätz, Austria-Hungary still seemed rather strong "so that Bismarck was indeed not interested in seeking political adventure, over the head of Austria-Hungary so to speak, in places where Germany had no business (yet)."[759]

Thus Germany did not play a major role on the Balkans, simply because it did not want to.

In Berlin obviously no one realized that the role it took without any particular display of actions (i.e. as a back-up for the Austrian Balkan policy) was still sufficiently significant to - if unintentionally - influence the decisions of other European or Balkan states.

The fact that the German Reich as a monarchy dissociated itself from all sorts of liberation movements and endeavours of independence (especially the revolutionary ones), must have hurt the Macedonians at the end of the 19th century. Berlin rejected anything related to parliamentarians and democracy, as they meant the disturbance of the proven system, - although tolerance and human rights were developed much earlier and more exemplary than in most other European states.

(The following should not be forgotten: Shortly after Louis XIV's historical misdemeanour of revoking the Tolerance-Edict of Nantes in 1685, Frederick William decreed the (Tolerance-) "Edict of Potsdam": quite something for the "Soldier-King". Prussia was the first country in the world to abolish torture in 1740. Ten years later Prussia passed a law on religious freedom. In 1717/1750 general compulsory school attendance was introduced for boys and girls [in France this was done in 1880, and in England in 1884.][759a]).

Having said that, the role of Germany was expressed in a form that it might not have been aware of: the role of a giant shadow and protector of Austria, - despite the traditional rivalry between Hohenzollern and Habsburg. That effect might be ascribed to the centuries of communal life of both of them within the Holy Roman Empire of the German Nation.

In any case, the image of the disinterested and moderate German Reich in the Balkans must perforce be rendered invalid. What matters is not just the way a state sees itself, but the way the others see it. Obviously, Germany had misjudged Ambassador von Marschall's analysis of his astute report to the Kaiser stating that economic activities, too, could have political consequences. Later in 1910 he wrote:
> "In former times, we have been rather generous in making declarations about our political abstinence. That way, we intended to protect our economic interests without running the risk of getting involved in political bargaining. ... I (have) fought the sentence based on a misunderstood word by Bismarck. This sentence has become a weapon for our enemies, who are causing the Turks to believe that we are only after their money without lifting a finger to protect them in case of need and danger." ... "This sentence ... does not only damage us, it is also false. Just imagine the consequences we would have to face if England and Russia succeeded in depriving the Turkish Empire, like Persia before, of its independent existence by means of a

slow vivisection." ... "Nowadays we can only develop economically in the Orient if the Turks are convinced that we have a political interest in the existence and independence of their country."[760]

In fact, the relations to *Turkey* had been of a rather friendly nature for a long time, - although not in the sense spread by the English press at that time, in order to stir up the anti-German mood in Great Britain. (See also above, ch. 4.3.1) In 1761 (i.e. during the Seven-Years' War) the first Treaty of Friendship and Trade had already been signed between Prussia and the Porte.[761] A hundred years later, in 1860, the penultimate year of the reign of Frederick William IV, the Austrian engineer and entrepreneur Baron Hirsch, began constructing the 364 km long Turkish railway line in Macedonia from Thessaloniki to Mitrovica via Skopje (completed in 1870). In spite of the endeavours of keeping up good relations with the Porte, the Prussians, having after the Crimean War participated in the Paris Peace Treaty of 30 March 1856 alongside Russia, Austria, England, France, Sardinia-Piedmont (and of course Turkey) did not close their eyes to the misery of the "14 million Christian subjects" that were subjugated in Turkey under cruel tyranny. Logically consistent, Count Ruth-Volmerstein pointed out in a report by the Prussian Foreign Ministry that there had never been

> "a more suitable moment to overthrow the Ottoman throne and to push the Crescent out of Europe."[762]

But meanwhile England had turned against Russia, which resulted in the English participation in the Crimean War and later in the status quo policy.

The next railway line was also built by a German company in the years 1892-94: it, too, was located in Macedonia and with a length of 220 km it connected Thessaloniki with Monastir. (Further details about the German railway construction in Macedonia under Turkish rule can be found in Fritz Fischer: Der Erste Welkrieg ... l. c., p. 268, footnote 25.)

In 1867, still Prussian King, William I had met with the Turkish Sultan: in "Coblenz" – (as spelled in file R 12136). In this context, the two visits of Kaiser William II to Constantinople in 1889 and 1898 should also be mentioned.

Talking about William II:

In the past 85 years the mistakes and deficiencies of William II have been exploited in Germany and the world. Critics of Kaiser William have no scruples about throwing the first stone without analysing the facts and obviously without making any attempt to understand him – and above all understand him as a child of his times.

William II loved to boast, and he was pompous. He was also known to be impatient and unfortunately rather temperamental in his moods as well as his judgements. And he was probably much too honest. (Some years ago a famous book was published in Germany about the consequences of this character trait by Ulrich Wickert.) He was too credulous and occasionally even naïve. But he was also a bright (Kennan states: "occasionally even brilliant"), knowledgeable and variedly interested observer of Germany's home and foreign affairs. With an open mind and with much enthusiasm he followed both industrial and technical progress and - like his predecessors - he supported culture and science with lasting effect. Stürmer, who otherwise hardly misses an opportunity to paint the monarch in the darkest colours, phrases the following with much appreciation:

> "Supporting modern natural science with enthusiasm, the Kaiser ..." (p. 132) "... was a restless friend of educational progress." (p. 139)

(Bismarck, on the other hand, lacked the open-mindedness required for "modern times", so that Kennan characterized him as follows: "Like Kaiser William I, whom he loyally served for such a long time, he was in many respects a child of the 18th century."[763])

This was not true for William II.

In contrast to his reputation, he dedicated himself to social issues as well as to reforms in society, and this was highly unusual for his aristocratic background.

Summarising, Jürgen Zimmermann comes to the conclusion that "the German Empire was modern, cosmopolitan and innovative in many areas, in many ways more cosmopolitan than what came later", ... "the empire was not something which suffered from early globalisation; it was an important actor". ("Fragen an die 'transnationale Geschichte des Kaiserreichs'. [Questions on the 'Transnational History of the Empire"] In FAZ 11.07.2007)

As a child of his times, Kaiser William was convinced of the principle of the divine right; however, less so than his Habsburg colleague and the Russian Tsar. And he was very pious, he was so filled with the Christian belief that he even held sermons himself.

The principle of the divine right goes back to ancient constructions of power.

As a reminder, the derivation in brief according to Edgar Hösch:

> "In early medieval society there is a discernible causal connection between the conversion work of Christian missionaries ... and the establishment of sovereignty. The church blessing gave divine authority to the sovereign power and with regard to foreign affairs granted relative protection against attacks by Christian neighbours."[764]

José Ortega y Gasset wrote about this: the European states believed "the 'kings of God's grace' had to command. They believed this because they ... believed in the existence of God. ... As the general public stopped believing in God, so the kings lost the grace they had owned and the hurricane of the revolution swept over them." (On the Roman Empire. Stuttgart 1942, p. 17 f)

William's father Frederick III would probably have possessed the farsightedness to grant the people's representation more democratic rights in time, if his personal fate had given him the necessary time for such an undertaking. The history of Germany, and Europe, would have taken a different turn if the fatally ill Kaiser Frederick had not been called to meet his Maker so soon. Three more years of governing - instead of three months of suffering - or better yet ten years would have given the boisterous Crown Prince William enough time to mature, in order to live up to the weight of such a heavy burden. "Would have" ...

Thus, the unerring observer Winston Churchill could eloquently express his scepticism on the concentration of governmental power and representation in one person:

> "But uniting pomp and power in a single state function makes every human being subject to burdens that reach far beyond his natural abilities and tasks, even far beyond the strength of the worthiest and the greatest of men."[765]

Kaiser William attracted many noble figures, however, also flattering courtiers and overpraising insinuators, among them the so-called "Junker".

William II liked being a soldier, and he loved uniforms, but his pomposity and passion for decorations and uniforms did by far not come close to that of his uncle, King Edward, in London (let alone Edward's numerous love affairs). Nor was he the infatuated militarist presented in caricatures. Quite the reverse: even if his enemies will dislike this, he was particularly peaceable, if not peace-loving. Those that dump their frustrations about the old system on him - as if William had established it in the first place - and blame him for the Prussian militarism as well as other unbearable conditions, not only of his time, look for a whipping boy in a handy simplification according to the clichés of the propaganda of both the later victorious powers and the entire political left.

Count von Krockow profoundly called the "objects", i.e. the ships that William loved with an almost youthful or child-like passion (just as he admired any technical innovation) "gigantic toys".[766] This is exactly what they were for him. And, in fact, B. Tuchman repeats Wilhelm's almost congenial memories (loc. cit., p. 331) in which he publicly announced in Kiel that "the construction of the German navy resulted from his admiration for the English fleet which he had visited during his childhood accompanied by <good aunties and friendly admirals>" (English, of course). But even this almost sympathetic picture was painted black – otherwise it might just have been possible to discover human traits in the Teutonic monster.

Tragically, this technical category not only encompassed cruise liners (a. o. to Norway and Corfu) and barges (on the Rhine), but also battle ships. And they were bound to be taken as a special sign by the other side, especially by an island, and one island in particular. At least that is how the English government presented it (but see ch. 5).

It is rarely mentioned that, from the English point of view, the greater evil was that the Wilhelmine Germany started to become too successful and too strong on the continent.

Indeed, William dreamed of bringing the German Reich closer to the state of a world power and he did not have the slightest doubts that he would be able to keep the peace at the same time, particularly with "his" England.

A total misjudgement of the exclusive English urge to (world) hegemony!

His rivalry with England actually spurred him on, so to say, to enter into a sports competition with the British Empire, - the rivalry having been constantly stirred up by his rather insensitive English mother his whole life. Like many non-Englishmen he must have completely misunderstood the so-called English fairness in sports as an outstanding character trait of the English gentleman, - even today a widespread misapprehension. Instead, the English philosophy of life seems to be characterized by an extreme realism (might this be the reason for the compensating joy in drolleries?), as illustrated in the motto of English Air Marshal Brian Burridge:

"If you happen to find yourself in a fair fight, you must have made a mistake in planning it."[767]

Knowledge about this English leitmotif, which will be exemplified sufficiently in chapter 5, would have spared the partly English William (disregarding the fact that a large part of the English Royal family had German ancestors), like many other Germans and continental Europeans, illusions about their relatives or neighbours across the Channel.

That is what caused William's mistakes. Mistakes, as always in history - goodness gracious - that cannot be reversed:

The German naval programme of 1898 (ff.), for example, had allegedly made an approach towards England difficult (as it represented a serious pretext for England), but not totally impossible, because according to Niall Ferguson: "Tirpitz's naval programme did not necessarily mean war." (l. c., p. 86).

Is it not schizophrenic that William did not interfere when Admiral Tirpitz is said to have made the famous Haldane-mission fail, but during the war attempted to keep his battle ships undamaged? A Wilhelmine gigantic toy after all? V. Krockow:
"At least this dreamlike construction ... was not to be destroyed."[768]
The failure of the Haldane-mission, on the other hand, was not Kaiser William's fault alone, for it is known that in 1912 Poincaré objected to this peace initiative in London. With success – obviously.
(Details will be given in chapter 5, providing examples of major doubts about the significance of the issue of the navy (apart from propaganda) for the anti-German position of the English leaders.)

The rather worrying speech (if perhaps dramatized) on the occasion of his second journey to the Middle East in Damascus is just as unforgivable as his "Nibelungen loyalty" towards the Habsburgs, guaranteeing Austria support against Russia in case of conflict (How could he!); in addition to that, the notorious Daily-Telegraph interview in 1908. But in this case, too, crucial details were kept from the German public:
The Chancellor, according to his own statement, can, for example, not be relieved from the burden of responsibility for the catastrophe in the press, as the Kaiser had *previously* sent him the rather long text for approval. The Chancellor, however, did not read it himself as he normally did, but due to some carelessness (on holiday) and permanent strain, passed the review on to his relevant higher officials in the Auswärtiges Amt. In this rare case, however, Prussian reliability proved insufficient. This chain of misfortunes was exploited by the English press; it was like handing it down to them on a plate. William was the one who suffered most from the unintentional and unpredictable effect of the press campaign that followed, which was manifested in an illness, - while von Bülow tried to talk himself out of it.
There are but few historians who abstain from following the given trend to present William II as the first show-off of his time. Stürmer, e.g., describes his „boasting ruler's self-consciousness", but at the same time compares it with his „romantic softness". (p. 239) The historian Henry C. Meyer represents a different approach. According to his explanations in "Propyläen Weltgeschichte" (l. c.), William's statements were practically harmless compared to the agitations of Admiral Philip Howard Colomb – to mention only one of Meyer's listed examples.
All publications and documentations cite Kaiser Wilhelm's - admittedly unforgivable - Huns' speech ("Hunnenrede"), but is the following, barely less martial call of the well-respected First Admiral of the Fleet in Great Britain, Sir John Fisher, "His official slogan in case of war was 'nothing spared, no prisoners, sink everything, no time for mercy'" also written down in all of the school text books of the free and democratic nations? Of course, Fisher, in comparison to Wilhelm, could count on Barbara Tuchman as a reporter, who understood how to place his blood-thirsty speech in a favourable light; so she "fairly" and gentlemanly waves it aside: "This was intended more as a moral signal than as a serious tactic" (loc.cit., p. 308).
This type of charitable understanding has never been found for the German Kaiser.
A propos Fisher. The anecdotes are repeated over and over again about the Kaiser who was well pleased on his ships amongst his officers and enjoyed playing so much. This meant that it was easy to imply a certain type of abnormality. In comparison, one rarely reads about similar (definitely harmless) cockiness of Admiral Fisher. Of course, it is perfectly admissible for Fisher to have passion for dancing and to dance everything from sailor's hop to waltzes. But one can imagine the English (if not glob-

ally) organised malice if one were to read about Wilhelm II, or the often maligned Admiral Tirpitz, the same as one could read about Fisher: "If there was no lady to hand, then the fellow officers had to fill in" (loc.cit., p. 307). (See also the cites about Captain Mahon and Beveridge in ch. 5.1.3.4)

Doubtlessly, the Kaiser was popular with "the people", even after the Daily Telegraph affair and even up until the first years of the war. The people's participation in his birthday celebrations are not at all comparable with the ordered parades of modern-day potentates. In those days, the people saw a deeper meaning in honouring their monarch on his birthday,[769] as seen today in the monarchies of 'old Europe'.
It goes without saying that losers stop being popular. As in ancient rites, which can already be found in the Old Testament, people are always looking for a scapegoat.[770] In England and the rest of the world (after the war also in Germany) this scapegoat was represented by the Kaiser – and he was thoroughly slaughtered. During his time in office, the Kaiser was known to show affability towards his "subjects". At times, though, he behaved overbearingly, which was interpreted by some (also English!) critics as a sign of insecurity. In private he was a helpful, loving, yes, even tender-hearted member of the family, being generous and far from unforgiving. Nevertheless, he was also vain, (Stürmer: "in public admiration prancing like a cavalier", p. 241) – but if the author attempts to compare some of the smug and self-righteous characters he met in his own professional life (nationally as well as internationally) with William and tries to imagine that they could bask in William's throne, it becomes obvious that William would clearly have been overshadowed by them. The Kaiser's vanity, though, went back to unfortunate circumstances and seemed rather artificial – and therefore occasionally so ridiculous. V. Krockow looks into these circumstances in William's biography sensitively as well as convincingly:
From the beginning his relationship towards his mother was problematic as she was unable to accept the fact that his left arm was handicapped due to birth complications. She therefore rejected her son. (Not the other way round! He always wanted to be near her and yearned for her affection.) The years of medical ordeal through operations, stretching devices and other painful methods to treat the handicapped arm as well as the merciless, cruel and even bullying education by the pedagogue Dr. Hinzpeter (even Chancellor v. Bülow commented on Hinzpeter's methods as devastating[771]) could not have remained without consequences. His father, too, should have thought twice before uttering the fatal judgement on his son and accusing him of "over-assessment and presumptuousness" without considering the parents' contributions.
V. Krockow sums up:
"In the Kaiser's childhood all that could be bungled, actually had been bungled."[772]
And Paul Sethe states:
"Is it any wonder that the Prince's self-assurance was disturbed and always irritated as a result of his wrong education – at times being harshly subdued and then again strongly spurred on, but always unsteady?"[773]
P. Zolling describes the rack and other painful methods (he calls them "torture equipment") "which tormented the child but brought no healing". His conclusion:
"These treatments certainly formed Wilhelm's character and caused lasting psychological damage." (loc.cit., p. 48)
This makes it even more difficult to understand why even our democratic and socially aware post-fascist times do not allow a fairer judgment on the fate of the former Kai-

ser. Any scoundrel, any criminal, even murderers are granted mitigating circumstances because of serious childhood traumas. Only a German emperor is not! It is obviously impossible to get away from the ideological prejudice as a consequence of permanent propaganda that he did not deserve any sympathy.
Of course: Quod licet bovi, not licet Jovi!

> It can only be called historic irony that one of William's many merciless, if not brutal, opponents in England, Winston Churchill, had also suffered under deprived affection and rejection by his parents; so much so that he did not only have a lisp but even developed a stutter as a schoolboy. (Massie, p. 625-29)

It is exactly this – almost Faustian – ambiguity that cannot be avoided in the characterization of William II. Again Stürmer accurately points out:

> "Sensibility and prudence are opposed to one another without cancelling each other out." (p. 240) "Fear and arrogance influenced him alike." (p. 239)

It would have been desirable for the Kaiser and, above all, for the Germans, if a greater part of that human nature had taken effect in the person of William, what Stürmer describes so unbeatably and almost touchingly with regard to the fate of Germany:

> "Did he understand the central position that advised him to be cautious and that made each of those loud words that he so loved dangerous?" "Throughout his lifetime he lacked Bismarck's premonition of the German tragedy that he had presided over for such a long time." What is especially tragic, but occurs often with famous historic personalities, "… is their lack of awareness of their own limits." (p. 240-243)

This concludes the "enumeration" - as it is actually impossible to do justice to such a complex character in only a few lines, a character that in an addition to his own iridescent diversity was demonised by both accidental and intentional falsifications.
However, a final view must be cast on *the* crucial issue of the whole German history of the 20th century which, at the same time, leads back to the Balkans: *the outbreak of the First World War.*
To begin with, the following example illustrates William's active readiness to keep the peace, which is incompatible with the common cliché of the Prusso-Teutonic militarist, a condemnation that only wants to see the jeering German soldiers on the front, but ignored the cheering English and enthusiastic French or the Russians that were practically on their knees in anticipated joy awaiting the war. Kennan provides a further example:

> "And one must not forget the hysterical mass enthusiasm that had already been present at the mutual visits of the Franco-Russian fleets in the early nineties."[774] (That was in the 19th century!)

Initially, in the Serbo-Austrian Sarajevo affair the Kaiser had reacted aggressively – as was his habit. However, when it became apparent that more was involved than just dramatic threats, he was *the only* one, of those gambling for a war, who did not only make a show of advising prudence. William II was relieved about the quick Serbian reply to the Austrian ultimatum and wrote:

> "… thus any reason for a war ceases to exist."

(Even Fritz Fischer admits that Kaiser William II tried to avoid a war despite the "Prince's assassins" in Serbia. In: "Weltmacht oder …", p. 51. In contrast, Hermann Kantorowicz likes to spitefully discredit this statement by the Kaiser and, at the same time, all those critics that would eventually be willing to see at least *a little bit* of good in William II.)

This was another occasion for the Kaiser (he of all people!) to call for moderation as he had often done whenever the situation "threatened to become dangerous". He instructed Foreign Minister Gottlieb von Jagow to telegraph to Vienna:

> "The few retentions that Serbia still made could be settled by negotiations, and he himself was prepared to lead the peace negotiations." (!)

Today it is still moving to read Graf Krockow quoting from the relevant documents:

> "Too late: the governments in Vienna and Berlin were already determined on war. Therefore, Bethmann Hollweg delayed the transfer of the Kaiser's message until he was sure that Austria was about to declare war on Serbia, "mitigated" the text according to his ideas and instructed the German Chargé d'affaires in Vienna: 'You are asked to .. carefully avoid creating the impression that we wish to hold Austria back.'"[775]

The author's assessment of this process coincides completely with Fritz Fischer's opinion:

> "Bethmann Hollweg's decisions ... were conscious political decisions rather than fate or disastrous tragic."[776]

This again was not a case of Clio's assistance. This was the sole misdeed of a politician. But still it was not Bethmann H. who was being "judged", but the Kaiser (and a thousand times condemned) – contrary to the wish in his well known biblical epitaph. Maybe a simpler epitaph would have suited William much better, like the one Carl Zuckmayer had read at the grave of a great Indian Chief during his American emigration:

> "He had the mistakes of a human being and the virtues of a nation."

4.4.1.2 A look back at the Congress of Berlin and its consequences

- After the risings of the oppressed nations against Turkey in 1875/76,
- after the failed Conference of Constantinople and
- after the 8th Russo-Turkish War;
- after the Preliminary Peace Treaty of San Stefano
- and the following reactions of England (and Austria),
  all was set for a peace conference in Berlin.

> "As Austria-Hungary itself was among the potential enemies of Russia, the Congress could not be held in Vienna, let alone London. For similar reasons Constantinople and St. Petersburg were out of the question, too. Berlin was considered suitable, as the capital of a Great Power which did not have any immediate interests[777] on the Balkans, but possessed enough power and was geographically close enough to the Balkans. Thus, all participants deemed Berlin sufficiently neutral and influential to promote a peaceful solution."[778]

As expected, in their presentation of the past history and the progress of the Congress, Craig and Maurois showed Germany and Bismarck in particular in a rather bad light. Maurois admitted reluctantly that the Russians only consented to participate in the Congress after England had threatened them with war, and only after

> "the quietly summoned Indian troops had begun to land." (p. 323 ff.)

Even though Andreas Hillgruber concedes that the *Congress of Berlin* can be regarded as the successor of the Conference of Paris after the Crimean War, he makes, however, a remarkable distinction:

> "One cannot speak of actually ... resuming the great congresses of the European nations, as only the situation in southeast Europe, in the strictest sense of the word, rather than Europe as a whole was subject to debate."[779]

The tensions of the Congress arose from the conflict

"between the rising national movements on the Balkans and the contrasting interests of the Great Powers."[780]

Geiss subsumed the whole complex under the term "Oriental affairs", that was common at that time; this did not include the problems in the Near East, though, i.e. in Persia, Armenia and Egypt etc, but foremost on the Balkans: 57 out of the 64 sections of the Treaty of Berlin dealt with issues of the Balkans. In addition, there was mention of the search for a permanent home for the Jewish diaspora in Palestine.[781]

It is true that the Congress succeeded in peacekeeping as its most significant achievement; a peace which lasted longer than the participants of the Congress had anticipated.

"But in the long run, the problems were not solved but postponed at the expense of the declining Turkish nation and the rising South Slav national movements."[782]

One of theses movements was the Macedonian one.

"Due to the return of Macedonia to Turkey, the Congress of Berlin once more postponed the great Balkan conflict around this region. ... Later, Macedonia turned out to be the great conflict matter."[783]

Geiss proceeds – in complete understanding with the panel of the highest European statesmen:

"Surely the problems that had accumulated in centuries of Ottoman supremacy could not be solved promptly, because they were much too complicated;"[782] "...they can actually only be dealt with by experts."[784]

After all, Bismarck succeeded in convincing the other participants of the peaceableness of the German policy.

"On the Congress of Berlin Germany turned from a disturbing factor to a peacekeeping element of inner-European politics."[785]

But at what costs!!

Paris had surely drawn a totally different picture of the German Reich and was hardly willing to change that. And Russia blamed Germany for its allegedly disadvantaged position in Berlin, although

"the main conflict (was) .... between England and Russia" and "although Bismarck did indeed support Russia's interests in essential issues."[786]

Kennan quotes from documents that even the Russian Ambassador Count von Shuvalov had defended Bismarck against the Tsar's accusations:

"Throughout the Congress Bismarck ... supported the Russian interests in a discreet but effective manner."[787]

Some of the Russian demands had to be enforced by Bismarck - e.g. towards England - even with threats of his resignation (from chairmanship). But neither Bismarck's attempt at appeasement nor Schuwalow's correction were of any use. Therefore, according to Th. Schieder, Germany was forced to make a decision;

"created by the strong reactions on the containment of the Russian Balkan expansion, that the Tsar and his counsel blamed Germany for. In the so-called "Ohrfeigenbrief" [a letter resembling a slap in the face] of Alexander II to William I of 15 August 1879 the Russian rage was expressed impressively."[788]

Andreas Hillgruber comments:

"The burden on the Russo-German relations from the Congress of Berlin could never be eliminated."[789]

To make matters worse: since Bismarck had taken Tsar Alexander's letter as a sign of an irreversible destruction of the Russo-German relations (and forever lost his trust in Alexander II[790]) he decided in the following year to enter into the *Dual Alliance* with Austria, which Craig rightly called a "milestone in European history" (l. c., p. 137). It is on record, how difficult this decision had been for Bismarck. Did the great man, who until then had sought his well-being - Germany's well-being - in (military) independence (i.e. no alliances or leagues, but this does not exclude treaties), not suspect that he thus paved the way for Russia to enter into other leagues or alliances and for France to move out of isolation? How did he manage to assert himself against his admired Kaiser, who despite Alexander's unsettling letter would have preferred to maintain the Prusso-Russian alliance?[791] Rather a farsighted move of William I ...

> In this case Craig tries to sympathise with Bismarck, who had used the Dual Alliance only as a trigger to revive the old Triple Alliance with Russia and Austria, which really was successful in 1881. (P. 138)
> However, this was only of a superficial and temporary nature.

The severity of the dispute between the two men is reflected by the fact that the Kaiser threatened to abdicate and the Chancellor threatened to resign.[792] It is not clear why William I did not assert himself despite his good arguments, as his reaction resembled the proverb: once bitten twice shy.

Stürmer illustrates his attitude as follows (p. 236):

> "The bloody defeat of Frederick's army in 1806 ... became his lifelong trauma. The Russians as his brothers in arms were political necessity for Prussia: without Russia, Prussia was alone, against Russia, Prussia was lost."

Fritz Fischer described the critical situation of Germany more generally acceptable:

> "Despite the artistic system of alliances, Germany's political self-isolation was already apparent in Bismarck's times: the option of the problematic form of the dual monarchy of Austria-Hungary in 1879 constituted a first step in this direction, ..."[793]

And who did the German Reich get in return? A senile reactionary with a megalomanic cabinet and a Foreign Minister who was constantly craving for appriciation ("sensitive to prestige"). And in 1882 the unreliable Italy was added. Not exactly the sort of company worth envying Germany for. When the Entente later also attempted to have Italy as an ally,

> "British diplomats were joking that it would be all the better if Italy remained in the Triple Alliance and be a source of weakness." (N. Ferguson, l. c., p. 99)

After that, the Russo-German relations approached the crucial cross-road that can only be called tragic:

On 16 June 1890, after a three-year period of validity, the renewal of the *Reinsurance Treaty* of 1887 was due that Chancellor von Caprivi had rejected despite constant Russian efforts. (The author is aware of repeating himself: How could he!, - as his argumentation complied with neither the psychological nor the military dimensions of the treaty, taking into account the alleged advantages of public economic and trade agreements rather than the "secret forming of alliances".[794]) This decision is especially frustrating because it is supposed to go back to the recommendations of a diffuse existence in the Foreign Service, i.e. the Head of the Political Department von Holstein, who wrongly thought the Anglo-Russian divergence unbridgeable.

> "The chance of an agreement between Great-Britain and Russia seemed small. The antagonism was deeply rooted; German statesmen thought it was irreconcilable."[795] Von Holstein even assumed that "an Anglo-Russian war was unavoidable."[796]

A misjudgement of historic dimensions!

It is unbelievable what surprises history has in store or, in other words: how small a straw is necessary to actually break the camel's back:

On 1 July the governments in London and Berlin performed the exchange of the island of Zanzibar for Heligoland (including the famous "corner" in the south of Africa – at that time "Caprivi" was German Chancellor). This minor Anglo-German approach caused the Russian government - unwilling to be isolated - to finally yield to the year-long French wooing and enter into negotiations to form an alliance.[797] In 1892 these negotiations led to the Franco-Russian military convention (after a first success: the Consultation Agreement of 1891).

This marked the beginning of the decline of Bismarck's system of securing the alliance policy of the German Reich, - a process chosen by George F. Kennan as a title for his complex work: "The Decline of Bismarck's European Order."

After all, the old Treaty of the Three Emperors of 1873 still existed. In 1881 (this time the matter was secret, top secret) it was reissued as the Treaty of the Three Emperors and was signed by the new Tsar, Alexander III, (according to Kennan, out of unending sympathy and respect for his great uncle William I).

In 1884 the League of the Three Emperors was even renewed.[798] And what can be found there? Is it possible that Bismarck missed precisely this detail? Or did he deliberately let the amendment pass? In that document Austria reserved the right to annex Bosnia and Herzegovina at a convenient time. This was contractually veiled imperialism. Where was Bismarck's objection!?

The second amendment, however, was, as mentioned above, comparatively close to reality:

> "The three powers shall not oppose the eventual unification of Bulgaria and Eastern Rumelia, should this question arise through the force of the circumstances (par la force des choses)."[799]

This "force" became evident already a year later, in 1885. (See above, ch. 2.1.2) In this context it is important to mention:

On the one hand, it is now easy to explain, why not a single European state reacted, in order to stop Bulgaria when it undertook the unification of the two parts of its country and thus violated the principle of status quo, and only Serbia prepared itself for a war against Bulgaria. Austria of all states, one of the signatories of the treaty, had to "save" Belgrade from the Bulgarian claims for territorial "compensations" after the defeat, - naturally: as it had incited Serbia to this war!

According to Imanuel Geiss, the Serbo-Austrian "coalition" was essential for the decision of Bulgaria to ally with the Central Powers (i.e. Germany) in the First World War in 1915,

> "and thus accepting an alliance with the actually despised Ottoman Empire."[800]

This line of argument is only sound in relation to the constellation that, during the First World War, Bulgaria could for security reasons not be simultaneously opponent to both Austria-Hungary in the north and the Ottoman Empire in the south. This decision had, however, nothing to do with the "Serbo-Austrian coalition" of 1885 since, in the meantime, the Bulgaro-Serbian relationship had developed into opposition (not least because of the assassination of the pro-Austrian Serbian King Alexander on 10 June 1903), in particular once the co-operation in the first Balkan war had changed to open hostility in the second Balkan war.

On the other hand, the argument of an insult of Russia as a result of the Bulgarian high-handedness - that has already been questioned in the chapter on Bulgaria - is becoming doubtful, as the unification with Eastern Rumelia, evidently, had not only been realized with Russian knowledge but in fact with previous approval. Thus, in the eyes of Russia, the accusation gains credibility that the many years of ill-feeling at the Tsar's Court were indeed a result of the presumptuous wish of the Prince of Bulgaria, the German Alexander von Battenberg, to marry the Hohenzollern Princess Viktoria, the later Kaiser William's II sister (as well as of eventual incalculable personal animosities of the Tsar).

4.4.1.2.1 Background information (8)
The chain of events around the Balkan League with the cause of the First World War and the question of the war-guilt

As already mentioned in the introduction, the documents of the political archives provided surprising information about the significance of the Balkan League as an instrument of the Entente powers in staging a great war against the German Reich and Austria-Hungary. Enriched by relevant quotes from historiography, the documents reveal interesting insights into the processes that eventually led to the outbreak of the First World War.

This paragraph, that closes the chapter on the German Reich, contains some of the evidence gathered in the research on this particular issue. It is true that this evidence is mainly used for the discussions on Germany's alleged sole responsibility for the outbreak of the First World War. However, this has no influence on the inseparable connection between the fate of the Macedonians and the Entente-policy of the encirclement of Germany with the help of the Balkan states, whereby - as a price for the latter's accession - the Entente powers sacrificed the Turkish provinces of Thrace, Macedonia and Epirus.

1.)
The propaganda of the Entente against anything German, in particular against the Kaiser and other German state representatives, was not only continued in the same way after the First World War, but even increased.

Later, not even scholars expressed the necessary doubts concerning the allegations of the Entente. Among them was the famous historian Fritz Fischer. In his works he neither mentions the Anglo-Russian convention of Reval of 1908, nor the *Secret Agreement* of Russia with Serbia and Bulgaria of 1911 before the formation of the Balkan League. Nor did he acknowledge the secret Anglo-Russian *Naval Agreement* of spring 1914. This had to result in a, from his historical perspective, serious misinterpretation. Furthermore he took the publicly reported information about the Sazonov/Grey meeting in *Balmoral* in September 1912 *unreservedly at face value*[801], - rather than searching for the "story behind the story".

Can true historiography include uncritically taking a simple press release for undisputed fact?

Fischer was in good company. The lawyer Hermann Kantorovicz did not even cover Reval in his book with the meaningful title: „Der Geist der englischen Politik und das Gespenst der Einkreisung Deutschlands". Berlin, 1929 [The Spirit of English Policies and the Ghost of the Encirclement of Germany.] This book is in desperate need of details such as the Anglo-Russian convention of 1908, which could either have confirmed the justified Germans' fear of *encirclement* by England and Russia that later turned out to be justified – or simply cleared up any doubts. Although he mentions the convention (p. 389 and 228), he quotes the two state representatives Hardinge and Izvolsky in his unbeatable manner in order to prove, by simply naming these honourable men, that this "<talk>" of encirclement was nonsense. Well, if that is the case...

Unfortunately, 30 years after Kantorowicz, Hans Herzfeld, too, disregards the background to the convention of Reval in his standard work "Die moderne Welt" [The modern World]. Although he emphasizes that the Anglo-Russian Entente of 1907 created "the basis for a positive cooperation", he defines the "potential of this development ... between England and Russia" as more limited than the one between England and France (of 1904),[802] – similar to the way the situation was seen by part of the contemporary politicians (see also the discussion concerning Herzfeld in ch. 5.1.1 and 5.1.3.4). Von Holstein, too, had succumbed to the deceptive hope for an irreconcilable dissent between England and Russia – and influenced Kaiser William accordingly.

Herzfeld's attitude was shared by others; even some English supported a similar opinion. Niall Ferguson thus quotes the Liberal politician Sir Charles Dilke, who in 1888, as a challenge for England, only saw "Russia and France" as potential foes:

> "Between ourselves and France differences are frequent, and between ourselves and Russia war is one day almost certain." (Ferguson, l. c., p. 45)

In Germany many observers gave in to this delusion (probably supported by England). Ferguson confirms the misjudgement and characterizes the situation at that time as follows:

> "If there was a war which imperialism should have caused, it was the war between Britain and Russia, which failed to break out in the 1870s and 1880s; or the war between Britain and France, which failed to break out in the 1880s and 1890s. These three powers were, after all, the real imperial rivals. ... Few contemporaries in 1895 would have predicted that they would end up fighting a war on the same side within twenty years." (p. 39)

Robert K. Massie was the only one to mention Reval in his book about the dreadnought ships and the eve of the First World War, published another 30 years later. However, neither does he refer to the reported connections between Reval (or Balmoral) and the First World War. After all, Massie names Grand Duchess Olga as being among the participants of the convention of Reval – however, without any reference to Greece. Massie does not even mention her "role" as wife to George I, and thus as Queen of Greece.[803]

It makes one think when a phalanx of such highly esteemed representatives of historiography completely disregards the convention of Reval. There are grounds for the assumption that Reval might not have had the same tragic significance as a location for a bilateral meeting at the highest level for the preliminary planning of the First World War, as it evidently had (due to the expansion policy of Greece) for Macedonia.

Consequently, one might come to the conclusion that it was not necessarily the convention of Reval that became the key event in the future policy of the Entente towards Germany and Austria. The agreement on a joint belligerent act against Germany (via Austria) could have been made at any other place or on any other day, and still have led to the same effect and left the same mark. Indeed, there are some indications that the basis for the Anglo-Russian agreement was not established in Reval in June 1908, but had perhaps been laid as early as 1907 (as a marginal note of the treaty of the so-called "Triple-Entente" that was allegedly negotiated only to deal with colonial issues), or much earlier still in the preliminary negotiations, namely 1906 or even 1905, i.e. in the talks following the Entente Cordiale of 1904.

It would have also made sense if the Tsar's indignation after the unexpected annexation of Bosnia by Austria early in October 1908 and the Russian Foreign Minister Izvolsky's anger, caused by Aehrentals's (alleged) infamous breaking of his word, had first been directed by Edward VII and Foreign Minister Grey towards the mills of an anti-German coalition (see also above ch. 4.2.6 and no. 4 in this chapter).

Regardless of the time (and place) of the agreement on a joint course of action against Germany, crucial evidence for the responsibility for the outbreak of the First World War leads to Great Britain.

After all, not much time had passed since the English newspaper "Saturday Review" of September 1897 and its sensational article "Germania esse delendam" [that is what the text says]

> "kept on (inciting) competition against Germany by stating that every Englishman would be richer, if the German Reich was extinguished."[804]

It should be mentioned that in 1983 M. Stürmer, in his highly esteemed fundamental work, also mentions this altered statement of Cato the Elder regarding Carthage as an English motto "Germaniam esse delendam". (l. .c., p. 333)

> This particular quote from the 1897 "Saturday Review" by an English academic makes life a lot easier for today's - at least the unknown - authors, for in the last decades a German would never have been allowed to quote such a detrimental comment on a friend and ally. It would certainly have been considered as an abusive and thus improper use of the argument "tu quoque". Any discussion of propaganda or misdeeds, let alone crimes committed by anyone other than Germans would have been stifled behind the convenient wall of crimes of the Nazi regime in an attempt to pass on or at least reduce Germany's sole guilt for the First World War. Because in addition to this, for German speaking areas rather unusual quote, the British historian Ferguson went on to publish other important research results on the causes of the First World War, it may now be permitted to use other quotes.
>
> And this seems even more pressing now, since in 2002 the German Chancellor mentioned "en passant" the sole responsibility of Germany for *both* World Wars.

It is astonishing to read in Ferguson that by 1902 the English Foreign Minister Sir Charles Grey, who is highly praised in German historiography, was already of the opinion "that Great Britain should align itself against Germany."[805] A year later he even said: "I have come to think that Germany is our worst enemy and represents the greatest danger." Consequently in 1905, before his entry into the government, he added in the presence of a Liberal Member of Parliament if "any government drags us back into the German net":

> "I will oppose it openly at all costs."[805]

When the government under Balfour was voted out in October 1905 the Liberals formed the new government. Ferguson calls Prime Minister Asquith, Foreign Minister Grey and Minister of War Haldane "*a de facto imperialist government.*"[806] He provides evidence for this straight away as "the plans for a naval blockade against Germany were taken as given". However, it was not before September 1905 (!) that the General Staff first began to think seriously of sending an 'expeditionary force' to the Continent in the event of a war between France and Germany. It was in this context (In the year 1905!) that the question of Belgian neutrality came up"[807] and regarding this issue, Ferguson sums up:

> "If Germany had not violated Belgian neutrality in 1914, Great Britain would have. This puts the British government's much vaunted moral superiority in fighting for 'Belgian neutrality' in another light."[808]

Soon after the Liberals had come into power, an Anglo-French military convention about these land assault forces was held, and "by February 1906 the Anglo-French talks were already well advanced, the number of troops promised by the General Staff had risen to 105,000 and senior officers ... were beginning to regard 'armed collision' with Germany as inevitable"[809] (see also Stürmer, p. 333).
In addition, the impediment that Grey had erected against the Germans in his speech in November 1905 regarding the issue of Morocco (as reported by Ambassador v. Metternich, Germany had to "swallow the French Morocco-policy without complaint"[810]), appears to be a measure of *preventing* a political solution with Germany rather than promoting one (if seen from the above mentioned point of view).
This explains why the reigning French Prime Minister Delcassé, who had just been brought down by the first Morocco-crisis, spread indiscretions about the English promises in the "Matin", having been angered by the failure of his war plans against Germany (because the French Cabinet had in fact agreed to the German conference proposal):

> "In case of a German attack, England would mobilize its naval force, occupy the Kiel Canal and land 100,000 men in Schleswig-Holstein." In order to provoke this situation, he supported the "rejection" of the German proposition to hold a conference on the (first) Morocco crisis.[811]

As Kaiser William II wrote in his above mentioned letter of New Year 1905 to the Chancellor, he had denied in the presence of the London banker Beit that this had only been a "ridiculous threat", ... "but, considering the immense numeric superiority of the English navy, this could well have been put into practice". (v. Bülow, l. c., p. 194) In the previous year William had agreed with the assessment of the Head of his Admiral Staff, who regarded the "movements in the [English] navy since November 1904 as preparations for a war and not simply as the usual dislocations." (v. B., p. 195)

> *It seems worth repeating that this had been in progress between 1904 and 1906 and therefore throws a clear light on the English long-term plans against the German Reich.*

Ferguson continues:

> "Thus, within half a year of coming into office, Grey had presided over a transformation of the Entente with France," which had begun life as "an attempt to settle extra-European quarrels in a *de facto* defensive alliance."[812] More precisely, as he states a couple of pages earlier: "Grey encouraged ... the evolution of a military 'annotation' to the Anglo-French Entente." (l. c., p. 62)

Therefore, Grey's promise to Ambassador v. Kühlmann at the end of 1912 that

> "England's foremost interest was to keep the peace among the Great Powers; it pursued no privileges ..."[813]

is no sign of fairness, as eagerly claimed by the English. It is rather another *deceit* making the reported gesture of "détente" not really worth a penny. (Consequently, Secretary of State v. Kiderlen reacted reservedly and advised the Ambassador to practice careful scepticism.)
Regarding this situation from a German point of view, one cannot but contradict Henry C. Meyer, who granted the steadfast and alert English Foreign Minister

> "to have honestly (tried) to bear in mind the German position, too."[814]

Honestly? Was it honest to simply put the blame on his deputy Eyre Crowe instead, who was known to get his information on the "foreign policy of Imperial Germany" from the "aggressive all-German press" rather than the government and whom even the anglophile Kantorowicz (avoiding the term "anglo maniac") had to call germanophobic? (Matrimony does not seem to support international understanding: Crowe was married to a German. And his mother was German, too!) And what does Kantorowicz have to say about Grey? He praises his "absolute peaceable nature" and also mentions the politician's "uncompromising righteousness".[815]

In contrast to this, Foreign Minister Grey - unlike his Russian colleague Sazonov - expressed himself clearly and unambiguously at times, despite all the concealing and misleading remarks that he was known for. [Ferguson called him "enigmatic". On another occasion he mentions Grey's "tactic of studied ambiguity." L. c., p. 156].

In January 1906 Grey told the German Ambassador in London, Count Metternich:

> "If France got into trouble over Morocco, for example, "feeling in England and sympathy for France would be (...) so strong that it would be impossible for any Government to remain neutral." (N.F., l. c., p.63)

He repeated a similarly honest warning when early in December 1912, i.e. during armistice in the first Balkan War concerning Macedonia, he informed the German Ambassador that Germany

> could "not count on Britain's neutrality in case of a continental war."[816]

Fritz Fischer provides similar examples from Prince Lichnowski's time in office as Ambassador in London (i.e. from the end of 1912). The prince had repeatedly warned the Auswärtiges Amt,

> "that in order to <maintain the balance of the groups to some degree, English politics could by no means tolerate a suppression of the French [as in 1871]>". "England did not want to ... be confronted with a united continental group led by a single power."[817]

This may have been nationalistic, if not chauvinistic; and it was certainly imperialistic and anything but fair; and maybe it was not even wise [Ferguson, therefore, comes to the conclusion that in their patriotic arrogance the English leaders had backed the wrong horse. This could explain the German translation of the title of his book "The Pity of War" into "The 'wrong' war" (Der falsche Krieg)]. But it was clear, almost recklessly clear!; it was absolutely inadmissable and inexcusable for Kaiser William and the German leaders to cling until the very end to false hopes about English neutrality in an unrealistic and almost childish manner.

(Fritz Fischer does not tire of rightfully repeating von Bethmann's illusions regarding England's approach to Germany that never actually occurred. "Weltmacht oder ...", p. 54 ff.)

> The question the author asks himself (which, however, due to its function as a "supporting role" cannot be dealt with here) is whether or not England had not already been so deeply entangled in its destruction plans [„...delendam esse"] that, even if the Germans had practised moderate restraint, it would have insisted on its imperialist tradition towards the German Reich – of course under the pretext of having been forced into the war. According to the author, this was the case.

2.)

The author is of the impression that regardless of the circumstances, *"Reval"* still has priority over any other explanation for England's and Russia's joint plans, not least because the Entente kept on denying vehemently the existence of an *agreement to encircle* Germany – even without any immediate cause. Thus it is indispensable to mention a number of sources concerning the "encirclement" theory. Examining the accessible English sources it is exactly these vehement denials that attract one's attention.

Sir Arthur Nicolson, at that time English Ambassador in St. Petersburg (and known for his friendly feelings towards Russia; it was *he* who accomplished the Anglo-Russian Entente in 1907), had of course participated in the conference between King Edward

VII and Tsar Nikolas II before Reval on 9/10 June 1908. In his report he mentions (as quoted later by his son, Harold Nicolson, in his book) that the German press had wanted to take a secret agreement *"for the encircling and isolation of Germany"* as a reason for as well as a result of the conference.[818] Arthur Nicolson denied this. According to him, the two sovereigns did not discuss any political issues, and the meeting was simply a family reunion. Secretary of State Hardinge had

> "talked to the Russian Foreign Minister Izvolsky about reforms in Macedonia and several other issues; no decisions were made, though."

In that era Macedonia obviously constituted a cardinal issue of international foreign policy, which doubtlessly required a conference of the Monarchs on the Baltic Sea!

Arthur Nicolson's son Harold made a subtle remark on this topic in his own commenting text; according to him, it is certainly true that no agreement was made in Reval [is that so?], but it is also true that on the English side next to Sir Arthur Nicholson and Hardinge the presence of the Russian Prime Minister Stolypin and the Foreign Minister Izvolsky along with two of the highest military figures of army and navy, French and Fisher, would inevitably have caused suspicion that there must have been more to the visit than simply a family reunion.[818] On the next page Harold Nicolson continues:

> "Therefore, it is not surprising that the Germans, who had taken the Anglo-Russian Convention [of 1907] rather calmly, were alarmed about the convention at Reval. Even a careful and unprejudiced historian such as Erich Brandenburg <fixes upon Reval as a turning-point in European diplomacy>..."[819] (L. c., p. 275)

Hans Alfred Steger describes the reaction of the historian and publicist Hans Delbrück in similar words:

> Although he had commented on "the conclusion of the Anglo-Russian Agreement of 1907 with a rather defiant optimism, after the Reval convention of Edward VII and Nicholas II of June 1908 he writes: <What is the obvious encirclement of Germany supposed to mean?>..."[819]

Delbrück's answer to this question will be dealt with below.

Kantorowicz is again unbeatable in denying any anti-German tendency in the Anglo-Russian Agreement of 31 August 1907 with the at least informative explanation:

> "The Anglo-Russian Entente was Edward's doing to a much greater extent than an Anglo-French one, and this alone is enough to doubt that it was formed with the intention of endangering the peace."[820]

However, the crucial role that Edward VII played in the foundation of the Entente Cordiale as well as the Triple Entente was also confirmed by a grandchild of the English King, the Count of Harewood. But in contrast to Kantorowicz, he did not doubt the fact that these alliances were endangering the peace. (Danish documentary "Royal Family", part 4 on Arte, 2 January 2007).

Arthur Nicolson's anti-German policy did not remain unnoticed. Chancellor von Bülow wrote that it did not escape his attention that Nicholson

> "(had) incited the Russians not only against Austria but even more so against Germany and was not exactly sparing with suspicions as to our intentions nor with intrigue and slander."
> "And King Edward had watched this game with a smile on his face, and even favoured and supported it. ... He loved seeing frictions and mistrust between the two great Nordic Empires."[821]

There are similar remarks in a report about the Reval convention by State Secretary Sir Charles Hardinge, who elaborates in detail on the "reforms in Macedonia", despite his initial intent to deliver only a short report, in his paper he keeps on returning to this issue almost completely out of context, since he is covering totally different topics that he had discussed with Foreign Minister Izvolsky, e.g. Persia, Afghanistan, the Baghdad-railway, Crete, etc. It seems as if it was important for him to mention Macedonia repeatedly in his text in order to create the impression that Macedonia was the red thread that ran through the whole text, and thus through the discussions and consequently the Reval convention as well.

It is easy to see through his intention: after all, it was well known that Germany showed no interest at all in the Balkans. There may have been hope then of stifling the German mistrust by constantly emphasizing the issue of "Macedonia" and drawing off attention from the main topic of the convention, i.e. completing the encirclement and the plans for a war against Germany. However, in his paper, there is still mention of the German sensitivity that was apparent on the visit of the King of England in Reval. This was the reason why Foreign Minister Grey in his last "speech recently in front of the House of Commons" carefully maintained by way of precaution, "that it was not proposed to negotiate a new treaty or convention at Reval", a remark he had included into his speech in order to spare Russia the problems with Germany, which it might have to face after the Reval convention.[822] How very prudent of Mr. Grey.

The same thoughtfulness under his own, English name, would have been taken amiss, as it would have been unworthy of the world power Great Britain, which, at the beginning of the 20th century, Albert Ritter once called "World Britain".[823]

Due to the significance of this issue, it is essential to let a politician of the opposite side get a word in edgeways. Chapter XXI of Volume 2 of (then former) Chancellor von Bülow's memoirs begins with the meaningful sentence:

> "Looking back at the political affairs of the year 1908, we find in the centre the convention "at Reval between King Edward and the Russian Emperor and his wife on 9 and 10 June ["July" in the original text is a misprint]. Needless to say that I did not have the slightest doubts about the significance and ... about the tragic consequences."[824]

This shows that the Chancellor considered Reval as so crucial for the future of Germany - at least in retrospect - that for him it was more significant than e.g. the revolution of the Young Turks and the Austrian annexation of Bosnia in October 1908.

However, unlike Kaiser William, von Bülow did not attach more importance to the obvious *encirclement* of Germany. This can easily be explained, because – following Bismarck, whom he held in high esteem – he was of the opinion that Germany had already been encircled since the Treaty of Verdun of the 9th century.[825] Therefore, he focussed on the "aggravated opposition" of Russia towards Austria – and thus towards Germany -, after the Russian expansion in the Far East was defeated by Japan. His contemporary Hans Delbrück also examined the effects of "Tsushima" on the position of Germany within the context of *Europe as a whole*. As quoted by A. Steger, Delbrück had clearly drawn up the consequences of the defeat of Russia – and of course regretted them:

> "<As long as Russia was strong, the balance between the powers was certainly maintained>; the <most important result of the Russo-Japanese War> was the fear of Germany "being considered generally dangerous."[826]

The correct analysis of the "return" of a defeated Russia to Europe together with the long-term abolishment of the Anglo-Russian antagonism regarding the Straits on the Black Sea Conference in London of 1871 had already revealed what would influence the Anglo-German relations in the future. All measures of England's foreign policy until the outbreak of the (world) war, which the British government deemed necessary

for the re-establishment of the shifted balance, originated in this insight, i.e. the operations in the Far East.
An early approach by Hans Delbrück to the "global" interdependency.

Regardless of this, England had already considered *Germany as the trouble maker* on the Continent for one generation, to be precise: since the unification of the German Reich, as it had interfered with the English ideas of "balance" in Europe. (See below) From the aspect of the Austro-Russian relations, v. Bülow (together with most European politicians) foresaw that Russian interests would inevitably be re-directed towards the Balkans, e. g. Macedonia. Therefore, as a practical man the Chancellor was able to see some benefit in the Macedonian reforms - although only put forward in Reval as an excuse - as he was among those politicians who were convinced of the (doubtlessly exaggerated) argument (rather: were taken in by the ruse) that the "Turkish Revolution" was "partly caused by the Macedonian reform plans announced at Reval by Russia and England."[827]

Reality, however, probably looked like this: Even if in June 1908 at Reval there had actually been talks of plans for division [there is evidence for this] and for reforms for Macedonia - at least in passing (in order to feed the press and divert the Germans) - four months later, after the revolution of the Young Turks, all those reform plans were obsolete. And the fact that the Russian Foreign Minister Izvolsky, continued shifting the issue of reforms around like a piece on a chessboard, was evidence enough that this was only a game. In addition to that, the Chancellor feared real Austro-Russian frictions as a consequence of the "curtailing of power of the Sultan" after the revolution of the Young Turks (l. c., p. 325). The Chancellor was aware of the risk of "exposing Vienna to the danger of a conflict with the powers of the Entente ... because of its strong interests on the Balkan Peninsula" (l. c., p. 327).

From the point of view of the opposite party, it had to be concluded that the Entente acted logically when choosing Sanjak as a mine, in order to draw Austria on the Balkans first into a minor war against Serbia and after that automatically into a major war together with Germany (see below).

Therefore criticizing Chancellor von Bülow to a certain extent cannot be avoided: keeping in mind Prince Bülow's otherwise prudent behaviour, it is painful to notice that he – out of his admiration for Bismarck (and also because of the small significance of the double monarchy of the Habsburgs for the Dual Alliance) – did not dedicate more attention to *the* main emphasis of Bismarck's foreign policy, namely the absolute prevention of the *isolation of Germany*. After all, often enough he had written that "the encirclement" *and* "the isolation" of the German Reich had been, and remained, England's prime concern for *decades*. For decades!

Some specific cases leave the impression that the Germans had been worked on at all levels in order to prevent them from realizing the real threat of "Reval". Even the circular decree the Chancellor addressed to the Royal Prussian missions in the German Reich in order to cool down feelings, despite the "gravity of the situation" could not fulfil this intent. Thus Chancellor von Bülow writes that the Russian Foreign Minister explained to the German Ambassador in St. Petersburg

> "that at Reval no agreements were made on issues other than the ones treated in the Anglo-Russian Agreement of the previous year... Least so anything ... that could be directed against

Germany in any way, ... Later Izvolsky had his department head ... in Berlin give assurances that the Reval convention would not influence the Russo-German relations in any way."[828]
This could not have been more conspicuous!

Foreign Minister Sir Edward Grey had also held forth in London "that at Reval nothing whatsoever had been agreed upon or planned against Germany." (l. c.) Were these trivial belittlements not reason enough for Germany to become suspicious!?

A certain justification for this suspicion can also be drawn from a note of a secret report about Russo-German relations sent by the Royal Ambassador D. Popovic from St. Petersburg to the Serbian Prime Minister Pasic, where Popovic mentions Russia's "*secret memorandum* of June 1908!"[829]

On 11 June, namely shortly after the Reval convention, even the Tsar had sent a telegram to the Kaiser in Potsdam informing him "that the convention had <in no way> influenced the political situation."[828]

The plans against Germany formed at Reval must really have been drastic, taken that, a year later in June 1909 when meeting with the German Kaiser again in the Finnish skerries, Tsar Nikolas gave him his

> "honest and sacred word" never to give in to any unreasonable demand of the French or the English that was "directed against Germany ... or sprang from any intent against Germany."[830]

It is doubtful whether Nicholas still remembered this sacred oath precisely five, respectively eight years later.

(Or is it possible that the peace-loving Tsar was tricked by his government and his military - remember e. g. the general Russian mobilization at the end of July 1914 - just like Kaiser William? Hard to believe.) (See below, ch. 5.1.3.4)

His untiring Foreign Minister Izvolsky also informed the Chancellor through Foreign Secretary Baron Schön

> "about the assurance that the Anglo-Russian Agreement exclusively covered the known issues of Central Asia... With his understanding with England he did not intend to dig at Germany. The Triple Entente was a fabrication of the press."[830]

One should not have believed this ruthless schemer a single word!

As the process of history always depends upon persons who act, a remark containing von Bülow's misgivings needs mentioning in this context:

> "The fact that ... in 1910 Nicolson replaced Hardinge as Subsecretary of State in the Foreign Office, was a symptom almost as bad as the delegation of Delcassé to St. Petersburg as Ambassador three years later in 1913."[831]

As v. Bülow recalls on another occasion, the latter had resigned as Foreign Minister in 1905 when the French Council of Ministers decided to participate in the Morocco Conference against Delcassé's advice.

> "Even if in 1905 he had tried in vain to either cause the war of revenge or a deeper humiliation of Germany, in 1913 he was the storm bird that preceded the thunderstorm that broke out a year later." In St. Petersburg he "moved heaven and earth ... to win Russia for the war against Germany and push it into this war." (l. c., p. 119)

Finally von Bülow quotes from an article of the "Berliner Tageblatt" after Delcassé's death in 1923:

> "The career of this arsonist began with the conclusion of the Entente, but came to a sudden interruption, when Delcassé, swollen with hatred and ambition and inciting a war against Germany with all his strength, had been overthrown in 1905. Nine years later Delcassé saw his dream of the ignition of a world fire come true, after he had prepared the First World War as delegate to his friend Poincaré in St. Petersburg."

It should not be forgotten that at that time Izvolsky, of all people, was Russian Ambassador in Paris!

In this regard, too, a conspiring phalanx had closed around Germany like an iron ring.

3.)

What about King Edward? Did he stay passive? In no way. In August he went to Ischl, where Kaiser Franz Joseph was staying for a cure. V. Bülow writes:

> "My circular decree of 25 July 1908 ..." [that had also been sent to Vienna] "assisted His Imperial and Royal Apostolian Majesty more in showing stronger resistance, when approached by the seducer King Edward in Ischl on 13 August, than our ancestor Eva did with the serpent in paradise."[832]

This English attempt to woo away the Austrians came to nothing. Later, however, in the First World War, there were some Austrians who would have liked to turn their back on the Germans, who had been foolish enough to stand by Austria. [Revenge for Sadova!]

In this context it is useful to look at Kantorowicz as he actually lists a number of occasions on which Edward VII "was said" to have made similar offers to Franz Joseph, namely in Vienna 1903, in Marienbad in 1904 and once again in Ischl in 1905 – but Kantorowicz certainly shrugs off these attempts of wooing away Austria as mere "court gossip"![833]

Von Bülow's use of the biblical metaphor matched the picture he drew of the English King on another occasion:

> "Edward VII ... was a skilful preparer of poison." In April 1905 he did "all in his power to enrage the Franco-Prussian dispute [on the issue of Morocco]. Even so, three years later, during the Bosnian crisis he made great efforts to incite Russia against Germany." (l. c., p. 114)

In this context von Bülow also comments:

> "During the whole Bosnian crisis King Edward was busy adding fuel to the fire. His indulgence in political intrigues and his talent for political trouble-making were shown at their best." (l. c., p. 399)

It was then that v. Bülow noted an enlightening explanation for this conspicuous attitude of the King:

> "During the Prusso-Danish War, the Prusso-Austrian and especially the Franco-Prussian War Edward had "...openly shown his personal dislike of Bismarck's Germany, the strong and powerful Germany. (l. c., p.30)

Particularly, Edward's anti-German attitude in the Prusso-Danish War is understandable as only a year had passed since Edward, as a Crown Prince, had married the beautiful Danish Princess Alexandra, who never grew tired of acting against the victor of the Battle of Dybbol. And what was more obvious than using her feminine influence against the Germans when opportunities arose, e.g. regarding Königgrätz and Sedan. Then again, Alexandra's anti-German intrigues were well received by Edward who, as Crown Prince, in *1874*, i. e. before the exaggerated war-in-sight crisis, had already drawn attention through his premature anti-German warning letters to the Paris address (a process sufficiently proved by George F. Kennan). Edward could not have been motivated by his dislike of his nephew William (II) as, at that time, he was only 14 years old. (It is more likely that Edward pitied him for the hard times he had in his childhood and adolescence.) It must have been his hatred against the recently unified German Reich, which Edward already saw rising as England's competitor. At the same time, Edward had, at one point, called himself and his sister Victoria, William's mother, a "Coburg", in other words, a German. (Edward's and Victoria's father, Albert, had his origins in the House of Saxe-Coburg and Gotha, as did their mother Queen Victoria's female ancestors.)

In his above quoted decree, the Chancellor had carefully added:
> "Even if we do ... not have cause to attach to the Reval convention ... the character of an immediate threat for us and Austria-Hungary, it would still be a fatal error to trust in the promises given to us and thus to ignore that the Ententes and agreements, that are yet loose and vague, could actually become solid alliances..." (In the original, the latter half of the sentence is printed in italics.)[834] "Perhaps they might ... not hesitate to take aggressive steps against us and even bring us down if they were confident that they had the power to do so." (ibid.)

England had made *extensive* preparations to win this "confidence":
For once, there were the well-known treaties with France and Russia. Moreover, London had made an agreement with Japan just on time, i.e. in 1902, (namely before Russia was defeated by Japan, revealing that the English war plans against the German Reich reach far back into the 19th century). Furthermore, England had, with great foresight, or more precisely, in realistic assessment of the situation, continuously improved its relations to the United States (as well as Canada), although it disliked their aggressive "colonial policy" at that time (one should not forget the Philippines, Puerto Rico, Hawaii, and Cuba, for example). The basis for Great Britain's future was founded in 1901 with the Hay-Pauncefote Agreement about the anglo-american friendship, which allowed England to continue making its preparations against Germany totally relaxed until 1914.

In his review "Fundamentale Harmonie" (FAZ, 25 August 2006) of Magnus Brechtken's book of the Balfour/Roosevelt era Klaus Schwabe mentions another case that supported the Transatlantic-Anglosaxon solidarity "when Great Britain ... in her boundary dispute with Venezuela, that had been supported by the U.S., withdrew all along the line. (Brechtken: "Scharnierzeit 1895-1907. Persönlichkeitsnetze und internationale Politik in den deutsch-britisch-amerikanischen Beziehungen vor dem Ersten Weltkrieg.") This was a good basis for London to use America's strength profitably for the British interests. This happened, although not long ago, in 1895, "The Times" had felt compelled, in response to a self-assured remark of President Cleveland, to write in an arrogant condescension:
> "The English, and not the inhabitants of the United States, are the strongest force on the American continent, and none of the republican dogs can open their muzzle and bark without our permission." (B. Tuchman, loc. cit., p. 50 and p. 169)

England itself would probably never have forgotten a humiliation like this in a similar situation.

As stated in a report by Count v. Metternich, back in 1904 the former Liberal politician Grey had used as justification to the German Ambassador the rather artificial argumentation, these "foreign policy principles that the whole of England wishes to maintain" were only natural.[835]

Finally England had developed a fundamental strategy in the Balkans and was tirelessly busy flanking the Russian measures, in order to close a complete ring around the two German states in southeast Europe and thus isolate them hermetically. This was done together with the Balkan states using Macedonia as a lure.

Last but not least, despite all complaints about the insubordinate Germany, the English Navy was twice the size of the hated German one.[836]

Robert K. Massie sums up:
> "Great Britain had decided not to tolerate German hegemony on the Continent. From this vague but powerful instinct flowed the entente with France, the rebuilding of the Royal Navy, and the entente with Russia."

And, in the same context:
> "The German Chancellor and Wilhelmstrasse had failed to realize the [Anglo-Russian] convention's deeper significance."[837]

However, he adds that the German Ambassador had at least issued a warning, and the Kaiser agreed with him in a note to the Ambassador's despatch stating that the balance is "directed against us."

Indeed Massie writes (l. c.) that Nicolson later admits
> "<that thereby we were securing some defensive guarantees against the overbearing domination of one power.>"

Regarding the "entente with France" mentioned by Massie, that in analogy might also be called an "Anglo-French *balance*", the English weekly newspaper "Spectator" had reported on 9 May 1904 that Kaiser William's speeches of 1 and 8 May - that seemed (once more) martial but rather helpless - were a *"consequence of the isolation"* of Germany that William II had finally come to recognize.[838]

On this basis England was insured against a variety of risks and in association with the giant Russian Empire and France, which was eager for revenge, was thus "confident" of staging a war against Germany and triggering it via Serbia and Austria.

American President Woodrow Wilson's envoy in Berlin, Colonel House, reported on this issue to Washington: "Whenever England consents, France and Russia will close in on Germany and Austria". N. Ferguson quotes this sentence and mentions further that although House obviously criticized the mood of glorification of the war in Germany, he admitted "that German security interests had indeed been threatened."[839]

When the Reich government finally decided to accept the English proposal of an ambassadorial conference on 29 July 1914, it was impossible to stop Austria, though (after it had declared war on Serbia the previous day).

In this light Haldane's or Grey's eagerly preached attempts to negotiate (in the very last minute, on 31 July 1914 towards Ambassador von Lichnowski) were nothing but shadow-boxing and manoeuvres to cause delay, in order to conceal from Germany the gravity of the situation until the very last moment – i.e. England's true attitude. (Yet another example of the Macchiavelian rule: keep your plans secret long enough so that your opponent is faced with a fait accompli.)

One could have been tempted to hope that with his decades of practising campaigns of hatred against Germany, Edward formed an exception in the English Royal House. This was an illusion. Apparently, the whole monarchy joined in the anti-German war plans of the British government and of the House of Lords and the press. This emanates from a remark of King George V. As late as 26 July 1914 he had informed the German Crown Prince about his doubts concerning the option of England to stay neutral in a continental conflict, but at the same time he confirmed his and the Germans' hopes and tried to nurture false hopes of security:
> "Together with my government I will undertake all that is necessary to prevent a European war...,"[840]

Instead, they had been determined for years to destroy the Wilhelmine Germany and the Habsburg Empire: *Ceterum censeo Germaniam delendam esse!*

William's desperation - as well as helplessness - is revealed by the fact that it was only on 2 August 1914 that he had "inquiries" made in London, whether Great Britain would, on certain conditions, stay out of the conflict. As a reaction to the article "Diese Marine" (FAZ of 30 May 2006) Jens Freese writes: "They saved themselves the trouble of answering the question and declared war on the German Reich on 4 August 1914." (FAZ, 16 June 2006) This arrogance again proves how William utterly misjudged the destructive aims of both his relatives and the British government against the Wilhelmine Reich.

William II must have had iron nerves not to have turned mad over the disloyalty and perfidy of England declaring war on the German Reich - he, who despite his boasting mania, that England was well familiar with, never intended to attack "his beloved England" (quoted in the ZDF- (and Arte-) documentary "History" by Guido Knopp).

When England on that very 4 August had finally reached its long-desired aim of declaring war on Germany, Prime Minister "Asquith and his wife 'could not speak for tears'" (N. Ferguson, p. 177). The text seems to insinuate that those were tears of shock and sadness, - thus a skilful creation of prestige for the history books. As sentimentality, however, is probably not among the most striking characteristics of the British "Imperialist" Asquith, this author tends to take them for tears of joy when going through the finishing line, which is what the Prime Minister had been working on for such a long time.

Churchill on the other hand was less prone to emotional fuss and acting. Quite the contrary, half a year later his remark to Lady Asquith of 22 February 1915 was kept for posterity:

> "I *love* this war. I know it's smashing & shattering the lives of thousands every moment – & yet – I can't help it – I enjoy every second of it." (ibid.)

Jörg Friedrich comes to be understood better and better.

4.)
As far as the issue of *"encirclement"* is concerned, Henry C. Meyer's view of 1960 must be subject to contradiction:

> "In a rather exaggerated manner the Germans got excited about the alleged encirclement by the Entente."[841]

This means that Meyer was either uninformed or he was openly prejudiced (despite the certainty, which he should have had, that the encirclement was in no way "alleged", nor was the excitement of the Germans in any way exaggerated).

The prejudice in Hermann Kantorowicz's work, however, cannot be surpassed, as he displays his partiality already in the title of his above mentioned book entitled "Der Geist der Einkreisung Deutschlands" ("The Spirit of the Encirclement of Germany"). The chapter on England's "absolute peaceable nature" in his so-called "expert opinion" bears the characteristic heading "Das Märchen von der Einkreisungspolitik" (The Fairy-Tale of the Encirclement Policy).[842] Outrageous.

Fischer, too, deems the German fear of "being encircled" of course exaggerated for publicity reasons. ("Weltmacht...", p. 52)

The fact that Anglo-Saxon historians today see and write about the matter differently to their colleagues or the responsible authorities at that time, does them credit. After a thorough examination of the underlying facts of this period Ferguson concludes:

> "All this makes German fears of encirclement seem less like paranoia than realism. When Bülow denounced in the Reichstag the efforts to <build a circle of powers around Germany in

order to isolate and render it impotent> he was not - as British statesmen subsequently insisted in their memoirs - fantasizing."[843]

Apart from its scientific merit, this is an analysis that can only be acknowledged with relief. (It was this kind of objective argumentation that had been deemed undesirable for decades by foreign countries as well as the German left, the east Germans and the international Left alike.)

At this stage Chancellor von Bülow should once more be allowed to speak, as a short additional remark (not quoted by Ferguson) reveals his main concern:

> "On 14 November 1906, I held ... one of the longest speeches of my life about our foreign affairs. I spoke offhand ... At first I illustrated our relations to France stating that we should not have any illusions about its irreconcilability, in view of our vivacious neighbours' traditional and brilliant characteristics, their lively patriotism, and their high and strong ambition. To the issue of the Entente I added gravely that a policy that aimed at encircling Germany, building a circle of powers around us, to isolate us and to paralyse us was a *precarious policy to keep the peace in Europe.*"[844] (Italics by the author)

Regardless of these objections, England proceeded with its war policy against Germany until the bitter end. Of course it did – as this was its long-term strategy.

To complete the picture, von Bülow's remark about England itself must be quoted, as it touches one of the allegedly *neuralgic* points in the bilateral relations:

> "With regard to England, I strongly emphasized that we did not intend to build a navy as strong as the English one. We had the right and the duty, however, to keep a navy of the size suitable for our trade interests, whose only task would be to protect our overseas interests and defend our coasts." (l. c., p. 263)

The fact that England denied the German Reich this "right and duty" and reserved both exclusively for itself, should soon become evident.

In one of his endless discussions with the Kaiser about this issue, von Bülow again confirmed this line in front of William II:

> "I fail to see why we should not try to come to an understanding with England on the basis of a slower progress in the naval expansion." (l. c., p. 320)

This will be examined in detail below.

It is also interesting to take a look at the Russian reports at that time. Thus, Benno von Siebert, who had been Counsel to the Russian Embassy in London for many years, quotes from a report the Russian Foreign Office of 10 February 1909 (a few months after the Reval convention) taken from his extensive collection of documents:

> "Grey ... is hoping that the feeling of isolation in Germany will abate", "a war would be ... unavoidable if Germany was really isolated or had reached European hegemony, the latter danger is now extinct."[845]

The only possible conclusion would be: as the danger of German hegemony had already been declared extinct by Grey himself in 1909, the only cause (of war) that existed was the isolation of Germany (according to plan) – thus, according to Grey, a war against the *isolated* Germany would be "inevitable".

And that is what actually happened.

Nevertheless, an additional remark:

Having said that, the author feels his opinion is confirmed: the obvious intent of the Entente to *encircle* Germany had been agreed upon in Reval after all, even though – in view of the numerous critical moments in those years – there had been plenty of other opportunities for England, France and Russia to form a coordinated, permanent alliance. The unmistakeable signs and the results should carry the greatest weight.

Which of the Entente members would today be willing to accept a confession of its assistance in having started the war (let alone its partial guilt), taking into account the betrayal through the obsessed, vitriolic Georges Clemenceau? After all, he had even slated the American President Wilson and made him look ridiculous and thus pushed through the totally unjustified section 231 of the Treaty of Versailles dealing with Germany's sole guilt. No, even when confronted with the text of a treaty itself, no one would make this confession.

This explains why the author was denied access to the Reval convention records in the Royal Archive of Windsor Castle, - but this is of course farce.

It was a much noticed gesture of Lloyd George to admit that we all seemed to slide into the First World War. But that, of course, was not enough for Fritz Fischer. In the continuation of his self-mortification he insisted in his book "Juli 1914 – Wir sind nicht hineingeschlittert" (July 1914 – we did not slide in) that Germany had exclusive responsibility. (Even the idea of the concept of looking for the causes of the First World War in the events during the month of July 1914, only, is a system error in reasoning, which many historians have made and which had to lead down the wrong path.)

More recently, the view of this part of history has been changing. In his review of David Stevenson's book (1914-1918. Der Erste Weltkrieg. Düsseldorf 2006), Michael Salewski provides the latest developments:

"Nobody today believes in the helpless 'sliding theory'." (FAZ, Stillstand und Eskalation. 10.06.06, p. 8)

5.)

The Reich government together with the Kaiser (who had called the annexation of Bosnia "a piece of brigandage"[846]) had not been informed beforehand about Austria's outrageous and outrageously unwise step. Nevertheless, they were compelled to side with Vienna. Even today it is impressive to read the rather long indignant note Kaiser William wrote in Rominten on 6 October 1908, taken aback by the dangerous situation solely created by Austria:

"My personal feelings and my feelings as an ally are deeply hurt, because no one had the least confidence in me."[847]

Yet, the Kaiser and the Reich government had no other choice but to remain friendly with Vienna; very much like the creditor with his debtor if he intends to regain some of his capital (of trust).

The Achilles heel of Bismarck's Dual Alliance!

(In this case Kaiser William I must have turned in his grave, because despite strong opposition he had followed Bismarck when he agreed to the Dual Alliance with Austria, leaving Russia aside.)

In Petersburg the English Ambassador Nicolson had spread the lie that in the annexation affair Russia had to yield to German pressure, - a version that entered the history books without a clear denial from Germany, although it was pure invention, as later proved by George F. Kennan. The Russian set-back against Austria had actually been caused by Foreign Minister Izvolksy himself. (See above, ch. 4.2.6)

In the context of the alleged exercise of German pressure on Russia, Robert K. Massie quotes from a 1908 letter of Tsar Nikolas (II) to his (Danish) mother:

"The German action towards us has been simply brutal, and we won't forget it."[848]

This subtle threat might allow the conclusion that the poison of hatred that the Danish Princess Dagmar, as Tsarina Maria Feodorovna, had poured on her son all her life, did not seem to be without effect despite his happy marriage to a German.[849] Otherwise there would be no reason for the actually good-natured Tsar to let himself be tempted to start such an adventurous war, - even if he did not like the German Kaiser, or feared him, as Hardinge remarked in his report on Reval: "He felt an anxiety all the time as to what might be unexpectedly sprung upon him."[850]

In this context it is essential to remind once more of the fact that Dagmar's sister as wife of Edward VII had been Queen of England (since 1901). Having said that, the assumption of an anti-German league formed by the descendants of the Royal House of Denmark together with the European dynasties (including France) gains a considerable degree of credibility.

Are the Germans (or is the author) *imagining* things again? Their imaginings could be illustrated by two examples:

1.)
Chancellor von Bülow mentioned in his memoirs on the Doggerbank incident of 6 November 1904 when, on their way to Japan, the Russian fleet (risking its destruction) "sank several harmless English fishing boats" in the North Sea due to a misjudgement. The English press made a big fuss of it, insulting the Russian Admiral, demanding compensation and declaring "that a war could hardly be avoided." At the same time, the English government is said to have "quietly attempted to prevent a war with Russia." And the main point concerning this case is that

> "the two Danish sisters, Tsarina Maria Feodorovna and Queen Alexandra of England made even more eager efforts in this direction, having contributed to the understanding between 'whale and bear' during the Afghanistan crisis back in 1885."[851] (1885! Constant dripping wears away the stone.)

Imaginings? Phantoms?
Of course Paris, too, was concerned about a war between England and Russia, - exactly as expected by many Englishmen and many Germans. These two states, with which France had been able to form friendly alliances, were the only ones eligible for a coalition against the despised Germans. Consequently, Delcassé did his best to mediate between Russia and England.[852]

2.)
During a visit of the German Kaiser in Copenhagen in 1905, William had bombarded the aged King Christian IX with half-baked ideas so vehemently that when the news had reached London, Christian's daughter, at that time Crown Princess Alexandra of England, was "quite horrified" and asked her father "whether he intended to <betray> England." This letter even induced him to send Foreign Minister Count Gaben to London,

> "in order to ensure Denmark's strictest neutrality under all circumstances."[853]

Are these supposed to have been phantoms?
Probably not. More likely, they were the persistent attempts to settle a 40-year-old debt, - which should finally satisfy their thirst for revenge precisely 50 years after the Prusso-Danish War of 1864. The price for this satisfaction, however, was high: complete ruin. The Tsar and his whole family were slaughtered, after England had (as already mentioned in ch. 4.3) refused to accord them asylum. This incredible interdependence leaves room for speculation that this solution may not have been unwelcome in London. Otherwise an old ally and good friend, apart of being a relative as well, as a survivor might have asked one day for the fulfilment of the Entente promise concer-

ning Constantinople and the Straits, which after all, according to the fundamental English way of thinking, belonged to Britannia.

Tsar Nikolas' II (Danish) mother, Dagmar/Maria F. of all people, escaped this fate: a year after the assassination of the Romanovs, the Bolshevists handed her over to a British ship on the Crimea. Due to a quarrel with her sister Alexandra, she returned from London to Denmark, where she died in 1928. Following her last will, her mortal remains were brought to St. Petersburg to be buried next to Tsar Alexander III in the Peter-and-Paul-Cathedral as late as September 2006.

Of course, the Soviets had dealt quite differently with a German relative of the Romanovs: another member of the Tsar family, princess of the Grand Duke of Darmstadt, Alice's sister, was killed in an atrocious manner and was canonized as a martyr by the Orthodox church in 1992 (as reported by Lorenz Jäger in the FAZ on 28 September 2006). She had been married to the Grand Prince Sergej (one of Tsar Nicholas' II uncles), who had already been the victim of an assassination in 1905.

By the way, in the course of history even Denmark, was subject to the stereotypical selfish representation of exclusively national interests. Denmark, too, was far from remembering self-critically its centuries as an imperialistic and exploiting Great Danish nation (a fact that today one is reluctant to hold against this easy-going people). Denmark, quite confidently, had occupied not only large parts of Germany but the whole of Sweden, Norway, Iceland and Greenland (Greenland until today! – now it is associated, though) and was conceivably outraged that all these nations reclaimed their freedom and property. It is all a question of perspective; see Alsace, Macedonia, Gibraltar, Ceuta and Melilla, Corsica, Northern Ireland, etc. In so far it appears rather subjective, when the (Danish) Tsarina Dagmar/Maria Feodorovna, as quoted by George F. Kennan, said to the French Ambassador's wife in Petersburg when they bade farewell:

"She would never forget what the Germans did to her native country, Denmark."[854]

In a typical mechanism of repression, Dagmar evidently did not want to accept that her father, Christian IX, immediately after ascending the thrown in 1863 had annexed the Dukedom of Schleswig "and breached a Treaty" (R. K. Massie, l. c., p. 57), namely the London Protocol of 1852. In the same way the Danish Royal Family and with it the whole nation for generations were outraged that the German Confederation had marched into Schleswig-Holstein in 1864 and – the oh so militant Prussians – had taken back the Dukedoms two years later.

On the other hand, the Great Powers did not regard the Prusso-Danish War as a war of conquest (Stürmer, p. 18). Therefore, the British fleet this time, in 1864, did not appear at the German coast as it had done in 1848, when the parliamentarians at Frankfurt Paul's Church "threatened" to agree on a free and democratic path to a united Germany. (Imagine, this happened in 1848!) Neither did the Russians menace in 1864 the Prussians with intervention as they had done in 1848.

Anti-German influences were, however, not only exercised by former enemies. Even Tsar Nikolas' wife of Hessian, i.e. German descent, possessed a deep hatred against the German Reich. In the context of the convention of the monarchs in Reval, Chancellor von Bülow reports:

"King Edward ... with his great art of dealing with people ... [was] (supported) by his niece Empress Alexandra Feodorovna of Russia, who, despite being the daughter of an ancient German royal house had strong pro-English but anti-German feelings, to get the Russian Emperor on his side."[855]

As clearly illustrated by Paul Sethe, the former Princess Alice of Hesse-Darmstadt, even as Tsarina Alexandra, had obviously been unable to overcome the loss of Hessian sovereignty and the special privileges after the unification of the Reich in 1871. Early in the 19th century, Napoleon had just promoted Hesse-Darmstadt to the status of a Grand Duchy (as he had similarly made Bavaria and Württemberg the so-called "Parvenu-Kingdoms"[855a]); all of them, in their vanity, seemed to have shut their eyes to the high price: total submissiveness. In a review, Michael Salewski quotes David Stevenson ("1914-1918. Der Erste Weltkrieg"), who described Alice/Alexandra even as lusting after war.[855a]

William's II remark about the inclination of German princesses to turn against their native country once they are abroad, even tempted this author to smile at his patriotism (see above, ch. 2.3.9.2). Obviously quite unfounded.

And Izvolsky? Massie writes about him after the failed trade of "Bosnia for the Black Sea Straits" and the following manoeuvre of deceit against his Austrian colleague Aehrenthal:

> "Although he remained Foreign Minister for three more years, his effectiveness was diminished. In 1911, he resigned and was appointed Russian Ambassador to France. In Paris, he worked vengefully day and night to strengthen the Franco-Russian alliance. When war came, Alexander Isvolsky boasted: 'This is my war! My war!'"[856]

(By the way: Izvolsky closely cooperated with Raymond Poincaré – the man from Lorraine!)

Personally Izvolsky could not enjoy his intrigues. In this case history simply overran the guilty one: As von Bülow notes in his memoirs concerning his last conversation with Izvolsky in 1909, he remembers to have quoted Bismarck who once had talked about the possible consequences of a "guerre entre les trois empires": <Ce seront ... les trois dynasties qui payeront les pots cassés.>

(This will be taken up again later.) Von Bülow proceeds:

> "Izvolsky has lived long enough to experience for himself the righteousness of [this] prediction. He had to ... watch the defeat, ... He died sick and embittered in poor lodgings in a small town in the south of France, where he received a modest pension from the French government, a poor reward for his inflammatory agitations ... compared to the millions that Russia had paid for decades to greedy French journalists and politicians."[857]

6.)

This still leaves the subject of "naval expansion".

The question of the causes of the First World War is unthinkable without the German naval expansion programme. Countless numbers of bookshelves are filled with treatises on this issue. In other words, there is no need for more. Therefore, only a few reminiscences are added here:

Chancellor v. Bülow evidently had numerous disputes with the Kaiser about making him reduce the naval expansion. Without success. And there are just as many allegations of English politicians who have based their alleged fear of Germany on the supposedly superior German Navy.

According to v. Bülow, the Earl of Crowe, Lord Chancellor of the Privy Council and former Foreign Minister as well as Prime Minister, had told him in an Anglo-German Royal convention in 1909 that

> "he fully admitted that the English fear of the much weaker German Navy was exaggerated. I should not forget, though, that not only the English Empire but also the English mother country depended upon its absolute security on sea, its supremacy over the oceans and its un-

assailability. ... As the Germans, however, had an extraordinary talent for organisation and as the young German Navy was considered excellent, the English did not want to have the same experiences with the Germans at sea as the Austrians and the French had done with the Germans on land in 1866 and 1870." (v. Bülow: l. c., p. 426)

With that Crowe had expressed England's recurring motive that was emphasized by Prime Minister Asquith in similar form five years later:

"We cannot allow Germany to use the Channel as a hostile base."[858]

It was also against British interests if France should be wiped out as a Great Power. With regard to France, Foreign Minister Grey was of the same opinion:

"Britain could not risk a German victory because such a victory would have made Germany <supreme over all the Continent of Europe and Asia Minor>." (l. c., p. 169)

Ambassador v. Metternich had made it clear to his government in Berlin that these statements were unambiguous. In August and November 1908 he reported:

"No one will be able to make the English believe that a German Navy ... is a mere triviality for them."[859]

"The Englishman is a matter-of-fact person. For him our naval expansion programme ... constitutes a danger", ... "England is preparing itself in military as well as political respect, ... The best thing for us is to anticipate this as a definite and absolute fact." (l.c., p. 417)

In this case, the modest advice of the former Ambassador von Metternich meets the quintessence of the contemporary research of the historian and the Count's later colleague, Hans Alfred Steger:

"All that remained for Germany to do was ... to maintain the semi-hegemonial position of the Empire on the Continent as under Bismarck's rule..." At the same time Steger states critically that "neither official diplomacy nor the nation's self-confidence was willing to be satisfied with that."[860]

And yet!

Yet Niall Ferguson uncovered many of the above mentioned arguments as pretexts. His research provides evidence that neither Germany's striving for colonies nor the continuously growing navy, which actually reached half the strength of the English one when the war started, can be considered crucial causes![861]

Ferguson leaves no doubt about the real reasons: At the beginning of his time in office, namely at the end of 1905, Grey found "support from Colonel William Robertson of the War Office Intelligence Department, who commented on the continental threat, "as Germany was the more serious military threat" (than e.g. Persia or Afghanistan):

"For centuries past we have thwarted ... each and every power in turn which has aspired to continental predominance; ... and as a consequence, we have enlivened our own sphere of imperial ascendancy ... A new preponderance is now growing, of which the centre of gravity is Berlin. Anything ... which would assist us in opposing this new and most formidable danger would be of value to us."[862]

Repeated in 1905!

The comments by the First Lord of the English Admiralty made in a memorandum late in 1904 were basically in the same direction. According to v. Bülow, the Admiralty aimed at

"having the whole English Navy prepared for war, in the sense that it is at all times ready to attack immediately." This was a "concession to the public opinion in England that was increasingly upset by our" [the German] "naval expansion."[863]

Shortly before, an article was published in the "Army-and-Navy-Gazette" that expressed unequivocally:

"In former times England would simply have destroyed a fleet that we suspected of possibly being used to our detriment... The other powers would probably watch such an act with badly disguised pleasure if not with open approval." (ibid.)

In the following year the Calendar of European History published the almost identical comment of the Lord of the Admiralty Lee of January 1905 about the advantages of a preventive strike against Germany:

> "The English Navy could have struck a terrible blow against the German one, before the German citizen even read about the declaration of war in the newspaper."[864]

Such remarks show where Churchill got his ideas for his book "The Gathering Storm" from, which in the end he wrote after the Second World War.

It could easily have come to a military action by the British Navy. After all, it was just a short way (by water) to the resumption of Admiral Nelson's tactic, who had attacked and sunk the Danish fleet in Copenhagen at the beginning of the 19th century without declaring a war, (in order to prevent it from being of use to Napoleon). This par force attack has become an established political term in British history, so that the Chancellor could write about (the notorious) Lord Fisher that he constantly nagged the English King Edward VII to allow him to "<copenhagen> ... and to destroy the German fleet before it is to late." (l. c., p. 84)

[This term reminds one of the terrible word "magdeburgisieren" (to "magdeburg") from Tilly's campaign in the Thirty Years' War in 1631.]

Thus, it is not surprising that Admiral Tirpitz could say to Chancellor v. Bülow years later:

> "The Kaiser is worried that the English would <Copenhagen> his great battle ships (using a term coined by Lord Fisher), should we send them out of our native seas." (p. 320)

In view of Lord Fisher's unambiguous encouragements it seems like a confirmation when the historian Henry C. Meyer fairly maintains that in 1906 Great Britain

> had given "the signal for a further acceleration of the naval expansion and ... in the statements of First Admiral Sir John Fisher, (was) just as war-mongering as the most quarrelsome German navy propagandist."[865]

Hans Delbrück had similar "fears of an English pre-emptive strike", especially during the Bosnian crisis of 1908/09.[866]

Also in 1908 (in December) the English Admiralty was of the opinion

> "that <in a protracted war the wheels of our sea-power (though they would grind the German population slowly perhaps) would grind them 'exceedingly small' – grass would sooner or later grow in the streets of Hamburg and widespread dearth and ruin would be inflicted.>"[867]

"The fire" of the Second World War at the beginning of the 1940s was theoretically anticipated in 1908!

Sönke Neitzel puts the English naval policy into a historical context:

> "The putative danger of a powerful German fleet of battle ships on England's doorstep must be seen in the context of the traditional English fear of the second strongest naval power. The 1830s saw the debate on the Russian Baltic Sea Fleet, and at the end of the 1850s the discussion on the French naval plans under Napoleon III reached its peak. From 1906 the German battle ships inspired the imagination of the English press." ... "It is true that in connection with the naval expansion the German Reich was presented as a Great Power, rarely, however, as a World Power."[868]

This is all well and good – yet "fear" was certainly the least of the English motives.

In contrast to the above mentioned and various other statements of British politicians, N. Ferguson comes to a conclusion that, from the German point of view, is sensational:

> "Traditionally, Grey's anti-German policy has been justified by historians because Germany's Weltpolitik had come to be viewed in London ... as a growing threat to British interests in Africa, Asia and the Near East."

Then Ferguson sums up his findings in the following almost succinct sentence, considering the historical significance of this revolutionary thought:

"Yet, on close inspection, neither the colonial issues nor naval issues were leading inevitably to an Anglo-German showdown before 1914."[869]

Excerpts from his argumentation:
Even Churchill and Grey had no objections to the German colonial expansion. Furthermore, "it is quite misleading to see the naval race as a 'cause' of the First World War." (l. c., p. 70) Regarding the efforts to make naval agreements, in contrast to the traditional propaganda against the politics of the German Reich, Ferguson enumerates eight proposals made between 1907 and 1914, five of which were made by the Germans, two by the English and one was made mutually. (l. c., p. 70) Ferguson also treats the failure of the Haldane mission of February 1913 with scepticism, as the actual reason for this failure was not the Germans' refusal of a naval limitation, but the unwillingness of the British to come to terms with the neutrality issue, ... (p. 62) (The author is inclined to add: ... because neutrality would have tied their hands for the much desired war against Germany.)

Ferguson himself offers a relatively simple but amazingly convincing explanation for the position of Britain:

"Not surprisingly, as it was based on unassailable strength. As Grey put it in 1913, 'if you are going to have an absolute standard superior to all the other European navies put together ... your foreign policy is comparatively simple.' His view was accordingly uncompromising," ...
"As Grey's private secretary Tyrrell put it, ... why should Britain bargain for something she already possessed?" (l. c., p. 71)

This naval standard thus surpassed the ancient English principle of the two-power-standard, requiring England to be always stronger than the next two navies together. (Stürmer, p. 195)

As early as in 1912, the Foreign Office under Foreign Minister Grey and State Secretary Nicolson "opposed the idea of an agreement with Germany" (Ferguson, p. 72), because it would result in impairing the English relations with France and Russia. This argument, too, does not convince the British historian, as "Grey's reasoning was deeply flawed." (l. c.)

"The strongest justification" of the policy of England was based on the assumption "that Germany had megalomaniac ambitions". ... (l.c., p. 74) [Probably – horribile dictu – similar to England.] It was insinuated that "Germany would attain to that dominant position " ... stated to be inimical to the interests of this country. (p. 74)

As the above mentioned fact was only an "assumption", Ferguson applies the argumentum e contrario:

"Precisely because they (Grey and the Foreign Office) wished to align Britain with France and Russia, it was necessary to impute grandiose plans for European domination to the Germans." (p. 76)

Therefore, in 1911 Grey warned of a threat to Europe that was of "Napoleonic extent". Thus it is only logical that he was willing

"to make military commitments (with France) which made war with Germany more rather than less likely,..." (p 73 ff.)

For the same reason, England wanted to reinforce Russia's position against Germany (p. 61). And for the same reason again the suspicion of "war-mongering" was thrown onto Germany.

Otherwise it would have been revealed that it was not the high-ranking convention summoned by Kaiser William II on 18 December 1912 that was crucial for the outbreak of the First World War, - although later the member states of the Entente eagerly propagated this as the decision-making "war council" and forever held it against the Germans without giving them the chance to prove them wrong.

The convention that was actually an immediate cause of a great war had been held in England 16 months before: on 23 August 1911 the conference of the CID, the Committee of Imperial Defence, had already set the course for a military confrontation with Germany![870]

August 1911! England had immediately reacted after the secret agreement between Russia and Serbia/Bulgaria and summoned the CID.

This date renders valuable an information taken from the Serbian files seized in 1917, which would seem less plausible without these revelations. The report of Ambassador Dr. Gruitsh to the Serbian Prime Minister Milovanovich reveals that, on the basis of the decision in August 1911, the English government promptly demonstrated their determination

> "to show immediate and complete solidarity with France in case of conflict. The officers on leave (were) ordered back ... and an enormous amount of coal was bought and taken to the depots of the northern fleet with special trains." "Most important among the secret measures are the preparations that were met for the fastest possible transport of 40,000 soldiers to France. ... The destination of these men was Boulogne, where all the necessary preparations were made for their further transport to Amiens."[871]

In 1911 !

The Kaiser had summoned his conference only after the German ambassador had telegraphed a message of the British War Minister Lord Haldane to Berlin:

> "Britain could not allow Germany to become the leading power on the continent and it [the continent] to be united under German leadership." (N.F., p. 68)

December 1912.

> *As Fritz Fischer treats Kaiser William's "war council" in the sense of his well-known hypothesis,[872] but never even mentions the* real *war council in England, his conclusions were bound to go only against Germany, in other words pronounce Germany's sole guilt for the war.*

After the above quoted irrevocable English guideline Ferguson concludes that "the Kaiser's inference": <that England would fight on the side of France and Russia out of envy and hatred towards Germany>, "was not wrong". (p. 68)

In this respect the Kaiser and his former Chancellor were obviously in absolute agreement, because Stürmer quotes (p. 145) from a letter of Bismarck to his wife,

> "that we do not live alone in Europe, but with three other powers that hate and envy us."

George F. Kennan described Russia's envy of Germany's military success in a similarly free way.[873]

Ferguson as well puts himself in the position of all non-Englishmen. He demonstrates the situation at that time by means of a literary figure. (As in chapter 1 shown at the example of Albania, a literary presentation can illustrate historical facts, if not surpass them in its meaningfulness.) Thus Ferguson quotes a character of Erskine Childers:

> "We can't talk about conquests and grabbing. ... We've collared a fine share of the world, and they've every right to be jealous." (p. 38)

But so much insight was only possible in a novel.

In real life, with very few exceptions, the English as a rule would never tolerate a similarly powerful - let alone equally powerful - state on the continent! One of those exceptions to the rule was Lord Sanderson, who not only politically drew logical conclusions but also had the human greatness to ask

> "why... in the course of the 20th century (should) the Germans not take predominance on the continent, as the British did before?" (Stürmer, p. 328)

This attitude, however, would have been totally incompatible with the English self-conception as a "dominating" nation (which is what they call themselves even today) and their imperial position of strength as an unalterable fact. Other nations had to accept England's power and wealth, - and if they tried to emulate England, they would simply be destroyed.

The inevitable counter-question
("If it were neither the German Navy nor the colonies that provoked England's ill-humour: what was it then?") is thus answered.
Nevertheless Ferguson provides his answer to this and consequently many other questions:

> "...but in reality it (those people's acting) is rooted in their compulsive *Germanophobia*." (l. c., p. 69) (Author's italics)

This is also the place to provide the answer to the question Delbrück asked himself ("What does the ... encirclement of Germany mean? ... Where does the essence of this World War come from?"):

> "The ultimate cause is neither Morocco nor Turkey – the ultimate cause is also no longer the French thirst for revenge" [is that so?] "or the Russian greed for Constantinople: The ultimate cause is nothing but England's jealousy of Germany."[874]

One should be grateful to Henry C. Meyer that he revealed in such a radically honest way the reason why Germany got into this situation:

> "The Germans had made their country a European centre of industry and commerce."
> "The great skill they applied to make natural science and technology profitable for the industry, justified their reputation in the world." "But this same Germany was a new-comer to the family of European Great Powers, a trouble-maker, who questioned guaranteed interests and well-founded sovereign rights."[875]

"Guaranteed ... and well-founded ... sovereign rights." How scornful! 'The arrogance of power'.

B. Tuchman also provides a reason which must convince absolutely everyone as to why the Germans are so totally disliked in the world:

> "The presumption with which the Germans consider themselves to be leaders in the music had slowly started to annoy other peoples." (L.c., p. 380)

Occasionally, even in Great Britain a courageous and level headed voice could be heard (and this was apparently easier once the British King Edward VII had died). This meant that e. g. George Bernard Shaw came to the conclusion that there was an "anti-German hysteria" in Europe. (Tuchman, p. 397)
After the First World War, the victorious powers continued their propaganda with similar hate campaigns, including one against the German language. German was declared an "enemy language" almost everywhere. In North America "they stopped teaching (it) in schools", in Great Britain and France "(it) was stigmatised as a language of the Barbarians" and "in Russia (its use) was forbidden".[875c]
So, Germany was a trouble-maker in the eyes of those who considered the world their own personal property. Consequently, the Germans would have done better to stay the defenceless supplier of land and people for states with more power – and more "rights"!
For whoever is in power, ...

Labelling Germany as a new-comer and a troublemaker, some neighbours, above all England, created a convenient auxiliary construction to help them suppress all memory of the facts of the almost 900-year-old history of the German Reich. According to Helmut Plessner, the term "late nation" is therefore a myth. This view was also shared by Georg Schmidt, whose thesis is rendered in Caspar Hirsch's report about a conference in Oxford, according to which the "old Reich" was supported by "a strong German sense of a common nation holding values such as freedom, pacifism and legal certainty and fitted into <early modern Europe with its liberal-republican community>."[875a]

(See also the comments on the Holy Roman Empire under ch. 4.4.1.1)

Even today the situation looks depressing for Germany, considering the fact that 50 years after the Second World War in London a monument was erected to honour the notorious "Bomber-Harris" and that at the unveiling ceremony none other took part than the English institution, if not icon, despite her biblical age and forever smiling: Queen Mum. This, too, might be an example of the influence "of the unbeatable hatred of the English media towards the Germans..."[875b]

After this clear analysis it is quite simple to draw a parallel to *Macedonia*:
Achieving the status of a nation rather late, Macedonia would have disturbed the "guaranteed interests and well-founded ... sovereign rights" of the Greeks, the Bulgarians and the Serbs to Macedonian territory! I.e. the Macedonians would have curtailed their neighbouring nations without so much as a by-your-leave in their holy right to an increase of power by expansion. What a way to behave! It is understandable that the neighbours could not tolerate such unreasonable behaviour. The better alternative then was to do good works that please God: to attack the Christian Macedonian land in the Balkan Wars, to free the people from the Islamic yoke – and divide both into three parts, or to be more precise: into four parts, and to subjugate them! In this inelegant, but common way, one simply disposed of the "Macedonian trouble-maker". The powers of the Entente gave their assistance the English way to the best of their ability, as much as it lay in their interest.

It is by no means true that the Germans needed foreign countries to describe their situation to them, in order to realize how critical it was at the beginning of the 20 th century.
Chancellor v. Bülow repeatedly pointed out, in this case in a speech in the Reichstag in November 1908 that
> "Upstarts ... were generally unpopular. The German Reich, the latest member of the European Union of States, had since its foundation enjoyed more respect and even fear than affection. Germany, the formerly convenient gathering place for foreign interventions, has become an inconvenient competitor." (l. c., p. 382)

Many years before in 1904, on the occasion of the launching of a ship of the line named "Preußen", he had stated:
> "From the very start, Prussia was threatened, feared and hated..." .."Those who envy and despise us will not get us down, as long as we are true to ourselves and the spirit of Prussian history. With firm courage, cold blood and a flexible hand we will manage to get through honourably." (p. 69)

With these principles v. Bülow might have succeeded in keeping the peace if he had stayed Chancellor...

But had not England's determination to wage war on Germany become too strong now? The author repeats himself: yes, it had!

But then again, all England ever did was to continue her well-known power politics exclusively according to her own interests. (But what if everyone acted thus?) If the English government could have relied on the opinion of the general public in the world, just as it could rely on its own population after years of propaganda, it would, according to the standards of that time, have led an open pre-emptive war against Germany without hesitation. And this war had indeed often been dreaded by Kaiser William and other leading public figures. It would have been quite possible for the world, however, to get the impression that England was waging a kind of colonial war in Europe (on Germany) so that its population, as recommended by the "Saturday Review" in 1906, could become even richer. The government, however, did not want to be reputed thus, mostly because it was actually true; the war therefore had to be initiated in some other way, and in order to destroy the German Empires, and at the same time put the whole blame on them – and despite all this (at least) stay ... wealthy.

That explains the yearlong careful construction of the worldwide alliance system around Germany and Austria. It also explains the setting of a trap over the Balkan connection that would actually unleash the war (see below). This way England would be able to fabricate that it had actually been "forced" to go to war, - and at the same time be allowed to realize its above mentioned real interests (to destroy "Germaniam") without fear of punishment in the opinion of world public. In a way, an ideal construction.

Consequently, Churchill could have written his book "The Gathering Storm", that Jeffrey Herf wrote about in the FAZ in February 2003, already in the First World War rather than after the Second. After the Second World War the victorious powers were no longer in need of a German acceptance of guilt; therefore, they could simply wipe off the reproach of a violation of the "Hague Conventions respecting the laws and customs of war on land" according to Jörg Friedrich's documentation.

The situation was different after the First World War. At that time it was still important to conceal England's real motives from general public, - while at the end of the Second World War the victorious powers could even permit themselves to enact a law that prevented the indictment of their own criminals for their war crimes.[875d]

With regard to the shifting of the "sole guilt", Ambassador von Metternich clearly prephrased the expected situation and construction in a report as early as 1904. In a dialogue with Haldane, who at that time was not yet a member of Asquith's later Liberal government, Metternich had expressed the concern

> "that the French would go further than they were entitled to by right and equity if they felt incited by England." [From Delcassé's indiscretions] the German nation had to derive with bitterness that England, "a country we had never been at war with", was prepared to fight against us with the French, at their free will and without ever entering into any previous obligations."
> ... "No one who was familiar with the public opinion in this country should have any illusions concerning the hedging by clauses of this attack. Should the French cross the German border tomorrow, the day after tomorrow news would be spread all over England that they had been forced to do so by Germany's provocative position."[876]

Thus v. Metternich rationally, and with an objective and almost cynically English view, uncovered the old question of guilt "Who started it?" as an instrument for a ruse.

> *By means of propaganda both the English government and the monarchy as well as the press held the British people at a very tight grip and manipulated them.*

This is illustrated clearly in a report by the Serbian Ambassador in Paris, Dr. Milorad Wessnitsch, to Prime Minister Pasic in 1913. He had heard from a reliable source that the positive effect,

> "which the presence of the English royal couple would have at the wedding of the German Kaiser's daughter should soon be paralysed by another manifestation in accordance with the Triple Entente, and that the latter would have much greater political significance."[877]

Isn't it rather typical of the imperialist, and thus unfair, British government to fear its people's reaction because it (correctly) assumed the obviously harmonious family party in Germany would lead to positive conclusions to the peaceful agreement between their own monarchy and the related German one? The British government, however, did not exactly embrace this reaction, as at the same time plans were being made to lead the British people under the English King to war against the German part of the family.

The government's main fear was that the British people's reaction would be according to their reputation: fair and just. The above mentioned "manifestation" against the risen sympathy towards the German Kaiser and his family was meant to prevent precisely this.

This obviously planned malicious campaign did not constitute a new anti-German policy, though. Quite the reverse, it was a continuation of the aggressive line which had been exercised by England since the unification of the Reich in 1871, or, even earlier, since 1848 (British naval deployment!) when a totally peaceful, legal and democratic movement - at that time unsuccessfully - struggled for the German unification. The consequence of this malicious instigation was that in Britain even people with a fundamentally noble mind were filled with hatred and envy and had let themselves be abused by their leaders. In other words, they had drifted into a war that they, knowing the truth, never would have gone to. (No isolated case, evidently.)

The outbreak of the First World War revealed what the experienced English propaganda was further capable of: One of the disparagements was not only directed against the Germans in general but against the person of Kaiser William II in particular – and has been continued ever since. Until today.

Only on one occasion there were serious doubts in England whether government, monarchy and press would be able to remain in control of public opinion in Britain: This was when the Soviet revolutionary government under Trotzki and Lenin began to publish the documents of the Tsar's secret agreements with the other imperialist powers, - an operation that is also mentioned by Fritz Fischer.[878] The political archive harbours an excerpt from a report of the Chief of Naval Staff stating:

> "Besides, influential circles fear mostly that the English nation is deprived of their moral reason to fence. For them the publication of the secret agreements by Russia was rather embarrassing. ... It would be a major blow to the morale of the English people that has only artificially got worked up by Belgium, the Lusitania etc. Signed Dr. Forkel"[879]

Concerning the topic of "Belgium", i.e. Belgian neutrality, it should be added that according to the American author Terence Zuber, *"no Schlieffenplan" existed*, as he explained in the journal "War and History". This also disproved "the main evidence for the German aggression in the First World War". It is therefore no wonder (as revealed by Eberhard Kolb's review of the anthology "Der Schlieffenplan" by Hans Ehlert, Michael Epkenhaus and Gerhard Groß) that some historians, including Germans, reacted rather upset when confronted with these implications.

The mention of the sinking of the Lusitania by a German torpedo in 1915 suggests that this incident, too, had been exploited for propaganda. Many incongruities, however, had led to speculations about whether or not "the First Lord of the Admiralty, Winston Churchill, might have deliberately exposed the Lusitania to this danger, in order to bring off a propaganda coup". In her review of Diana Preston's book Miss Urbach inter alia quotes the following sentence by Churchill: "The poor infants, who died in the sea, gave a more deadly blow to the German army than the sacrifice of a hundred thousand soldiers at war."

Klaus-Jürgen Bremm comments on this in his analysis of the propaganda of the "most powerful press in the world" in the First World War, England:

> "Particularly Great Britain was in desperate need of a moral reason for the military intervention on the continent. The quickly waning readiness to enter into a war present in the United Kingdom had to be enhanced again by a systematic defamation of the enemy. As "Huns" and "murderous barbarians", the Germans were "expelled from the circle of the civilized nations" without further ado." "… for the first time in the First World War the allies actually perfected it" [the propaganda] "to a real weapon for war." "In the words of the British Member of Parliament Arthur Ponsonby, this lie became a <patriotic virtue>."[879a]

This shows that the English people could be - and were - seduced by propaganda just like any other nation, as long as the government was sufficiently cunning (or in other countries: sufficiently brutal and terrifying); it also shows that the English people would have had the potential to act according to their reputation without the propaganda of their government and press. Just like any other nation.

Quintessence:

> For decades the British leaders had not only deceived and lied to the German people; for base motives, they also misled their own population to unnecessarily entering into a catastrophic war.

Germany was by no means the only nation to enjoy defamation as a specific British fair play treatment. During the Crimean War, e. g., the British press did not only blame the Tsarist regime as "enemy of mankind" but demonized even the orthodox religion as backwardly barbarian.[879b]

It is only logical that in her latest book Brigitte Hamann takes an English image of that time "where the German enemies are represented as bloody monsters" as an opportunity to quote from "Mein Kampf",

> "where Adolf Hitler recognizes German propaganda as sentimental and praises the English one that he also used as a model for his own propaganda."[880]

As a matter of fact, even Paul Kennedy is generous enough to objectively admit that

> "newspapers and pressure groups … were often effective instruments for the articulation and intensification of feelings against foreign 'foes'." I. e. the German foe!

Regarding the "public opinion" in England mentioned by Metternich, it is clear that he knew what he was talking about. Others were aware of that, too. Walther Rathenau, at that time Chief Executive of AEG in Berlin, remarked on the Anglo-German relations in a memorandum that had been forwarded to the Chancellor by the director of HAPAG Lloyd, Albert Ballin, in Hamburg in 1909:

The English concerns were constantly directed towards Germany. "This is where the competitor and the rival sits. It is implied in every conversation with educated Englishmen, either as a compliment or as a reproach or irony: you will surpass us, you have surpassed us." ... "Thus English dissatisfaction is substantiated and localised with the name Germany. And what the educated class expresses as motivated conviction, is turned into prejudice, hatred and fantasy by the common people, and the young in the provinces, by far surpassing our journalistic apperception." (v. B., p. 428)

As the background and the motives leading to the First World War were exactly as foreseen by v. Metternich and interpreted by Rathenau, the Chancellor could repeat a remark by Roosevelt "who at that time could still be seen as pro-German", according to which the German nation

"was held responsible for the World War and its consequences far beyond any justification. And it is being exploited with a brutality unseen in history for reparations to which it was bound by coerced signature." (v. Bülow, p. 238)

George Clemenceau could be proud of himself.

In contrast to him, the world renowned member of the British delegation in Versailles, John Maynard Keynes, resigned his office as a protest against the allied conditions of the "punitive peace"; and even Lenin called the Treaty of Versailles an "imperialistically" dictated peace, against which it was his duty to fight.[880b] In this Arte documentary, Jäger also quotes the remark of a French historian according to whom the French aim of the Treaty of Versailles had been the elimination of Germany: "éliminer l'Allemagne". In this context George F. Kennan emphasizes that the Second World War was a direct continuation and consequence of the First World War, a result of the unwise, humbling and punishing peace of 1919. The treatment of the defeated enemy by France and Great Britain had practically caused the extremism that hardly gave democracy a chance.

According to French propaganda, the First World War was led on behalf of the human rights, though!

"The Prussian militarism was the only obstacle that stood in the way of the realization of freedom and eternal peace."[880a]

You can be as aggressive and brutal as you want, you only have to have a good pretext.

7.) At the end of this chapter, the comments of another historian, who has been repeatedly mentioned, have to be aired, for he reached the summit of dialectic argumentation. In one of his comprehensive works he investigates the increasing antagonism between Greatbritain and Germany in the years 1860 - 1914. In sound analyses he goes into topics such as bilateral trade, the influence of newspapers and pressure groups, the cultural, religious and dynastic relationship, the ideological and colonial rivalry and many other aspects. The results are by no means always unfavourable to Germany – just the opposite. One of them says that the outbreak of the First World War was not at all unavoidable. Nevertheless, he comes finally to the conclusion that in two points the German Reich delivered the decisive prerequisites giving the English (who, after all, have always been used to placing their own interests at the forefront) no other option than once again to intervene on the continent; this time against the Germans, or rather against the "Huns" (it is tempting to use this descriptive, traditional and in England still ineradicable popular word).

The first point was the geography. This geographical proximity! If only this bustling German Reich had been a bit further away e. g. in the Far East, like Japan, or in the western hemisphere, like the USA, then it would have bothered the afflicted English less and would have been unlikely to provoke such an immediate British response (P. Kennedy, loc. cit., p. 465). But no, the Germans had, of course, to live right close to Great Britain. Or when they at least would have given into their "Drang nach Osten", then no-one in White Hall would have been the slightest bit interested and the British could have continued not caring less. But no – they had to attack the west.

With this cue Kennedy manages to open another field of argument. He points out that the Germans had been guilty of wars in Europe, they fought against Austria (see ch. 4.4.1.1) and forcibly expanded towards Denmark (see ch. 4.4.1.2.1, No 4) and France (see ch. 4.4.1.1. The forcible French expansions towards Germany through the centuries – again: who could care less!) With this accusation Kennedy appears to want to underline the difference to the fair and cultural aware English, - perhaps trying to portray English colonialism and slave trading outside Europe as negligible and therefore not worth mentioning. If one remembers Ireland's dreadful fate under English rule, then one appears to consider its history as if this country belonged to the African continent; this is not even inconsistent considering that, during his rule, PM Salisbury had already called the Irish Hottentots (cf. quote from B. Tuchman).

The British Empire, in which innumerable peoples loved to labour exclusively for the prosperity and wealth of the British, could have continued unabated if only these German barbarians had remained in their "insignificance" (loc. cit., p. 464). (A propos: in the vocal world of the English aristocracy, the word "insignificant" appears to have had, and to have, a particularly magical sound when connected with the German Hun.) But no, they simply were brazen enough to try to copy other European people. Even worse, "Germany was not only growing out of its skin" [The fact that for generations England had been entitled to grow out of its "European" skin was, so to say, its traditional right], "but was also acquiring the early attributes of a world power …". Here Kennedy comes to the gist of the matter: "All this necessarily implied a *relative diminution* in Britain's own commercial/colonial/maritime position …" (p. 465). Is that not enough reason to start one more in a long series of wars?

The second point was ideological in nature. Great Britain apparently felt called to crusade against the Huns. This meant that the English automatically considered it to be their right and obligation through "British intervention to maintain 'the liberties of Europe' from the Junkers". However, this presumptuousness almost automatically brought with it the British fear that Germany, too, was probably planning a similar coup [which certainly was not the case], to take measures to break the British efforts "to preserve their unwarranted global hegemony and the artificially frozen European equilibrium". Convincing, isn't it?

This is no historical science and no correct judgement of the German Reich but is a continuation of the – albeit masterly – dialectic and the widely known propaganda used to supply an artificial reason to construct a war against this damned Germany.

On the other hand it has to be agreed that Kennedy does permit self-critical arguments since the Germans would not without reason provide the appropriate arguments:
- that Great Britain itself had already conquered an unreasonably large area of the globe
- that Harold Nicolson had admitted that Britain, after its own predacious period between 1500 and 1900, would first have to make their own Elizabethans responsible, before they blame Germany

- that even Churchill in the middle of 1913/14 had willingly admitted: "We have got all we want in territory, and our claim to be left in unmolested enjoyment of vast and splendid possessions, mainly acquired by violence, largely maintained by force, often seems less reasonable to others than to us" (p. 467).

Kennedy's work, however, would hardly have been so successful if he had not been able to immediately provide the British nation with convincing explanations. Should it really be the case that one is allowed to excuse the German desire for power (and particularly "at the expense of its neighbours") by pointing out the misdeeds of others?! One can vividly imagine the general sigh of relief throughout the whole UK: of course, one cannot do that! Just look at the (virtually Shakespearian) phrasing, whether England could "excuse" this unbearable desire of an insignificant upstart; and psychologically even more effective: whether England "could be allowed" to excuse. No, under no circumstances; there are unnatural appearances in life against which all decent Englishmen had to battle wit hviolence. Great Britain has always been ready (and quick) to launch a war – up till now. (Luckily, in the European Union today wars take place only on the market and in the sportfields.)

Even if England had not enjoyed applying moral measures, "there remains the question of whether it was prudent for the German leaders to appeal so often to the code of *naked* Machtpolitik", where the clever English diplomacy had always been able to so pleasantly "disguise" its own power claims throughout the centuries. "Britain, by contrast, had indeed carved out a colossal world empire; but by emphasizing the right of European peoples, ... it had manged ... to harmonize [its national policy] with the general desires and ideals common to all mankind." (P. 468) Thank God for England.

Once he had trodden this path, then the following *anachronistic* argument must have almost thrust itself onto the historian Kennedy as the peak of the art of producing a fable at the end of his 500 - 600 page analysis: "It is impossible for the person who knows the post 1914 course of German history, not to take an ethical stand".

Clearly, in expectation of what would happen to the world one day under Hitler in the Third Reich (to which one, incidentally, had contributed through the Versailles Treaty in 1919), the cultivated, moral and ethical English, who were above all others, simply were justified, no, forced, to start a preventive war already in 1914 against the barbaric Huns.

What a wonderful comfortable English philosophy and lifestyle: Since centuries they staged, declared - or didn't declare but waged - innumerable wars, and from the middle of 19 th century they needed nothing else but some lies and dodges to lead a propaganda campaign of hatred against the Germans to indoctrinate their own people and to please others. Perfect performance – albeit a typical case of measuring with two standards. It is, therefore, small wonder that this morbid atmosphere gives rise to abnormal practices: so it happened in the year 8 of the 21st century that a book could appear in the exemplary European state of Greatbritain, where Messrs Dan Karlan, Allan Lazar and Jeremy Salter are not ashamed to write down, that <Siegfried, the hero of nationalism, is one of the main responsibles of the German inclination to unleash world wars>.
880c

4.4.2 France

"In the Orient France had a traditional interest as Catholic protector of the holy places and for centuries had been an ally of the Ottoman Empire since Francis I (1536)."[881]

This did not prevent France from securing their share of the Turkish heritage in time – Russia having increasingly gained new territory up to 1830. Together with Britain and Russia, France had just defeated the Turko-Egyptian Armada at Navarino in 1827. Furthermore, the 5th Russo-Turkish War had ended with the Peace of Adrianople and the independence of Greece, when France subdued Turkish Algeria in fierce fighting since 1830 – a war which after all lasted forty years. (One of the beneficial consequences was the smoking out of the hiding places of the corsairs, who had terrorized the European coasts for centuries by taking Christians as slaves and treating them with indescribable brutality. (Robert C. Davis: Christian slaves, Muslim masters. Basingstoke 2004)

Although this war against the Ottoman Empire lasted until around 1870, Paris urged the Turks to declare war on Russia in 1854, and together with England and Sardinia-Piedmont France itself sided with Turkey in the Crimean War. The main reason for the French interest in this war against Russia was their hope that in the event of a Russian defeat, they would be able to declare obsolete the Vienna Treaties of 1815 resulting from the Napoleonic Wars.

And this is exactly what happened.

A few years later, Napoleon III used the Italian War of Unification of 1859 (whereby Italy gained Lombardy [which had until then been Austrian] and Venetia), in order to annex the Italian province of Savoy (and Nice) in the most western part of northern Italy.

The French defeat in the Franco-Prussian War of 1870/71 and the return of Alsace-Lorraine to the German Reich left Paris deeply wounded – as if Germany had robbed an integral part of French soil, rather than returning it to formerly German territory.

"The dreams of revenge, the desire of regaining hegemony that it had held in Europe for two centuries, and the desire for the Rhine as its border (are) not extinct yet in France."[882]

"According to Bismarck, that would have likely and no less so happened even if the Germans had not insisted on annexing Alsace and Lorraine; but now this territorial loss turned into a convenient symbol and focus of all discontent."[883]

It took French diplomacy more than 40 years to finally give France the prospect of quenching its thirst for revenge. But first it was imperative to find an ally. At that time France inevitably looked towards Russia, as its relations to England would not have allowed any joint actions. The preparations were lengthy, difficult and expensive; and they proved rather delicate, because the French could not achieve their aim without the use of perfidious methods. George F. Kennan describes in detail how France used any kind of trick and did not even recoil from lying. He also mentions the forgeries of 1875 and the (forged) "Ferdinand documents" of 1887.

At the Congress of Berlin France still remained in the background. Then again, Paris held no immediate territorial interests in the Turkish part of the Balkans. But when the news came to light about the British occupation of Cyprus, Paris at once demanded compensation for this "insult affecting world politics as well as colonial politics" at the Congress of Berlin.[884] And compensation was obtained by the occupation of Tunisia in 1881. The following chain reaction is well-known: as a compensation for this the British occupation of the Suez Canal zone as well as Egypt in 1882 gave France on the other hand the pretext to seize Morocco.

When in 1879 Bismarck finally decided to enter into the Dual Alliance with Austria and in 1890 a putative Anglo-German approach occurred with the Heligoland/Zanzibar exchange, but particularly after Caprivi's crucial mistake of not renewing the Russo-German Reinsurance Treaty in 1890, the path for France to St. Petersburg was clear after years of trying, which included a number of intrigues.

The starting-point for the French rapprochement to Russia was the instrument of capital export to a market which was starved of capital, where demand knew no bounds. French strategy was clear: first Russia was to be fed and softened up with small portions, in order to lure the gigantic Russian Empire to France, which was at that time completely isolated – only to use it when needed (imperceptibly) for French interests (that is: for its plans of revenge). With success:

> "Indeed, French diplomats and bankers began to discuss the possibility of a Franco-Russian entente based on French capital as early as 1880." ... "The first major French loan to Russia was floated on the bourse (in Paris) in the autumn of 1888. The following year, the Paris Rothschilds agreed to undertake two major Russian bond issues with a total face value of some £ 77 million, and a third £ 12-million issue followed the next year. In 1894 a further loan worth around £ 16 million was issued; and there was another for the same amount in 1896."[885]

Thus George F. Kennan could claim:

> "Russian debts towards France [were] at that time (the) highest international debts of all times."[886]

Even today, on 15 November 2002, the FAZ reported from London that Russian plans to pay off loans of the Soviet Union were interrupted because the rouble loans of the Tsarist era had not yet been redeemed or reimbursed, and looking far back it continues:

> "Early in 1900 France was the central market for Russian loans. At that time France had intended to win over Russia as an ally against the German Reich."

This aim was pursued rigorously, but rather cunningly by means of forgeries, lies and money, - money that the Russians now have to pay back after they were asked to take the risks for England and France in the First World War. Bolshoj kapitalist.

(Other branches were also profiting from trade expansion: the Tsarist court was one of the best clients of Louis Roederer champaign company in Reims. The Russian revolution, however, plunged this enterprise into a severe crisis.[886a]

As early as 1891, a seemingly harmless Franco-Russian consultation agreement was concluded, - but for France this meant a breakthrough. In 1892 this loose form was tightened up into the Franco-Russian Entente, which was followed in 1894

> "by the Franco-Russian alliance ..., one of the main elements... that led to the fatal situation of 1914."[887]

As a matter of fact, the Franco-Russian alliance of 1894 was cause for great concern in Britain at that time! (Henry C. Meyer, l. c., p. 31)

Nevertheless, the French alliances with Russia constituted the first step towards the Entente Cordiale with England of 8 April 1904 – officially (allegedly only) formed for reasons of colonial policy. Regarding its historical significance, the Entente is

> "one of the essential historical causes of the First World War, which completely destroyed the order of the Congress of Berlin."[888]

One of the initially inconspicuous but grave consequences of this alliance was that it

> "(demoted) the importance to Britain of good relations with Germany."

Because of the largely improved Franco-Russian relations it (the Anglo-French entente) implied better Anglo-Russian relations.[889]
This led almost inevitably to the culmination of this triangle in 1907: St. Petersburg entered into the so-called Entente Cordiale that was from then on to form the Triple Entente.
The nightmare of Bismarck and all other classical strategists regarding the encirclement of Germany had come true.
The Balkan monarchies took the developments within the European "concert" as a "role model" for the formation of a Balkan League and used them to improve the consolidation of their own starting position to gain Turkish - i.e. Macedonian - territory.

4.4.3 Italy

After the formation of the Italian nation in 1859/61 the Congress of Berlin was the first international conference where Italy was present. (At the Paris Conference in 1856 after the Crimean War, one of the participating victorious powers was still "Sardinia-Piedmont".)
Among others, Germany supported the establishment of a French protectorate over Tunis, which consequently could no longer serve as a colony for Italian settlers. Angered by this, "Italy - also motivated by the opportunism of its foreign policy - becomes a rather doubtful member of the Triple Alliance in 1882."[890] (According to Hillgruber's definition, this alliance constituted a new formation rather than an extension of the Dual Alliance of 1879.[891])
A year after the Congress of Berlin the German Embassy in Rome reported Italia's "incurable distrust towards Austria-Hungary,"[892] caused by the shock of the Austrian occupation of Bosnia. This again extended the part of the coast on the eastern Adriatic Sea which was under Austrian influence and thus left less room for a long hoped-for Italian Albania. The Embassy quoted from a section of the official "Diritto" of 20 October 1879, which recommended a league of all Balkan states including Greece as a "joint defence" against the "position of Austria-Hungary, which was nothing short of threatening".[892]

Since 1887 Prime Minister Crispi had practised the "grand policy" of Italy by occupying the ports of Eritrea and establishing the protectorate of Italian Somaliland. The conquest of Ethiopia, however, failed in 1896. (In 1935 Mussolini launched another attempt: the King of Italy was pronounced Emperor of Abyssinia. The new Emperio Romano made progress.)
The Italian animosities against Austria did not remain unnoticed in Vienna; even more so when they were not even mitigated by the above mentioned Triple Alliance of Italy with Germany and Austria in 1882. After all, the Franco-Italian Neutrality Agreement of 1902 made Italy a "dead weight" in the Triple Alliance.[893] Vienna was also irritated by the conclusion of the military convention between Italy and Montenegro of 1905 – in the event of a war between Austria and Italy! By means of an offensive and defensive agreement as well as the formation of a customs union between Serbia and Bulgaria, according to the "Vossische Zeitung" a chain was forged
"in order to destroy the influence of Austria-Hungary in the Balkans completely."[894]

It seems as if no one wanted to notice that this network under Russian and English control was completed in order to close the ring around the two German states. (The Serbian files captured in the First World War reveal that the Italian Prime Minister Tittoni had already harmonised his Balkan policy with that of the Russians in 1908 – despite Italy's membership of the Triple Alliance.) But not even these obvious signs of danger could prevent Austria from annexing Bosnia and Herzegovina in 1908!

After the crisis year of 1908 it was evident that the future of the Turkish colonies on European soil - including Macedonia - became more and more gloomy. After talks with the Italian Ambassador Panso in the Auswärtiges Amt in Berlin, Secretary of State von Schön mentions a Russo-Italian agreement, according to which

"in the event that the status quo in the Balkans cannot be upheld, <de favoriser le développement des Etats Balcaniques d'après le principe des nationalités.> [895]

The Macedonians could easily have been among these "nationalités", had not Athens successfully wrested support for the Greek expansion from the Great Powers, using its dynastic connections to the European courts.

The monarchistic background is also the reason for the astonishing fact that Britain and Russia, according to the wishes of Greece, modified the principle of the status quo in the Balkans, which had until then been defended so vehemently, - if only the coalition against the German Reich and Austria would be accomplished. However, the above mentioned consultation between the Russian Foreign Minister Izvolsky and his Italian colleague Tittoni is significant for other reasons: the aforementioned Russo-Italian conference took place in Racconigi in 1909. This name is famous for many records and historical works, but only rarely is the significance of the consultation as clearly pronounced as in the above mentioned records of the Auswärtiges Amt. And only in these records is the consultation of Racconigi described as the extension of the Anglo-Russian plans of June 1908 at Reval!

How did the Italian ambassador interpret the "principle of the nationalities" during his démarche? It seems sufficiently worthwhile to list the few clauses:
1. "Should the status quo in the Balkans collapse, ..." i.e. more precisely: should there be war in the Balkans against Turkey over Macedonia,
2. "... the natural course of action would be to leave it to the Balkan states to defend their position." In other words: The Balkan state which enjoys the greatest dynastic protection and is capable of conquering the largest part of Macedonia will have the natural advantage of being allowed to keep this part. Whoever is in power, is in control. In brief: might is right.
3. "Both powers, Italy as well as Russia, would not intervene nor would they claim any advantages for themselves." Of course not, as Greece was to be the one to benefit most from the advantages and – as a fig-leaf if it proves unavoidable – to some extent Serbia and Bulgaria. Every sacrifice of the parties to the agreement (Italy and Russia) was acceptable as long as the ring around Germany became tighter and closer.
4. "This would constitute a further peacekeeping element."[895] Even at that time this kind of mendacity could practically be found in any diplomatic action. So the sentence should read as follows: peace would only be threatened if a third power (in this case Austria and Germany) was so unreasonable as to disagree with this ideal solution.

Further explanations by the Italian ambassador make all too obvious the attempt by Russia and Italy to conceal their ulterior motives despite their protestations of peaceful intent:

"Incidentally the fact that Tittoni informed Vienna about that programme of national development provides sufficient evidence that he and Izvolsky did not have any ulterior motives."

Only a fool would believe such a swindle.
Rather than fulfilling Panso's expectations, von Schön, on the other hand, drew his own conclusions:
> He perfectly understood "if the programme that more or less resulted in the patronizing of a Balkan League by Russia and Italy was not welcomed by Vienna." And he concluded by adding: "We would have preferred not to have been apprised of the existence (of the programme) by circuitous routes."[895]

All in all, however, the Entente plan was perfect:
Thanks to the dynastic protection, a prevention of an intervention of "other" Great Powers (such as Austria) in the war of the Balkan states against Turkey for Macedonia - which had already been sanctioned by Russia and Britain - would not only give the Greeks free rein against Macedonia. At the same time, the other Balkan states would be bound to the Entente, or even committed. Furthermore, Turkey's position as a possible ally to Germany and Austria would be weakened considerably – and that, without having to dissociate itself totally from the principle of the status quo in the Balkans (a principle meanwhile reduced, but of utmost importance to Britain). In summary:

-- Reval provided the Anglo-Russian preliminary plan of winning the Balkan states as allies for a concealed preventive war against the Dual Alliance. This again required an agreement made in 1911 beneficial for the Balkan states but detrimental to Macedonia. (compare ch. 5.1)

-- Racconigi included Italy in this conspiracy. The conclusion of the "Quadruple Entente" with Italy on 26 April 1915, its termination of the membership of the Triple Alliance together with the declaration of war on Austria-Hungary one month later and on the German Reich in 1916 had evidently been prepared on a long term basis. Confirmation of all this can be found in the reports (seized in 1917) by the Serbian Envoy to France and Belgium, Dr. Veznic, no. 557 from Paris of 10 November 1912 (R 20728-1, sheet 35).

As France had actually founded the anti-German coalition, it did not need to be forced to participate in an undertaking that it had been planning for decades, in order to gather joint forces against Germany.

Thus the ring around the two German states had long been closed before the threat of Germany's and Austria's escape from the ring was to be feared. In addition, that very wedge had already been driven between the Dual Alliance and Turkey which had been so urgently recommended in the "Fortnightly Review" in 1906! Now the members of the coalition could wait for something to happen. And something did happen:
on 13 March 1912 Greece, Serbia and Bulgaria formed the Balkan League as a prelude to the Balkan Wars. For Serbia, Russia, France and England the shots were fired in Sarajevo on 28 June 1914 as the prelude for the great war against the two German states.

Further fundamental significance of Italy for the formation of the Balkan League and the outbreak of the Balkan Wars - and thus for the fate of Macedonia - could be found in a different and rather unexpected region:
In view of the successes achieved by the other colonial powers and the diminishing Turkish legacy, after several rather unconvincing attempts Italy had rushed at the remains of Turkish Africa in panic and had begun a war for Tripoli and the Cyrenaica in 1911 (in 1912 also for Rhodes).

The Balkan states used this event for the formation of the Balkan League in 1912 (precipitously, after the preparations had been going on for decades). This league, however, would have been unthinkable without the back-up of the Russians on the instructions of the Entente. This meant the fulfilment of what Chancellor von Bülow had briefly described a couple of years before in a directive to the German Embassy in Vienna:

> "The Italian aspirations (could) be directed towards Tripoli, which would be equally inconvenient for both England (because of Egypt) and France (because of Tunis)."[896]

What he had not thought of was, however, that the Italian aspirations in connection with the Balkan League's plans against Macedonia turned out to be even less convenient for Austria and Germany!

In the same directive von Bülow remarked: "It would be best to refer Greece to Albania…" The German Chancellor had clearly underestimated, however, the territorial insatiability of Athens. As if the Greek hunger for land could have been satisfied with another small piece of Epirus!

Only the long-term political plans of the powers of the Entente for a preventive war against Germany could provide a basis for the Balkan states to declare war on Turkey and openly subdue the Christian nations of Macedonia and Thrace.

5 THE BALKAN LEAGUE AND THE BALKAN WARS

5.1 The Formation of the Balkan League

5.1.1 Russia provides the indispensable prerequisite for the formation of the Balkan League

1.
Several external factors influencing the formation of the Balkan League have already been determined, such as:
- the failure of the Mürzsteg reforms in Macedonia,
- the persistent plans of Greece to annex Crete,
- the repeated riots in Albania as well as
- the immediate cause: the Italian campaign against Turkish Libya.
- Furthermore, the accelerating effect of Sultan Hamid's sudden eagerness for reform on the Young Turks and thus on the actual date of the formation, which have already been explained.

In retrospect, the Greek newspaper "Ephimeris" described the situation presenting itself to the government in Athens as follows:
Only the Young Turks' policy had actually "managed to bring about a complete change of attitude in influential circles ... in Greece" and "made its participation in the Balkan League appear worthwhile".[897]

All these influences, however, were not sufficient to put the Balkan League into effect. Although it had been planned and announced again and again for decades, it had just as often been utterly rejected. The plan of the Balkan states to seize Macedonia could only be carried out in a joint effort. However, they never managed to negotiate a sufficiently satisfactory consensus. If they had ever succeeded, there still would have been one thing they had not reckoned with: none of the potential aggressors could be sure whether Austria-Hungary (and to a certain extent Romania) would not intervene in case of conflict and possibly overpower the aggressors together with Macedonia. After all, Austria was just as interested in gaining additional territory on the Balkans (above all the Sanjak and Macedonian territory, including possibly Saloniki) as the proximate neighbouring states in that region. According to Henry C. Meyer, the Austrian Sanjak Railway between Bosnia and Saloniki left no possible doubt as to eventual future expansion plans of the Dual Monarchy.[898] Especially among the Russians there was a constant feeling of suspicion. Thus, Under-Secretary Sir Charles Hardinge reported that the Russian Foreign Minister Izvolsky had told him in Reval:
> "the completion of the Austrian schemes" [of the Sanjak Railway] "would mean the Germanization of Macedonia."[899]

It required a sharper sword than what their own sables would have accomplished against the Austrian weapons to remove the existential fear felt by the bellicose Balkan states in such a threatening situation. Such a sword was found in St. Petersburg (not without prior consultations of Russia with England and France within the Entente). Only the protecting - albeit controlling - hand of the Tsar enabled Macedonia's neighbouring states to focus their attention jointly and simultaneously on the object of their desire.

The archives contain a press release providing a plausible explanation for this approach. Due to strict secrecy, it was only as late as January 1913, i.e. ten months after the formation of the Balkan League and three months after the outbreak of the First Balkan War, that the "Vossische Zeitung" managed to get information and published an article providing a deep insight into the *indispensable prerequisite* for the actual formation of the Balkan League:

The final "go ahead" to set up the Balkan League and attack Turkey (more precisely: Turkish Macedonia) was given to the Balkan states by means of a *secret agreement* concluded by Russia with Serbia and Bulgaria in 1911, - a key event for the whole Macedonian conflict up to the present day! In this agreement Petersburg committed itself to

> "making sure that the military operations of the Balkan League against Turkey would not be disturbed or influenced by the intervention of other Powers."[900]

"Other Powers" doubtless only meant Austria and Germany.

This again provided an answer to the question asked by everyone in connection with the Balkan states :

> "Who is behind this? Who managed to ... suddenly unite such contrasting and hostile interests to joint actions?"[901]

A few days later the German Embassy in Petersburg reported about Russian Foreign Minister Sazonov's denial of any secret agreement; according to Ambassador von Lucius, however, the Minister had not denied an oral agreement and had confirmed that "Russia would certainly have protected Serbia from an 'écrasement'." And repeating the wording used by the Austrian press he had even employed the German expression "zerquetschen" (to crush).[902]

The relevant information in Fritz Fischer's book "Krieg der Illusionen", however, was not at all up-to-date even in 1967 (or 1977) as he wrote:

> "Russia had learned about the Serbo-Bulgarian negotiations" of 1911/12 only "when they were almost completed" (p. 218).

An error of grave consequences. More so, considering that Fischer thought that the Balkan League was formed without Russian support, thus grossly underestimating the role of Russia – especially its function as the spearhead of the Entente.

Equally untrue is his remark that Russia had won Bulgarian consent to the Balkan League "by hinting ... that Bulgarian territorial demands would be largely satisfied" (l. c., p. 216). After all, it was chiefly Bulgaria that spurred the others on to form the Balkan League. It seems that Fischer never asked himself why Russia tried to press for the formation of the Balkan League by baiting Bulgaria.

The development outlined here leads to the conclusion that Serbia, Bulgaria, Greece and Montenegro might have formed the Balkan League. However, no matter how much they may have coveted Macedonian territory, they would *never* have dared to declare war on Turkey had they not felt encouraged by Russia's promise to provide protection, their respect for Austria (and its protector Germany) being too great. Consequently, the fate of Macedonia, Thrace and Epirus would in all probability have taken a totally different turn without the Russian Agreement. The doubtless anti-Austrian and anti-German motivation behind these plans is also confirmed by the initial Russian proposal that pro-German

> "Turkey (should) join Bulgaria, Serbia and Montenegro, and that together they should form a Balkan League under the protectorate of Russia and England."

The fact that England was mentioned explicitly is extraordinarily significant.

What is astonishing with regard to Macedonia is that:
> "According to this plan, Albania and Macedonia would gain independent administration" and join the (Balkan) League.[903]

This kind of "Balkan League" would have meant a historic opportunity for Macedonia, - but as the interests of Greece, Bulgaria and Serbia ran absolutely counter to this plan, and these countries were needed by the Entente against the Triple Alliance, the original idea was never executed.

Further conclusions can be drawn from the Russian Secret Agreement:

Russia together with Britain and France in the background must have had a very strong interest in the Balkan League. This interest must have been so strong that in concurrence with the Entente, Russia agreed to, as well as supported, the union of the Balkan kingdoms in full awareness of the aggressive aims of the League – i.e. of the inevitable result: the Balkan War.

This strong interest of the Entente, however, can not only have been focussed on the (relatively insignificant) Balkan League as such, not even the Balkan War and least of all on the remainder of Turkey on European soil. It goes without saying that the Balkan states pursued their aims to their own benefit, which was the only way for the Entente to instrumentalize them for its own purpose. Thus, there can only be one reason that justifies the whole effort of the Entente – that is to say the desire to build a closed front *against Austria and Germany. For the Entente, the Balkan League was therefore only a means to an end, a tool.*

The so-called "closed front", of course, only represented the small southern part of the complex ring of the Entente around the Dual/Triple Alliance, gone down in history under the term of "encirclement". At that time, the "encirclement" played a major role between the two parties. For a closer examination see below.

A successful inclusion of the Balkan League in such a "closed front" would enable the Entente at any time to drag both German states into war without having to fear the Balkan states changing sides and going over to the Central Powers, i.e. as long as they were securely attached to the fish-hook of the Entente.

The bait for this line was *Macedonia*.

One of the most important elements of this concept was of course the strategy to provoke the Dual/Triple Alliance into declaring war and thus adroitly conceal the fact that the Entente itself had started the war; this would make it possible to put the whole blame on Germany – which is exactly what happened later.

The only successful way for the Entente to trigger off a conflict would be by way of Austria's expansion interests. (Therefore the use of the Balkans!). The Entente was fully aware that in case of danger, despite his boasting and sabre-rattling ways, Kaiser William would *shrink back from any war*. The Kaiser's readiness for peace (a fact that the distorted image, drawn of the Kaiser before, during and after the First World War, did not allow for) was proved convincingly by Chancellor von Bülow in his "Denkwürdigkeiten" by means of many examples.[904] Thus von Bülow comments on a letter he received from the Kaiser in 1906:
> "Each line ... revealed the Kaiser's fear of war. ... He was almost too pacific, in so far as his reluctance to enter into a serious conflict was too obvious to any sharp observer." (l. c.)

(This relatively positive assessment did not prevent the Chancellor from telling the Kaiser what to do when it came to his more awkward character traits.)

But also the British historians Niall Ferguson and Gordon Craig as well as their American colleague Robert K. Massie (and even Fr. Fischer!) confirmed this assessment from their point of view.[904] Coming from former "opponents", the confirmation of the Kaiser's peaceable attitude is of considerable value.

The Entente, however, also knew that the weak spot of William II was his "Nibelungen loyalty", going back to his appallingly thoughtless and unnecessary consent to support the Habsburgs, - a crucial mistake that his grandfather, who had very reluctantly agreed to the Dual Alliance with Austria in 1879, would probably never have made.

Consequently, the Entente had included a kind of chain reaction in their strategy concept: In order to challenge Austria by means of effective provocation, use was to be made of a prominent weakness of the Habsburgs: their insatiable greed for Turkish territory on European soil, - a principle the Entente powers themselves had pursued for centuries in their colonial policy. By satisfying this same insatiable longing, the Entente was able to use the Balkan states for its own purposes.

> It hardly needs confirming that the aggressive policy of the Entente was subject to the strictest secrecy under any circumstances – and it was to stay that way forever. Therefore, it is no wonder that the measures accompanying the preparations for war were carried out in extreme confidentiality. Even today the Archives of Windsor Castle did not allow the author to research on the "Macedonian Question".

2.

It was due to Russia's clever management that the events around the Balkan League, which were tragic for Macedonia, presented themselves initially in a rather harmless way: the Russian Foreign Minister Sazonov (Austria's greatest opponent, - fully equal to his predecessor Izvolsky) for tactical reasons only named security and joint commercial and trade interests of the Balkan states as motivation for forming a league.

The external setting, too, presented itself rather innocuously: On the day of the Bulgarian Crown Prince Boris' coming of age, on 2 February 1912, the Crown Princes of all neighbouring states were present in Sofia, – as customary, they were accompanied by distinguished political figures, of course. On the occasion of a normal conference the final agreements were made.

> In spite of the strict secrecy the reviewed original records and the commentaries of the files "Die Große Politik der Europäischen Kabinette" reveal that "the text had not remained unknown in Berlin." (See below, ch. 5.1.2)

This "ordinary" conference resulted in two separate agreements.

1. The *Serbo-Bulgarian Agreement* on the formation of the Balkan League was signed on 13 March 1912. (In August Montenegro joined the agreement.) The agreement is unmistakeably clear about its plans for Macedonia: the territory north of the Shar mountain range, i.e. the old kingdom of Serbia and the Sanjak together with Novi Pasar were to go to Serbia, and the territory south and east of the Rhodope mountains and the river Struma was to become part of Bulgaria; the territory in between, i. e. *what is known today as Republic of Macedonia, was to gain autonomy*.[905]

This might theoretically have been another starting-point for Macedonian independence. But (in order to prevent this outcome nevertheless) the two contracting parties had as a precaution constructed a back-up position: in case the autonomy for Macedonia proved impossible to achieve, the two parties would probably have to make a personal sacrifice and annex even larger territories, meaning:

The area northwest of Kyustendil up to Struga with Kratovo, Veles, Monastir and Ohrid would go to Bulgaria, - whereas the districts north of that line and south of the Shar mountains (namely Kumanovo, Skopje, Krushevo, Dibra and Struga) would fall under the jurisdiction of the Tsar, who had accepted this function.[905]

> After the secret agreement with Russia this regulation constitutes a further *sensation*: for the Tsar had not only accepted this function, he had actually *notified* his acceptance to both parties late in April 1912.

This seemingly harmless procedure, however, represents a significant milestone in the history of Macedonia:

> *The Tsar "notified" his consent to act as arbitrator at the partition of Macedonia should problems arise!*

This again underlines the significance of this procedure: precisely one year later, in April 1913, Foreign Minister Sazonov denied the existence of this note in front of the German ambassador; for Count von Pourtalés repeated the minister's remark that until that time Russia had not been asked to act as arbitrator for the conclusion of the Balkan agreements.[906]

This was indeed a lie.

It is true that outwardly the Tsar agreed to the *partition of Macedonia* among Greece, with which he was dynastically related, and, like it or not, to the other Balkan kingdoms.

The deeper meaning of this "generous" gesture, however, can be found in the long-term plans of the Entente regarding the two German states, as will be illustrated in detail in this work. This reveals why Russia pursued the project of a Balkan League so persistently – and so secretly.

More than 45 years later Hans Herzfeld summed up the events around the Balkan League in his fundamental work as follows:

> "Besides the dynamics immanent in the national movement in the Balkans there is the ... unquestionable fact that this alliance would never have been formed without the determined negotiations and encouragement of the Russian diplomats in the Balkans. The public section of the Serbo-Bulgarian alliance agreement of 13 March 1912 contains a defence agreement for the protection of their territorial integrity and for the maintenance of the status quo in the Balkans (against a possible expansion of Austria-Hungary). In its secret amendment" [of 2 July and 28 Sept.] "it contains an offensive alliance for the time when Turkey would be unable to stand up against internal or foreign conflicts. This agreement would have been unthinkable had Russia not adopted this position, especially since the partition of Macedonia as planned would never have been implemented without the agreement containing a reservation to the effect that Russia act as arbiter concerning the disputed Vardar zone, which was initially neutralized. The same goes for the Bulgaro-Greek Agreement of 29 Mai 1912."[907]

This is all quite correct and scientifically well put, - but it contains no trace of any reference to the Balkan League and the Balkan War being part of a strategic plan of the Entente against Austria and Germany... Thus it also lacks the conclusion that it was the intent of the Entente to hold the Dual Alliance responsible for the imminent war at all costs.

2. *The Greco-Bulgarian Agreement* for the formation of the Balkan League was concluded two months later, on 29 May 1912. In contrast to the information available even in standard historiography, Athens had not entered into the bilateral Serbo-Bulgarian Agreement, but had concluded a separate one with Bulgaria. (Fritz Fischer, too, claims that Greece "had joined" [the already existing one].[908]) Compared with the decades of unsuccessful squabbling, these negotiations proceeded relatively fast, almost promptly,

under the pressure of the events, although they too went through phases of disagreement and were almost broken off completely. From the very beginning Athens had made clear that it would only agree to negotiate with Bulgaria "if the aim of the Balkan states was to drive the Turks out of Europe for good". However,

> "Bulgaria broke off negotiations when, in the event of a partition of the European part of Turkey, Greece demanded from Bulgaria a border line north of Vallora, Monastir, Vodena and Serres" and as a border to the east demanded "the river Nestos beyond Cavalla", and made these demands "a condition for further negotiations" on this line.[909]

The Greek demands concerning the desired position of the border might have been extensive, later, though, in the Balkan Wars, Greece indeed took Vodena and Serres. It was, however, unable to annex the other two towns: Valora, today known as Vlora in Albania, and Monastir, today known as Bitola in Macedonia.

Only one year later, when the first Balkan War had almost ended, the German ambassador in Vienna learned from his Greek colleague von Streit that during negotiations with Bulgaria regarding the Balkan League Greece had demanded a defence alliance with a programme designed to carry out reforms in Macedonia. Acting as negotiator for the Greeks, von Streit had chosen this harmless wording, because, when Prime Minister Trikupis was in office, the Bulgarians had once before disclosed the contents of their conversation with the Greeks to the Turks. Therefore, he had

> "drawn up the agreement so carefully that even the Turks would not have been able to take offense."[910]

The fact that the Greek government had done the same to the Bulgarians once, Ambassador v. Streit had been careful to conceal.

> "Greece had no particular agreement with Serbia. There had only been negotiations, put down in an exchange of notes."[910]

As late as May 1912 Bulgaria made a new attempt. The Greek newspaper "Ephimeris" reported: Although, due to international implications in this matter, Sofia rejected the Greek request to include Crete in the planned agreement, the two countries did in fact enter into negotiations on concrete terms.

The Greco-Bulgarian Agreement, too, began with a surprising concept:

> "If autonomy was achieved for Macedonia and Albania, ..."[909]

By the way: These names were written in a Greek agreement in 1912, - and not in 1944!

Interesting! So interesting indeed that it could only have been this text that later caused "The Times" to praise the aim to apply the "fundamental principles of international law", that was pursued on behalf of the Christian population of the European part of Turkey, - and at the same time enthuse about the defensive character of the agreement.[911]

The Bulgarian government had actually provided one of many examples of this aim, i. e. to

> "improve the living conditions for the suffering Christians in Turkey."[912]

On another occasion the Balkan correspondent for this newspaper stated: The liberation from tyranny and oppression ...

> "has been achieved by the unaided strength of the young Balkan kingdoms united for the purpose of liberating their oppressed kindred – for that was the real object of the war."[913]

Thus it seems that even "The Times" had been deceived by the nice wording regarding the liberation of the Christians, which in fact only served to gloss over the Greek and Bulgarian greed for land.

Or did the "Times" only pretend to be taken in?
It is possible and quite likely that the newspaper was protecting the British government and at the same time the Balkan states and supporting them in their concealment tactics. In that case we would not speak of self-deception but deliberate misleading.

Thus the Greco-Bulgarian Agreement reveals that in May 1912 Greece still expected *autonomy for Macedonia* (and Albania)! The wording of the agreement does not create the impression as if Greece had at that time regarded Macedonian territory as Greek property. This position was only taken *after* the Balkan Wars when it turned out to be necessary to convert wrong into right by subsequently declaring the territory originally Greek, and supporting this idea (as part of the Megali Idea) with all rigidity available.

> *This meant that in the summer of 1912 the Macedonian path to independence – however hard it may have been – beginning with autonomy, had not yet been completely closed.*

This does not prevent Greece today from continuing to deceive all its "friends" and allies in the EU, the USA and the UN with forged historical data.
Nevertheless: In May 1912 Greece and Bulgaria finally signed an agreement similar to the Serbo-Bulgarian one. Their military convention followed on 5 October 1912 (i.e. four days after their official mobilization)!
One year later, after the Preliminary Peace Treaty, concluded on 30 May 1913 in London, the Greek Ambassador in Berlin, Rhangabe, complained to State Secretary von Jagow that when Bulgaria signed this treaty it concealed the fact that it had already made an agreement with Serbia, making certain promises "about the partition of the territory to be conquered. He thus claims to have been deceived by Sofia."[914] Can this be true or did the ambassador simply complain about two horse-traders seeing each other for what they were? Where did the truth lie? Considering the fact that soon after the First Balkan War the second one was already in preparation psychologically, the answer is quite obvious.
As stated in a report in the newspaper "Ephimeris", the willingness of the Greeks to enforce autonomy for Macedonia and Albania depended on the expectation that

> "it (would) fall to Bulgaria to ensure "hellenization" as well as to enforce Greek claims to Epirus."[915]

The Hellenic Republic of today quite likely prefers not to be reminded of this appeal to their arch-enemy Bulgaria in May 1912, to *"ensure the hellenization as well as to enforce Greek claims on Epirus"*. The question arises as to the actual nature of those claims, taking into account that Greece entrusted their enforcement to a Slav adversary that it had always regarded as extremely unreliable!
The press article further reveals that in 1912 the Greek government tried to impress the Bulgarians with a reference to the famous Treaty of Berlin of 1878 and thus pretended that their own treaty had a basis in international law. This way the Bulgarians would not dare to dispute the Greek proposition that Bulgaria and Greece should jointly determine the Macedonian border. The reference went as follows:

> "Greece was to be granted the border line as determined in the Treaty of Berlin."[915]

What a surprise! The ancient conjuror's trick of hoodwinking the audience worked well: The Bulgarians were taken in by the ruse. They had obviously forgotten that "Macedonia" was never actually mentioned in the Treaty of Berlin.
All this might have had quite a different outcome for the Greeks: if the Bulgarians had at least been marginally familiar with the content of the Treaty of Berlin or taken the

care to re-read it, they might have been rather amused (at least at the fact that the Greeks had fallen into their own trap). For according to Minutes No. 13 of the conference of 5 July 1878 with reference to section 24 of the Treaty of Berlin, the rectification of the border to the benefit of Greece might

> "follow the valley of Salamyraias (formerly Peneus) up to the Aegean Sea as well as the Kalamas up to the Ionian Sea."[916]

The Bulgarians, however, did not remember that, at the time, the ideas of the Greeks on the rectification of the border only included the border with Turkey in Thessaly and South Epirus. (Apparently the Greeks themselves had also forgotten this: for them the historical reminiscence was only a question of choosing the right negotiation tactics from a bag of tricks anyway.)

At that time they considered themselves fortunate to obtain support from the Powers of the Congress of Berlin for their territorial expansion to the detriment of Turkey. At one of the two conferences he was permitted to attend, the Greek Foreign Minister Delyannis had gone so far as to claim that gaining Crete and the aforementioned provinces

> would bring "peace and stability to the kingdom." ... "The annexation of the provinces also lay in the interest of Turkey." [!] "It would rid them of any further causes for riots in the future."[917]
>
> *And who ever took the Greeks at their word, when they presented new demands backed by the same old arguments – and promptly broke their promises?*

Clever Greek politicians of the Venizelos type have repeatedly managed to twist the truth. To be precise, Delyannis, at that time Greek Foreign Minister, showed enough insight to concede in 1878 that these wishes were all "that can be achieved for Greece at the moment."[917]

The Italian attack on Tripoli as well as the Cyrenaica in October 1911 was, as mentioned before, enough to cause great unrest among the Balkan states. In truth, the Italo-Turkish War had triggered a veritable war psychosis. Now that Greece was safeguarded by means of its treaty with Bulgaria, the Greek government could afford to take the appropriate steps: Athens mobilized,[918] – discreetly, of course, and secretly. Yet, the Greek government had imposed upon itself a certain restriction: in the face of the severe problems that the "Military-League" had caused the government as well as the King only recently, Prime Minister Venizelos did not yet dare provide the Greek army with weapons for the general mobilization in September 1912.[919] (On 1 October the four Balkan states mobilized officially, and on 17 October the First Balkan War began.)

In May 1912 Crown Prince Constantine had told the Imperial Envoy in Athens, von Wangenheim, that the Italian Military Attaché had informed him that if Athens now announced the annexation of Crete,

> Turkey (still being weakened by the war against Italy) would not be able to take action against Greece, because Bulgaria would be sure to attack its flank."

Baron von Wangenheim commented on this rather blunt demand of the Italians that Greece should wage war against the Ottoman Empire, adding that he relied on "Venizelos' prudence."[920]

Hoping for pacifism in Venizelos seems rather naïve for such a wise and careful diplomat, - in this particular case there might be a justification. However, not because Venizelos wanted to prevent the war by all means, as was soon to be revealed, but because he was waiting for an even better opportunity - and for the strong Bulgarian ally.

5.1.2 The strict secrecy of the plans for the League conceals further intentions of the Entente

Thus the contractual foundations of the Balkan League for the campaigns of the Balkan kingdoms were laid. For decades the potential aggressors had collaborated in the preparation of a joint imperialistic crime, for which each single neighbouring state of Macedonia alone would not have been strong enough. *Even all of them together could not have risked the war without backing by the powers of the Entente.*
The imperial embassies of Austria-Hungary and Germany had not heard a single word about these agreements from their "friends" in the Balkan states nor in the capitals of any of the other Great Powers.
Why should anyone have exercised such secretiveness "among friends"!?
And "secretiveness" it was, taking into consideration that the government of the German Reich had to find another way of getting hold of a copy of the Serbo-Bulgarian agreement and the appendant military convention. Berlin was also aware of the fact that the agreements *"had not only been made with the previous knowledge of the Russians but also at their instigation"*.
It seems as if the German Ministry of Foreign Affairs had drawn the conclusion that the planning could not only have affected the Balkans (the Balkan League). However, Germany did not take any specific action.
After all, the secrecy of the League Agreement worked so well that it took another three months after the news about the formation of the League actually reached the press. Even "The Times" launched an extensive series of articles on the Balkan League and its preparations on 4 June 1913, i.e. only four days after the Peace Treaty of London (the official end of the First Balkan War), noting with respect that the considerations and negotiations were highly confidential. So much so that - as even ministers and other members of the government were kept in the dark - hints of this development were not published before "the summer of the previous year", that is 1912, and even then their significance was still underestimated.[921] Coming from a traditional newspaper such as "The Times", this confession is even more remarkable, as other papers talked as well as wrote rather openly and at a relatively early stage about these plans for a League. ("The Times" might have considered it safe to publish some confidential information a couple of days after the war ended, without expecting the Balkan states to continue the war in a second armed conflict.)
Even well-informed circles may not have shown the League the interest it deserved. Due to the frequent circulations of vague hints at the possible conclusion of a Balkan League, in the end hardly anyone believed it when it was actually put into practice. To demonstrate the precautionary measures that were taken by Greece alone (e.g., in spring 1911) in order to conceal its approach of Bulgaria, "The Times" describes how the proposal of the Greek Prime Minister Venizelos reached Sofia:

> "The document was sent under seal in the hands of a trustworthy person via Corfu to a well-known Englishman in Vienna, who delivered it to the Bulgarian Legation, whence it was transmitted, still under seal, to Mr. Gueshoff. At Sofia, as at Athens, complete secrecy was maintained ... The two Prime Ministers ciphered and deciphered their messages themselves, and no subordinate was allowed to see them."[922]

Were these precautions only taken in order to prevent Turkey from being warned in advance? This can be ruled out – as it would be completely out of proportion.
The planning must have been made with much wider aims.

The only one to be quicker on the uptake than the "Times" was Ambassador von Tshirshky with his above mentioned report to the Auswärtiges Amt by virtue of a remark by his Greek colleague (see ch. 5.1.1). He was able to clarify part of the League's history already six weeks before the Peace of London:

It is true that the Italo-Libyan War basically acted as a trigger for the members of the Balkan League; the decision to act soon, however, was made in Belgrade, Sofia and Athens only after

> "the Albanians had required the Porte to put the four Vilajets [districts] inhabited by Albanians under Albanian administration, which had been already been granted in Constantinople by the appointment of Albanian Valis for Mitrovitza and Janina." Only then did Athens conclude "a military convention with Bulgaria." (see footnote 910)

Von Streit's unusual communicativeness might partly have been motivated by gratitude for his German colleague's visit at his bedside. Another reason might be found in his allegation that shortly before the foreseeable end of the first Balkan War the high level of secrecy that had been kept in this matter until then, was no longer needed. This again showed that the Greek Ambassador was obviously not familiar with the actual reason for this maximum degree of confidentiality, i.e. the plan of the Entente to use the Balkan states as allies in a *greater war* than purely and simply against the Turks.

The threatening nature of the far-reaching strategy pursued by the Balkan League, or to be more precise by the Entente, emanates from the fact that all information about the various stages of development of the Balkan League was withheld systematically. On top of that, the participants even took the trouble to run a consistent misinformation policy of deception and concealment under the direction of the Russian Foreign Minister Sazonov. Thus on 25 June 1912, the German Embassy in Vienna forwarded to the Auswärtiges Amt excerpts from the text of a circular note sent by the Serbian government to their representatives abroad, stating:

> "According to current opinion in the circles of European diplomacy, the Slavic states of the Balkan Peninsula are negotiating the establishment of a Balkan League on a Slavic foundation, and in the relations between Serbia, Bulgaria and Montenegro a complete agreement has already been reached ... and the new Slavic group is under the protectorate of Russia."[923]

The Serbian Foreign Office thus provided a true picture of the situation. But what did they make of it?

As mentioned above, the Serbo-Bulgarian Balkan League was signed on 13 March 1912. The attempt to play the matter down, i.e. to issue a démenti which was more of a confirmation than a denial to its own staff, was thus still considered necessary and expedient three months later. This was allegedly done in order to prevent Greece, Romania as well as "Turkey and other powers from developing distrust and animosity towards us, ..." which might "result in serious damage to our own interests". Greece of all nations?

> This sounds more like a confession. The dispatchers in the Serbian Foreign Office obviously did not worry much about the fact that "distrust and the animosity" were bound to erupt once all this deception was uncovered. But is it not legitimate to deceive one's own staff!? And in the end, it is the winner who decides what is right or wrong. After all, who would dare then to entertain doubts about the illegitim ... pardon legitimacy of the government!

Any way, most of the information contained in the note was formally correct:

-- It is true that there was no understanding between Serbia, Bulgaria and Montenegro, at least not when the Agreement was signed in March or when the note was sent in June 1912, as Montenegro only joined in August.
(According to a wire from the Embassy in Constantinople, Montenegro had not been asked to join in the negotiations of the Balkan representatives "in various capitals, but mainly in Paris", because of King Nikita's habitual indiscretion.[924])
-- Furthermore, there was no Balkan League on a Slavic foundation, as Greece, having signed its part of the agreement in May merely with Bulgaria, did not consider itself to be a Slavic state, [925] so that in that respect, too, the note contained the "truth".
-- Nor was there, of course, a "complete" understanding reached between the contractual parties. This is rarely the case!
-- And the disputes between the parties had been known for decades, - in particular regarding the partition of the Macedonian territory.
-- However: The denial of Russian patronage remained a walloping lie. So far, this book has repeatedly shown Russia's persistency in achieving its aim of a Balkan League as complete as possible. Being in line with the traditional Russian foreign policy regarding Islamic Turkey, these constant efforts could not even be considered unusual. But why then was it denied so vehemently?

Apart from such obvious exaggerations, there were too many odd occurrences happening at the same time for anyone to assume that all this was solely about the liquidation of the Ottoman Empire on European soil.
Ambassador v. Wangenheim's telegram was remarkable in that it expressed his absolute certainty that "Russia was informed about the plans", or "had its hand in them,"[926] so that one must come to the conclusion that the information was quite new to him and that he obviously had not been aware of the fact that Russia had not only known about the formation of the Balkan League aimed against Austria – and thus against Germany –, but had actually promoted it.
As mentioned above, William II had met with Tsar Niko (as he amicably called his relative) in the summer of 1912. Nicholas had not informed William about the Balkan League that had been set up in the spring (although William obtained this information from other sources without ordering any steps to be taken). The Kaiser must have regarded the concealment as a bitter rejection, legitimately nurturing the alert distrust that he was always accused of (because it is rather troublesome, if your "opponent" sees right through you).
The Russian position towards France is of course quite contrasting. When Prime Minister Poincaré visited St. Petersburg in August that year because of the Naval Convention, he was of course informed about the project; and he immediately recognized its significance for the French plans of revenge which were over 40 years old – and made use of it.
It should have been noted as equally conspicuous that as early as August 1911 the Bulgarian parliament had granted the King (Ferdinand) the right to conclude secret agreements. Should not someone at least have asked: why? But not a single foreign observer became suspicious.
It is essential to quote the embarrassing final words of the dishonest circular note:
"Thus we consider it necessary to let you know for the purpose of your personal information that neither are we planning the establishment of a Slavic Balkan League nor do any precondi-

tions or foundations for such a close alliance of Serbia, Bulgaria and Montenegro exist in actual fact."⁹²⁷

"Personal information" sounds nice; but the misinformation was meant for the Austrians and Germans to hear (ostensibly for the Turks), which is why very soon it was common knowledge. A dirty business.

So, the English papers had been the first to report on this, followed by the French. Then the "Kölnische Zeitung" published the news about the "entry" of Greece. Anything was expected to happen in the event of "military complications" on the Balkan Peninsula.⁹²⁸

The "Wiener Allgemeine Zeitung" disbelieved the horror scenario. After all, the Balkan press had constantly ensured the public that such an alliance only served the purpose of defence, - and a Turkish attack was hardly to be expected. How innocent!

Should not Vienna have reacted nevertheless when there were actual signs of a war intrigue, namely a war that reached far beyond the comparatively "harmless" Balkan War? Were the people on the Ballhausplatz really so slow-witted?

Austria was known to be constantly on the look-out for an opportunity to annex more Tur-kish territory on the European Continent after Bosnia – if possible close to its own borders. (After all, "Austria-Hungary ... was the only great power neighbouring the Balkans."⁹²⁹) Was not that where the Sanjak was situated that Austria had already once occupied in 1878, only to release it again?

> *The Sanjak in Russia's belligerent plans will later turn out to play the tragic role of a trap. Albania was intended to be used as an instrument to make this trap work. (See below)*

No wonder that in such a gamble everything was kept strictly secret.

Nevertheless, State Secretary von Kiderlen-Wächter must have 'smelled' this subterfuge despite its complexity. Or did anyone give him a hint? That remains to be seen. In any case, Berlin finally reacted. More on this below.

How effective the *information blockade* actually was, is revealed in a report from the German Embassy in Constantinople of 6 October. In this report the Ambassador forwarded the message of his Austrian colleague, Margrave Pallavicini, that according to Turkish information "the Balkan Entente had been formed in Paris about three weeks previously."⁹³⁰

"About three weeks previously" would mean: mid-September 1912. But the agreement had been signed in mid-March! The contents of this report were again the consequence of misleading information!

One should not forget: The German and Austrian embassies were not informed by any of the other embassies, nor did any of the various spies around pass on the news. The only one who actually shared the information was the equally unsuspecting Porte – although with the delay of six months. The relevant report could only have been written two days before the first declaration of war and was nevertheless on a completely wrong track, because a false scent had been laid for Germany and Austria.

And all that was supposed to have been arranged for the benefit of the Balkan states? Impossible!

The Chargé d'Affaires von Biel then reported from Athens:

> "We are expecting the outbreak of Turko-Greek hostilities any day now."⁹³¹

He turned out to be right.

In contrast to what was generally expected, it was not Bulgaria who made the first move against Turkey.
In fact, *Montenegro* (it is tempting to write Great Montenegro!) will be the first country to declare war on the Ottoman Empire *on 8 October 1912*. (See below.)

5.1.3 Elements of the Entente's intrigues

On the eve of the Balkan War it seemed as if the Great Powers undertook various efforts in order to prevent the crisis from breaking out.
The Great Powers? That would include *all* the Great Powers! Indeed, apparently – or only seemingly?
In the face of the general excitement caused by the approaching conflict on the "Balkan Orient" as well as the humane policy of pacifism jointly exercised by all Powers, one might easily forget that the formation of the Dual Alliance in 1879 (and later on the Triple Alliance) as well as the Entente in 1904 and even more so the Triple Entente in 1907 had produced a *major revolution* in the relations between the Great Powers.
The Anglo-Russian *Secret Understanding* concluded in 1908 (in Reval) laid down the age-old English aim ("Germaniam delendam esse"), which the Triple-Entente from then on had pursued imperturbably, until the plan was finally put into practice on 31 July and 4 August 1914.
Despite the irreversible struggle to realize its destructive aim, the task and the art of the Entente consisted of provoking Austria into starting a war, and at the same time feigning harmony, filling the divide between the two "blocks", levelling out the differences, and building up new friendly relations across all gaps in order to create the impression of a climate of collaboration and trust among the Great Powers. (One should not forget the friendly and relaxed atmosphere that prevailed when the English Royal Family and the Russian Tsar's family attended the wedding celebrations of Kaiser William's daughter in Germany. What base-mindedness!)
In the slipstream of this new climate England and France intended to carry out their respective plans of achieving hegemony and of taking revenge, - that is to say *by all possible means!*

> The powers of the Entente were in absolute need of Macedonia, Thrace etc., - but only in order to sacrifice them as pawns. To further their plans against Germany and Austria by sacrificing the freedom, and even the existence, of three nations, the monarchs of the Entente, who had been hassled by King George of Greece for decades, gained the submissiveness of the Balkan states, i.e. their membership in the Entente. Thus, without hesitation they sold off cheaply the possible autonomy of Thrace, Macedonia and Epirus, and in the interest of their "higher" aim to provoke a great war, they laid these regions at the feet of the Balkan kingdoms as a reward.

5.1.3.1 Cheap propaganda the Russian way

1). The Russian Foreign Minister Sergej D. Sazonov was the exponent as well as executor of the Entente's plan.
In the course of its implementation he paid visits both to England and France early in October 1912.
Meanwhile the four Balkan states had announced their *mobilization* (on 1 October).

That is when it all started: who would have thought of associating Sazonov with this carelessness of Russia's vassals in the Balkans? He was not even at home at the time in question. Therefore, he could not have had anything to do with it.

On 8 October, when the news of Montenegro's declaration of war on Turkey reached the Auswärtiges Amt, the very same Sazonov was actually in Berlin. (Compared with the foolhardiness of the mobilization of Russia's vassals – especially because it was supposed to appear as if it had been carried out without the knowledge and even against the will of Russia – the declaration of war by the small state of Montenegro on the Ottoman Empire was actually sheer madness. And madness it would indeed have been without the protective paw of the Russian bear!)

It does not take much imagination to realize that Sazonov's stay in Berlin was planned and fully intended. His absence from St. Petersburg was meant to feign Russian neutrality and indifference at the "critical time" when the news broke, but at the same time to be present at one of the neuralgic places, in the lion's den so to say, in order to be able to act as regulator if necessary. When at a dinner party his host remarked to him ["remarked" rather than throwing it right into his opponent's face as Sazonov would probably have done, had he been in this situation] "that the game Russia had played had been a rather dangerous one, 'de patroniser l'alliance des Etats balcaniques' ", Sazonov had the nerve to lie to the State Secretary (von Kiderlen)

> "that Russia had explicitly required the Balkan states to refrain from any aggressive tendencies."[932]

It is hard to believe but in his report to the Kaiser (at Rominten), that had been signed by the Chancellor, State Secretary von Kiderlen indeed recorded that

> "Montenegro's declaration of war clearly had made a depressing impression on the Russian Minister", as in the afternoon he had expressed "that the maintenance of peace in the Balkans was not only his urgent wish but his sincere hope."[932]

What a good person he was.

One must not forget either that von Kiderlen had been influenced accordingly by the German Ambassador v. Lucius, as the latter had shortly before reported from St. Petersburg that he "(thought) Mr. Sazonov's concern at the outbreak of a Turko-Bulgarian war was sincere."[933]

It is still painful to read about how an experienced ambassador with many years of diplomatic service to his standing was able to form such a credulous and charitable – but rather naïve – opinion of this villain.

This misjudgement was the result of the diplomatic subtlety and great acting skills of the Russian Foreign Minister, - who had actually initiated the whole scenario (most likely including the date and the wording of Montenegro's declaration of war).

Early in October the "Deutsche Tageszeitung" had already reported:

> "The King of the Black Mountains recently claimed that he would not make a single move without Russian approval."[934] Almost a month before, a similar remark was made in the report from St. Petersburg just quoted from above: "King Nicholas of Montenegro is said to have publicly declared recently that he would not do anything against the will of Russia."[933]

This is complemented by a document from the opposite side. According to a report sent by the Serbian Ambassador Popovic from St. Petersburg to Prime Minister and Foreign Minister Milovanovic referring to King Nicholas's reaction to the Russian admonitions received during his visit to Russia, to the effect that he "should not engage in an adventure":

> "He told Mr. Sazonov that his position towards Russia resembled that of the soldier and his superior." ... "In Montenegro I am King, but in Russia I only follow orders from above."[935]

In the meantime, in Cettinje, the capital of Montenegro, the atmosphere was almost that of an operetta. A telegram from the Envoy, von Eckardt, revealed that his Russian colleague had told him "subject to strict confidentiality":

> "he had promised the Prime Minister of Montenegro financial help if everything remained calm and had declared adamantly that Russia would not support Montenegro should it attempt to start a war."[936]

Wicked Montenegro!
Taking into account the "financial aspect" makes it easier to believe what Major Ali Riza Bey, a Turkish delegate in Cettinje, told the German Ambassador. He was going to suggest to the Porte to

> "offer Montenegro financial compensation in order to induce it to give up its claim" to a particular Turkish territory, "violently defended by the Albanian tribe of the Rugowi."[937]

(Was that a policy motivated by personal interest? Was the Major a Rugowa himself? His first name "Riza" as well as the name of the tribe suggest Albanian nationality.)
After all, the Turks were not at all famous for the humane and careful treatment of their subjects. (Thus, it was too late for that now.) Apart from that, this process interestingly reveals that at this early stage, i.e. late in September 1912, when neither mobilization had been announced nor any (of the four) declarations of war had been made, the inevitable consequences of the war were actually being discussed in detail ("territorial cessions", "financial compensation").

The report mentioned above was forwarded to the Kaiser at Rominten where, as a passionate hunter, he went deer hunting in the autumn.
(This hunting ground obviously existed long before the times of Göring and Gomulka. The latter two and many other potentates could easily have been the subject of Michael Stürmer's accusation of "neurotically shooting all the game" as was William II, - and perhaps with more justification. (l. c., p. 240)
William was advised by his counsellors to remain at Rominten in order to avoid misinterpretations and possible ensuing agitation.
Anyway, the stock markets had already reacted in panic. And as stock markets tend to react seismographically, St. Petersburg[938] as well as Paris[939] had already experienced slumps soon after the official news of the mobilization of the four Balkan states on 1 October. The Berlin stock exchange was the only one not to suffer great losses despite the "enormous sales" (particularly by Austria). The explanation is quite simple: in contrast to Paris and St. Petersburg (and perhaps in Vienna ?!) nobody in Berlin suspected that a major war was being stage-managed. Quite the contrary; according to a letter by an executive of the Deutsche Bank to the envoy extraordinary in the German Foreign Office, Baron von Stumm, "the market had good buyers, including ... some from St. Petersburg."[940]
This blind confidence was widespread in the German-speaking countries. The "Berliner Lokalanzeiger", too, had let itself be used as a medium for the Russian Foreign Minister, after its correspondent, Baron von Behr, who spoke Russian fluently, had completely fallen for the "courteousness" of "His Excellency Sazonov", "representative of the Tsarist Empire" – which showed that he was a typical figure of the vast majority of Austrian as well as German politicians and members of the press. Thus he reported:

> "To shrug his shoulders was the statesman's only response to the premature action by Montenegro, which was pursuing a policy of surprise warfare on its own responsibility and against

the will of Europe and its friend Russia, thus making an illusion of the struggle for peace by European diplomacy."[941]

In the attempt to remove Russia from the line of fire Sazonov was careful to mention Europe first.

Kaiser William, however, remained unmoved and unimpressed by Sazonov's hypocrisy! He annotates the sentence that the League of the Balkan states should "refrain from any aggressive tendencies" as follows:

"Russia knew that they would not take this seriously."[941]

Why did the Chancellor not realize these interconnections? And why was not more attention paid to Kaiser William's doubts? (Was it still because of the Daily-Telegraph affair?) The chapter on the German Reich (ch. 4.1.1) described how in 1914 the Kaiser had been tricked by politicians, mainly by Chancellor v. Bethmann Hollweg, in an even more dramatic situation.

2). The Russian Foreign Minister's coordination seemed to work out perfectly; each Balkan state was involved and had to play its part. On the day of mobilization the German Embassy in St. Petersburg reported that Sazonov had spread the news

that he had "told the Bulgarian Ambassador that Bulgaria could not count on help from Russia and (had) strictly warned Belgrade, Cettinje and Athens."[942]

Surely, that is all that can be done to keep the peace, is it not?

Although it was closest to the Tsar, Greece remained in the background and was astonishingly reserved, but planned to give up this reticence at the right moment, as will be revealed later.

Serbia was, like Bulgaria, kept by Russia as a vassal and thus acted accordingly.

Even the Austrian Foreign Minister, otherwise extremely credulous, finally had

"doubts about the honesty of the Russian policy, considering the fact that an official Russian envoy like Mr. Hartwig, could act as he wished in neighbouring Serbia, completely unchecked by his go-vernment. Mr. Hartwig was nothing but a pan-Slavistic agitator, and knowing how this man, who acted as a Russian viceroy, had Serbia under control, where not a single note was written without his approval, the question presents itself whether this official Russian envoy had not also had a hand in the latest development in Serbian politics."[943]

Mr Sazonov seemed to be involved in some double dealing, a belief that he (Count Berchthold) did not want to share... Further on, the same report states that

"he was not willing to credit any suspicions that Russia was behind the actions of the Balkan states; he preferred to trust in the honest pacifism of the Russian statesmen."[943]

Exactly! He should have been suspicious, because these circumstances were the subject of lively discussions, but he did not wish to. This course of action can only lead to disaster.

Three weeks later Berchtold's scepticism had further increased. He still was not sure whether or not Sazonov intended to take late revenge on him as successor to Baron Aehrenthal, sworn enemy of the former Foreign Minister Izvolsky (Sazonov's predecessor until 1910). He also wondered whether or not this was *a trap, "set for Austria-Hungary by the whole Triple Entente.*"[944]

A light in the dark. Because this is exactly what it was. That way all the requirements for the revelation of this gigantic swindle would have been fulfilled.

Unfortunately, this light was extinguished later on. In 1914 at the latest.

In view of Serbia's total dependence on Russia, it cannot have escaped the observers' notice that Serbia all of a sudden seemed to defy completely all demands made by Russia. Thus, on the day, the four Balkan states officially announced their mobilization the "Neue Freie Presse" in Vienna commented with growing distrust:

> "Is there ... an explanation for the strange incident that Serbia, whose leading figures at court and in the government crawl on their knees before Russia, nevertheless dares to set its army in motion against the Tsar's will and attack Turkey?"[945]

At last, here was someone who had actually given the matter some thought and was expressing his concern and suspicion publicly. A lonely voice in the desert.

With growing scepticism the "Neue Freie Presse" reported that at the beginning of Foreign Minister Sazonov's circular trip news had come from Balmoral late in September

> "that there had been a fraternization between England and Russia for the sake of peace. But what happens some hours" later? "Serbia, who has taken a pride in being the lackey of every single Russian cabinet, starts mobilizing in order to begin a war of aggression. Such experiences ... make the world lose confidence in the politics of the Great Powers." The newspaper suspected too that the conference "at Balmoral had almost turned the Entente into an alliance."[945]

"Fraternization of England and Russia for the sake of peace": a prime example of Anglo-Russian propaganda in preparation of a major war – and a model for countless slogans of future generations of hypocrites and liars.

This was obviously not an exception. Everywhere "The Times" appeared as a willing accomplice and acted on behalf of the British government as propagandist and "agent provocateur", behind which the government in London tried to cultivate its reputation of being a fair and credible negotiating partner for the Germans. The large number of Embassy reports on *rabble-rousing articles of the "Times* - and various other papers - *against Germany"*, however, paints a completely different picture.

Especially the London editors Moberly-Bell and Harmsworth and above all the Berlin correspondent of the "Times" Saunders had excelled in this fateful occupation. The well-known New Year's letter sent by the Kaiser to Chancellor von Bülow in 1905 reveals this, following hours of talks with the banker Beit, who resided in London. The latter was not only compelled to confirm the subversive activities of the "Times", but also knew about the financial support given by Britain to Russian, French and Belgian papers to ensure the publication of *anti-German inflammatory articles*, and he was even able to confirm the sums involved. In view of the obvious damage to Germany's reputation in Europe [as well as the United States!] caused by this smear campaign as well as the serious burden it placed on Anglo-German relations, Beit had agreed to plead with the relevant authorities in London on behalf of the Kaiser to tone down this war-mongering psychosis.[946] The Chancellor also wrote that the "Times" was threatening and abusing Germany.

> "Other papers such as the "Daily Chronicle", the "Standard" and above all the "Daily Mail" raged in the same direction." (ibid., pp. 114 and 237)

This occurred around the years 1905 and 1906! The propaganda of the English press against Germany started soon after 1871 (actually soon after 1848), - and without interruption has continued in waves - up to the present day.

In his report on the visit of King Edward VII to Kiel in July 1904 Ambassador von Metternich made some remarks of general validity about the influence of the press on public opinion in England at that time:

> "Englishmen in general, including the educated ones, are inclined to assume that their monthly papers do not exercise any political influence, because only few people read them. I do not agree. Only a few provide the impulse which is then transmitted to the masses." (Ibid., p. 35)

As far as the Chancellor's criticism of the English press is concerned, it goes without saying that von Bülow also criticized the German press organs, i.e. the German newspapers, declaring that they were very much given to regarding matters from the point of view of a Great Power, thus actually providing the grist for the mills of the foreign press:

> "A large part of the ill-feeling that foreign countries bear towards us and attempt to turn into political action goes back to manifestations of our press and public opinion in our country, which do not take sufficient account of the mental outlook and the way of thinking of other nations." (l. c., p. 329)

In a letter to his brother, the Chancellor could express himself more openly and be more straight-forward:

> "Large German papers ... (are wagging their tongues) about alleged German militarism, whereas the French ... are much more militaristic than we are! What is all this clamour about German 'Imperialism' supposed to mean, which is quite harmless compared with England's imperialism and obsession with its navy! Our exaggerated and unbridled self-criticism constantly provides other countries with weapons ... against us." (l. c., p. 237)

Niall Ferguson adds an example from critical days about ten years later (this shows how long the "heavy barrage" of the English press against Germany had been going on):

> "On 31 July [1914] Rothschild" [the London Rothschild of course, not the Vienna or the Paris or the German branch] "implored *The Times* to tone down its leading articles, which were 'hounding the country into war'; but both the foreign editor Wickham Steed and his proprietor Lord Northcliffe regarded this as 'a dirty German-Jewish international financial attempt' ..."[947]

Strange – who in Germany after the Second World War would have dared to think let alone quote these words from honourable English gentlemen.

Agreements, bans as well as propaganda and psychological warfare were perfectly coordinated.

An example taken from the time between the two aforementioned dates (1905 and 1914) demonstrates the duration of these "heavy broadsides": as already implied, the Russian press did not only receive financial means from London for their anti-German inflammatory articles; Russian sources, too, paid large sums for such publications in the French press. In the famous Reval convention of 1908 Tsar Nicholas regretted very much that due to the "freedom of the press" he was unable to interfere with the press campaign against Germany; in view of these activities, however, this regret appears cynical. He must have been aware of the fact that the Russian press was overstepping the mark in its own country. Thus the British Under-Secretary Sir Charles Hardinge reported on the Tsar's delicate sense of humour [that he could obviously still afford at that time]. (Memorandum, l. c., p. 6):

> "The Emperor admitted that ... (he) and his Government (had) considerable embarrassment, since every incident that occurred in any distant province of the Empire, such as an earthquake or thunderstorm, was at once put down to Germany's account and serious complaints had recently been made to him and the Government of the unfriendly tone of the Russian press."

The Russian Foreign Minister Izvolsky had made a similar remark to Under-Secretary Hardinge in which he left no doubt that "the hostility of the Russian press towards Germany ... reflected their true feelings." (l. c., p. 2)
Almost six months later the French paper "Matin", too, did not hesitate to write about the Balkan League "que le traité d'alliance avait un caractère purement défensiv."[948] (The paper only attributes an additionally offensive trait to the Bulgaro-Greek military convention.)
Dust thrown in the eyes of Austria and Germany.
This course of action was relatively harmless, though. Things were going to get much worse later:
A long time after the First World War England, for example, apologized for the notorious anti-German agitation (the German soldiers were said to have eaten Belgian infants and caught with their bayonets children who had been thrown up in the air). At the same time, however, Britain tried to justify this slander as war tactics. (Arthur Ponsonby: Falsehood in Wartime. London, 1928)

5.1.3.2 The trick of presumably localizing the Balkan War

After Foreign Minister Sazonov, organizer of the whole crisis, had reaped enough sympathy in Germany and Austria for his concern about the insubordination of the Great Power Montenegro, which having wantonly taken its energies out on the small country of Russia with their (allegedly unauthorized) declaration of war on the Ottoman Empire on 8 October 1912 and the impending Balkan War, he obviously felt the time was right to point out to the Germans and the Austrians some of the presumably rather harmless consequences of Montenegro's declaration of war. Having come to know him better, a rough extrapolation of his argumentation can be made. Maybe in the following fashion: What significance can Montenegro's declaration of war possibly have in the great mechanisms of our universe? And indeed: In the aforementioned interview v. Behr hastened to quote H. E. Sazonov (spelling his name 'Ssasonow' thanks to his linguistic abilities in the phonetically correct way):

> "The small Balkan kingdoms" were in a state, "in which they took the disentanglement of the Balkan problem into their own hands, going against the advice of the Tsardom and Europe, its solidary partner; and unless he was completely mistaken, one was now on the verge of events, the avoidance of which had until recently been the prime object of the Cabinet of St. Petersburg."[949]

All lies!
Without Russia, or rather: without the Entente the Balkan states would not have taken *anything* into their own hands, - maybe with the exception of some minor border skirmishes.
Of course, Sazonov did not explicitly mention the despicable word "war", but playing the situation down he at first spoke of "events" or "eventualities". As everything had run smoothly for Sazonov without his having attracted undue attention, he was able to reel off what he considered important in his future strategic plans. See also this passage in v. Behr:

> "However, not even this eventuality seemed to put the minister in a pessimistic mood, and with firm inner conviction he pointed at the undeniable fact that the Great Powers were determined to localize the war" [it was obviously impossible now to avoid that disgusting term] "with all

political means and if necessary military 'art'" [the Russian Foreign Minister must have been a true friend of the arts, if not a classical scholar]. l.c.

Now, he had let the cat out of the bag.

With this ingenious *trivialization* of the Balkan League, which he himself had organised with the inherent consequence of the Balkan war as a prelude to a great European confrontation, he baffled outsiders so convincingly that in one of Kiderlen's records even Kaiser William II noted down "correct" in the margin. William, however, did not exactly require someone like Sazonov to convince him of the benefits of "localizing" the Balkan War, as despite his occasional thoughtless comments, this attitude had already been part of his political maxim for a long time.

Countless documents reveal that the Kaiser either approved of limiting the war entirely on the Balkans, decreed it himself or at least made affirmative comments. One of these documents from those days, a paper submitted to the Kaiser by the Auswärtiges Amt dated 9 October 1912 stated:

"Following Your Majesty's Most Gracious Directives, the main focus remained on the fact that ... we ... would be willing to join any demarche that is guaranteed to localize the imminent war and ensure that the Great Powers will stay out of this conflict."[950]

If the Russian Foreign Minister Sazonov had known that with his above mentioned proposal he would actually be preaching to the converted as far as one of his potential opponents/victims was concerned, he could have saved a lot of his tricks and lies.

For every leading politician the ideal solution was:
"if far away in Turkey
the nations clashed." (Goethe, Faust)

The Powers of the Entente pretended to be extremely concerned that the Great European Powers, woe betide! could actually be drawn into the Balkan conflict, - although their plan was aimed at precisely that. If only the Austrians and the Germans had developed a better perception and distrust of what the French and the Russians together with England were really planning behind this Potjemkin-like façade of trust, they would have been able to make political preparations accordingly; in that case, there would have been enough time to condemn Sazonov's infamy and/or admire his enormous cold-bloodedness as well as callousness. If only ... would have ...

In the meantime, Sazonov further claimed:

"The basis of this determination on the part of Europe, however, was not only the solidarity of the Great Powers that became evident in those days, but above all the established Russo-Austrian understanding."[949]

That was the limit! Considering the fact that because of the general Balkan involvement of all countries, it was Austria (maybe even more so than Germany) that was Russia's real enemy and that needed to be destroyed, Sazonov obviously had no choice but to resort to this degree of shameless exaggeration in order to appear truly credible. In another part of the interview he indeed did not hesitate to emphasize his old "friendly relations" with the Austrian Foreign Minister, Count Berchtold. That was actually too much of a good thing!

For in contrast to Russo-Austrian enmity, friendly relations between Russia and Austria were by no means of long standing, and the personal relations between the foreign ministers were also heavily strained.

Thus, Sazonov had eventually succeeded in pretending that Russia was seriously trying to prevent the Balkan War after all. In his role with the halo of an honest man, who was responsible for the unselfish Russian peace policy, he earned great praise, even affection or at least sympathy everywhere. He even succeeded together with Austria, which with this minor preliminary war was to be lured into the deadly trap of a truly great European war, in establishing a common demarche between the Balkan states in order to create the impression of urging those to keep the peace whom he had originally incited to start the Balkan War (and more). In so far one has to concede that Sazonov's aforementioned remark concerning the "Russo-Austrian understanding" was even accurate in terms. The chances of lulling Austria's vigilance this way were thus increased.

The personal interest of the Balkan states joining in the war plan and its expected result was so great that they all participated willingly.

In his note of refusal, however, (which was doubtless issued with previous Russian consent) the King of Montenegro took the liberty of acting on his own initiative – at least in a small detail: Despite the whole put-up job, there were more grains of truth to be found in his reaction to the preconceived demarche of the Russian (and Austrian) envoy than in the show staged by the Russians. King Nicola a. o. wrote:

"I regret that the intervention of the powers comes so late. ... Europe remained silent, and I believed to have been forgotten. In the last 34 years Turkey has done us so much injustice. ... After all, not even the massacres wreaked on our Christian brothers in the border regions of Montenegro have stopped and have broken my heart."[951]

In his respective report from Cettinje the envoy also incidentally mentions that "the local representatives of the other Balkan states were not informed" about the fact of Montenegro's declaration of war. As in all likelihood they had indeed not been informed, they were able to claim convincingly that their governments had no intention to start a war and that "Montenegro had not [even] entered into negotiations with Serbia, Bulgaria and Greece."[952] Even ten days before Montenegro's declaration of war this was still true of Cettinje, because the secret negotiations took place in other capitals, above all in Paris.

Furthermore, in contrast to his reputation, even the King of the Black Mountains was able to keep mum. (Also in September) von Eckardt reported that

„the King and the Prime Minister ... (remained) strictly silent about their plans and aims".[952]

He even went further than that: in the interest of the cause the King lied to the German envoy claiming that Crown Prince Danilo

"(had) originally only wanted to stay in Dalmatia and Venice, ... but (had) then gone to Paris in order to visit the Russian Grand Prince Nicolai."

Of course, the King did not mention the fact that Nicolai had come to Paris to attend the decisive negotiations of the Balkan states (lasting a week) before the declarations of war.

With the information concerning his son, King Nicola incidentally stuck quite close to the truth, as his relative, the Grand Prince Nicolai, was married to one of Montenegro's two Princesses, who lived at the Tsar's court. They would eventually have lived their life totally unnoticed by history, if the two of them had not introduced the healer Rasputin to the desperate (last) Tsarina Alexandra, the former Princess Alice of Hesse-Darmstadt, in order to help her haemophiliac son.[953]

At any rate, the German envoy had to admit that

"it had not been possible to ascertain the true purpose of [Danilo's] seven-day journey ... as yet."[952]

> Danilo, by the way, had been married to Princess Jutta, the daughter of Duke Carl of Mecklenburg-Strelitz since 1895. They were King and Queen of Montenegro for a short time in 1921, although the country was no longer kingdom since 1918.

The fact that his Russian colleague also pretended to be ignorant, either represented a more sophisticated form of deception, or it shows how "waterproof" Foreign Minister Sazonov's plot actually was.

The Grand Prince's visit to the German border was played down by both the Russians and the French as being simply a routine trip, but it was once more impossible to pull the wool over Kaiser William's eyes. On the contrary, he noted in the margin of the respective report (from Constantinople!):

> "... the whole affair at our border ... was ... no longer a comedy, but a preparation for deadly earnest."[954]

Once again he was to be proved right. (See also ch. 5.1.4 and 5.4)

Sazonov's deception tactics, however, had not come to an end:

> "A Balkan War is not a European war, unless it can be prevented at the last hour".

Until the outbreak of the war, this was the pacifying phrase continually used by every politician in Petersburg, Paris and London as well as by their representatives abroad. It sounded good: beguiling music in the ears of the Viennese and in those of Berlin. Nobody seemed to be aware of the treacherous content of this actually harmless remark: Whatever gave the Russian Foreign Minister the idea that such a minor skirmish <far away in Turkey> could turn into a "European war", - unless he had previous knowledge that led him to use such a revealing term!

Sazonov knew this; "the Germans" did not. That explains his - unfortunately successful - attempt of a precautionary appeasement.

Thus the story goes on in this unbearable manner:

> "In solidarity, Europe can .... observe the war with her arms crossed."[955]

As a European, one ought to be ashamed to confront modern-day Macedonians with this quotation. Furthermore, the reference to "solidarity" in this context shows the deep depravity of the imperialistic way of thinking as well as acting. In fact, nobody showed any kind of solidarity with the Thracians and the Macedonians.

And where is today's solidarity with Macedonia?

5.1.3.3 The alleged refusal of territorial changes after the Balkan War

1).
As the German speaking listeners practically hung on the Russian Minister's lips while he purred phrases of peace, Sazonov saw no reason to stop his lullaby. In contrast, he heralded the next stage of his peaceful war strategy, or rather his belligerent peace strategy.

Attempting to measure this fiend's true dimensions, it is necessary to recall with each of his actions and practically every single word of his that this man travelled through Europe in order to carry out his mission of starting a war – and that he proceeded so unobtrusively that afterwards all the world was to think that the Germans were the evil ones. (The Germans were indeed foolish enough to provide him with the material for his plan.)

Thus, he proceeded with his stratagem in a carefree manner:

> "A few weeks hence, and everything will be as it has been, and the map of Eastern Europe will retain its former face. Neither victors nor defeated will experience any territorial changes on the Balkans." [955]

This would have been an opportunity to expose this play-acting diplomat as a clown. But nobody actually thought of asking him about the emperor's new clothes in order to find out why on earth the Balkan states had gone to war in the first place if afterwards all was to remain the same!

All just for fun!?

Meanwhile, the Russian credo of the alleged prevention of "territorial changes" again seemed to be a rather convincing trick to lull the German-speaking politicians' attention so that they obviously did not want to hear anything else.

As early as mid-September 1912 according to a telegraphic report of the Embassy in Vienna, the Austrian Foreign Minister had been concerned about

> "the threat of serious complications, should the Balkan states attempt to obtain territorial expansions in a possible war with Turkey,"[956] because Austria could not tolerate "any western expansion of Serbia", i.e. towards Bosnia.

A Serbian expansion towards the Sanjak too could "under no circumstances be permitted" by Austria.[957] The Royal Imperial General Staff as well as the Austrian "Evidenzbureau" were of course equally determined to take military steps as soon as

> "Montenegro or Serbia or both of them together were to march into the Sanjak."[958]

From a strategic point of view this was understandable, as Vienna did not want its only land bridge to Turkey blocked by a wilful Serbia (or Montenegro). This precaution, however, proved once more that the strategic considerations of the Entente had actually started at the right place by setting the Russian trap with the help of the "Sanjak" as a bait! (See below)

The Kaiser could only complacently comment on this legitimate Austrian position by saying: "Aehrenthal had solemnly renounced it" [the Sanjak].[958] This was a bait that even Kaiser William II had not got wind of.

So many different theories about the motives of the Balkan Kingdoms have been spread abroad, mostly lies, the most significant of which - and the most perfidious one - was the *liberation of the Christian nations* in Macedonia and Thrace from the Turkish yoke that a responsible politician would be completely justified to start thinking. It was especially "perfidious", because the pretext of aspiring noble humanist ideals concealed nothing but naked *violence and expansionism*. I.e. the respective peoples were not only abused as victims – before that they even had to serve as the fig leaf for the noble convictions of their butchers: the Balkan states and the Great Powers.

The "Freie Presse" in Vienna had seen through all this, as it wrote the following:

> "The allied (Balkan states) want a degree of independence and autonomy granted for Macedonia, Albania and Old Serbia, which the Porte considers to be an actual break-away. Turkey believes that an autonomy forced upon their provinces by the allies would be nothing else but cutting the portions which each Balkan state would like to swallow. Turkey will most determinedly answer in the negative. That is almost the beginning of the war, if not the war itself."[959]

This might be an opportunity to emphasize once more that the planned Balkan War was clearly a *war of conquest,* and not a war of religion – possibly in the interest of other Christians. Absolutely not.

The Bulgarian King did indeed shamelessly "proclaim a war of religion", as Secretary v. Kiderlen regretfully remarked in a directive to the Embassy in Vienna.[960] This appeal might have helped to motivate his Christian soldiers, whose fathers and forefa-

thers had for centuries suffered under the Turkish Crescent like slaves, but it was surely not the aim of *this* war.
Its aim was rather the greed for more land, for greatness and imperial power.

Meanwhile the polite Russian Foreign Minister allayed any fears on the part of his Austrian colleague concerning any radical changes on the Balkans, by categorically ruling out any territorial changes. Instead, as illustrated above, he continued his stratagem of placing special emphasis on the "carrying out reforms in Macedonia".
After all, it was not Sazonov's fault that the Foreign Minister of the Habsburg Dual Monarchy believed his Russian colleague's assertion.
Even the newspapers wrote that
> "the distrust of the announced reforms felt by the Macedonian population" was actually one of the reasons for the "agitation on the Balkans."[961]

By the way, this is another instance in which the Macedonians themselves are referred to as being active. Apart of that, the Macedonians, the Thracians and the Epirotes mainly appear as objects, keeping in mind that they did not possess statehood (yet). A confirmation of the resounding effect of this red herring can be found in a report from Sofia, in which the embassy categorically rules out the threat of war almost three weeks before its declaration, despite signs of "extreme nervousness" in Bulgaria. The only circumstance that seems to have weakened their conviction, were "certain elements" that "now once again" chose to speak "of the powder keg and the spark":
> "These elements are the Macedonians, the most agitated ones and worst in the country, who with their goings-on have caused unpleasant problems for some governments in the past and even now consider the moment to be suitable to ... fan the flames of war."[962]

From the point of view of the *history of Macedonia*, this is (further) impressive and respectable proof of the tireless activities of the Macedonians (in exile), to finally secure the longed for *autonomy* for their people and country.
Promptly, Secretary v. Kiderlen noted down in his records for the Kaiser in Rominten,
> "that, whatever the end of the conflict may be, the powers will not tolerate any territorial changes." This is followed by the incredible sentence (signed by the Chancellor): "The enemies of Turkey" [namely those Balkan states willing to start a war] "will be able to raise less objections against this, as they are the ones who declare that they are only interested in reforms."[963]

Of course, if that is what they said, then it must be true - knowing the Balkans and international diplomacy!
The degree of stupid, Teutonic naiveness is becoming almost unbearable.
On another occasion the nonsense about the existence of symptoms is even repeated in that
> "the Balkan states are not serious about their armaments."[963]

A directive to the Embassy in Vienna reveals that even after the official mobilization, the Secretary still believed that all the Great Powers were opposed "to the authorization of territorial changes."[964]
That was indeed too much ignorance! Kaiser William must have been almost desperate in the face of such irresponsible credulousness. He had his envoy, Baron von Jenisch, answer from Rominten by return of post:
> "His Majesty does not believe that the Balkan states can be fobbed off with the Turkish promise of reforms."[965]

Realistic, crystal clear and precise. Were there serious reasons to see this differently in the Chancellery?

Did the Europeans not anticipate (what the people on the Balkans already knew), what the Turkish "gesture of good will" regarding the *reforms* actually looked like even in this hour of danger? It was actually the following: Under the pressure of a Muslim demonstration the Porte withdrew a law it had discussed for decades and announced in a communiqué that the "reforms had to be studied first and depended upon the approval of the Chambers as well as the Sultan."[966] In this connection the Kaiser's marginal notes were once more concise and to the point:

"Total misjudgement of the situation." And: "When the battle is on our doorstep!!!"

A few days later, in its official answer to the proposal note of the Balkan states demanding autonomy for Old Serbia (Kosovo), Macedonia, Albania and Crete, the Porte indeed rejected "any foreign interference in the execution of the reform plan."[967]

In the early days of October 1912 "The Westminster Gazette" had already called the collective note of the four Balkan states a manoeuvre

"to close the door upon peaceful negotiations" adding that this was "the boldest 'bluff' ever played in history."[968]

What is of interest here is not the (typically?) Anglo-Saxon exaggeration, but indeed the early date of the statement as well as the fact that the "Gazette" had obviously not been brought into line.

Despite all the criticism of the existing system in Turkey, occasionally a certain kind of sympathy for the situation of the Porte became apparent. Thus, the "Tägliche Rundschau" wrote:

"The Ottoman Empire is confronted with an extraordinarily difficult decision..., as the damaged self-confidence of Turkey will refuse to agree to the demands of such opponents, who a relatively short time ago had actually been dependent on the Ottoman Empire."[969]

In addition, "The Times" wrote that in the event of humiliating concessions revolution might eventually break out in Turkey. (As in 1908 this actually happened again in 1913.) But "The Times" also stressed the significance of a satisfactory solution for Macedonia, as otherwise there was the danger of a revolution in Serbia, Bulgaria and Greece instead. The constellation had come to such an impasse and had become so hardened that a war was the only means to force the relevant population to bow to the inevitable and to even accept bitter results.[970]

2).

In Vienna Ambassador von Stolberg quoted the Austrian Foreign Minister's statement in a wire, according to which Sazonov had promised him to exert pressure on the Balkan states in a peaceful sense of the word ..."[971]

In order to demonstrate how much pleasure the Russian chief diplomat must have felt, in duly fulfilling his delicate (and malicious) task, but at the same time leading the credulous Austrian and German opponents up the garden path, it is necessary to quote also the second part of the telegram according to which Russia

"...even frightened [the Balkan states] by mentioning a possible move of Austria-Hungary against them."

Lies to make Vienna feel safe and lead it to disaster, - and at the same time on top of that to make cynical jokes. The success proved Sazonov right. In one respect, however, Berchtold seemed to have been not entirely deserted by his sense of reality, as he appeared convinced that what mattered to the Balkan states were no longer Turkish reforms in Macedonia, "but instead obviously only territorial expansions."[971]

When the Count as a final resort suggested that the Great Powers should explain to the Balkan states "that they would not tolerate any changes of the geographical map", he himself already "doubted whether Russia would actually agree to that." (l. c.)

Count Berchtold obviously thought that "the other Great Powers", namely France and England (in contrast to Russia) would have agreed to his idea.

Touching – as if the Entente that had been sending fateful signals to the central powers for years had ceased to exist! Berchtold could have followed the example of the Austrian Head of the General Staff Schemua, who in September had already expressed his strong fears about the

> "strong pan-Slavic trends in the Russian Empire, risking a fire on the Balkans, in silent anticipation that the fire would not remain limited to its original setting." His conclusion: "A very likely outbreak of a war on the Balkans (can) easily develop into the great European war…"[972]

Well! Why didn't anyone listen to such warnings?!

In St. Petersburg in mid-October, the German Ambassador tried to analyse and thus solve the dilemma between the pressure of the growing realization into the dimension of the increasing threat of war and the duty to take the resulting warning signals seriously, as well as the hope that the Russian promises could be trusted, which led everyone to believe in peace. To achieve this, Pourtalès' used the construction of distinguishing between the appeasing statements of the Russian government and the pan-Slavist threats - as well as the resentment growls of the Russian Orthodox Church - that could not be ignored. At first sight, he thus managed to present a relatively good assessment of the actual situation at the time. Unfortunately, he was wrong, as the government offices did not deserve his trust, because they permanently concealed the truth. However, he did not let himself be lulled completely, but also warned of possible (self-)deceptions.[973]

His colleague in France was even less fortunate. During Sazonov's stay in Paris Ambassador v. Jagow had even come under fire from two sides. On the one hand, Prime (and Foreign) Minister Poincaré let off his intelligent fireworks to deceive the leaders in Berlin and Vienna. To quote just a small example from one of the many reports: On 1 October, the day mobilization was officially announced, the representatives of the Balkan states in the Quai d'Orsay

- "[had been] told explicitly that the French government could only deeply regret and disapprove of this step. It was a fatal mistake, if the Balkan states cherished hopes to reach the object of their desires this way. France was said to be asserting its whole influence in order to prevent a territorial gain at the cost of Turkey."
- "On the following day at the diplomatic reception, Mr Poincaré had firmly warned the Balkan envoys of pursuing the path taken. As Poincaré told me immediately afterwards, he had accused them, in unusually harsh language, of having formed a league of evidently aggressive nature behind the backs of the powers, of wantonly playing with fire" and expressing demands which could not be approved by anyone.[974]

On the other hand, in this well staged play, in which all figures united against Austria and Germany und everyone played their part perfectly, even the director appeared on stage personally. When Foreign Minister Sazonov arrived in Paris coming from London (Balmoral), he told the German Ambassador besides many other hypocrisies:

> "It seems that a great aim, the unity of Europe, has practically been achieved thanks to the German and French endeavours." … "During his five-day stay here Mr Sazonov has received many diplomats, among them repeatedly so the representatives of the Balkan states. As I was able to ascertain without any doubt, he made quite serious propositions to them." (l. c.)

Without any doubt?

Poincaré and Sazonov were said to have "uttered in confidential conversations afterwards that the Balkan diplomats had left them in a totally shattered state of mind."[974] Congratulations! The performance was a great success!

Looking back, it is depressing to realize how utterly the German (-speaking) conference partners had one by one been taken in by the polite pretences of their foreign colleagues.
Then again, one should to a certain degree try to understand the inclination of the German and Austrian politicians and civil servants not to respond to the friendly promises from abroad with constant distrust. A reason for that was not only their foremost duty to improve bilateral relations; after decades of propaganda full of hate they were hoping to gradually achieve a genuine alignment of the different positions. Each sign of "reduced tension" seen on the horizon was consequently welcomed with a sigh of relief. Why then should they have suspected such an excessive amount of treachery and intrigue?
They should at least have been on the alert, though.

In addition to that, the Entente powers were constantly juggling around in public with hypothetical plans of how to make the naughty Balkan states see sense, (who on the other hand, regarding their internal relationships, were expected to perform their task. As a reward they would obtain their shares of Macedonia, - according to the principle of territorial expansion, which was only seemingly rejected.) Thus, they skilfully fed each other's lines around the credulous Germans and Austrians.
When, for example, the Russian Ambassador in Paris, Izvolsky - besides Baron Hartwig in Belgrade one of the major supporters of Sazonov and his war strategy - made the suggestion (intended solely for German ears) that
> "the powers should calm [the] Balkan states down by guaranteeing the realization of reforms in Macedonia", the French Prime Minister Poincaré regarded this suggestion, which was new and worth discussing, as "too long-winding."[975]

Perfect staging: Both German states were once again a little bit more convinced of the alleged goodwill of the other Great Powers; Russia and France had both cut a good figure, and nevertheless the good idea was out of the way, i.e. their protégés on the Balkans would not be hindered in their striving for expansion.
An additional example affording further proof: Ambassador von Jagow reported almost emotionally about the praise that Prime Minister Poincaré and even the "anti-German 'Matin'" (after forty years of preaching hatred) had showered upon the sympathetic Germans.[976] Is it any wonder then that it was so easy to gain his trust – and abuse it?
(The long sleepless nights must have been numerous, in which v. Jagow later blamed himself for these traumatic experiences, after having realized how meanly he had been deceived. Tragically enough, nobody playing an active part in the course of history is immune to such experiences.)

Interjection!
Can all these peace-loving and credulous people in Germany and Austria really be identical with that pack of belligerent monsters and Prussian militarists with spiked helmets, as they were demonised in and after the First World War by the victorious powers, i.e. the former liars and deceivers – and still are today?!

No! The continued deception on the part of the active participants at that time as well as the slandering of the whole German population was only possible with the help of the despotic rule enforced after the war.
Once more: Vae victis.

According to Henry Cord Meyer's references to the nationalists and chauvinists in England, Karl Pearsons e.g. would have been the one to be condemned as a warmonger rather than the Kaiser and the other German Spectres. And it would have been understood that Admiral Tirpitz's ideas would at that time have been unthinkable without the publications of the American "Captain Alfred T. Mahan ... about the naval power in Europe's colonial heads.[977] His books "The interest of America in Sea Power" and "The influence of Sea Power in History" were similarly instructive and laid the basis for the expansive imperialism of the United States. In his strong desire to increase power, he had the assistance of famous Americans such as Theodore Roosevelt and William T. Bryan. The "eruption of chauvinism, jingoism and general desire for war" (Barbara Tuchmann. l.c., p. 185 and 162 ff) were the breeding grounds on which Hawaii's annexation, the war against Spain and the Philippines, the Panama Canal project and the struggle for Venezuela and the sugar island Cuba (let alone the opening of Japan by force) could flourish. One of the most aggressive representatives of American imperialism was Alber Beveridge who Tuchmann cited as saying: "We are a people of conquerors ... We have to follow the call of our blood, conquer new markets and, if necessary, new countries ... In the infinite world plan of the Lord ... the lower cultures and the races which have fallen into decay" are damned to make way for "a higher culture of a more noble and stronger race" (loc. cit. p. 189). No wonder that the Pan-Germanists in Berlin mimicked this theory. In comparison to this, Joseph Chamberlain in London was hardly in need to learn any new tricks with which to convince others about the superiority of the English race and the resulting necessity for a large British empire. The self-esteem of "God's Englishman" (loc. cit. p. 297) could hardly be beaten. But even the English, who considered the treasures of a vast colonial empire to be their natural right, were surprised by the extremism of their American friends, which, for example, caused the English representative at the (first) Hague Peace Conference to say about his American colleague Mahan: "When he raises his voice, then Christ's Kingdom on earth turns pale." (l. c. p. 322)
The continuity of the traditional expansion strategy on the American continent itself at the price of the extinction of millions of Red Indians is evident.
Likewise, there were enough imperialists and warmongers in Russia and France, who could easily be a match for the German "Junker", the All-German Association and the officer corps. That way, the fateful role of the English bestseller of the year 1907: *"The Clash of Empires"* (!) would also have been exposed, in which Rowland Thirlmeres "painted the Germans blacker than black" and denounced the allegedly threatening ambitions of Berlin.[978]

In order to complete the confusion, the powers of the Entente made great efforts to spread contradicting rumours:
> "With regard to Montenegro's declaration of war on Turkey", the Ambassador wrote from Paris, "most of the press expresses the assumption that Montenegro has been induced to this course of action by Bulgaria. Some papers, however, see Italy as the instigator, [and one] ... paper even tries to make Austria-Hungary out to be the driving force."[979]

Brilliant! That way they were sure various kinds of speculation would circulate – with the exception of the truth.

At this point Sazonov's perfect coordination once more becomes very obvious; because Ambassador von Lucius had shortly before reported from St. Petersburg that Prime Minister Kokovzov had told him that the Russian government had warned Montenegro's King Nicola "(not) to let the Bulgarians use him as a front man."[980]

What a meticulous plan!

3).

With regard to Bulgaria, it is now time to mention two documents enlightening the *identity of the Macedonians*:

1. The Serbian envoy in Vienna assessed the situation in Bulgaria on the basis of his knowledge:

> "The leading personalities in Sofia are seriously endeavouring to keep the peace, but it is doubtful whether they are actually able to stand up to public opinion in the country, which is being stirred up by the many Macedonians in the army as well as in the administration."[981]

It is absolutely understandable that the Macedonian refugees in Bulgaria were not interested in a settling of the crisis. They possessed enough visual evidence to know that the Turks could only be dealt with by means of violence. They hoped to finally gain their *autonomy* with the help of the imminent *war of "liberation"*. Of course, they had not been informed about the fact that the Balkan states only intended to betray them, attack them from behind and enrich themselves at the cost of Macedonian territory. (Nevertheless, it is interesting to note that in the course of their exile in Bulgaria the Macedonian refugees had managed to hold positions "in the army as well as in the administration".)

2. Similar reports came from the Envoy von Below directly from Sofia. In a conversation with the Head of the Royal Cabinet, Dobrowitsch, even on the very day after mobilization the possibility had not been ruled out that should Turkey promise reforms in Macedonia to be guaranteed by the powers, Bulgaria might actually demobilize. However, the envoy seemed to have serious doubts about the remarks of his opposite number. He expressed these doubts in his report with the following interesting explanation:

> "It is not clear, however, ... in how far the King actually has the power to ... oppose the demands of the army and the Macedonian element behind it."[982]

Present-day Bulgarians will have to face these facts about an independent Macedonian nation ("element").

Another popular method to create confusion consisted of the fact that the Entente powers spoke disparagingly to German and Austrian politicians about other members of the Entente. They criticized them and doubted their reliability, in order to blur the impression of monolithic unity and the intended agreement. Thus, Ambassador von Jagow dedicated many passages of a report to the peaceable nature of the French statesmen as well as their complaints about England and Austria, but even more so about Italy and its "frivolous adventure of Tripoli". This meant a good opportunity to accuse Rome of inciting the "Balkan states, and in particular Montenegro ... to their aggressive course of action".

The Kaiser (who else!) did not agree, noting:

> "It was Barrère who stirred up (Italy)."

[Barrère was the French Ambassador in Rome.]

Von Jagow continued:

> "Even allied Russia is not treated by the French press with the usual almost obsequious friendliness. Often one cannot help suspecting that Russia is playing a double game."[983]

As the special peace concluded between Russia and Germany in 1917 showed (which was not allowed according to the Entente treaty), this line of reasoning could indeed not be denied. In his aforementioned book, Ferguson has shown convincingly that the English in particular were not sure whether or not they were also being deceived by the other Entente members, seeing that they themselves were often inclined to deceive others. The curse of the evil deed ...

4).

With regard to the frequently mentioned *"reforms in Macedonia"*, Sazonov's readiness to deceive went so far that he even included them (together with the idea of autonomy for the Turkish provinces) in the aforementioned notes, which were exchanged between Russia and Austria on the one hand and the Balkan states on the other.[984] Germany and England did not play any part in this show. Kaiser William, who due to his honest nature did not see through the deceptive intention of the English reluctance this time, even noted down in the margin of a relevant file:

> "The very reserved and disapproving position of England and Germany is the only right one to adopt."[985]

As mentioned above, Austria was nurturing the belief that it was part of the "Russian note to the benefit of the Christian peoples in Macedonia" (just as in the Punctation of Mürzsteg previously).[986]

What despicable treachery by the Russians, and what naivety of the Austrians!

Even *after* the declaration of war by Montenegro (8.10.), Russia for several days kept up the illusion towards Turkey and Germany that the Turkish guarantee of the status of autonomy for their European provinces accompanied by real and fast reforms could prevent the military action.

In quite a matter-of-fact manner, as was the English habit, Sir Edward Grey told the German Ambassador:

> "The only true possibility to keep the peace would have been an armed forced intervention by the powers. But nobody had been prepared to take such a step."[987]

Another example for Kaiser William's politically alert instinct in this context: When Chancellor v. Bethmann Hollweg finally remarked in a report that "a military confrontation ... was not only likely but also probable" and added:

> "We can await this matter calmly. Everyone is working towards localizing the war,"

the Kaiser woke up and noted in the margin:

> "Thus, it seems that others have expected this before us."[988]

Did Mr. von Bethmann at least feel exposed?

5.1.3.4 Mobilization(s)

Mr. Sazonov eventually had a third favourite idea. In the past, the Iron Chancellor would surely not have ignored the Russian excuses, provided that Sazonov had at all dared to trick the Chancellor so obviously. With this set of politicians, however, he could easily afford to play cat and mouse unscrupulously:

> "When I ... recalled ... the alleged mobilization of Russian troops," ...

It was not Foreign Minister Sazonov, however, who dared to address this way to Baron von Behr – on the contrary, the journalist zealously relieved his eminent guest of this unpleasant task. Thus Behr continued:

>..."the minister took up the subject with a vivacity that showed that he was pleased to respond to the manifold misinterpretations of this rule, which was within the usual scope of the Russian Military Act."⁹⁸⁹

This constitutes another of Sazonov's successful theatrical scenes. Given so much subservience he did not even need to take the initiative himself.

The only question that remains is what Mr. v. Behr might have thought (and *written*) after a number of disclosures by the press in November 1913, but at the latest in June/July 1914, when he learned that the so-called *Russian trial mobilization had* in fact been a *real troop deployment* on the Austrian border, in order to be able to attack Austria immediately, as soon as the trap snapped to, - which at that time, however, State Secretary v. Kiderlen was still able to keep open.

Is it any wonder that, in view of such an excessive degree of credulity and bootlicking, the Head of the Russian Foreign Minister's chancellery, Baron Schilling, had the devil in him?

When during the departure of the Russian delegation from "Friedrichstraße Station on the following day at 11.41 a.m.", one of those staying behind waved good-bye as good friends do and called out to one of the travellers "requesting" him "to get in touch soon", Mr. von Schilling called back:

>"Oh no, I won't have any time to write, only to act."⁹⁸⁸

Baron Schilling will probably have regretted this arrogant cynicism, but not before 1917 in Brest-Litowsk, - if at all.

What he actually meant by "act" will be the subject of the following discussion. A foretaste of this "acting" was provided by the only man of stature, who kept a cool head during all this simple-minded flattery: Kaiser William II.

Before that, it is necessary to take a discriminating look at the question of the *mobilization*. For in this matter a distinction must be made between *two totally different operations*.

1.)
After Russia had laid the foundation for the long-desired Balkan War of the Balkan League members against Turkey over Macedonia in 1911 by providing a guarantee, it was necessary for the four kingdoms to make military preparations. In this context, the rumours, allegations and denials had been raging back and forth in the diplomatic communication with the Porte for weeks, with each side trying to surpass the other in accusations. Under cover of this turmoil, however, each side did precisely that of which it accused its opponent: they secretly armed and concentrated their troops.⁹⁹⁰

On the basis of promises from Bulgaria, Ambassador von Below in Sofia initially believed in a mere act of demonstration.⁹⁹¹ His Austrian colleague, Count Tarnowski, too, had

>"the deepest trust in the loyalty of the Bulgarian government" ... and "during the whole crisis " he had "never believed in a warlike engagement..."⁹⁹²

The only one among his circle of colleagues to view "the situation pessimistically" was interestingly enough of all people the Russian Envoy von Nekljudov. [Sic, not just one of Tolstoj's fictional characters.] As a result of these continual deceptions, it was inevitable that von Below should report about the one colleague who was closest to the

truth, that he was "known to have repeatedly alarmed his government needlessly." (l.c.) However, it can be assumed that using his common sense, Gospodin N. assessed the situation almost correctly on the strength of his knowledge and belief, although he had been given as little information as his colleagues by his government, which also applied to the national, i. e. Bulgarian politicians. (This is comparable with the situation of the British Ambassador Cartwright on the occasion of his farewell visit to Baden-Wuerttemberg and Vienna. See above section 4.2.6).
In carrying out the mobilisation, Turkey was at a definite disadvantage, as it had to ship the main part of its troops in from North Africa and the Middle East. Among other things, this circumstance led the "four Christian Balkan states" to believe that "together they were superior to Turkey".[993]
Thus, the Balkan states (doubtless only after authorization or by order of St. Petersburg) *officially* announced *their mobilization on 1 October 1912.*[994]

A report from London of the following day emphasizes how perfectly secrecy had been maintained everywhere so far. In it Ambassador von Kühlmann did not report what he had heard in Buckingham Palace or in Downing Street or at least in Whitehall ..., but he writes the following:
> "Reuters have been informed that the simultaneous mobilization of Bulgaria, Serbia and Greece was the result of a previous understanding of the relevant states."[995]

Excellent! As if in such a historically significant matter as the imminent outbreak of a coalition war, there could actually have been such a thing as the accidental coincidence of all mobilization orders! As he was obliged to resort to a press release in this crucial matter, did the ambassador not at least notice the English restraint in comparison with their general generosity when it came to exchanging information?

Afraid of being left high and dry, the Turks tried to make use of the influence of the Great Powers on the Balkan states at the last minute by making suggestions in particular to Germany and Austria, asking them to persuade the Balkan states to call off the mobilization. Among other things, the Turks would have been willing to demobilize their own troops too, although they (as well as their opponents) had repeatedly claimed not to have mobilized yet.[996] Their offers to the Greek government were more realistic, hoping to deprive the war coalition of an important partner from. On 1 October Ambassador v. Wangenheim had wired that the Porte had recognized the gravity of the situation and assumed that "Greece intended to unite with Crete."[997] Early in October, Athens had indeed planned to challenge the Porte by soon admitting representatives from Crete to the Greek Chamber. Thus, in his wire the ambassador quoted his Turkish colleague correctly by saying:
> "This circumstance would be considered by Turkey as a casus belli."[998]

The official reaction from Constantinople, however, was rather a different one: After Montenegro's declaration of war on 8 October 1912, but before that of the Greeks (17 October), the Porte sought an understanding with Greece "on the basis of Crete becoming Greek, while Greece should renounce its demands on Epirus".[999] (Were the particular interests of eminent Albanian dignitaries once more behind this astonishingly generous offer?)
The Embassy in St. Petersburg had reported about Russian Foreign Minister Sazonov's suspicion
> "that ... by surrendering Crete to Greece, Turkey would buy that state's neutrality."[1000]

This idea seemed to resemble a kite that the Greek Prime Minister Venizelos had already been accused of flying in mid September. At that time, he was said to have played with "the idea of offering Turkey the exchange of part of Thessaly for Crete."[1001] That was probably a feint. One may assume that Sazonov had provided the Greeks with this idea in order to unsettle the Turks.

But the Turkish proposal, too, was not free of traps. After all, v. Wangenheim also stated in his aforementioned wire that Foreign Minister Kiamil Pascha had made the attempt to reach an understanding (allegedly) without the knowledge of the Grand Vizier. Consequently, they both left themselves a way out according to a well-tried pattern, in order to let their own initiative fall through should things get critical and disavow their negotiating partners.
Apart from that, the Turks should have known the Greeks better, who in case of doubt would take the risk, let the bird in the hand fly away and wait for the other two in the bush. As it actually happened...

On 1 October, the day of the official mobilization, Ambassador v. Wangenheim reported from Constantinople that the Grand Vizier
> "for the first time considered the situation to be extremely grave; without doubt, this was 'un coup concerté' of the Balkan states." "There were plans to establish autonomous Serbian, Bulgarian and Greek territories and furthermore to unite Crete with Greece."[1002]

Correct and absolutely to the point – but once again this realization came much too late.
Likewise before the war began, the ambassador mentioned in addition that in view of the disadvantageous military situation of Turkey the Grand Vizier showed an emotional reaction in the council of ministers:
> "When the situation was discussed, Noradungian cried."[1003]

There have never been reports, though, about any grand vizier's sympathy during the 500-year reign of terror during the Turkish conquest or punitive campaigns in Europe involving murders, pillages and violation of women and boys.

2.)
There must be a clear distinction between the mobilization of the Balkan states and the *Russian* mobilization with its *troop deployment* on the Russo-Austrian border in Galicia. Russia in fact mobilized "its army on the borders of Austria-Hungary" (as well as Romania) immediately on the very day Montenegro declared war on Turkey on 8 October.
Did not anyone ask why Petersburg was actually able to react so quickly, although "all the other governments - meaning in Austria and Germany - were taken completely by surprise and needed weeks, if not months for this operation?
The attempt to minimize the matter by referring to a *"trial mobilization"* in a communiqué issued by Russia later, in April 1913, was designed to hide the fact that Russia was actually seriously planning a confrontation with Austria.[1004] (Compare below, sections 5.1.4 and 5.4)
(This deliberate act of deception - because it can hardly be called a mistake - is even continued in the 21st century by the British historian Hew Strachan in the special edition of the SPIEGEL I/04. See below)

For the *Balkan War,* that was soon to break out (in about ten days), a Russian mobilization would not only have been irrelevant, but also completely inappropriate, as Russia no longer planned any military involvement on the Balkans nor did Russia actually need any – at least certainly not at the Austrian border, provided that it wanted to avoid the risk of serious misunderstandings on the side of the Austrians or the Germans. The troop deployment only made sense if it was meant as a preparation for the Russian *invasion* of Austria in expectation of the Austrian occupation of the Sanjak.

That is exactly why the Russian government worked so hard - and thus made it so obvious - to trivialize the troop deployment, by which the Germans nevertheless were once more taken in.

Especially the so-called *"trial mobilization"* was originally supposed to represent the starting point of a full-scale European upheaval. Compared with this *outrageous provocation*, the cynical gaiety of the Russian foreign minister in Berlin in response to the enquiry of the journalist v. Behr about the Russian deployment on the Austrian border acquires with hindsight a particularly malicious and deceitful tinge.

There was not a single politician or statesman - except for Kaiser William II - who made an attempt to interpret the situation; only a journalist of the newspaper "Der Tag" did so:

> "Naturally everyone looks towards the east with suspicion. ... Scarcely noticed at first, the trial mobilization of parts of the Russian army (had) all of a sudden become enormously significant, and the situation ... could ... not have been seen more pessimistically."[1005]

And indeed: it could not have been more pessimistic!

In St. Petersburg, after his return from Berlin, Sazonov's numerous audacities reached another climax in a conversation with Ambassador von Pourtalès. He explained his view on the "eventualities" on the Balkans so objectively that no one would have suspected that Sazonov had set an existential snare, personally constructed for Austria in particular; for the most important aspect of the question of "whether or not the war on the Balkan Peninsula would lead to further complications", remained the position of Austria.[1006] (In the meantime, Montenegro had issued its declaration of war and therefore he had no difficulty uttering the word "war".)

An Austrian "concentration of troops at the Serbian border" would be "understandable" should the war break out, Sazonov said:

> However, "he attached great importance to a previous public announcement ...(perhaps by an official communiqué).[1006]

Well done!

In diplomatic poker this is called making the most of one's hand. He, himself, had almost been caught at wisely concealing the Russian deployment at the Austrian border, hoping to be able to hush up the real purpose of the Russian mobilization. Nevertheless, with the greatest casualness, he expressed his expectation that the Austrians should do exactly what he was not prepared to do, should they deploy at the Serbian border. The reasoning behind this expectation (in the event of a factual dispute) was, in principle, as justified as if it had been an Austro-German one. An advance announcement would

> "appease public opinion" [in Russia] ... "which still greatly mistrusted Austria and could not be dissuaded from the idea that this power wanted to take the opportunity to again occupy and usurp the Sanjak of Novi Bazar."[1006]

As already quoted above, Russia had sworn never to let itself be duped by Austria again.

With his next argument, Sazonov proves that great and successful diplomats can also make annoying blunders. (Thanks to their reputation, however, nobody would ever think of doubting or verifying their statements. Added to this, when things get critical, they skilfully work their way around any further questions, and would never admit to any irregularities anyway.). Thus:
> "Marching into Sanjak would indeed lead to Austria-Hungary's participation in the war; on Turkey's side."[1006]

It remains a mystery, where the logic was supposed to be in Sazonov's conclusion that Austria would stand beside the robbed and defeated state should it again annex a section of the European part of Turkey. The only plausible reason might be that Sazonov was looking for any trivial argument he could use as propaganda for accusations against Austria. This would allow him to pretend that the Austrian "annexing to the benefit" of Turkey, which he, himself, had proposed, meant that he had to side with the Balkan states, (allowing him, once again, to disguise the fact that he had been on their side for a long time and had set the trap himself).

Apart from that, his repeated mentioning of the Austrian invasion of the Sanjak make it appear as if he actually had to physically point out to the Austrians their desired object so that they finally realized what they had to undertake, thus giving Russia the required pretext to shut the trap and march into Austria.

The whole web of lies and the range of deceptive intrigues of the Entente were thus perfectly collusive and so effectively staged by Sazonov that decades later even eminent authorities such as Hans Herzfeld allowed the Russian foreign minister
> to vacillate uncertainly "between the need for prestige and the wish to keep the peace out of fear of responsibility".[1007]

Sorry – this is either pure euphemism or absolute gullibility.

Herzfeld doubted that the question had been conclusively answered as to whether Sazonov
> "had clearly been determined to unleash the war in the Balkans in order to re-establish Russian prestige, which had been severely damaged in 1909."

In principle, any kind of doubt is justified. In view of both the above mentioned and the following discussions, this doubt, though, can probably be dispelled. Herzfeld's instinct for a lasting uncertainty is the sign of the careful historian, but it is also not surprising in view of the fact that he was not aware of the effects of the Anglo-Russian agreement of Reval in June 1908 (or wherever and whenever).

On the other hand, he emphasizes that the *Balkan League,* meaning the Bulgaro-Serbian League of 13 March as well as the Bulgaro-Greek one of 29 May 1912,
> "would never have been formed without the decisive negotiation and encouragement of the Russian Balkan diplomacy (Hartwig in Belgrade, Nekliudow in Sofia)."[1007]

With this description, Herzfeld makes an essential contribution to explaining the reasons for the crucial role of the Russian government in enabling the formation of the Balkan League as well as in causing the Balkan War. However, he fails to draw the necessary conclusions with regard to the consequences concerning the First World War.

But then again, the revealing fact that the Russians actually agreed to accept the role of mediator for the "planned partition of Macedonia" was a fixed date for Herzfeld, too! (l.c.) All the more does it set one thinking that he does not draw the obvious, yes, inevitable conclusion concerning the imminent risk of war for Austria-Hungary and for Germany, even though he takes into consideration the memorable occasion of the above mentioned visit of the French Prime Minister Poincaré to St. Petersburg in August 1912 with its surrounding potential for danger. In Herzfeld's opinion, after Sazonov had informed Poincaré about both agreements that had led to the foundation of the Balkan League, he had "appeased" (!) the "concerned" prime minister with the argument that the Balkan League

> "contained the seed for a war not only against Turkey but also against Austria-Hungary."[1007]

Was that still not enough for Herzfeld!?

Finally, it is important to mention that Herzfeld was not alone in his considerate overestimation of the qualities of the Russian foreign minister's character. Peter Count Kielmansegg, too, for example, (due to the false information in historiography) cannot but consider Sazonov to be benevolent and trustworthy, when he writes about the July 1914 crisis:

> "...Sazonov, too, now seems to have been convinced that a European war was inevitable,"[1008]

... *a war, which Sazonov himself had for years been influentially helping to stage for the Entente.*

Neither German statesmanship nor historiography has learned anything from the shameful debacle of the *misinterpretation of the Russian mobilization in 1912.*
It is incredible.

Two years later Russia did not even need to change its tactics, - let alone its strategy: for the credulous German or German-speaking lambs it was perfectly sufficient in July 1914 to once again use the same trick of the previously successful *trial mobilization*.

Mentioning "July 1914" suggests
looking at the cause of the First World War:

In such situations, the question of which side was the first to initiate mobilization plays a fundamentally crucial role. So it did in the outbreak of the war of 1914. It was of utmost significance for the cause of the war and thus for the question of responsibility.

As the real development, however, could not remain unnoticed and the reality did not fit into the concept of the Entente, the facts were later "re-allocated" by the victorious powers – and any mention of different versions was prevented.

In this matter, even Niall Ferguson, who otherwise tries to be objective, initially vacillates between the Triple Entente and the Triple Alliance. However, he clearly records the "first espionage success" of the "German military intelligence delivering evidence of Russian mobilization", as a result of first indications reaching Berlin from Russia "that the period preparatory to war had been proclaimed on the night of 25 July 1914", and "reports that general mobilization had been ordered by the Tsar arrived in Berlin on the evening of 30 July", though it was not until the following morning that Moltke was convinced of their correctness.[1009]

This clear constellation in favour of the German wait-and-see policy is diluted by Ferguson initially using restrictions regarding the process of the Russian mobilization. Later, however, due to his source research, he cannot avoid confirming

> "that Sazonov and his colleagues tried to persuade the vacillating Tsar to agree to a full mobilization. He finally did so at 2 p.m. on 30 July ..." (l.c., p. 157)

This supports the idea that the German leaders had already been informed about Russian mobilization on the evening of 30 July, but just to be quite sure, Moltke, nevertheless, withheld confirmation until the following morning, before the Germans made their decision which depended on the conduct of Russia.

Moltke knew why he was so very carefully watching the precise point of time of the Russian mobilization, before, with a clear conscience, he called for the "defensive war": he would have been thinking about his own memorandum from 14 April 1866 in which he had written to the king "in case we mobilize (we cannot) balk at the accusation of being aggressive".[1009a] Moltke was obviously living within the Prussian code of honour without being in the slightest bit aware of the hate and perfidy of the Entente opponents. These opponents, of course, knew about the logic behind the sequencing of the Russian mobilization and the German declaration of war but were, nevertheless, striving for a preventive war while at the same time wanting to lay the blame for the war solely on the German Reich.

Furthermore, Ferguson mentions the significant detail that because of appeals by European monarchs the Russian leaders refused to

> "suspend their military operations." (l. c.) As "Russia continued to mobilize, the Germans insisted that they had no other option but to do the same. ... The <war according to schedule> between the four continental powers commenced the moment Russia decided on full mobilization." (l. c., p. 158)

None of this actually helped, because later, after war had ended, nobody was interested in the facts anymore. Nobody dared ask the question of who mobilized first. Everything was done according to the principle: power beats justice. With this power, pressure was exerted, regardless of the fact that Germany "had not started all this", in order to hold Germany alone responsible for the outbreak of the war and thus for the war itself.

One should assume that this dispute has today come to an end, even if large parts of Germany and other countries still use the old clichés. As early as 1983 Michael Stürmer had commented on the Russian mobilization (p. 371) on the basis of Peter Count Kielmannsegg

> that it "had been started quite unobtrusively already one day after the Austrian ultimatum; not unobtrusively enough to deceive the Germans, though."

In contrast to this ultimately clear and precise description of the operations at that time, Kantorowicz - who obviously disagreed with the positive outcome for Germany which arose from the objective description of the course of events - favoured introducing his interpretation of the tragic events around the crucial question of the outbreak of the war, that the Entente had been planning over so many years, with the "convincing" remark:

> "Losing track in *the world of history* and thus in pure facts shows after all the enormous overestimation of the question of the Russian mobilization..."[1010] Pure facts!

Of course – otherwise the only thing left for him to do would have been to admit that Russia, rather than Germany, had started the war. And what else could have been more convincing in Kantorowicz proving the German untruth than by turning into ridicule "history" and "pure facts".

Fritz Fischer, too, persists in contradicting what the facts show, *believing* that Russia had not announced the general mobilization before Germany. ("Weltmacht ...", p. 48) How, then, could he have judged the situation correctly!

Although on other occasions Gordon Craig has not shown any willingness to diverge from the well-worn path of the exclusive responsibility of the Germans (l. c., p. 257-260), he at least mentions the irrefutable fact that the Russian general mobilization was first, - unfortunately without drawing the logical conclusions.

Not so his colleague Hew Strachan, who in the 21st century - unimpressed by new research results, in particular from his own country - falls back into the old days by stating the following under the polemic title of "Der Krieg des Kaisers" [The War of the Kaiser]:

> "In its attempts to re-allocate the responsibility for the war, Germany later made a lot of fuss about the Russian mobilization."[1011]

Does the author want to express that the fact that Russian mobilization occurred before the German one is irrelevant? How much fuss would he have made, had the situation been the other way round? Or is he concerned that a discussion of this essential detail is prevented in order to protect England from becoming an object of criticism itself? A few lines further down:

> "For Russia mobilization did not yet mean war."

This statement is wrong and totally detached from any historical context and from international law.

But it gets even more frivolous:

> "For Germany, however, the mobilization did indeed mean war..."

Of course: German readers can be expected to swallow anything. (Kantorowicz sends his regards.) Some more examples?

> "England did not deny Germany its place in the sun."

On the contrary: precisely because Great Britain denied Germany this place, it spent decades preparing the ground for a (preventive) war against the German Reich, beginning, among others, with the Balkan War.

> "The wars in Libya and in the Balkans were waged by smaller nations who could influence the great powers by making use of their growing disagreement."

This description resembles a total misjudgement of the true relations between the Entente and the Balkan states. This author fears that this was not simply misjudging but deliberate misleading, making it part of the well-tried English concealment strategy. (Apart from that, it is very unlikely that Italy was willing to be categorized under the heading of "smaller nations".) Further on:

> "In 1912, Belgrade – as well as Sofia and Athens – (directed) the whole matter according to their wishes."

Precisely, - they directed "the whole matter" over the heads of the small nations of Russia, Great Britain and France, which were in dispute within the Entente and had been pushed aside by the Balkans!

Prof. Strachan even came up with the old hat of the Austro-Russian tug-of-war for the annexation of Bosnia and the acquisition of Constantinople. [He better should have referred to the corresponding arrangement between Russia and Britain in the frame of the Entente.] In order to get the relevant information, he could simply have consulted the documents of the former English ambassador in St. Petersburg, Arthur Nicolson, or convinced himself of these forgeries by reading George F. Kennan.

With the greatest confidence, Hew Strachan again mentions the so-called war council of Kaiser William of December 1912, without wasting a single syllable on the crucial war council, meaning the one of the English CID of August 1911. (See also section 4.4.1.2.1, Nr. 5)

> Some things don't change: the great powers, and above all the victorious powers, write their own history – and other nations' history, too.

He is not alone: Peter Zolling, also, mentions only the German (war) Council of 1912 in his book (Deutsche Geschichte, loc.cit. p. 75f) without the slightest comment. Is this typical for LSE where Zolling studied? His book leaves this impression.

Another example: In Strachan's analysis the greatest imperial power of the last centuries, i.e. England, appears but once, and, then, only befittingly in the margin: on 29 July 1914.

What Prof. Strachan's text seems to be targeted at is clearly exposed when one reads that in the fourth year of the 21st century he digs out Fritz Fischer's antiquated hypotheses again. *Those were the days when it was easy to hide behind the Fischer controversy. When reading Fischer's theses, no fair Englishman could have the slightest doubt about the Germans' sole responsibility, no, guilt, for the First World War.*

How might H. Strachan have reacted to David Stevenson's conclusion in the book "1914-1918. The First World War" (Düsseldorf 2006) in which Fritz Fischer's bizarre assertion (Germany "reaching for world power") was banned to the *land of fables*.[1011a]

Needless to add that P. Zolling also prejudicely indulges in Fischer's outmoded "Griff nach der Weltmacht" (p. 82)

At that time, the German Reich was not at all striving to become a world power. However, in spite of Great Britain's world hegemony claim, it believed it had a right to what the Reich's Chancellor had called the "place in the sun". Since there was no way England would be prepared to accept this idea, but did not want to openly admit to this refusal, the Germans were referred to as a bogy who wanted to capture and command the world. In a constant propaganda campaign, the German Reich was being accused in the public eye of exactly the type of thing the Entente members had been doing for a long time themselves.

The editors of the "SPIEGEL", too, give Fischer the chance to speak again, although this author has the impression that Fischer's account lacks the consideration of *the other great powers'* war plans and aims - *of England, in particular*. It would have been academic procedure for Fischer to adapt his theories regarding Germany's role to the policies of other combatants of the World War. Only in his anthology of *1977* does it seem as if Fischer has finally come to the conclusion that it was high time

> "to complete the contemplations, which until then had been restricted to Germany, to an overall picture of imperialism" ... "by including all states from before and during the war", ... and "present the aims and methods of imperialism of the other great states..."[1012]

Pardon! No, it is not high time, - it would have been high time long ago...

In his documentary as part of the ZdF series "History", one could have expected Guido Knopp, at least, to have an objective attitude towards Kaiser Wilhelm II. Once he had confirmed, as if it was the most natural thing in the world that in July 1914 Russia was the first state to mobilize, he should consequently have come to the logical conclusion that Germany could not be made solely guilty for the First World War – but no!
Nothing.

The SPIEGEL editors further repeat the well-known misinterpretation that Bethmann Hollweg's notorious programme of the aims of the war of September 1914 can be taken as an irrevocable proof that the Germans are responsible for the outbreak of the war, without taking into consideration that the September programme was not written until five weeks *after* the war had started. A case of anachronism.

Since a taste of Hermann Kantorowicz's barely digestible historical views have already been provided, it is indispensable to mention another one:

As late as the 1960s Kantorowicz had heedlessly tried to play down the renewed Russian troop deployment - again disguised as a so-called trial mobilization - at the Austrian border in July 1914 with trite arguments. In order to qualify the accusation of likely 'aggressive behaviour' by the Russians, he goes so far as to actually include in his "report" the statements of the ones accused: "… according to the firm conviction of the Russian military…"[1013]

Of course – if one cannot find a more suitable witness for one's preferred view, the only option is to take the statement of the accused for fact. This is logical, for if the quoted Russian officers had indeed been "guilty", they would certainly have admitted this truthfully in front of the whole world.

However, in his lengthy report, as soon as Kantorowicz cannot avoid permitting the question of a possible Russian aggressive intent, he quickly hides behind the excuse that "this question … hypothetically as well as psychologically cannot be answered with full certainty."[1013] It is as easy as that. And regarding the German argumentation, he takes an even easier way out. From the beginning he simply calls it "propaganda" as if it was the most natural thing in the world. (l. c.)

It is not astonishing that he speaks of the Russian foreign minister as the "peace-loving and reserved Sazonov". (P. 121) When it came to the critical incorporation of an eventually unavoidable accusation of Russia of also having viewed *Constantinople* as a *war target*, Kantorowicz willingly relieves the Russians of this expansionist burden: "… Once … despite Sazonov's desperate peace-keeping attempts … the European War had started, the possession of Constantinople of course became an aim of peace." (P. 122) *Of course!*

> (In exactly the same manner he juggles dialectically between not viewing "Alsace-Lorraine" as the French reason for war, but rather viewing it as the natural French aim of peace.)

Is it, indeed, legitimate to make an accusation so severe and serious as the Germans' sole guilt for the war so frivolously?

Peter Zolling goes even further: not only does he repeat without comment and without reaching any conclusions the fact of the first Russian mobilization (loc.cit. p. 78), but also he goes as far as to argue the then development had been a "German razzle-dazzle" (p. 82), and to rake up Fischer's old theory.

Is the London School for Economics and Political Science in this way of arguing, which comes closer to propaganda than to science, representative for the English faculties of history?

In order to emphasize the diversity of historical processes and their interpretation, it seems adequate in this context to quote from a report of a member of the Military Attaché Staff of the Embassy in Vienna, Lieutenant von Bülow, who was able to acquire private information about the mobilization issue from an unexpected point of view, namely the inner circle around the Tsar, - in case it was not forged.

During his former posting in the Embassy in Athens, he had been able to keep close associations with the Greek royal family. This personal relationship led to his being appointed from Vienna to Zurich in 1917 after complicated secrecy measures (which were necessary, in order to avoid nurturing the propaganda of the Entente against the Germans and the Greek King Constantine, who at that time lived in Swiss exile with his family). This appointment meant, that the Attaché was the first to contact the royal family again. Thus, in December 1917 he had several opportunities to talk to Prince Nicholas' wife, the Grand Princess Helena. Three and a half years after the outbreak of the war (and immediately after the October Revolution and Brest-Litowsk [the treaty was not signed, however, until 3 March 1918]) she was said to have still been struck by the tragic days of July and August 1914.

From her accounts Lieutenant v. Bülow learned that the Minister of War Sukhomlinov ordered the mobilization "behind everyone's back" [what she probably meant was "behind the Tsar's back, meaning 'without his approval']. Among other things v. Bülow reported:

> "The princess ... especially complained about how badly she had been deceived in Russia at the beginning of the war by unscrupulous people. Thus, she mentioned the day of the declaration of war, which she spent with the Tsar and the Tsarina in Zarskoje Seelo. In the last few days, due to the worsening situation in Europe, the atmosphere there had been rather alarming. In the eyes of the Tsar's family, this concern, however, was completely removed again by the very friendly and reassuring exchange of despatches[1014] with our most eminent Kaiser. As on the previous days, the atmosphere at the dinner on that significant evening in August was rather elated, and remained that way after dinner, too, until Grand Prince Boris was called to the telephone by the foreign office [in St. Petersburg] and returned as pale as a ghost with the message: "Germany has declared war!" Totally unaware of Sukhomlinov's unauthorized order of mobilization and believing to have been deceived by Germany, the agitation was first directed against His Majesty, as nobody knew what had really happened, and thus everyone felt deceived."[1015]

First of all: the question of the time of the *(general) mobilization* played the traditionally *overriding role in the outbreak of the war also for the Russians* (in contrast to what Kantorowicz, Fischer and many others want to believe)!

Apart from that, it seems to be quite a touching story that any naïve German would almost be inclined to believe in again ... But wasn't this more about the attempt to take the Tsar out of the line of fire and beg for fair weather, i.e. sympathy in Germany, or rather from the Kaiser?

For, soon after the October-revolution, Trotzki had several secret files of the Tsar published in the Russian press; the minutes of a secret conference on 21 February 1914 (i.e. five months before the outbreak of the war!) were printed in Maxim Gorki's paper "Nowaja Shisnj": with Foreign Minister Sazonov presiding, the operation programme of the Russian government was accepted. According to this document, the Russian reasoning for the war was clearly determined as the *conquest of Constantinople and the Straits*. But above all: what is more significant here is the fact that this aim could not be reached without a European war against Germany. In his own hand writing Tsar Nicholas II had post-scripted the original document with the following approval:

> "I fully agree with the decisions of this counsel."[1016]

Now then, Grand Princess Helena, what about the evil Minister of War, Sukhomlinov? (Back to the chronology of the Balkan League.)

5.1.4 William II sees through the trap of the Entente

As mentioned above, in 1912 Sazonov talked to the German Ambassador in Petersburg about parameters (which were basically elements of his trap for Austria) as reservedly as if they did not exist at all. At the same time, he immediately took the opportunity to establish a fall-back position that was, however, just as dangerous for Austria and

Germany as his original basic idea. That is to say; he would prefer Austria to adopt a different position:

> "Even if troops from Serbia or Montenegro should enter the territory of Sandzak in the course of the war" [how elegantly reserved: "enter"], Austria-Hungary would have no reason to be concerned that one of these states could take up its position there permanently", [He cannot be serious!] "as the whole of Europe has guaranteed to maintain the status quo."[1017]

Was there not a single German or Austrian politician or senior official who was irritated by this aggressive cynicism? Did no one anticipate the danger? It would have been sufficient for them to use their own brain, but they did not even reflect, let alone think ahead. Only one of them remained on the 'qui vive'.

In the relevant record for the Kaiser, in which Sazonov's idea was further enhanced by the following addition from another report of the same kind...

> "if the Serbs took up their position in Sandzak, (Austria could) drive them out of there by force, that is to say, as executor of the powers' expressed intent not to tolerate any territorial changes,"

...William added to his exclamation "Mephisto!" (describing the Russian foreign minister and his plan perfectly) the following marginal note:

> "and then the all-Slavs would release such a scandal in Russia that Russia would be forced to take action anyway."[1018]

Thus, William II gave a precise description of the real constellation. The Kaiser obviously knew the general opinion in Russia and the Russian leaders' way of thinking better than his representative there and than the chancellor. He was fully and clearly aware of the anti-German aggressiveness of the pan-Slavism, the Russian Orthodox Church and the relevant press.

Considering how fast Austria and Germany had to adapt themselves to the power of facts after the victories of the Balkan states – keeping in mind that the whole of the Entente plan had been aimed precisely at this outcome, even though Russia, France and England tried to create the impression that they were extremely unwilling to accept this plan – one cannot but appreciate without reservation William's feeling for political relations. For, if the Kaiser had agreed to this truly "Mephistophelian" plan, the automatism constructed by the Entente would, as he predicted, ('Russia would have to proceed then anyway') already have taken effect in 1912 and would have resulted in a great European war.

After Bismarck's death, which other German-speaking politician lived up to William's ability to assess each political constellation both systematically and analytically? Chancellor von Bülow did, but he had resigned in 1909. The question, however, whether his high standing abroad and his level-headed diplomacy would have been sufficient to resist the iron will of an imperialist group in England, that tried to destroy the Wilhelmine German Empire through war, will remain historical speculation.

> By the way: the compelling and justified mentioning of additionally positive, partly brilliant qualities of Kaiser William II negates neither his repeated unchecked boasting nor the dangerous effect of these attitudes on politicians of other countries, - especially if they were interested in using his often tactless blustering against him and the German Reich.

Robert K. Massie writes for instance that the First Lord of the Admiralty, Sir John Fisher, was also known for his tactless behaviour; furthermore, he describes him as a "ruthless character" and as unscrupulous. (l. c., p. 404 ff.)

Kaiser William II was in no way like that. Nothing could have been further from the nature of this man, who possessed such a high degree of decency and human dignity.

But victors will be honoured, - and they let the losers be condemned, and the deceived losers will be condemned even more vigorously, so that, if possible, any attempt of elucidation can already be nipped in the bud.

When von Kiderlen-Wächter wrote (in the above mentioned record) in an incomprehensibly appeasing manner that it was "in no way surprising" that the Balkan states had "just ignored the Russian orders", as four countries "were much more difficult to control once they had formed a union, however temporary, than each state individually", although they had "explicitly been ordered" "not to take any crucial steps without permission from Petersburg", Kaiser William noted down on the margin:

> "and the [permission] would only have been given if Russia had been "ready" against us and had thought that the right moment had come to launch its attack!"[1019]

And it is this second marginal note which leads to the very centre of the Balkan conflict, which had been planned by Russia, France and England as a preparation and reasoning for a European war, which makes the Kaiser's remark historically significant: The Kaiser had seen through the strategy of the Entente. The state secretary had not.

As the Balkan states, however, took "the crucial step" anyway, Russian permission "to launch an attack" must have been given. Without permission, which was in fact an *order*, the small Balkan Kingdoms would obviously never have risked their existence for such an adventure.

That was not all. The *actual highlight* is still to come.

The perfect clarity of Kaiser William's political understanding is particularly emphasized by the fact that he linked his comment to a report that at first sight seems almost irrelevant: in chapter 5.1.3.2 the visit of the Russian Grand Prince Nicolai in Paris is mentioned, which the King of Montenegro tried to make out as harmless by relating it to his son's journey to France. The German Ambassador in Constantinople wrote about this incident that his Austrian colleague, Margrave Pallavicini, accused Russia "of having been informed about the Parisian conferences of the Balkan representatives."[1020]

In the telegraphic directive (wire decree) no. 74 of 4 October 1912, which was especially intended as information for the embassies in Vienna and Petersburg, the Reich Chancellery had prepared quotes of the reports and - due to their significance - the relevant marginal notes made by the Kaiser. According to these notes, Kaiser William had inferred from the incident involving the Russian Grand Prince that Nicolai had not only "been informed about the intentions of the Balkan states", but had even presided over the conferences in Paris (as he adds from an unnamed source in Rome).

Then William outlines the Russian strategy in the following words:

- *"Austria will launch an attack against Serbia,*
- *which will make Russia intervene,*
- *and thus trigger the casus foederis for us,*
- *upon which Gaul should immediately attack us from behind."*[1021]

To the ears of us future generations all this sounds too familiar, even boring. However, in contrast to all the other political leaders in Berlin and Vienna the Kaiser had already seen these connections during the crisis of 1912, i. e. 95 years ago. (So, the strict principles of the Iron Chancellor had left their mark on him after all.)

It was just that *(behind his back)* his uncle Edward, both the King of England and brother of his mother "Vicky" and son of Queen Victoria (who died in William's arms

and not in her son's arms), was going to be standing as an active leader on the side of his opponents, who were planning (and executing) the war, - for the decent Prussian William, it was too outrageous to imagine such a degree of falseness and hatred.
But this was precisely what happened, as the Amsterdam "Standard" wrote on 1 December 1917 basing it on a number of secret files of the Tsar, which had been published in revolutionary Petersburg. A few days later, the "Norddeutsche Allgemeine Zeitung" quoted the text of the Dutch newspaper:

> It was assumed that the Entente had "agreed upon their course of action in case of war long before 1914. But however ruthless one had imagined the greed of the alliance" [the Entente] "no one had remotely dared to think that England, France, Italy and Russia - at a time when the German Kaiser was received in London as well as in Petersburg in the most friendly manner – would literally conspire behind his back in order to attack Germany in due time."[1022]
> "Attack!"

Do we need more definite proof?

In this context, Bismarck might have referred to the fatal influence of the former Danish Princess Alexandra, the wife of the King of Great Britain. Is it possible that William thought of that, too?
The author tends to doubt this, as despite his occasional unbearable boasting and other tactless behaviour, words like honour and loyalty were not just empty phrases for the Kaiser, - qualities that he (unfortunately) also granted everybody else.
In order to be able to honour the exceptional quality of the Kaiser's analysis properly, one must consider the fact that he had already come to his conclusion on 4 October 1912; i.e. a few days after the coordinated mobilization of the four Balkan states on 1 October, but in fact, before Montenegro's declaration of war on 8 October. And certainly before the war actually started with the announcement of the other three declarations of war on 17 October 1912.
In contrast to this, the general public learned about these connections just one year later as a result of a (Bulgarian) indiscretion through a press release of the text of the Bulgaro-Greek agreement of the formation of the Balkan League as well the military convention on the conquest of Macedonia, which will be dealt with in the chronological course of this chapter. (See chapter 5.4 and in particular 5.4.2)

> (Apart from that, the above mentioned scenario of the Entente inciting Austria to launch an attack, and thus start a great European war, is not yet complete, as will be explained later.)

And let it be mentioned now that there are further opportunities for documenting *Kaiser William's unconditional willingness to keep the peace* – despite his occasional martial language – which Chancellor v. Bülow often referred to in his "Denkwürdigkeiten" (e.g., p. 198). In his biography of William II, Christian Count v. Krockow also gives evidence of this same quality of the German Kaiser, and he does not fail to remind his readers that it was exactly this quality that made certain German circles consider him a nuisance. Thus, for example, the Kaiser had briefly added to the quote of the Russian military attaché in a report from Constantinople "if Austria attacked Serbia":

> "There is no reason for that."[1021]

Not even Kaiser Franz Josef, let alone Foreign Minister Count Berchtold, would have dared to consider ignoring this verdict.)
Even Gordon Craig, who otherwise only restricts himself to showing William II in a negative light (p. 252-258) admits that

> "even the Emperor, with his lack of self-control, ... surely never wanted a war." (l. c., p. 365)

Only Mr v. Bethmann H. considered himself authorized to change a directive of the Kaiser that had been aimed at keeping the peace.
Only a man who "knew nothing about foreign policy"[1023], as Prince Bülow wrote later, could act that way. (This represents v. Bülow's general opinion about his successor, which is not exactly flattering,[1024] – while both R. K. Massie and Michael Stürmer are less critical of v. Bethmann Hollweg.)
Was von Bethmann ever held responsible for his policy? Or did he at least receive one of the countless heaps of scorn that were poured upon William II? He would have deserved it.
It is rather unfortunate that von Kiderlen did not share the Kaiser's scepticism towards the person and the policy of the Russian Foreign Minister, but succumbed to Sazonov's friendly charm like many others. William II, on the other hand, wrote in the margin the rather apt addition to Sazonov's characterization that he was "false" and "cunning".[1021]
This false, but cunning, minister could return from Berlin to Petersburg early in October 1912, convinced of having properly led the Germans and the Austrians by the nose. For the Kaiser's discoveries had had no effect, as the political leaders in Berlin did not understand them and thus did not exploit them in any way.
Or did they? More of this later.

Therefore, after his return, Sazonov could take as long as he wanted to sound the bell for his next phase, i.e. to give the three Balkan states of Serbia, Bulgaria and Greece the signal *to declare war on Turkey*.
It is only at this point that it dawns on the observer, why of all states it was Montenegro – rather than, as everyone had expected, Bulgaria – that was given the task of being the first to declare war: as the talkative King of Montenegro (who, as described above, could also be discreet), carried out this step, he appeared almost theatrical to the Triple Alliance and much less explosive than if one of the other three Kingdoms had started the war.
Further proof of Sazonov's meticulous General Staff operation.
Whoever finds this too straightforward, remember the joint, meaning coordinated, mobilization on 1 October. An Austrian newspaper commented on 5 October:

> "We see a plan arranged down to the smallest detail. The allied Balkan states mobilized simultaneously, marched simultaneously and operated like a unity organized by a single leader not discernible to the outside, as if they were of one mind and body."[1025]

They surely did not have a single body, - but they were indeed of one mind: the Russian mind, or that of the Entente.
Such evident conspicuousness set one or any other alert contemporary thinking, and thus, a journalist of the "Tägliche Rundschau" asked sceptically:

> "Isn't it possible that the Tsar's Empire is in fact the great manipulator, having the Balkan groups dance at its bidding..?"[1026] And he goes on: "..because it .. wants to redeem the legacy of Peter the Great and secure the free passage to the Mediterranean?"

This addition is in no way unfounded: after all, the "Neue Freie Presse" of the same day reminded of the occasion when Tsar Nicholas (I) virtuously

> "asked of the British Ambassador Seymour that England should share the legacy of the sick man with him."[1027]
> "Such signs indicate that secret threads connected Russia with the Slavic Balkan states." "That, however, would mean that the prospects of Turkey were rather bleak, if not hopeless." ... "That way, at least, the European territory" [of Turkey] "would fall prey to the Slavic states."[1028]

In view of all the other uncertainties, this was a precise prediction.
However, so outrageous was the actual core of the Entente's plan, or the resultant plan, namely the staging of a world war, that obviously nobody even dared to think of it, let alone make it public.
Whether it was planned or not: the paper nevertheless issued a warning that had, in fact, been hanging around since 1871: it was obvious

> "that together with Austria-Hungary the German government spares neither trouble nor expense to stifle or at least restrict in good time the fire flaring up in the Balkans, which could easily develop into the dreaded 'global fire'. (l. c.)

As mentioned above, *Montenegro* had declared *war on Turkey* on 8 October. As a curiosity, the author would like to add that the ministers' residence in Cetinje reported how the King of Montenegro financed the war expenses: at least 300,000 crowns came from the "Russian quarterly subsidy". Already two weeks before, information from Cetinje that put "the Russian policy in a strange, ambiguous light, even for the credulous Count Berchtold, had been made public in Vienna:

> "Three days before the declaration of war [of Montenegro] half a million roubles (have) arrived from Russia ..."[1029]

Another 1 to 1.5 mill. crowns were still available from the Austrian loan, and also the Bulgarian envoy regarded payments from his government as "likely".
Furthermore, Mr von Eckart (but only ten days after the war broke out) was able to confirm the correct date of the Bulgaro-Serbian treaty of March 1912.[1030] In contrast to that, the date of the Bulgaro-Greek agreement (of May) remained unknown; July was just a guess.

> "On 13 October", [the three remaining allies] "had delivered identical notes in Constantinople and to the Great Powers, in which they demanded from Turkey a complex reform programme within its European territories. When on 15 October Turkey did not reply to these notes and called back its representatives from the Balkan states, Bulgaria, Serbia and Greece also declared war on Turkey on 17 October."[1031]

The *First Balkan War* had broken out. (Continued in ch. 5.2)

In this context, it is useful to refer once more to Fischer's "Krieg der Illusionen" (p. 215 ff.):
After many other inconsistencies, Fischer assumed that the declarations of war on Turkey by the three allies on 17 October 1912 would remain unsupported by Russia, - more than that: he knew so little of the intense relations between them and Russia that he insinuated wrongly that Russia had even tried to prevent the four league allies from fighting a war against Turkey. Further on, he (correctly) writes that Russia nevertheless wanted to prevent interventions (from other powers) against the four Balkan states. If this controversial policy represents a mystery in itself, it remains completely inexplicable how Fischer can claim that Russia had tried to prevent the "Great Powers" (i.e. also England and France?) from intervening.
Russia's special relations and - in the background - also those of the Entente to the Balkan states with their (subordinate) aim against Turkish Macedonia, but with the main force directed against Austria and thus against Germany, are completely ignored by Fischer and thus had to lead to grave misjudgements of the assessment of guilt or innocence, respectively partial guilt, regarding the outbreak of the First World War. But even today, Fischer is - of course - highly respected as a reliable source by British historians, such as John Röhl and Hew Strachan. (See above)

5.1.5 The German Kaiser, the Greek Crown Prince and Macedonia

The number of Kaiser William's marginal notes (in the records of the Auswärtiges Amt alone) are legion. Innumerable treatises have been produced about their content and interpretation. However, the author has rarely noticed any texts by the Kaiser himself (apart from letters). Could it be possible that of all countries *Macedonia* that, just like the whole Balkans, in Bismarck's days was so alien to the German Reich [there is as little need at the end of this book as there was at the beginning, to illustrate this point by quoting Bismarck's famous saying (about the bones of any Prussian grenadier)] – that this Macedonia, of all states, or rather of all the remaining European provinces of Turkey, would become the subject of a separate *directive* of the German Kaiser?

In fact, neither Macedonia, nor any other Balkan state, is mentioned once in the multiple-page document, - and yet, this region was doubtlessly the reason, and even the immediate cause, for him to write down his thoughts about the Turkish Balkans. The reason for William to leave specific names out of his concept was, of course, not ignorance or political caution but was rather for psychological reasons: he might not have considered it opportune to specify his very general political ideas about the structure of the Balkans by giving names. Therefore, he certainly did not give the name of the state which actually caused his change of attitude and thus the presentation of his policies.

The Kaiser, in fact, never mentioned Macedonia because in his – unfortunately it is necessary to call it by its name – antiquated, i.e. still monarchist world view (what other view could he possibly have?) it was practically non-existent. The failure to mention it was by no means meant as undervaluation or depreciation, but it was a fact that the Macedonians did not live in an acknowledged state, and thus the German Reich, as all the other Great Powers at that time, only perceived the Macedonians as being at their disposal. For reasons of pedagogic strategy, William did not give the name that was *really* important to him and that was the actual reason for him to go to the trouble of properly elaborating; it would be more precise to say that he suppressed the name, or even practically concealed it, in order to hide the true origins of his interest – his *personal* interest – from the public, or rather from the administration. This was obviously successful. No one was supposed to gather a deeper purpose from his text, with which he eventually intended to deliver a general political message. Or, in other words, he simply did not want to announce which *private motives* had led him to suddenly support the cause of the Balkans. After all, his exposé contains a, for him, rather "revolutionary" idea:

His renunciation of befriended Turkey and turning to the Christian-Orthodox Balkans!

In this context, though, it is important to consider Fritz Fischer's remark that WilliamII
"anyway had a negative attitude towards the Young Turks, because for him they were the symbol of the despicable 'revolution',"[1032]

"His friend" the Sultan, on the other hand, was still in office.

There is no need to talk around the matter any longer: Kaiser William's personal motive was, of course, *Greece*. After disclosing this name, it is only a short way to inferring that only Prince Constantine can have been the cause of this turn of his. And who stood behind, or rather next to - or even in front of -, the heir to the throne? Of course, ... the Crown Princess, William's sister Sophie! This is the only explanation.

So what was it all about?

There is no need to repeat what a prominent role Germany played behind Austria-Hungary in the historical development before the outbreak of the First World War. But even in the Balkan conflict itself, although not recognizable at first sight, Germany was decisively involved – even if one disregarded, in this context, the disastrous combination of the fate of Germany with that of Austria regarding Bosnia. This role became rather obvious in the German relations to Turkey, particularly in the relations of the imperial family to Turkey, meaning the Sultan. For many decades, the German Reich and its emperors had endowed their relations towards the Ottoman Empire a formidable role within the German foreign policy; never destructive or to the detriment of third parties (in contrast to France, which had formed alliances with the Sultan since the 16th century in order to annex German territories in the western parts of the German Reich by wilfully attacking or by tricking with the so-called "réunions"), but out of conviction about the important, especially economic, function of Turkey in South-East Europe as well as in the Near East.

In view of the presumptuous way Great Britain ruled over a vast empire, the occasional boasting speeches of the Kaiser, e.g. about the German relations to the Islamic world, should be seen more as a naive attempt to pretend that, if he could not be a "ruler", he was, at least, a *friend* of a great commonwealth. In that respect, his swaggering speeches would have been similar to those, which, according to Henry Cord Meyer, English politicians blazoned out more often and in a much blunter way. In this context, it is also important to name Admiral Philip Howard Colomb, mentioned by Meyer[1033], against whose agitations the Kaiser and Tirpitz appeared almost harmless. Lloyd George's notorious threatening speech against Germany during the 2nd Moroccan crisis on 21 July 1911 in Mansion House, which is mentioned by N. Ferguson[1034] and many others, did not exactly contribute much to keeping the peace either. Here, on the other hand, one would have to agree with Fritz Fischer's opinion that with this speech on foreign affairs England clearly came out of its otherwise preferred shell.[1035]

It was London's intention to spare France a humiliation and at the same time demonstrate the significant role of the French Entente-partner in the English concept of balance, thus leaving no doubt that an English rather than a German hegemonical stance was intended. The success confirmed that England had taken the right course of action: Kaiser William and Chancellor v. Bethmann H. did indeed draw back, when they had to admit their underestimation of the gravity of the pro-French policy of England.[1036]

Nevertheless, there must have been at least a dent, if not a breach in the good relations between Kaiser William II and Turkey. For, in his report to the Chancellor of 2 October from Rominten (that had more resemblance to a private service note), Jensch took up the eloquent complaint:

"I have repeatedly tried to explain to His Majesty" [Tiens, tiens!] "that maintaining and establishing the state of Turkey in Europe is indeed of interest to us. His Majesty, however, ... lost interest in Turkey a while ago."[1037]

Evidently, these circumstances were correctly reported by Baron v. Jensch, there is no doubt about that. But it seems that he was not aware of the reasons that led the Kaiser to change his attitude "a while ago", as William withheld them even from his liaison man to the chancellery.

By the way, in the same letter the envoy - probably unaware - confirmed the high standard of the Kaiser's political intuition when he wrote:

"H. M. ... is very critical of Russia and England ... and doubts the Great Powers' honest intentions to restrain the Balkan fire."[1037]

Brilliant! The Kaiser was right after all. Despite the general mobilization of the Balkan Kingdoms Mr v. Jensch was still of a different opinion. Today we ask ourselves: How could he *not* doubt the "honest intention" of the Entente?
Once everything had been revealed, did the Baron or any other member of the Kaiser's or the government's staff eventually mention it to him again or, to call it by its proper name, apologize or at least ask for understanding?

Indirectly, the Kaiser's interest in the Balkan war was closely connected with *Macedonia*, but directly it was exclusively connected with *Greece*. His change of sympathy can only be explained against the background of his personal relations to the Greek Crown Prince, his brother-in-law Constantine (or Tino to him and his family). In the years when the development of the Balkan League was dragging on with minor success, the husband of William's sister must have managed to convince the German Kaiser to give up the principle of sanctity of the status quo in the interest of a re-Europeanisation and division of the remaining Turkish provinces and to relocate his sympathies from Turkey to the Balkan states: meaning *Greece*.
It is inconceivable that the two men could have considered that the expansion aimed at by Greece could be a solution without a war, because after 500 years of experience with the Turks, and after the last 230 years in particular, this was simply impossible. Thus, the Greek appeal to the imperial brother-in-law to agree to a violent solution to the otherwise endlessly smouldering problem of the European provinces under the Turkish crescent was probably just directed from *the soldier Constantine to the soldier William*. For in the imperial directive there are - and it can only be interpreted this way - hints at these (with respect) simple military doctrines that are, after all, hundreds or even thousands of years old. For the Kaiser actually wrote:

"The situation, as it is now, must definitely lead to a clash of the Balkan states with the remaining Turks in Europe. (Ch. 2, p. 3)
As this cannot be solved peacefully, there will be fighting. (Ch. 3, p. 4) And:
It is all right if a war breaks out. That way, the Balkan states will show what they are capable of, and whether they have a right to exist. If they defeat the Turks decisively, they were right, and they deserve a certain reward. If they are defeated, they will shrink and keep the peace for a long time, and the territorial question will be dropped." (Ch. 4, p.5)[1038]

However, the likeable, handsome Constantine, who had undergone a Prussian education with a German private tutor and in the German army must have taken exactly this last chain of arguments as reason enough to place his honour as a soldier to the benefit of the whole Greek army and thus, at the same time, challenge the Kaiser's honour as a soldier, whereby the decision is taken through action on the battlefield, in which "the stronger secures victory". It is rather obvious that William's text is characterized by his sympathy for the anti-Turkish plan developed by Constantine, when he writes:

The *will of the people*, who want the war for territorial expansion, is not sufficiently taken into consideration [oh, look at that, the good monarch!]; otherwise the people would probably be outraged and

"surrender the rulers to the revolution. ... For they are ... rather likely to be expelled or even murdered by the population", which includes the "eventual fall of the Balkan Dynasties". (Page 1-3)[1039]

William's fear was in no way out of the blue. Its source can be tracked precisely, - it remains in the family, so to say: A few days before, the Chargé d'affaires in Athens, v. Biel, telegraphed that he had been "ordered to the Crown Princess":

> "The noble lady is in a rather depressed mood", as the Greek army "was insufficiently prepared for war." And then the crucial sentences: "In case of a defeat of Greece, a revolution is sure to follow." "The noble lady finally expressed the urgent wish that we should, just in case, send battleship for her protection."[1040]

No wonder then that her brother at home was so concerned and pronounced himself against a revolutionary solution (by the Young Turks). He would neither let his brother-in-law, the future heir to the Greek King George, nor his beloved sister suffer this, as they would then probably never rise to the honour of a ... Unthinkable! Therefore, he preferred to (secretly) put his good relations to the Sultan at risk. And he did so consistently. For on 5 October an Austrian newspaper wrote about the dangers of the impending war and stated:

> "The fate that urges the Turks to this war is logical, because they have not been able to catch up with European civilization and have missed the opportunity of making citizens out of their subjects and of giving them the benefits of an ordered legal certainty." Kaiser William's lapidary marginal note: "Crete's connection to Greece is also logical."[1041]

Thus, times, attitudes and interests can change. Blood is thicker than water, - and particularly so in royal houses.

With this line of argumentation, William II by no means took up an extreme position. Rather, it was nearly identical with the policy of the English, as described by Ambassador von Kühlmann in a conversation with Foreign Secretary Sir Edward Grey, according to which the solution to the problem of Crete

> "(could) either consist of an affiliation with Greece ... or autonomy for Crete."[1042]

The difference lies in William's turning away from the Sultan, and thus from Turkey, - which, for England, was only of functional interest.

It is about time once again to remember Bismarck's ingenious foreign policy (setting aside all the inexcusable mistakes he had made in German national and cultural policy which had led to serious disruptions in the German Reich, and in the economic policy – take for instance the failed protective duty policy and the Lombard policy – that caused a disastrous deterioration of the German relations to the one state that Bismarck was especially concerned about: Russia). Did the Iron Chancellor in 1888 not warn Sophie's brother, the recently appointed Kaiser in a report (which was almost too elaborate for the small country of Greece that one tended to smile upon in the chronology of the introductory chapter) of the unforeseeable consequences of a German involvement in Greek matters through Princess Sophie marrying into the Royal House in Athens?

Bismarck had foreseen this.

With any other opponent of the future Greek King Constantine, it would have been possible to limit the negative consequences, - but with a prime minister like Venizelos...!?

Now the time had come. Germany was right in the middle of the Balkan intrigues.

To the benefit of the Kaiser, one limit has to be set. It was part of the concept of William II that his readiness to first and foremost give Greece a free hand against Turkish Macedonia had an absolute limit, even against the Crown Prince. The four Balkan

Kingdoms might have been willing to wage a war against Turkey to achieve their imperialistic aims; but they had to bear the risk of a defeat themselves, for the Kaiser categorically rejected an intervention by the Great Powers, including, and particularly so, Germany and Austria (see also the text of his directive). Because of the strict policy of secrecy it was impossible for the Kaiser to know that the principles of the Entente members were by no means as stand-fast as his. For example, as has already been discussed, they guaranteed the Balkan states their military support in a secret agreement!

William probably had detailed information about the standard policy that Christian territory, once liberated from the Turkish yoke, should never again fall under the suzerainty of the Sultan. Eventually, he had been able to read in many reports from his representatives in the Balkans and in the press that the Balkan states had always relied upon the idea that they "could only gain from victories, but could hardly lose anything from defeats."[1043] State Secretary von Kiderlen had phrased this in a directive to the embassy in London:

"... The whole world agreed that it was unthinkable that Christian provinces that had once torn themselves free from Turkey, ... should again be under Turkish rule."[1044]

At the Congress of Berlin, on the other hand, - at England's and Austria's urging - some provinces had in fact been returned to the Ottoman Empire! This means that completely different, stronger interests must have been able to exert themselves over normal "customs and practices". Nevertheless, for the Kaiser - in contrast e. g. to the Tsar - *his* war against Turkey was out of the question. This conclusion is indeed significant, as a victory of the Balkan states against Turkey, meaning the "liberation" and annexation of Macedonia, had by no means been guaranteed initially. (How could he have known that, instead, it had been guaranteed by the Entente!)

Russia, for example, was apprehensive concerning its promise that

"in case of a Bulgarian defeat, it would eventually be forced to an armed intervention for the sake of the relations."

Despite the Russian concern or rather because of the promised military help, the Bulgarians, on their part, would not

"refrain from starting a war", because they might say to themselves "that without the loss of its whole prestige on the Balkans, Russia cannot abandon to their fate the Slavic states, which were once protected and established by Russia itself."[1045]

Doesn't this argumentation evoke the memory of the cunning Serbian King Milan?

It is inevitable to conclude: the Kaiser's directive also contains mistakes – and thus misjudgements.

1.
To explain his attitude in favour of a military campaign led by Greece (and the other Balkan states) against the still Turkish Macedonia, William even made use of examples from Prussian history on its way to the unification of the Reich:

"Just as little as we allowed others to interfere with our 'justified development' in '64, '66 and '70, I cannot and do not want to hinder others or interfere with their affairs, now."[1046]

This argumentation of the Kaiser was improper, as he overlooked the difference between his grandfather's - if late - unification of the German nations that belonged together ethnically, linguistically, culturally, historically and politically, and the conquering and plundering military campaigns of the Balkan states leading to the annexation of Macedonia; to which they did not have any rightful claim at all.

The explanation is rather simple: it is so easy to see through the nature of William II that, even without much empathy, it is clear that with his historical reminiscence the Kaiser made the clumsy (and thus foredoomed) attempt to justify to himself his brother-in-law Constantine's planned military campaign against Macedonia. It cannot be ruled out, though, that Constantine also made use of untruthful arguments in front of the Kaiser, - similar to what the Greek governments did at that time, and are still doing today.

2.

Judging from what his text says, William at that time assumed that the Entente-powers had seriously considered preventing the Balkan war, as they repeatedly claimed, and they were even supposed to have thought about using violence against the Balkan states (in order to enforce this concept). Among other things, this is revealed by a long marginal note of the Kaiser on a press-clipping of 1 October 1912.[1047] But this assertion of the Entente, as presented in detail above, was by no means in accordance with the truth. Instead, it was a red herring, and in this case the Kaiser was again the victim. Furthermore, William seemed to be so filled with the hope that his sister's husband would, as a successful commander, win this war for Greece (he would doubtless have felt the same way, had his sister Sophie been married to any other crown prince, e.g. of Romania or Italy etc., provided that he would have liked him as much) that he strongly refused to deny his brother-in-law – and thus at the same time the other Balkan states – the disposition of the territories that were to be annexed, as was said in Russian (as well as French and English) statements in pretence. (As already mentioned in another context, William was much too honest, and in contrast to his uncle Edward, he made no bones about it.) There is, for example, a wire from the embassy in Belgrade (no. 36 of 25 October 1912), regarding the situation at the end of the first week of the war, which

> "reports that the Serbs had captured the whole Sandzak of Novi Pazar".

In addition to that, there is a memo in the files stating clearly that the Kaiser had noted down in the wire's margin

> "that he would absolutely vote against any attempt of denying the Balkan League the conquered Turkish territory."[1048]

That way, the other Balkan states, too, were able to benefit from Kaiser William's sympathy towards Greece, and respectively towards Sophie & Co.
To the detriment of Macedonia.

This definite determination of the German Kaiser made clear that an Austrian attack on Serbia was out of the question. (One and a half years later, in summer 1914, the Kaiser's willingness to keep the peace, no longer had a regulative effect on Austria's and v. Bethmann's unauthorized behaviour!)

The *irony* in this was that the following can almost certainly be assumed: neither did Kaiser William anticipate that the Entente-powers had exactly the same attitude in favour of Greece (and the other three Balkan states) - considering that they always claimed the opposite (which again the very Germanic Kaiser believed) -, nor did they know that the Kaiser in this respect had become their closest ally. (Unless the Greek Crown Prince had from the beginning driven on two tracks. But this can only be examined once the states concerned have opened their own archives.)

Particularly this constellation reveals the tragedy for the Macedonians: the fate of Macedonia was actually determined by decisions of the German Kaiser that were based purely on his family or private matters.
> This means that *Germany today* has a duty to accept special political responsibility and stewardship for Macedonia, - although very much less than the former Entente members have.

If the course of history was straightforward and easy to see through, which it is not, the Macedonians would have to mark as one of the (many) black days in Macedonian history that one day in April 1888, when Princess Sophie of Hohenzollern met the Greek Crown Prince Constantine.

It is certainly impossible to prove that William II would have supported autonomy for Macedonia, Thrace etc. if he had *not* felt bound to the Greek dynasty. It is even highly unlikely, since, being ignorant of the true situation on the Balkans, he would probably *not* have acted to the benefit of Macedonia. But it can by no means be ruled out that a situation could have arisen where the Reich government, or any other Great Power, would have initiated support for Macedonia, - just like Austria in the imminent Balkan war manages to clear the conquered Albanian Skutari of Montenegro's military forces. (See below)

Apart from that, there is every reason to believe that the Kaiser – who without his sister Sophie and his brother-in-law Constantine would have had no argument to abandon the Sultan and expose him to a war of aggression – for these overriding reasons alone, would have put his foot down against the planned Balkan war! In this case, the First Balkan War (regardless of the Russian secret agreement with Serbia and Bulgaria and regardless of the respective part of the Anglo-Russian understanding of Reval) would *not* have broken out in October 1912 any more than it did in the 34 years since the Congress of Berlin. Since no Entente in the world would have started a war against the German Reich, just in order to induce the Kaiser to allow the Balkan states to march against Turkey and thus annex Macedonian and Thracian territory. In this case the Entente would have had to wait to be able to entice the Balkan states in another way, with another bait into their coalition against Germany and Austria, and find another reason to start the full war.

That way, the remaining Christian nations would still have remained under Turkish rule, but their final destiny would never have been irreversibly determined then by conquest and annexation by the Bulgarians, the Greeks and the Serbs, - at least as far as the Thracians, Epirians and the Macedonians in Greek Aegean-Macedonia and in the Bulgarian Pirin-Macedonia were concerned.

> The *history of Macedonia* and South-East Europe, or the Central Balkans, would have taken a totally *different turn.*

The Entente was interested in more than just the Balkan League and Macedonia. Its aim was a European war against the German Reich and Austria-Hungary. To achieve that, it desperately needed the participation of he Balkan Kingdoms, - and this was only to get by sacrificing Thrace, Macedonia and the Epirus. Therefore, the Balkan League was so important for the Entente as an indispensable instrument for its plans in the South-East – and in the centre of Europe.

5.2. The First Balkan War
5.2.1 The end of the territorial status quo – and of the Berlin Treaty

One week after the beginning of the war and the victorious course of the battles in favour of the Balkan powers, Paris was still mainly pleading for the "maintenance of the territorial status quo" and was allegedly considering the eventual use of "instruments of power rather than powerful words" on the part of the European Great Powers. Only London initiated its "verbal" retreat. The British Foreign Minister Grey, in fact, told the German Ambassador:

> "It must be considered as a supreme principle to maintain the territorial status quo of Turkey *by all means*."[1049] (Author's italics)

Despite all uncertainty, there was again just one realist on the side of the Germans (and the Austrians), - and it was always the same one. William II noted down on the margin of this report: "No longer possible!"[1050]

One could not comment on the situation at that time in a more precise and concise way. The false reports and tricks were repeated over and over again by the members of the Entente like a mantra, until Mr Sazonov thought (that now, since the victories of the Balkan states had become obvious on all battle fields) the time was right to present to the German states - that were not even amazed - the next phase. This phase was the opposite of what he had previously claimed, - of course on the basis of "a strong inner conviction", as the journalist v. Behr had put it then. But he proceeded patiently and without haste: step by step. That way, he did not ask too much of his opponents by making unreasonable approaches. Instead, he made a restriction that was almost inviting and inspired confidence:

> "Should [Russian] public opinion after a Turkish defeat demand territorial expansions for the Balkan states, it will simply get the reply that Russia was not in a position to help them achieve such aims. Only Europe could do that, and Russia had declared its solidarity in this issue."[1051]

Of course – after all, it was supposed to seem as if this was an all-European initiative rather than one taken by the Entente alone.

Thus, ten days after the outbreak of the war, Ambassador v. Kühlmann, for example, reported following a conversation with FM Grey that meanwhile London had also promptly gone along with the new line:

> "No change of whatever nature of the territorial conditions on the Balkans could in any way affect the English interests so much that an intervention of the English power could be justified, except, of course, the question of Constantinople. The English public would never agree to the use of English instruments of power, in order to relieve the Balkan states of their conquests. Constantinople was a European question of utmost importance. He did not take into consideration the possibility of its being dealt with now, as he certainly believed that all powers would wish to see the status quo there maintained."[1052]

Grey already knew that, even before the outbreak of the Balkan war, but who would have been so rude as to remind the English of the contrary promises they had only recently made!

Towards the end of October, Paris also expressed feigned consent

> "that one way or other, ... one would be forced to abandon the plan of the maintenance of the status quo."[1053]

Even though, these were only crocodile tears, William II noted down "correct" on the margin. After all, the French position fitted his concept of favouring his Greek brother-in-law.

The Kaiser cannot have been presented with the report on the same day by the major and aide-de-camp in the staff of the military attaché of the Embassy in Vienna, Count Kageneck, who had written:

> "A defeat by the Balkan states of the Turkish armies, ... which were also on the main war stage in Thrace, would render a maintenance of the 'status quo' on the Balkans impossible."[1054]

Von Kageneck, too, was bound to have considered this eventuality at a time when his English and Russian colleagues were still going on about the maintenance of the territorial status quo.

Even the Austrian Foreign Minister Berchtold succumbed to the purring tones, "tones of friendly disposition towards Austria", that even came from Serbia, "unheard in this way for a long time." Thus, he seemed to seamlessly throw out an old Austrian principle:

> "We definitely have to reckon with a territorial expansion of Serbia."[1055]

Some things don't take long!

The Austrian press as well began "to bury the status quo in the Balkans;" and wrote elsewhere:

> "The empty promises of the status quo ... have ... become pointless. Europe has to get used to the idea of fundamental changes in the Orient..."[1056]

Back in October, on mobilization day, the "Neue Freie Presse" in Vienna had already expressed a recommendation to treat the Balkan states carefully:

> "Wasting our soldiers' lives and our taxpayers' money, in order to forcibly take the hope for a better future from the oppressed nations in Macedonia and Albania, would constitute a vile relapse into the aberrations of Prince Clemens Metternich, which have burdened the Austrian name with so much anger."[1057]

The "better future" for Macedonia and Albania was just an illusion, the insight in Metternich's aberrations and the burden for Austria was extremely late, albeit very true.

At first sight, one hardly notices that these relatively simple statements at the end of the territorial status quo mark a *historical turning-point* in the existence of several forgotten Christian nations. They are symptomatic for the whole of European politics at that time (and today), and they pass judgement on the fate of a large part of the Macedonian population for the next 30 years and of an even larger part (in the Greek and Bulgarian part of Macedonia) for ever. The readiness to abolish the status quo policy also sanctioned the destruction of the results of the Congress of Berlin by the European dynasties, - that is, not only by the ones of the Entente-powers, but also by the imperial courts of the two German states.

5.2.2 Solun/Saloniki – a Greek city?

Although the German Embassy in Athens only had bad news to tell about the condition of the Greek army, the insufficient equipment, the deficient means of transport, and even about the lack of the soldiers' enthusiasm, the chargé d'affaires was able to report to everyone's great surprise by the end of October that

> "the events ... (have been) progressing fast and Greece ... (has) listed one success after the other."[1058]

Bulgaria, too, which carried the main burden of the war, was at first victorious, when it occupied Thrace and besieged Adrianople. But then the Bulgarian advance was stopped before the Tshataldsha line, the Turkish stronghold around Greater Constantinople (on the basis of the Byzantine fortresses). Serbia took Skopje, Bitola, Durazzo and the province of Sandzak with Novi Pazar. To the Bulgarians' great annoyance, Greece additionally conquered Epirus and occupied *Saloniki* on its own account and outside what had been agreed.

Saloniki, the old Macedonian *Solun*, not only played a major role in the political and military struggle during the last third of the 19th century and at the beginning of the 20th century. Although it fell into Greek hands in 1913, it still represented a trouble spot in the new relations between Macedonia and Greece at the end of the 20th century, after 1991.

When a few Macedonian squallers in their enthusiasm for the newly achieved independence of the Republic of Macedonia also called out for the return of the old Slavic city of Solun, it would perhaps have been understandable if the Greeks had shown a certain degree of agitation, - but surely not the *hysteria* that broke out in the whole of Greece after that; keeping in mind that such a faux pas was exposed to ridicule in view of the democratic constitution of the Republic of Macedonia as well as the protection of the EU and the NATO for Greece. The Greek government, on the other hand, welcomed such notes of discord, as they enabled the government - together with the Orthodox Church - to make an example of the unloved new state in their neighbourhood, (with which they had not yet arranged themselves as comfortably as with communist Yugoslavia in the past, although *the Republic of Macedonia of today has born the same name within the same borders* since the foundation of the federal state of Yugoslavia in 1944). Greece has discredited Macedonia in front of the world where-ever possible and at the same time has stirred up public opinion in favour of the "Greek" Saloniki.

On the other hand, the Greeks consider a comparison with their own 150 years of calling for the return of Constantinople into the empire of the Hellenists as inappropriate: after all, those calls were directed at Turkey, which makes them something totally different. An example taken from that time will illustrate this: After Crown Prince Constantine succeeded in conquering the Albanian South-Epirus from the Turks, an indescribable jubilation broke out in Athens. In absence of the "Generalissimo"[1059], the Greek people at least wanted to give their ovations to the "victorious prince's" wife. In an assembly in front of Crown Princess Sophie's palace, the mayor closed his address with cheers – and with the words:

"And then in Constantinople."[1060]

On this occasion, the president of the Association of Epirus in Athens also happened to express "the gratitude of the people of Epirus to his liberator and future king", - in Athenian eyes the unbeatable and irrefutable proof for the whole world that Epirus must "always" have been Greek! But every time after 1991 that the media in the Republic of Macedonia showed photographs of the famous "white tower" of the former Macedonian Solun or a map with the historic borders of Macedonia before 1912, an (organised) storm of national indignation broke out in Greece. What an outrageous provocation of the Macedonians in their "Republic of Skopje" to abuse the picture of an edifice from a city of the sublime Hellas, which did not have the least connection with a succession state of Yugoslavia!

> This *terrible simplification* practically cries out for some quotations from the relevant documents. (See also the following chapters 5.2.2.1 and 5.2.2.2)

After the Greek propaganda, one was supposed to think - then as well as today - that, with Saloniki, Greece had conquered, or even re-conquered, a Greek city. But what was the real picture?

In a secret mission, the High Porte had sent a delegation to Athens, consisting of the previous "Turkish" representative of Saloniki, Honeos, (his mandate had expired after the Greek conquest of the city) and the journalist Vokraftyros, in order to "sound out" the attitude of the Greek government towards a
> "future confederation of the Balkan states under the hegemony of the Sultan."[1061]

Unconvincable! The fact that the Sultan and his Grand Vizier still cherished the grotesque hope that the admission of Turkey into the Balkan League was possible, as long as "Turkey" ... yielded "to the harsh peace terms",[1062] can only be explained by a total loss of a sense of reality. The Grand Vizier still dreamed of the "creation of a Balkan League with Turkey", although in the meantime the Bulgarians had even begun negotiations with the Porte about the evacuation of Adrianople.[1063] The Greek Prime Minister, the cunning Crete Venizelos, notified the Turkish envoy anyway by putting him off. Why should he reject a Turkish plan that would never be put into practice anyway? Honeos returned with the impression that
> "the exaggerated demands of Bulgaria and Serbia impeded the peace agreement, which was desired by the saturated Greece."[1064]

Pardon?
Greece was already "*saturated*" with the conquest of South-Epirus and Saloniki? This can only mean that the territorial expansion to (South-)Epirus and Saloniki with its harbour was a totally sufficient war aim for the Greeks.
No mention of the rest of Macedonia!

Another surprising case of irony in history. At that time, a few days before the armistice (on 3 December 1912) and before the beginning of the two London Balkan Conferences on 18 December 1912, Greece did not anticipate a second Balkan war, which would bring Greece even more spoils in the form of foreign land, - meaning half of the Macedonian territory and in addition West-Thrace!

This, on the other hand, leads to the conclusion that even in this state of development there was still a chance for *Macedonian autonomy* and that the Macedonians could, in this case, have kept a larger part of their country than in 1944 or 1991, - albeit without Saloniki.

It was completely in line with the previous Greek strategy when furthermore the former Turkish representative Honeos returned to Constantinople with the information that it would be in the interest of Greece, should Turkey achieve a weakening of these enemies on the Bulgarian and Serbian front through incessant resistance![1064]

Mr. Honeos' impression
> "that there was no agreement at all among the Balkan states about the future territorial expansions;" (l. c.) cannot in the least astonish.
>
> *This development has been foreseen for decades by everyone, without exception: all statesmen of the region as well as all foreign observers of the Great Powers. There was no other possibility: for none of the neighbouring states possessed a single piece of Macedonia, therefore, they fought to get hold of a preferably large share of this foreign territory.*

It was this disagreement about the division that led to the continuation of the conflict (in the Second Balkan War) the following year.
But it had not yet come to that.
There was no need to explain to the Greeks that the taking of Saloniki was an international injustice. One was not allowed to talk about it, though, (this strategy has re-

mained the same until this very hour.) Athens increased its efforts to make the world believe that this injustice was, in fact, in accordance with Greek law by using all sorts of tricks.

> *One hundred – more precisely: ninety – years seem swept away. One might think the time had stood still then. Today's attempted deceit of the Greeks regarding the enforcement of unjustified imperialist claims for Macedonia with its name and its history are very similar to, or even identical with, the ones of the past.*

This was the reason why the anti-Macedonian propaganda machine in Greece ran so smoothly after 1990 under Prime Minister Mitsotakis. One had been practicing for a long time!

5.2.2.1 Solun as a Germano-Greek source of friction

In the light of these efforts, Athens was also not about to shrink back from abuse. Bismarck was among the few who, 25 years earlier, had already expressed that he considered the Greeks capable of any irregularity. In this affair between Germany and Greece, the Greeks finally began to confirm Bismarck's analysis.
1.)
After the Greek capture of Saloniki, the Embassy in Athens reported on false news that had reached the Greek press, in which following the capture the Kaiser was said to have sent his sister, the Greek Crown Princess Sophie, a telegram containing "three cheers". On the one hand, such "praise" on a private basis from the soldier William to the soldier Constantine would have been typical of the Kaiser. On the other hand, in view of the present critical situation, the author only needs to quote the monarch himself, who in a report had once remarked on a similar allegation regarding his person: "No, he is not such a donkey!"
Nevertheless, the Greek Foreign Minister Coromilas continued the notoriously self-perpetuating diplomatic process by treating as a fact the false report he had possibly even started himself. At a suitable occasion he even sold this story as true to, of all people, the German Ambassador - and it was only with him that his plan would work out - stating:

> "He was glad to be able to gather from this telegram that Germany acknowledged the Greeks as the rulers of Saloniki."[1065]

Since the Greeks themselves knew best that in the course of the last 2000-3000 years they had never been the "rulers of Saloniki", they needed the testimony of a sufficiently respected, and at the same time respectable great power, upon which they could actually impose this trick, and thus provide themselves with the missing legitimisation to the rest of the world. They could rely on the fact that Kaiser William II considered himself to be above paying them back in the same way and thus, possibly, bringing his relatives of the Greek Royal House in Athens into discredit through a public correction. (Bismarck had also foreseen such dilemmas.)
Envoy v. Quadt, who "of course protested violently against this misrepresentation", did, in fact, see through the Greek tactics. However, even then, he added, almost resignedly:

> "All these small nuances show the means with which Greece attempts to achieve its aims."[1065]

Until today this description holds true.
So far so bad. But the "donkey business" was not without consequence.

A few weeks later, a report from Constantinople revealed that, this time, the Greek government was totally innocent. William had indeed sent his sister such a telegram. The circumstances that brought this information to light were especially embarrassing. The ambassador had a denial published in the "Ottoman Lloyd" immediately after the appearance of this rumour, but soon after this he had to learn from his Austrian colleague, Margrave Pallavicini, that

> "the wife of the local Spanish Ambassador, who lives in Athens, wrote in a letter posted there that the Greek Crown Princess herself had shown her His Majesty's congratulation telegram."[1066]

Reading this report, the Kaiser (as usual, only temporarily) became seriously angry. But he did not want to blame his sister, Sophie, even though she would have deserved the scolding. Therefore, the poor ambassador in Athens got the full blow, while at the same time William tried to shift the blame from himself:

> "If my ambassador is so stupid as to foolishly pass on my coded congratulations, i.e. which were <u>meant to be kept secret</u> – otherwise I would not have sent them via the anyway indiscrete Auswärtiges Amt – so that they become public, let him go to the devil or run off to Guatemala." (l. c.)

However, the Kaiser himself had to bear the actual damage, because the Turks, who were still befriended (and would soon also be allied!) with Germany, could have drawn their conclusions from William's sympathies for his brother-in-law's victory, which had, after all, led to their defeat. On the other hand, the Turks knew of the family relations for a long time – and in this respect they were in no way narrow-minded.

And the Greeks? Did they make use of the benefit of their innocence to gain prestige? At first they were patient, but they could not resist making use of this mistake and damaging the Germans at a time when no one would have believed a denial any more. Thus, a few months later, in the first year of the war in 1914, two telegrams were published in the international press. The first contained a boasting report from the Kaiser about German victories over the Russians, and the other one contained wishes for the recovery of his severely ill brother-in-law "Dino" [isn't that commendable?] – and this without any proof of them having been written by the Kaiser nor of them having arrived at his sister, (who had meanwhile become) the Greek Queen Sophie.[1067]

2.)
The Greeks' propaganda machinery was still working at full steam: the dynastic relations of Greece with the German Imperial House were to be squeezed out like a lemon. (And again Bismarck ...) Two weeks later, Baron v. Wangenheim reported (from Constantinople) that the "Crown Princess of Greece was to spend the winter in Saloniki". Von Wangenhem's clear conclusion:

> "Greece obviously intends to construct a German interest in leaving Saloniki with Greece."[1068]

Of course, only a (false) "construction" could help the Greeks, as they were unable to prove any natural, historical, lawful, ethnic or otherwise political right to Saloniki.

The prudent ambassador had carefully suggested a "timely change of place" to the Crown Princess; in vain, the Greek government remained firm.
But neither did von Wangenheim give up. Two weeks later (after New Year 1913), his wife sent an (open) telegram to the Crown Princess in Saloniki, offering her to accompany her to Berlin, where she

> "was expected at His Majesty the Kaiser's birthday in his jubilee year" [25 years of reign].

Mrs v. Wangenheim, however, only received the answer: "Journey unfortunately impossible", which led the ambassador to the conclusion

"that very strong influence was exercised upon Her Majesty, in order to tie her to Saloniki."[1069]

At that time, "Saloniki remaining with Greece" was by no means secure. As mentioned above, a sufficiently strong objection by the (or one of the) Great Powers might have induced Greece to return its spoils – just as it had done several times before in the past decades.

> The history of Macedonia would have taken a totally different course – maybe even the history of Serbia, Austria and the Balkans and, who knows, Europe, too.

But, in 1913, the threads that led to the European catastrophe of 1914 had long been made into ropes and fastened so tight that the question: "Saloniki – Greek or not?" remained only marginal in the context of the situation all over the Balkans and, above all, Europe. To the Macedonians' disadvantage …

5.2.2.2 King George I and Saloniki

It hardly needs mentioning that working with false reports was not an exception (nor was it restricted to Greece). The following intrigue may serve as an additional example.

Since, in the First Balkan War the Greek Crown Prince Constantine had begun – after severe set-backs – to distinguish himself through shining victories, the desire arose in the political scene of Athens, and in army circles in particular, for King George to resign in favour of his son. (Only Prime Minister Venizelos uttered that he would have preferred governing with the "convenient" King to cooperating with the eager Crown Prince, as the latter would almost have been tantamount to a sharing of power.) Although George I had often juggled with the instrument of resignation during the decades of his reign, his mind was not set on it at the time of the Greek military success. For him this was an hour of victory (after all, Saloniki had already been conquered) since, in fact, he had politically prepared this successs himself in permanent, persistent struggle with the governments of all European Great Powers using his monarchic family ties.

Regardless of all this, the news emerged in the Greek press that "after the fall of Jannina" in Saloniki [where, as the reader will recall, his son, Prince Nicholas, resided as governor[1070]],

> "the King had given a dinner party and pronounced a toast saying that the only means of rewarding the Crown Prince for His good behaviour was to let Him ascend the throne of Greece, whereas He, the King, would resign from state business."[1071]

It is true that FM Coromilas had to deny this news in front of the German Ambassador when asked, but interested circles had given the now 68-year-old king a clear signal – and, in view of the events that were still to come, almost a deadline.

Talking about *Jannina:* the kings fortune in war did not, however, smile upon the Crown Prince in the same way. Exactly one month before, the envoy still had to report that

> "a bad state of affairs" … would [not: could] "arise from the circumstance that the Crown Prince will probably return from Jannina without having achieved anything."[1072]

On this occasion, Envoy v. Quadt also reported of the uncertainty in Athens whether or not the London Conference would "reclaim" Saloniki from Greece.

In this case, the joy of the Greeks over the conquered Solun would have proved rash. The envoy had already compiled a detailed and, as far as can be judged, an exhaustive analysis of the "possibilities .. for the future of Saloniki", which culminated in the summary:
> "Either Saloniki will become Greek or Bulgarian or Serbian, or Saloniki will become internationalised or autonomous."[1073]

The doubts of the Greeks were reasonable despite their military success. In case Athens "won the bid" [like at a cattle market], the envoy had assumed two definite consequences:
> We "must not expect Saloniki's hinterland to become Greek, too." But even without this hinterland "Bulgaria would take the first opportunity offered... to snatch away Saloniki from the Greeks." And that would "infallibly ... mean a war between Greece and Bulgaria."[1073] (This actually happened later.)

The Greek Ambassador in Vienna, von Streit, saw this in a totally different light. In a fundamental political conversation in February 1913, he explained to the German Ambassador, von Tshirshky, the Greek request regarding Saloniki and "the islands". In doing so, he used the same arguments - as if he had taken them from a standard catalogue -, and sometimes even the same phrasing, as one of his predecessors, Count Ypsilanti, had used when talking to the Austrian politicians 30 years before (1883). (Compare above ch. 2.3.3)

The solution to the problem of the islands was
> "of eminent importance for the country and a permanent guarantee of peaceful conditions in the Near East."[1074]

This audacious claim reminds one of the objections which had already been raised by Foreign Minister Delyannis at the Congress of Berlin.
> "Leaving those islands in the possession of Turkey would create a furnace for permanent unrest. Following the example of Crete, the people of these islands would keep on working with all possible means for their annexation into the much larger Greece."

This is followed by a well-tried but false promise:
> "If Greece obtained these islands, any reason for hostilities between Greece and Turkey would cease to exist," ... "but otherwise a thorn would remain, and these islands would collaborate with the Greeks at any time and would always be ready for possible operations against Turkey."

The change between flattery and threat, too, seems to have been practised by the Greek Ministry of Foreign Affairs following a certain pattern:
> "Turkey would not be capable of preventing this." ... "Nor would the Entente powers interfere, and thus violent measures of the Triple Alliance powers would eventually become necessary, which, in view of the opposition of the Entente, might lead to very dangerous situations."

Finally, like a record which is stuck, the following melody is repeated, which Ypsilanti had already played in the past regarding the Ottoman Empire:
> "For Germany, however, he considered it important to be on good terms with the Greek element, which it will need desperately in the pursuit of its interests in Asia Minor."

He obviously wanted to say that Greece in turn would not need Germany in such a way. Although this might sound strange: this was indeed fact. For in the long term, i.e. beyond the limited Balkan war, the Entente powers, as already mentioned several times, attached great importance to a preferably complete *encirclement of the two German states*. With its long coasts and great number of harbours, it was necessary to win Greece for the Entente, especially if the Entente could not be sure of the Ottoman Empire, - which was exactly what happened. At the London Conferences, the Entente held several trump cards they could use, in order to place Greece under obligation to thank the Entente. This can lead to the conclusion that the chances for a fulfilment of the territorial aspirations of the Greeks were extremely favourable.

Who in London, Paris or Petersburg took any interest in the fact that this horse-trading was to the detriment of Thrace, Epirus and Macedonia?

Regarding Saloniki, the envoy told Mr von Tshirshky that he did not believe

> "that Bulgaria regarded their possession of Saloniki as vital." "The Bulgarians were a nation of peasants ... As lords of Saloniki they would introduce a strict, but intolerant rule and make life for the other nationalities and foreign tradesmen as difficult as possible. The Greeks were, after all, a nation of tradesmen; they understood the conditions required for international trade much better."

Then von Streit continued almost verbatim like his famous predecessor:

> "If Greece attaches crucial importance to the possession of this city, this emerges from the consideration that, in the future, Greece will have to bury all its dreams of a 'Greater Greece' with Constantinople as a centre. With the crushing of Turkey and the advance of the Slavic element to the Aegean Sea" [compare Ypsilanti] "this hope, too, will be gone forever. Greece is fully aware that what it has not achieved yet, it will actually never achieve."

The most interesting part, though, was the revealing description, the envoy gave of the city that Greece later got into the habit of presenting as "historically Greek", after having longed for it and then winning it quite unexpectedly:

> "Saloniki was neither a Bulgarian nor a Serbian city, and even if a large number of Jews were living there, the whole character and spirit of the city was still Greek."[1074]

The envoy did not even mention by the bye that surely Greeks were living there, too, which was doubtless the case. He preferred concentrating on "character and spirit" – a hardly convincing explanation for the Greek right to an annexation of the Macedonian city.

But even this shortened description of Saloniki did not hold out in reality. For what did the German Consulate in Saloniki report in May 1914, when King Constantine (together with his family) paid the new Greek city of Saloniki an informative visit after the end of the Balkan wars at the beginning of a first consolidation phase?

> "Saloniki will probably change its Jewish-Turkish character soon. Compared to former times, more Greek is spoken and it seems that everyone is eager to learn this national language. King Constantine is said to have looked for a long time at the improvement plans presented to him and expressed that they should be put into practice soon, to help the city lose its Turkish character."[1075]

Can one wish for a better chief witness than the Greek King? Regarding the "Jewish-Turkish" character of the city, Consul Walter had already reported from Saloniki a few weeks after the end of the Second Balkan War (see ch. 5.5) that

> "a large number of rich Jewish and Turkish families ... are (leaving) the country out of fear of the extremely prevalent dreadful concomitants of murder and robbery." It is feared that there may be more "fights between Turks and Greeks, Albanians and Serbs."

It is said that Turkey received financial support from the non-Turkish Islamic world [History repeating itself !] and from Jewish high finance for the "war of the movement aimed at the autonomy" of West-Thrace and Macedonia,

> "in order to prevent Saloniki, this gathering point of an ancient Jewish population, from remaining Greek."[1076]

Supporting this, a specific number: Edgar Hösch mentions in his book "Geschichte des Balkans" (C. H. Beck, München 2004, pg. 23) that Saloniki had 120.000 inhabitants at the end of the 19 th century, only 14.000 of which were Greeks.

Occasionally, one gets the impression of a free reign of history:
Or what else could it mean when King George, six months before the 50-year anniversary of his reign and after his decades of persistent and at times (as already mentioned in another chapter) almost pushing efforts on a dynastic level in favour of Greece, in the hour of his triumph, or at least partial triumph (as he could not know anything about the Second Balkan War and the Greek conquest of half of Macedonia) meets such a sudden end, in a city symbolising the achievement of an important aim, *Saloniki*.
In Saloniki on 18 March 1913, King George I was the victim of an assassination.[1077]

Was the Greek military in such a hurry to heave the Crown Prince to the throne? The authorities were able to present the assassin, but there was no way of changing the fact that he had a Greek name. No problem: with impunity, he could be identified as a Bulgarian subject, and thus suspicion as well as hatred was drawn towards the next potential enemy, Bulgaria. Someone even claimed to remember that two weeks before the murder of the King the (Macedonian) revolutionary, *Jane Sandanski*, had already announced an event "which would mess up all combinations."[1078]
The revolutionary jargon might have been true. And the Macedonians, who had fought in the Balkan war with the one belligerent party that had made them the greatest false promises regarding their autonomy, had reason enough to be angry with the Greek King, - but did they know anything about his activities at all, as not even the members of the Greek parliament were always informed about George's "travelling-diplomacy"? And which "combinations", that would have changed the fate of Macedonia, were "messed up" by his death?
No, the scam rather resembled a mode of distraction carried out by those who really had a plausible motif for the deed...

>Apart from that, Sandanski was called Bulgarian (in order to turn the Greek's anger on Sofia), although he was Macedonian. This fact can be taken as another confirmation of Torsten Szobrie's (re)discovered explanation (compare the discussion in chapter 1.2.2) that at the time of the century-long Bulgaro-Greek church dispute it was customary to call all Christians/Rajah who were not Greek, "Bulgarians".

5.2.3 The intermezzo between armistice and the Peace Treaty of London

It was during those weeks that the public began to understand the deep sigh that the "Wiener Sonn- und Montagszeitung" had made when writing: in the past there were discussions

> "that the Balkans had united, in order to protect themselves from foreign attack plans," "at present it seems as if ... one tends to be searching for the trouble spot that is affecting the whole of Europe in the Balkan states."[1079]

This analysis of the situation at that time could not have been more precise.
On 3rd December 1912, an armistice was eventually achieved. One of the conferences that were consequently convened in London

> "consisted of delegates from Turkey, Serbia, Bulgaria, Greece and Montenegro, and the other one summoned the ambassadors of the European Great Powers under the chairmanship of the English Foreign Minister Sir Edward Grey."[1080]

The difficult negotiations lasted several months. However, the bone of contention, the *"question of Macedonia"*, remained *untouched*. Of course, the Macedonians, who were directly affected, were again not present. Dynastic agreements had taken care to prevent their attendance. And why should the powers, which all agreed on giving each Balkan state its share of the Macedonian bear's fur, actually permit the Macedonians' participation in the first place? To sanction their death sentence? Thus, Stojcevski can rightly complain that

> "at important negotiations, the Macedonians ... were passed over by the great powers."[1081]

However, the negotiations in London failed after the Young Turks' coup d'état, who refused "to hand over the still defended Adrianople."

After the fights resumed on 3rd February 1913

> "the last Turkish bastions of Joannina, Adrianople and Skutari (which after 14 days under Austrian pressure the Montenegrins had to leave again) fell."[1082]

As one can see, with the help of a protest against Greece regarding Saloniki, a liberation (of the city) might have been successful!

As far as *Jannina* was concerned, there was a peculiarity. It has been mentioned further above that initially the city had successfully resisted the Greek siege. Now surprisingly, to the great joy of the Greeks, Jannina had fallen! The German Embassy was able to offer an explanation for this unexpected turn of events, which was, however, carefully declared as a rumour. (But where there is smoke, ...)

> "The unexpected handing over of Jannina has been explained by the rumour that its commanding officer had been given the order for this from Constantinople. It is said that Turkey was still trying to win [the sympathy of] Greece, eventually in order to aggravate the Bulgaro-Greek conflict."[1083]

(Until a few years ago, Sultan Hamid had always greatly succeeded in doing so.) This news enhanced the arising impression of new coalitions and of a totally changed course of the frontline in the imminent new conflict. Neither did the opposition remain inactive: even before the above mentioned armistice, Bulgaria had offered Turkey an "offence and defence alliance", in order to obtain privileges from this step. In return Sofia would undertake to

> "abandon interest in the unresolved questions between Turkey and the remaining allies."[1084]

The other members of the Balkan League had always feared such treacherousness, - even though none of them was actually free of such disloyalties and thus had no reason to reproach any of the others. Therefore, it only seemed logical, when the German Embassy in Athens reported that "the bitterness towards the Bulgarians ... (was) constantly increasing."[1085] This was, among other things, reflected in relevant newspaper articles. The Embassy actually reported one of them. The "Ephemeris" wrote:

> "If the Greeks believe that the Bulgarians are the Greeks' allies, they are very much mistaken. The Bulgarians are a greater enemy than the Turks or any other nation." Mr von Quadt had heard similar opinions coming from private sources: "It is actually preposterous that the Greeks are fighting with the Bulgarians against Turkey. It would be much more natural ... for the Greeks to fight with Turkey against the Bulgarians."[1085]

This was indeed about to happen in the near future.

Two further opinions regarding the deteriorating Bulgaro-Greek relations:

> "The hatred against the Bulgarians in Greece can hardly be described", the correspondent of "Nowoje Wremja" said to the German Ambassador in Constantinople in April 1913, so that "a war of the Greeks against the Bulgarians would be much more popular" than the one against the Turks.[1086]

The possibility of such a combination was also mentioned by Prince Heinrich of Prussia in a letter to his brother William (II) from Athens, where he had been delegated to represent the German Kaiser at King George's funeral. He had added that Crown Prince Constantine had taken this eventuality into consideration and added that he "did not have to fear such a war, as his troops were now well trained and accustomed to fighting." (Constantine did not even rule out the possibility of a Greek alliance with Turkey.)[1087]

This war, in fact, started three months later.

On 30 May 1913, the great powers succeeded in negotiating *a peace treaty in London*, which later, when a second Balkan war started – and there was eventually a final peace treaty (in Bucharest) - would have to be called a "preliminary" peace treaty. Turkey lost all territory west and north of the Enos-Midia line (i.e. beginning at the mouth of the Maritza on the Aegean coast in a curve up to the town of Midia on the Black Sea, - meaning also Albania, whose independence was enforced against Russia by Austria, Germany and Italy) and the Aegean islands. This, however, thwarted the hopes of Serbia and Montenegro of an access to the Adriatic Sea. Only East-Thrace and Constantinople remained Turkish.[1088]

As far as *Albania* is concerned, Niall Ferguson reminds us that in the autumn of 1912, the Austrian FM Count Berchtold demanded an independent Albania, which, as "a surprise to the Albanians", actually became reality.[1089]

The regret in Europe over the Turkish losses seemed to keep itself within limits.
Even before the outbreak of the war the "Westminster Gazette" wrote:

"The Turks have tried to reform themselves and evidently failed ... and the Macedonian chaos still continues. ... If Turkey cannot govern decently and keep order in her European provinces, Turkish power is doomed in those regions."[1090]

But at least the paper concedes:

"The European powers, too, had failed to enforce the promises made in the Treaty of Berlin and thus solve the in fact feasible problem of providing Macedonia with a proper government," adding ironically: "Every experienced Indian official of the border-administration would have been able to cope with such a problem within a few months."

To the disadvantage of the quoted Indian official, one has to say that he would have failed just the same if he had been forced to assert himself against the delaying resistance and the constant empty promises of the Greek King, who permanently tried to convince his relatives that the Greeks, respectively the Balkans, would solve these problems themselves – i.e. more precisely: in their own interest.

The "Westminster Gazette" continued criticizing the obvious fact that:

"Some (Balkan states) have ... bitterly disappointed us. ... The Bulgarians and the Greeks with their desires and the ruthless warfare of their gangs in Macedonia." (l. c.)

This insight is supported by an article in the Austrian "Reichspost":

"The pro-Turkish diplomacy of Europe did Turkey a bad service when it ... tried to avoid any vigorous action, any strong pressure on Turkey, in the question of reforms."[1091]

At the end of the month of October, when crucial military successes had already been achieved but peace negotiations had not even begun, the Austrian "Neue Freie Presse" commented on the military *situation of Turkey* in an unusually prosaic, and almost lyrical, form and thus delivered an impressive description (excerpts):

- "The wan dusk of doom is spreading over Constantinople."
- "In the government palaces, the Pashas are whispering quietly of the lost battle and of the defencelessness of the country that has lost all strength and hope of support."
- "The army (is) a heap of rubble and the Empire is crushed."

- "A lost campaign is not a passing misfortune as it used to be."
- "This empire is dying because it did not know how to adapt to a time that is forced to anticipate the reawakening and the upswing of the national awareness. Turkey is going to pieces and is withering away because it managed to satisfy neither the spiritual nor the economic needs of the subdued nations, brought misery upon them and did not even offer them the usual legal certainty, and, of these people, those who have relatives the other side of the border, are regarded as the strongest obstacle for progress."
- "Reflection is needed in the face of this pile of fragments, which is the site of the ruins of a state which once held the world at terror..."[1092]

The resignation in the surviving, inwardly ruined and now also outwardly decaying empire was so profound that in clear view of their general backwardness - if discernible -, the Turks did not even look for someone to blame and let heads roll as they used to in the past. (Again "hüsün"?)

Even more so did France enjoy the Turkish defeat:

"The admiration for the victorious offensive of the armies of the Balkan League ... is clearly accompanied by a certain satisfaction that the Turkish army leaders, who had been trained by the Germans, are obviously not up to their task. With particular complacency it is pointed out that the Balkan Slav's artillery, which has proved their superiority so brilliantly, was of French origin, whereas the Turkish artillery was made by Krupp."[1093]

Later, in Gallipoli, another member of the Entente (GB) cost dearly this pride.

On the other hand it seems that the triumph of the cannon factory of Creusot over that of Krupp was not completely unjustified, as even Chancellor v. Bülow occasionally remarked that despite all "shining advantages" of the Prussian army, the old-fashioned code of honour had led to "prejudice and self-deceptions".[1094]

Despite the defeat of Turkey, their neighbouring states, i.e. the former fellow sufferers under the scimitar of the Ottoman Empire, were still feeling the horror of the past in their bones so strongly that even months after the Balkan wars, there were discussions in the chancelleries, of whether or not "Turkey would go to war against Greece."[1095]

The threat of Turkish re-conquests was regarded as even greater when Bulgaria with its revision plans became known as a potential coalition partner of Turkey.

Therefore, it is no surprise that in the great struggle following 1914, both states found themselves as allies on the side of the two German (minus Italy) central powers.

It was even thought

"possible that the Macedonian committees have come to an agreement with the committee of the Young Turks." (l. c.)

Thus, another chance for the Macedonian autonomy emerged.

Little prophetic talent is needed, however, to imply that the Young Turks would once more have let the Macedonians down at the crucial moment, as they had already done in their first revolution in 1908.

How deep the "star of the crescent" had already sunk, is revealed among other things by a report of Ambassador v. Wangenheim: in Constantinople on 27 October 1912, the council of ministers had "decided upon the eventual *transfer of the Khalifat* to a city in Asia Minor."[1096] This decision was a result of the misjudgement of the aims of the European powers regarding the Golden Horn and the Straits.

(On the other hand, the distrust of the High Porte - and the opposing frust of the Europeans - was not unjustified, as experience had shown.)

Mark Mazower wrote about the time after the (preliminary) Peace of London on 30 May 1913 by quoting the American Frederick Moore:

Now "[the Turk] will return to Asia, where he came from centuries ago, hardly altered by the contact with the European nations – that he left the way he had found them, in a medieval state." And in the words of the Polish historian Oskar Halecki he writes: "The Ottoman Empire – whose origin, tradition and religion is totally unknown to its European subjects – did by no means (let) them rise in a new type of culture, ... but (brought) them nothing ... but a degrading foreign rule interrupting their participation in European history for almost four hundred years."[1097]

First and foremost, Halecki probably thought of the renaissance, the reformation and the enlightenment.

Even "The Times" rose to higher realms of deep reflections about the *historical dimension* of the operations on the Balkans. There might not be a better way of expressing what moved the era at that time:

"The year 1912 witnessed the extinction of the Asian rule in Europe and will be remembered thus forever." "And an end has been put to a ... régime of tyranny and oppression."[1098]

5.3 Another sensation: Russia pursues a *new* Balkan League

After the above mentioned armistice on 3 December 1912 interrupted the First Balkan War, which had erupted two months before, the Russians immediately resumed their attempts at looking for other allies, - or at least neutralize the one or the other uncertain candidate before the big fight began.

The Russian Tsar sent his brother, Grand Prince Nicolai Mikhailovich, to *Romania,* in order to present the Field Marshal's baton to King Carol in commemoration of the jointly achieved victory of Plevna on 11 December 1877 35 years before. (This time, the Tsar "only" sent his brother ahead; a few months later, in June 1914, when the Entente undertook every effort to alienate Romania from the Triple Alliance, Tsar Nicholas travelled to Constanza personally to visit King Carol, bringing along considerable "compensations, which were meant to corrupt the Hohenzoller".[1099] With success.) The Field Marshal's baton was a great honour for the Romanian King. But Carol was familiar with such dubious gifts. Under the impression of his experiences, Kaiser William also noted down on the margin of the wire, in which this honour was described as a Russian "sign of confidence in Romania":

"Bluff. Simply .... hoping to paralyse Romania."[1100]

And when Envoy von Waldthausen quoted the Romanian Foreign Minister Majorescu, stating that he

"considered an agreement between Germany, Austria and Russia to be for the best", because the latter was suitable "as a bridge between the Triple Entente and the Triple Alliance",

William's whole bitterness arising from the disappointments with Tsar Nicholas was expressed in his marginal notes:

"Utopia." And: "I would rather swim than step on a Russian bridge." (loc. cit.)

The Romanian King was indeed soon to discover that the handing over of a present was only a superficial motive. The actual reason for the visit was a number of questions, e. g., whether or not Romania would be willing *to enter into the Balkan League*! This question should have hit Vienna and Berlin like a bomb and set all the alarm bells ringing!

To what end did Russia want to forge a new Balkan League between the armistice and the already foreseeable date for a Balkan peace!? The purpose of the previous league was as good as fulfilled anyway! Thus, the Balkan states did not need a new league.

Did the Entente perhaps need the new league!? And against whom?

The answer to the last question – if one considers it necessary to actually pose it at all – settles itself...

King Carol could easily reject the Russian request for Romania to enter into the Balkan League by referring to the foreseeable Bulgaro-Greek disagreements as well as the circumstance that the present members were not even sure themselves whether or not they should continue with the league.[1101] However, the King is supposed to have "talked around" the matter, when the Grand Prince was anxious to know why the Austrian Chief of the General Staff Conrad Count von Hötzendorf had come to Bucharest. For having Romania on the side of Austria and the German Reich would have been a coalition, which for obvious reasons went absolutely against the concept of the Entente regarding their war plans.

> Thus, it was not just about the continuation of a simple Balkan League against the Turks! In such a secondary Balkan war, it would not have mattered to the Russians at all, whose side the Romanians were on.

King Carol, on his part, expressed great concern about the Serbian agitation in the Austrian provinces of *Bosnia* and Herzegovina. The agitations, as the Romanian King put it, had to stop by all means,

> "and Serbia should finally abandon the plan to expand its borders further than its present state. If that did not happen, Austria would not show such patience again next time, as it did now, and in a few years an all-out European war would doubtless break out."

The Romanian King can hardly have guessed how crucially significant his prediction about the anticipated attitude of Austria would be for his interlocutor, the representative of the Entente, - considering that the whole success of their war plans depended upon the conduct of Austria.

The German Embassy in Bucharest had reported meticulously what they had heard from King Carol about this conversation, containing inter alia the following:

> "The Grand Prince has noted down the King's words, in order to pass them on to His Majesty the Russian Emperor,"[1102] –

while he might have thought: 'This is going well! Exactly what my "little brother" is hoping to hear. Now all the Tsar needs to do is to loosen the reins a little more for the Serbs – and Austria would walk right into the trap without Russia having to start the great war itself ... !'

This clearly shows the long-term planning of the Entente with the help of Serbian agitators, - consequently leading to Sarajevo.

Later - although not very much later, meaning towards the end of the year (1913) - it would turn out that Russia did in fact not only slacken the reins for the Serbs, but they promised to give them an almost princely reward.

Why?!

Why should it be worthwhile to *promise the Serbs Albania*, when the Balkan war had already ended, – and ended successfully?!

This was not meant as a reward for a further joint attack on the battered remains of the Ottoman Empire, after (South-)Epirus, Thrace and Macedonia had already been conquered in the past anyway. And Constantinople was off-limits for Russia, - *still*.

-- Had Albania not declared itself independent, by the way?

-- And how was it possible that despite the Russian promise Albania still managed to escape its demise by a hair's breadth in the end? The Macedonians were less lucky.

-- Why was Serbia treated so favourably?
-- Or was this just some kind of compensation? Was Greece rewarded even more generously?
Questions upon questions, - which will be referred to in chapter 5.4. (esp. 5.4.2)

For its grand plan, the Russians also had to make an effort to treat the Bulgarians whom they had ignored for quite a while in favour of the Serbs, in a much more friendly way. This line was contrary to the trend of the other Balkan states, but Ambassador v. Pourtalés found an explanation for this new Russian course:

> "It almost seems as if they are trying to prevent King Ferdinand from giving in to the temptations of the Viennese Cabinet and seeking the support of Austria-Hungary."[1103]

This fear was in no way groundless, as Bulgaria would – [would?] – have entered into an alliance with any state if this could help Sofia increase its position of power and thus reawaken the dream of the greatness of Bulgaria in medieval times, as it had almost been achieved in 1878.

Indeed, this is the reason why the Bulgarian switch to Austria and Germany would soon be undertaken.

The perforce increased Russian sympathies for the Bulgarians are so remarkable because Russia obviously needed Bulgaria as an important chess piece, although only recently Russia had had to defuse the Bulgarians' excessive demands, - just as in the past (despite all kinsman-like understanding for the Greek desire for expansion) it had flatly rejected similar suggestions by the Greeks:

After the visit of a high Bulgarian guest in St. Petersburg, the German Ambassador closed his report on this subject by stating:

> "Many people think that General Dimitriev has made the futile attempt to demand the consent of Russia for the Bulgarian march on Constantinople."[1103]

How could King Ferdi and General Dimi have achieved what neither the Tsars of the First (842-971) nor of the Second Bulgarian Empire (1185-1393) had been able to achieve before them?

And now, to ask permission from the Russians of all people, who in 1878 had been prevented from making this tempting move by Britain and Austria-Hungary (but not by Bismarck!). This was presumptuous of Bulgaria, to say the least. Thus, this démarche was bound to fail.

For now, 30 years later, the situation was completely different: Russia was about to plunge into a new war against Germany (see also ch. 5.1.3.4, no. 2). The Entente Cordiale must have made the tsar an almost incredible offer to lure him into the "Triple" Entente (1907). True, Tsar Nicholas II's Danish mother had spent her entire life preaching to her son her hatred for the Germans, who had simply taken back the province of Schleswig which had been illegally occupied by her father Christian IX. Yet, in order to entice Nicholas into a war against Germany and his relative (William II), Britain and France must have offered something which was simply irresistible, – this can have been exclusively *Constantinople and the Straits*. Only from reading between the lines and nuances in the interpretation of the relevant texts can it be inferred that Britain was prepared to sacrifice the choice prize coveted for centuries to Tsar Nicholas for the priceless advantage of being able to use the enormous Russian Empire as its ally.

How fascinating to find specific details over above these elements, as when Alan Palmer quotes from secret Soviet sources from the beginning of the communist revolutionary government, referring to the "Constantinople Agreement of March 1915", "in which the Ottoman capital and the Straits were assigned to the Russian Empire".[1103a] (l. c., p. 344) [It seems to have taken long, though, to work out specifications of the bait – apparently Russia's 'friends' in London and Paris wanted to wait for the general mobilization of the Tsarist army and the actual attack on Austria.]

It is completely another question whether the Tsar would really have been permitted to pocket the promised reward after Germany had been defeated. Would King Edward VII have kept his word, which he had no doubt given in 1907, or in 1908 at the latest, during the Reval meeting?

How great were Nicholas's prospects of success when we read in Barbara Tuchman that Edward remarked about him in connection with the Peace and Disarmament Conference at The Hague (i.e. about ten years before he met the nephew of his wife Alexandra at Reval in 1908) that he would easily be able to rope in Nicholas for his purposes, since he "[was] a weakling ... and lacks character"? (Loc. cit., p. 298)

> It should be remarked in passing that Kaiser William II wrote, in a letter to Theodore Roosevelt about Edward's attitude to the (Second) Hague Conference, that the latter "had himself taken the initiative in 'tell[ing] me that he regarded it as humbug'." (B. Tuchman, loc. cit., p. 335. Of course, Tuchman is enough of a master of her field to represent Edward's [in principle unacceptable] attitude, so to speak, as an endearing quirk in his attempt to create a harmonious atmosphere for his conversation with a nephew he despised!)

It became evident that the activities of the Entente, represented by Russia, were focussed on the formation of a new Balkan League, which pursued an aim on a higher, European, level. The idea was that Russia's new favourite, Serbia, in particular, should be rewarded far beyond its share of a Macedonia, which was no longer Turkish, and at the same time Serbia should serve as a spearhead aiming at Austrian territory, in order to provoke and weaken the Dual Monarchy of Habsburg.

This plan was a provocative challenge to the Empire of Austria-Hungary and could only be achieved at the cost of a critical worsening of relations on an international scale. Would Russia, would the Entente risk this? It seems that on the basis of the joint hatred in London and Paris for the German Reich, the certainty of having developed a realistic plan had matured to the point of complete confidence.

This, however, raises the question why St. Petersburg did not consider the price calculated to be too high; and why did it not also reckon with the failure of its belligerent feelings. Did the warmongers in Russia, especially in Moscow (the anti-German press, the officers' corps and the Orthodox Church) really have enough reasons for being convinced of a Russian victory?

Or were they - perhaps encouraged by generous admissions of their Entente partners - pushed into thoughtlessness, i.e. into doom?

Poor Tsar Nicholas, -
who let himself be misused by England and France as a naïve continental ally and by the Russian pan-Slavists as well as the Russian Orthodox Church as a spear head against Germany. He must have had enough time to often think about his meeting with his uncle Willy in Björkö in the summer of 1905. True, William was impetuous, - but wasn't he in the right?

Poor Alice-Alexandra,

poor children ...

In this context it must be permitted to raise a crucial additional question:
Is it possible that in 1913, as indeed experienced in Europe at the end of the First World War, (these dates consequently comprise a relatively short time) France in its pathological craving for admiration and revenge and Britain in its megalomaniac world-wide pursuit of hegemony, have anticipated and thus included in their plans the power shifts, so that not only the German and the Habsburg empires but *all three European empires would fall* at the same time? This would have at last enabled them to destroy the institution of the unloved German Empire in central Europe and to sink it finally to the bottom of history, and thus ease the deep wounds to their self-love and ambition a little, which have caused them pain for 400 years, when in that distant century neither the French King, Francis I, nor the English King, Henry VIII, became "Emperor of the Holy Roman Empire" (with the in no way groundless addition: "of the German Nation"), but both candidates had to make way for a German of all people, Charles V.
(And neither the Corsican-Napoleonic Emperor nor the exotic Indian Empress proved to be an adequate substitute.)

The reference to the *Holy Roman Empire* is too far fetched? Modern English historiography is of a different opinion:

In 1912, Balfour published an article on "Anglo-German relations, in which he explicitly accused the German government of planning a war of aggression; its aim was the re-establishment of the Holy Roman Empire on the continent as well as the extension of its Empire overseas."[1104]
As far as stirring up the British public against Germany and systematically preparing for a war was concerned, no cliché was too far-fetched for the British warmongers.
Although the Conservative Balfour must have been just as aware as the governing Liberals at that time that this absurd idea was simply untrue, the British imperialists did not hesitate in their propaganda battle against all things German to use any unfounded nightmare possible for their ideological explanation for a potential preventive war against Germany. That way, they would not only destroy the German Empire at last, but *at the same time extinguish the successful, progressive and thus much envied Wilhelmine Age.*
As mentioned above, the conditio sine qua non remained just as irreversible as this aim:
The English preventive war had to appear as a German war of aggression!
If necessary, it would have to be presented as such – which is what actually happened.

Considerably more substance than Balfour's propagandistic attack is provided in the analysis by the famous French historian, Duc de Broglie, who had the greatness to write that France's envy of Germany was not due to the constant to-ing and fro-ing linked to Alsace, nor even to the rivalry for the Holy Roman Empire, since in fact it went back even further into history, to the time when the East Frankish Empire (the later German Reich) was assigned the larger part of the Lotharingian Middle empire, the inheritance of Charlemagne's third grandson, - and particularly: *"the crown"*!

5.3.1 The formation of a new war-coalition in the Balkans

Analogous to the deterioration in, or rather the breakdown of the Bulgaro-Greek relations, the ones between Serbia and Bulgaria were also getting worse. Major von Massow, Military Attaché at the Embassy in Sofia, repeated in a report what the Serbian Envoy Spalaikowitsch told him about this matter:

> "Before the beginning of the war, [the Bulgarians] had boasted, promising their allies the earth. The siege of Adrianople had only been possible with the aid of Serbian troops and artillery. The world only ever mentioned Bulgarian successes and forgot that at Kumanovo and Monastir the Serbs achieved a destruction of the [Turkish] Vardar army, whereas in Thrace no decisive result had yet been reached. The Bulgarians did not make any progress because their war preparations had been incomplete."[1105]

Once on this track, the Serbian Envoy added

> - "that as the war progressed, the relations between the Serbian troops and the Bulgarians experienced a further deterioration. His fellow countrymen preferred their own enemies, the Turks, to the inapproachable, xenophobic Bulgarians, who he called 'Tartars';"
> - that the Serbs "(considered) themselves to be pure Slavs, but called the Bulgarians half-breeds with a strong Mongolian element. Therefore, they would not willingly grant them supremacy in the Balkans as a dominant Slav power;"
> - that over the years, in Belgrade "the military preponderance of Bulgaria was felt oppressively", which goes back to the defeat in Slivnitsa and Pirot in 1885.

Similar complaints about the Bulgarians reached Berlin from Belgrade itself: As Ambassador von Griesinger put it, the Serbs were filled with bitterness about the

> "openly practised ruthless propaganda, initiated by the Bulgarians all over the occupied territory. This includes the establishment of bank branches in the locations conquered by the Serbs such as Monastir and Prilep, the deployment of the Komitadzhi to exercise political influence on the population according to the principle: 'if free you'll not come, I will use force', as well as the opening of schools and churches wherever the existence of Bulgarians can be proved."[1106]

Even if this was in accordance with a clause of the Serbo-Bulgarian Balkan League Treaty, the Serbs no longer kept their promise, as the real situation at the front turned out to be quite different. In view of the military successes of Serbia, the Serbian government demanded a revision of the partition agreement.

> "According to the wording of the treaty, Monastir, Prilep and Ochrid would in fact not fall to Serbia", as the "border line ... had already been defined."[1107]

The Bulgarians, on the other hand, assuming that, according to the agreement, the mentioned cities would be theirs, even if they were conquered by the Serbians, who would consequently concentrate on their own section of the front, did not even think of complying with the Serbian wishes, even if the agreed line was no longer identical with the real position of the front. Sofia instead dismissed the Serbian application for revision in a note which was 45 pages long.[1108]

Consequently, the semi-official newspaper "Samouprava" announced

> "that if Bulgaria did not give in, a belligerent confrontation would be inescapable."[1109]

As a result of this discord, both quarrelling parties tried to win Romania as a possible ally. In addition, Serbia talked of a "separate alliance" with Athens.

This clearly marked the formation of a new circle of aggressors, whose aim was *once more Macedonian territory*, which at that time was in the hands of Bulgaria, though.

In fact, the intensity of the Serbo-Greek relations rose to unexpected heights. During a stay in London on the occasion of the conference

> "the Serbian representative Novacovich and Prime Minister Venizelos are said to have entered into extremely cordial relations" and laid the foundation for a "Serbo-Greek alliance".[1110]

Although the date of the peace agreement of the First Balkan War had not been fixed yet, Serbia and Greece already agreed that

> "both states could together oppose the absurd demands of over-zealous chauvinists in Sofia."

Despite the enthusiastic Serbo-Greek promises of friendship (the Encyclopaedia Britannica even mentions their anti-Bulgarian alliance of 1 June 1913), this new relationship also retained a familiar uncertainty:

> "The difficult question of the allocation of territory among the allies has not yet been dealt with."[1110]

After he had "vented his displeasure about the greediness and arrogance of Bulgaria", the Serbian Envoy in Sofia told his German colleague von Below about "already binding agreements with Greece".

Furthermore, he even mentioned the plan of an

> "alliance of protection and resistance with Turkey, which would be quite easy to achieve, as there had never been any deep antagonism between Turkey and Serbia." (loc. cit.) (Sic?)

Over dinner, a different story was told; but as a German book of (gallows) humour puts it so nicely: Pain once endured is pain now cured. (Wilhelm Busch)

Von Below's comment:

> "The whole idea looks like a deliberate encirclement of Bulgaria, which has always been good at making itself unpopular and is today rightly considered by all those closely affected as the future trouble-maker in the Balkans."[1111]

This sounds rather too general and prejudiced; however, it fits in with a (later) quote about the year 1941:

> "The Bulgarian occupation" [of Macedonia] "is often interpreted as a final stroke of Macedonian sympathy for Bulgaria, as the Bulgarians do not behave as liberators but as radically assimilating occupiers." (At that time, the Bulgarians also handed over the Sephardic Jews from Vardar-Macedonia to the Germans, which they did not do to the Jews from Bulgaria itself.[1112])

In this circle of new allies all that was missing was - what the Russians had long since felt as a disturbing deficiency - another Bulgarian neighbouring country: *Romania*. Indeed, as Major Massow put it in one of the final sentences of his report: "Negotiations with Bucharest are in progress." (See footnote [1105]) It was known that the Romanian government was constantly concerned about the well-being of its Vlach-Aromanian fellow tribesmen in Macedonia. After a conversation with the Russian Envoy Misu, the German Ambassador in London, von Lichnowsky, reported in March (1913) that in the interest of the Kutzo-Wallachians Misu had agreed to a subordination of that tribe, whose unified majority was in Epirus and Southern Albania, to Albania, which granted the tribe more reliable protection

> "than the Greeks, who were determined to hellenize all foreign parts of the nation." "Due to the continuous hellenization, namely by the Church, the anger against the Greeks should not be underestimated in those regions and no one had confidence in Greek promises."[1113]

The Greeks, too, were similarly concerned about Bulgaria. Therefore, a new front line seemed to be taking shape in Greece. Envoy von Quadt repeats Prime Minister Venizelos' remarks:

> - "... With regard to the present war, which presented Turkey as a Greek enemy, it is regrettable that 700,000 Greeks alone would fall under Bulgarian rule. While under Turkish rule they would have remained Greek, they would now be made Bulgarian within a short period of time and thus be forever lost for Greece.[1114]

(How promptly a hellenizer was able to see through a bulgarianizer.)

> - "The (Balkan) League has only been formed for the war and terminates with the end of the war." "Beyond the war", Greece was "in no way bound to its allies." "But until peace was made, Greece would remain loyal to its allies."

So much for the officially pronounced sense of justice and moral standards of the "loyal" Greek Prime Minister Venizelos – in theory. In practice, however, in those days the German Embassy reported by wire:
> "In Macedonia there seems to have been a serious armed confrontation between Greeks and Bulgarians."[1115]

This closed the ring of the members of the previous Balkan League and the First Balkan War as new war-time enemies in the Second Balkan War: *around Bulgaria*.
(To be continued: chapter 5.5)

5.4 On "the brink of disaster"
5.4.1 The Russian communiqué of April 1913

The conclusion of the Ambassadors Conference in London after the end of the war of the Balkan states against Macedonia in April 1913 was followed by an even more significant event than the (preliminary) Peace Treaty of London at the end of May, which is known to have lasted only a few weeks.

After the absolute ban on information by the Entente regarding the preparations and the eventual formation of the Balkan League as well as the resultant (First) Balkan War, in April, the world was unexpectedly informed about the content and the course of events of the London Ambassadors Conference as well as the political aims of Russia by means of a long *communiqué* by the Russian government. This created the impression that the insinuations, assumptions and speculations about the uncertainties of the role of Russia in the context of the Balkan League and the First Balkan War would finally come to end.

The *sensational* text of the communiqué revealed
- that Russia intended to safeguard their victorious allies' military successes,
- that their allies "were only able to achieve their successes due to the non-intervention of other powers" and
- that these two measures were the only way to localize the war.[1116]

In view of the previous secretiveness, deceptions and lies this *publication* was tantamount to a real revelation.

All of a sudden, all uncertainties, which were still very much in the air, seemed to be swept away. At least this was what St. Petersburg tried to make the world believe.

> *However, this lengthy text did not contain a single word about the involvement of the Entente powers and their actual aims, of course.*

After all, with this note Russia had admitted to having pursued individual as well as Balkan-related aims, whereas on the eve of the First Balkan War Russia had gone through all kinds of contortions to disguise those aims:

1.)
It now emerged that St Petersburg indeed intended to or (by order of the Entente) was asked *to help the four Balkan states to make territorial gains and guarantee their protection*. This was simply denied until the declaration of war by Montenegro and the other three countries by means of many treacherous tricks. (It was not without reason that in this book the "invalidity of territorial changes" was dealt with in a separate chapter! Compare ch. 5.1.3.3)

2.)
As far as the *"non-intervention of other powers"* is concerned, this could only have referred to Germany's and Austria's abstention from an intervention, - as the Entente

powers were all hand in glove with each other anyway, although this was of course not admitted in the note. This, therefore, was the reason for this enormous effort involving countless intrigues, deceptions and lies, - which even from today's point of view (after 90 years have elapsed) was excessive. This also confirms that Germany and Austria might indeed have been able to avert the imperialistic war of conquest of the Balkan states against (the still Turkish) Macedonia, - but from ignorance or self-interest, they abstained from intervening. (This will be referred to below.)
3.)
These two concessions are presented in the communiqué with such adulation, as if the only possible way *to localize* the Balkan war had been with their help alone. It seems as if in Berlin and Vienna people believed this argument of the Russians, assuming that the Entente powers, too, had seriously desired a localization of the conflict.

> *This shows that "the Germans" still did not see through the infamy of the Entente's plan.*

According to the communiqué, the settlement listed was achieved in "complicated and difficult" negotiations at the above mentioned conference, which had been especially convened for this purpose (on 18 December 1912).
Furthermore, the communiqué extensively explains the reason for the solution of the "difficult task" of the demarcation of *Montenegro* [Pardon!?] and the independent *Albania*, whose interests had especially been "protected" by Austria-Hungary. (Quite an unexpected praise of the despised enemy.)
In that way, the "northern and north-eastern border of Albania" had been determined, too,

> "which was prevented by the interests of Montenegro and Serbia with their natural aspirations for expansion." The conference has also shown this understanding for the Albanian "aspirations ... to ... find a way to expand their borders", which is why "Russia (believed)" "that it was obliged to grant Albania the annexation of Skutari" ... "after long and difficult negotiations and mutual concessions", which, however, led to the "gaining of Prizrend, Ipek, Diakova and Dibra for the Slavic states."[1116]
>
> *So – this was what the understanding for the "natural aspirations for expansion" meant at that time. However, due to the Entente powers' own interests, the Greek objection and the compliance of the European dynasties, there was no understanding for the natural aspirations for freedom, independence and statehood of the latecomers Macedonia, Thrace and Epirus.*

Looking at the prudent and dispassionate style of the communiqué, one might almost have taken this for an objective presentation of the facts. However, it would have been advisable to ask, why the settlement was so important for Montenegro that out of the total of 130 lines of the communiqué, 74 alone are dedicated to this subject, about 30 to the issue of Albania and almost the same number to the basic description, -- but not a single line covered the Serbian, Bulgarian and Greek demarcation. Only then might one have realized that the style and the scope of the text created the impression of a means of deception or represented the attempt not to admit any other version of the content and the course of events of the conference other than its own, i.e. the Russian one.

> *Thus, the lengthy communiqué concealed more than it revealed at first sight.*

What had actually caused the unexpected publication of details of the London Balkan conference? The following provides an attempt of a reconstruction:

As was mentioned above (compare ch. 5.1.4), William II had seen through the trap of the Entente. In contrast to what was feared after the first impression, the Kaiser's warning did not go unheard. This enabled the *Wilhelmstrasse to prevent Austria from falling into the trap*, which had already caused a major conflict in the past. Permanent Secretary von Kiderlen, however, seems to have had great difficulties in persuading Vienna (and Petersburg) to participate in the conference.

According to the customs of diplomatic intrigue, it may be assumed that the Russian government could only be made to agree to go to London and to display peaceful behaviour on condition that after the conference they would have the right to publish their own version of the conference's deliberations. For only this would explain why Sazonov was allowed to write and publish his communiqué of April in that form without any objection, which except for some disclosures concealed more than it revealed.

> In this way, the Russian deception of Germany and Austria was unabatedly continued with the help of the maintenance of the web of lies of the Entente regarding the aims against the Dual Alliance which went beyond the Balkan League.

This was the basic condition enabling the Entente to continue with its war plans –with the result that it did not even need to change its strategy.

Only the Second Balkan War had to break out and end, and then another three months had to pass until (almost) the whole - sad - truth about the double game of the Russians, the French and the British against the Germans came to light.

5.4.2 A Bulgarian act of revenge brings the truth to light

Only six months later [in this paragraph several comments need to be made prior to discussing the Second Balkan War], the Russian communiqué also turned out to be once more nothing but a hotchpotch of justifications and misrepresentations as well as concealments and deceptions:

The bombshell dropped when the French newspaper "Le Matin" published the texts of the Bulgaro-Greek alliance agreement of 16 May 1912 and that of the military convention of 22 September 1912 towards the end of November 1913.[1117] The search for the leak quickly led to *Bulgaria*. For apart from the actual victim of the Balkan wars, Macedonia, which had been attacked and quartered completely without defence and whose population was facing the bitter fate of the Serbization, Graecization and Bulgarization (the "visible", violent Albanization of the western part of the Republic of Macedonia - after the gradual one in previous decades - only commenced with the beginning of the new millennium), thus, apart from Macedonia, Bulgaria was the state to gain least from the two Balkan wars and their conferences in London and Bucharest. Therefore, the Bulgarian disappointment about Russia was great, which explains the desire to at least snap at the heels of the Great Power which had destroyed all Bulgarian visions.

> The result of this frustration was the publication by "Le Matin", which was so extremely embarrassing and degrading for Russia.

In addition to the texts of the agreement from Paris, the "Frankfurter Zeitung" promptly published an elucidation, which was possible so soon because "the essential matters of these disclosures for months ... (had) remained not unknown",[1118] so that consequently all it had to do was wait for a confirmation and the right time.

And now the time had come.
The new and additional sensation of the disclosures consisted of three fundamental clarifications:
1. Embarrassingly, the Russian government was exposed to the world as the one who *had pulled the strings for the Balkan League* and the Balkan war, - although for years it had presented itself as being interested, but not involved. The trick with the *localization of the Balkan war* was thus only one of the many means of deception. The reported pursuit of the maintenance of the *status quo* turned out to be a downright lie.
2. The Entente had built a network, in order *to engage Austria in a war*.
3. The Russian *mobilization on the Galician border was not a test-mobilization at all*, as Foreign Minister Sazonov had – with great success – made the world believe. It was not "simply a peaceful demonstration, but instead it was seriously calculated as an *attack against Austria*."[1118]

What bizarre contortions Russia [and subsequently later historians] had gone through for this mobilization, in order to make Austria and the German Reich believe that it was merely a harmless and on top of that legal routine measure! And what an undignified role the Russian Sazonov had played in this malicious game. Only later was it all exposed as a web of lies.

The idea was to appeal to the Habsburgs' greed for land, which Vienna was notorious for – not without reason. (We can now at least specify what was previously only hinted at):
The Sandzak was chosen as a *bait*. As a *trap*, the Entente had puzzled out the following construction, which after a pre-calculated automatic process was supposed to start a *chain reaction* and eventually use Austria to also engage Germany in a great war:
To this end, "treaties for the *acquisition of Albania for Serbia* were made" under Russian "patronage"! As soon as the Austrians got wind of this outrageous coup - according to the Anglo-French-Russian calculation - they would (without waiting for the reaction of the Italians, who would probably be enraged) immediately try to secure their own interests in a knee-jerk reaction and march into the *Sandzak*. For Serbia this would have been a casus belli. In this case, the next step would be the application of a clause of the Bulgaro-Greek alliance agreement,
> "committing Bulgaria, in the event of the occupation of Turkish territory (meaning the Sandzak of Novi Pazar) by a third power (Austria-Hungary, of course), to accept the clause of mutual defence."[1118] [The content of the brackets is part of the original text.]

Due to the existing European alliance system, this still relatively limited war of Serbia and Bulgaria against Austria would automatically escalate into a major European war, for the obligations of Germany towards Austria on the one hand, and Russia towards Serbia on the other hand, were known world-wide, as were those of France towards Russia.
Although *France* gave the appearance of "showing a rather peaceful face during the crisis" it led the way in the secret agreements.
> "The Balkan League was even a pet of French diplomacy, which had made great sacrifices for the Balkan League and thus wanted to use it to strike hard not only Austria-Hungary but also the German Reich."

"The stage ... was set for a European conflict."[1118]

Due to the fact that the clauses of the agreement were also binding for *Greece*, the Greek government was fully included in the planning as well as execution and even served as the most important anti-Austrian and anti-German agreement partner. The Greek breach of loyalty against Germany - despite the coveted dynastic relations - shows that the Russian promises of enormous territorial gains must have been part of the game, without which it might not have been possible to bait even the unscrupulous Venizelos and make him turn against Crown Prince Constantine, who was married to a German.

This furtiveness, which had been planned long beforehand, also explains the *extreme secrecy*, so obviously practised by Prime Minster Venizelos before the formation of the Balkan League, which is clearly exemplified by the quote of "The Times" mentioned above (ch. 5.1.2).

Thus, everything was contrived exactly as described by Kaiser William.
What he could not anticipate in his political analysis was the perfidy of the Albanian trap with the Sandzak bait. It would have been beneath the dignity of this often boisterous, but inwardly honourable man.

> "The careful position of Germany and Austria alone" [Despite the Austrian resistance, the positive mentioning of the Habsburg monarchy was obviously due to a diplomatic euphemism.] "which England was so kind as to join" [dito], "has prevented the belligerent confrontation." "For Kiderlen-Waechter did not only lead Austria-Hungary but also Russia to the London conference against their will" and thus caused "the controlling position of Russia, which was assisted at the conference by England", and by which means Russia could be made to abandon the plan of giving Albania to Serbia.[1118]

Only in view of this explanation it is possible to expose as one of many lies the cynical presentation in the Russian communiqué of April 1913, in which Russia pretended to be full of concern for Albania.

> (It is no wonder then that the Russian assignment of blame was once more directed against the German Reich, as was the case in 1878 after the Congress of Berlin, and again this time after the London Ambassadors' Conference, and just as unfair, - although the disclosure had obviously come from Bulgaria.)

At the London Conference in 1913, the German delegation had thus succeeded in defusing the detonator of the *chain reaction planned* by England (together with France and Russia): i.e. for the provocation of Austria and thus for *precipitating* at first an Austro-Serbian and as a result *a European war of the Entente against the Triple Alliance*.

This time after the crisis of 1912/13 the "world war" sought by the Entente could be averted.

Basically, Austria and - on its coat-tails, partly depending, partly dominating - the German Reich should later also have been able to recognize and avoid the trap of 1914, as in 1912, until the instigators had revealed themselves – or kept the peace, even if that peace was unstable.

As one of many examples, the remark by the Austrian Foreign Minister, quoted by Ambassador v. Tshirshky in a report, proves that the principle of these "rules of the game" were also known to the German-speaking leaders of the Dual Alliance at that time (even though they obviously did not know how to play the game): Graf Berchtold had not intended to adopt a negative position,

> "in order to show Russia his goodwill and not to be regarded by the world as a peacebreaker."[1119]

This noble gesture was not worth it.

For Germany and Austria, the disclosures, however complex they might have been, suffered from the deficiency that they did not go far enough and that they did not make public all that was planned against the Triple Alliance, - least of all the basics.

> *Despite the exposure of Russia, the Entente had managed to save their conspiracy, which lay behind the Russian activities throughout the course of the London Conference, and keep it secret.*

An attempt at an explanation leads to the conclusion that this result was due to cold-blooded double-cross played by *the English*, who succeeded in pretending to the central powers the *illusion of its real willingness to reach an understanding* and to create the impression that London (at least temporarily) stood on the side of Germany and Austria against *Russia*, at the same time managing to pretend that Russia had acted independently all the time: this meant that Petersburg was forced to adopt the role of the scapegoat. But all in all, this was an ingenious construction.

Regarding the third cornerstone, the British government also managed to pretend that it was in no way necessarily bound to *France*, although Britain, as was set out above (ch. 4.4.1.2.1) had from the very first (i.e. at least since the turn of the century, if not after 1871) been determined to join France against Germany. In order to maintain its *world hegemony*, London showed the greatest interest in a new *Continental* balance on a lower level. To that end, the two German Empires had to be destroyed; not necessarily by England herself, but, as usual, preferably by other Continental powers: the notorious Continental force. As Prince Bülow put it in his memoirs:

> "England is seeking ... alliances (or) maybe friendships, always led by her customary policy of sending others to fight for her."[1120]

(Poor Tsar Nicholas.)

Brief retrospect:

Nicholas was simply among the many people abused and cheated (by the British), as the pattern of this British policy was well known and had often been practiced.

William Pitt the Elder, for example, had used the principles of this English policy. At that time, however, England was not fighting against the Hohenzollern dynasty, but against Bonaparte. Pitt financed the Russians and the Austrians, and in return they were to keep France at bay for him; despite their superiority, the Russians and Austrians were absolutely no match for the ingenious Corsican strategist. In the battle of Austerlitz, for instance, they were completely bowled over by the smaller French army, which by means of astute tactical moves caused a shocking high number of victims.

After that, the Prussians fared even worse; instead of joining their neighbours right from the start or at least taking the obvious lesson from the embarrassing beating that the Russians and the Austrians had suffered, they actually possessed the clumsiness and arrogance of confronting Napoleon at Jena and Auerstädt on their own and thus allowed the French to rout them.

At any rate, at that time the three continental powers decimated their forces as planned and at the same time pulled the chestnuts out of the fire for the English, who, after the brave victory at Trafalgar and Napoleon's first defeats in Spain (Vitoria), did not have to stand their ground again before Waterloo.

There is no doubt that from the beginning England had played a decisive role in the plans and put them into practice step by step (1904, 1907 and 1908 etc.). (The murder of the Serbian King Alexander in 1903 might have been carried out by Russia alone, so as to entice Serbia away from Austria and onto the Russian side, - but not the secret agreement of 1911 with Serbia and Bulgaria.)

In 1912, the trap of the Entente could not close over Austria, because the Kaiser had warned the Auswärtiges Amt and the German government held back the Habsburgs, and because furthermore the Kaiser was willing to yield and was not interested in a belligerent confrontation and probably even dreaded the war (in contrast to his occasional boasting).Thus, in the attempt to protect the whole plan of the Entente against the Germans and at the same time to save her neck quickly, at the London Conference together with Germany and Austria (doubtless after an agreement with Russia and thus again for tactical reasons rather than fairness, - at least not towards Germany), England was *for the time being* forced to agree to a peaceful solution: *against Russia*!

Due to this precarious situation, Russia was forced to play the role of the "scapegoat", in order to leave Germany and Austria in the dark. In the botched issue of Albania in particular, all that Petersburg could do was to assume responsibility. This was already rather embarrassing, as it was accompanied by a loss of face, - but after all the war plans against Austria and Germany remained secret, or at least cloaked in ambiguity, e.g. as far as the Russian troop deployment on the Austrian border was concerned.

The cold-blooded, strong-nerved calculation of an Entente guided by England turned out to become a success.

A *masterpiece*: despite the embarrassing disclosures.

Is there no one to stand up for the poor English who have once again been "unfairly" victimized by this author? But of course – and with unbeatable proof:

Even in 1912, Hermann Kantorowicz (as a precaution?) did not even take notice of the countless lies of the English, the Russians and the French regarding the trap laid for Austria and Germany to make them start a European war. However, it can easily be interpolated what his justification of the English would have looked like in such a case, as he constructed a similar one for the year 1914:

In this context he praises the British "Blue Book" of the year 1925 as well as the "British Documents of the Origins of the War 1898-1914", the publisher of which vouched "for a formally and materially faultless work" *with their name alone*. Even though the author considers it inevitable to discuss *"problematic"* deficiencies in these documents, they are immediately, in the same sentence, or in the very same line, played down as "obviously harmless".[1121] Nevertheless, the author could not avoid investigating in detail some likely "deliberate misrepresentations". Some highlights of legal sophistry must not be omitted from his manifestations of harmlessness:

> One of the misrepresentations "had to be labelled as a falsification in a broader sense, but in the sense of the question of the responsibility for the war, it is none; after all, the idea was not to conceal a motive for the war but for peace."

He stated that, in a second example, too, one could not speak of an actual misrepresentation (as in Germany no injustice was done by leaving out part of a document),

> "for there was no attempt made to withhold a fact, which was taken for the truth, but to nip an opinion in the bud, which was considered false."[1121]

The text in question was only left out under the "aspect of preventive counter-propaganda" anyway. So – there …!

Hundreds of pages further down, when the slightly disturbing impression of this argumentation might have been assumed to have faded, the report closes this issue quite insouciantly:

> "Today we no longer assume English responsibility for the war in the sense that the English government brought about the war by positive actions."[1122]

However, should this be the case, contrary to all reason, Kantorowicz provides impeccable relief by stating:

> "Whoever wishes to render homage to this madness, only needs to read the >British documents< now,"[1122]

- which he himself had been forced to declare to be dubious earlier in the text.
This proves how easy life can be with the help of historical misrepresentation.

A comparison of von Kiderlen's readiness to trust and Chancellor v. Bethmann Hollweg's credulousness with the Kaiser's sceptical and politically wise attitude, which had matured in the course of 25 years of experience, allows the following statement:
In a situation in 1912, which historically endangered the existence of both Austria and Germany, William II had drawn the attention of the élite of the German government as well as the Austrian government to the dangers of the planned war so that the state secretary of the Foreign Ministry was able to avoid the actual problems by clever arrangements (however, only with the help of the English upholding the deception behind the façade) as well as to defuse the impending conflict at the London conference.
For the last time ..., since the next time the bullets would be flying from the start – in Sarajevo.
Consequently, Kaiser William's early warnings had an effect on the events after all.
However, William would not in his worst nightmares have imagined that his beloved England, above all, King Edward, despite his constant promises, would treat him with such hostility and conspire behind his back with the French and the Russians, in order to destroy Germany in a concealed preventive war.
His awakening must have been terrible. In his work "Griff nach der Weltmacht" (p. 78), Fritz Fischer quotes a marginal note by the Kaiser on the report by Prince Lichnowsky of 30 July 1914:

> "Even after his death, Edward VII is stronger than I am, and I am still alive!"

(King Edward had died in 1910.)

A few months after the events of 1912 and 1913, when Britain, France and Russia launched their next coup against the two German Empires with the same "trick", William II could no longer assert himself against the belligerent Austria and the German government led by von Bethmann Hollweg, although he again ordered the policy of the maintenance of peace (as described in the chapter on Germany, ch. 4.4.1).

In various of his works, Fritz Fischer puts it thus:

After William's reaction to the Serbian response concerning the Austrian ultimatum ("With that every reason for war ceases to exist."), he writes correctly:

> - "In the eyes of the Auswärtiges Amt and the military this was the dreaded moment, in which the weak-nerved monarch - as in 1906 and 1911 - would shrink back from war at the last minute, and this is the reason why it was now covered up."("Griff ...", p. 69)

- "But the crucial matter is that ... the statesman formally responsible, Chancellor von Bethmann Hollweg, also decided in favour of the hard line ... and even stopped the Kaiser when he threatened to become weak again." ("Der Erste Weltkrieg...", p. 311)
- "As in 1905 and 1911, he had shrunk back from the danger of belligerent confrontations. This is why he was deprived of his power ... by the Chancellor in the July crisis." ("Juli 1914. Wir sind nicht ..., p. 46 ff)

At that time, Turkish Macedonia (and Albania) was no longer available as a trap, nor was the Sandzak available as a bait, as these problems had been "solved" in favour of the Balkan conquerors (except with regard to Albania).

Therefore, the Entente, together with those Balkan states in their debt as a result of the sacrifice of Macedonia by the Great Powers, Serbia in particular, used further violent provocations to winkle out the Austrians and - together with their protector - lure them on to destruction:

After the Germans and the Austrians did not react in any way to the *six assassinations* of Austrian governors in Croatia and in Bosnia during the previous four years,[1123] the final provocation was successful with the assassination in Sarajevo on 28 June 1914.

How great is Hermann Kantorowicz's range of argumentative art in the case of Serbia?
"The numerous claims of a Serbo-Russian >conspiracy< against Austria-Hungary (1908-1914) ... are dissolving into thin air." ... The accusations ... against Serbia would involve "the danger of suspecting innocent people or assuming their guilt as too grievous" ... "as there is no reliable record of the trial."[1123]

How unfortunate for the discovery of the truth that Mr Kantorowicz absolutely refused to accept *un*reliable trial reports.

However, some documents, the existence of which Kantorowicz had not considered, although they represented a sensation for every German, have survived nevertheless. The text of a telegram is as follows:

"According to the information of Mr von Dobrowitsch, a letter from the former Russian Consul in Nish" [Mr Tshakhotin] "to the deceased Envoy von Hartwig has been found among the captured records in Serbia, stating that the Russian government was not only informed about the assassination in Sarajevo, but even supported the undertaking financially. Michahelles."[1124]

"Thus, in 1912, Europe was close to an abyss and would indeed have fallen into it, if things had gone according to the plans and agreements" of France, Britain and Russia. (see note [1118])

It is remarkable that Gordon Craig (l. c., p. 363), even if he does not admit the whole truth, at least acknowledges that the Serbian Government was "involved" in the Sarajevo murders. Thus he goes further than Fritz Fischer and many others of his colleagues.

Remembering the impending catastrophe of 1912, the almost identical operations around the traps of 1912 and 1914 could have put Austria-Hungary and the German Reich in a position to avoid the tragedy on their own authority, as suggested by the Kaiser. Instead, in its impudence, Austria ran into destruction with open eyes – assisted by the German Chancellor v. Bethmann H.

And once more, it was not just "fate", nor inevitable "history", but the work of people, - the work of egocentric, vain and irresponsible people.

Postscript:
Thus, *Albania* owed the maintenance of its newly created national sovereignty and independence to the German government, - in the persons of Kaiser William II and (on the side of the government) State Secretary v. Kiderlen-Wächter.
But the world pays with ingratitude. For since the Albanians, like all Europeans, have had access to unexpected flexibility after the beginning with the German reunification in 1989/90, they have exported all their crimes abroad, including to Germany. To record a relevant remark, in June 2002, the UNMIK chief Michael Steiner possessed the courage to face the truth and even pronounce it openly, which in our society - burdened with lobbyism - is hardly ever practised ["The truth" is no longer discussed, "because it is considered politically incorrect"[1125]]:

> "The population of Kosovo cannot expect the Europeans to show any great interest in investing in their region, unless Kosovo stops exporting crime to Europe."[1126]

Just so that we are not mistaken: if the Albanians can go on operating undisturbed in Switzerland, Germany and other countries, they are rather unlikely to show any great interest in European investments in their region, as this would only disturb their circles. This assessment confirms the experience that the reputation of well-meaning people - as in any other nation - always suffers from the deeds of the villains.

5.5 The Second Balkan War

> "In May 1913, the Russian Foreign Minister Sazonov wrote to Belgrade: 'Serbia's promised land is located in the area of what is today Austria-Hungary'; ..."[1127]

However, things had not got as far as that yet. First, the Second Balkan War broke out. Only three weeks after the (Preliminary) Peace of London (of 30 May 1913), the four Prime Ministers of the Balkan League member states said at a conference in St. Petersburg that "there was only talk of war ... everywhere".[1128]
The Bulgarian Envoy to Belgrade, Toshev, had described the situation at that time to his German colleague von Griesinger by saying:

> "The chances of a peaceful argument (have) almost reached rock-bottom now".

On this occasion, Mr Toshev had still made an optimistic remark:

> "In the event of a war, which will probably be rather bloody and of short duration, Serbia will not only be left with nothing, but will also lose territories around the borders at Pirot and Vranje."[1128]

The negotiations of the four Balkan powers were observed from Vienna "not without some concern".

> "The plan of the formation of a new permanent Balkan League in particular is taken as a direct affront to Austria-Hungary."[1129]

This was doubtless the case.
It was obvious: although the aim of driving the Turks out of Macedonia, which had been pursued for decades, was finally achieved, Russia still did not cease from its efforts to form a new alliance! Therefore, Vienna had good reason to be concerned.
In order to produce a minimum of constructive Austrian policy, Ambassador von Tshirshky had advised the Austrian Foreign Minister Count Berchtold at least

> "to settle the South-Albanian border dispute amicably as soon as possible, in order to prevent Greece from being sacrificed to the Entente powers and thus also to the Balkan League."[1129]

A well concerted plan, but too late – much too late. As if Greece had not been the prime mover in direction of a second Balkan war – against Bulgaria.

It is rather astonishing that *Bulgaria* had actually still been invited and admitted to the St. Petersburg conference! Its task cannot have been to announce to the other participants that it was soon to start the Second Balkan War, can it?! But this is exactly what Bulgaria did, because Serbia and Greece disputed its right to the sole possession of Macedonia.

This is at least the usual historical version, which in this case was also how it was portrayed by the victorious powers. There are indeed doubts; because why should Bulgaria have started a war after it had already annexed the lion's share of the Thracian and Macedonian territory?

The Serbian secret files consistently reveal that Bulgaria was by no means willing to accept the blame for having started the war. In contrast, Sofia asserted and claimed to have proof that the Greeks and the Serbs had started the war, in order to take from the Bulgarians their share of Macedonia, which at that time was considered too large. Have the defeated in this case once more been treated according to the principle of "might is right"?

The history books therefore aver that one month after the Peace of London (30 May), there was an outbreak of violent clashes between Bulgaria and its former allies Serbia and Greece on 29 June 1913.

This marked the beginning of the *Second Balkan War*.

It was important for Greece and Serbia to attain their new objective of driving the Bulgarians out of Macedonia. They have almost succeeded. Even today the situation on the central Balkans is influenced by the result.

On 10 July, *Romania* as well, claiming South-Dobruja with Silistra, interfered in the war and marched on Sofia. This initiated what the Bulgarians had feared for generations. On the previous day, the Envoy, von Waldthausen, had reported from Bucharest that he had been informed by the Romanian prime minister that the latter was in the process of negotiating a military agreement with the Greek delegation, at that time staying in Bucharest (in order to announce the ascent to the throne of the new Greek King Constantine I).[1130]

Finally, "the Turks, too, ... did not run from the opportunity for revenge..."[1131] (Warnings had constantly been issued about this danger.) They indeed succeeded in reconquering Edirne (Adrianople) and achieving further demarcation corrections in their own favour.

By this superiority Bulgaria was defeated.

> "On 10 August 1913, it was forced to make peace in Bucharest and surrender further territories, which it had already conquered in the First Balkan War."[1131]

In addition to South Dobruja and Adrianople, Bulgaria lost Vardar-Macedonia and the Aegean Macedonia with Cavalla (i.e. its direct access to the Mediterranean Sea). All that was left to Bulgaria was Pirin-Macedonia (about 10% of Macedonian territory).

It was of crucial significance to crushing the Greater Bulgarian idea that Bulgaria also "*lost the exarchate in Macedonia*".[1132]

With a share of about 38%, Serbia received the whole of *Vardar-Macedonia* (the territory of *today's Republic of Macedonia*) and was considered the strongest power in the Balkans, although with 51% Greece had annexed the largest part of Macedonia, and was additionally granted the Aegean Islands and thus almost doubled its national territory.

Although the present conflict was limited to the countries involved, there were forebodings unmistakeably pointing to *Sarajevo*. It was only a year until the carefully planned shots were fired on the Austrian heir to the throne.

At the beginning of the 20th century, the often quoted Edith Durham was perhaps the best independent Balkan expert. In her later field report, she mentioned a remark by the Serbian Prime Minister Pasic, which he had made after the signing of the Bucharest Peace Treaty in August 1913:

> "The first match has been won; now our task is to prepare the second one against Austria."[1133]

This was unmistakable.

And this was supposed to have been a subtlety invented by the Germans?!

(Hermann Kantorowicz also lists a number of such quotations, but he tries very hard to trivialize them in dialectical somersaults by means of dubious arguments.)

At that time (as before the Balkan wars[1134]), the Double Monarchy had intended to take belligerent action against Serbia, but was prevented by Germany and Italy. Vienna was rather concerned about the activities it had noticed between France and Russia on the one hand and Serbia on the other hand.

Also the

> "relations between Romania and Serbia (are) closer and more intimate ... than Bucharest is willing to admit. Now Romania does not even seem to be considerate of friends of the Triple Alliance, by at least informing them about its political decisions. Under these circumstances, the likelihood of the plan of the formation of a great Balkan League - still eagerly pursued by Russia and France - is rising again, and despite the fact that it is not formally directed against Austria-Hungary, it would still be an instrument in the hands of France and Russia."[1135]

> (It may be regarded as a sign of extremely ingenious use of tactics by the British that in his short but principally precise analysis Berchtold only speaks of "France and Russia", without ever mentioning Britain, which was pulling the strings in the wings.)

This time, the Austrian Foreign Minister listened to his instincts. If only he had made use of it a year later!

Count Berchtold would have been in dire need of his instincts, as once again the three Entente powers got out their old tricks of *trivialization and deception*.

The Envoy to Athens, Count von Bassewitz, reported that the three prime ministers of Greece, Serbia and Romania continued the collaboration they had begun in Bucharest, founded a postal union and intended to make numerous trade agreements. Had his conversational partner, the Greek Foreign Minister, divulged secret information? After all, the report closes with the repetition of his statement that

> "the treaties about eventual trade agreements and economic agreements for the time being (make) way for more important matters."[1136]

With hindsight, it is easy to reconstruct what exactly these "more important matters" were.

Had not the "Tägliche Rundschau" already reported from Russia in September 1912 that the most significant and most agitating paper, the "Novoje Vremja", which was said to be very close to the Orthodox Church,

> "wrote almost every day" ... "that Germany – sometimes it mentions Austria to avoid boredom – was the actual war-monger in Europe?"[1137]

A few days later, the "Kölnische Zeitung" was even able to specify this by quoting a Russian evening newspaper, where General Batjanov, the former "leader of the Third Manchurian Army" had written:

> "the Balkan war will be followed by another one between Austria-Hungary and Russia, and this one will end with the destruction of Austria, and after that it will be Germany's turn."[1138]

This general was vilified and ridiculed by the pro-government press in Russia, in order to label him as untrustworthy, but as he was actually right in the end, one will have to make up one's own mind about the trivialization by Russia, when it was put quite harmlessly:

> "The idea of revenge by the French left the Russians quite unmoved." (l. c.)

Can the reader be asked to read about one more argumentation by Hermann Kantorowicz regarding this matter? "Revenge" did not mean vengeance but retaliation...! *Oh, so this is what it means*! Alsace-Lorraine was not war aim for French politics (maybe for the French, but never for French politics), but, if at all, a peace aim, meaning as a "price for victory" in a war "in case it should break out nevertheless."[1139]

Happy France, to have such a convincing advocate!

It is known that the three Balkan states of Greece, Serbia and Romania later indeed entered the Entente. At first, the Greek Ambassador to Vienna, von Streit, had still resisted the persuasiveness of the French Ambassador Dumaine, - but Mr Venizelos will doubtless have put that right. Even the Serbs were initially reluctant to give in to French wooing, - surely only in order to force up the price. Is it possible that the French were assisted in their negotiations by a bit of horse-trading?

> "Serbia was supposed to grant Bulgaria the districts of Istip and Kotschana in return for the promise that Bulgaria supported Serbia in acquiring the Serbian territories of Austria-Hungary."[1140]

This proposal, too, left nothing to be desired with regard to the precision of its aim. This proposal was actually made in December 1913.

Meanwhile, Bulgaria sought its luck (in the revision of territorial boundaries) with the central powers, - as did Turkey, by the way. Sofia had even swallowed the bitter pill of forming a secret military convention with the despised Turks, in order to prevent possible attacks by Greece and Serbia. In the event of a fortunate outcome, Bulgaria would have received "territorial compensation in western Thrace up to the river Mesta".[1141]

They never give up!

But after the enormous losses of the Ottoman Empire in the past 230 years, that small piece of land would not have mattered to the Turks at all.

Under these circumstances, it did not exactly help much that the "Wiener Sonn- und Montagszeitung" - inspired by "Ballhausplatz" - buoyed the Austrians up:

> "The retreat of Turkish power of course requires Austria to be even more alert. [The Austrians] have succeeded in preventing the Russians from replacing Turkish rule, ..."[1142]

Did they - really? If only Vienna had kept its feet on the ground.

And Macedonia? In those unfortunate days, which are still influencing the fate of the Macedonians even today, Prince Lichnowski reported from London about an event which like an ancient fairy tale must make Macedonian readers nostalgic for the past. The question asked by an MP in the British Parliament three weeks *before* the Peace of Bucharest, which ended the Second Balkan War,

> "whether out of consideration that Bulgaria was claiming a large part of Macedonia occupied by Greece and Serbia, he wanted to suggest to the Great Powers the creation of an independent Macedonian state ,"

was answered by Foreign Minister Sir Edward Grey as follows:

> "he did not think it possible to carry out this suggestion, and he did not believe that it would actually be supported by anyone."[1143]

So considerately, objectively and *fairly* did the politicians in London determine the fate of another non-British but at least Christian nation.

On the other hand, in view of the mostly depressing development for Macedonia, one would scarcely have dared to hope that in July 1913 there was actually a single international politician left to consider the political future of Macedonia and put the issue of the independence of a Macedonian state up for discussion in a debate in the mother of all parliaments, - and even using the correct name, of course.

Two further reports, this time from Sofia, reveal that the Macedonian people had reason enough to complain about the new occupying forces. Envoy von Below wrote:

> "It is characteristic that the [Macedonian] petitioners emphasized the fact that such conditions, as can currently be observed, did not even prevail in the cruellest times of Turkish rule in the Macedonian territories now occupied by the Greeks and the Serbs, and never before has such a considerable number of refugees come to Bulgaria to seek refuge."[1144]

And a few days later, shortly *after the Peace of Bucharest of 10 August 1913* he reported:

> "The Macedonian refugees in Bulgaria have now formed a special committee. This has in turn directed the petition - a copy of which is respectfully attached - of the 13th of this month to the present representatives of the Great Powers, in order to protest against the result of the Peace of Bucharest and repeat the request that Macedonia be made into an autonomous province under the protection of the Great Powers."[1145]

Deceived, betrayed, oppressed and exploited, these people did not give up their hope for their small share of justice.

None of the Great Powers, including Germany, can claim not to have known about the injustice that occurred in Macedonia.

> "After the Peace Treaty of Bucharest ... Austria-Hungary was the only European Great Power which repeatedly mentioned a revision of this treaty in diplomatic circles."[1146] Vienna represented its own interests, though: "The Balkan Wars and the Peace Treaty of Bucharest weakened the Austrian ... position in the Balkans... The lost access to both of the Macedonian Mediterranean ports of Cavalla and Saloniki was a heavy blow. Therefore, Austrian ... diplomacy made several attempts to once more bring up the 'question of Macedonia' and achieve a discussion of a revision of the Peace Treaty of Bucharest." (l. c.)

Yet after decades of lobbying by Greece, the Entente-powers had presumably not allowed *the sacrifice of Macedonia* to be wrung from them (profiting from this themselves in the process), only to reopen the whole question.

> "Even at that time it became obvious that the European consensus was disturbed and against this background a solution to the 'question of Macedonia' was no longer to be expected."[1146]

This had to wait until the historic change at the end of the 20th century.

5.5.1 The Greek greed for land: a hubris

A few lines above, the Macedonian city of *Cavalla* on the Aegean coast was been mentioned again, as it was at the beginning of chapter 5.5 with reference to the issues of the Peace Conference of Bucharest. There has been constant struggle for that city, which also involved the German Reich through its dynastic relations with Greece.

Despite the unexpectedly large increase in land and people for Greece in Macedonia and Thrace, Athens moved heaven and earth to get the port of Cavalla across from the island of Thassos as well. The Greeks were obviously not interested in being able to look their opponents, the Bulgarians, in the eye again after the war; instead, it was clear that the Greek government and the Greek King also intended to humiliate Sofia by taking away the last access to the Aegean Sea. When the Greeks needed help for their unjust claim in Bucharest, the new King Constantine (who was still at the front) sought contact to the German Kaiser: of course via his wife, Queen Sophie. And when Sophie telegraphed to her brother,

> "Tino just wired begging me to telegraph you that most important would be ein gutes Wort einzulegen" [to put in a good word for] "King Romania to support claims Greece on Cavalla,"[1147]

William, as was to be expected, could not resist and telegraphed back to his cousin, King Carol, (after all, also a Hohenzollern and furthermore married to another cousin of William II's):

> "Sophie has just telegraphed ... < text > ... Can you do something about Cavalla? I would look favourably on the issue. Kindest regards..."[1148]

But Sophie does not seem to have felt very comfortable about her request; for she closes with the sentence:

> "Please excuse forwarding this important message."

It speaks for the political alertness of the high officials of the German Reich that they by no means agreed to Kaiser William's intervention. A sentence from the letter of the "Imperial Ambassador in the most eminent entourage (on H.M. yacht Hohenzollern)", von Treutler, to the relevant recipient in the Auswärtiges Amt, gives a clear idea of the precarious situation:

> "Dear Jagow, ... I have endeavoured to formulate the text in a manner that no partiality can be read into it that goes beyond the natural and thus justified feelings of a brother and brother-in-law."[1149]

This German commitment to Greek excesses (which the ancient Greeks would have no doubt called "hubris" in their writings) does not become any more bearable by the fact that once more the Tsar was roped in for the Greeks' interests, and Athens took severe action: above all, the King's mother, Grand Princess Olga, argued against the Bulgarians [irrespective of Pan-Slavism or Orthodox belief] in a telegram to her nephew, Tsar Nicholas.

> "Mr Zaimis, the former Prime Minister, who in St. Petersburg is announcing King Constantine's ascent to the throne, also has special instructions regarding the issue of Cavalla."[1150]

There was resistance, however: The former Russian Foreign Minister Izvolski, Ambassador to Paris at the time, immediately saw the advantage for Russia if Bulgaria should control ports in the Black Sea as well as the Mediterranean. Despite massive threats, Izvolski was defeated in this tug of war by the cliquishness of dynastic relations: *Cavalla became Greek.*

Looking into the future:

This time, Grand Princess Olga had been able to achieve a triumph. The next - and last - time, when her name came up in this series of files, she appeared as a petitioner under extremely tragic circumstances in the last year of the First World War. Eating humble pie cannot have been an easy task for this proud and occasionally even arrogant woman. But she was also aware of the German Kaiser's noble character and knew that she could rely on him. Although the Russian Empire, and especially her own family,

had done great injustice to Germany and in particular the Kaiser personally, William II could not help but react to her cry for help with human sympathy:
In summer 1918, the newspaper "Berliner Zeitung am Mittag" had still respectfully reminded the people of the arrival of the widow of the Greek King in Switzerland that
> "during the war ... (she was staying) in St. Petersburg, ... in order to prevent measures against Greece and her son. She knew very well the strength of her influence on the Tsar and the imperial family, and she knew how to use it properly. Of course, this changed when Tsar Nicholas was overthrown" [resignation in March 1918] "and the Republic of Russia was created. Nevertheless, the Queen remained in St. Petersburg under the Kerenski government, and she was forced to remain there under the Bolsheviks."[1151]

However, among the files there is a telegram sent by Grand Princess Olga to the wife of the German Kaiser in August, despite the necessary brevity showing desperation in the hour of human tragedy and at the same time exuding the miasma of world history in an era of radical change:
> "My brother Dimitri, my son-in-law George and many of my cousins are imprisoned in Petrograd in greatest desperation and in danger of their lives. As I am convinced that the Kaiser could have them all transported to Reval, Pskov or some other safe place, I beg for your assistance and would be forever grateful."[1152]

Three weeks later, her despair seems to intensify as the catastrophe unfolds:
> "My last brother, both sons-in-law, heads of the family and other relatives are threatened to be shot dead. I instantly beg you to put in a rescuing word for them. Olga."[1153]

Of course – William II tried to help, as is revealed by a telegram from the Kaiser to the chancellor to be forwarded to Queen Olga ("Measures have been taken in the direction requested ...., the success of which is yet to be seen."[1154]) By contrast, Britain's King George V rejected the request for asylum by the Tsar's family, who were also related to him – and (so-called) allies!
At that time, however, nobody knew that when Olga's *first* cry for help arrived, Tsar Nicholas and his family had already been dead for more than five weeks and also an unknown number of other members of the dynasty had been murdered (on 17 July 1918).
(This short historical anticipation of future events, however, precedes the chronology by five whole dramatic years.)

Back to the Second Balkan War, which was almost at an end in the summer of 1913. It was extraordinarily successful for Greece.
Joy and gratitude bubble forth from Sophie's last two telegrams on this subject to her brother:
> "Intensely relieved. Thankful overjoyed. Peace at last. Know what we owe you. Thanks again. Kisses. Canons firing rejoicing in Athens. Sophy."[1155] [Original text.]

Could the Greek Queen Sophie have been expected to think of the people of Thrace, Macedonia and Epirus, who have been oppressed in Greece since that time until this very day... ?
> [It is conspicuous that Sophie who probably had communicated with her parents-in-law, her numerous sisters-in-law and brothers-in-law etc. in English in the previous quarter of the century, permits herself to use also English in her correspondence with her brother. William, of course, wrote his answers in German, although he (in contrast to many presidents and heads of governments today – even in the EU) was fluent in several languages. It is remarkable though that Constantine always wrote in German to his eminent brother-in-law William.]

A few days later, after the King's return from the front, the breathlessness of wife, mother, queen and sister can still be felt – like in a good book rather than a historical document – who still thinks about her brother and protector in Berlin, despite the celebrations of victory:

> "Our thoughts with you full of gratitude. Grateful joy during Tino's splendid, touching, enthusiastic reception with soldiers. ... Tino and boys well, but look very tired and thin. Joy in the kingdom indescribable. Such a relief to have them home again. Best love. Sophie."[1156]

Joy and grief are constant bedfellows: *Happy Sophie, poor Macedonians. The poor defeated, - poorer still the deceived defeated.*

5.5.2 Constantine I continues the Greek expansion policy

The Greek greed for foreign territory did not abate. In that respect, King Constantine proved to be a worthy successor to his father George.

After the tug of war for the Macedonian port of Cavalla, Constantine continued his efforts without a break. Almost one month after the Peace of Bucharest (10 August 1913), which presented Greece with an enormous increase of power, Constantine had the nerve to "energetically" complain to the German Chancellor on the occasion of a visit to Berlin

> "that the Albanian state was going to be founded at the expense of Greece and the former was poised to annex many Greek communities."[1157]

He was especially concerned about the city of *Koritsa*.

This time, however, the German government stayed firm: The King was asked not to be "intransigent in the South Albanian issue" but to

> "yield to the decision of the powers ... in Greece's own interest. His resistance would only ... compromise his future policy," as he was seeking support from the Triple Alliance. Even "His Majesty, the Emperor, (has) advised him strongly to give in."[1157]

Vienna too adopted an identical position towards the latest Greek demands – referring to the decisions made in London.[1158]

The Austro-German admonitions referred to the bad habit which can often be observed and which the Turks had also been guilty of many times (considering the return of Thessaly and South Epirus, which had been delayed for years), namely to disregard the fulfilment of international obligations or to fulfil them only reluctantly. This time, the Greeks were the ones who did not withdraw from North Epirus.

In a report, the German delegate in the "South Albanian border region", formed on the basis of the London Conference after the Second Balkan War had ended, complained about the incorrect procedure of the Greeks, which actually damaged their reputation:

> "The whole commission – even the Russians – are disgusted by this tactic of lies."[1159]

Just like his father – Constantine did not give up: With reference to the allegedly "spontaneous" pro-Greek opinion among the Epirot population living in Albania, he did not hesitate to play the Triple Alliance off against the Entente in front of the German Envoy. He claimed to feel pushed "forcibly onto the other side", especially by Austria and Italy.

> "Germany, too, sat back passively and watched, it was asserted, as far as Albania was concerned." Regarding "the islands of Asia Minor" he also hoped "that the issue would be dealt with ... in Greece's favour."[1160]

Until then, however, another five years was to pass.

With regard to Koritsa, an interview which Prime Minister Venizelos shortly afterwards granted the Romanian newspaper "Universul" reveals that Greece had to withdraw from the region in question "after the 14 months of occupation"[1161] after all.

Nevertheless, Constantine's successes were rewarded by a considerable donation by the Greek state: he was granted the "state forest of ... Golema Reka ..., situated in the centre of Macedonia, with all rights of possession and beneficial use."[1162]
(The consequences of this donation for Constantine's heirs are discussed below in ch. 5.6.4.1)

5.6 Bits and pieces
5.6.1 An unexpected Turkish proposal speaks volumes

In his report of November 1914, the German Ambassador to Vienna, von Tshirshky, repeated an interesting proposal by the former Turkish governor of Macedonia:

> "Concerning the still reluctant attitude of Bulgaria, which anyway counted on pocketing its profit in Macedonia without any active participation after the end of the war" [in the meantime, the First World War had broken out], "Hilmi Pasha mentioned to me that there was a good way of ruining this business for the Bulgarians. In the peace agreement, the Bulgarians should only be granted the smallest part of Macedonia which was exclusively populated by Bulgarians, and make an independent state out of Macedonia proper. With a population of about two million, this state would be almost equal to Albania. Greece will not reject this solution, once the victorious powers have accepted it in the peace agreement, especially if Greece was granted the possession of the city district of Saloniki. This would provide the Greeks with the further advantage of not having any direct borders to Bulgaria, but instead there would be a buffer state between them"...[1163]

Astonishing! Who could have been better at judging the situation in the Balkans than a high Turkish official? Consequently, he was even capable of making a constructive proposal regarding Macedonia even at such a late hour.
But as it came much too late and was made too quietly, it died away unheard...
And when a few years later, the proposal was once more taken up, it was still too soon: the French newspaper "L'Action Francaise" had published the following prophetic sentences: bearing in mind that Macedonia has been the greatest bone of contention between Greece, Bulgaria and Serbia,

> "<pourquoi ne pas ... créant une Macédoine indépendente?>, considering that the Macedonians themselves accepted no other nationality but the Macedonian one." <Salonique, qui n'est pas plus grecque qu'autre chose, en deviendrait la capitale.> "A Macedonian buffer state would be a preventive measure, which one day people would congratulate themselves on."[1164]

How right the newspaper turned out to be.

5.6.2 A Balkan's expert demonstrates her objective eye for historical coherence

1). The often quoted author and consultant, Edith Durham, made a historical comparison, in order to prove how one conflicting party used the tactics of operating with double standards, when seeking to enforce a pretext for a confrontation at all costs:
When in 1904 the Russian Consul Rostowski was ambushed and shot by an Albanian soldier "through his own fault", as Durham put it, (because the former had whipped him the day before with a riding crop), Russia demanded

> "satisfaction and compensation from the Turkish government." But in 1914, "Russia [had] ... mobilized, when Austria insisted in the investigation of a murder of an archduke."[1165]
> (In the original text, the last sentence is given special emphasis.)

2). Another significant sentence by this honest lady again from the year 1914 is mentioned in chapter 21 (of the same book) called "Die Kriegsjahre" (meaning again the years of the First World War rather than the Balkan Wars):

> "The first thing I did in London was to return to King Peter of Serbia the medal of the Sacred Sava which he had awarded me and write to him that in the previous year I had heard openly discussed the attack on Austria and that I thought he and his people were responsible for the most grievous crime in history."[1165]

Even though this accusation, which was perhaps exaggerated in an Anglo-Saxon way, contained a great deal of truth regarding the cause of the First World War, the Serbian King can hardly have been impressed, - but for us descendants it is another indication of the *injustice of section 231 of the Treaty of Versailles.*

This attitude of a really fair-minded Englishwoman is even more remarkable as she was probably not aware then of the actual background: the Russians' knowledge and financing of the assassination of Sarajevo (see also chapter 5.4.1).
It is characteristic of the psychological warfare of the British that in her home country Edith Durham was disparaged and her book was put down as unreliable, in order to conceal the truth about the actual cause of the First World War.

5.6.3 The Entente continues to mould a Grand Balkan League

The hope of the Great Powers and the Balkan States that the end of the Balkan Wars would also mean the answer to the *question of Macedonia* was - of course - just an illusion. Such excessive injustice could under no circumstances be a permanent solution.
> "The refusal of the Turks to finally conclude the peace treaty [of Bucharest] with Serbia," was noted in Belgrade with great concern. "The meetings and agreements of Young Turk committee members with delegates from the Bulgaro-Macedonian revolutionary organisations as well as the implementation of permanent committees in Sofia and Constantinople with a view to joint actions in bands, aimed at creating an autonomous Macedonia, caused even more concern."[1166]

The Macedonian Liberation Organisation VMRO – perfidiously, as usual, "supported" by Bulgaria – persistently tried to revive the old plan of an *autonomy for Macedonia.* As was mentioned above, Bulgaria had already irritated the other two states which were interested in Macedonian territory, namely Serbia and Greece, with this idea before the Balkan wars.
As Envoy von Scharfenberg further reported from Belgrade in January 1914, Russia must have attached great importance to establishing good relations between Bulgaria and Serbia after the Balkan wars, as the *"re-establishment of the old Balkan League"* mattered a great deal to the Russians!

Finally, the Second Balkan War had ended, too, – and Russia was still pursuing the construction of a Balkan League, to which end it even issued invitations to a conference in St. Petersburg once more.
Was this not a *clear indication of the "encirclement" of Germany*?
At this point, Fritz Fischer finally mentions a warning from a report by the Envoy v. Waldthausen from Bucharest, going beyond the "Balkan" dimension of the Balkan League. As if a sub-clause was the right place for fundamentally significant and, particularly for Germany, tragic information, Fischer quotes (without any commentary) that
> "the Prime Ministers of Serbia (Paschitsch), Greece (Venizelos) and Romania (Take Jonescu) ... (are uniting) in a new anti-Austrian and anti-German Balkan League."[1167]

Nevertheless, it seems that this sensation did not mean much to Fischer. Therefore, he totally disregards the dangerous consequences for the Dual Alliance, emerging from the obvious indications of a long-term plan by the Entente for a war against the German states. Instead, in his controversy, with Egmont Zechlin for example, he tries to put this danger into perspective by arguing that German foreign policy had tried "to form ... a Balkan League itself."[1168]
Under the heading of prejudice, it is quite easy to return a verdict of guilt.

According to the Greek newspaper "Hestia", as stated in a report from Athens, the Bulgarian King Ferdinand had left no doubt that any Bulgarian participation in a (new) Balkan League required "the revision of the Treaty of Bucharest ... through diplomatic channels."[1169]
Furthermore, the envoy reported from Belgrade that, as an important result of his observations and information, with this project of the new Balkan League, Russia believed that it had "a *battering ram in readiness against the Austro-Hungarian monarchy.*"[1166]
Even the German press wrote that the true purpose behind the conference in Petersburg was

> "to unite the Christian Balkan states in a Balkan League under Russian protection and with a military spearhead against Austria-Hungary and its allies."[1170]

The undisguised threat obviously did not trouble anyone in Berlin or Vienna. It is shocking to realize that the disillusioning experiences of Germany and Austria with the lies and deceptions of the Entente powers were still not enough for the former to become wise to the latter.
Thus, in those days (in February 1914!), Ambassador von Pourtalès closes a report from Petersburg with the hardly bearable sentence:

> "The efforts of Mr Sazonov, who I think is honestly trying to prevent a new conflict in the Balkan peninsula in the near future, must have been aimed at supporting joint agreements between Romania, Serbia and Greece, in order to control Bulgaria."[1171]

Unbelievable! As if the true reason had not already been published in the press!

The political analysis of the "Fortnightly Review", which was mentioned above (compare ch. 4.3.1 and 4.3.2), shows the full gravity of the strategy, stating that the Entente did not intend to create a tight ring around the two German states, but instead to drive a wedge between the Balkan neighbours Austria and Turkey.
Thus, after Sarajevo and the tragic Austrian ultimatum of 23 July to Serbia, the Austro-Serbian war was inevitable, which could by rights have been called the Third Balkan War, if it had not in fact been the beginning of the First World War.
The commentary of former Chancellor von Bülow regarding this issue is rather revealing:

> "... The name Theobald von Bethmann Hollweg ... will forever be connected with ... the ridiculous ultimatum to Serbia."

On another occasion he repeats the words of a prominent German entrepreneur:

> "In the words of Albert Ballin", von Bethmann's conduct made "us <stumble into the most unnecessary of all wars and on top of that it made us lose this war>..."[1172]

5.6.4 Greece continues to work on its increase in power

In his persistence, Constantine (compare above, chapter 5.5.2) was perhaps only surpassed by Prime Minister Venizelos.

It is true that after the Greek elections in December 1915, Venizelos was overthrown and left Athens, but in the very same month he landed in Saloniki with his rebels.

During the First World War, several waves of military actions swept across the Balkans. In 1916 large parts of Aegean Macedonia (except for Saloniki, which was still occupied by the French) became Bulgarian by the invasion of the Austro-Bulgarian army, which was also supported by *German* troops.

> The remark that German soldiers participated in this action, reminds the author of his period of service in the Republic of Macedonia. At that time, he often experienced the people's willingness to take care of the war graves, (which was strictly forbidden during the Tito regime). The Macedonians assured him that they only had good memories of the German soldiers.
>
> It seemed as if a circle was finally closed: some time ago in the church of the town of Barth (on the German Baltic coast between Rostock and Stralsund), the author noticed a small marble tablet among the ones put up in memory of the soldiers of that parish who had been killed in action, commemorating a soldier who has rested in Macedonian soil since 1916. The inscription goes:
> Albrecht Dau
> 10.11.1916
> in Macedonia
>
> The author hopes that the "German National War Graves Commission" (Volksbund Deutsche Kriegsgräberfürsorge) will also be able to sponsor the restoration of the graves in Macedonia, in order to give the individual suffering a fitting place and a name.

This new front line brought King Constantine into a difficult situation. For in Macedonia (as well as on Crete), Venizelos did not only organize a pan-Hellenic uprising but also one against the pro-German King Constantine himself. With the help of Franco-English intervention, Constantine was forced into exile in 1917. (Together with his family and a staff of counsellors he went to Switzerland, as Germany remained closed to him due to the propaganda that could be anticipated from the Entente powers. If Germany had offered refuge to the Greek royal family, the Bulgarians' anger would inevitably have been provoked, which would have increased the risk that the Entente could achieve their aim of drawing Bulgaria into the Entente to an irresponsible degree.)

Venizelos took this opportunity to proclaim Constantine's second son, Alexander, king. Incidentally, he sided openly with the Entente.

According to Mark Mazower, it took Athens quite a while "to bet on what turned out to be the right horse":[1173]

In summer 1917, Greece entered into the First World War. The government in Athens declared war on several states, which it obviously intended to defeat, i.e. the Ottoman Empire, the Habsburg Empire, the German Reich and Bulgaria. Thus, Venizelos gave political expression to his hatred of Germany following the same motto that he is reported to have quoted in 1915:

> "It is better to perish with France than to triumph with Germany."[1174]

Deprived of power, King Constantine meanwhile attempted to engineer his return to the Greek throne, hoping that Kaiser William could help him regain his exalted position. However, the latter had in the meantime (despite the affection towards his sister Sophie) other matters to worry about. Besides Turkey, Bulgaria was, after all, the only ally the Central Powers had in the Balkans; and therefore, the German General Staff

and the Kaiser had to take special care in their treatment of this ally. There was no longer any scope for representing family interests.
Consequently, a record in Berlin from the end of the year 1917 reads as follows:

> "... (Bulgaria) considers itself ... at war with Greece. If there was any reduction in the Sarrail expedition" [i.e.: in the event of a withdrawal of the French expedition troops from Saloniki] "the Bulgarians would doubtless claim Saloniki, which has always been the object of their desires, but would by no means agree to support an operation with the purpose of returning King Constantine to power in his country and thus to rule this city."[1175]

A relevant detail is added in the context of a name mentioned further above:

> "Bulgaria is ... not of a mind to return Drama, Seres and Cavalla, and together with Austria-Hungary we have explained to the Bulgarian government that according to ... our agreements, we will not raise any objections against the acquisition of this territory." (l. c.)

A conversation which the military attaché of the Embassy in Bern, Major von Bismarck, was allowed to have with the Greek Queen Sophie six months later after endless precautionary measures and which was kept secret, contains the following interesting revelation:

> "Her Majesty ... mentioned ... that she had the fullest sympathy for our situation towards the Bulgarians and believed ... that Greece would have to renounce Cavalla."[1176]

Although the tables have obviously been turned again in favour of Greece and the status quo was once more re-established after the First World War, it was important to demonstrate that under the circumstances at that time, even the Greek royal house had realized that Greece would not be able to keep all the foreign territory it had once annexed.

Constantine himself had already resigned a year before. When the chief editor of the newspaper "Die Vossische Zeitung", Dr. Emil Ludwig, reminded him in summer 1917 of the fact that in February 1915 he had still been prepared to wage a war against Bulgaria for Monastir (and North Epirus), he now admitted shamefacedly: "Monastir is a pium desiderium."[1177]

After the war, Venizelos stayed in Paris for two years, because he did not want to miss any of the long and tough peace negotiations. With success, - which not least traces back to his radical methods in dealing with the Americans, above all Woodrow Wilson himself: threats and shouting as well as his sarcastic scepticism, openly displayed, towards the success of Wilson's pet project, the League of Nations:

> "Another war (would) break out in the Balkans... if the United States did not support (the Greek claims to Thrace)."[1178]

Venizelos' additional remark: if Greece was granted Thrace, "a war in the Balkans would be prevented for at least 15 (?) years...", particularly discouraged the "American supporters of the League of Nations."

Thus, Venizelos had enforced his success with the same methods as the ones used by the unscrupulous tiger Clemenceau, who also clashed with US President Wilson, to carry out his "programme of hatred" against the Germans.

Venizelos celebrated his triumphs in Greek participation in the treaties with *Bulgaria in Neuilly* of 1919 as well as with *Turkey in Sèvres* of 1920.

> "The Peace Treaty of Sévres ... (divided) almost all of the Sultan's territory among the victorious Great Powers [of the Entente] and the neighbouring states. Besides Great Britain and France, Italy, Greece and the Republic of Armenia (founded in 1918) were also granted large parts of the Ottoman core region of Anatolia."

In that way, Greece, Romania and Serbia were able to base their territorial expansions on international law.[1179]
Furthermore, Venizelos managed to get the Dodecanese islands from Italy.
Only one of these territorial gains turned out to be a Trojan horse for him as well as for Greece: the right to extend Greek occupation to the *Anatolian mainland*.
But that is a different story.

5.6.4.1 *Background information (9)*

1.The end of the dynasty in Greece
After King Alexander's premature death, his father Constantine (I) was reinstated by a referendum and was enthroned for another two years before his remaining two sons George II (1922 and 1935) and Paul I (1947) succeeded him to the throne.
As the last Greek king, the grandson of Constantine I (and great-grandson of George I), Constantine II ascended the throne at the age of 24 – until he also had to go into exile after the military coup of 1967. (In 1973/74 the Republic of Greece was proclaimed and confirmed by a referendum.)
The dutiful slave had served his purposes and could be cast aside ...
Precisely 20 years later, "the slave" was even dispossessed by means of a new special Greek law. Ingratitude is the law of life.
Only in November 2002 did the European Court of Human Rights decide that Greece had to pay to the former Greek King Constantine II the amount of 12 million euros compensation.[1180]

2. From Sophie to Sofia
When Queen Sophie wired to her brother William the above mentioned telegrams after the Second Balkan War, her third son (the fourth out of five children), Paul, was twelve years old. At the age of 37 – rather late considering the custom of that time – Paul married Friederike, Princess of Hanover and Great Britain and Duchess of Brunswick. (In 1692, the Guelphs had received (more precisely: purchased) the status of electoral princes under Emperor Leopold I, which they were entitled to, however, because of their close relations to the English dynasty.) In 1962, their eldest daughter Sofia married the Spanish Infante. When the latter became King Juan Carlos I of Spain after Franco's death in 1975, the Greek Queen Sophie, sister of William II, became the grandmother of the present Spanish Queen "Sofia". (However, Sophie did not even live to see Sofia's birth in 1938, as she had already died six years before, aged 62.)

5.6.5 Further proof of Macedonian's separate identity

In the context of the post-war order (after the First World War) "politicians, scientists, analysts and journalists ... thought about the problem of Macedonia as well as ... the nationality of the Macedonian population."
> "The allies employed a group of French experts to survey the ethnic-national composition of the Macedonian population, undertaking a field study in Aegean Macedonia. They came to the conclusion that the population was neither Serbian, nor Bulgarian, nor Greek, but instead a special Slav nation with its own language and culture. British and Italian studies came to the same results."[1181]

Quod erat demonstrandum.

CONCLUSIONS

With a view to the history of the Balkans, the question was initially asked, why, of all Southeast-European states, Macedonia in particular had to deal with such a difficult background so that even in retrospect
- on a national level the application of the metaphor of the legendary Gordic knot seems justified and
- on an international level the Macedonian question of politics is still setting us riddles even today.

It is only a reappraisal of the past which could provide an explanation for the framework surrounding the situation. Historical oblivion, or even the absence of historical awareness, would on the other hand lead to permanently incurable state of tension, perhaps covering forever all traces of understanding under the quicksand of history. Something many parties want. In unusual constellations, the tides, however, could set them free again.
Such a gate was opened by the revolutionary turn in the history of the world of 1989/90, once more uncovering the past – and making it virulent.
What, in the course of the 20th century, had been pushed to the edge of general perception by the turbulences of the tragic events in central Europe, could, in the quiet after the storm, be subjected to a systematic examination. The original files of the Auswärtiges Amt from the times of the German Reich served as reliable and almost perfect material for a reference to the origins of these turbulences. Naturally, those files contained more than the "congealed history" in the standard volumes of historiography could offer.

While light was slowly being spread on Balkan history allowing an increasingly clearer view of the various connections it became obvious that the *"Macedonian knot"* was certainly not a phenomenon being protected by the Norns. Instead the responsibility for its existence – and maintenance – lay in the simple work of man. This meant it had to be possible to *disentangle* the knot.
This "work of man" originated in the imperialist era, the forces of which are obviously still at work until this very day. Even today, they still prevent an unimpaired, successful and peaceful development in the Republic of Macedonia.

The years of combing through the old (unprinted) reports of the German embassies containing descriptions of the events of those decades have revealed the tool which the neighbouring states of Macedonia used to enforce their imperialist aims:
They denied the identity of the Macedonians!
Furthermore, they believed they could provide themselves with a vague basis for their claim by referring to medieval, and in the case of Greece, even ancient history.
In the truest sense of the word, they forcibly took possession of Macedonia in the Balkan wars 1912/13 and since then have pretended to the world public that the Macedonians are not what they used to be, but what they intended to make them, namely Bulgarian, Greek and Serbian subjects, or to be more precise: Bulgarianized, Hellenized and Serbianized "state property". (The Albanians, though, were clever enough not to

fall into *this* trap – which does not mean that their specific strategy was less perfidious and violent.)

In addition, in the last decade, the four neighbouring states once more made use of a well known method of the past:

One part of this work (chapter 2.3.) refers back to the report of the Royal Prussian Embassy in Constantinople No. 161 of 28 October 1868, quoting the Bulgarians' complaint that the Greek clergy had attempted to Hellenize the Bulgarian population by means of schools, masses etc, in order to make them forget that, before Turkish times, the Bulgarian Church itself had once been independent. According to the reporter, the Greek counsellors of the High Porte, the so-called Phanariots, had

> "used their influence and the ignorance of their Turkish masters to free the Church of the national-Bulgarian element."

A similar form of a lack of knowledge was used by the Greek government on 26 June 1992 in the Council of Ministers of the EU in Lisbon and on 8 April 1993 in front of the whole League of Nations of the UN in New York, in order to foist the totally unjustifiable (allegedly provisional, thus temporary) name of "FYROM" for the Republic of Macedonia on their European and international "friends". And this was done under false pretences, - namely in the repeated attempt to deny the Macedonians their identity and thus gradually deprive the new state of its means of existence. This policy is still being pursued today, - with the approval and even support by the European Union.

In view of such methods and due to the lack of precise information at that time, no contemporary and politically active person could be expected to have at his disposal a sufficiently rational basis for the judgement of the present decisions made with respect to the Republic of Macedonia. In good faith, the international community of nations could only come to the conclusion that the information given by the Greeks, the Albanians and the Bulgarians (and before that the Serbs) was reliable. Abusing this faith, Macedonia's neighbours made the international world believe that they had certain rights to the language, the name and the territory of Macedonia, right up until the 21st century.

The main concern of this work could therefore only be to disclose the neighbouring states' <red herrings> since the Congress of Berlin of 1878 and uncover the *Macedonians' own identity* to the eyes of the public that until now has not been informed correctly.

In the course of this, it has been quickly revealed that the cardinal error was made after the last Russo-Turkish war of 1877/78, when at England's urging during the Congress of Berlin some of the provinces, which had already been liberated from the Ottoman rule, were returned to Turkey instead of granting the Macedonians and the Thracians the benefits of their long-desired autonomy, or in the latter's case, independence. It was only this "original sin" which enabled the already independent (at least autonomous) states of the region to direct their attention (of the usance of imperialism, i.e. in the footsteps of the Great Powers) to the Macedonian-Thracian region, which - thrown back to the status of a colony of the Ottoman Empire - was practically "up for grabs".

Once it came to implementing the expansion plans, the iron-clad axiom became clear that for the most dubious of reasons every state neighbouring Macedonia claimed the now again Turkish Macedonia for itself. Nevertheless not even their immense greed for territory and consequently for power could hide the fact that none of these states on its own would ever have dared to attack Turkey, in order to conquer and annex Macedonia. They could not even have taken the existential risk of beginning a war against the Ottoman Empire *jointly*. Therefore, for decades, the attempt of forming a league of all contemporary Balkan Kingdoms had failed, - and thus the formation of a "Balkan League" against Turkey. When negotiations actually commenced, none of the parties was spared the immanent dilemma, which Prof. Troebst summarized thus:

"Each individual gain (meant) a loss for the enemy, each weakening of one's own position ... a strengthening of one rival or both of them."[1182]
(In this quote, the order of the listing was changed.)

In the course of this work, unexpected interdependencies have become obvious:
Without the promise of support that was made by Russia in a secret agreement in 1911, the three Balkan states of Bulgaria, Greece and Serbia would never have been able to make their annexation dreams come true in the end, if their territorial demands had not concurred with the long-term plans of England, France and Russia of isolating the German Reich and Austria-Hungary.
This was the indispensable step of the Entente-powers in their preparation of a great European *preventive war aimed at the destruction of both German Empires*.
As accomplices to the Entente, and in return for the protection against a possible military intervention of the central powers, the Balkan states, on the other hand, had to fulfil the task of completing the iron ring around the German Reich and the Habsburgs in Southeast Europe. As blood money, under the protection of the Entente, they were authorized to lead their war of conquest against Turkey for the defenceless Macedonia.

Nevertheless, all these meticulously elaborated plans would have failed if the German Kaiser – in a remarkable historical coincidence – had not, for private reasons, revised his policy of the rejection of a war of aggression against Turkey to the benefit of Greece.
It can hardly be called irony – at best sarcasm – of history that in consenting to a war against Turkey, Kaiser William II assisted England, Russia and France of all states in securing their belligerent preparations against "his own" Wilhelmine Germany. These preparations included binding the Balkan states to the Entente by means of sacrificing Macedonia and thus adding them to the list of their accomplices who would assist them in their future aggressions against the central powers and, at the same time, provide them with unfailing support in Southeast Europe.
The blind confidence, the credulousness and, yes, even the naivety of the Germans towards the treacherous operations of the Entente, as well as an extreme short-sightedness when it came to recognizing the ambush which the Triple-Entente had set for the Dual Alliance, made it much easier for the Entente to carry out its plans.

In contrast to the propagandist accusations made by the later victorious powers, William II had, in 1914, indeed tried to prevent the Austrian war against Serbia, just like in 1912 for example, when he had successfully mitigated conflicts at the edge of disaster. Unlike the English and the Entente, which in 1914 thought the time was right, he had actually shrunk from a preventive war already in 1905 and 1909 (1911). But in

July 1914, the Kaiser was outplayed by other forces, which were actually prepared to go to war.

As a result of the world-famous alliance systems of Austria-Germany, France-Russia, France-England and England-France-Russia as well as Serbia-Russia, every European was well aware of the predictable chain-reaction:
When the Entente advised Serbia to reject the Austrian ultimatum, it was following its long-time plan, which had already failed several times and was specifically aimed at starting a war. Even though Kaiser William had clearly seen through this plan, Austria declaring war on Serbia meant that, on 27 July 1914, the Entente-powers had achieved their aim of a great European war. The rest would be left to combat operations - as well as to propaganda.

Compared to the fact that England, France and Russia had deliberately prepared the war against the German Reich very carefully, the details that the First World War began on 27 July with Austria's declaration of war on Serbia rather than later on 1 August, when the German Reich declared war on Russia as a reaction to the Russian general mobilization on the previous day, can almost be called irrelevant. What actually happened between St. Petersburg and Berlin did in no way coincide with the plan of the Entente, the idea of which was *to put all the blame for the war on the German Reich alone.*
Therefore, these facts were suppressed and modified, in order to feed historiography with false data against Germany causing the German governments, which in future decades would certainly insist on corrections, to come away with empty hands. This was the only way to humiliate and exploit the German Reich by means of severe und unheard of terms, bringing about its destruction, or at least damaging it long-term.

Meanwhile, the Macedonians were freed from the Turkish yoke, with their country divided into three (in fact: four) parts, and forced under the Christian-Orthodox yoke - which was even worse - of the neighbouring states of Greece, Bulgaria and Serbia. (Albania, too, was presented with a piece of Macedonian land by the Entente – perhaps due to the attempt of compensating for the Albanian region ceded to Montenegro.) For almost 30 years, Northern Macedonia, which had been annexed by Serbia in 1912/13, was part of Serbia in the Kingdom of the Serbs, the Croats and the Slovenes, and, since 1929, in the Kingdom of Yugoslavia.
After the Second World War, the liberation of Yugoslavia from the Bulgarian and German occupation of 1944 led to an *independent Macedonia*, which after extensive internal counselling decided in favour of an alliance with the Yugoslavia of Tito. The majority of the Macedonians were fully aware of the fact that a principally possible dependency on Bulgaria would sooner or later have led to the total loss of their national identity. Tito, on the other hand, granted the Macedonians (as well as the other five Slavic nations) the status of a nation and at the same time their membership in the Federal Republic of Yugoslavia as the 6th federal state. (Needless to repeat that this "republican status" could only be measured on the communist scale of "democracy". In this, all six federal states were in the same boat.)

It was only in 1990, when the Yugoslavian federation collapsed in the face of their internal contradictions that history also offered the path to independence also to those Macedonians who had survived as a nation under the roof of Yugoslavia for more than 45 years.

It is admirable how systematically and carefully the statesman Kiro Gligorow, the first President of the Republic of Macedonia, "with wisdom, sense of proportion and personal courage", as the German President Roman Herzog commented on his Macedonian colleague on the occasion of his state visit to Skopje on 9 September 1996, began to solve the problems of the Macedonian knot (unlike Alexander the Great dealing with the Gordic knot) in the conflict area of the still envious and power-hungry neighbours.

In view of the heavily burdened legacy, which was brought about by the neighbouring states and which the Macedonians today still have to bear, and with regard to the above mentioned indifference of the governments in Europe and the United States about the true situation in and around Macedonia, this Sisyphean task could not be fulfilled by a single human being alone. Part of this task of liberating the country and its people from the unjustified Albanian, Bulgarian, Greek and Serbian claims will obviously have to be executed by future governments.

This is where responsibility begins - or rather: the obligation - of those European states, without whose assistance the Macedonians would never have got into this miserable situation: Great Britain, France, Russia, Austria, Germany and Italy.

It is the task of the EU, the USA, the NATO, the Council of Europe, the OSCE and the UN to avoid any further injustice on the basis of the old degenerate foundation of the 19th century!

Therefore, the European Union is obliged to give Macedonia the same chance - if not preference - of entering into the EU as any other Balkan state. Macedonia should be accepted together with Bulgaria (as well as Croatia and Romania). With respect to its scale of values, Europe, must not allow Greece and the other neighbouring states to use their blockade to continue the policy of the imperialist age in the 21st century.

There is still one spark of hope for all present and future members of the European Union:

The desire of all Balkan states to enter into the European Union shows that the role of the borders - even if they are still maintained - is constantly losing significance in Europe.

Notes

Introductory remarks
1 Basic information and current situation

1 In spelling the name „Macedonia", (Macedonians, Macedonian), the author adheres to the regulations of the Auswärtiges Amt (German Ministry of Foreign Affairs).
In quotes - for all names - the spelling of the original text has been kept in each case; this is the reason why spelling may often differ.
2 Fikret Adanir also quotes this report and the title of the article: Die makedonische Frage. Ihre Entstehung und Entwicklung bis 1908. Wiesbaden 1979, p. 153, footnote 357
3 Imanuel Geiss: Der Berliner Kongreß 1878. Protokolle und Materialien. Boppard 1978, p. XI
4 If an incoming report was likely to be of interest for further topics, or had to be sent on to other embassies, copies in Sütterlin script were still prepared. Because of the scripts (and the differences between them) deciphering the texts was often difficult and slow; an additional difficulty that was, however, compensated for by the invaluable impression of directness and authenticity.
5 Hermann Kantorowicz: Der Geist der englischen Politik und das Gespenst der Einkreisung Deutschlands. Berlin 1929, p. 19 sq.
6 E.g.: Hans Herzfeld: Die moderne Welt 1789-1945. II. Teil: Weltmächte und Weltkriege. (Reihe: Geschichte der Neuzeit. Ed. Gerhard Ritter), Braunschweig 1960, p. 85
7 H. Herzfeld: Die moderne Welt. ... loc.cit., p. 78
8 Wiener Sonn- und Montagszeitung on 23.9.1912, enclosure of report No. 275, Vienna, 14216
9 Brockhaus, 20. edition, Leipzig-Mannheim 1996, vol. 2, sub voce „Balkanbund", p. 535
10 Brockhaus, loc.cit., vol. 2, sub voce „Balkankriege", p. 536
11 Th. Schieder: Europäisches Staatensystem und Gleichgewicht. ... loc.cit., p. 31
12 Brockhaus, Die Enzyklopädie, 20. edition 1997, vol. 9, sub voce „Griechenland", p. 117
13 Michael Wood in WDR III television on 7.7.2000
14 Letter from Dr. Ivan Minev to the Head of the Foreign Politics department of Bayerisches Fernsehen, Bergmann, on 2.4.1992, p. 3
15 Cf. footnote 57
16 Georg Stadtmüller: Geschichte Südosteuropas. Munich 1950, p. 95 and p. 111
17 Klaus Steinke: Sprachen. In: Hatschikjan/Troebst (ed.): Südosteuropa. ..., p. 402
18 Brockhaus, 20 th edition 1998, vol. 14, sub voce „Makedonier", p. 83
19 M. Weithmann: Die slavische Bevölkerung auf der griechischen Halbinsel. Ein Beitrag zur historischen Ethnographie Südost-Europas. Munich 1978, p. 132
20 Risto Kuzmanovski: Ohrid – und seine Kunstschatzkammer. Ohrid 1994, p. 13
21 Günter Prinzing: Die umstrittene Selbständigkeit der MOK in historischer Sicht. In: Walter Althammer (ed.): Makedonien. Probleme und Perspektiven eines jungen Staates. Südosteuropa-Gesellschaft, Munich. Aus der Südosteuropa-Forschung, vol. 10, p. 39/40, incl. footnote 15
22 Brockhaus, 20. edition 1998, vol. 14, sub voce „Makedonien", p. 79
23 G. Prinzing: Die umstrittene Selbständigkeit ..., loc.cit., p. 42
24 Prinzing: loc.cit., p. 39
25 Prinzing: loc.cit., p. 40
26 Prinzing: loc.cit., p. 41
27 W. Oschlies: Republik Mazedonien ..., loc.cit., p. 30/31
28 Hans-Dieter Dörpmann: Die religiöse Entwicklung Mazedoniens. Kurzfassung eines Vortrags anläßlich der II. Deutsch-Mazedonischen Konferenz in Jena vom 29.11.-01.12.2001
29 Vera Bojic/Wolf Oschlies: Lehrbuch der mazedonischen Sprache. Munich 1984, p. 11 (also fig. 8)
30 Andreas Raab: Dürfen Makedonen Makedonen sein? Der Streit um die makedonische Identität. In: Elke Lorenz/A. Raab (ed.): Makedonien. Reiches armes Land. Ulm 1997, p. 132-133
31 Ch. Voss: Der albanisch-makedonische Konflikt ..., loc.cit., p. 274
32 Ch. Voss: Der albanisch-makedonische Konflikt ..., loc.cit., p. 276
33 Theodor Schieder: Staatensystem und Gleichgewicht. In: Staatensystem als Vormacht der Welt 1848-1918. Propyläen Geschichte Europas, vol. 5. Reprinted in: K. O. Frhr. v. Aretin (ed.): Bismarcks Außenpolitik und der Berliner Kongress. Wiesbaden 1978, p. 28
34 I. Geiss: Der Berliner Kongress 1878. Sicherheit und Zusammenarbeit in Europa vor 100 Jahren. Aus Politik und Zeit-Geschichte. Beilage zur Wochenzeitung „Das Parlament", R. 41/78, 14.10.1978, p. 7

35 Jutta de Jong: Die makedonische Nationswerdung – eigenständige Integration oder künstliche Synthese? In: Klaus-Detlev Grothusen (ed.): Jugoslawien. Integrationsprobleme in Geschichte und Gegenwart. Göttingen 1984, p. 164, footnote 2)
36 V. Meier: Wie Jugoslawien ...loc.cit., p. 323
37 Giorgi Stojćevski: Makedonien in den internationalen Beziehungen (1878-1919). In: Walter Lukan (ed.): Österreichische Osthefte. Ost- und Südosteuropa Institut. Year 40, vol. 1/2, p. 170
38 Reichs-Gesetzblatt Nr. 31. Reprinted in: I. Geiss: Berliner Kgs. ... Prot. u. Mat. ..., loc.cit., p. 387
39 I. Geiss: Berliner Kongress. Prot. u. Mat. ..., loc.cit., p. 18
40 Richard von Mach: Die macedonische Frage. Vienna 1895, p. 12
41 R. v. Mach: Die macedonische Frage. ... loc.cit., p. 19
42 R. v. Mach: loc.cit, p. 13
43 J. de Jong: Der nationale Kern ..., loc.cit., p. 8
44 G. Stojćevski: Makedonien ..., loc.cit., p. 173
45 Torsten Szobries: Sprachliche Aspekte des nation-building in Mazedonien. Die kommunistische Presse in Vardar-Mazedonien (1940-1943). Stuttgart 1999, p. 55
46 Brockhaus, 20 th edition 1997, vol. 4, sub voce „Bulgarien", p. 118
47 Vera Bojic/Wolf Oschlies: Lehrbuch der mazedonischen Sprache. Munich 1984, p. 9
48 M. Weithmann: Die slavische Bevölkerung auf der griechischen Halbinsel. ... loc.cit., p. 93
49 J. de Jong: Der nationale Kern ...loc.cit., p. 6
50 Manolis Andronicos: Museum Thessaloniki. Ektodite Athenon 1990, p. 27
51 Hans-Wilhelm Haussig: Kulturgeschichte von Byzanz. Stuttgart 1959, p. 354 and 548
52 Karl Kaser: Raum und Besiedlung. In: Hatschikjan/Troebst (ed.): Südosteuropa ..., loc.cit., p. 61
53 Edgar Hösch: Kulturen und Staatsbildungen. In: Hatschikjan/Troebst (ed.): Südosteuropa ..., loc.cit., p. 41 sq.
54 M. Weithmann: Die slavische Bevölkerung auf der griechischen Halbinsel. ... loc.cit., p. 165 (Further names of Slavic tribes frequently mentioned by Weithmann are: Belegeziten, Baiuniten, Berziten, Strymoniten, Milingen and Ezeriten.)
55 Klaus Steinke: Sprachen. In: Hatschikjan/Troebst: Südosteuropa ..., loc.cit., p. 402
56 K. Steinke: Sprachen. In: Hatschikjan ..., loc.cit., p. 398
57 T. Szobries: Sprachliche Aspekte ..., loc.cit., p. 49
58 T. Szobries: Sprachliche Aspekte ..., loc.cit., p. 50
59 T. Szobries: Sprachliche Aspekte ..., loc.cit., p. 50
60 T. Szobries: Sprachliche Aspekte ..., loc.cit., p. 57 and 59
61 T. Szobries: Sprachliche Aspekte ..., loc.cit., p. 54
62 T. Szobries: Sprachliche Aspekte ..., loc.cit., p. 61
63 T. Szobries: Sprachliche Aspekte ..., loc.cit., p. 51
64 J. de Jong: Der nationale Kern des makedonischen Problems. ...loc.cit., p. 287
65 T. Szobries: Sprachliche Aspekte ..., loc.cit., p.50
66 T. Szobries: Sprachliche Aspekte ..., loc.cit., p. 51
67 K. Steinke: Sprachen. In: Hatschikjan ..., loc.cit., p. 406
68 Brockhaus, 20. edition 1997, vol. 4, sub voce „Bulgarische Sprache", p. 124
69 K. Steinke: Sprachen. In: Hatschikjan ... loc.cit., p. 405
70 K. Steinke: Sprachen. In: Hatschikjan ..., loc.cit., p. 401
71 C. Hopf: Sprachnationalismus in Serbien und Griechenland. ... loc.cit., p. 19
72 Francisco R. Adrados: Geschichte der griechischen Sprache von den Anfängen bis heute. Tübingen, Basel 2001, p. 284
73 Eric J. Hobsbawm: Nations and Nationalism since 1780. Programme, Myth, Reality. Cambridge 1995. Quoted by Claudia Hopf: Sprachnationalismus ..., loc.cit., p. 149, footnote 362
74 F. R. Adrados: Geschichte der griechischen ...loc.cit., p. 285
75 C. Hopf: Sprachnationalismus ..., loc.cit., p. 148-149 sq.
76 For more detail, see C. Hopf: Sprachnationalismus in Serbien und Griechenland. ... loc.cit.
77 C. Hopf: Sprachnationalismus ..., loc.cit., p. 136, footnote 328
78 R. 29 Athens 20.4.1877, 7328
79 F. R. Adrados: Geschichte der griechischen...loc.cit., p. 289
80 K. Steinke: Sprachen. In: Hatschikjan/Troebst ..., loc.cit., p. 401
81 K. Steinke: ..., loc.cit., p. 409
82 K. Steinke: ..., loc.cit., p. 412
83 T. Szobries: Sprachliche ...loc.cit., p. 61
84 For detailed information, cf. V. Meier: Wie Jugoslawien ... , loc.cit., p. 381 sq.

85 Christian Voss: Der albanisch-makedonische Konflikt in der Republik Makedonien in zeitgeschichtlicher Perspektive. In: Südosteuropa Mitteilungen 2001, No. 3, p. 276
86 M. Weithmann: Makedonien ... loc.cit., p. 265
87 Klaus Schrameyer: Das Verbot der Partei der Makedonier in Bulgarien durch das bulgarische Verfassungsgericht. In: Südosteuropa 2000, volume 5-6, p. 283
88 K. Schrameyer: Das Verbot ..., loc.cit., p. 289
89 Gerhard Seewann: Minderheiten und Nationalitätenpolitik. In: M. Hatschikjan and S. Troebst (ed.): Südosteuropa. Gesellschaft, Politik, Wirtschaft, Kultur. Ein Handbuch. Munich 1999, p. 188.
90 K. Schrameyer: Das Verbot ...,loc.cit., p. 288 and p. 283
91 Viktor Meier: Wie Jugoslawien verspielt wurde. Munich 1995, p. 334
92 Magarditsch A. Hatschikjan: Tradition und Neuorientierung in der bulgarischen Außenpolitik 1944-1948. Die „nationale Außenpolitik" der Bulgarischen Arbeiter-Partei (Kommunisten). Munich 1988, p. 246
93 V. Meier: Wie Jugoslawien ... loc.cit., p. 335
94 Michael W: Weithmann: Makedonien – „Land zwischen vier Feuern", Außenpolitik III/93, p. 265
95 Claudia Hopf: Sprachnationalismus in Serbien und Griechenland. Theoretische Grundlagen sowie ein Vergleich von Vuk Stefanović Karadžić und Adementios Korais. Balkanologische Veröffentlichung, vol. 30, Wiesbaden 1997, p. 306
96 Ch. Voss: Das slavophone Griechenland – Bemerkungen zum Ende eines Tabus. In: Südosteuropa-Mitteilungen, 2000, No. 4, p. 351
97 Ch. Voss: Minderheiten in Griechenland. In: Pogrom. Gesellschaft für bedrohte Völker. Volume No. 153, May/June 1990, p. 22-3
98 V. Meier: Wie Jugoslawien ..., loc.cit., p. 337
99 M. Weithmann: Makedonien ..., loc.cit., p. 268
100 V. Meier: Wie Jugoslawien ..., loc.cit., p. 320 sq.
101 See also Wolfgang Höpken: Staatensystem. In: M. Hatschikjan and S. Troebst (ed.): Südosteuropa. Gesellschaft, Politik, Wirtschaft, Kultur. Ein Handbuch. Munich 1999, p. 270
102 Rainer Hermann: Die Geschäfte der Embargobrecher. Vorwürfe des Haager Kriegsverbrechertribunals gegen Griechenland. In: FAZ on 26.6.2002
103 Nada Boškovska: Sein oder nicht. Ein Staat ringt um Anerkennung. In: NZZ-Folio, September 1992, p. 44
104 Ch. Voss: Der albanisch-makedonische Konflikt ..., loc.cit., p. 276
105 W. Höpken: Staatensystem. ...loc.cit., p. 271
106 Marie-Jeanne Calic: Außen- und Sicherheitspolitik. In: M. Hatschikjan, S. Troebst (ed.): Südosteuropa. ... Handbuch. ... loc.cit., p. 294
107 W. Höpken: Staatensystem ..., loc.cit., p. 271
108 Ch. Voss: Der albanisch-makedonische Konflikt ..., loc.cit., p. 281
109 G. Seewann: Minderheiten ..., loc.cit., p. 190
110 G. Seewann: Minderheiten ..., loc.cit., p. 196 and 177
111 Quoted in ZDF television, in Frontal 21 (Theo Koll) on 7.8.2001
112 M. Weithmann: Makedonien ..., loc.cit., p. 269
113 Stefan Troebst: IMRO + 100 = FYROM? Kontinuitäten und Brüche in den makedonischen Nationalbewegungen in historiographischer Perspektive. In: Walter Lukan/Peter Jordan (ed.): Makedonien. Geographie, Ethnische Struktur, Geschichte, Sprache und Kultur, Politik, Wirtschaft, Recht. In: Österreichische Osthefte, Year 40, Vienna 1998, p. 220
114 S. Troebst: Politische Entwicklung in der Neuzeit. In: Hatschikjan/Troebst (ed.): Südosteuropa. ... Handbuch. ... loc.cit., p. 80
115 Jutta de Jong: Der nationale Kern des makedonischen Problems. Ansätze und Grundlagen einer makedonischen Nationalbewegung (1890-1903). Ein Beitrag zur komparativen Nationalismusforschung. Frankfurt/M, Bern 1982, p. 5 sq.
116 Ch. Voss: Der albanisch-makedonische Konflikt ..., loc.cit., p. 274
117 G. Seewann: Minderheiten ..., loc.cit., p. 178
118 Ch. Voss: Der albanisch-mazedonische Konflikt ..., loc.cit.: 1.) p. 278, 2.) p. 273
119 G. Seewann: Minderheiten ..., loc.cit., p. 178
120 Wolf Oschlies: Republik Mazedonien. Report of the BIOst No. 14/1994, p. 23
121 G. Seewann: Minderheiten ..., loc.cit., p. 186
122 Ch. Voss: Der albanisch-makedonische Konflikt ..., loc.cit., p. 273
123 Luan Starova: Zeit der Ziegen. Zürich 1999, p. 46 and 51

124 Ch. Voss: Der albanisch-makedonische Konflikt. ..., loc.cit., p. 278, incl. footnote 32
125 Stefan Troebst: Kommunizierende Röhren: Makedonien, die Albanische Frage und der Kosovo-Konflikt. In: Südosteuropa Mitteilungen 1999, No. 3, p. 216 and 224
126 L. Starova: Zeit ..., loc.cit., p. 42 sq.
127 Ch. Voss: Der albanisch-mazedonische Konflikt ..., loc.cit., p. 277
128 Matthias Rüb: Schießerei unter Albanern. In: FAZ, No. 73 on 27.3.2002, p. 8
129 Matthias Rüb: Haager Tribunal ermittelt in Mazedonien. In: FAZ, 10.04.2002, p. 2
130 W. Höpken: Staatensystem. In:... Südosteuropa ..., loc.cit., p. 272
131 M. Martens: Den Haag ist voreingenommen. Ein Gespräch mit Koštunica. In: FAZ on 1.8.2002
132 Hans-Dietrich Genscher: Erinnerungen. Berlin 1995, p. 668
133 Stefan Troebst: Präventive Friedenssicherung durch internationale Beobachtermissionen? Das Beispiel der KSZE-Spillover-Monitormission in Makedonien 1992/1993 vom 25.10.1993. Stiftung Wissenschaft und Politik, Ebenhausen, Nov.1993, p. 14
134 C. Hopf: Sprachnationalismus in Serbien und Griechenland..., loc.cit., p. 305

2 The development of the Balkan League in the Balkan States
2.1 Serbia

135 Concerning the southern position of Greece, we can see the Ottoman withdrawal line as an almost concentric circle with an ever-diminishing radius around the former centre Constantinople, from which the western coast of Greece is as far removed as the northern border of Serbia.
136 K. Kaser: Raum und Besiedlung. In: Hatschikjan/Troebst (ed.): Südosteuropa-Handbuch. loc.cit., p. 56 sq.
137 K. Kaser: ..., loc.cit., p. 60
138 E. Hösch: Kulturen und Staatsbildungen. In: Hatschikjan/Troebst (ed.): Südosteuropa-Handbuch. loc.cit., p. 43
139 E. Hösch: ..., loc.cit., p. 44 sq.
140 Brockhaus, 20. edition 1998, vol. 14, sub voce „Makedonien", p. 79
141 V. Meier: Wie Jugoslawien ..., loc.cit., p. 50
142 E. Hösch: Kulturen und Staatsbildungen. In: Hatschikjan/Troebst (ed.): Südosteuropa-Handbuch, loc.cit., p. 40
143 E. Hösch: ..., loc.cit., p. 52
144 K. Steinke: Sprachen. In: Hatschikjan/Troebst (ed.): Südosteuropa-Handbuch. ... loc.cit., p. 405
145 Because Southeast Europe was isolated for centuries, cultural epochs such as the Reformation or the Enlightenment had in any case passed the peoples who were living under Turkish rule by.
146 The author adheres to the method of counting in I. Geiss: Der Berliner Kongress. Prot. u. Mat.., loc.cit., p. 3.
147 Georg Stadtmüller: Geschichte Südosteuropas, Munich 1950, p. 342
148 Mark Mazower: Der Balkan. Kleine Weltgeschichte. Berlin 2002, and
Aug. Heinrich Kober: Europäische Fürstenhöfe – damals. [vol. 3] Zwischen Donau und Bosporus. Frankfurt/M. o. J. (probably also 1937, like the two volumes in the same series by Paul Sethe), p. 12
149 G. Stadtmüller: Geschichte ..., loc.cit., p. 359
150 I. Geiss: Berliner Kgs. ... Prot. u. Mat., ... loc.cit. p. 5
151 Idem, loc.cit., p.6
152 Idem, loc.cit., p.7
153 I. Geiss: Berliner Kgs. ... Prot. u. Mat., ... loc.cit., p. XV
154 R. 55 Belgrade 18.10.1880, 14400
155 Alfred Cattani: Die Geschichte eines Hasses. NZZ-Folio, Sept. 1992
156 R. 55 Belgrade 18.10.1880, 14400
157 A. Hillgruber: Bismarcks Außenpolitik. Freiburg 1972, p. 177
158 R. 100 Bucharest 14.10.1886, 14401
159 R. 84 Belgrade 16.10.1886, 14401
160 R. 98 Belgrade 29.11.1886, 14401
161 R. 84 Bgd. 16.10.1886, 14401
162 R. 40 Sofia 25.3.1891, 14401. (The Serbian wish for "revenge for Slivniza" encumbered the bilateral relations between Serbia and Bulgaria for years, although Serbia could not support its claim on Rumelia either historically, or legally, or ethnically. Such catchwords seem to have been the vogue, cf. the legendary Austrian (and French) slogan „revenge for Sadova" (Königgrätz) 20 years before or, only approx. 15 years before, the „revenge" for returning „French" Alsace.)

163 R. 40 Sofia 25.3.1891, 14401
164 T. Szobries: Sprachliche Aspekte des nation-building in Mazedonien. ... loc.cit., p. 52 sq.
165 T. Szobries: Sprachliche ..., loc.cit., p. 53
166 Aug. Heinrich Kober: Europäische Fürstenhöfe ... ,loc.cit., p. 19 sq.
167 A. H. Kober: Europäische Fürstenhöfe ..., loc.cit., p. 48 sqq. (Maria Fagyas in „Der Tanz der Mörder. Reinbek/HH 1976, rororo 4011" describes Draga as Alexander's former nanny who became his lover and from whom he could not separate himself for the rest of his life.)
168 T. 416 Den Haag 13.6.1917, 7492
169 Gotthold Rhode: Der Berliner Kongreß und Südosteuropa. In: Karl O. Frhr. v. Aretin (ed.): Bismarcks Außenpolitik ..., loc.cit., p. 122
170 R. 170 Belgrade 14.10.1897, 14402
171 Johannes Lepsius, Albrecht Mendelssohn Bartholdy, Friedrich Thimme (ed.): Die Große Politik der Europäischen Kabinette 1871-1914. Berlin 1924, vol. 12/I, p. 549 (R. 73 Sofia 26.7.1899)
172 This was a usual term (not only for businessmen but also for dipomats) which bore no negative connotations at the time and was thus not considered to be defamatory.
173 R. 197 Belgrade 28.10.1903, 14402
174 M. Edith Durham: Die slawische Gefahr. 20 Jahre Balkan-Erinnerungen. Stuttgart 1922, p. 122
175 E. Durham: Die slawische Gefahr ..., loc.cit., p. 117
176 Brockhaus, 14. edition 1908, sub voce „Orientfrage"
177 R. 124 Bgd 27.9.1904, 14402
178 On the subject of "self-caused" misery, the ambassador may have thought of the regicide of Alexander Obrenović in the previous year (1903) which brought Prince Peter Karadjordje himself to power and impaired his reputation with the European dynasties for years – although this murder was "only" one of many between the two families. One could even think of the "curse of the misdeed", i.e. the murder by Miloš Obrenović of "Black George" Karadjordjević, his godfather, in 1815.
179 F. Adanir: Die mazedonische Frage ..., loc.cit., p. 57, footnote 289
180 Brockhaus, 20. edition 1998, vol. 14, sub voce „Makedonier", p. 83
181 M. Weithmann: Makedonien ... In: Außenpolitik ...loc.cit., p. 265
182 G. Stadtmüller: Geschichte Südosteuropas. Munich 1950, p. 376
183 R. 92 Belgrade 25.7.1904, 14402
184 J. de Jong: Der nationale Kern ..., loc.cit., p. 10 (Karl Hron: Das Volkstum der Slawen Makedoniens 1890. Skopje 1966 (reprinted in Macedonian), p. 58
185 R. 34 Bucharest (!) 7.2.1906, 14403
186 The author's contemporaries used to hold the opinion that the singularized plural was a bad, derogatory language habit of the III. Reich. But in earlier times, this seems to have been common usage – also in other languages, e.g. the Turk (the Turks), l'Allemand (the Germans).
187 R. 3 Belgrade 4.1.1907, 14403
188 Bernhard v. Bülow: Denkwürdigkeiten. Berlin 1930, 2. vol., p. 330
189 R. 193 Belgrade 30.12.1908, 14403
190 R. 191 Vienna 30.5.1909, 14403
191 Enclosure with B. 226 Belgrade 9.11.1909, 14403
192 R. 226 Bgd. 9.11.1909, 14403
193 R. 354 Constantinople 27.11.1909, 14403
194 R. 379 Vienna 30.11.1909, 14403
195 R. 237 Bgd. 6.12.1909, 14403
196 R. 5 Bgd 17.1.1910, 14404
197 The Times (A 11234) 4.6.1913, 14405
198 R. 72 Co'ple 6.3.1910, 14404
199 R. 38 Bgd. 27.3.1910, 14404
200 R. 105 St.P'bg. 24.3.1910, 14404
201 R. 106 St.P'bg. 25.3.1910, 14404

2.2 Bulgaria
202 Stadtmüller: Geschichte ..., loc.cit., p. 67
203 E. Hösch: Kulturen und Staatsbildungen. In: Hatschikjan/Troebst: ..., loc.cit., p. 38
204 K. Kaser: Raum und Besiedlung. In: Hatschikjan/Troebst: ...,loc.cit., p. 56
205 E. Hösch: Kulturen ..., loc.cit., p. 36
206 Stadtmüller: Geschichte ...loc.cit., p. 121

206a H.-Dieter Dörpmann: Das alte Bulgarien. Leipzig 1973, p.. 32
207 Stadtmüller: Geschichte ... loc.cit., p. 123
208 E. Hösch: Kulturen ... In: Hatschikjan ... loc.cit., p. 38
209 M. Weithmann: Die slavische Bevölkerung auf der griechischen Halbinsel ...loc.cit., p. 166
210 A memo: In 925, after deposing Frankish rule, the Croatian Tomislav founded the first Slav Catholic kingdom in the Balkans.
211 In the description of an earlier siege of Constantinople in the year 626 when the Bulgarians did not yet have their own state and could therefore not yet have been assimilated, they were listed separately next to the other besiegers – Avar, Slavs and Gepids.
212 E. Hösch: Kulturen ..., loc.cit., p. 36
213 Brockhaus, 20. edition, Leipzig/Mann. 1998, vol. 18, sub voce „Russland", p. 677 sq.
214 Stadtmüller: Geschichte ... loc.cit., p. 126
215 E. Hösch: Kulturen ... In: Hatschikjan ... loc.cit., p. 44
216 Brockhaus, 20. edition 1997, vol. 4, sub voce Bulgarien, p. 118
217 Stadtmüller: Geschichte ..., p. 373
218 Stadtmüller: loc.cit., p. 360
219 Stadtmüller, loc.cit., p. 361
220 Bojic/Oschlies: Lehrbuch ... loc.cit., p. 11, fig. 7
221 Bojic/Oschlies: Lehrbuch ... loc.cit., p. 11, fig. 8
222 J. de Jong: Der nationale Kern ..., loc.cit., p. 9
223 Stefan Troebst: Die makedonische Antwort ... In: Südosteuropa 41, 1992, p. 431
224 Stadtmüller: Geschichte ... loc.cit., p. 362
225 Stadtmüller: loc.cit., p. 374
226 K. Steinke: Sprachen. In: Hatschikjan/Troebst: ..., loc.cit., p. 406
227 M. Edith Durham: Die slawische Gefahr ..., loc.cit. p.116
228 Bojic/Oschlies: Lehrbuch ... loc.cit., p.11, fig.9. Thus, next to the patriarch of Constantinople and the Metropolitan bishops of the Orthodox sister churches in Antiochia, Alexandria, Jerusalem and Cyprus, there was also the Exarch of Bulgaria.
229 Lepsius u.a.: Große Politik ...loc.cit., vol. 12/I, p. 148 (R. 249 Co'ple 28.4.1897)
230 Report from Athens of January 1877, R 7328 (No. of report and date unfortunately lost)
231 George F. Kennan: Bismarcks europäisches System in der Auflösung. Die französisch-russische Annäherung 1875-1890. Frankfurt/Main 1981, p. 79
232 K. O. Frhr. v. Aretin: Bismarcks Außenpolitik ...loc.cit., p. 87
233 I. Geiss: Berliner Kgs. ... Prot. u. Mat., ... loc.cit., p. XVI
234 I. Geiss: Berliner Kgs. ... Prot. u. Mat., ... loc.cit., p. XXIV
235 I. Geiss: Berliner Kgs. ... Prot. u. Mat., ... loc.cit., p. 373
236 Th. Schieder: Europäisches Staatensystem und Gleichgewicht ..., loc.cit., p. 23
237 R. 578 Vienna 11.12.1880, 14400
238 G. F. Kennan: Bismarcks ... System ..., loc.cit., p. 151 and 157 (also 159 and 161)
239 T. Szobries: Sprachl. Aspekte des nation-building in Mazedonien. ... loc.cit., p. 52, footnote 146 a
240 „The Times" on 4.6.1913, A 11234, 14405
241 Paul Sethe: Europäische Fürstenhöfe – damals: Berlin/Vienna. Frankfurt/M. 1937, p. 20
242 F. Adanir: Die makedonische Frage ..., loc.cit., p. 105, footnote 42
243 R. 57 Bucharest 19.6.1886, 14400
244 R. 73 Sofia 11.7.1886, 14400
245 Instruction No. 472 to the embassy in St.P'bg. of 21.7.1886, 14400
246 Instruction to the embassy in Vienna No. 373 of 5.7.1886, 14400
247 P. Sethe: Europäische ..., loc.cit., p. 21-22
248 P. Sethe: Europäische ..., loc.cit., p. 42
249 Sethe; loc.cit., p. 22
250 Enclosed with report No. 170 from Belgrade of 14.10.1897, 14402
251 Münchener N. Nachrichten of 6.4.1897, A 4567, 14402
252 R. 148 Bgd. 26.8.1898, 14403
253 I see with regret that the otherwise highly respected "Herzfeld", in his basic historical work (which I have quoted frequently) „Die moderne Welt 1789-1945" Part II, Braunschweig 1960, p. 28, interprets the „I" in IMRO as meaning „international" (instead of "inner"), fails to account the „M" (for Macedonian) altogether and finally even defines this *Macedonian* liberation organization as *Bulgarian*.
254 Heinr. Müller: Die Slavomazedonier in Griechenland. Gesellschaft für bedrohte Völker,1992, p. 2

255 V. Meier: Wie Jugoslawien ..., loc.cit., p. 325
256 J. de Jong: Der nationale Kern ..., loc.cit., p. 1
257 E. Durham: Die slawische Gefahr ..., loc.cit., p. 114
258 Brockhaus, 20. edition 1997, vol. 10 sub voce IMRO, p. 442
259 J. de Jong: Der nationale Kern ..., loc.cit., p. 7
260 J. de Jong: Der nationale Kern ..., loc.cit., p. 290
261 J. de Jong, loc.cit., p. 284
262 Jutta de Jong: Die makedonische Nationswerdung ... In: K.-D. Grothusen (ed.): Jugoslawien. Integrationsprobleme in Geschichte und Gegenwart. Göttingen 1984, p. 167
263 J. de Jong: Der nationale Kern ..., loc.cit., p. 285
264 Loc.cit. (A 'millet' is a "national group" organized according to religion, as a basis for the Turkish administrative system)
265 The Times on 5.6.1913, A 11234, 14405
266 R. 138 Sofia 26.11.1908, 14403
267 B. 1449 Sofia 14.12. 1908, 14403
268 R. 45 Sofia 3.2.1909, 14403
269 R. 96 Bgd. 27.4.1909, 14403
270 R. 178 Sofia 2.12.1909, 14403
271 R. 29 Belgrade 9.3.1910. In: J. Lepsius et. al.: Große Politik der europäischen Mächte. vol. 27: Zwischen den Balkankrisen 1909-1911, Berlin 1925, p. 182 sq.
272 loc.cit.: footnote
273 R. 237 Bgd. 6.12.1909, 14403
274 Chr. Voss: Der albanisch-makedonische Konflikt ..., loc.cit., p. 273, footnote 175 a

2.3 Greece
276 K. Kaser: Raum und Besiedlung. In: Hatschikjan/Troebst (Hg.): Südosteuropa-Handbuch, ...a.a.O., S. 60
277 Stefan Weidner: Bruder, wo bist du? In: FAZ vom 14.06.2002
278 K. Steinke: Sprachen. In. Hatschikjan ...a.a.O., S. 401
280 Stadtmüller: Geschichte ...a.a.O., S. 88
281 Hans-Wilhelm Haussig: Kulturgeschichte von Byzanz. Stuttgart 1959, S. 182
282 M. Weithmann: Die slavische Bevölkerung der griechischen Halbinsel ...a.a.O., S. 133 und S. 132
283 M. Weithmann: Die slavische Bevölkerung ...a.a.O., S. 167
284 Haussig: Kulturgeschichte ... ,a.a.O., S.184
285 M. Weithmann: Makedonien – Land zwischen ...a.a.O., S.274 f.
286 M. Weithmann: Makedonien – Land zwischen ...a.a.O., S. 268
287 R. 11 Athens 16.1.1904, 7483
288 E. Hösch: Kulturen u. Staatsbildungen. In: Hatschikjan ... a.a.O., S. 37
289 K. Steinke: Sprachen. In: Hatschikjan ... a.a.O., S.400 f.
290 Lorenz Jäger: Wie Japhet nach Europa kam. Epochenschwelle zwischen 1500 und 1800. FAZ vom 12.12.2001, S. N 5
291 F. R. Adrados: Geschichte der griechischen Sprache ..., a.a.O., S. 286. Vgl. auch C. Hopf: Sprachnationalismus in Serbien und Griechenland, ...a.a.O., S. 137
292 Stadtmüller: Geschichte ..., a.a.O., S. 275
293 Rainer Hermann: Im Zeichen des Doppeladlers. In: FAZ vom 9.8.2000
294 C. Hopf: Sprachnationalimus ...,loc. cit., p. 155
295 C. Hopf: ibidem, p. 142
296 C. Hopf: ibidem, following Th. Schieder, p. 142, footnote 344
297 Stadtmüller: Geschichte ..., loc. cit., p. 360
298 Th. Schieder: Nationalismus und Nationalstaat. Göttingen 1991, S. 93, zitiert von C. Hopf: Sprachnationalismus ..., p. 159, footnote 389
299 E. Hösch: Kulturen ... In: Hatschikjan ..., loc. cit., p. 51
300 R. 161 Constantinopel 28.10.1868, 12377
301 R. 39 Athens 8.5.1877, 7328
302 R. 17 Co'ple 25.2.1870, 12136
303 R. 35 Athens 22.7.1876, 7326
304 R. 1 Athens 12.1.1877, 7328
305 Enclos. of 5.11.1876 from Saloniki to R. 247 Co'ple 20.11.1876, 7327

306 R. (A 5904) Corfu 16.10.1876, 7327
307 R. 5 Athens 22.1.1877, 7328
308 R. 16 Athens 2.3.1877, 7328
309 R. 30 Athens 22.4.1877, 7328
310 R. 16 Athens 2.3.1877, 7328
311 Internal record (Nr. 672 ?) Berlin 13.8.1876, 7326
312 R. 56 Athens 16.6.1877, 7329
313 Just as a memo: in his second marriage Wilhelm II was married to the widowed Princess Hermine, née Reuß. (Incidentally, Prince Reuß signed his reports, when he added his first name at all, with a Roman seven without a dot.)
314 R. 186 Co'pel 28.6.1877, 7329
315 R. 66 Athens 20.7.1877, 7329
316 This strategy was to become a cherished habit: remember summer 1917, whwn Greece declared war on those countries which it apparently intended to defeat, namely the Ottoman Empire, the Habsburg Empire, the German Empire and Bulgaria. It paid off another time: as a "victorious" power in the First World War Greece had its 1913 annexation of Macedonia and parts of Thracia and Epirus attested in the treaties of the suburbs of Paris (and received several islands).
317 Im. Geiss: Berliner Kgs., Prot. u. Mat., ...loc. cit., p. 304
318 Im. Geiss: Berliner Kgs., Prot. u. Mat., ...loc. cit., p. 306
319 R. 106 London 26.7.1876, 7326
320 Im. Geiss: Berliner Kgs. ... Prot. u. Mat., ... loc. cit., p. 12 a. p. 304 and Brockhaus, 14. ed. 1908, sub voce: „Orientfrage" („Oriental Question")
321 Im. Geiss: Berliner Kgs. ... Prot. u. Mat., ... loc. cit.; p. 261
322 P. Sethe: Europäische Fürstenhöfe – damals. 2. Vol.: Der russische Zarenhof, . loc.cit., p. 11
323 R. 187 St. P'bg. 9.8.1876, 7326
324 R. 257 Vienna 23.10.1876, 7327
325 R. 25 Athens 13.4.1877, 7328
326 R. 19 Athens 22.4.1880, 7337
327 R. 314 Co'ple 10.9.1880, 7337
328 R. 142 Athens 26.9.1886, 7422
329 R. 55 Athens 4.6.1887, 7472
330 R. 407 Vienna 5.10. 1887, 7473
331 R. 61 Athens 19.7.1888, 7473 and R. 355 and R. 357 Vienna 30.7.1888. 7473
332 Internal record, Nr. 26 of 28.8.1888, 7473
333 R. 24 Athens 5.4.1888, 7473
334 Internal record (v. Kiderlen), A 11087 of 9.9.1888, 7473
335 Cutting A 11075 of 7.9.1888, 7473
336 R. 106 London 26.7.1876, 7326
337 Internal note of the Reich's Chancellor for an instruction of thee Auswärtigges Amt Nr. A 11241 of 10.9.1888, 7473
338 „Politische Correspondenz" Nr. 3938 of 15.9.1888, (A ...482?), 7473
339 R. 84 Athens 5.9.1888, 7473
340 R. 92 Athens 10.10.1888, 7473
341 R. 71 Cop.hgn. 23.10.1888, 7473
342 P. Sethe: Europäische Fürstenhöfe – damals: Der russische ..., loc. cit., p. 11/12 and p. 15 ff.
343 R. 71 Cop.hgn. 23.10.1888, 7473
344 R. 95 Athens 12.10.1888, 7473
345 R. 95 Athens 12.10.1888, 7473
346 K. Kaser: Raum u. Besiedlung. In: Hatschikjan/Troebst: SO-Europa. ...loc. cit. p. 50
347 R. (A 13378) Dresden 2.11.1887, 7473
348 R. 95 Athens 12.10.1888, 7473
349 R. 113 Athens 18.11.1888, 7474
350 R. 77 Athens 30.7.1889, 7474
351 R. 92 Athens 13.9.1889, 7474
352 R. 120 Athens 27.11.1889, 7475
353 R. 111 Athens 20.10.1889, 7475
354 R. 54 Athens 16.6.1889, 7474
355 R (A 12923) Athens 16.7.1889, 7474
356 Enclosure to the report from Athens of 6.7.1889, 7474

357 R. 121 Athens 30.11.1889, 7475
358 R. 15 Piräus 3.2.1890, 7475
359 R. 121 Athens 30.11.1889, 7475
360 R. 119 Athens 22.11.1889, 7475
361 „Kölnische Zeitung" of 13.4.1891, 7496
362 T. 6 Athens 16.4.1891, 7496
363 J. Lepsius a. o. (Ed.): Die Große Politik ..., Vol. 12/I. (R. 96 Sofia 25.10 1899), p. 552/3, footnote
364 R. 16 Athens 9.1.1891, 7496
365 R. 84 Athens 1.6.1898, 7480
366 R. 75 Athens 17.10. 1899, 7481
367 R. 39 Athens 28.5.1909, 7485
368 R. 26 Athens 2.4.1909, 7485
369 R. 220 St. P'bg. 21.9.1888, 7473 and T. 16 Athens 10.11.1888, 7474
370 R. 55 Athens 6.5.1883, 14400
371 R. 92 Co'pel 31.5.1883, 14400
372 „Kölnische Zeitung", Nr. 143 of 23.5.1883, 14400
373 R. without Nr. (A 3003) Athens (Corfu) 27.6.1883, 14400
374 Compare also „Die Post" of 22.1.1901 from Vienna (A 1181), 14402
375 R. without Nr. (A 3003) Athens (Corfu) 27.6.1883, 14400
376 R. 159 Vienna 30.6.1883, 14400
377 „Kölnische Zeitung", Nr. 143 of 23.5.1883, 14400
378 H. Herzfeld: Die moderne Welt.loc. cit., p. 73
379 St. Troebst: Die makedonische Antwort auf die Makedonische Frage....loc. cit., p. 15
380 R. Nr. 245 of 7.7.1883, 14400
381 R. 71 Athens 14.7.1883, 14400
382 R. 112 Co'ple 27.7.1883, 14400
383 V. Meier: Wie Jugoslawien ..., loc. cit., p. 124
384 Ordinance Nr. 79 of 30.1.1886, 14400
385 R. 147 Athens 3.10.1886, 14401
386 R. 301 Vienna 10.10.1890, 7475
387 R. 288 Vienna 5.11.1891, 7476
388 R. 178 Athens 18.12.1886, 7472
389 R. 92 Athens 10.10.1888, 7473
390 R. 105 Bukarest 8.11.1887, 14401
391 M. Weithmann: Makedonien – „Land zwischen vier Feuern", loc. cit., S. 263
392 Christian Voss: Die slawische Minderheit. Liberalisierung in Ägäis-Makedonien und Politik der kleinen Schritte. In: Pogrom. Gesellschaft für bedrohte Völker. - Minorities in Greece. Vol. 209, 2/2001, p. 18 f.
393 R. 107 Sofia 27.6.1891, 14401
394 R. 96 Co'ple 14.7.1891, 14402
395 R. 387 London 29.6.1891, 14401
396 R. 38 Bgd. 21.6.1891, 14402
397 Confirmation of his journey to France (Aix-les-Bains) in R. 46 Athens 5.6.1890, 7475
398 R. 84 Athens 8.3.1897, 7479
403 R. 58 Vienna 29.3.1897, 7479
404 R. 103 Athens 14.11.1895, 7478
405 R. 84 Athens 24.11.1891, 7476
406 R 45 St. P'bg. 30.1.1896, 7478
407 R. 282 St. P'bg. 10.5.1900, 7481
408 R. 325 Athens 8.11.1897, 7480
409 R. 421 St. P'bg. 21.11.1897, 7480 and R. 10 Cop.hgn. 28.1.1898, 7480
410 R. 282 St. P'bg. 10.5.1900, 7481 and R. 16 Athens 22.5.1900, 7481
411 R. 102 Cop.hgn. 16.9.1896, 7479
412 R. 17 Athens 24.3.1896, 7478
413 R. 66 Athens 24.10.1911, 7487
414 R. 31 Cop.hgn. 14.3.1897, 7479
415 R.911 London 7.9.1909, 7485
416 R. 120 Athens 20.11.1909, 7486
417 R. 40 Cop.hgn. 20.3.1897, 7479

418 R. 20 Athens 16.2.1910, 7486
419 R. 65 Athens 19.8.1890, 7475
420 R. 126 Athens 15.4.1897, 7479
421 R. 20 Athens 22.2.1887, 7472
422 R. 25 Athens 10. 3. 1887, 7472
423 R 54 Athens 16.6.1889, 7474
424 R. (A 12923) Athens 16.7.1889, 7474
425 R. 57 Athens 8.6.1891, 7475
426 R. 38 Athens 10.4.10, 7487
427 R. 79 Athens 19.8.1896, 7479
428 R. 362 Vienna 18.11.1903, 7483
429 R. 94 Cop hgn. 2.9.1896, 7479
430 R. 21 Cop.hgn. 18.2.1897, 7479
431 R. 15 Tokio 19.2.1891, 7475
432 R. 66 Athens 12.7.1891, 7475
433 R. 51 Athens 17.5.1891, 7475
434 R. 74 Athens 16.8.1891, 7475
435 R. 44 Tokyo 10.6.1891 7475
436 R. 82 Athens 16.11.1891, 7476
437 Since the founding of the German Empire there had been relics of a degree of autonomy reflected in the relations between several states (and one Free City) and the central governmant of the Reich, which were set out in contractual agreements with the result that the records also contain reports from the capitals of the following "missions": Darmstadt, Dresden, the Hanseatic City of Hamburg, Karlsruhe, Munich, Stuttgart, Weimar, Oldenburg.
438 R. 16 Munich 20.2.1897, 7479
439 R. Athens 27.1.1898, 7480
440 T. 114 Athens 29.4.1897, 7479
441 T. 180 Athens 30.5.1897, 7479
442 R. 38 Athens 27.9.1898, 7480
443 R. 190 Athens 24.5.1897, 7479
444 T. 26 Athens 26.2.1898, 7480
445 R. 39 Athens 27.2.1898 7480
446 Fikret. Adanir: Die makedonische Frage. ...a.a.O., S. 123, Fußnote 168 (aus: W. L. Langer: The Diplomacy of Imperialism. New York 1951, p. 377
447 Brockhaus, 14. Ed. 1908, sub voce Kreta
448 R. 33 Cop.hgn. 3.5.1898, 7480
449 R. 86 Athens 9.8.1895, 7478
450 R. 117 St. P'bg. 17.5.1898, 7480
451 R. 36 (63 ?) (A 5849) Cop.hgn. 11.5.1898, 7480
452 R. 280 St. P'bg 3.7.11898, 7480
453 R. 279 Rome 5.12.1900, 7381
454 Letter of Envoy v. Wangenheim of 8.9.1910 (A 15342) from Oberhof to the Chancellor, 7487
455 R. 67 Athens 17.9.1899, 7481
456 R. 68 Athens 23.9.1899, 7481
457 Private letter (A 14569) Baden-Baden of 12.10.1900, 7481
458 Joh. Lepsius a. o. (Ed.): Die Große Politik der Europäischen Kabinette 1871-1914. Berlin 1924,12. Vol., 1. half, S. 141 (Ordinance Nr. 76 v. 4.3.1897 to Ambassador Prince v. Radolin, St. P'bg.)
459 R. 246 Athens 2.8.1897, 14402
460 M. Edith Durham: Die slawische ..., loc. cit., p. 115 (Durham was thus articulating what at about the same time the organ of the Serbian young radicals, ODJEK, had written: "For as long as [the Slav peoples] have been known to history, they have never maintained amicable relations to each other or entered into alliances with one another; instead they have warred with each other and one has vanquished the other. If there were rulers who intended to unite all the Balkan states, the aim was oslely to conquer and subjugate." From: R. 49 Belgrade, June 9, 1911, 14404
461 Enclos. to R. 170 Bgd. 14.10.1897, 14402
462 R. 148 Cop.hgn. 23.8.1903, 7482
463 R. 55 Cop.hgn. 21.8.1903, 7482

464 R. 8 Athens 26.1.1903, 7482 and R. 18 Athens 6.3.1903, 7482 (Princess Alice was the daughter of Grand-Duke Ludwig von Battenberg and Princess Victoria of Hesse and at Rhine)
465 R. 54 Athens 30.10.1901, 7482
466 R. 55 Cop.hgn. 21.8.1903, 7482
467 R. 201 Athens 25.9.1903, 7483
468 R. 362 Vienna 18.11.1903, 7483
469 R. 4 Athens 8.1.1904, 7483
470 R. 70 Athens 28.9.1906, 7484
471 Private diplomatic correspondence from the envoy in Athens to the Undersecr. of state in the Auswärtiges Amt (A 16215) of 27.9.1909, 7485
472 R. 18 Athens 6.3.1903, 7482
473 R. (A 18188) Athens 10.10.1905, 7484
474 R. 36 Athens 14.11.1900, 7481
475 R. 97 Athens 28.6.1903, 7482
476 T. 43 Corfu 11.4.1905, 7483
477 R. 22 Athens 23.2.1891, 7475
478 R. 887 London 25.7.1905, 7483
479 R. 155 Co'ple 31.8.1905, 7484 and R. 175 Co'pel 1.9.1905, 7484
480 R. 175 Co'ple 1.9.1905, 7484
481 R. 162 Athens 29.9.1905, 7484
482 Annex to R. 172 Athens 5.11.1905, 7484
483 R. 401 Vienna 9.12.1905, 7484
484 R. 100 Vienna 9.3.1906, 7484
485 R. 841 Paris 8.11.1906, 7484
486 R. 255 Rome 10.11.1906, 7484
487 R. 266 Rome 25.11.1906, 7484
488 R. 268 Rome 28.11.1906, 7484
489 „Tägliche Rundschau" (A 19949) of 30.11.1906, 7484
490 T. 22 Athens 23.4.1907, 7484
491 R. 35 Athens 8.6.1906, 7484
492 „Neue Freie Presse" (A 9260) of 11.6.1907, 7484
493 R. 35 Athens 15.6.1907, 7484
494 R. 35 Athens 15.6.1907, 7484
495 R. 27 Athens 11.5.1907, 7484
496 R. 35 Athens 15.6.1907, 7484
497 R. 83 Athens 10.9.1907, 7484
498 R. 104 Athens 18.11.1907, 7485
499 R. 90 Athens 9.12.1908, 7486
500 R. 124 Athens 30.3.1915, 7497
501 T. 375 Athens 18.6.1916, 7491 and T. 1581 Cop.hgn. 13.11.1916, 7491
502 T. 552 Madrid 13.12.1916, 7492
503 R. 2963 Bern 29.12.1916, 7492
504 R. 259 Bukarest 21.8.1913, 7489
505 R. 3943, 28.12.1917, 7491
506 R. 185 Cophgn. 31.7.1918, 7495
507 Robert K. Massie: Die Schalen des Zorns. Großbritannien, Deutschland und das Heraufziehen des Ersten Weltkriegs. 2. Auflg. Frankfurt/M. 1993, S. 498
508 P. Sethe: Europäische ...(Zarenhof), loc. cit., p. 47
509 R. 36 Athens 20.6.1908, 7485
510 „Berliner Lokalanzeiger" of 17. and 18. 11. 1908, 7485
511 R. 462 St. P'bg. 12.10.1908, 7485
512 R. 54 Athens 14.8.1908, 7485
513 R. 119 Athens 20.11.1909, 7486
514 Letter from Oberhof to the Chancellor of 8.9.1910, (A 15342), 7487
516 R. 37 Athens 25.5.1911, 7487
517 R. (A 14304) Athens 22.8.1909, 7485
518 R. 1067 London 30.10.1909, 7486
519 Berliner Lokal-Anzeiger (A 17815) of 30.10.1909, 7485
520 R. 5 Athens 21.1.1909, 14403

521 R. 129 Athens, 11.12.1909, 14403
522 „The Times" of 5.6.1913, A 11285, 14405
523 J. Lepsius u.a.: Die Große Politik ..., loc. cit., 12. Vol. p. 138 (Internal record, without Nr. of 21.1.1897)
524 R. 32 Athens. 8.5.1911, 14404
525 R. 180 Cophgn. 5.10.1911, 7487

2.4 Romania

526 Stadtmüller ...,loc. cit., S.393
527 Im. Geiss: Der Berliner Kgs. .., Beilage/Parlament, loc. cit., p. 7
528 Im. Geiss: Der Berliner Kgs. .., Prot. u. Mat., loc. cit., p. 366 ff.
529 Im. Geiss: Berliner Kgs. .., Beilage/Parlament, loc. cit., p. 14
530 R. 101 Bukarest 18.12.1879, 14400
531 The Aromanians are called Kutzovlachs by the Greeks and also by the Romanians themselves, Tsintsars (or Tzintzars) by the Serbs, Chobans (or Chobani) by the Turks and Rumeri (or Remeri) or Latinci by the Albanians. From: Edgar Hösch: Kulturen u. Staatsbildungen. In: Hatschikjan/Troebst (eds.): Südost-Europa. ..., loc. cit., S. 37
532 R. 309 St.P'bg. 5.9.1886, 14400
533 R. 147 Athens 3.10.1886, 14401
534 R. of 22.8.1887 from Bukarest, in the ordinance (A 10408) of 27.8.1887, 14401
535 R. 107 Bukarest 17.6.1888, 14401
536 R. 182 Bukarest (Sinaia) 6.10.1888, 14401
537 R. 80 Vienna 19.3.1891, 14401
538 R. 63 Bukarest 13.5.1896, 14402
539 R. 86 Bukarest 8.7.1896, 14402
540 Brockhaus, 14. ed. Leipzig 1908, sub voce. „Rumänien", p. 20
541 „The Times" of June 4, 1913, A 11234, 14405 (The Times subsequently explained the breaking off of the relations as follows: since the uprising in Macedonia in 1903 gangs of Greeks had attempted to convert the Vlakhs (Aromanians) to become Greeks. The Greeks in turn were persecuted by the Bulgarians – in Macedonia and in Bulgaria. This constellation proved to be extremely detrimental to the Greek aims when another rebellion broke out in Crete in 1905 and Greece was in sore need of allies.)
542 R. 55 Bukarest 5.4.1897, 14402
543 „The Times", 4.6.1913, A 11234, 14405
544 R. 48 Bukarest 25.4.1904, 14402
545 Gotth. Rhode: Der Berliner Kongreß und Südosteuropa. In: K.O. Frhr. von Aretin: ... loc. cit., p. 123
546 R. 34 Bukarest 7.2.1906, 14403
547 R. 370 Vienna 5.12.1908, 14403
548 R. 78 Bukarest 22.12.1909, 14403
549 R. 49 Bukarest 12.4.1911, 14404
550 „The Times" of 4.6.1913, A 11234, 14405
551 R. 32 Athens 8.5.1911, 14404

2.5 Albania

552 E. Hösch: Kulturen u. Staatsbildungen. In: Hatschikjan/Troebst (eds.): Südosteuropa-Handbuch, ...loc. cit., p. 51
553 K. Kaser: Raum und Besiedlung. In: Hatschikjan/Troebst ...loc. cit., p. 55
554 Stadtmüller: Geschichte ..., loc. cit., p. 203
555 Stadtmüller: ibidem, p. 97
556 Stadtmüller: ibidem, S. 202
557 E. Hösch: Kulturen ... In: Hatschikjan ... loc. Cit., p.. 40
558 F. Adanir: Die makedonische Frage. ...loc. cit., p. 22, footnote 52
559 K. Kaser: Raum und ... , loc. cit., p. 69
560 K. Kaser: ibid., p. 64 (In this connection one further consequence of the social and legal system of the Ottoman Empire may be quoted: „Most of the Roma [Romanis, Gypsies] reached South-East Europe during Ottoman rule. Their ancestors had probably left India between the 9th and 11th centuries, emigrating to Persia, Asia Minor and Syria. From Syria ... they reached Spain via Egypt and North Africa, from Asia Minor ... they came to South-East Europe." (Kaser, p. 67) So

not as part of the entourage of the returning army of Alexander the Great, in whose glory they too are fond of basking, roughly implying: ‚We were in the Balkans even before the Slavs arrived!')

561 Turkish special forces (and civil servants), formed from abducted Christian children who were forcibly converted to Islam (in German „Knabenlese", in Turkish "Devshirme") and former Christian prisoners of war.
562 F. Adanir: Die makedonische Frage. Ihre Entstehung und Entwicklung bis 1908. Wiesbaden 1979, p. 84, footnote 469
563 V. Meier: Wie Jugoslawien ..., loc. cit., p. 50
564 From: „Politische Correspondenz" Nr. 918, Vienna, 10.8.1878, 12425
565 Stefan Troebst: Politische Entwicklung in der Neuzeit. In: Hatschikjan/Troebst (eds.): Südosteuropa-Handbuch. ... loc. cit., p. 95
566 Stadtmüller: Geschichte ... loc. cit., p. 276 f.
567 The name „Shqiptars" is a very beautiful, almost mystical and exotic name from ancient Europe but the Albanians insist that only they have the right to call themselves Shqiptars; whenever the Macedonians use this name they consider it as an insult.
568 R. (no Nr.) Ragusa 6.8.1865 (transferred by the German Embassy Vienna on13.8.1865), 12136
569 R. (no Nr.) Ragusa 17.5.1865, 12136
570 R. (no Nr.) Vienna 5.8.1868, 12136
571 R. 57 Ragusa 5.8.1868, 12136
572 Brockhaus, 14. ed. 1908, Vol. 11, p. 92
573 ZdF: 37° on 02.05.2000

3 Ottoman Empire

574 The following remarks are largely based, if not otherwise accounted for, on: Imanuel Geiss, in: Der Berliner Kgs., Prot. u. Mat., loc. cit. and in: Der Berliner Kgs., Parlamentsbeilage, l. c. and in: v. Aretin: Bismarcks Außenpolitik, l. c.;likewise on: Brockhaus, 14th ed. 1908, vol. 17 s. v. „Orientalische Frage" u. Brockhaus, 20th ed. 1999, vol. 22, s. v. „Türkei"
575 The naval battle of Lepanto. Documentation. ZdF am 30.6.2002, 19.30 Uhr
576 Austria had already inherited Hungary in 1526 when Louis II of Hungary had died in the battle of Mohács, but was not in a position to exercise its right to rule Hungary until the Turks had been expelled. As is well known, the Dual Monarchy was not established until 1867.
577 Im. Geiss: Der Berliner Kongreß 13. Juni – 13. Juli 1878. In: K. O. Frhr. v. Aretin: Bismarcks Außenpolitik und der Berliner Kongress. Wiesbaden 1978, p. 86
578 R. 57 Ragusa 5.8.1868, 12136
579 Rainer Hermann: Kreuzberg in der Türkei. FAZ, 06.06.2002, S. 12
580 Richard von Mach: Die Macedonische Frage. Vienna 1895, p. 4 und 5
581 K. Kaser: Raum u. Besiedlung. In: Hatschikjan/Troebst (Hg.): SO-Europa ..., a.a.O., S. 65
582 Ludwig Dehio: Gleichgewicht oder Hegemonie. Betrachtungen über ein Grundproblem der neueren Staatengeschichte. Zürich 1997, p. 22
583 E. Hösch: Kulturen u. Staatsbildungen. In: Hatschikjan/Troebst: SO-Europa, ...l. c., p. 50 f.
584 There is a – dare I say it – typically English ironical metaphor from a report on the visit by Lord Salisbury to Athens in January 1877 after the unsuccessful ambassadors' conference in Constantinople which aimed at defusing the conflict that was brewing about the rights of the Christians in the European part of Turkey. By pointing to the unanimity of Europe in this matter he surprised the Greek politicians "who, with reference to the relationship between their own political parties, are inclined to conclude that the European Concert is a bellum omnium contra omnes". R. 8 Athens 28.1.1877, 7328)
585 It is evident from special files in the Political Archives on this subject that the Porte could only be induced to bring the guilty to justice by means of drastic threats – French, Austrian, Russian, German and English gunboats off Saloniki ! In spite of this, the penalties were provokingly mild, and their implementation was extremely lax. Apparently, the present-day Turkish modus operandi has a long tradition.
586 Brockhaus, 14th ed. 1908, vol. 17, s.v.. „Orientalische Frage"
587 Im. Geiss: Der Berliner ..., in: v. Aretin: Bismarcks Außenpolitik ... l. c., p. 85
588 St. Troebst: Politische Entwicklung ..., In: Hatschikjan/Troebst: ...l. c., p. 85
589 Like note 586
590 R. 4 Athens 20.1.1877, 7328
591 R. v. Mach: Die makedonische Frage. Vienna 1895, p. 4

592 K. Kaser: Raum u. Besiedlung. In: Hatschikjan/Troebst: SO-Europa-Handbuch, ... l. c., p. 65
593 Rhea Galanaki: Das Leben des Ismail Ferik Pascha. Frankfurt/Main 2001
594 Aide-Mémoire of 3.5.1883, (A 2009), vol. 14400
595 R. 89 Co'pel 21.5.1883, 14400
596 „Norddeutsche Allgemeine Zeitung", Nr. 220 of 16.5.1883, 14400
597 Holm Sundhausen: Die serbische Frage. Lecture held on 5.2.1993 at the Osteuropa-Institut of the Freie Universität Berlin (published as a brochure). Cited in: Claudia Hopf: Sprachnationalismus ..., l. c., p. 147, footnote 357
598 Michael W. Weithmann: Makedonien – Land zwischen vier Feuern, in: Außenpolitik III, 1993, p. 261 ff.
599 R. 84 Belgrade 16.10.1886, 14401
600 R. 63 Bukarest 13.5.1896, 14402
601 Joh. Lepsius a.o. (eds.): Die Große Politik der Europäischen Kabinette 1871-1914. 12th vol.: Alte und neue Balkanhändel 1896- 1899. Berlin 1924, p. 538 f.
602 St. Troebst: Politische Entwicklung ..., in: Hatschikjan/Troebst ...,l. c., p. 85 and p. 78
603 Joh. Lepsius a. o. (eds.): Die Große Politik ...l. c., vol. 27 Zwischen den Balkankrisen 1909-1911, Berlin 1925, p. 153 (R. 40 Athen 31.5.1911)
604 J. de Jong: Die makedonische Nationswerdung ...l. c., p. 174 f.
605 T. Szobries: Sprachliche Aspekte des nation-building in Mazedonien. ... loc. cit., p. 60
606 R. 1094 London 14.11.1908, 14403
607 R. 298 Co'ple 21.11.1908, 14403
608 R. 112 Co'ple 27.7.1883, 14400
609 R. 347 Co'ple 22.11.1909, 14403
610 Joh. Lepsius a. o. (eds.): Die Große Politik ...vol. 27, Zwischen den Balkankrisen ...loc. c., p. 178 (R. 207 Athens 30.12.1909)
612 R. 360 Co'ple 4.12.1909, 14403
613 R. 4 (?) Bukarest 11.1.1910 (A 673), 14404
614 R. 8 Bukarest 6.2.1910, 14404
615 Stephan Stuch: Statistisches Profil. In: Hatschikjan/Troebst (eds.): SO-Europa, ...l. c., p. 502 f.
616 Christian Voss: Der albanisch-makedonische Konflikt ..., l. c., p. 276
617 R. 8 Bukarest 6.2.1910, 14404
618 R. 29 Bgd. 9.3.1910, 14404
619 R. 113 Co'ple 4.4.1910, 14404
620 R. 114 Co'ple 5.4.1910, 14404
621 Ibidem
622 R. 14 Co'ple 5.4.1910, 14404
623 Austrian defeat against Prussia at Königgrätz (Sadova) on 3.7.1866
624 R. 114 Co'ple 5.4.1910, 14404
625 R. without Nr. (A 6497) Wien 14.4.1910, 14404
626 R. 43 (?, illegible) Bgd 20.4.1910, 14404
627 R. 179 Co'ple 30.5.1910. 14404
628 T. 330 Co'ple 23.10.1911, 14404
629 T. 397 Co'ple 1.12.1911, 14404
630 Brockhaus, 20th ed. 1997,vol. 11, s. v. „Jungtürken", p. 308
631 „The Times", 5.6.1913, A 11285, 14405

4 The European Great Powers

4.1 Russia

632 This was already the 2nd Holy League. The first one had been founded before the naval battle at Lepanto in 1571.
633 Venice had already fought six wars against the Ottoman Empire alone. Russia would exceed this number by another two wars (not mentioning the ones, it did not fight alone against Turkey).
634 Im. Geiss: Der Berliner ... In: K. O. v. Aretin: Bismarcks Außenpolitik ..., l. c., p. 72
635 In contrast to the latter, the intellectual movements of Western Europe, such as reformation and enlightenment, did practically pass over those nations, which were isolated under the rigid Islamic rule of Turkey.
636 According to Imanuel Geiss, the upcoming Oriental question only represented a further dimension for the great powers' rivalry, for historically it was a lot older „and at least since the conflicts of

reformation and counter-reformation, it must be dated to the beginning of the early modern times in the 16th century." As corner stones, Geiss mentions the Treaty of Westfalia of 1648 and the Treaty of Utrecht of 1712. (I. Geiss: l. c., Parlamentsbeilage ..., p. 5)
637 Stadtmüller: Geschichte ..., l. c., p. 344
638 Richard Nürnberger: Das Zeitalter der Französischen Revolution und Napoleon. In: Golo Mann, Alfred Heuss (ed.): Propyläen Weltgeschichte. Das 19. Jh. Frankfurt/Main, Berlin 1960, vol. VIII/1, p. 144
639 K. O. Frhr. v. Aretin: Bismarcks Außenpolitik ...l. c., p.79 f.
640 Th. Schieder: Europäisches Staatensystem ... In : K. O. Frhr. v. Aretin: Bismarcks ..., l. c., p. 21
641 Reichs-Gesetzblatt Nr. 31. In: Im. Geiss: Der Berliner Kgs. Prot. u. Mat., l. c., p. 387
642 Gotth. Rhode: Der Berliner Kongreß und Südosteuropa. In: K. O. Frhr. v. Aretin (ed.), Bismarcks Außenpolitik ... l. c., p.114
643 Enclosure to R. 325 St. P'bg. 30.10.1879: „Russische St. Petersburger Zeitung" of 27./15. 10. 1879, 14400
644 Encl. to R. 325 St. P'bg. 30.10.1879: „Neue Zeit", No. 290 of 28./16. 10.1879, 14400
645 R. 325 St. Petersburg 30.10.1879, 14400
646 From: „Kölnische Zeitung", No. 143 of 25.5.1883, 14400
647 J. Lepsius a. o. : Die Große Politik ..., l c., vol. 12, p. 551 (R. 96 Sofia of 25.10.1899)
648 Decree No. 858 to the Embassy St. P'bg. of 27.12.1885, 14400
649 R. 309 St. P'bg. 5.9.1886, 14400
650 R. 102 Co'ple 8.6.1890, 14401
651 B. v. Bülow: Denkwürdigkeiten. ...l. c., p. 44
652 R. 154 Rome 21.5.1890, 14401
653 R. 357 London 29.6.1891, 14401
654 R. 341 St. P'bg. 6.8.1896, 14402
655 Gotth. Rhode: Der Berliner Kongreß und Südosteuropa. In: K. O. v. Aretin (ed.):... l. c., p. 114
657 R. 381 St. P'bg. 14.9.1898, 14402
658 R. 396 Vienna 16.12.1908, 14403
660 R. 26 St. P'bg. 18.1.1909, 14403
661 R. 219 St. P'bg. 11.6.1909, 14403
662 Bernhard Heimrich: Die Krämer-Tugend. FAZ of 08.01.2002, p. 1
663 T. 378 Co'ple 7.12.1909, 14403
664 Quote from Schamonis about Kaiser William II
665 Paul Sethe: Europäische Fürstenhäuser – damals. Der russische Zarenhof. ... l. c., p. 56 ff.
666 R. 456 St. P'bg. 27.12.1909, 14403
667 Regarding Izvolsky, Robert K. Massie, however, also tells an amusing anecdote from the time, when he was appointed Foreign Minister (1906): When he was still Envoy to Copenhagen, ("for Russia, known as a family embassy and career springboard for future ambassadors". From: v. Bülow: Denkwürdigkeiten. .., p. 293) he learned about an imminent reshuffle in the Russian FO. As he was expecting a post in Rome or in Berlin, he asked a friend to find out more about this and wire back to him: if the posting was to be Italy, he was to write the code word „Macaroni", if Berlin „Sauerkraut". When Izvolsky received a telegram with the word „Caviar", he knew what this meant. From: R. K. Massie: ..., l. c., S. 596.
668 R. 5 Wien 2.1.1910, 14404

4.2 Austria-Hungary
669 K. Steinke: Sprachen. In: Hatschikjan/Troebst: SO-Europa ...,l. c., p. 402 f.
670 Alfred Cattani: Die Geschichte eines Hasses. NZZ-Folio, Sept. 1992
671 E. Hösch: Kulturen u. Staatsbildungen. In: Hatschikjan/Troebst ... l. c., p. 45
672 These and the following discussions are mainly based on the sources already used further above: Hans Herzfeld, l. c.; I. Geiss: l. c. (three sources) and Brockhaus, 20. ed. 1998, vol. 16, subject index „Österreich"
673 A. Hillgruber: Bismarcks Außenpolitik. Freiburg 1972, p. 43
674 Im. Geiss: Der Berliner Kongreß, Parlamentsbeilage, ... l. c., p. 7
675 Im. Geiss: Der Berliner ..., Prot. und Mat. ..., l. c., p. XV
676 Im. Geiss: Der Berliner Kgs., Parlamentsbeilage, ... l. c., p. 9
677 Im. Geiss: ibid, p. 7
678 A. Novotny: Quellen und Studien zur Geschichte des Berliner Kongresses 1878. Graz-Köln 1957, p. 17, quoted in: Im. Geiss: Der Berliner, ... Prot. u. Mat. ..., l. c., p. XXII, footnote 65

679 Im. Geiss: Der Berliner Kgs., Parlamentsbeilage, ...l. c., p. 12
680 Im. Geiss: Der Berliner Kgs., Parlamentsbeilage, ... l. c., p.15
681 Im. Geiss: Der Berliner Kgs., Parlamentsbeilage, ... l. c., p. 12, including footnotes 26 and 27
682 R. 447 Co'ple 10.11.1879, 14400
683 R. 455 Vienna 11.11.1879, 14400
684 R. 55 Belgrade 18.10.1880, 14400
685 Im. Geiss: Der Berliner Kgs., Parlamentsbeilage, ... l. c., p. 7
686 Im. Geiss: Berliner ..., Prot. und Mat., ...l. c., p. XIX
687 Im. Geiss: Der Berliner Kgs., Parlamentsbeilage, ... l. c., p. 13 (21)
688 Im. Geiss: Berliner ..., Prot. u. Mat., ...l. c., p. XXVI and Th. Schieder: Staatensystem und Gleichgewicht ... In: v. Aretin: Bismarcks Außenpolitik ..., l. c., p. 25
689 Geoffrey Barraclough: Das Europäische Gleichgewicht und der neue Imperialismus. In: Golo Mann, Alfred Heuss (ed.): Propyläen Weltgeschichte. Eine Universalgeschichte. Das neunzehnte Jahrhundert. Ulm 1976, vol. VIII / 2, p.733
690 G. Barraclough: Das Europäische Gleichgewicht ... In: G. Mann: Propyläen ..., l. c., p. 734
691 Th. Schieder (l. c., p. 25) summarizes that the basic treaty with Romania was made by Austria; Germany entered this alliance later, and Italy joined in 1888.
692 G. Barraclough: Das Europäische Gleichgewicht ... In. G. Mann: Propyläen ..., l. c., p.735
693 Im. Geiss: Der Berliner Kgs., Parlamentsbeilage, ... l. c., p. 13
694 G. F. Kennan: Bismarcks europäisches System ..., l. c., p. 14
695 Henry C. Meyer: Das Zeitalter des Imperialismus. Propyläen Weltgeschichte, vol. IX / 1, Das 20. Jh., p. 37
696 R. K. Massie: Dreadnought. Britain, Germany, and the Coming of the Great War, 1st ed. Random House, New York 1991, p. 342
697 Fr. Fischer: Der Erste Weltkrieg und das deutsche Geschichtsbild. Beiträge zur Bewältigung eines historischen Tabus. Düsseldorf 1977, p. 257
698 Brockhaus, 20. ed. 1998, vol. 16, subject index „Österreich", p. 370
699 Im. Geiss: Der Berliner Kgs., Parlamentsbeilage, ... l. c., p. 15
700 R. 478 Vienna 27.10.1886, 14401
701 Joh. Lepsius a. o. (ed.): Die Große Politik ..., l. c., vol. XII, 1. half, p. 130 (directive no. 988 of 16.12.1895)
702 Joh. Lepsius a. o.: Große Politik, ... l. c., p. 131 (T. 11 Vienna 23.1.1896)
703 Joh. Lepsius a. o.: Große Politik, ... l. c., p. 132 f. (T. 16 Vienna 28.1.1896)
704 R. 112 Cophgn. 20.10.1887, 7473
705 Joh. Lepsius a. o.: Die Große Politik, ...l. c., p. 121 (R. 58 Co'ple 23.5.1895)
706 Im. Geiss: Der Berliner Kgs. ..., Prot. u. Mat. ..., l. c., p. 18
707 Joh. Lepsius a. o. : Große Politik, ... l. c., p. 121 (R. 58 Co'ple 23.5.1895)
708 T. Szobries: Sprachliche Aspekte des nation-building in Mazedonien. ...l. c., p. 59
709 Joh. Lepsius a. o. : Große Politik ..., l. c., p. 121 (R. 58 Co'ple 23.5.1895)
710 B. 584 St. Petersburg 13.7.1904, 14402
711 Directive no. 362 of 26.10.1904, 14402
712 R. 56 St. P'bg. 7.2.1906, 14403
713 R. 3 Belgrade 4.1.1907, 14403
714 Im. Geiss: Der Berliner Kgs., Parlamentsbeilage, ... l. c., p. 14
715 H. Herzfeld: Die moderne Welt. Die Geschichte unserer Epoche. ... l.c., p. 61
716 Henry C. Meyer: Zeitalter ... Imperialismus. In: Propyläen Weltgeschichte, ... l. c., p. 42
717 B. v. Bülow: Denkwürdigkeiten. 2. vol., l. c., pp. 337 and 400 ff.
718 R. 366 Vienna 3.12.1908, 14403
719 T. 18 Stuttgart 5.12.1908, 14403
720 Directive no. 1825 of the Auswärtiges Amt to the Embassy in Vienna of 6.12.1908, 14403
721 H. Herzfeld: Die moderne Welt. ... l. c., p. 61
722 R. 385 Vienna 8.12.1908, 14403
723 Directive of the AA no. 1844 to Embassy in Vienna of 12.12.1908, 14403
724 Directive of the AA no. 1946 to the Imperial Ambassador to Vienna, von Tschirschky, of 28.12.1908, 14403
725 R. 193 Belgrade 30.12.1908, 14403
726 Record (A 21773) of 27.12.1908, 14403
727 The summarizing term „German" for „Austrian", but often also for „Austrian *and* German" was at that time widely spread and quite common and is even today still a frequently used expression

and way of thinking on the Balkans, reflecting the people's view of the centuries-old joint Austro-German identity within the Holy Roman Empire of the German Nation.
728 R. 178 Rome 26.11.1909, 14403
729 R. 179 Co'ple 30.5.1910, 14404
730 P. Sethe: Europäische Fürstenhöfe ... Berlin/Wien, l. c., p. 128 and p. 130
731 R. K. Massie: Dreadnought. ... l. c., p. 860, 863 und 864

4.3 Great Britain
732 L. Dehio: Gleichgewicht oder Hegemonie. ... l. c., p. 153 and 162
733 L. Dehio: Gleichgewicht oder Hegemonie. ... l. c., p. 22
734 Gotth. Rhode: Der Berliner Kongreß und Südost-Europa. In: ..., l. c., p. 114
735 L. Dehio: Gleichgewicht ..., l. c., p. 147
736 L. Dehio: Gleichgewicht ..., l. c., p. 177
737 Im. Geiss: Der Berliner Kongress. Protokolle u. Materialien. Wiesbaden 1978, p. XII (or p. XV ?)
738 R. 106 London 26.7.1876, 7326
739 Im. Geiss: Der Berliner ..., Prot. u. Mat., ... l. c., p. 9
740 Im. Geiss: ibid, p. XIV
741 G. Rhode: Der Berliner Kongreß ... In: v. Aretin: Bismarcks Außenpolitik ..., p. c., p. 102 f.
742 R. 106 London 26.7.1876, 7326
743 R. 158 Co'ple 7.6.1877, 7329
744 Closely connected with this tactic was a speculation of English politicians about the idea of implementing a compliant Greek regime in Constantinople, as a front man so to say – taken that England would not be in a position to occupy or possess it herself – (just like Bulgaria, that was supposed to play governor for Russia). The report states that these politicians had considered giving Greece the opportunity „to develop such an abused and run-down nation (to) help them produce their own food", as Greece cannot „live or ... historical memories alone". Even the Byzantine idea of the removal of the „Greek throne to Constantinople" was taken into consideration, because „in many respects the Greeks were closer to the Turks than any other nation." ... „And once the Sultan and the Turkish element were replaced, the Turkish subjects who would then be able to stay, would find it easier to get used to the Greek rule than to the Slavic one or any other foreign rule. In: R. 106 London 26.7.1876, 7326, pp. 4 a. 5
745 Letter of Envoy v. Winckler of 12.10.1900 from Baden-Baden to the Chancellor, 7481
746 R. 936 London 5.10.1906 (Fortnightly Review), 14403
746a From FAZ issue No. 129 of 6 June 2006, p. 41
747 R. 61 Belgrade 21.5.1906, 14403
748 R. 237 Bgd. 6. 12. 1909, 14403
749 R. 179 Co'ple 30.5.1910, 14404

4.4.1 The German Reich
750 I. Geiss: Der Berliner Kongreß .. In: K. O. v. Aretin (ed.): Bismarcks Außenpolitik ..., l. c., p. 71
750a Andreas Kilb: (...) Wie die Briten ihren Festlandsdegen verloren und ein Weltreich gewannen. FAZ, 12.09.2007, S. N 3
751 Andreas Hillgruber: Grundzüge der Außenpolitik Bismarcks von der Reichsgründung bis zum Abschluß des Dreibundes 1882. In: K. O. Frhr. v. Aretin: Bismarcks Außenpolitik ... l. c., Wiesbaden 1978, p. 129 f.
751a Gina Thomas in F.A.Z. of 10 June 2005, p. 31
752 Im. Geiss: Der Berliner Kgs. Parlamentsbeilage ... l. c., p.7
753 G. F. Kennan: Bismarcks ... System ...l. c., pp. 24 a. 35
754 G. F. Kennan: ibid, p. 35
755 G. F. Kennan: ibid, p. 118
756 G. F. Kennan: ibid, p. 18
757 Im. Geiss: Der Berliner Kgs. Parlamentsbeilage, B 41/78, p. 7
758 Im. Geiss: Der Berliner ..., Prot. u. Mat., ... l. c., p. XIV f.
759 K. O. Frhr. v. Aretin (ed.): Bismarcks Außenpolitik ..., l. c., p. 82
759a Prof. W. Stibrny in F.A.Z. of 24.2.2004
760 R. 179 Co'ple 30.5.1910, 14404
761 Preußisches Geheimes Staatsarchiv. Deutsches Zentralarchiv: Roem. 1/Rep. 89. Histor. Abtlg. 11:2,2.1, Nr. 13340: Türkei, years 1835-1910, vol. II: Auswärtige Sachen. Sheet 16: Record of 25. 7. 1840

762 Preußisches Geheimes Staats-Archiv. ...l. c., sheets 51 and 78
763 G. F. Kennan: Bismarcks ..., l.c., p. 119
764 Christian Graf von Krockow: Kaiser Wilhelm II. und seine Zeit. Biographie einer Epoche. Berlin 2002, p. 218
765 E. Hösch: Kulturen und ..., In: Hatschikjan/Troebst ... l. c., p. 41
766 C. Graf v. Krockow: Kaiser Wilhelm II. ... , l. c., p. 127 ff.
767 Quoted by Bernhard Heimrich, in: FAZ of 22.03.03, p. 12
768 C. Graf v. Krockow: Kaiser Wilhelm II. ..., l. c., p. 236
769 This was also true for diplomatic receptions at the embassies for the Germans abroad. The relevant report of the Ambassador in Athens, von Radowitz, mentions such a birthday party (however, only for William's grandfather, William I., in the year 1879) and its description resembles a passage from a novel (maybe by Alexandre Dumas), rather than the quote from a factual report of days gone by. After the description of the reception programme, the reporter characterizes some of his guests: At the top was „the honorable former general doctor of the Greek army, the 83-year-old Dr. Treiber, who had come to Greece already in 1819 and later was a fellow of Lord Byron and witness to his death. In 1824, Dr. Treiber embalmed the body of the British poet using the same scalpel that had served to dissect the body of Emperor Napoleon on St. Helena three years before. An English doctor had brought it to Greece. Dr. Treiber is the living chronicle of modern Greek history. " (From: R. 16 Athens 23.3.1879, R 7335)
770 C. Graf v. Krockow: Kaiser Wilhelm II. ... , l. c., pp. 256 and 15
771 B. v. Bülow: Denkwürdigkeiten. 2. Bd. Berlin, l. c.
772 C. Graf v. Krockow: Kaiser Wilhelm II. ..., l. c., p. 29
773 P. Sethe: Europäische Fürstenhöfe ..., l. c., pp. 31 and S. 29
774 G. F. Kennan: Bismarcks ... System ..., l. c., p 14, note
775 C. Graf v. Krockow: Kaiser Wilhelm II. ..., l. c., p. 220/21
776 Fr. Fischer: Der Erste Weltkrieg und das deutsche Geschichtsbild. ... l. c., p. 312
777 What is meant here are *terrtitorial* interests.
778 Im. Geiss: Berliner Kgs. ..., Parlamentsbeilage, ... l. c. p. 7
779 A. Hillgruber: Grundzüge ... In: K. O. v. Aretin (ed.): Bismarcks ..., l. c., p. 53
780 Im. Geiss: Der Berliner ..., Prot. u. Mat.,... l. c., p. XII
781 Im. Geiss: ibid, p. XXVI
782 Im. Geiss: Berliner Kgs. ..., Parlamentsbeilage ..., l. c., p. 11
783 K. O. Frhr. v. Aretin (ed.): Bismarcks Außenpolitik ..., l. c., p. 9
784 Im. Geiss: Berliner Kgs. ... Prot. u. Mat., ..., l. c., p. XXVI
785 Im. Geiss: Berliner Kgs. ..., Prot. u. Mat., ... l. c., p. 3
786 G. F. Kennan: Bismarcks ... System ..., l. c., p. 87
787 G. F. Kennan: Bismarcks ... System ..., l. c., p. 88
788 Th. Schieder: Europ. Staatensystem ..., In: K. O. v. Aretin (ed.): Bismarcks ..., l. c., p 25
789 A. Hillgruber: Grundzüge ... In: K. O. v. Aretin: Bismarcks ..., l. c., p. 54
790 G. F. Kennan: Bismarcks ... System ..., l. c., p. 90
791 Im. Geiss: Berliner Kgs. ..., Parlamentsbeilage ..., l. c., p. 13
792 G. F. Kennan: Bismarcks ... System ..., l. c., p. 91
793 Fritz Fischer: Griff nach der Weltmacht. Die Kriegszielpolitik des kaiserlichen Deutschland 1914/18. Düsseldorf 1977, p. 23
794 C. v. Krockow: Kaiser Wilhelm II. ..., l.c., p. 119
795 R. K. Massie: Schalen des Zorns. ... l.c., Frankfurt/M., 1993, p. 491
796 Henry C. Meyer: Zeitalter des Imperialismus. ..., l.c., p. 39
797 Horst Joachim Lieske: Preußen auf einen Blick. Die Könige von Preußen, ihre Zeit und Bauten. Lieske Verlag Langelsheim, 2001, paragraph: „(um) 1895"
798 A. Hillgruber: Grundzüge ..., l.c., p. 62 ff.
799 A. Hillgruber: Grundzüge ..., l.c., p. 64
   Chapter 4.4.1.2.1
800 Im. Geiss: Der Berliner Kgs. ..., Prot. u. Mat. ..., l.c., p. XIV
801 Fritz Fischer: Krieg der Illusionen. Die deutsche Politik von 1911 - 1914. Düsseldorf 1969, p. 220
802 H. Herzfeld: Die moderne Welt 1789-1945. II. Teil, Weltmächte und Weltkriege. Braunschweig 1960, p. 60
803 Robert K. Massie: Dreadnought, Britain, Germany, and the Coming of the Great War, 1st ed., New York 1991, p, 602

804 Sönke Neitzel: Weltmacht oder Untergang. Die Weltreichslehre im Zeitalter des Imperialismus. Paderborn, München, Wien, Zürich 2000, p. 233
But decades before, H. Kantorowicz had already quoted the „Saturday Review" in his book „Der Geist der englischen Politik und das Gespenst der Einkreisung Deutschlands" (Berlin 1929, p. 346), - but presented the expression as completely harmless; in the same manner as he glorifies the English virtues everywhere in his book, and instead minimizes their vices and shifting them onto the Germans.
805 N. Ferguson: The Pity of War ... , l.c., p. 57
806 N. Ferguson: ibid, p. 58
807 N. Ferguson: ibid, p. 62
808 N. Ferguson: ibid, p. 67
809 N. Ferguson: ibid, p. 63 und M. Stürmer, l.c., p. 333
810 B. v. Bülow: Denkwürdigkeiten. ...l.c., p. 202
811 B. v. Bülow: Denkwürdigkeiten. ...l.c., p. 167
812 Ferguson: The Pity of War. ...l.c., p. 64
813 R. 1003 London 25.10.1912, 14243
814 H. C. Meyer: Das Zeitalter des Imperialismus. In: G. Mann a.o.: Propyläen ..., vol. IX/1, p. 41
815 H. Kantorowicz: Gutachten zur Kriegsschuldfrage 1914. Frankfurt/M. 1967, pp. 346 ff. a. 349
816 Brockhaus, Wiesbaden 1999, vol. 24, subject index: Erster Weltkrieg, p. 27
817 F. Fischer: Griff n. d. Weltmacht., ... l.c., p. 33
818 Harold Nicolson: Sir Arthur Nicolson, Bart., First Lord Carnock. A study in the Old Diplomacy. London 1930, p. 274
819 Hans Alfred Steger: „Deutsche Weltpolitik" bei Hans Delbrück 1895-1918. Marburg 1955, p. 63
820 H. Kantorowicz: „Der Geist ... und das Gespenst ...", l.c., p. 387 f.
821 B. v. Bülow: Denkwürdigkeiten. ... l.c., pp. 399 and 416 f.
822 Hardinge-Memorandum vom 12.6.1908, Royal Archives Windsor Castle, RA vic/x 22/44, p. 6
823 S. Neitzel: Weltmacht oder Untergang. ... l.c., p. 336 f.
824 B. v. Bülow: ... l.c., p. 316
825 B. v. Bülow: ... l.c., pp. 83 and 318
826 H. A. Steger: „Deutsche Weltpolitik" bei Hans Delbrück 1895-1918.Marburg 1955, p. 63
827 B. v. Bülow: ... l.c., p. 330
828 B. v. Bülow: ... l.c., p. 326
829 R. from St. Petersburg to Belgrade of 18.3.1911, 20728-2, sheet 107 f.
830 B. v. Bülow: ... l.c., p. 481 f.
831 B. v. Bülow: ... l. c., p. 399
832 B. v. Bülow: ibid, p. 330
833 H. Kantorowicz: Der Geist d. engl. Politik ..., l.c., p. 393
834 B. v. Bülow: ibid, p. 326 f.
835 B. v. Bülow: ... l.c., p. 203
836 N. Ferguson: The Pity of War. ... l.c., p. 38
837 R. K. Massie: Dreadnought. ..., l.c., p. 600 f.
838 F. Fischer: Krieg der Illusionen ..., l.c., p. 96
839 N. Ferguson: The Pity of War. ... l.c., p. 153
840 N. Ferguson: The Pity of War. ... l.c., p. 155
841 H. C. Meyer: Zeitalter des Imperialismus, ... l.c., p. 45
842 H. Kantorowicz: Gutachten zur Kriegsschuldfrage 1914. Frankfurt/Main 1967, p. 112 f.
843 N. Ferguson: The Pity of War. ... l.c., p. 68
844 B. v. Bülow: Denkwürdigkeiten. ... l.c., p. 263 f.
845 Benno v. Siebert (ed.): Diplomatische Aktenstücke zur Geschichte der Ententepolitik der Vorkriegsjahre. Berlin und Leipzig 1921, p. 61
846 R. K. Massie: Dreadnought. ... l.c., S. 607
847 B. v. Bülow: ..., l.c., p. 303 f.
848 R. K. Massie: Dreadnought. ... l.c., p. 608
849 Paul Sethe: Europäische Fürstenhöfe. Der russische Zarenhof. Frankfurt/M. 1937, a. o. p. 12
850 Hardinge-Memo: ..., l.c., p. 7
851 B. v. Bülow: Denkwürdigkeiten. ... l.c., p. 66
852 H. C. Meyer: Zeitalter des Imperialismus. ... l.c.., p. 39
853 B. v. Bülow: ... l.c.., p. 145
854 G. F. Kennan: Bismarcks ... System ..., l.c., p. 187

855   B. v. Bülow: ... l.c., p. 325
855a Stevenson, David: !914-1918. Der Erste Weltkrieg. In F.A.Z. of 10 June 2006
856   R. K. Massie: Dreadnought. ... l.c., p. 608
857   B. v. Bülow: Denkwürdigkeiten. ... l.c., p. 404
858   N. Ferguson: The Pity of War. ... l.c., p. 163
859   B. v. Bülow: ... l.c., p. 321
860   H. A. Steger: Deutsche Weltpolitik ... l.c., p. 166
861   N. Ferguson: The Pity of War. ... l.c., p. 38
862   N. Ferguson: The Pity of War. ... l.c., p. 60
863   B. v. Bülow: ...l.c., p. 71
864   H. A. Steger: Deutsche Weltpolitik ... l.c.,pS. 63
865   H. C. Meyer: Zeitalter des Imperialismus. ...l.c., p.41
866   H. A. Steger: Deutsche Weltpolitik ... l.c., p. 64
867   N. Ferguson: The Pity of War. ... l.c., p. 86
868   S. Neitzel: Weltmacht oder Untergang. ... l.c., p. 239
869   N. Ferguson: The Pity of War. ..., l.c., p. 68
870   N. Ferguson: The Pity of War. ..., l.c., p. 65 and 68
871   R. 170 of the Serb. Embassy in Paris of 19.10.1911, 20727-2, sheet 98 f.
872   F. Fischer: Krieg der Illusionen ..., l.c., p. 232 f.
873   G. F. Kennan: Bismarcks ... System ... l.c., p. 456
874   H. A. Steger: Deutsche Weltpolitik ... l.c., p. 63 f.
875   H. C. Meyer: Das Zeitalter des Imperialismus. ... l.c., p. 45
875c Helmut Glück: Sprachfreies Denken gibt es nicht. In F.A.Z., 25.04.08, p. 39
875a Wolfgang Burgdorf: Das alte Reich starb in den heißen Sommerferien. In: FAZ, Nr. 174 of 29.07.2006, p. 41
875b H. Ulrich Gumbrecht: Rezension über das Buch von Mattias Matussek: Wir Deutschen. In: FAZ of 26.05.2006, p. 37
875d Sieghard v. Pannwitz: Die Treue der Kosaken. In F.A.Z. of 23 July 2005
876   B. v. Bülow: ... l.c., p. 203
877   R. of the Serb. Envoy in Paris to Belgrade, no. 177 of 27.3.1913, 20728-2, sheet 124
878   F. Fischer: Der Erste Weltkrieg u. d. dt. Geschichtsbild. Düsseldorf 1977, p. 116 f.
879   Record of the Admiral Staff in Berlin of 26.4.1918, A 18647, 20734-1, sheets 6 a. 7
879a Eberhard Kolb: Kein Siegesrezept, aber eine Notlösung. In: FAZ of 04.10.2006, p. L 42, and Karin Urbach: Enorme Wirkung. Besprechung von Diana Restons Buch: Wurden torpediert. Schickt Hilfe. In: FAZ of 03.12.2004, and
      K.-Jürgen Bremm: Krieg der Welten. In: FAZ of 17.08.2006, p. 8
879b Jäger, Lorenz: Interessen? Wir? Glucksmann und Levy über Georgien. In: FAZ of 16.08.2008
880   Karsten W. N. Kurze: review of the book of „Brigitte Hamann: Der Erste Weltkrieg. Wahrheit und Lüge in Bildern und Texten. München 2004" in Generalanzeiger of 19.10.2005, p. 14
880a Aus: FAZ of 24.06.2006
880b Jäger, Lorenz: "Der Patenonkel. Arte erklärt den Versailler Vertrag." F.A.Z. of 4 August 2004, p. 34
880c See F.A.Z., 18.06.2008, p. 38

4.4.2 France

881   Im. Geiss: Der Berliner Kgs., ... Parlamentsbeilage ..., l.c., p. 15
882   B. v. Bülow: Denkwürdigkeiten ..., l.c., (a. o.) p. 328
883   Niall Ferguson: The Pity of War. 1914-1918, London, 1999, p. 54
884   Im. Geiss: Berliner Kgs. ..., Parlamentsbeilage, ... l.c., p. 15
885   N. Ferguson: The Pity of War. ...l.c., p. 43 f.
886   G. F. Kennan: Bismarcks ... System ..., l.c., p. 427
886a V. Hiller, Christian: Wir investieren nur in Spitzenqualität. FAZ, 19.03.2007, p. 17
887   G. F. Kennan: Bismarcks ... System ..., l.c., p. 14
888   Im. Geiss: Berliner Kgs. ..., Parlamentsbeilage, ..., l.c., p. 16
889   N. Ferguson: The Pity of War. .. , l.c., p. 54

4.4.3 Italy

890   H. Herzfeld: Die moderne Welt ..., l.c., p. 72
891   A. Hillgruber: Grundzüge ... In: K. O. v. Aretin: Bismarcks Außenpolitik ..., l.c., p. 64

892 B. 130 Rom 30.10.1879, 14400
893 A. Hillgruber: Grundzüge ..., In: K. O. v. Aretin: Bismarcks ..., l.c., p.
894 R. 53 Vienna 5.1.1906, 14402
895 Record (A 19303) Berlin 23.11.1909, 14403
896 Directive no. 1844 to the Embassy in Vienna of. 12.12.1908, 14403

5 The Balkan League and the Balkan Wars

897 Attachment (A 23227) to R. 156 Athens 15.12.1912, 14404
898 Henry C. Meyer: Das Zeitalter des Imperialismus. In: G. Mann a. o.: Propyläen ... vol. IX/1, p. 42
899 Charles Hardinge: Memorandum. London 12.6.1908, Royal Archives Windsor Castle, RA vic/x 22/44, p. 5
900 „Vossische Zeitung" (A 361) of 6.1.1913, 14404
901 „Der Tag" (A 16905) of 1.10.1912, 14238
902 R. 11 St. Petersburg 10.1.11913, 14404
903 R. of the Serb. Envoy in London no. 71 of 20.10.1911 to Belgrade, 20727-2, sheet 99
904 Bernhard von Bülow: Denkwürdigkeiten. 2. vol., 1.ed., Berlin 1930, l.c., pp. 210 a. 298
Dito: Niall Ferguson: The Pity of War. 1914-1918, London 1999, und R. K. Massie: Dreadnought ... l.c., pp. 710, 685 a. 801 and 843 (with reservation) and 850 f. as well as even Fritz Fischer: Krieg der Illusionen. ... l.c., p. 100, 129, 250, 290 (and 293)
905 „The Times" (A 11373) of 6.6.1913 and (A 11769) of 11.6.1913, 14405
906 R. 136 St. P'bg. 26.4.1913, 14405
907 H. Herzfeld: Die moderne Welt ..., l.c., p. 85
908 Fritz Fischer: Krieg der Illusionen. Die deutsche Politik 1911 bis 1914. Düsseldorf 1969, p. 216
909 Attachment to R. 156 Athens 15.12.1912, 14404
910 R. 157 Vienna 19.4.1913, 14404
911 „The Times" (A 11373) of 6.6.1913 a. (A 11769) of 11.6.1913, 14405
912 R. 68 Sofia 20.9.1912, 14216
913 "The Times" of 4.6.1913, (A 11234), 14405
914 Record no. (A 12455) Berlin 22.6.1913, 14405
915 R. 156 Athens 15.12.1912, 14404
916 Im. Geiss: Der Berliner Kongreß. Protokolle u. Materialien. No. 9 of 29.6.1878 , p. 303 f. and p. 388
917 Im. Geiss: Der Berliner ..., Prot. und Mat. ... l.c., p. 261
918 T. (A 16313) Corfu 12.10.1911, 7487
919 Minutes of Prof. Jäckh of 5.9.1912, 7493
920 T. 5 Corfu 3.5.1912, 7487
921 "The Times" of 4.6.1913, (A 11234), 14405
922 "The Times" of 5.6.1913, (A 11285), 14405
923 R. 182 Vienna 25.6.1912, 14404 (also published in „Die Große Politik". vol. 27, 1. Half: Zwischen den Balkankriegen 1909-1911. Berlin 1925, p. 191)
924 T. 346 Co'ple 6.10.1912, 14404
925 Rainer Hermann: Griechenland will zur Balkanstabilität beitragen. FAZ, 26.03.2001
926 T. 346 Co'ple 6.10.1912, 14404
927 R. 182 Vienna 25.6.1912, 14404
928 „Wiener Allgemeine Zeitung" of 19.9.1912 as attachment to R. 273 Vienna, 14404
929 R. 282 Vienna 28.9.1912, 14216
930 T. 350 Co'ple 6.10.1912, 14404
931 R. 56 Athens 5.10.1912, 7488
932 Record of the Chancellor : no Nr. (A 17495) or date (probably of 9. or 10. October 1912)
933 R. 273 St. P'bg. 19.9.1912, 14216
934 „Deutsche Tageszeitung" (A 17379) of 8.10.1912, 14239
935 R. of the Serb. Envoy in St. Petersburg no. 24 of 17.2.1912, 20729-2, sheet 98
936 T. 32 Cettinje 21.9.1912, 14216
937 T. 33 Cettinje 28.9.1912, 14216
938 „Kölnische Zeitung" (AS 16448) of 5.10.1912, 14238
939 R. 361 Paris 13.10.1912, 14242
940 Letter of the Deutsche Bank (A 16983) of 2.10.1912, 14217
941 „Berliner Lokal-Anzeiger" v. 9.10.1912, 14242

942 T. 217 St. P'bg. 18.9.1912, 14216
943 R. 291 Vienna 11.10.1912, 14242
944 R. 341 Vienna 31.10.1912, 14243
945 „Neue Freie Presse" (A 16904) Vienna of 1.10.1912, 14238
946 R. von Bülow: Denkwürdigkeiten. 2.vol., Berlin, 1. ed. 1930, p. 195 (and 192 ff.)
947 N. Ferguson: The Pity of War. ... l.c., p. 195
948 "Le Matin" of 26.11.1913, (A 23554), 14405
949 „Berliner Lokal-Anzeiger" of 9.10.1912, 14242
950 Record (no no.) Berlin 9.10.1912, 14242
951 Attachment to R. 77 Cettinje 9.10. 1912, 14242
952 R. 43 Cettinje 27.9.1912, 14217 and B. 73 Cettinje 27.9.1912, 14217
953 P. Sethe: Europ. Fürstenhöfe-damals. Der russische Zarenhof. L.c., pp. 32 a. 78 ff. (One of Sethe's sources could have been report no. 290 from St. Petersburg of 12.10.12, vol. 14242)
954 T. 74 Constantinople (exact date and volume number are unfortunately lost) [1st and only case !]
955 „Berliner Lokal-Anzeiger" of 9.10.1912, 14242
956 T. 79 Vienna 20.9.1912, 14240
957 R. 280 Vienna 27.9.1912, 14240 and R. (A 17877) Vienna 14.10.1912, 14242
958 Mil.-Att.-R. 56 Vienna 27.9.1912, 14216
959 „Neue Freie Presse" (AS 1647) of 4.10.1912, 14238
960 Decree no. 100 to the Embassy in Vienna of 3.10.1912, 14240
961 „Wiener Sonn- und Montagszeitung" of 23.9.1912, attachment to report 275 Vienna, 14216
962 R. 69 Sofia 20.9.1912, 14216
963 T. 74 Berlin (to the Kaiser in Rominten) of 2.10.1912, 14217
964 Decree 100 Vienna 3.10.1912, 14240
965 R. (of the special envoy) 5 (A 17086) from Rominten 3.10.1912, 14217
966 T. 357 Co'ple 8.10.1912, 14242
967 T. 396 Co'ple 14.10.1912, 14242
968 „The Westminster Gazette" (AS 1640), London of 3.10.1912, 14238
969 „Tägliche Rundschau" (AS 1632) of 1.10.1912, 14238
970 „The Times" (AS 1643) of 4.10.1912, 14238
971 T. 83 Vienna 26.9.1912, 14240
972 Mil-Att.-R. 56 (A 16790) Vienna 27.9.1912, 14216
973 R. 290 St. P'bg. 12.10.12, 14242
974 R. 348 Paris 7.10.1912, 14242
975 T. 294 Paris 2.10.1912, 14240
976 R. 351 Paris 9.10.1912, 14242
977 H. C. Meyer: Zeitalter des Imperialismus. In. Golo Mann: Propyläen Weltg.,l. c., pp. 34, 36 a. 41
978 S. Neitzel: Weltmacht oder Untergang. .. l.c., p. 235
979 R. 351 Paris 9.10.12, 14242
980 T. 219 St. P'bg. 20.9.1912, 14216
981 R. 281 Vienna 27.9.1912, 14216
982 T. 46 Sofia 5.10.1912, 14241
983 R. 361 Paris 13.10.1912, 14242
984 T. 25 Bgd 13.10.1912, 14242 and T. 60 Sofia 14.10.1912, 14242
985 R. 5 (A 17086) Rominten 3.10.1912, 14217
986 T. 357 Co'ple 8.10.1912, 14242
987 R. 965 London 14.10.1912, 14242
988 T. 71 Berlin 1.10.1912, 14217
989 „Berliner Lokal-Anzeiger" of 9.10.1912, 14242
990 R. 60 Belgrade 30.9.1912, 14217 and T. 57 Athens 2.10.1912, 14240
991 R. 71 Sofia 25.9.1912, 14216
992 T. 34 Sofia 28.9.1912, 14216
993 R. 60 Bgd 30.9.1912, 14217
994 T. 37 Sofia 30.9.1912, 14216 and T. 34 Sofia 28.9.1912, 14216
995 R. 940 London 2.10.1912, 14241
996 T. 57 Athens 2.10.1912, 14240 (and correspondg. directive of 3.10.1912)
997 T. 315 Co'ple 1.10.1912, 14217
998 T. 57 Athens 2.10.1912, 14240 (and 14217)
999 T. 372 Co'ple 10.10.12, 14242

1000 R. 279 St. P'bg. 28.9.1912, 14240
1001 T. 289 Co'ple 18.9.1912, 14216
1002 T. 315 Co'ple 1.10.1912, 14217
1003 T. 338 Co'ple 5.10.1912, 14242
1004 Wolff's Telegraphic Office of 11.4.1913, 14404
1005 „Der Tag" (A 16905) of 1.10.1912, 14238
1006 R. 288 St. P'bg. 12.10.12, 14242
1007 H. Herzfeld: Die moderne Welt. ... l.c., p. 85
1008 Peter Graf Kielmansegg: Deutschland und der Erste Weltkrieg. Frankfurt/Main 1980, p. 16
1009 N. Ferguson: The Pity of War. ... l.c., p. 150
1009aCol. Dr. H.J.Rautenberg, in FAZ of 28.09.2006, p. 10
1010 H. Kantorowicz: Gutachten zur Kriegsschuldfrage 1914. ..., l.c., p. 103
1011 SPIEGEL Special I/04 (a. o., p. 13)
1011aMichael Salewski: Stillstand (Deadlock) und Eskalation. Review in FAZ, 10.06.2006, p. 8
1012 F. Fischer: Der erste Weltkrieg u. d. dt. Geschichtsbild. ... l.c., pp. 12 a. 13
1013 H. Kantorowicz: Gutachten ..., l.c., pp. 329 ff. and 335 f.
1014 Massie talks about the „Willy-Nicky-Telegrams". L.c., p. 870 f.
1015 R. 2812 (?) (illegible) Vienna 21.12.1917, 7493
1016 Minutes of the secret conference of Tsar Nicholas II of 21.2.1914, 20734-1, sheet 324/5-326
1017 R. 288 St. P'bg. 12.10.12, 14242
1018 Records of the Reich Chancellery (A 17495) of 9.10.1912, 14242. Similar thoughts of the Kaiser, however, can also be found in the report of his envoy v. Jenisch no. 5 of 3.10.1912, 14214(7) as well as in decree no. 100 for the Embassy in Vienna of 3.10.1912, 14240
1019 „Berliner Lokal-Anzeiger" of 9.10.1912, 14242 and R. 5 Rominten 3.10.1912, 14214(7)
1020 T. 325 Co'ple 3.10.1912, (A 17074)
1021 T. (wire decree) 74 Berlin 4.101912, A 17074-76
1022 The „Amsterdamer Standard" of 1.12.1917, published in the „Norddeutsche Allgemeine Zeitung", no. 270 of 6.12.1917, 20733-2, sheet 111
1023 B. v. Bülow: Denkwürdigkeiten. ... l.c., p. 416 (not very flattering characteristics of that kind on pp. 103 and 246)
1024 B. v. Bülow: Denkwürdigkeiten. vol. 3, Berlin 1930, p. 160
1025 „Neue Freie Presse" (AS 1647) of 5.10.1912, 14238
1026 „Tägliche Rundschau" (AS 1632) of 1.10.1912, 14238
1027 „Neue Freie Presse" (A 16904) Vienna of 1.10.1912, 14238
1028 „Tägliche Rundschau" (AS 1632) of 1.10.1912, 14238
1029 R. 291 Vienna 11.10.12, 14242
1030 R. (A 19070) Cettinje 27.10.1912, 14404
1031 Fr. Fischer: Krieg der Illusionen. ... l.c., Düsseldorf 1969, p.218 f.
1032 Fr. Fischer: Krieg der Illusionen. ... l.c., p. 225
1033 H. C. Meyer: Zeitalter des Imperialismus ..., l.c., a. o. p. 36
1034 N. Ferguson: The Pity of War. ... l.c., p. 69
1035 F. Fischer: Griff nach der Weltmacht. ... p. 27
1036 F. Fischer: Krieg der Illusionen ..., l.c., p. 126
1037 Report (private service letter) (AS 1637) Rominten 2.10.1912, 14238
1038 Directive of the Kaiser (AS 1650) Rominten of 4.10.1912, 14238
1039 Record (no no.) Berlin 9.10.1912, 14242
1040 T. 60 Athens 4.10.1912, (AS 1645)
1041 „Neue Freie Presse" (AS 1647) Vienna 5.10.1912, 14238
1042 R. 1003 London 25.10.1912, 14243
1043 „Neue Freie Presse" (AS 1647) Vienna 5.10.1912, 14238 and
1044 Decree no. 1207 to the London Embassy of 20.10.1912, pp. 4-5, 14243
1045 R. 279 St. P'bg. 28.9.1912, 14240
1046 Directive (AS 1650) Rominten of 4.10.1912, 14238
1047 „Der Tag" (AS 16905) of 1.10.1912, 14238
1048 Memorandum (A 18581) of 25.10.1912, 14243
1049 R. 1003 London 25.10.1912, 14243
1050 R. 369 Paris 25.10.1912, 14243
1051 R. 288 St. P'bg. 12.10.12, 14242
1052 T. 169 London 28.10.1912, 14243

1053 R. 372 Paris 26.10.1912, 14243
1054 Mil-Att.-R. 69 (A 18714) Vienna 26.10.1912, 14243
1055 R. 340 Vienna 31.10.1912, 14243
1056 R. 331 Vienna 26.10.1912, 14243 and B. 327 Vienna 26.10. 1912, 14243
1057 „Neue Freie Presse" (A 16904) Vienna of 1.10.1912, 14238
1058 Private service letter (A 19089) of the envoy in Athens to the StS in the FO of 26.10.1912, 7488
1059 R. 897 Athens 23.4.1913, 7488
1060 R. 80 Athens 9.3.1913, 7488
1061 T. 560 Co'ple 27.11.1912, 14404
1062 T. 120 Athens 28.11.1912, 14404
1063 T. 526 Co'ple 15.11.1912, 14404
1064 T. 560 Co'ple 27.11.1912, 14404
1065 T. 152 Athens 13.12.1912, 7488
1066 Private service letter (AS 341) Co'ple 12.3.1913, 7497
1067 T. 1003 Athens 30.7.1915, 7491 and T. 279 head quarters 8.8.1915, 7497
1068 T. 617 Co'ple 27.12.1912, 7488
1069 T. 16 Co'ple 12.1.1913, 7488
1070 R. 125 Athens 9.4.1913, 7488
1071 R. 93 Athens 16.3.1913, 7488
1072 R. 50 Athens 20.2.11913, 7488
1073 R. 20 Athens 31.3.1913, 7488
1074 R. 73 Vienna 21.2.1913, 7488
1075 R. 105 Saloniki 27.5.1914, 7490
1076 R. 179 Saloniki 2.10.1913, A 20059, 14236
1077 „Reichs-u. Staats-Anzeiger", no. 68 of 19.3.1913, 7488 and „Norddeutsche Allgemeine Zeitung", no. 67 of 20.3.1913, 7488
1078 T. 164 Co'ple 19.3.1913, 7488
1079 Attachment to report 275 Vienna („Wiener Sonn- u. Montagszeitung" of 23.9.1912), 14216
1080 G. Stojćevski: Makedonien in den internationalen Beziehungen. In: W. Lukan (ed.): Österreichische Osthefte. 40th year, 1998, issues.1 a. 2, p. 180
1081 G. Stojćevski: Makedonien ..., l.c., p. 180
1082 Brockhaus, 17. ed 1966, subject index „Balkankriege", p. 251
1083 T. Athens 10.3.1913, 14404
1084 T. 566 Co'ple 29.11.1912, 14404
1085 R. 156 Athens 15.12.1912, 14404
1086 R. 102 Co'ple 8.4.1913, 7488
1087 Letter of Prince Heinrich of Prussia (A 7316) from Athens of 29.3.1913, 7488
1088 „Der große Ploetz", 32. ed. Freiburg 1999, chronological table „30.5.1913", p. 712, and Brockhaus, Leipzig 1929, 2. ed., subject index: Balkankriege, p. 248
1089 Ferguson: The Pity ..., l.c., p. 147
1090 „The Westminster Gazette" (AS 1640) of 3.10.1912, 14235
1091 R. 332 Vienna 27.10.1912, 14243
1092 „Neue Freie Presse" (A 192123) of 31.10.1912, 14243
1093 R. 372 Paris 26.10.1912, 14243
1094 B. v. Bülow: Denkwürdigkeiten. ... l.c., p. 228
1095 R. 42 Bucharest 3.2.1914, 7489
1096 T. 451 Co'ple 28.10.1912, 14243
1097 M. Mazower: Der Balkan. ... l.c., pp. 41 f. and 44 f.
1098 „The Times" (A 11234) of 4.6.1913, 14405
1099 F. Fischer: Der Erste Weltkrieg. ... l.c., p. 272/275
1100 T. 30 Bucharest 3.10.1912, 14217
1101 R. 162 Bucharest 15.12.1912, 14404
1102 R. 170 Bucharest 22.12.1912, 14404
1103 R. 136 St. P'bg. 26.4.1913, 14405
1103a Alan Palmer: Verfall und Untergang des Osmanischen Reiches. Munich/Zurich 1994, p. 344
1104 N. Ferguson: The Pity of War. ... l.c., p. 163 f.
1105 Military report no. 40 (A 3184) Sofia 7.3.1913, 14404
1106 R. 39 Belgrade 9.3.1913, 14404
1107 R. 41 Bgd. 11.3.1913, 14404

1108 R. 127 Sofia 21.6.1913, 14405 and R. 97 Bgd. 21.6.1913, 14405
1109 T. 35 Bgd. 17.4.1913, 14404 and R. 66 Bgd. 17.4.1913, 14404
1110 R. 39 Athens 13.2 1913, 14404
1111 T. 52 Sofia 3.3.1913, 14404
1112 Ch. Voss: Der albanisch-makedonische Konflikt ..., l.c., p. 277 (including footnote 28)
1113 R. no. ? London 28.3.1912, 14243 (?)
1114 R. (A 5605) Athens 15.3.1913, 14404
1115 T. 18 Athens 10.3.1913, 14404
1116 Wolff's Telegraphic Office, Berlin, 11.4.1913, 14404
1117 „Le Matin" (A 23554) of 26.11.1913, 14405
1118 „Frankfurter Zeitung" (A 23614) of 27.11.1913, 14405
1119 a R. 291 Vienna 11.10.12, 14242
1120 B. v. Bülow: Denkwürdigkeiten. ... l.c., p. 327
1121 H. Kantorowicz: Gutachten zur Kriegsschuldfrage. ...l.c., pp. 71 and 78 f.
1122 Kantorowicz: Gutachten ..., l.c., p. 345
1123 Kantorowicz: Gutachten ..., l.c., pp. 125 and 354
1124 T. 112 Sofia of 8.1.1916, 20727-1, sheet 41
1125 Frank Pergande, in: FAZ of 31.01.2003
1126 Michael Martens: Waffentragende Esel. In: FAZ of 22.06.2002
1127 E. M. Durham: Die slawische Gefahr. 20 Jahre Balkanerinnerungen. Stuttgart 1922, p. 9
1128 R. 97 Belgrade 21.6.1913, 14405
1129 R. 191 Vienna 3.6.1913, 14405
1130 T. 123 Bucharest 9.7.1913, 7489
1131 Gerhart Binder: Epoche der Entscheidungen. Eine Geschichte des 20. Jahrhunderts. Stuttgart 1964, p. 44
1132 Encyclopaedia Britannica (CD ROM) 1994-2001, subject index: „Balkan Wars"
1133 E. M. Durham: Die slawische Gefahr. ... l.c., p. 9
1134 In his book „Krieg der Illusionen. ..." l.c., p. 225 Fr. Fischer writes: „Berchtold's memoirs still echo the bitterness about the fact that the position of Germany before the outbreak of the war had prevented Austria-Hungary from an active policy towards the Balkan states." Despite all sympathy for Kaiser William's willingness to keep the peace, this case must allow the speculative question: (looking back at the consequences) is it possible that his reluctance was a mistake, considering that England had been successful with the same policy?
1135 T. 174 Vienna 22.7.1913, 14405
1136 R. 1969 (?), (A 17636) Athens 23.8.1913, 14405
1137 „Tägliche Rundschau" (A 16664) of 28.9.1912, 14239
1138 „Kölnische Zeitung" (AS 1648) of 5.10.1912, 14238
1139 H. Kantorowicz: Gutachten ..., l.c., p. 114
1140 R. 387 Vienna 9.12.1913, 14405
1141 RB. 233 Bgd 20.11.1913, 14405
1142 R. 326 Vienna 13.10.1913, 14405
1143 R. 421 London 18.7.1913, 14405
1144 R. (no. unknown) Sofia 5.8.1913, 14405
1145 R. (no. unknown) Sofia 16.8.1913, 14405
1146 G. Stojćevski: Makedonien in d. internation. ...In: W. Lukan (ed.): ÖOH, 40th year. 1998, p. 174
1147 T. 234 Athens 31.7.1913, 7489
1148 T. 56 Balestrand 1.8.1913, 7489 (A 15656)
1149 Private service letter (A 15588) of 28.7.1913(?), 4789
1150 R. 303 Athens 3.8.1913, 7489
1151 „Berliner Zeitung am Mittag" vom 10.6.1918 (A 24757), 7494
1152 T. 468 from Castle Kassel-Wilhelmshöhe 25.8.1918, 7495
1153 T. 1451 Bern 16.9.1918, 7495
1154 T. 561 Hofzug 19.9.1918, 7495
1155 T. 77 Swinemünde (as Envoy v. Treutler forwarded the text of the telegram from Athens, which had directly been sent to the Kaiser, to the Auswärtiges Amt as well) 9.8.1913, 7489
1156 T. 19 (almost illegible) (A 16964) Tatoi (country estate of the Greek King close to Athens) 8.1913, 7489
1157 Record (and decree) to Vienna and Rome (AS 1073) of 10.9.1913, 7489
1158 R. 296 Vienna 25.9.1913, 7489

1159 R. 13 Monastir 28.9.1913, A 19811, 14236
1160 R. 382 (386?) Athens 5.11.1913, 7489
1161 R. 107 Bucharest 1.5.1914, 7490
1162 R. 1489 Athens 20.11.1914, 7490
1163 R. 360 Vienna 6.11.1914,
1164 „L'Action Française" no. 209 of 29.7.1919, A 21122, 22027
1165 E. Durham: Die slawische Gefahr. ... l.c., pp. 121 and 342
1166 R. 10 Belgrade 30.1.1914, 14405
1167 F. Fischer: Griff ..., l.c., p. 41 f.
1168 F. Fischer: Juli 1914. Wir sind nicht ..., l.c., p. 14. Similarly in: Der Erste Weltkrieg ..., l.c., p. 279
1169 R. 41 Athens 9.2.1914, 14405
1170 „Magdeburgische Zeitung" (A 2290) of 3.2.1914, 14405
1171 R. (no. illegible) St. P'bg. 14.2.14, 14405
1172 B. v. Bülow: Denkwürdigkeiten. ... l.c., pp. 246 and 103
1173 Mark Mazower: Der Balkan. Kleine Weltgeschichte. Berlin 2002, p. 180
1174 T. 666 Copenhagen 21.4.1915, 7490
1175 Record no. 1951, Berckheim (for Berlin) (A 40785) of 7.12.1917, 7493
1176 R. 1606 Bern 28.6.1918, 7494
1177 Memo of Dr. Ludwig from St. Moritz of 1.6.1917, 7493
1178 Radio message from Lyon of 24.7.1919, A 20907, 22027
1179 St. Troebst: Politische Entwicklung in der Neuzeit. In. Hatschikjan/Troebst: ..., l.c., p. 86
1180 Note in FAZ of 29.11.2002
1181 G. Stojćevski: Makedonien in den internationalen ... l.c., ÖOH 1998, p. 182
1182 St. Troebst: IMRO +100 = FYROM? In: ÖOH 1998, p. 219

Bibliography

Adanir, Fikret	Die makedonische Frage. Ihre Entstehung und Entwicklung bis 1908. Wiesbaden 1979
Adrados, Francisco R.	Geschichte der griechischen Sprache von den Anfängen bis heute. Tübingen, Basel 2001
Andronicos, Manolis	Museum Thessaloniki. Ektodite Athenon 1990
v. Aretin, K. O. Frhr.	Bismarcks Außenpolitik und der Berliner Kongress. Inst. Für Europäische Geschichte. Wiesbaden 1978
Barraclough, Geoffrey	Das Europäische Gleichgewicht und der neue Imperialismus. In: Golo Mann, Alfred Heuss (ed.): Propyläen Weltgeschichte. Eine Universalgeschichte. Das neunzehnte Jahrhundert. Ulm 1976, vol. VIII/1
Binder, Gerhart	Epoche der Entscheidungen. Eine Geschichte des 20. Jahrhunderts. Stuttgart 1964
Bojic, Vera/ Oschlies, W.	Lehrbuch der mazedonischen Sprache. München 1984
Boškovska, Nada	Sein oder nicht. Ein Staat ringt um Anerkennung. In. NZZ-Folio, Sept. 1992
v. Bülow, Bernhard	Denkwürdigkeiten. (4 volumes), Berlin 1930
Burckhardt, Jacob	Weltgeschichtliche Betrachtungen. Berlin, Stuttgart 1905
Calic, Marie-Jeanne	Außen- und Sicherheitspolitik. In: M. Hatschikjan, St. Troebst (ed.): Südosteuropa. Gesellschaft, Politik, Wirtschaft, Kultur. Ein Handbuch. München 1999
Cattani, Alfred	Die Geschichte eines Hasses. NZZ-Folio, Sept. 1992
Craig, Gordon	Deutsche Geschichte von 1866 bis 1945. Vom Norddeutschen Bund bis zum Ende des Dritten Reichs. München 1980
Davis, Robert C.	Christian slaves, Muslim masters. Basingstoke 2004
Dehio, Ludwig	Gleichgewicht oder Hegemonie. Betrachtungen über ein Grundproblem der neueren Staatengeschichte. Zürich 1997
Döpmann, Hans-Dieter	Das alte Bulgarien. Ein kulturgeschichtlicher Abriß bis zum Ende der Türkenherrschaft im Jahre 1878. Leipzig 1973
Döpmann, H.-Dieter	Die religiöse Entwicklung Mazedoniens. Kurzfassung eines Vortrags anläßlich der II. Deutsch-Mazedonischen Konferenz in Jena vom 29.11.-01.12.2001
Durant, Will	Kulturgeschichte der Menschheit. Bd. 5: Weltreiche des Glaubens. (New York 1950), Köln/München 1977
Durham, M. Edith	Die slawische Gefahr. 20 Jahre Balkan-Erinnerungen. Stuttgart 1922
Fagyas, Maria	Der Tanz der Mörder. Reinbek/HH 1976, rororo 4011
Farmakis, Constantinos: *)	
Ferguson, Niall	The Pity of War. 1914-1918, London 1999
Ferguson, Niall	Der falsche Krieg. Der Erste Weltkrieg und das 20. Jh. Stuttgart 1999
Fischer, Fritz	Griff nach der Weltmacht. Die Kriegszielpolitik des kaiserlichen Deutschland 1914/18. Düsseldorf (1961) 1977 Fischer, Fr. Weltmacht oder Niedergang. Frankfurt/Main 1965
Fischer, Fr.	Krieg der Illusionen. Die deutsche Politik 1911 bis 1914. Düsseldorf 1969 und 1978
Fischer, Fr.	Der Erste Weltkrieg und das deutsche Geschichtsbild. Beiträge zur Bewältigung eines historischen Tabus. Düsseldorf 1977
Fischer, Fr.	Juli 1914: Wir sind nicht hineingeschlittert. Das Staatsgeheimnis um die Riezler-Tagebücher. Eine Streitschrift [über die Fischer-Kontroverse]. Reinbek bei Hamburg, 1983
Galanaki, Rhea	Das Leben des Ismail Ferik Pascha. Frankfurt/Main 2001
Geiss, Imanuel	Der Berliner Kongreß 1878. Protokolle und Materialien. Boppard 1978
Geiss, Im.	Der Berliner Kongress 1878. Sicherheit und Zusammenarbeit in Europa vor 100 Jahren. Aus Politik und Zeit-Geschichte. Beilage zur Wochenzeitung „Das Parlament", B 41/78, 14.10.1978
Geiss, Im.	Der Berliner Kongreß – 13. Juni bis 13. Juli 1878. In: Karl O. Frhr. v. Aretin (ed.): Bismarcks Außenpolitik und der Berliner Kongress. Wiesbaden 1978

Genscher, H.-Dietrich	Erinnerungen. Berlin 1995
Große Konkordanz	zur Luther-Bibel. Stuttgart 1979
Hamann, Brigitte	Rudolf. Kronpriz und Rebell. München, Zürich 2003 (1978, 1987)
Hamann, B.	Der Erste Weltkrieg. Wahrheit und Lüge in Bildern und Texten. München 2004
Hardinge, Charles	Memorandum. London 12.6.1908, Royal Archives Windsor Castle, RA vic/x 22/44
Hatschikjan, Magarditsch	Tradition und Neuorientierung in der bulgarischen Außenpolitik 1944 1948. Die „nationale Außenpolitik" der Bulgarischen Arbeiter-Partei (Kommunisten). München 1988
Hatschikjan, M./Troebst, St.	Südosteuropa. Gesellschaft. Politik. Wirtschaft. Kultur. Ein Handbuch. München 1999
Haussig, H.-Wilhelm	Kulturgeschichte von Byzanz. Stuttgart 1959
Heimrich, Bernhard	Die Krämer-Tugend. FAZ vom 08.01.2002
Hermann, Rainer	Die Geschäfte der Embargobrecher. Vorwürfe des Haager Kriegsverbrechertribunals gegen Griechenland. In: FAZ of 26.6.2002
Hermann, R.	Griechenland will zur Balkanstabilität beitragen. FAZ, 26.03.2001
Hermann, R.	Im Zeichen des Doppeladlers. In: FAZ of 9.8.2000
Hermann, R.	Kreuzberg in der Türkei. FAZ, 06.06.2002
Herzfeld, Hans	Die moderne Welt 1789-1945. II. partl: Weltmächte und Weltkriege. (Series: Geschichte der Neuzeit. ed. Gerhard Ritter), Braunschweig 1960
Hillgruber, Andreas	Bismarcks Außenpolitik. Freiburg 1972
Hillgruber, A.	Grundzüge der Außenpolitik Bismarcks von der Reichsgründung bis zum Abschluss des Dreibundes 1882. In: K. O. Frhr. v. Aretin: Bismarcks Außenpolitik und der Berliner Kongress. Wiesbaden 1978
Höpken, Wolfgang	Staatensystem. In: M. Hatschikjan u. St. Troebst (ed.): Südosteuropa. Gesellschaft, Politik, Wirtschaft, Kultur. Ein Handbuch. München 1999
Hösch, Edgar	Kulturen und Staatsbildungen. In: Hatschikjan/Troebst (ed.): Südosteuropa. ... Handbuch, München 1999
Hopf, Claudia	Sprachnationalismus in Serbien und Griechenland. Theoretische Grundlagen sowie ein Vergleich von Vuk Stefanović Karadzić und Ademantios Korais. Balkanologische Veröffentlichung, Bd. 30, Wiesbaden 1997
Jäger, Lorenz:	Wie Japhet nach Europa kam. Epochenschwelle zwischen 1500 und 1800. FAZ of 12.12.2001
de Jong, Jutta:	Der nationale Kern des makedonischen Problems. Ansätze und Grundlagen einer makedonischen Nationalbewegung (1890-1903). Ein Beitrag zur komparativen Nationalismusforschung. Frankfurt/M., Bern 1982
de Jong, J.:	Die makedonische Nationswerdung – eigenständige Integration oder künstliche Synthese? In: Klaus-Detlev Grothusen (ed.): Jugoslawien Integrationsprobleme in Geschichte und Gegenwart. Göttingen 1984
Kantorowicz, Hermann:	Der Geist der englischen Politik und das Gespenst der Einkreisung Deutschlands. Berlin 1929
Kantorowicz, H.:	Gutachten zur Kriegsschuldfrage 1914. Frankfurt/M. 1967
Kaser, Karl:	Raum und Besiedlung. In: Hatschikjan/Troebst (ed.): Südosteuropa. ... Handbuch, München 1999
Kennan, George F.	Bismarcks europäisches System in der Auflösung. Die französisch-russische Annäherung 1875-1890. Frankfurt/M, Berlin, Wien 1981
Kennedy, Paul M.	The Rise of the Anglo-German Antagonism 1860-1914. London, 4th ed., 1993
Kielmansegg, Peter Graf:	Deutschland und der Erste Weltkrieg. Frankfurt/M. 1980
Kober, Aug. Heinrich:	Europäische Fürstenhöfe – damals. [vol. 3] Zwischen Donau und Bosporus. Frankfurt/M. o. J. (probably also 1937, as the two volumes of this series by Paul Sethe)
von Krockow, Christian Graf:	Kaiser Wilhelm II. und seine Zeit. Biographie einer Epoche. Berlin 2002
Kuzmanovski, Risto:	Ohrid – und seine Kunstschatzkammer. Ohrid 1994

Lepsius, Johannes, Mendelssohn Bartholdy, Albr. Thimme, Friedrich (ed.):	Die Große Politik der Europäischen Kabinette 1871-1914. Berlin 1924
Lieske, Horst Joachim:	Preußen auf einen Blick. Die Könige von Preußen, ihre Zeit und Bauten. Lieske Verlag Langelsheim, 2001
Lorenz, Elke/Raab, Andreas:	Makedonien. Reiches armes Land. Ulm 1997
Mazower, Mark	Der Balkan. Kleine Weltgeschichte. Berlin 2002
von Mach, Richard:	Die Macedonische Frage. Wien 1895
Martens, Michael:	Den Haag ist voreingenommen. Ein Gespräch mit Koštunica. In: FAZ of 1.8.2002
Martens, M.:	Waffentragende Esel. In: FAZ of 22.06.2002
Massie, Robert K.:	Dreadnought. Britain, Germany, and the Coming of the Great War, 1st ed., New York 1991
Massie, Robert K.	Die Schalen des Zorns. Großbritannien, Deutschland und das Heraufziehen des Ersten Weltkriegs. 2. Aufl., Frankfurt/Main 1993
Maurois, André	Benjamin Disraeli. Lord Beaconsfield. Sein Leben. Berlin 1929
Meier, Viktor	Wie Jugoslawien verspielt wurde. München 1995
Mendelssohn Bartholdy, A:	Siehe Lepsius
Henry Cord Meyer:	Das Zeitalter des Imperialismus. Mann/Heuss (ed.): Propyläen Weltgeschichte, Das 20. Jh., Bd. IX/ 1,
Müller, Heinrich:	Die Slavomazedonier in Griechenland. Gesellschaft für bedrohte Völker, 1992
Neitzel, Sönke:	Weltmacht oder Untergang. Die Weltreichslehre im Zeitalter des Imperialismus. Paderborn, München, Wien, Zürich 2000
Nicolson, Harold:	Sir Arthur Nicolson, Bart., First Lord Carnock. A study in the Old Diplomacy. London 1930
Novotny, A.:	Quellen und Studien zur Geschichte des Berliner Kongresses 1878. Graz-Köln 1957, quoted in: I. Geiss: Der Berliner Kgs. Prot. u. Mat. Boppard 1978
Nürnberger, Richard:	Das Zeitalter der Französischen Revolution und Napoleon. In: Golo Mann, Alfred Heuss (ed.): Propyläen Weltgeschichte. Das 19. Jahrhundert. Frankfurt/Main, Berlin 1960, vol. VIII/1
Ortega y Gasset, José	Über das Römische Imperium. Stuttgart 1942
Oschlies, Wolf:	Republik Mazedonien. Report of the BIOst No. 14/1994
Oschlies, W.:	see also: Bojic, Vera
Palmer, Alan	Verfall und Untergang des Osmanischen Reiches. München, Leipzig 1994
„Ploetz, Der große",	32. ed. Freiburg 1999
Prinzing, Günter:	Die umstrittene Selbständigkeit der MOK in historischer Sicht. In: Walter Althammer (ed.): Makedonien. Probleme und Perspektiven eines jungen Staates. Südosteuropa-Gesellschaft, München. Aus der Südosteuropa-Forschung, vol. 10
Raab, Andreas:	Dürfen Makedonen Makedonen sein? Der Streit um die makedonische Identität. In: Elke Lorenz/A. Raab (ed.): Makedonien. Reiches armes Land. Ulm 1997
Rhode, Gotthold:	Der Berliner Kongreß u. Südosteuropa. In: Karl O. Frhr. v. Aretin (ed.): Bismarcks Außenpolitik und der Berliner Kongress. Wiesbaden 1978
Rosen, Klaus	Die Gründung der makedonischen Herrschaft. Chiron 8, 1978
Rüb, Matthias:	Haager Tribunal ermittelt in Mazedonien. In: FAZ of 10.04.2002
Rüb, M.:	Schießerei unter Albanern. In. FAZ, no. 73 of 27.3.2002
Schieder, Theodor:	Europäisches Staatensystem und Gleichgewicht. Aus: Staatsystem als Vormacht der Welt 1848-1918. Propyläen Geschichte Europas, vol. 5. published in: Karl O. Frhr. v. Aretin (ed.): Bismarcks Außenpolitik und der Berliner Kongress. Wiesbaden 1978
Schrameyer, Klaus:	Das Verbot der Partei der Makedonier in Bulgarien durch das bulgarische Verfassungsgericht. In: Südosteuropa Mitteilgn. 2000, issue 5-6

Schrameyer, K.	Makedonien: das neue Gesetz über die territoriale Organisation und das Referendum vom 7. November 2004. In: Südosteuropa Mitteilungen issue 1, 2005
Seewann, Gerhard:	Minderheiten und Nationalitätenpolitik. In: M. Hatschikjan und St. Troebst (ed.): Südosteuropa. Gesellschaft, Politik, Wirtschaft, Kultur. Ein Handbuch. München 1999
Sethe, Paul:	Europäische Fürstenhöfe – damals: Berlin/Wien. Frankfurt/M. 1937
Sethe, P.:	Europäische Fürstenhöfe – damals: Der russische Zarenhof. Frankfurt/M 1937
v. Siebert, Benno (Hg.):	Diplomatische Aktenstücke zur Geschichte der Ententepolitik der Vorkriegsjahre. Berlin und Leipzig 1921
Stadtmüller, Georg:	Geschichte Südosteuropas. München 1950
Starova, Luan:	Zeit der Ziegen. Zürich 1999
Steger, Hans Alfred:	„Deutsche Weltpolitik" bei Hans Delbrück 1895-1918. Diss. Marburg 1955
Steinke, Klaus:	Sprachen. In: Hatschikjan/Troebst (ed.): Südosteuropa. ... Handbuch. München 1999
Stojćevski, Giorgi:	Makedonien in den internationalen Beziehungen (1878-1919). In: Walter Lukan (ed.): Österreichische Osthefte. Ost- und Südost-Europa-Institut. 40th year, issues 1 u. 2
Strachan, Hew	Der Krieg des Kaisers. SPIEGEL Special I/04
Stuch, Stephan:	Statistisches Profil. In: Hatschikjan/Troebst (ed.): Südosteuropa. ... Handbuch, München 1999
Stürmer, Michael:	Das ruhelose Reich. Deutschland 1866-1918. Berlin, Darmstadt, Wien (1983), 1994
Sundhausen, Holm:	Die serbische Frage. Vortrag gehalten am 5.2.1993 am Osteuropa-Institut der FU Berlin (published as a brochure)
Szobries, Torsten:	Sprachliche Aspekte des nation-building in Mazedonien. Die kommunistische Presse in Vardar-Mazedonien (1940-1943). Stuttgart 1999
Thimme, Friedrich:	siehe Lepsius
Todorova, Maria:	Die Erfindung des Balkans. Europas bequemes Vorurteil. Darmstadt 1999
Toynbee, Arnold	Menschheit und Mutter Erde. Die Geschichte der großen Zivilisationen. Wiesbaden 2006 (Mankind and Mother Earth. A Narrative History of the World.)
Trautmann, Reinhold	Die slavischen Völker und Sprachen. Eine Einführung in die Slavistik. Leipzig 1948
Troebst, Stefan:	Die makedonische Antwort auf die „Makedonische Frage": Nationalismus, Republiksgründung und nation-building in Vardar-Makedonien 1944-1992. In: Südosteuropa 41, 1992
Troebst, St.:	IMRO + 100 = FYROM? Kontinuitäten und Brüche in den makedonischen Nationalbewegungen in historiographischer Perspektive. In: Walter Lukan u. Peter Jordan (ed.): Makedonien. Geographie, Ethnische Struktur, Geschichte, Sprache und Kultur, Politik, Wirtschaft, Recht. In: Österreichische Osthefte, 40th year, Wien 1998
Troebst, St.:	Kommunizierende Röhren: Makedonien, die Albanische Frage und der Kosovo-Konflikt. In: Südosteuropa Mitteilungen. 1999, no. 3
Troebst, St.:	Politische Entwicklung in der Neuzeit. In: Hatschikjan/Troebst (ed.): In: Südosteuropa ... Handbuch. München 1999
Troebst, St.:	Präventive Friedenssicherung durch internationale Beobachtermissionen? Das Beispiel der KSZE-Spillover-Monitormission in Makedonien 1992/1993 vom 25.10.1993. Stiftung Wissenschaft und Politik, Ebenhausen, November 1993
Troebst, St.:	Von der „Mazedonischen Frage" zur „Albanischen Frage". Der Balkan am Ende des 20. Jahrhunderts. In: FAZ of 31.07.1996
Troebst, St.	See also: Hatschikjan, Mag.
Tuchman, Barbara	Der stolze Turm. Ein Porträt der Welt vor dem Ersten Weltkrieg. 1890-1914. München/Zürich 1969

Vasmer, Max:	Die Slaven in Griechenland. Abhandlungen der Preußischen Akademie der Wissenschaften, Bd. 12, Berlin 1941
Voss, Christian:	Das slavophone Griechenland – Bemerkungen zum Ende eines Tabus. In: Südosteuropa-Mitteilungen, 2000, no. 4
Voss, Ch.:	Der albanisch-makedonische Konflikt in der Republik Makedonien in zeitgeschichtlicher Perspektive. In: Südosteuropa Mitteilungen 2001, no. 3
Voss, Ch.:	Die slawische Minderheit. Liberalisierung in Ägäis-Makedonien und Politik der kleinen Schritte. In: Pogrom. Gesellschaft für bedrohte Völker. Minderheiten in Griechenland. Issue 209, 2/2001
Voss, Ch.:	Minderheiten in Griechenland. In: Pogrom. Gesellschaft für bedrohte Völker. Issue 153, Mai/Juni 1990
Weidner, Stefan:	Bruder, wo bist du? In: FAZ of 14.06.2002
Weithmann, Michael W.:	Die slavische Bevölkerung auf der griechischen Halbinsel. Ein Beitrag zur historischen Ethnographie Südost-Europas. München 1978
Weithmann, M. W.:	Makedonien – „Land zwischen vier Feuern", Außenpolitik III/93
Zolling, Peter	Deutsche Geschichte von 1871 bis zur Gegenwart. Bonn 2005

*) The author cannot help mentioning the political propaganda publication of C. Farmakis: „Die makedonische Frage in der deutschen Politik" (Frankfurt/M. 1994.) He refuses, however, to discuss this work in an academic context and is rather irritated by the fact that the university of Bonn did not regard it as beneath its dignity to accept such a pamphlet as a dissertation, - which, by the way, only marginally mentions the "German policy" of the title in the text.

Abbreviations

The majority of the abbreviations are only used in the notes.

A	Aufzeichnung (record)
AA	Auswärtiges Amt (Ministry of Foreign Affairs)
A. a. O., a. a. O.	l. c., loc. cit.
ALB, alban.	Albania, Albanian
Austr.	Austria, Austrian (Österreich, österreichisch)
Bgd.	Belgrade
B. (R.)	Bericht (Report)
Berlin Cgs.	Berliner Kongress (Congress of Berlin)
Bo.	Botschaft, -er (Embassy, Ambassador)
BOS, B u. H	Bosnia and Herzegovina
BUL, bulgar.	Bulgaria, Bulgarian
byzant.	Byzantine
Ch.	Chancellor
Co'ple	Constantinople
Cophgn.	Copenhagen
c, ct.	century
DÄN, dän. (Den., Dan.)	Dänemark, dänisch (Denmark, Danish)
DR	Deutsches Reich (German Reich, German Empire)
D	Deutschland (Germany)
E, (ENG), Engl.	England, English
Ed.	editor
e. g.	exempli gratia (for example)
Emp.	Empire
F, franz. (French)	Frankreich, französisch (France, French)
FM	Foreign Minister, -stry
FO	Foreign Office
F.A.Z.	Frankfurter Allgemeine Zeitung
GB	Great Britain
Geh. Rat	Geheim(er) Rat (Privy Council)
GK	Generalkonsul (Consul General)
Ges.	Gesandter (envoy)
GRI, griech.	Griechenland, griechisch (Greece, Greek)
I, ital.	Italien, italienisch (Italy, Italian)
Jh.	Jahrhundert (century)
KWII.	Kaiser Wilhelm II (William II)
KOS	Kosovo
l. c., loc. cit	locus citatus
LR	Legationsrat (legation councillor)
MAZ, mazedon. (MAC, Macedon.)	Mazedonien, mazedonisch (Macedonia, -n)
Min.Präs.	Ministerpräsident (Prime Minister, PM)
MOC	Macedonian Orthodox Church
MonteN, Montenegrin.	Montenegro, montenegrin.
ÖST, österr.	Österreich, österreichisch (Austria, Austrian)
Ö.-U.	Österreich-Ungarn (Austria-Hungary)
O. R., (O. E.)	Osmanisches Reich (Ottoman Empire)
P., Pg. (p., pg.)	Page
PM	Prime Minister
Prinz.'in	Prinzessin (Princess)
R.	Report (meaning: written report)
Reg.	Regierung (government)
Rk v.B.	Reichskanzler von Bülow (Chancellor)
Rep.	Republic
ROC	Russian Orthodox Church
Rom., Roman. (RUM, rumän.)	Romania, Romanian, (Rumänien, rumänisch)
RUS, russ.	Russia, Russian

RVV	Rückversicherungsvertrag (reinsurance treaty)
SER, serb.	Serbia, Serbian
St. P'bg.	St. Petersburg
StS	State Secretary (Undersecr.)
T.	Telegram (wire)
TOP	Tagesordnungspunkt (agenda item)
TUR., Turk. (TÜR, türk.)	Turkey, Turkish, (Türkei, türkisch)
UÇK	National Liberation Front Kosovo
v. B.	von Bülow
1. WK	Erster Weltkrieg (First World War)
1.WW	First World War

Technical Remarks

- The source references of quotations from the reports of diplomatic missions of the Auswärtiges Amt are made up of the following components (not separated by punctuation except for abbreviations, dates and between numbers):

    - B. (R.) for Bericht (report) or T. for telegram
    - Number of the report. If a B. (R.) number is missing, the Journal number (in brackets) is listed instead, where available. These numbers from the Journal in the Foreign Ministry, which were noted on the first page of every incoming report and were arranged strictly according to the numerical order of the arrival of the reports in the Ministry, began in each calendar year [not in every volume of records] with a "1".
    - Name of the source location. (The Embassy in Constantinople is a special case: the embassy distinguished the location of the source precisely according to the name of the district of the city in which the office was located or that of the suburb in which the summer residence was situated or that of the Ambassador's Residence. So as to avoid confusion the name of the capital, Constantinople, has been used rather than that of the exact geographical locations Bujukdere, Therapia and Pera. Similarly in the case of Romania no difference has been made between the summer residence of Sinaia and the capital Bucharest.)
    - Date (of compilation of the report). Day and month are written without zero in the case of one-digit numbers, with the name of the month also being given as a number rather than being written out in full, although this was the general convention at that time in the reports.
    - Number of the volume in the Political Archives of the Auswärtiges Amt (albeit without the prefixed letter "R", which is used without exception in the archives).

Quotations are given in smaller print in the text and are additionally indented (normally only in the case of complete sentences).

The spelling of names (and technical terms) has not been standardized, but follows the (often varying) forms used in the reports over decades.

The map showing the political boundaries of the modern Balkan states is published by the kind permission of the Westermann Schoolbook Publishing Company Brunswick.
The historical map is taken from the "Institut Historique Macédonien" in Sofia. According to the Bulgarian Encyclopedia (Enciklopedija Bulgarija) of 1984 the Institute existed from 1923 to 1947. As far as the author was able to establish, there is no successor organization which has the licensing rights. The map shows the borders of the three (in fact: four) parts of Macedonia after the Balkan Wars of 1912/13 as they were confirmed in the treaties signed in the suburbs of Paris, in the case in question the Peace Treaty of Neuilly between Bulgaria and the Entente powers.

Index of Names

The names of contemporary authors are mentioned only in the text and/or in the notes and in the bibliography; likewise, the names of the numerous Ambassadors/Envoys are not included in this index. (With very few exceptions).

Aali Pascha (Grand Vizier) 110
Aarifi Pascha (Turk. FM) 194
Abdul Hamid II. (Sultan) 78, 98, 113, 190, 194, 202, 241, 255, 295, 358
v.Aehrenthal, Count (Austr. Chanc. a. FM) 195, 226 f, 228 f, 231, 261, 276, 299, 310, 317
Ahmed Abdallah (Director, Cairo) 107
Albert, Prince of Saxe-Coburg a. Gotha (Queen Victoria's husband) 268
Alexander, the Great 13, 21, 34, 48, 124, 163, 257, 395
Alexander I (Tsar) 206
Alexander II (Tsar) 110, 115 f, 152, 164, 185, 245, 247, 256
Alexander III (Tsar) 68, 92, 115, 118, 120, 140, 145, 152, 258, 275
Alexander v. Battenberg (Bulg. Prince) 70, 91, 93, 127 f, 138, 164, 219, 259
Alexander Obrenović (Serb. King) 68, 71, 258, 374
Alexander, Prince a. King of GRE (Son of Konstantin I) 388, 390
Alexandra (Tsarina, Princess Alice v. Hesse-Darmstadt) 115, 288, 315, 343
Alexandra (Danish Pr., Pr. of Wales) 114, 142, 147, 153 160, 168, 268, 274, 287, 338
Alexandra (Greek Princess, Great Pr.) 126, 145
Alice v. Battenberg, see Viktoria Alice
v. Andrassy, Count (Austr. FM) 218 f
Andrew/Andreas (Prince of GRE) 125 f, 153, 160
Andriskos 22
Andronicos, Manolis 35
Antigonos II. Gonatas 21
Aristotle 21, 40
Asen, Peter, Ivan (a. Ivan II) 86
Asparukh (Bulg. Khan) 84
Asquith (PM) 261, 271, 277, 283 f., 289, 295
Lady Asquith 271
Assim Bey (Turk. FM) 201
Attila 22
Badinter Robert (Law-Commission) 48
Bajazeth I (Ott. Sultan) 26
Balfour (PM) 261, 275, 365
Ballin, Albert 285, 387
Balugdjic 74 ff
Basileios II (Byzant. Emperor) 25, 86
Batjanov, Russ. General 380
Battenberg, see Alexander or Ferdinand
Beaconsfield, Earl of, see Disraeli

v.Behr, Frhr. (Journalist) 271, 296, 307, 310, 327
Beit (Banker) 262, 276, 311
v.Berchtold, Count (Austr. FM) 217, 257, 272, 310, 314, 320, 338, 340, 349, 359, 372, 377
Berovski (Mac. Patriot) 27 f, 31, 222
Bertie, s. Edward
v.Bethmann Hollweg (Chancellor) 80, 246, 255, 263, 271, 277 f, 310, 324, 333, 339, 342, 375 f, 387
v.Bethmann Hollweg iun. (Envoy) 160
Beverage, Albert 322
Bib Dada (Prince of Alban. Meridites) 180
v.Bismarck, Otto Prince 64, 90, 99, 109, 119, 124, 130, 133, 156, 186, 208 f, 216 f, 220 f, 225, 227, 229, 235 ff, 243 ff, 246 f, 250, 254 ff, 257, 265 ff, 276, 280, 289, 291, 315, 317, 320, 323, 336 ff, 341, 344, 352 f, 363
v.Bismarck, Herbert Graf 119, 124
v.Bismarck (Major, Mil.-Att.) 389
Bomber-Harris 293
Boris (Bulg. Tsar) 85, 258
Boris (Bulg. Crown Prince) 94, 125, 298
Brandenburg, Erich 264
Bratiano, sen. a. iun. (Roman. PM.s) 92, 170ff, 172, 195 ff
Briand, Aristide (French PM) 159
de Broglie, Duc 365
Bryan, William T. 322
v.Bülow, B. (Chanc.) 74, 77, 79, 155, 209, 225 ff, 226, 244 ff., 254, 257, 265 ff, 268, 271 f, 274 ff, 277 ff, 282, 286, 290, 294, 311 f, 339, 360, 373, 387
Burridge, Brian (Brit. Airmarshall) 243
Busch, Wilhelm (Cartoonist) 367
v.Caprivi (Chanc.) 67, 209, 258, 290
Carol v. Hohenzollern-Sig. (Roman. King) 90, 92, 170, 174, 361 f, 382
Cartwright (Engl. Amb.) 229 f, 230, 326
Catherine II, the Great 150, 206, 233
Cato, the Elder 261
Chamberlain, Joseph 322
Charlemagne 365
Charles V 242, 343
Charlotte, Princ. of Preußen (Tsarina) 152
Chilandarski, Paisij 39
Childers, Erskine 280
Christian IX (Dan. King) 92, 114, 124, 148, 274 f, 287 f., 295, 363
Christopher (Greek Prince) 126, 162, 168
Churchill, Winston 45, 242, 250, 254, 271, 278 f, 283, 285, 288, 290 f., 295

431

Clarendon (Engl. FM) 245
Clemenceau, Georges 157, 229, 273, 286, 389
Cleopatra VII (last Ptolemae. Pharaoh) 22
Cleveland (US-Pres.) 269
Clio 255
Colomb, Philip H. (Admiral) 252, 342
Conduriottis (Greek Amb. a. FM) 88, 127, 132, 237
Constantine I (Greek Crown Pr. a. King) 69, 119, 124, 131, 134, 149, 151 f, 155, 158 ff., 264, 302, 334, *341*, 346, 350, 352, 354, 356, 372, 378, 382 f, 384 f, 388 ff
Constantine II (Greek Prince a. King) 388, 390
Constantine (Russ. Grd. Pr., Olga's father) 123
Contostavlos (Greek FM) 128 f., 132
Coromilas (Greek FM) 352, 354
Cortéz 257
Craig, Gordon 244, 247, 255 f, 298, 331, 338, 376
Crispi (Ital. PM) 208, 252
Crowe, Eyre Earl of (Undersecr.) 262, 276, 289
Cvijić, Jovan 38, 43, 76
Cyrill a. Methodius (Apostles) 36
Dagmar/Maria Feodorowna (Dan. Pr., Tsarina 92, 115, 118, 121, 124, 140, 142, 147, 152, 168 273 ff, 287 f.
Dahn, Felix 14
Danilo (Prince of MonteN) 315 f
Davis, Robert C. 289
Décazèz, Duc de 237
Dehio, Ludwig 184, 229
Delbrück, Hans 238, 264, 278, 281, 293
Delcassé (French PM a. FM) 221, 262, 267, 274, 283, 287, 295
Delćev, Goce 37 f, 96
Delyannis (Greek FM a. PM) 114, 146, 152, 155, 263f, 302, 355
Demosthenes 46
Dendramis, Vasilis 49
Derby, Lord 113
Descartes 230
Dimitriyev (Bulgar. General) 88, 363
Dimitrov, Georgi M. (Bulg. Communist Leader) 45
Diocletian 22
Disraeli, Benjamin 182, 233, 235 ff, 244 f
Djuvara (Roman. FM) 173
Dreyfus 239
Drummond, J. Erik 49
Dschingis Khan 257
Dürrenmatt 187
Durham, Edith M. 72, 88, 97, 152, 157, 379, 385 f
Durant, Will 188
Dušan, Stefan D. Urosh IV, the Powerful (Serb. Tsar) 25, 61, 65, 174

Edward VII, ("Bertie") 115, 117, 124, 158 ff, 261, 264, 268, 270, 274 f, 278, 281, 290, 312 f, 337, 346, 364, 375
Elisabeth zu Wied (Roman.Queen) 169
Elisabeth (Princess of ROM) 161
Elizabeth II, Brit. Queen 154
„Empress Friedrich", see „Kaiserin Fr."
Enver Hodscha 178
Ermanarich (Gothic King) 84
Eugen, Prince of Savoye 181, 213
zu Eulenburg, Count (Undersecr., Amb.) 219
Fallmerayer, Jakob Ph. 105
Ferdinand I, of Saxe-Coburg and Gotha (Bulg. Prince a. King) 78, 83 f, 94 f, 100 f., 125, 150, 198, 224, 232, 267, 305, 317, 387
Ferguson, Niall 243, 248, 260 f, 262 f, 270, 277 f, 280, 285, 290 ff, 298, 312, 324, 330 f, 342, 359
Fest, Joachim 238
Fischer, Fritz 228 f, 239, 247, 254 f, 257, 259, 263, 271, 280, 284, 292, 296, 298 f, 331, 333, 340 ff, 375, 386 f
Fisher, John (First Lord of the Admiralty) 252, 264, 278, 290 f., 336
Francis I (François I, Valois) 181, 242, 289 343
Franco 390
Franz Ferdinand (Austr. Crown Pr.) 228
Franz Josef (Austr. Emp.) 134, 157, 232, 268, 281, 317, 326, 281, 338
Frederick, the Gr. 244
Frederick III (Emp.) 119, 250
Frederick William (the"Soldier King") 248
Frederick William IV. 241
French (Engl. Commander-in-chief) 264, 278
Friederike, Princ. of Hannover u. GB a. Duchess of Brunswick (Greek Queen, 1947) 390
Friedrich, Jörg 271, 284, 291, 295
Galanaki, Rhea 55, 104, 106, 187
Garašanin (Serb. Min. of Inter.) 64
Garibaldi, Ricciotti 173
Genscher, H.-Dietrich (FM) 59
George V (Brit. King) 383
George I (Dan. Pr., Greek King) 28, *104* a. whole chapter 2.3, 234, 260, 307, 344, *354, 357* f, 384, 390
George (Prince of GRE) 125 f, 148, 153, 160 f, 238; (as King Georg II:) 170, 390
Georg Mikhailovich (Great Prince) 140, 153
v. Giers (Russ. Chanc.) 209
Gladstone (PM) 245
Gligorov, Kiro (President of the Rep. of MAC) 189, 395
Goethe 178, 314
Goluchowski, Count (Austrian Chanc. a. FM) 157, 222
Gomulka 309
Göring 309
Gorki, Maxim 335

432

Gortshakov, Prince (Russ. Chanc.) 90, 247
Grekov (Bulg. FM) 94
Grey, Edward (Brit. FM) 259, 261 ff, 267, 269f, 272, 277 ff., 279, 281 ff., 285, 289, 291 f, 324, 344, 348, 357, 380
Grigorios V. (Patriarch) 107
Gruev, Dame 96
v.Habsburg, see Habsburg Empire
Haldane (Brit. War Min.) 261, 270, 279 f, 283, 291 f., 295
Hamann, Brigitte 232, 239, 285,
Hamid, Sultan, see Abdul H.
Hardinge, Charles 259, 264, 267, 274, 278, 284, 287, 295, 313
Harmsworth, editor 311
Harris, see Bomber
Hartwig, Baron (Russ. Consul) 310, 321, 329, 376
Hatsiskos, Dr. (Greek doctor a. MP) 144
v. Haymerle, Baron (Austr. FM) 219
Henry VIII 343
Heinrich, Prince of Preußen 358
Helena Vladimirnova (Great Princess) 153, 161, 312, 335
Heraclius (Emp.) 105
Herzfeld, Hans 18, 227, 230, 260, 329
Herzog, Roman 48, 395
Hilmi, see Husni
Hinzpeter, Dr. (Pedag.) 253
Hirsch, Baron 241
Hitler 238
Hobsbawm, Eric J. 28, 106
Hohenzollern 216, 248, 373
v. Holstein 239, 246, 257, 260, 273
Homer 40
v.Hötzendorf, Conrad Count (Aust. Chief of Gen. Staff) 362
House, Col. (Pres. Wilson's contact person in Berlin) 270, 283
Hoxha, Enver 180
Husni Hilmi Pascha 192, 385
v.Ignatieff, Count (Russ. Amb. a. FM, "Father of Lies") 90
Ipek (Metropolitan) 77
Isidor, Bishop of Sevilla 105
Ismael Pascha, Khedive 185
Ivan IV (The Terr.) 205
Izvolski, Alexander P. (Russ. Amb. a. FM) 78, 84, 90, 100, 195, 215, 227 f, 252 f., 259 f, 260/1, 264 ff, 267 f, 273 f, 276, 280 f., 284, 286, 288 f., 292, 295, 298, 310, 313, 321, 382 a. note 667
v.Jagow, Gottlieb (Amb. a. Secr. of State) 228, 246, 262, 301, 320 f, 323 f, 382
John of Thessalonica 34
Jonescu, Take (Roman. PM) 162, 386
Juán de Austria 181
Juán Carlos I (Span. King) 390

Jutta, Princess of Mecklenburg-Strelitz, "Queen of MonteN" 316
Kadaré, Ismail 58
„Kaiserin Friedrich"("Empress Frederick", daughter of Qu. Victoria, mother of William II) 93, 124, 144
v.Kálnoky, Count (Austr. FM) 118, 129 ff, 134, 222
Kanaris (Greek PM) 211
Kantorovicz, Hermann 34, 211, 245, 259, 264, 268, 271, 331 f, 334, 374 ff, 379
Karadjordje (Black George) 62 a. note 178
Karadjordje, Peter (Serb. King) 69, 73 f.
Karadzić, Vuk 53
Karavelov (Bulg. Komitadji a. PM) 92, 96
Karl I v.Hohenzollern-Sigmar., see Carol
Karlan, Dan 288
Kemal Atatürk 193
Kennan, George F. (American Amb.) 91, 93, 239, 242. 245, 247, 250, 254, 256, 258, 268, 273, 275, 280, 286, 289 f, 332
Kennedy, Paul M. 242, 246, 285, 287 f,
Kerenski 383
Keschko, Natalia (Serb. Queen) 63, 68
Keynes, John Maynard 286
Kiamil Pascha (Turk. FM) 327
v.Kiderlen-Wächter (Amb., Secr. of State) 144ff, 170, 190, 268, 270, 276, 296, 306, 308, 317 f, 337, 339, 345, 370, 372, 375, 377
v.Kielmannsegg, Peter Count (Prof.) 330 f
Kollar, Jan 51
Koneski, Blaze 38, 52
Korais, Ademantios 40, 108
Kostopoulos, Tasos 136
Koštunica, Vojislav 59
Krasniqi, Jakup 54
v. Krockow, Christian Count 243 ff., 246, 338
Krum (Bulg. Khan) 85
Kumunduros (Greek PM) 112
Lahovary, Alexander (Roman. FM) 191
v. Lam(b)sdorf, Count (Russ. Chanc.) 211, 226
Lasker, Eduard 238
Lazar, Allan 288
Lee, Lord of the Admiralty 278, 290
Leeds, Mrs., née Stewart 162
Lenin 284, 286
Leo XIII (Pope) 159
Leopold I (Austrian Emp.) 47, 181 f., 390
Lesseps, Ferdinand de 236
Levski (Bulg. Komitadji) 96
Louis II of Bohemia a. Hungary (Yagiellone) 216
Louis XIV 181, 240, 248
Louise (Danish Queen) 118, 124
Lloyd George, David 342
Ludwig Wilhelm I, Margrave of Baden („Turk-Louis") 213
Luther, Martin 33, 199

Macchiavelli 242, 270
Mahan, Alfred T. (Captain) 253, 322
Mahmud II, Sultan 178, 182, 192
Majorescu (Roman. FM) 361
Mann, Golo 238
Maria Feodorowna, Tsarina, see Dagmar
Maria Louise von Parma (Bourbon Princ.) 94
Marie (Greek Princess) 141, 149
Marie Bonaparte (Princess) 160, 168
Marko (Serb. King) 61
Marschall v. Bieberstein, Frhr. (Secr.of State a. Amb.) 81, 191, 196 f., 208, 219, 228, 236, 241
Mashin, Draga (Serb. Queen) 68, 72 a. see note: 167
Massie, Robert K. 228, 232, 253, 260, 269f, 273, 276, 283, 286, 288 f, 298, 336, 339
Maurois, André 182, 233, 247, 255
Mavromichali (Greek FM) 167
Max Emanuel, (Prince Elector) of Bavaria 213
Medschid, Sultan 184
Mehmed Ali Pascha (Egypt) 175, 184, 234
Menschikov, Prince (Russ. Amb.) 185
Metaxas (Greek. PM) 21
Methodius (Apostle) 36
v.Metternich, Clemens, Prince 349
v.Metternich (Amb.) 311
Meyer, Henry C. 252, 262, 271, 278, 281, 285f, 290, 295, 322, 342
Michael III (Byzant. Emp.) 36
Michael, Archbishop of Ohrid a. Makedonija 24, 35, 38
Milan, Obrenović (Serb. King) 68, 100, 163, 190 f., 345
Milošević, Slobodan 47, 66
Milovanovich, (Serb. PM a. FM) 242, 280, 308
Miovski, Mito (Mac. Prof.) 38, 51
Misirkov, Krste Petkov 37
Mitsotakis (Greek PM) 47, 82, 352
Moberly-Bell (editor) 311
v. Moltke (Gen.Fieldm.) 311
Moore, Frederick 360
Munir Pascha (Vezier) 164
Muravieff, Count (Russ. FM) 143, 150
Mussolini 291
Mustafa, Sultan 38
Napoleon Bonaparte 62/3, 181, 206, 213, 232, 242, 276, 278, 290, 373
Napoleon III 217, 237, 246, 278, 289
Natalie (Serb. Queen) 68
v. Nekljudow (Russ. Envoy) 325, 329
Nelson, Admiral 278
Nemanja, Stefan (Great Zupan) 61, 73
Nicholas I (Tsar) 152, 206, 339
Nicholas II (Tsar) 94, 115, 121, 124, 150 153, 162, 214, 221, 264, 267, 273, 275, 281, 286, 305, 335, 361, 363 f, 373, 382 f
Nicholas (Greek Prince) 148, 153, 156, 161, 312, 334, 354

Nicolai Michailovich (Grt. Prin.) 298, 315, 361
Nicolson, Arthur (Brit. Amb.) 228, 263, 267, 270, 273, 279, 283 f., 286, 292, 332
Nicolson, Harold 264, 287
Nik(c)ola/Nikita/Nicholas (Prin./King of MonteN) 266, 270, 297 f., 305, 308, 315, 323
Noradungian (Grand Vizier) 327
Northclifffe, Lord 312
Novaković (Serb. PM) 69 f.
Obrenović (Serb. Kings):
  Alexander 68, 70, 72 a. note 178
  Michael 63
  Milan 63, 71
  Miloš 63 a. note 178
Olga (of Kiev) 86
Olga (Great Princ., Greek Qu.) 110, 115, 116, 118, 123, 125, 143, 145, 151, 156, 162, 165, 260, 274, 382 f
Ortega y Gasset, José 250
Otto v. Wittelsbach/Bavaria (Greek King) 28, 108, 114, 121 f, 142, 148
v.Pallavicini, Margrave (Austr. Amb.a. Undersecr.) 268, 306, 316, 337, 353
Papandreou (Greek PM) 47
Papakonstantinou (Greek FM) 46
Pašić (Serb. PM.) 77, 226, 379, 386
Patriarch of Const. (Greek) 25
Paul (Tsar) 152
Paul (Great Prince) 126, 141, 145
Paul I (Prince a. King of GRE) 366
St. Paul (Apostle) 47
Pearsons, Karl 322
Peter, The Gr. (Tsar) 205 f, 229, 233, 241, 339
Peter, Karadjordje (Serb. King) 72, 84, 198, 386
Philipp v. Battenberg (Duke of Edinburgh) 154
Philipp II (King of Makedonia) 21, 34 f
Piccolomini (General) 33
Pitt, the Elder, William 343
Pius V, Pope 181
Pizarro 257
Plato 40
Poincaré, Raymond (PM a. FM) 252, 267, 276, 284, 289, 305 f, 320 f, 330
Ponsonby, Arthur 313
Ponte, Carla del 30
Poulianos (Greek Historian) 106
Potyemkin 205
Presyan (Bulg. Tsar) 23, 85
Preston, Diana
Princip, Gavrilo 232
Ptolemaeans 21 f
Pulevski, Georgi 38
Putin Vlad. (Russ. Pres.) 91
Queen Mum 293
Rakovski (Bulg. Komitadji) 96
Rastislav (Great Prince of Moravia) 36
Rasputin 315
v. Rathenau, Walther 285 f

Reuß, Prinz Heinrich VII 112, 118, 130 f, 218, 233 a. note 313
Rhallis (Greek PM) 145
Richelieu 242
Rifaat Pascha (Turk. FM) 195
Ristić (Serb. Regent) 63, 68
Robertson, George (NATO, Secr. Gen.) 29
Robertson, William (Col.) 277
Röhl, John (Prof.) 340
Roland (French Prince) 160
Romanov 211, 275
Romulus, the Gr. 187
Roosevelt, Theodore 286, 322, 364
Rothschild, (a.o. Baron Albert) 140, 290, 311
Rudolf (Austrian Crown Prince) 232
Rugowa 309
v.Sabourov (Russ. Amb.) 109, 111
Sacred Sava 386
Safvet Pascha (FM) 112
Salihu (UCK-Leader) 54
Salisbury, Lord (PM a. FM) 113, 235, 287
Salter, Jeremy 288
Samuel (Prince, Tsar) 23 f
Sandanski, Jane 193 f, 211, 357
Sanderson, Lord 280
Saunders, corresp. 311
Sazonov (Russ. FM) 90, 259, 268 f., 271ff, 277, 296 ff, 299, 304, 307 ff, 310 f, 313 ff, 316, 318 f, 320 f, 324 ff, 328 ff, 334 ff, 339, 348, 370 f, 377, 387
Schmidt, Helmut (Former Chancellor) 50
Seeley, Robert 233
Shuvalov (Russ. Amb.) 132, 208, 256
Selim III, Sultan 178, 182, 192
Seymour, Engl. Amb. 318
Shaw, George B. 281
Silvestrelli (Ital. Amb. in Athens) 106
Simeon (Bulg. Tsar) 85 f
Simić (Serb. PM.) 69
Simitis, Konstantin (Greek PM) 19
"Sissi", Austr. Empr. 156, 232
Sobieski, Jan (Polish King) 181
Sofia (Greek Princess a. Span. Queen) 366
Sophie(Princ. of Preußen, Greek Qu.) 119f, 122, 124 ff, 144, 152, 159 f, 341, 347, 350, 352 f, 382 f, 388, 390
Stalin 45
Stambulov (Bulg. PM.) 93, 138 f., 171
Starova, Luan 55
Stefan Dušan Uroš IV (Serb. King) 61, 73, 176
Steger, Hans Alfred (Amb.) 264 f, 277 f., 289
Steiner, Michael 377
Stevenson, David 273, 333
Stoel, Max van der (High Comm.) 48
Stoilov (Bulg. PM) 208, 222
Stolypin (Russ. PM) 264, 278
Stone, Oliver 21
Stone, Norman 113
Strachan, Hew (Prof.) 327, 332 f, 340

Stürmer, Michael 217, 237, 244 f, 247, 249, 252 ff, 257, 261 f, 275, 279 ff, 331, 339
Sturdza, Gregor (Roman.Pri.) 170, 172
Sukhomlinov (Russ. War Min.) 312, 335
Suleyman, The Magnif. 113
Svyatoslav (Prince of Kiev) 86
Tamerlane 26
Thaci, Menduh 54
Theotokis (Greek Ex-PM) 168
Thirlmeres, Rowland 322
Tilly 278, 290
Tirpitz (Admiral) 252 f., 278, 290, 294, 321, 342
Tito 32, 38, 41, 43 f, 46, 56, 74, 88, 120, 198, 388, 394
Tittoni (Ital. FM) 158 f, 252 f., 292
Tolstoj 307
Toynbee, Arnold 33
Treiber Dr., (Doctor of Greek Army a. „living chronicle" in GRE),see note769
Trikupis (Greek FM a. PM) 112, 122, 124, 127, 132, 138, 260
Trotzki 284, 335
Tshakhotin 376
v. Tsharykov (Russ. Chanc.) 213, 228
Tsochatzopoulos (Greek Min.) 19
Tuchman, Barb. 55, 235, 239, 252, 269, 281, 287, 322, 364
Vance, Cyrus 35
Venizelos, Eleftherios K. 40, 159, 161f, 165, 174, 264 f, 302 f, 327, 344, 354, 367 f, 372, 384, 386, 388 ff
Victoria, Queen 93, 115, 117, 144
Victoria ("Vicky", Brit. Princ., daughter of Queen Victoria, mother of Kaiser Wilhelm II.), see "Empress Friedrich" 93, 166
Viktor Emanuel (Ital. King) 158 f
Viktoria, v. Hohenzollern (Princess of Preußen) 93, 259
Viktoria Alice v. Battenberg 125, 153, 160, 276
St. Vladimir (Kiev) 86
Volkashin (King of Prilep) 61
Waldemar (Dan. Prince) 135, 150
Wallenstein 218
Watt, W. Montgomery 188
Wickham Stead (ed.) 312
Wilhelm I (William I) 93, 111, 119, 220, 227 239, 241 f., 247, 249 f, 256 ff, 273
Wilhelm II 69 f, 78, 81, 93, 100, 113, 119f, 124 ff, 139, 141, 144, 156 f, 162, 164, 203, 214, 221, 229, 231 f., *249*, 254, 259, 262 f, 268, 270 ff, 273 f., 276, 279, 283 f., 285 ff., 289, 292, 294 f, 297 f, 305, 307, 309 f, *314,* 316 f, *324 f,* 328, 332 f, *335,*338, *341,* 344, 348, 352 f, 358, 361, 363 f, 370, 372, 375, 377, 382 f, 388, 390, 393
Wilhelm II (King of Württemberg) 229
Wilson, Woodrow 270, 273, 389

Wimmer, Willy (MP) 26
Witte (Russ. PM) 209
Xenia (Great Princess) 150, 168
Ypsilanti, Count/Prince (Greek Amb.) 118, 129ff, 132 f, 355
Zaimis (Governor of Crete, PM) 153, 359
Zankov, Dragan (Bulg. PM.) 70, 94
Zechlin, Egmont 387
Zinovieff (Russ. Amb.) 208 f.
Zuber, Terence 285
Zubkov, Alexander 94 f
Zuckmayer, Carl (emigrated author) 255

Index of Keywords

ABeCeDar (Greek primer for macedon. children in North-Greece) 49
Abyssinia 291
Achilleion 156
Achilles heel (of Bismarck's Dual All.) 273
Acropolis 21, 203
Adria (-tic Sea) 75, 158, 178, 214, 239, 291, 359
Adrianople (also: Peace of) 33, 108, 169, 178, 183, 206, 249, 349, 351, 358, 366, 378
Adyghe (also troops) [Cherkess] 89, 177
AEG 285
Aegaean (Sea) 27, 77, 132, 174, 207, 214, 239, 263, 202, 382
Aegaean Macedonia (North Greece) 31, 42, 55, 214, 347, 378, 388, 390
Aegaean Islands 378
Afghanistan 221, 239, 265, 274, 277
Aix-les-Bains 116, 139 f, 143
AKSh, (successor of UÇK) 57
Albania, Albanians 17, *51*, 53, 59, 106, 130, *174*, 187 f, 189, 212, 215, 230, 240, 252, 254, 268, 291, 294, 297, 300, 304, 306, 356, 359, 362, 369, 372, 374, 377, 385, 391, 394
-ancient 173
-"belligerent Mountain tribes" 177
-demand f. independence 359
-islamisation of ALB 174
-Italian 251
-oppressed nation 349
-as "Present" to Serbia 362, 371
-Russ. cynicism: ALB 350
-in Serbia 62
-South-Albania 345, 378
-as a "trap" 372
Albanian -
-autonomy 25, 158, 317
-census 51
-communism 55
-ethnic cleansing 190
-immigration in GRI 174 ff
-independence 53, 219 (see Independence)
-expansionism 190
-extremists 53 f, 55
-flag (in MAC) 52
-homeland 105
-Illyrian origin 175
-language *41*
-League/Liga (Convention) 179
-loan words (from Slavic languages) 175 f
-minority 48, 51, 53, 57 f
-nationality 178
-neutralität 176
-population in MAC 55 f
-question 77, 351
-refugees (15th a. 20th cent.) 47, 56
-Republic Ilirida 52
-revolts 166, 201, 295
  (student revolt 1981) 56
-secession plans 52, 190
-South Epirus 350
-territorial goals 190
-terrorism (in history) 177
-terrorism (UCK-Terr.) 48, 54, 59
-Turkicized 177
-unification (with KOS) 52
Albanization 177, 370
Algeria 183, 186, 289
Al-Jeel Centre Cairo 107
All-German Association 322
Alliance system 394
Al-Qaida network 59
Alsace (Lorraine) 203, 275, 289, 334, 365, 380
a. note 162
Alvensleben Convention 238
Ambassador Conference
-in Constantinople 183
-in London 177, 346
Ambush of the Triple Entente 343
America, s. USA
American
-expansion/imperialism 322
-war against Spain a. Philippines 322
-Panama Canal project
-Struggle Cuba a. Venezuela 322
"Amselfeld" (Kosovo) 56, 62, 73, 107, 181
Anatolia 26, 109, 133, 186
Trans-Anatolian railway 238
Anglo-
-American friendship 269
-French Military Convention 262
-German relations 311, 365
-Japanese Alliance 221, 282
-Russian antagonism 200, 248, 265
---arrangement/meeting 246 f
---Convention 264
---Entente 260
---fraternization 311
---Naval Agreement 259
---propaganda 311
---Secret understanding (1908) 307
-Turkish Trade Agreement 234
Ankara (Battle of Angora) 168
Annexation
-BOS (by Austr.) 69, 75, *77*, 83, 95, 98, 130, 164, 173 f, 193 f, 198, 208 f., 212, 214, 225 f, 228 ff, 231 f, 258, 261, 265, 273, 291, 332
-Crete (by GB) 153
-Crete (by GRE) 159, 255, 264, 302
-"French" Alsace (by Germany) 221
-German territory (by France) 342
-Hawaii (by USA) 322

437

-MAC (by BUL) 42, 92, 345
-MAC etc.(by GRE) 42, 65, 137, 141, 170, 302, 345, 392
-MAC (by SER) 42, 65, 345
-Saloniki/Solun (by GRE) 356
anti-Austrian coalition 198 f
anti-German
   -aggressiveness (by Pan-Slavism etc) 336
   -baiting by English press 261
   -coalition 198, 261, 293
   -hysteria 281
   -inflammatory press articles 311
   -policy (in GB, by FM Grey) 239, 247, 250, 278, 291
   -policy in FRA 247
   -press in Russia 364
   -propaganda 122
anti-Macedonian policy/propaganda in GRE 130f, 207, 352
anti-Slav policy (of GRE) 129 ff
anti-Semitism 238
Apostles (Epistles of) 33
Arabia 239
Arabian Script 183
Archbishop Michael 24
Archbishop of Cyprus 24
Archbishopric of Ohrid 24 f
Archbishopric of Ohrid (Bulg.) 87
Archdiocese Bulgaria/Ohrid 24
Archives of Windsor Castle 273, 298
Armenia, Armenians 131, 177, 187, 192, 201, 222 ff, 256, 389
Armistice (between Balkan Wars) 357
Arnautes (Albanians) 106, 175, 181
Aromanians (see also Vlachs and Kutzo-Wallachians) 85, 104, 169 ff, 345. and notes 531 u. 541
Ashkenasi 131
Asenid (Kindom, rebellion) 24, 86
Asia Minor 65, 224, 239, 241, 355, 360
Asian/Asiatic rule in Europe 361
Asow 180
Assassination of Sarajevo 353
Assimilation policy (GRE a. BUL) 25 f, 137
Attica 107
   Albanian settlers in Att. 176
Attic dialect 40
Augsburg 46
Austerlitz 243, 373
Austria-Hungary 17 f, 31, 66, 73, 127, 129, 132, 169, 184, 186, 206, *216*, 236, 240, 245, 252, 259, 266, 268, 270, 273, 287, 291,295 ff, 299, 303, 305 ff, 309 f, 313 ff, 317, 319 f, 322, 324, 327, 329 f, 338, 362, 369, 371, 374 ff, 377, 379 f, 385 ff, 395
Austria as „peace breaker" 372
Austrian
   -annexation of BOS 164, 173 212 (see Annexation)

-attack on SER 346
-Balkan policy 216, 248
-expansionist policy 70 ff, 217, 225, 232
-occupation of BOS 207, 218
-resistance against Bosnian autonomy 231
-supremacy 217
-thrust to the Aegaean *131*
-Ultimatum 213, 375, 387, 393
-war against SER 393
Austro-
   -Austro-Bulgarian army 388
   -Hungarian Monarchy, see Austro-Hungary
   -Italian War 216
   -Prussian dualism 246
   -Russian war 206, 216
   -Serbian friendship treaty 66, 91
   -Serbian war 387
Autocephalous Bulg. Church, see Exarchat
Autocephalous Mac. Church *24*, 87
Autonom Province Kosovo (a. Vojvodina)
Autonom Province Salonica a. Monastir 235
Autonomy
   -Albanian 158, 260, 263, 300 f, 319
   -Bosnian 231
   -Bulgarian 29, 109, 186, 216, 327
   -Crete 149, 319, 327, 344
   -Danube Principalities 169
   -Epirus 307
   -Macedonia *26*, 29, 40, 45, *68ff,* 94 f, 96, 100, 138, 193, 223, 240, 258, 260 f, 263, 298, 300 f, 307, 317 ff, 323 f, 347, 351, 356, 360, 381, 386, 392
   - -for Macedonians a. Thracians 326
   -Oldserbia (KOS) 301, 319
   -Serbia 63, 327
   -Thrace (incl. West-Thr.) 307, 347, 356, 392
   -for Turkish regions 306
Avars 84, 104 f
"Backgroundinformation" 115
Badinter-Commission 48
Bagdad Railways 238, 241, 265, 278
Baiting against GER 343
Balance policy (Engl.) 200, 229, 234, 237, 279, 351
„balance of power" (continental) 78, 184, 204, 243 f
Balance in Europe 246, 248
Balfour-Roosevelt era 269
Balkan 202
Balkan Conference 208
Balkan countries (treated as colonies) 93
Balkan Federation/Alliance 16, 192
Balkan League *18*, *64*, 66 f, 71, 73, 76, 79 f, 83f, 91, *94*, *98*, 127, 130, 133 f, 139, 158, 163, *166*, 172 f, 188, 190, 198 ff, *201 ff*, 209 f, 212, 214 f., 216 f., 218 ff., 223, 230, 240 ff, 253 f., *259*, *264*, *295 ff*, - 393
   -anti-Austrian a. anti-German 95, 387

-„darling of the French diplomacy" 350
-foreign influence on *98*
-instrumentalization (by the Entente) 57
-re-establishment of the old Balkan L. 386
-Slavic Balkan League 212
Balkan League, new *361,* 377
Balkan League, new grand 386, *362*
Balkan War
 -First:
  18, 20, 31, 42, 65, 88, 101, 163, 166, 174, 192, 296, 301 ff, 317, 340, 347, *348,* 354, 367 f
 -Second:
  16, 172, 174, 195, 351, 356, 366, 370, *377,* 380, 383, 390
 -„Third": 387
Balkan War=war of conquest 317
Balkan War=European war? 298,302, 341
Balkan War=no religious war 317
Balkan Wars 123, 127, 139, 158, 161, 179, 219, 223, 196 258, 282, *295,* 385, 391
 -alleged localization *296*
 -alleged status quo *299*
 -imperialistic crime 303
Balmoral 259 f, 272 ff., 311, 320
Bar (in MonteN) 54
Battenberg affair 93 ff, 205 222
„Battle for Macedonia" 14, 39
Beirut 185
„Belgian Model" (for KOS) 52
Belgian neutrality 261, 285
Belgium 284
Benevolent neutrality 205
Berlin 239
Berlin, Congress of
 15, 19 f, 28, 31, 38, 44 f, 63 ff, 69, 74, 82 f, 89 f, 92, 110 ff, 113 f, 117, 126 f, 134, 169 f, 178, 186, *189, 194,* 207 f, 214, 217 f, 220, 222, 231, 236, *240 f,* 255, 289 ff, 302, 345, 347, 349, 355, 372, 392
 - failure of the Congress 218
Berlin, Treaty of
 29 f, 66, 70, 78, 90, 114, 130, 138, 159, *186,* 192, 207 f, 220, 223, 231, 256, 263, 301 f, *348,* 359
Bessarabia 169, 186, 206, 217
Bibel (in Turkish) 47
Bismarck's alliance offers (towards GB) 238
Bismarck's alliance system 218
Bismarck',s Dual Alliance 273
Bismarck's European order in decline 258
Bismarck's founding of the German Reich 238
Bismarck's Germany 268
Bitola 54, 193, 260, 300, 349
Björkö (German-Russ. Emp.'s meeting) 211, 364
Black Sea 185, 234
Black Sea Conference 245, 265
Bled 16

Boeotia (Albanian settlers in -) 176
Blockade, econ. (Greece against MAC) 77
Bloody Sunday (in St. P'bg.) 162
Bohemia 36, 105
Bolsheviks 383
Bomber-Harris 282, 293
Bonn 46
Bosnia a. Herzegovina 40, 63, 75, 88, 90, 100, 110, 127, 176, 186, 193, 198, 206 ff, 210, 217, 258, 276, 295, 306, 317, 342, 362, 376
Bosnian
 Crisis 268, 278
 Occupation (by Austria) 28, 70, 75
 Revolt 27, 110
 War 103
Bosporus (and Dardanelles) 17, 61, 85, 207
 --as Russian sphere of influence 210
Bourbon Kings 181
„Der Brand" (The fire, by Jörg Friedrich) 391
Brest-Litovsk (Peace of) 307, 312, 325
British-Blue Book 374
„British Documents" 194, 374 f
British Empire 206, 233 f, 229, 243, 287, 322
British Navy 278
British
 -financial press support (for RUS, FRA, BEL) 311
 -hegemony 233
 -imperialists 365
 -interests 277
 -intervention in Germany 287
 -psychological warfare 312
 -world hegemony claim 333
„Brotherly Teaching" (Korais) 40
Bucharest 169 ff, 171 f., 341, 363
 -Peace (1812) 202
 -Peace (1913) 338, 349, 355 f, 359, 379 ff, 384, 387
Buckingham Palace 112 ff, 203
Bukovina 216
Bulgaria, Bulgarians17 ff, 29, 36 ff, *42*, 49, 53, 63, 72, 79, *84,* 101, 103, 105, 109 f, 113, 116 f, 126 f, 133, 137, 154 f, 164, 166, 197, 202 f, 219, 202 f, 235 f, 239, 249, 280, 282, 292, 296 ff, 300 f, 303 f, 310, 318 f, 322, 325 f, 339, 345, 349, 358, 359 f, 362, 366, 371, 378, 381, 385 f, 388 f, 394 f and note. 211
 -Ancient BUL 84 f
 -BUL in First World War 99
 -Kingdom 94, 98, 162
 -as tributary Principality 90
 -Turkic (Turk-Tatar) Bulgars 23 f, 36, 85, 104
Bulgarian (see also Bulgaro-)
 -autoc. Orth. Church, see Exarchate
 -autonomy 39, 109 (s. Autonomy)
 -border demarcation 369
 -census 16

439

-Communist bureaucracy 45
-Document (important for MAC) *101*
-Bulgarian Empire:
---First 23, 109, 176, 363
---Second (Emp. of the Asenides) 86 f, 363
-expansion 138, 218
-Exarchate 97. See Exarchate
-External Mac. Revolut.Org. 96
-First Slavic Christian Orth. Kingdom 23, 84 ff, 173, 342
-hegemony 71
-horrors 89
-independence 78, 94, 98, 109, 164, 172, 193
-Kingdom 94, 98
-Kingdoms of Tarnovo a. Vidin 86
-language *39,*
-legion 96
-„Macedonian Committee" 96
-minority (in MAC) 193/6
-name 85
-National Day 90, 371
-National Liberation 89
-occupation (of MAC) 367
-Orthodox Church 25, 37, 51, 86, 97 f, 109, 392
-Proto-Bulgarians 36, 84
-revenge 370
-revolts, uprisings 27, 86 ff
-Supreme Committee 97
-Tartars 366
-Turkic tribes 84
-Unification (with East-Rumelia) 66
-Uprisings 86 f, 88 f
Bulgarization 37, 67, 89, 98, 127, 370
Bulgaro-
-Greek Alliance/League/Agr.mt. *259,* 299, 329, 338, 340, 348, 370 f
-Greek disagreements/relations 362, 366
-Serbian reaty/League *258,* 329, 340
„Bulgaroktonos" 86
„Bulgarophonoi Hellenes" (Bulgarians) 88
Byzantium, Byzantine Empire 22 ff, 34, 40, 61f, 84, 86, 128, 155 179
Calabria (Albanian refugees in -) 176
Califat 340
Candia (Crete) 112, 146
canon leca duqadini 56
Capital export (French to RUS) 250
"Caprivi corner" 258
Caribean 221
Catalaunian Fields 22, 104
Catholic Protector (FRA) 289
Caucasus 86, 201
Cavalla, see Kavala
Census:
-Albanians in MAC 51, 56
-Greek Orthodox 87
-Macedon. (a. Alban.) 51, 56

-Macedonians in Bulgaria 45 f
Central Powers 98 f., 171, 192, 210, 249, 257, 302, 351, 357, 365, 369, 393
Ceuta a. Melilla 275
Chain reactions (1914) 394
Chaironeia 35, 104
Chalkidike 55
Cherkess (Adygh) 177
China 230
Christian faith 187
Christianity/Christianization 105 f
Christian orthodox Balkans 341
Christian population (in Turkey) 147
CID (Com. of Imperial Defence) 332
Civil war:
 in Greece 82, 196
 in MAC 53
„Clash of Empires" 304
Clio (Muse of history) 246
Cold War 20
Colonialism (imperialist) 232
Committees, national (in MAC) 168
Communiqué, Russian (1913) 346
"compensation" (finance., territor.) 66, 309
Conference
-of Co'ple 63, 90, 185, 246
-of London (1912) 330, 334
-of Paris (1869) 109
Conquest (of MAC) 338
Conspiracy of the Entente 351
Constantinople
 17, 19, 61, 64, 75, 82 f, 86, 90, 116, 145, 185 f, *195,* 199, 201 f., 229 ff, 235, 241, 332, 334, 348, 350, 356, 359, 362 f
Constantinople Agreement (March 1915) 364
"Constantinople" as aim of peace 334
Constanza 361
Constitutional monarchy 144
Continental force, see mainland force
Conversion to Islam, forced 187
copenhagen, to 278
Corfu 107, 156, 239, 303
Corinth 106, 109, 176
Corinthian Alliance (Ancient Mac. Hegemony upon GRE) 21, 108
Corsairs 289
Corsican-Napoleonic Emperor 365
Council of Europe 136 f
Court of St. James's 233
Crescent 249
Crete (Ital.: Candia) 29, 31, 36, 43, 94, 109, 114, 134 f, 140 ff, 143, *146,* 150, 154, 164, 184, 207, 237, 239, 265, 278, 295, 300, 302, 326, 344, 355
Creusot 360
Crimea (and –n War) 26, 40, 86, 90, 109, 114, 169, 181, 185, 200, 206 ff, 217, 234, 241, 244, 246, 249, 255, 289, 291
Criminal Tribune, see: International …

Croatia, Croats 23, 36, 39, 43, 46, 376, 395
"The Crown" (of the Holy Roman Emp.) 365
Crusade 187 f
    The "Latin" crusaders 61
Cuba 322
Customs Union (SER/BUL) 222, 291
ČSSR (Soviet Invasion) 45
Cyprus (also Archbishopric) 38, 179, 186, 217, 236, 239, 289
Cyrenaica 154, 202, 254, 293, 302
Cyrillic alphabet 36, 50
Daily-Telegraph-Affaire 252 f, 309
Dacians 85, 172
Denmark 57, *288*
    Queen of Den.k 219
Dalmatia 104, 185, 244
Damascus 185, 252
Damocles 123
Danaergeschenk 166, 340
Danish –
--Court/royal house 121, 141
---Prussian war 245, 282
--Queen 219
Danube Monarchy 240
Danube Principalities 107, 169, 185, 206, 217, 234
Dardanelles (see Bosp.) 179, 181
--London Treaty of the Dard. 184
Debar 55
Deception (French/Engl.) 239
Declaration of War 257, 306
    Montenegrin (on the Ottoman Emp.) 269 f, 296 f, 308, 313, 315, 318, 322, 324
Demarcation line
    -Austro-Ottoman. 213
    -Serbo-Bulg. 81
Demotike 40
Denmark 57, 116, 121, 144, 219, *275,* 287, *288*
Depeschenwechsel (Willy-Nicky-Telegr.) 312
Desinformation policy of Entente 266, 304
Deutsche Welle 66
"Devshirme" (Turk. kidnapping) 187
Diadochoi 22
Dialects:
    Central-Macedonian 38
    Albanian (Kosovar) 41
Dibra u. Djakova 347
Diocese of MAC 34
Disguising tactics/strategy 210, 222
Divine right 242
Division, (partition) of MAC, 53, 55 ff, *68 ff,* 101 f., 126, 137, 170, 188, 259
Division of the Roman Emp. (395) 36
Djihad 185
Dobrudsha 92, 201
Dodecanese Islands 390
Doggerbank incident 162, 274, 287
Dolni Debar (Mac. revolt) 29, 42
Double game (Entente) 370

Double standards (by GRE) 49, 385
---by GB 234
Drama 42, 365
Dreadnought ships 260, 274
Dreyfus affair 238
Drugubites 36
Dual Alliance (GER/AUS) 73, 101, 162, *192,* 195, 197, 207 f, 220, *225,* 227, 256 f, 266, 273, 290 f, 293, 297 ff, 370, 372, 387, 393
Dual Monarchy (see Habsburg) 216, 257, 295, 318, 364, 379 and note 576,
Dubrovnik 177
Duma 206
Durazzo 349
Dybbol, battle of 268
Dynastic
    -agreements/arrangements 215, 358
    -assistance 110, 215
    -connections of GRE 115
    -favours 218 f
    -Greek Policy 33, 197
    -intervention 223
    -network 147, 172
Earthquake (Skopje 1963) 56
East-Bulgarian dialect (Varna) 53
East Francish Emp. 243, 365
Eastern Roman Empire 22, 105, 128
Eastern Rumelia 66, 68, 72, 91, 93, 132, 1524 186, 196, 193, 208 f, 222, 249
East-Thrace 83, 134, 236, 359
Ecumenical Council 38
Ecumenical Council Co'ple (8th) 24
Ecumenical Identity 103
Ecumenical Patriarchy (Greek) 86 f, 109, 165
Edict of Nantes (Tolerance) 248
Edict of Potsdam (Tolerance) 248
Edward's VII anti-German letters 268
    -as intriguing poisoner 281
Egypt 21 f, 183, 185, 187, 202, 217, 219, 235, 237, 239, 241, 256, 290, 294
„Ehrlicher Makler" 217, 231
Electoral reform in Prussia 142
Elias Day (Ilinden) 192
Elimination of Germany 286
Elysée 203
Embargo (Greek against MAC) 47
Emperor of Abyssinia (Ita) 291
Emperio Romano, new 291
Empress of India 115
Encirclement (of Bulgaria) 367
Encircling/encirclement (of German Reich) 214 242, 259, 263 ff, 271 f, 271, 283, 291, 297, 355, 386
England (refer to: Great Britain) 17, 19, 31, 75, 78, 84, 90, 99, 101, 108 f, 112, 117, 155, 162, 183 ff, 186, 206, 233, 243 ff, 246 ff, 255, 260, 269, 271 f, 283 f, 296 f, 313, 332, 336, 338 f, 363 ff, 372, 374 f
England's intrigues 229

441

England's jealousy 281, 293
E.'s psychological warfare 228
English (see also Anglo- and British))
    -anti-German agitation/propaganda *226*,
    -baiting against GER 343
    -balance policy 233, 239, 242, 265, 342
    -Balkan Committee 99
    -campaign of hatred against GER 288
    -colonial empire 239
    -colonialism 287
    -concealment strategy 332
    -continental (balance) policy 181, 373
    -continental supremacy 233
    -defamation (systematic) 285
    -democracy 235
    -dynastic protection 149
    -hegemonial policy 235, 342
    -imperialist (-ism) tradition 263, 312
    -jealousy 293
    -lifestyle/philosophy 288
    -neutrality 263
    -obsession (navy) 312
    -preventive war plans (see prev.) 283, 332
    -press (strategy) 249, 311 f (see: Fortnightly a. Saturday Review a. The Times)
    -propaganda 228, 284 f, 311 f, 333
    -responsibility for the war 375
    -superiority 322
    -supremacy policy 200, 239, 276
    -Turk. Trade Agreement 234
    -world hegemony (claim) 333, 373,
Enlightenment 340, 361 and note 145
Enosis 109, 146, 165
Entente
    -Policy/Strategy 13, 19, 33, 69, 73, 78, 80, 82 f, 99 f, 168, 172, 197, 199, 208, 212, 230, 240, 253, 259, *269*, 295, 297 f, *303, 307,* 313 f, 317, 320, 322 f, 329 f, 332, 334, 338, 343, 347 f, 362, 364, 370, 374, 384, 386, 393
    -powers 65, 72, 101, 186, 199 f., 253, 256 f, 296, 305, 325 f., 335
    -prevention of indictment for own war criminals 283
    -plan to stage a great war 340, 347
    -promise 274
    -propaganda 225
    -propag. against German language 281
    -screw of violence 353
    -"tissue of lies" 348
    -St. P'bg. as spearhead 192
    -Triple Entente, see Triple
    -trap for Austria 374
Entente (Cordiale) 99, 193 ff, 198, 201 f, 221, 230 f, 260, 262, 266 f, 269, 271 f, 282, 290, 293 f, 307
Ephesus 134
Epidauros (Greek constitution) 108

Epirus (South a. North) 20, 28, 30 f, 106, 108, 111, 113, 117, 122, 132 ff, 135, 149, 164, 169, 176, 212, 219, 230, 237, 259, 294, 296, 301 f, 326, 347, 350, 369, 383 f
Epirotes 318
Epistles of St. Paul 47
Equality (alleged) of Christians in Ottoman Emp. 138, 182
Erithrea 252, 291
Ethiopia 252, 291
Ethnic cleansing (Albanians in West-MAC) 55, 57, 59, 62, 190, 372
Eurasian nomad horsemen 61, 84
„European Concert" 185, 234, 291
European Council 32, 371
European Court of Human Rights (EMRGH) 15, 44, 366
EU (European Union) 32, 35, 42, 44 f, 46, 48 f, 56 f, 59, 91, 102 f., 137, 183, 288, 301, 350, 392, 395
"European war" 337 f, 347, 362, 372, 374, 394
Exarchate/Exarchy (Autoceph. Bulg. Orth. Church) 25 f., 37 ff, 51, 88, 97, 109 f., 128, 355
Expansionism (policy, strategy, efforts, etc) 38, 64, 66
    -Austrian 79, 210, 222, 228
    -Bulg. 44
    -Greek 28, 109, 127, 252
    -Imperialist. 32
    -Russian (Balkan) Exp. 247
    -Serbian 64
    -territorial 20
Fanariotes, s. Phanariotes
Fanatism 180
Falsifications
    -English 374
    -French 289
Far East (Russian interests) 206
Fashoda-crisis 221
„Father of Lies" (Ignatieff) 90
Father of Turkey: Kemal Atatürk 120
„Fatherly teaching" (Ecum. Greek Patr.) 40
Fehrbellin (Prusso-Swedish battle) 205
Ferdinand documents (French forged) 250, 289
Fischer controversy 363
Fleet, Brit. (Royal Navy) 275, 282 f., 304
Fleet constr. programme (German) 243, *289*
"Force before justice" 197
Forced conversion (Islam) 187
Forgeries
    in English documents 252
    in French documents 250
"Former Yugoslav Rep. of MAC" (FYROM) 32, 35, 46, 59, 135, 392
    "Preliminary" name as thumbscrew 29
Fortnightly Review (fundamental article on Brit. strategy) 238, 240, 242, 293, 387
France

17, 19, 75, 84, 90, 108 f, 122 f, 136, 181, 183, 185, 197, 206, 221, 230, 236, 238, 240, 242 f, 245, 247, 257, 261, 270, 272, 277, 280 f, 283, 287, *289,* 293, 320 f, 336, 338, 342, 360, 363 ff, 371, 388, 395
Frankfurt Pauls Church 275
Franco-
-English intervention 388
-Italian neutrality agreemt. 291
-Prussian War 206, 243, 245 f, 268, 289
-Russian Alliance 217, 221, 251, 276, 290
-Russ. Consultative-Agreemt. 221, 258, 290
-Russian Convention 140, 290
-Russian Entente 290
-Russ. Military Convention 138, 258
Freedom
     for MAC 154
     religious 248
     of a Christian 199
French
-capital export to RUS 250, 290
-"French intrigues" (Tsar) 94
-hegemony 217, 246, 289
-Naval Convention with RUS 305
-naval plans 278
-press 317
-"programme of hatred" 389
-propaganda 286
-war of revenge 267
French Revolution 36, 62, 98, 205, 207, 244
Friendship-Treaty (Austro-Serb.) 217
FYROM, see Former Yug. Rep. of MAC 29
Galicia (mobilization on Gal.border) 327, 371
Gallipoli 181
Gaul 18, 47
Gendarmerie (réforme) 190
General mobilization (RUS, 1914) 327 ff, 331, 335, 343
Georgia 202
Gepides (Note:) 211
German
-aggression 285
-Austrian War 213
-barbarians 287
-colonial expansion 279
-declaration of war 331
-defensive war 331
-"language enemy" 281
-Federation 288
-French war 202, 217, 238, 249
-hegemony 269, 272
-Huns 285, 287
-imperialism 312
-"inclination to unleash world wars" 288
-(Kaiser-) Reich 237, 388, 393
„leaders in music" 281
-militarism 312
-naivety 393
-naval expansion *276*

-National War Graves Commission 388
-propaganda 334
-relations to Islamic world 342
-Russian Neutrality Insurance Treaty (RVV) 205 f
-self-isolation 257
-Turkish Military Agreement 200
-"war of aggression" 365
-„War Council" 280, 332
„Germaniam delendam esse" (English motive) 261, 274, 277, 283, 307
Germanic migration 105
Germanization (of MAC) 211, 295
Germanophobia 121, 281
Germany, German Empire, German Reich 17, 19, 83, 120, 181, 186, 220 f, 238, 240, *242,* 246, 250, 256, 259, 261, 282, 296 f, 303, 305 ff, 313, 320, 340, 369, 371, 375, 377, 379 f, 395
Germany
-Germans as bogy 333
as (England's) „inconvenient competitor" 268, 282
as „parvenu" (upstart) 294
-'s sole guilt/responsibility 223, 333 f
as troublemaker and newcomer 228, 243, 266, 281 f, 292
Germany's "Weltpolitik" 278
Gheg 41, 180
Giaour 63
Gibraltar 275
Glagolithic Script 36
Gleiwitz 257
„God's Englishman" 322
Golden Horn 19, 57, 116, 161, 185, 199, 207, 234, 236, 360
Goli Otok, (Yugoslav concentr camp) 195, 198
Gordian Knot 13, 367, 391, 395
Gothic Empire 84, 104, 134
Graecization (Hellenization) 67, 70, 87 f, 106, 128, *135,* 137, 155, 168, 349, 367 f
Grand policy (of Italia) 291
Great Britain *233,* 261, 278, 281, 285, 289, 342, 379, 395
(Since practically all observers in those days, including the English themselves, used "England" instead of GB: see Engl. a. British)
Great (-er)
-ALB 52, 54, 57, 190, 372
-BUL 25, 30, 32, 81, 90, 95, 127, 186, 197, 207, 217, 219 f, 378
"Cutting up of Great-BUL" 44
-Denmark 275
-GRE (see also Megale Idea) 25, 28, 109, 134, 139, 166, 356, 372, note 744
-Hellenic Empire 194
-Kosovo 54, 190
-Moravian Empire 36

443

-Macedonia 44
-MonteN 307
-Moravian Kingdom 36
-policy of Italy 291
-power dreams 20
-Serbia 25, 66 f, 174, 232, 372
Great European confrontation/war 314 f, 337 f
"Great Politics" of Italia 252
Greco-
-Bulgarian Agr.mt. 300 f
-Bulgar. League and Military Conv. *166*, 265, 302, 348
-Bulgar. Rapprochement 202
-Turkish Convention (1880) 114
-Turkish Peace Treaty of Co'ple 148
-Turkish War 146, 152
Greece, Greeks
17 f, 37, *40, 45*, 51, 53, 59, 72, *104*, 108, 112, 123, 137, 170 f, 183, 186, 195 ff, 215, 222, 234, 282, 289, 291 ff, 294 ff, 297, 300 ff, 303 ff, 306, 310, 319, 326, 339, *341*, 346, 350 f, 353 f, 356, 359 f, 363, 367, 372, 378 f, 381, 383, 385, *388* ff, 391, 393 ff(a. note 316),
-slavicized Greeks 106
virginity of Greece 106
Greed for land/territory/power
-Austria/Habsburg 298, 371
-Balkan Kingdoms 392
-BUL 300, 318
-GRE *381*, 384
Greek
-annexation (of Crete) 109, 159
-assimilation policy 136
-Autonomous Republic 108
-blockade against MAC 19, 48, 77
-border demarcation 369
-Church tax 87 ff
-Civil War 45
-cruelties in MAC 174
-diaspora 48
-declaration of War 112, 365, and note: 316
-destroying Macedonian identy 137
-double standards 48
-Ecumenical Patriarch/at 26, 87, 89, 97, 109
-Empire 111
-expansion (policy/plans) 140, 157, 163 292, 384
-flight to Italy (from Slav settlers) 105
-folk mixture 106
-homeland 105
-hysterical nationalism 46
-hysteria 350
-imperialism 128, 164
-independence 108 f, 176, 206
-ingratitude (towards RUS) 114, 204 f
-Junta 41
-Kingdom of Byzantium 116
-language *40*,

-language nationalism 46
-Military League/Army L. (Hetaery) 163
-minority policy *134*
-monarchic family ties 354
-national feelings 124
-national vanity 142
-occupation (of Anatolia) 390
-Orthodox Church 25, 40, 87 f, 108, 138,
-orthodox New Year's celebration 145
-„pasta boycott" 46
-policy of deception 135
-Patriarchat, see: Ecum. Patr. or Greek Orth. Church
-plutocracy 107
-population in MAC 118, 134, 334
-revolts 107
-royal family 115, 120
-strategy *128 f.*, 135
Greenland 275
Gregorian(ic) calendar 27,
„Große Politik der Europäischen Kabinette" 15, 33, 223, 258, 298
Guilt allocation (of the Entente) 311
Guilt, sole German 33, 220, 275, 286, 292, 294, 312, 319, 370
Hague Convention on Land War 283 295
Habsburg Empire/Monarchy, Dual Monarchy 18, 27, 61, 76, 79, 177, 199, 201, 211 f, 214, 248, 252, 270, 283, 298, 374, 388
-supremacy 246
Hadrian's wall 47
Haemophiliac Tsarevich 315
Hague Peace Conference 322
Hagia Sophia 165, 212
Haldane-Mission 252, 279, 291
HAPAG Lloyd 285
Haus-, Hof- und Staatsarchiv Vienna 33, 100
Hawaii 269, 282
Hegemony
-Bulgarian 191
-German 269, 285
-English 233 f, 238, 243, 307
-French 233, 250, 307
-Greek 37, 191
-(ancient) Makedonian (on GRE) 21, 32, 35f, 104
-Russian 202
-Serbian 64, 191
-Turkish 191, 330
Hellenic cultural superiority 176
Helgoland/Zanzibar 258, 290
Hellenic cultural superiority 176
Hellenic Empire 118
Hellenism 21 f, 106, 110, 127 f, 130, 134, 152, 156, 168
Holy hellenistic interests 110
„Hellenic MAC-Hysteria" 50
Hellenization 39, 87 f, 98, 106, 129, 263, 301, 367, 392

--"hellenized Slavs" 106
Hellenization of MAC 136, 157, 170, 367
Hellenized slavs 106
Hellespontus 118
Henry-Martini rifles 186
Herzegovina (revolt) 27, 40, 89, 110, 116, 185, 235
High Commissioner f. National Minorities 20, 48
„Historian-Politician" 50
Hofburg 221
Hohenzollern 248, 373
Holstein 217
Holy League 61, 179, 205
Holy Roman Empire of the German Nation 205, 243, 246, 248, 365, also notes 636 a. 727
Holy Shrines (French protection) 249
"honest agent/mediator" (Bismarck) 220, 236
Human Rights 102
  In North-Greece 137
Hungarian rebellion (1848) >205
Hungary 17, 84, 131, 181 f, 213
Huns (Wilhelm's II speech) 22, 84, 104, 252, 285 f
Hüzün (s) 187, 360
hubris *381* f
Hysteria, Greek 50
Iceland 275
Identity
  -Macedonian 13, 20, 29, 37, 43, 60, 65, 74, 96, 103, 136 ff, 194, 323, 390 ff, 394
  -Persian 181
  -Serb., Croat., Bulg. 73 f
Ilinden (uprising) 21, 31 f, 37, 55, 59, *73*, 97, 103 153, 192, 208, 222, 224, 240
„Ilirida, Republic" 52
Illyria 104, 173
Illyrian language 54
Illyrians/Arnautes 106
Imperial Interests (ENG a. AUS-HUN) 181
Imperial and Royal Monarchy ("k.u.k." Monarchy) 116, 129
Imperialism 19, 28, 47, 65, 102, 128, 164, 248, 274, 298, 319, 367
  -"overall picture of imperialism" (Fr. Fischer) 333
Imperialist(ic)
  -Age/era 391, 395
  -aims/plans (Greek) 170 (See: motives)
  -aims of Balkan Kingdoms 345
  -arrogance of the Great Powers 184
  -clique/ tradition 277, 315, 344
  -crimes 264, 367 f
  -greed 207
  -Government, de facto (Cabinet Asquith) 261, 275
  -motives 199, 206 f, 222, 323
  -neighbouring states 191, 194

  -partition 263
  -presumptuousness of Grt.Powers 184
  -violence 76, 207
  -zeitgeist 81
„Imperialistically dictated peace" 286
IMRO, see VMRO
Independence
  -Alban. (also KOS) 53, 175 ff., 215, 354
  -Bulgar. 78, 94, 98, 109, 164, 172, 184, 193, 209
  -Egypt 185
  -Greek. 107, 109, 176, 249
  -Macedon. 43, 74, 87, 103, 152, 212, 215, 223, 235, 262, 269, 294, 298, 329, 370
      Declaration of indep. 358, 368
  -Montenegrin. 29, 186
  -Romanian 29, 169, 172, 186
  -Serbian 29, 63, 186
India 22, 184, 233 ff, 238, 241
  -Empress of India 115, 365
  -mutiny 234
Ingratitude of the Balkan states 205
"Insignificant" GER 287
Integrity,territor. (of ResidualTurkey) 183
Interim agreement (Greek-Macedon.) 35
International Criminal Tribunal f. the former Yugoslavia in the Hague 58
Intervention
  -eventual (of the Dual Alliance) 199
  -Soviet
Intrigues (French against D) 239
Ionian Islands/Sea 109, 302
Ipek 347
Ireland (Northern) 275, 287
„Iron Chancellor" 93,119, 222, 238, 324, 337, 344
Ischl, Bad 281
Islam
  and Christianity 188
  violent spreading 187
Islamic
  fundamentalism 31
  movement 184
  yoke 199, 282, 294
Islamic-Ottoman Empirial and Ruling System 182 f
Islamization 106 f, 178, 183
Isolation of Germany 240, 264, 266, 269 f, 272, 280, 283, 285, 393
Istanbul 108
Italy
  17, 22, 105 f, 173, 202, 216, 218, 225 ff, 240, 289, *291*, 302, 322 f, 332, 338, 379, 390, 395
Italian
  -attack on Tripoli a. Cyrenaica 302
  -campaign against Turkey 295
  -declaration of War (on Libya) 166
  -dignity and honour 158

445

-Irredentism 221
-sacro egoismo 173
-Somaliland 252
Italo-
-French Neutrality Treaty 252
-Libyan War 265
-Turkish War 166, 199, 264
J(o)anina 77, 123, 265, 332, 334, 337
Janissaries 178, 187
Japan 148, 165, 265, 269, 274, 286, 322
-Anglo-Japan. Alliance 218, 282
-Russo-Japan. War 218, 240, 279
Jassy (Peace) 180, 205
Jealousy (Engl.) 293
Jena and Auerstedt 38, 243, 373
Jewish Diaspora 246
Jihad 187
Julian Calendar 27
„Junker" 250, 322
Kaiser Proclamation 237
k.u.k. (Imperial a. Royal) Monar. 116 f, 129 ff
„Kampf um MAC" (battle for MAC) 14
Karlowitz (Peace) 205, 213
Karpoš insurrection 26, 33, 55, 179
Kazachstan 46
Katerini 55
Katharevusa 40 f
Kavala 42, 239, 300, 378, 389
„Kaviar", see: note 667
El Kebir (battle of) 237
Kephallenia 107
KFOR 180
Khalifat 360
Khedive 184 f
Kidnapping of boys (Devshirme), see Janitsharies 185 and note 561
Kiel (also canal) 262, 312
Kiev (Princes) 86, 205 f
Kingdom of Serbs, Croats a. Slovenes, (and Kingdom of Yugoslavia) 43, 96, 394
Kioto (Kyoto) 148
„Koburger" 83, 94, 101, 282
Koine 40
Königgrätz 217, 268
Kolossans, Epistle of St. Paul 47
Komitadjis 67, 72, 133
Kommuniqué, Russian (1913) *346*
Königgrätz 240, 282 a. note 162 a. 623
Konkordanz (Große) z. Luther-Bibel 33
„kopenhagen", to 290
Koran 185
Koritza 384
„Kosova, Republic" 58
Kosovo (also: - polje)
28, 43, 51, 56 ff, 59, 62, 70, *73*, 76 f, 176, 178f, 377
-Belgian Model 52
Kosovo-Albanians 41
Kowtow (BUL, SER) 84

Kresna (Mac. uprising) 29, 203
Krupp 360
Kruševo, Republic 32, 71, 192, 221
Kuban 26
Kurds ("belligerent mountain tribes") 177
Kütschük-Kainardschi (Peace) 33, 62, 182, 192, 201
Kutso-Wallachian 119, 170, 367
Lamian War 21
Language
-Albanian 41, 173
-Attic 40
-Bosnian 66
-Bulgarian *39*, 88
-Croatian 39
-Gheg 41
-Greek 40
-Illyrian 41
-Kosovar 55
-Latin (imperial language) 175
-Makedoromanian 168
-Macedonian *35*
-Old Greek 40 f
-Romanian 169
-Serbian *39*
-Serbo-Croatian standard 39
-Slavic 50
-Slavo-Bulgar. 39, 44
-Slav(on)ic, Old church 24, 37, 50
-Southslav 36
-Tosk 41
-Turkic 172
-ancient Albanian 173
Language codification 39
Latin (as imperial language) 175
Lauenburg 213
"Layered society" (BUL) 84
League of Nations 49
League of the three Emperors 92
League of Prizren 179
Lepanto 179
Lerin and Bitola Dialect 49
Lebanon 185
Liberation movement 188
Liberation of the Christian nation 317
Libya 168, 199, 255
Lies, as English „patriotic virtue" 285
Liga of Prizren 176
Localization (alleged) of the Balkan War 296, *313*, 368, 371
Lombard policy (Bismarck's) 344
Lombardy and Venetia 289
London
-Agreement (1827) 108
-Balkan Conferences 351, 370
-Black Sea Conference 238, 279
-Dardanelles Treaty 184
-Peace Treaty 303 f, 357, 359 f, 368
-Protocol (1852) 275

-Protocol (1877) 63, 111, 185
-School for Economics 334
-Treaty on the Dardanelles 181
Lotharingian Middle Empire 365
Luther-Bibel (Gr. Konkordanz) 33 (?)
Macedonia, Macedonians (also Anciant Mak.)
21, 23, 63, 72 f, 86 f, 93, 105, 113 f, 116 ff,
120f, 124, 128 f, 131 f, 134 f, 141, 146, 153
ff, 156 ff, 172, 184, *188*, 192, *195*, 207,
210, 215, 218, 222, 233 ff, 239 ff, 241, 248
f, 256, 259 f, 264 ff, 269, 275, 282, 291 f,
294ff, 297, 300, 307, 316 f, 321, 325, 340 f,
343, 347, 368, 370, 377, 380, 385, 393
-Aegaean MAC (in Greece) 347
-in the Bulgar. Orth. Church 98
-Core of European Turkey 183 (?)
-Free election 52
-free MAC 40
-as independent state 385
-"liberation" of MAC 345
-Non-interference into inner affairs (of MAC) 195
-Northern MAC 394
-oppressed nation 349
-Partitioning of MAC 138
-Pirin-MAC (Bulg.) 347
-Prima/Secunda Mak. 22
-as "special Slav nation" 390
-as troublemaker 294
Macedonia "proper" 385
Macedonian
 -agitation 221
 -ancient 86
 -Archbishopric of Ohrid 87
 -autochthonous population 85
 -Autocephalous Church (see Ortho.) *24*, 87
 -autonomy, pursuit of (see Autonomy) 26
 -census 45, 51, 56
 -committees 221, 360
 -constitution 48
 -dances 49
 -diadochoi 22
 -dialects, folklore 38, 49
 -emigrants 196
 -Empire 37 f
 -equilibrium 189
 -ethnic independence 39
 -ethnic tolerance 103
 -family names 49
 -folklore, dialects 38, 49
 -folksongs 52
 -freedom 101, 103, 182
 -frescoes 49
 -gravestones 49
 -grammar 39
 -hegemony 21, 104
 -icons 49
 -identity (see Identity) 13, 20, 29, 37, 43, 60, 74, 136 f, 323, 390
 -independence 43, 101, 103, 223, 298, 317, 350, 381, 392, 394
 -inner affairs 198
 -integrity 59
 -„Knot" 13, 99, 120, 367, 391, 395
 -komitadjis 67
 -language *35*, 49
  as „Bulgarian dialect" 44
 -minority (in GRE) 45 ff, 48
  (in BUL) 44
 -multiethnic population
 -music 49
 -mother tongue 46, 48
 -name *32*, 85
  Greek claim 85
 -nation(ality) 76, 385
  national liberation 89
  national movement 97
  national consciousness 74
 -non-interference in inner affairs 198
 -occupation (of antic Athens) 21
 -Orthodox Church (autocephalous) 23, *24 f,* 38, 87 f
 -Parliament (Sobranje)
 -partition 101, 329, 366
 -Ptolemaeans 21
 -Question
 29, 38, *42,* 74, 81, 137, 171, 208, 215, 218 f., 235 f, 298, 358, 381, 386
 -reforms 318
 -refugees 196, 323, 381
 -revolts (see Uprisings) 27
 -Self-determination 43, 102
 -separate identity 76, 87, 102, 136
 -separatism 38, 52
 -Slavic 86
 -Social Democrats 82
 -sovereignty 24
 -sphere of influence 101
 -„State, First" 23
 -State symbol (flag) 49
 -territory *42*, 137, 366, 378
 -Titular Nation 21
 -traditions 39
 -written language 38
 -uprising (ancient) 22
 -written language 38
Macedo-Romanian language 170
Macedo-Slavs 43, 56, 76
Macedo-Wallachians 134
"Machtpolitik, naked" 288
Madjaren (Magyaren) 84
 -fenno-ugric 104
„magdeburg" to 278, 290
Makedon. Organis. f. Balkan Prosperity (MAKIVE) 136
Mainland (continental) force (Festlandsdegen) 229, 343, 351
Mantzikert (Malasguir), Battle of 181

447

Marinovo (revolt) 40
Marmara Sea 185, 235
Marocco 277, 321
  -Question 276
  -Crisis (2.) 270
Mediterranean Sea 186, 234
Megale (- i) Idea 28, 42, 108 f, 114, 128, 13, 137, 168, 168, 189, 301
  -Serbian, Bulgarian Meg. Idea 189
Megalomania
  Greek 25, 133
  Austrian 63
Meglenites (Slav tribe)130
"Mein Kampf" 285
Meredites (Slav tribe) 177 f.
Mesopotamia 236
Mexico 183
Meyerling castle 232
"Might is right" 378
Migration of Peoples (-Age) 18, 22 f, 46, 84, 104 f, 129
  -Turkish migration 84
Milestone in Macedonian history 298
Miletus 134
Military Border
  -Croat.-Slavonian 62
  -Bosn.-Turk. 216
„Military Confrontation" (against GER, decision in GB 1911): 292
Military-Convention
  -Bulgaro-Serb. 79 f, 265, 301, 303
  -French-Russ. 248, 251
  -Greek-Bulgar. 262, 302, 304, 313, 338
  -Italian.-Montenegrin. 252
  -Serb.-Montenegr. 78 f, 291
  -Russ.-Roman. 167
Military League/Army Liga (Hetärie) 163, 302
Military Meeting, Anglo-French (1905) 275
Minority
  -Albanian in GRE 48, 130, 136
  -Albanian in MAC 51, 53, 57, 190
  -Armenians in GRE 131
  -Aromanian in GRE 48
  -Aromanian (Vlach) in MAC 51
  -Bulgarian in MAC 193
  -Greek in MAC 193
  -High Comm. f. National Minorities 20
  -Macedonian in BUL 44
  -Macedonian in GRE 47 ff, 136
  -National Minor.'s High Commiss. 29,
  -Pomak in GRE 48, 131
  -Turkish in GRE 48, 136
  -Turkish in MAC 51
  -Roma in MAC 51
  Vlach in MAC 51
Minorities in GRE 48, 131, 136
Minority protection in GRE 16
Minority rights
  -in BUL 44

  -in GRE 102, 137 f
Miraculi Sancti Demetrii 47
Mitrovica 241, 265, 304
Mobilization
  -of the Balkan States 269, 271 f., 301, 307, 309 ff, 318, 323 f, 326, 338 f, 343, 349
  -of GRE 117
  -of Russia 307, 309, 324, 326 f, 330 f, 334 f, 385, 394
  -alleged Russian "trial" mobilization 325, 327 f, 330, 334
Moesia 85, 91
Mohács (Hungary) 180, 216, a. note 576
Mohamedan(ian) occupation regime 211
Moldavia und Wallachia 107, 169, 214
Monarchic (dynastic) cooperation 115
Monastir 239, 249, 259 f, 300, 389,
  Albanian border 41
Mongolians, Mongol Tatars 26, 61
Montenegro, Montenegrins
  17 f, 26, 51, 53, 56, 63, 108, 116, 126, 176, 185, 202 f, 266, 268, 296, 298, 304 f, 307 ff, 315, 317, 322, 337, 347
  -declaration of war 308, 313, 322 ff, 327 f, 338 ff, 368, 394
  -Frontier adjustment 347
Moors, Saracenes 184
Morava-Vardar dip (line) 61, 77
Moravia 36
Morea (Italian.: Peloponnes) 176
Morocco (Crisis) 261, 268, 281, 290, 342
Moscow as third Rome 205
Moslems (Albanians a. Bosnians) 107
Moslem fanatism 150
Mostar 153, 190
Mother tongue (Macedonian) 46, 48
Multiethnic Population in MAC 23
Mürzsteg Punctation (reform plans in MAC) 192, 225, 228, 255, 295, 324
Name "Macedonia", Greek/macedon. dispute, („FYROM")
  30, 32 f, 46, 59, 135, 392
Napoleonic Invasion/Wars 62 f, 289
National consciousness (Balkan slavs a. Ro manians) 73 f, 87
National day (Bulg.) 91
Nation-State, -Idea 50, 73, 176
National State founding (GER) 238
NATO 32, 44, 46 ff, 57, 59, 91, 350, 371, 395
Naval blockade against GER 261
Naval Convention (FRA-RUS) 305
Navarino (Naval battle) 108, 181, 234, 289
Nemanyides 61, 65
Netherlands 57
Neo-Greek (language) 40 f
Neuilly (Treaty of) 42, 56, 365
Neutrality of Belgium 275
Neutrality, benevolent 205
„Nibelungentreue" (Nib. Loyalty) 252, 298

Nikolsburg (Peace reaty) 217
Niš 63, 176
Non-Intervention into inner-Mac. Affairs 198
North German Confederation 33, 109
North-Epirus, see Epirus 139, 163, 174, 361, 365
North-Greece 40, 55, 136
North-Macedonia 65, 370
Northern-Ireland 288
Normandie 84
Norway 275
Occupation
 -of Egypt (by ENG) 236
 -BOS a. Herc. (by Austr.) 28, 64, 66, 69, 75, 207 f, 215 f, 226, 251 f
 -Cyprus (by GB) 232
October-Revolution 312, 335
Ohrid 24, 37, 71, 179, 366
Ohrid, Archbishopric 37 ff., 87
Ohrid Lake 42, 55, 177, (344)
„Ohrfeigenbrief" of Tsar Alex II to Wilhelm I 256
Old Church Slavic 24
Old Greek 40 f
Old Serbia 71, *76 ff.*, 81, 100, 139, 177 f, 258, 317
 Oldserbian language 39
Olmütz Punctation 245
Olympic Games 21
Omladina (Great Serbia) 69
OMO-Ilinden (Mac. Party in BUL) 44
Opium War 234
Orthodox Church 74, 176
Ossuary (King Philipp II) 35
Oriental Question/crisis 64, 186, 248
OSCE 32, 46, 137, 395
Ottoman Capital 364
Ottoman Empire, Ottomans 17, 19, *26*, 28, 31 f, 62 f., 65, 69, 79, 84, 86 f, 91, 98, 101, 104, 107 ff, 112 f, 117, 127 f, 130, 137, 147, 149, 164, 172, *181,* 185 f, 188 ff, 191, 200, 206, 211, 216, 225 f., 229 ff., 233 ff, 236, 241, 258, 289, 305, 307 f, 319, 345, 355, 360 ff, 380, 388, 392 f
Ottoman
 -hegemony 247
 -imperial conscience 176
 -imperial Parliament 223
 -Millet system 98
 -moslems 107
 -multiethnic community 174
 -occupation 104
 -Turk-Tatars 65, 133
Ossarium (of Philipp II) 49
Pacifism 307
 Honest pacif. of Russia 310
Padisha 63
Palestine 105, 246
Pan-hellenic uprising 388

Panhellenismus 134, 364
Pan-Germanists 322
Panislam(ism) 234
Panslavism 67, 89 f, 127, 191, 203, 207, 211, 216, 302, 315, 343
Panslavonic 194, 320
Paris (Peace-)Treaty (1856) 90, 169, 182 f, 189, 206, 218, 241, 246, 255
Paris –Treaties 55 f, 386
Parliamentary system 144
Parliamentary election (in MAC) 23, 51
Partition, see division
Partition agreement 366
Partition(ing) (of MAC) 127, 139, 172, 191, 299
Passarowitz (Peace) 182, 216
„pasta boycott" 46
Patriarch
 -of Co'ple (Greek) 26, 97 f
 -of Tarnovo (BUL) 24
Peace (Treaty)
 -of Brest-Litovsk 324 f, 335
 -of Bucharest 338, 359, 379 ff, 384, 387
 -Jassy 205
 -of London (1913) 303 f, 336, 338, 357, 359 f, 368, 377 f
 -of Neuilly 42, 384
 -of Nikolsburg 217
 -of Paris, see: Paris
 -of Sèvres 42, 49, 365
 -of Versailles 386 (see Versailles)
  Readiness for peace by Emperor William II 317, 325, and note 1117
Peace a. Disarmement Conf., The Hague 364
Pelasgians 51
Peloponnes 22, 40, 105, 180
„Percentage Agreement" 16, 45
Persia 22, 114, 163, 221, 241, 248, 256, 265, 277
 Persian campaign (of Alexander) 21
 Persian Gulf 235
 Identity 183
Peru 183
Peterhof 113, 141, 203
Petarwardein 181
Petsheneges (Pechenegs) 84
Pharaoh 22
Phanariots 107, 109, 392
Philhellenism 144
Philike Hetairia 165
Philippines 269, 282
Pirin-MAC 42, 44 f, 55, 347, 378
Piraeus 109, 119, 124, 145, 155
Plevna (Festung) 112, 169 f., 340
Poland 201, 245
Polish rebellion 238
Pomaks 130
Pommeranian rifleman 221
Pontus clause 185, 206, 245

449

Porte (Sublime) 25, 29 ff, 63, 68, 91 94, 109 f, 112, 117, 128 f, 138, 146, 148, 166, 184 ff, 188, 190, 194, 198, 200 f, 249, 304, 306, 309, 317, 319, 325 f, 351, 360, 392
Potyemkin (Facade) >205, 314
Powder Keg (Balkan) 222, 318
Power Balance 181
Power vacuum
   in the Balkans 240
   in Germany 237
   in MAC 32
Preamble (Mac. Constitution) 32, 51
Preliminary Peace, London 262, 301, 338, 346
Prespa Lake 41, 179
Prevention of indictment for own war criminals 283
Preventive blow/strike/war against GER 244, 253 f, 278, 291/294, 332, 344, 353, 365, 369,
Prilep (Kingdom, revolt) 61, 344
Propaganda, Engl. 273, 294, 370
Propaganda (against GER) 291, 321, 344, 370
Propaganda (importance of) 394
Protection Letter (of Empr. Leopold I) 33
Proto-Bulgar(ian)s 36, 84 f, 175
Protocol of London
   -1830: 108
   -1877: 63, 90, 183, 235
Provisional name f. the Rep. MAC (FYROM) 32 f., 48, 368, 371
Prussia 144, 243, 248, 257, 282, 294, 373
Prussian
   -militarism 286
   -Seven Years War 243
Prusso-Austrian War 202, 245, 268, 282
Prusso-Danish War 246, 268, 274 f, 282
Prusso-Turkish Friendship a. Trade agr. 241
Pruth campaign 205
Psychological warfare (see Brit.) 312, 386
Ptolemaeens, Makedonian 36
"Public opinion" (in GB) 284
Puerto Rico 269, 282
Punitive peace 286
Pydna (battle of) 22
Quadruple Entente (with ITA) 293
Quai d'Orsay 320Queen Mum 282, 293
Quirinal 159
Racconigi (Russo-Italian Arr.mt.) 252 f, 291, 293
Ragusa (Dubrovnik) 177, 180
Railway lines (in MAC) 241
RAINBOW-Party (Ouranio toxo) 135
Raja(h) (non-Muslim subjects in Turkey) 31, 38, 108, 187
Raslovec (revolt) 27
Rascia 61
Razlog (uprising) 29, 42
Recognition (of Rep. MAC, e. g. by USA) 35
Reciprocity (of religious rights) 183

Reconquista 184, 322
Red Indians 322
Red Sea 234
Re-Europeanization 343
Reformation 340, a. note 145
Reforms
   - in MAC 29 f, 78, 138, 146, 163, 175, 182, 184 f, 192, 199, 221, 231, 260, 278, 280, 300 f., 318 f, 324, 340, 359
   - in Prussia 144
Refugees, Macedonian in BUL 323
Regicide (Serbian King Alexander) 69
Reinsurance Treaty 221
Religious Freedom in the Ottoman. Emp. 182
Renaissance 361
„Republica Ilirida" 52
Republic of Kosova 58
Republic of MAC 32
„Republic of Skopje" 35, 48, 350
Réunions (French) 342
Revanche/Revenge (-Policy), French 250, 289, 380 a. note 162
Reval (Anglo-Russian Monarchic meeting) 19, 78 f., 100, *162,* 165, 193, 197, 201 ff, 213 f, 229, 240 f, 259 f, 263 ff, 267, 269, 272, 275, 292 f, 312, 329, 347, 364
Revenge (for Sadova) 217, 268
Revisionism, (Bulgarian) 91
Rhine border 250
Rhodos 254, 293
"Ring" around GER 292
Rivalry (Austro-German) 248
Rome 21, 156, 158
Roma 130 a. notes 560, 769
Romaioi (Greek "Romans") 104
Roman Empire/rule 21, 40, 105, 175, 187, 234
Roman-Makedonian Wars 22
Romania
   36, 49, 53, 85, 88, 104, 114 f, 126, 135, 157, *169,* 195, 239, 225, 236, 295, 304, 327, 361 f, 366 f, 378 f, 395
Romanian
   -German Alliance 217
   -Independence 167
   -troops 112
Romanization 104, 171, 175, 177
Romans (Epistle of St. Paul to) 47
Rominten 273, 286, 308 f, 318, 342
Rostock 388
Royal Navy 269
Rumelia (also East) 26, 30, 33, 87
Russia 17, 19, 36, 81, 99, 101, 108 ff, 112, 118, 127, 155, 162, 177, 182 ff, 186, 196, 198 f, *205,* 221, 230, 232 ff, 240 f, 244 f, 252, 255 ff, 260, 268, 270, 272, 281, 289, 292, 295, 298, 303 ff, 313, 315, 319, 321, 324, 329 f, 338, 340, 344 f, 348, 359, *361,* 364, 368, 370, 374, 385 f, 395
   -and the Balkan League *207, 209 255*

-and the *new* Balkan League *346*
-and the new great Balkan League *362*
-as spearhead of the Entente 296
-as wire-puller f. the Balkan League 349
Russia, Republic of 383
Russia's vassals in the Balkans 296
Russian
  -Baltic Sea fleet 278
  -Church Slavonic 39
  -Communiqué (of 1913) *368*
  -debts 290
  -deceptions 211, 370
  -Empire 364
  -expansion (into the Far East) 265
  -"Freedom of the press" (in RUS) 312
  -free passage to the Mediterr. 339
  -hegemony 172
  -invasion into Austria 328
  -mobilization 267, *324*
  -Orthodox Church 27, 90, 320, 364, 379
  -pan-Slavism 217
  -pan-Slavista 364
  -press 312 f
  -propaganda *307*
  -Protectorate 200
  -Protectorship (for Slav Christians) 185
  -Romanian Convention (1877) 167
  -Secret Memorandum (1908) 261
  -Secret Agrmt., with security guarantees (for SER a. BUL) 202, 280, *295* f, 347, 374, 393
  -spearhead of Entente 296
  -strategy *212*, 337
  -supremacy 218, 222
  -"trial" mobilization 325, 327, 330, 334
  -troop deployment 325, 328, 334
  -war target (Co'ple) 334, 336
  -warmongers 364
Russification 204, 208 f
  in Latvia 162
Russo-Austrian deal 226
Russo-French Alliance 140
Russo-German Treaty (1887) 209
Russo-Italian arrangement 252
Russo-Japanese War 221, 236, 265, 279
Russo-Turkish Wars 19, 31, 40, 62 ff, 75, 88 ff, *111*, 117, 169, 182, 214, 231, 247, 392
Ruthenes 131
Rychines 36, 50
Sadova 199, 246, 268, 281 a. note 162
Safe conduct (Letter of Emp. Leopold I for MAC) 47
Salonica/Saloniki 36, 42, 75, 77 f, 81, 96, 100, 105, 128, 130, *132*, 164, 185 (a. note 585), 193 f, 202, 225, 231, 239, 241, 255, 295, *349*, 355 f, 358, 385, 388 f
  -Jewish-Turkish character 356
  -payments to prevent Greek Solun 356

Sanjak/Sandzak 196, 266, 258, 268, 280, 295, 298, 306, 328 f, 336, 346, 350, 371 f, 376
San Stefano (Peace Treaty, Prelim.)
  19, 30 f, 83, 90 f, 113, 169, 185, 200, 207, 218, 235, 246, 371
Sarajevo 98, 218 f, 232, 237, 245, 254, 293, 362, 375 f, 379, 386 f
  -Russian involvement in the assassin. 376
  -Serbian involvement in the assassin. 376
Sarakatschanes 131
Sarazenes 182
Sardinia-Piemont 289, 291
Saturday Review 261
Save-Danube line 61
Savoy and Nice 289
Schleswig (-Holstein) 245, 262, 275, 288, 363
Schlieffen-Plan 285
Sea Blockade, Engl. against GER 275
Sea-route (to India) 230
Secession, Alban. 51 ff, 187
Secret Agreement
  Russia with BUL and SER (1911) 256, 273, 280, 284, 296 f, 326, 374, 393
  Austro-Serbian 91
  Romania with the Dual Alliance 171
Security interests, German 283
Sedan 268, 282
Segudates 36
Self-administration (Statute f. Turk. Prov.'s in Europe) 220
Self-complacency (German) 239
Self-determination 43, 74, 102, 132, 215
Self-isolation (German) 247
Seljuqs (Rum-Turktataren) 84, 134, 181
Seperation (of Germany from Austria) 217
Separatism, Macedon. 38, 101
Sephardes 54, 131, 367
Serbia, Serbs 18 f, 23, 36 f, 39, *43*, 46, *61,* 72, 75, 78 f, 84, 101, 103, 108, 126, 137 f, 185, 197, 203 f, 208, 220, 229, 239 ff, 255, 266, 270, 280, 282, 292, 296 ff, 300, 304, 310 f, 317, 319, 326, 338 f, 349, 356, 362 ff, 366, 369, 371 f, 376 f, 378 f, 386 f, 394
Serbia (as spearhead against Germany) 67, 364
Serbian
  -agitation in Austrian provinces 362
  -attack on Austria 362
  -autonomy 63
  -border demarcation 369
  -culture "outside SER" 68
  -hegemony 64
  -independence 63
  -massacre 56
  -Omladina (Great Serbian Idea) 72
  -Orthodox Church 43, 88
  -Orth. Cathedral (Belgr.) 73
  -language *39,* 50,
    -border 75
  -rebellions 205

Serbification 67, 81, 95, 97, 370
   „serbisation brutale" 89
Serbo-
   -Austr. Alliance 217
   -Austrian „coalition" 258
   -Bulgarian demarcation line 81, 96
   -Bulgar. League/Agr. 265, 298 f, 303, 366
   -Bulgarian War 66, 68, 91
   -Croatian written language 39
   -Croats 43
   -European complications 231
   -Serbo/Greek Kingdom/Alliance 61, 367
   -Macedonian societies 68
   -Montenegrin. Military Convention 78
   -Russian conspiracy 376
   -Turkish War 207
Serdika 85
Seres-Group 211
Serres 300
Sèvres (Peace Treaty) 42, 49, 365
Sevastopol 185, 206
Seven-years war (see Prussia) 249
Shipka-Pass 113
Shism 89
Shqiptari 177
Sicily (Albanian refugees to -) 176
„Sick man" (at the Bosporus) 200, 230, 318
Siebenbürgen 175, 180
Silesia 105
Šišmanides 86
Skopje 33, 42, 46, 49, 55, 61, 64, 70, 240, 249, 349
Skutari 177 f., 180, 239, 326, 347, 358, 369
Skythic Slavs 106
Slav
   -controle of Greece 105
   -dialects 38, 136
   -dialects in North-GRE 136
   -hellenized 106
   -inscriptions 49
   -loan words 105
   -language schools (in North-GRE) 136
   -Liturgy a. official language 36 f
   -Macedonia 22 f
   -minority in GRE 48
   -settlers (a. settlements) in the Balkans 22, 36 f, 61, 105
   -Social democrats 82
   -State of MAC 137
   -Tribes 104, 110 f
Slav Apostles 36, 50
„Slavfree" (West MAC) 53
Slavia Orthodoxa 37, 50, 52
Slavicized Greeks 106
Slavinia 105
Slavism 106, 128 f
Slavonia 180
Slavonic, Old Church 21, 37, 39, 49

„Slavophone Greeks" (Slav minority in GRE) 136, 196
Slavoserbian 49
Slavs 22, 36, 84 f., *104*, 130
   -„graecizised Slavs" (Greeks) 106
Slavs in Austr. 131
Slivnica 66 f, 366 a. note 162
Slovenia, Slovenian (also constitution) 23, 43, 48, 56, 130
Sobranje (Macedon. Parl.) 25
„Soldier King" 248
Solomonic Judgement 71
Solun (the old, Macedon. Salonica) *349, 352*
Somaliland (Italia) 291
South-Africa 241
South-Dobrudja 169, 378
South-Epirus 117, 122, 133, 329 f., 342 (s. Epirus)
South Macedonia 81
„South Serbia" 43, 63, 215
South Tyrol 173
Soviet intervention (in Hung.) 45
Soviet Union (market f. French loans) 290
Spain 184, 242
Spanish Christian liberators 184
Sparta 105
„spill-over" (Serbo-Alb. conflict) 47
„splendid isolation" 221
staging a world war (by Entente) 340
Statistics:
   Albanians in SER 62
      in MAC 23 f., 27 f.
   -Bulgarians in MAC 196
   -Slavs in Austria 131
status quo 81, *82*, 89, 163, 195 ff, 199, 201, 207, 213, 236, 241, 249, 258, 292 f, *299, 335, 343, 348,* 371
   -territorialer status quo 316
Straits 28, 31, 35, 41, 45, 64, 90, 146, 183, 187, 199, 205 ff, 218, 229, *227*, 234 f, 265, 275 f, 335, 360, 364 See: Bosporus a. Dard.
Straßburg 181, 203
Struggle for MAC 76
Struma 258
Sublime Porte, see Porte
Suda Bay 155, 238
Sudan 221, 238
Suez Canal 187, 234 f, 236 f, 239, 290
Supreme "Macedonian" Comm. of Adrianople (BUL) 96 f
Sucerenity (Bulg.) 90
Sweden 201, 244, 275
Switzerland 194
Syria 22, 105, 187, 202, 236
Takiye (türk.), taqqijah (arab.) [officially legitimated betrayal, concealment, deception etc] 80, 102
Tarnovo (Revolts, Emp.) 36, 86, see Patriarch of T.

Tatars 84, 86, 344
Territorial cessations 309, 318 f
Territorial changes 299, *316*, 336, 347
Territorial Integrity of Turkey 181
Territorial expansion 28, 349
Tetovo 42, 54
Teutonic naiveness 318
Theben 32
Thessaloniki, see Salonica
Thessalonicans (Epistle of St. Paul) 47
Thessaly 30, 72, 89, 95, 109, 112 ff, 117, 132 f, 148 f, 164 f., 237, 239, 302, 327, 384
Third Reich 288
Thirty Years War 278
Thrace, Thracians (also Eastern T.) 20, 28 f, 30 f, 65, 85, 91, 95, 104 f., 113, 132, 134, 175, 190, 219, 236, 259, 294, 296, 307, 316 ff, 347, 349, 366, 369, 380, 382 f, 389
-West Thrace 351
Thracian ethnicity 85
Thracian liberation movement 45
Thracian territory 378
Three Emperors Agreement/League 92, 217, 248
-relations 214, 217
Tibet 221
„The Times" 174, 269, 301, 303, 311 f, 319, 361, 372
Timotheus (Epistle of St. Paul) 47
"Tissue of lies" 348
Titular Nation, Macedon. 25 f., 47
Tolerance 137, 187
Tolerance Edict of Nantes 248
Topkapi Palace 113
Torture abolishment (in Prussia) 248
Tosk 41
Trafalgar 373
Transanatolian railway 238
Transatlantic-Anglosaxon solidarity 269
Trapezunt 192
Trial mobilization (Russ.) 325, 327, 330
Tributary, tribut payments 63
    -BUL 90, 184
    -Byzantin. Emp. 179
    -SER 62
    -Crete 148
    -Moldavia a. Wall. 167
Trier 46
Triest 158
Triple Alliance (GER, AUS, ITA) 173, 198 f, 217, 230, 257, 269, 293, 297, 307, 330, 339, 361, 373, 379, 384
Triple Entente (GB, FRA, RUS) 98, 193, 196, 198, 200 ff, 213, 221, 240, 242, 259 f, 263, 267, 284, 291 f, 307, 310, 330, 361, 372, 393
Tripoli 202, 254, 264, 293 f, 302, 323
Trojan Horse 71
„Trouble maker" Germany 225, 246, 280, 292

Tsarigrad (Co'ple) 194
Tshataldsha-Linie 349
Tsherkesses (see Adyghe) 89, 130
Tsushima 265, 279
Tunis 186, 221, 236, 289, 291, 294
Turkey, Turks
    19, 67, 81, 83 f, 106 f, 114, 129, 171, 236, 239, 241, 248 f, 295, 297, 299 f, 302, 304, 315, 317 ff, 325 f, 329 f, 339, 341, 351, 356, 358 f, 367, 380, 388, 392 f
    -cutting up/parcelling out of Turkey 222
Turkic Bulgarian tribes 84 f
Turkinization 174
Turkinized Albanians (a. Bosmians) 177
Turkish
    -chauvinism 190
    -crescent 343
    -cruelties to Armenians 222
    -democratization 193
    -dominance 98
    -emigration 191
    -Empire 182, 248
    -European possessions/property 199, 201
    -German Military Agr. 197
    -hegemony 194
    -massacres 315
    -military frontier 219
    -minority (in GRE) 136
    -multiethnic state 194
    -rule 97, 103
    -Russian War (Crimea) 202
    -Tatar Bulgarians 104
    -territorial integrity 183
    -tolerance 137
    -tyranny 361
    -Venetian War 146
    -yoke 32 f, 53, 93, 317
Turkish War, great 201, 213
Turkization 172
Turk peoples 84
Turktatar Bulgarians 24, 84 f, 179
Turktatar name 44
Two-Power-Standard (Brit.) 279
UÇK-Terrorists actions 53 f., 57 f.
Üsküp/Uesküb (Skopje) 235, 241
Ukraine 26, 104, 180, 201
Ultimatum, Austrian 213, 254, 364, 370
UNHCR (UNO Refugee Commissioner 56
"Unification of all Albanians" 54
Unification (of BUL a. Eastern Rumelia 258
Unification (of GER) 266, 276, 284
Unification of the German Reich 213, 237, 280, 288, 345
Unification (of Italy) 289
United Nations 17, 32, 35 46, 48, 59, 102, 206, 262, 301, 392, 395
UNMIK 377
UN-Sanctions (against SER) 19

USA
    35, 47 f., 56 f, 135, 173, 262, 282, 301, 311, 322, 389, 395
Vacuum of power 242
Varangians 85 f
Vardar Macedonia 35, 42 f, 65, 197, 259, 299, 367, 378
Varna (also dialect) 36, 39
Vatican 18, 159 f
Vendetta 180
Venezuela 269, 322
Venice 116, 177, 201, 298
Verdun, Treaty of 265
Vergina, Star (or Sun) 35, 45, 49
Versailles, (Conference/Treaty) 15 f, 33 f., 223, 237, 243, 273, 286 f, 386
Vidin (Bulgar. Residual Emp.) 86
Vienna, Congress/sieges 17, 26, 35, 42, 181, 198, 205, 216, 243, 289, 337
Vinozito (Rainbow, Mac organis. in Northern GRE) 44
Vitoria 373
Vlachs 23, 85, 104, 135 f, 169, 175 a. note 531 (s Aromanians and Kutzo-Wallachians)
Vladivostoc 147
Vlora (Valora) 260, 300
VMRO (IMRO=Inner Macedon. Revolutionary Organisation) 37, *95*, 386
Voden(a) 300
Vojvodina 28, 57
Wallachia 69, 107, 169
Wallachian Romanians 85
War coalition, new Balkanic 366
War Council (Brit.) see CID
"War Council" (Wilhelm II) 280, 292
War guilt (as instrument of deception) 295
    -sole German 33, 200, 220, *273*, 292, 317
    -English 352
War-in-sight crisis 247, 268
Warmonger (RUS, GB) 343
Warmongering psychosis in London 311
„Warm Water" (Mediterranean) 89
Waterloo 63, 246, 373
West-Bulgarian Empire 24
Western MAC 52 f, 177
West-Thrace 140, 351
WEU 193
White Hall 287
Wilhelmian Age/Era/Emp. 78, 234, 238, 241, 277, 283, 365
Wilhelmine Reich 270 f, 336, 393
Willy-Nicky-Telegrams 312 a. note 1002
Windsor Castle (archives) 273, 298
„Worldbritain" 279
Worldhegemony, Engl. 181, 229, 243, 351
World War
    -First
    20, 43, 49, 55, 69, 109, 120, 127, 173, 195, 217, 219, 232, 254, 258, *259*, 267, 273, 279, 283 ff, 286, 290, 295, 313, 329, 333, 343, 360, 365, 382, 385, 387 ff, 394
    -Second
    15, 20, 43, 171, 278, 286, 394
Written (Macedonian) language 38
Yemen 187
Yifti u. Yürüken 131
Yoke
    -Christian Orthodox 394 a. note 460
    -Double (Ottoman. a. Greek) 88
    -Islamic 199, 294
    -Turkish 24, 45, 93, 127, 181 f., 211, 299, 345, 394
Yokohama 147
Young Turks (also revolution) 77, 94, 98, 146, 164 ff, 174, 187, 190, *192 f*, 200 ff, 211, 241, 265 f, 279, 295, 341, 344, 358, 360, 386
    -Reform Party 184
Yugoslav-Bulgarian agreement (1944) 44
Yugoslav constitution 56
Yugoslavia (communist) 55, 350
Yugoslavia (Kingdom, Federation)
    43 f, 47, 57, 59, 96, 190 350, 394
Zagreb 53
Zanzibar 248, 250
Zarigrad 191, 235
Zakynthos 107
zeitgeist 101, 133, 209
Zeta (battle) 181

www.ingramcontent.com/pod-product-compliance
Lightning Source LLC
Chambersburg PA
CBHW060910300426
44112CB00011B/1415